SHAW—"THE CHUCKER-OUT"

Allan Chappelow

"THE CHUCKER-OUT"
(*Shaw's Own Title*)

The last action photograph of Bernard Shaw
July 1950 – Aged 94

"This bright, nimble, fierce, and comprehending being."—Sir Winston Churchill

SHAW ~
"THE CHUCKER-OUT"

A Biographical Exposition and Critique

AND

A COMPANION TO AND COMMENTARY ON
"SHAW THE VILLAGER"

By

ALLAN CHAPPELOW
M.A., F.R.S.A.

FOREWORD BY
VERA BRITTAIN

AMS PRESS, INC.
NEW YORK, N.Y. 10003

By the Same Author
RUSSIAN HOLIDAY (1955)
SHAW THE VILLAGER AND HUMAN BEING (1961)

FIRST PUBLISHED IN U.S.A. 1971

First United States Edition 1971, AMS PRESS
Reprinted from the edition of 1969, London

Library of Congress Card Catalog Number:
74–152552

ISBN: 0–404–08359–5

Text printed by The Anchor Press Ltd., Tiptree, Essex
On paper specially made by the Inveresk Paper Co. Ltd., London
Blocks made by the Sun Engraving Co. Ltd., and John Swain & Son Ltd., London
Plates printed by The Anchor Press Ltd., Tiptree, Essex

PRINTED IN GREAT BRITAIN

THIS BOOK IS DEDICATED
TO
MY BROTHER PAUL

IN MEMORY
OF A POPULAR FIGURE
IN THE
BOOK TRADE
AND
HELPER IN MY WORK

The villagers [of Ayot St. Lawrence] thought he was a rum one—
a *very* rum one.

Mrs Edith Reeves in *Shaw the Villager*.

Look at me!   I seem a man like other men because nine-tenths of
me is common humanity.   But the other tenth is a faculty for seeing
things as they really are.

From *Back to Methuselah*.

'The Chucker-Out' . . . photograph . . . is extraordinarily symbolic—representing in aquiline fashion Shaw's spirit of 'divine
discontent', the fierce determination to throw out the dead wood,
the outworn traditions, and desiccated taboos of social decadence and
moral degeneration.

Professor Archibald Henderson in *Shaw the Villager*.

A great artist is not a lump of genius to be gaped at, but a combination to be analysed.

Bernard Shaw.

The business of the artist is to take facts out of the accidental
order in which they actually occur;   clear away the insignificant and
irrelevant facts which obscure them;   and arrange them so as to
reveal their true significance.

Shaw in a lecture on October 8th, 1908.

For mark you, Tavy, the artist's work is to show us ourselves as
we really are.   Our minds are nothing but this knowledge of
ourselves and he who adds a jot to such knowledge creates new mind
as surely as any woman creates new men.

From *Man and Superman*.

FOREWORD

By VERA BRITTAIN

Unlike Allan Chappelow and Dame Sybil Thorndike (who wrote a Foreword to this book's predecessor, *Shaw the Villager, and Human Being*) I never actually met Bernard Shaw, although as a young woman I was a fascinated member of the audience at several of his Fabian lectures. I recall especially his debate with G. K. Chesterton, organised by *Time and Tide* when Lady Rhondda was its editor.

But I had one indirect contact of which I have always been proud. In 1950, the year of Shaw's death, I published a book entitled *In the Steps of John Bunyan* in Britain, and in America *Valiant Pilgrim*. As Shaw had a devout admiration for Bunyan, whom he described in the *Saturday Review* during 1896 as "better than Shakespeare", my publishers sent him a copy of the book. They received in reply one of his famous postcards warmly thanking them for this new publication on "great Bunyan". As my book was published on June 29th and Shaw died on November 2nd, aged 94 years and 14 weeks, this postcard was clearly one of his last communications with the world outside Ayot St. Lawrence. Naturally the publishers would not part with it, but they sent me a photograph of it which is a treasured souvenir.

Twice during Shaw's final summer Mr Chappelow called on him, and through a combination of good fortune and persistence took the last photographs of him, as events proved. These pictures amounted to a major 'scoop' and later, when "Shaw's Corner" was opened to the public, large prints which Shaw had framed and hung on his walls became part of a national possession. On Mr Chappelow's second visit, a conversation occurred which gave him the title of his present book. Shaw took a special fancy to the picture (now reproduced as frontispiece and on the jacket of this book) showing him in his porch leaning on his stick and looking pugnacious. To Allan Chappelow he commented: "This is *alive*—this *ought* to be published. Call it 'The Chucker-Out'."

In *Shaw—"The Chucker-Out"* the reader will find (in addition to the opening chapter which presents Shaw's printed postcards and 'stock letter' replies) much valuable material on his 'new alphabet' and his succession of Wills, rare love letters and other evidence of Shaw's attitude to sex, and perhaps most important of all, a most fascinating panorama of Shaw's views on the full gamut of political themes. The subjects range through Socialism and Capitalism, Christian Economics, Democracy and Dictators (inevitably a controversial section which includes much of the material that caused Shaw to be criticised as a sympathiser with Fascism) to Equality of Income, Trade Unionism, and Communism—which term Shaw used in his own special sense.

Like so many people, I have often been perplexed by the contrast between the unquestionable brilliance of many of Shaw's views, and the sometimes facetious statements of the clown in him. When was he serious, and when was he 'talking with his tongue in his cheek'?

Mr Chappelow's book goes a long way towards providing the answer. It contains, apart from the other aspects of Shaw's character dealt with (and a great many interesting ones are) what must surely be the most thorough and detailed examination of Shaw's political, moral, and social views yet made by any biographer. Authenticity is given by frequent quotation from Shaw's pronouncements, and these include some of Shaw's finest and noblest, such as his "Christian Economics" speech, as well as his more controversial *obiter dicta*.

Mr Chappelow has ranged far and wide in what has obviously been most painstaking and conscientious research over a long period, and the fruits of it are extremely well integrated and presented. After spending several weeks on this book, my image of Shaw—hitherto always baffling and enigmatical—has become greatly clarified. I feel that Mr Chappelow's analysis is eminently fair and objective, and of the utmost value as a contribution towards our understanding of this fascinating but also extraordinarily complex man of genius.

I am certain that this is a book which no present or future student of Shaw and his time will be able to do without.

INTRODUCTION

The theme of this book was announced in the Introduction to *Shaw the Villager*, and also, in more detail, in "A Note to the Reader" at the end of it. For the benefit of those who have not read *Shaw the Villager*, or who may have forgotten the notes about this companion book in it, I will briefly recapitulate the background which has given rise to the present volume.

Shaw the Villager, and Human Being was a symposium of the reminiscences, based on their exceptionally close personal contacts, of some sixty-odd people who knew Shaw intimately—yet in some capacity *other* than as famous contemporaries in various fields, or as eminent members of his specialised circle of friends and associates in the theatre and literary worlds (to whom Shaw naturally appeared as 'G.B.S.'—the great dramatist and man of genius).

My aim was to see how Shaw appeared to these more ordinary folk—whose association with him was primarily due to incidental factors, such as their trade or profession, or simply because they happened to be his neighbours in the village of Ayot St. Lawrence or the surrounding Hertfordshire district. Reminiscences were given by his household staff (his gardeners, chauffeur, housekeeper, maid); and by the local publican, the apiarist who tended his bees, and the legendary village postmistress; also by local farmers, the district Conservative Party agent, the Rector of the Parish—and by private families such as the Tukes, the Vernon Sylvaines, and others living in Ayot St. Lawrence.

Then there were those whose professional client Shaw was—his doctors, dentist, barber, chemist; the printers and sellers of his books, and so on. And finally there were the residents of Wheathampstead, Kimpton, and other nearby parts of Hertfordshire, whom Shaw also regarded as his neighbours—including the people of Welwyn Garden City—with the development of which (pioneered by Sir Ebenezer Howard, Sir Frederic Osborn, C. B. Purdom, and others) Shaw was closely associated from the beginning. The Rector of Ayot St. Lawrence once said: "In our village Shaw could be himself", and indeed, the portrait which emerged from my investigation proved the existence of a humanity and humility in Shaw which few suspected to exist, and which was in complete contrast to his public 'G.B.S.' personality, and the 'sharp tongue', 'rapier-like wit', and predominantly intellectual approach to life usually associated with it.

Shaw the Villager fulfilled my best hopes in producing it, many reviewers making the point that our understanding of Shakespeare would have been considerably enhanced if some details of a similar kind had been collected and recorded about *his* everyday life amidst his neighbours and business contacts in Stratford-upon-Avon.   I take pride in the fact that even Shaw himself supported this view in the following words (from a draft in the British Museum) which could be taken to apply equally to the kind of intimate and authentic anecdotal material involved in *Shaw the Villager*:—". . . I would rather . . . have a collection of Shakespeare's washing bills and tailor's bills, or a verbatim report of what he said at rehearsal, than fifty essays on Hamlet".

Bernard Shaw, of course, never respected uncritical adulation, and when I interviewed those who were to form my symposium, I made every effort to obtain complete frankness in their reminiscences.   The corporate picture of Shaw which resulted was favourable and concentrated almost entirely, as I have said, on the part played by Shaw in the life of the village of Ayot and its environs, and his relationship as a human being with ordinary folk.   But it was nevertheless also true to say that— after purely personal memories had been recalled of Shaw's kindness, his way with children, his support of the village church, his regular visits to the 'pub', and so on—many of my subjects would conclude by voicing some criticisms of a much more general nature such as were, and still are, shared by a substantial section of the general public.   For example, Captain Ames, a next-door neighbour throughout the period Shaw lived in Ayot St. Lawrence from 1906 to 1950, qualified his numerous friendly personal reminiscences by expressing vigorously his opinion that: "Shaw was no Socialist! . . . He was Shakespeare's Puck fulfilled to perfection. . . . He was consistently unconvincing in the expression of his Socialism . . . a humbug." J. W. Sault, another member of the symposium, was particularly surprised that Shaw had never been a pacifist, which he felt inconsistent with his Socialism. He regarded Shaw's outlook as "one-eyed".

Others could not understand how Shaw's admiration for the Fascist dictators, Hitler and Mussolini, could be reconciled with Socialist beliefs. Then again, Shaw was frequently seen over the years being chauffeur-driven through the village in a succession of Rolls Royces, and this was felt to be inconsistent with his oft-repeated affirmations that he was a Communist. Then there was the village farmer, who "did not hold with" the view Shaw used to proclaim in his public utterances that the working class should be "exterminated". And others—after in every case telling stories (often amusing ones) of Shaw's simple humanity, his very real kindness, humour, and complete lack of egotism and 'side' to them—would end with some such words as: "But, of course, he did have some queer ideas which were beyond my ken. I *never* could fathom his new alphabet scheme, for example." And almost everyone expressed the opinion at some point or other that Shaw "said everything with his tongue in his cheek".

These criticisms were trenchant ones, and it will thus be readily appreciated that when I had finished collecting the many impressions of Shaw which made up the symposium *Shaw the Villager* I felt it desirable—and only fair to Shaw—to bring him back into the book at the end, and, by quoting selected statements made by him during his lifetime, to give him an opportunity of replying to his critics, and of clarifying his attitude on a number of topics of fundamental importance raised by the villagers on which not only they, but many other people besides, have often been perplexed and confused.

The original idea was to make this material a concluding chapter to *Shaw the Villager*, but as explained therein, it soon became clear that, although it was all too easy for people to pose questions and make criticisms of the kind I have mentioned, it was going to be a vastly more difficult matter to reply (or give Shaw an opportunity of replying) adequately and satisfactorily to them. For example, the only real way to answer the criticism "Shaw was no Socialist" is to try to analyse exactly what Shaw's political views were—and as his views were often of a contradictory and complex nature, this could never be an easy task. Particularly did this prove to be the case because one has to reckon not only with Shaw's Irishness and other (often unique) characteristics, but also with his quite exceptionally long working career. Shaw's first published writing (*i.e.* his first public expression of opinion—it was on a social subject) was in April, 1875, and his last in November, 1950—a span of *more than three-quarters of a century within his own lifetime*! Thus in considering, for example, Mr Sault's criticism that Shaw might have been expected to be a pacifist, one has to consider (if one is to do the job thoroughly) Shaw's position in relation not only to the First and Second World Wars, and to the present age of the atomic bomb into which he lived, but also to the Boer War of the turn of the century, and the Franco-Prussian War of the 1870s! (Indeed, Shaw was alive even in the era of the American Civil War, the Crimean War, and the Indian Mutiny, all of which were leading topics in the newspapers and conversation of his childhood!)

To sum up: *Shaw—"The Chucker-Out"* is an attempt to assist towards a better understanding of Shaw by clarifying Shaw's paradoxical character and attitude to life—with reference particularly to certain fallacies and misconceptions voiced by the villagers incidentally in the course of their reminiscences, but often shared and felt strongly about by the world at large. *Shaw the Villager* was a symposium demonstrating a little-known human side of Shaw. The present book is essentially a commentary on special aspects and topics arising out of that symposium, in which Shaw's views are presented and their controversial and paradoxical nature critically examined.

Hampstead,   ALLAN CHAPPELOW.
London, 1969.

ACKNOWLEDGEMENTS

It is a pleasure to acknowledge my indebtedness to the people and institutions who have assisted me in the production of this book.

Firstly, my deep gratitude is due to those friends who so kindly read drafts of the text at various stages, either wholly or in part, and made comments which I have often acted upon. In particular, I must thank Mr W. Branch Johnson (a writer himself and contributor to *Shaw the Villager*) and Mr John Sparrow, B.A. (Oxon), both of whom devoted extensive time and energy to such reading and subsequent discussions with me. I am also much indebted to my friend and fellow-author, Mr Michael Beresford, B.A., of Manchester University, who read the chapters on Politics and on War, and to Mr R. Howard Gordon, B.A., who read all the page proofs with a painstaking attention to detail which brought to light some points which had eluded previous readings. In addition Mr John Wood commented helpfully on certain aspects.

Secondly, I must thank the editors of newspapers and individual reporters who have allowed me to use or quote from newspaper articles, reports of speeches, or interviews lying in their copyright. As this book is, in the main, a discussion of Shaw's views, it would have been impossible to create it without their co-operation, and this was most generously given in every case without a penny piece being asked in fees.

Thirdly, I must express my thanks to Mr C. G. Allen, M.A., Sublibrarian of the British Library of Political and Economic Science, who went to considerable efforts to assist me in connection with the papers bequeathed by Shaw to that institution; and to members of the staff of the Manuscript Department of the British Museum, who—lovers of knowledge and research as they are—likewise evinced a courteous, friendly, and helpful spirit which was a source of encouragement as well as of technical assistance and was warmly appreciated. A particular debt of gratitude is due to Miss Yvonne Crossman, B.A.,

A.L.A., who by arrangement gave part of her spare time during several months to checking my transcripts of extracts from previously unpublished manuscripts with the originals in the British Museum, and certifying the accuracy thereof as required by the Shaw estate—to whom acknowledgement has elsewhere been made for permission to quote from Shaw's copyright writings. I must also thank Miss M. A. E. Nickson, B.A., A.L.A., of the same department, who kindly helped with this certification in Miss Crossman's absence.

The sources of illustrations are acknowledged where possible in the List given in the next few pages, and mostly *in situ* also.

I must especially thank Miss Barbara Smoker, sometime Secretary of both The Phonetic Alphabet Society, London, and the Shaw Society, England, for her contribution *G.B.S. and the A.B.C.*, and Miss Vera Brittain, the famous author of *Testament of Youth* and other works, for her kindness in writing a Foreword. I approached Vera Brittain in this connection because I had wanted to meet her ever since reading and receiving much early encouragement from her book *On Becoming a Writer* after coming down from Cambridge in 1948. I found it then, and still do, packed in every line with extremely wise and useful advice, and written in a pleasant and practical way which made me assimilate almost every word of it.

Finally, I must express my particular gratitude to Mr H. W. Hall and his colleagues of University Tutorial Press Ltd and to my friend Mr John Sparrow, whose patience and sympathetic understanding during times of production difficulties and delays have been greatly appreciated.

ALLAN CHAPPELOW.

CONTENTS

	PAGE
FOREWORD. *By Vera Brittain*	vii-viii
INTRODUCTION. *By Allan Chappelow*	ix-xii
ACKNOWLEDGEMENTS	xiii-xiv
ILLUSTRATIONS: *Plates*	xviii
Facsimile Line Illustrations	xix-xx
ENTER "THE CHUCKER-OUT"! BERNARD SHAW TAKES THE FLOOR, REPLIES TO HIS CRITICS, AND EXPLAINS HIMSELF	1
BERNARD SHAW'S PRINTED POSTCARDS AND STOCK LETTER REPLIES	6
ON HOW TO BECOME A MODEL PARENT	35
ON EDUCATION, CONDUCT, AND LIFE	36
ON THE LITERATURE OF THE THEATRE *The only lecture Shaw ever gave on this subject*	45
ON HIS AIMS AS A PLAYWRIGHT	58
ON STAGE MORALS AND CENSORSHIP, RELIGION, ART, AND SPIRITUAL AND PHYSICAL LOVE	61
ON LOVE, MARRIAGE, THE NATURE OF SEX, AND SEX ETHICS	78
ON SEXUAL REFORM	96
ON SOCIALISM	103
ON CHRISTIAN ECONOMICS. *Shaw's finest speech*	130

ON DEMOCRACY AND DICTATORS;   PAGE
COMMUNISM, SOCIALISM, CAPITALISM, AND FASCISM;
REVOLUTION, SEDITION, WOMEN IN POLITICS;
THE BRITISH LABOUR PARTY;
TRADE UNIONISM AND THE WORKING CLASS;
AND THE EQUALISATION OF INCOMES   162

*Poverty and democracy—Lincoln and democracy—Democracy and
despotism—Socialists should support Dictatorship—Autocracy,
idolatry, and democratic delusions—Educate the voters. Fabian
constitutionalism—Tyranny and slavery. The right sort of dictator—
Grades of slavery—The abolition of private property—Socialism and
civil war—Liberty and the voter. What is freedom?—Liberty and
leisure. Hitler, Fascism, and autocracy—Mussolini, Fascism, and
physical torture—British oligarchy compared to Fascist dictatorship—
Mussolini's success compared to Napoleon's—Shaw's Fascist
sympathies criticised—Free speech. Shaw's callousness—Fascism,
Nazism, and the British Labour Party criticised by Shaw—
Nazism and anti-Semitism—"Genuine democracy"—Democracy a
fraud. Political nomenclature—State and Private enterprise.
Socialism and Communism—Capitalism, Socialism, Communism,
and Fabianism—Plutocracy. Socialism the consummation of
Capitalism—Stalin not a dictator. Comparison with the Pope—
The Union of Soviet Fabian Socialist Republics—Karl Marx praised—
The middle-class origins of Socialist revolt—Fabians are State-
Socialists. Marx criticised—Marx not a Socialist. Merely anti-
bourgeois—Capitalism will not collapse of 'inner contradictions'—
Different sorts of Socialists. Jevons. Calvinism—Socialistic
illusions. British Fabianism non-Marxist—A Marxist criticises
Shaw—Shaw advocates violent revolution—Capitalists must be
reformed or killed—Russian and British Bolshevism—Shaw preaches
sedition—Ruskin and "Tory Communism"—Dickens and Ruskin not
democrats. The people cannot make their own laws—Equality of
Incomes—Debate with G. K. Chesterton: Socialism and the gentleman—Debate with Hilaire Belloc: Property and slavery—Belloc
opposes state-control—Does the artist need property in order to be
free?—'Infinite variety' v. Officialdom. Service v. Servitude—
Shaw's objections to inequality of income—Objections to Shaw's Equal
Incomes concept—Equality of Incomes controversy—A critic urges
Equality of Opportunity—Equal enjoyment of life not Shaw's aim—
Equality of opportunity incompatible with inequality of income to
Shaw. Professor L. T. Hobhouse's objections—Shaw: How can
individual remuneration be graded justly?—Professor Hobhouse's
last word—American sympathy for Shaw's view—Shaw admits the
conflict between equality and ambition—Shaw's 12-point later Equal
Incomes concept—Intermarriageability the test of social equality—
The ruling intelligentsia should get much more than the rest—The
difficulties of achieving Equal Incomes—Some will be 'more equal'
than others—Social equality: Shaw's final criteria—Women in
politics. The Labour Party criticised—Shaw criticises the working
class and the "parasitic proletariat"—Shaw's conception of "A Real
Socialist Party"—Trade Unions not Socialistic. The Labour Party
again criticised—Shaw condemns Trade Union strikes—The Trade
Unions are capitalistic. Socialism means compulsory labour—The*

absence of social friction in Russia—Shaw complains of being misunderstood—Shaw's "standard Socialist day". Life in his "One party or totalitarian State"—The poor are not free. Shaw praises Lenin and Stalin—Shaw's totalitarian sympathies criticised—Shaw replies to his critics and praises Russia—'Free' speech and social classes in Russia—Shaw praises Communist country 'elections': condemns free elections and adult suffrage—Can the artist flourish under totalitarianism?—Democracy and the monarchy. The two-Party system condemned—State-aided capitalism. Trade Unionism. Fabians are "a middle-class [not proletarian] lot"—Shaw on "The flop of Fabianism". Liberalism. Democracy re-defined—Shaw: "I am a Totalitarian Democrat"—Shaw advocates a blend of Communism, Conservatism, Liberalism, and Capitalism—Increased production urged. Functions of the "Democratic Aristocracy"—Shaw's social aims now partly achieved—Carlyle quoted. Shaw acknowledges that dictatorship as well as democracy has dangers—The precariousness of the dictator. Shaw praises General de Gaulle—Socialists will have some disappointments. Shaw described as "that fine old Tory"—Idolatry, Plutocracy, Oligarchy, and Democracy. The Protestant and the Priest—Tests proposed to establish fitness to govern or be governed. The $64 billion billion question—Shaw's views on Anarchy. He defines "the true Superman"—Civilisation ultimately dependent on the consciences of the governors and governed—Politics described by Shaw as "a religious vocation". Ibsen's non-Party attitude praised. The frequent misunderstanding of Shaw's views may be attributed to arguments obscured by his love of Rhetoric.

ON WAR AND PEACE   346

ON HIS PROPOSED NEW ENGLISH ALPHABET   413

G.B.S. AND THE A.B.C. *By Barbara Smoker*   423
    Editorial Comment   452

BERNARD SHAW'S WILLS: *Early Ones*   473
    His Last Will and Testament, 1950   499

MR JUSTICE HARMAN'S JUDGEMENT IN 1957, HOLDING INVALID THE ALPHABET TRUSTS IN SHAW'S WILL   518

APPENDIX. *Addendum to Chapter on War and Peace*   524

INDEX   528

ILLUSTRATIONS

(a) Photographs and Other Pictures

Shaw—"The Chucker-Out" (Shaw's own title). The last
action photograph—aged 94　　*(Allan Chappelow)* *Frontispiece*

FACING PAGE

Shaw posing as a statue between Virgil and Homer (who seem
less cheerful about life than he)　　42

A rare early cartoon by Sir Max Beerbohm. Page 43:
"School was to me a sentence of penal servitude. You see,
I was born with what people call an artistic temperament"　　43

A Cynic's Sketch of G.B.S.—with hat (pierced) for talking
through　　　　　　　　*(Victoria and Albert Museum)*　　43

The Bishop of Kensington, c. 1913
　　　　　　　　　　(National Portrait Gallery)　　64

Mlle Gaby Deslys, c. 1913　　　　　　*(Keystone Press)*　　64

Mlle Gaby Deslys. The voluptuous 'Toast of London'
　　　　　　　　　　　　(Keystone Press)　　65

Chinaman's dress. Shaw in Hongkong with leading Communist writers Lu Hsun and Ts'ai Yuan-p'ei
　　　　　　　　　　(Courtesy the Morning Star)　　65

The Happy Marriage. Mr and Mrs Bernard Shaw　　80

The Passionate Pursuer. Shaw's "luxurious young devil",
Miss Erica Cotterill　　80

Shaw warmly greeting the Director of the "Underground
Press" Section of the Museum of the Revolution in Russia　　228

Karl Marx (for whom Shaw had ambivalent feelings of
admiration and condemnation)　　228

Shaw in Russia with Lunacharsky and a group of 'hard core'
Bolsheviks　　229

Shaw with Hilaire Belloc and G. K. Chesterton　　252

Caricature by Harry Furniss. Shaw as he appeared to some of
his critics during the First World War, including Henry Arthur
Jones—who described him as "a freakish homunculus"
　　　　　　　　　　(National Portrait Gallery)　　387

xviii

(b) Facsimile Reproductions of Letters and Other Personal Writings, etc.

PAGE

Examples of Shaw's 'printed postcards'   13

Extract from Shaw's letter to Erica Cotterill of April 29th,
1908. "... if you dare to fall in love with a god, you must
be prepared for thunderbolts"   *Facing*   81

A flirtation begins. Shaw's telegram   *Facing*   81

Part of Shaw's letter to Erica Cotterill of April 22nd, 1908   85

Shaw's letter to Erica Cotterill of April 27th, 1908   88-9

Shaw's comments on the American Declaration of
Independence   164

Lecture card. "Our Attitude: Nationalization of Trade
Unions; Religion of State Supremacy; Stalinite
Nationalism", etc.   *Facing*   228

Lecture card. "The Terrible [Socialist] Responsibility:
1. Killing. 2. Inculcating the State morality in school",
etc.   233

Lecture card. "Excuses for Thieving—Requires certain
qualities of mind and body which ought not to be dis-
couraged"   *Facing*   252

A heavily corrected manuscript page from Shaw's article on
Marx quoted on page 220   *Facing*   253

Lecture card. "B[eatrice] W[ebb] took our breath away by
declaring that the Socialist State would retain the right to
strike—Under Socialism, it will be Criminal Direct Action"
                                                             Facing   294

"B[eatrice] W[ebb]'s plea that Compulsion is impossible
applies to all State Compulsion . . . Passive Resistance,
Conscientious Objection, Hunger Strike, and Civil War are
always possible; but they do not prevent effective compulsory legislation"   *Facing*   295

Lecture card. "The Socialist Plan"   300

Lecture card. "The Standard Socialist Day: Work 4 hours,
Wash and eat 4 hours, leisure 8 hours", etc.   *Facing*   302

Lecture card. "Compulsory Labor; Restriction of Inheritance; Teach Communism in Public Schools", etc.   *Facing*   303

PAGE

Lecture card. "Be Ready for Dictatorship . . . God fulfils
himself in Many Ways"   *Facing*   303

Shaw's shorthand draft of the letter quoted on the opposite
page. Note the neatness and steadiness of Shaw's handwriting in his 94th year   325

Lecture card. "If you have any business, GO AND DO IT,
if not, GET OUT OF THE WAY. Kitchener"   365

Lecture card. "Morals of War. The Gentleman's and the
Cad's. The Code of Decent Pugnacity—Not to Fight with
the Mouth", etc.   365

Lecture card. The Illusions of War (1915)   387

The words 'George Bernard Shaw' written in the prize-
winning phonetic British alphabets devised by (1) Mrs
Pauline M. Barrett, (2) Mr Kingsley Read, (3) Mr J. F.
Magrath, and (4) Dr S. L. Pugmire   440

Transliteration Key to the Shaw Alphabet (reproduced from
the bi-alphabetic edition of *Androcles and the Lion*)   450-1

Different standard type faces compared for scale with the
Shaw Alphabet type in the same 'point' size   456

The Complete 48-character Shaw Alphabet   457

Comparative handwriting tests of the normal and Shaw
alphabets   *Between* 457-8

Extracts from the first and last pages of Shaw's Last Will (his
"crowning masterpiece" as he called it)   517

ENTER "THE CHUCKER-OUT"!

BERNARD SHAW TAKES THE FLOOR,
REPLIES TO HIS CRITICS,
AND EXPLAINS HIMSELF

"Future generations will say: . . . who the devil was Bernard Shaw"? Thus did Shaw conclude his message to the Shaw Society of America, which I included at the end of my book *Shaw the Villager, and Human Being*—the symposium to which *Shaw—"The Chucker-Out"* forms a companion and sequel.

Who, indeed?!

It is naturally gratifying to me to record that—according to numerous kind reviewers and letters from readers—*Shaw the Villager* succeeded in throwing some new light on this question. Reminiscences and assessments were given by over fifty of Shaw's fellow-villagers and neighbours in Hertfordshire, and by his professional associates, with the aim of portraying the human, informal side of Shaw; whilst the text of Professor Henderson's fine speech lent perspective through a résumé of the other side—the great G.B.S.—the public figure, great man, literary genius, and so forth. What can usefully and appropriately be added now by way of enhancing the corporate picture of Shaw the man given by such a symposium, and making it more balanced and complete?

I think something can, for the reason that, as a vehicle for the delineation of character, a symposium has (as, indeed, a straightforward biography also has) the 'virtues of its defects and the defects of its virtues' as a literary form.

The strength of a symposium, in my belief (as I suggested in my Introduction to *Shaw the Villager*), is that it is relatively free from the element of bias from which the work of an individual biographer almost invariably suffers in some degree (no single person being capable of complete detachment and objectivity, or being in a position to see the subject in all the latter's moods and varying kinds of relationships). However, as a corollary to this, in a broadly based symposium the very diversity of impressions from many different people coming from many different trades, professions, and sections of society, inevitably results in conflicting opinions on certain aspects of the subject's character and outlook (which in Shaw's case were in addition of a particularly paradoxical and controversial kind).

The position with a symposium is to some extent analogous to that of a legal trial, in which witnesses are called giving both sides of the case (*i.e.* the defence and the prosecution). The members of the jury are then in a position to consider all the testimony and come to their own conclusions based thereon. Readers of *Shaw the Villager* will have formed their own mental images and tentative judgements in a similar manner.

We are not, of course, really concerned with a legal case here. But if one continues the analogy, there is, prior to the members of the jury retiring to come to their final verdict, usually the appearance of 'the prisoner in the witness-box'—which, when it occurs, is a most significant part of the proceedings.

Although the general picture of Shaw given by the contributors to *Shaw the Villager* is—as I trust readers of it will agree—a favourable one, there were inevitably a number of detractors, and in some cases one finds even the most friendly of Shaw's admirers supporting certain popular fallacies and widely-held criticisms. Shaw himself would not have expected it otherwise. In the preface to *The Irrational Knot* he wrote:

"As if people with any force in them ever were altogether nice!"

and in the course of a letter:

"Oscar Wilde said of me, 'An excellent man! He has no enemies; and none of his friends like him.' And that's quite true; they don't like me; but they are my friends, and some of them love me. If you value a man's regard, *strive* with him."

It has, therefore, seemed to me that it would be of real interest and value—and, indeed, essential in the interests of justice—if Shaw *himself* could now take the floor (or appear in the witness-box!) and give us all, in his own words and his own unique and entertaining way, his precise views in clarification of certain paradoxical aspects of his personality and attitude to life; in defence against fallacies and misconceptions about him raised by some contributors to *Shaw the Villager* and held by a section of the general public; and on certain associated topical and controversial subjects of wide human appeal.

So!—After the villagers and neighbours, after his professional associates, and after Professor Archibald Henderson (his 'authorised' American biographer), let us now hear . . . Shaw himself!

The following selection from Bernard Shaw's writings gives his own views, authentic and authoritative (and in many cases unabridged) on such controversial topics as democracy, dictatorship, war, Communism, capital punishment, equal incomes, vegetarianism, temperance, morality, love, sex, stage-censorship; his proposals for the reform of the British alphabet; his attitude to the numerous members of the public who wrote to him with requests of one sort or another; his various Wills, and his views on certain other germane subjects which I feel may help to round off the picture of Shaw the man with which the work as a whole is concerned.

The quintessential and little-known statements by Shaw which follow are, in the main, derived from sources other than his Prefaces. The material is collected together and published here in book form for the first time, and indeed, much of it—gleaned from original manuscripts bequeathed by Shaw to the British Museum and to the British Library of Political and Economic Science—is entirely new and hitherto unpublished material.

In addition to the work of selection, editing, and arrangement, I have provided commentary wherever I have felt it necessary, in an endeavour not only to relate the material to the earlier book which gave rise to it, but to assist the reader to the best of my ability towards a clearer appreciation and understanding of Shaw's fascinating, but at times highly complex personality. This particularly (but not exclusively) applies to the second half of this book where—after Shaw has been given a full opportunity (in the first half) of stating his basic beliefs and general views on a variety of important subjects—an opportunity is taken of examining specific details more closely, and, as far as possible, analysing, criticising, and drawing conclusions from them.

My overall endeavour has been to bring Shaw vividly to life for the reader. To this end I have drawn on his spoken words as well as on his written ones. In verbatim reports of speeches I have retained all the original style and interpolations, such as: '(Cries of "Hear, hear")' and '(Loud applause)', and something also of the Chairman's remarks, and of the questions and heckling at the end. I have specifically avoided the modern editorial practice, examples of which I have occasionally seen, of partly re-phrasing and re-writing reports of speeches into a 'literary' form prior to publication in a book, as this garbling, as I would call it, not only involves the real risk of altering the speaker's intended meaning, but the spontaneity and colloquial expressions of the actual language used are often lost in such a process—the impression gained by the reader being then merely of the subject's views in the abstract, rather than of him actually speaking and gesticulating on the platform.

In all quotations from Shaw's own writings I have followed his spelling and punctuation precisely—e.g. *labor* for labour, *-ize* instead of the more usual *-ise* in words such as anglicise. But in reports by other hands of Shaw's spoken words I have followed the forms used by the writers of the reports, and the same applies to invited contributions to this book, and to my own writing. Thus different spellings of the same word occasionally occur—sometimes even on the same page.

I hope above all that Shaw's abounding wit and humour, no less than his intellectual brilliance, will come through successfully in the following pages, and that at the conclusion the reader will have been entertained, as well as have gained a much clearer and more integrated picture of one of the most complex —though certainly very fascinating and quite unique— geniuses in literary history.

BERNARD SHAW'S PRINTED POSTCARDS
AND STOCK LETTER REPLIES

I propose to begin with the texts of Shaw's 30-odd 'printed postcards' and stereotyped letters—his stock answers to particularly frequent requests of various kinds from correspondents among the general public. These give, I think, some very interesting insights into Shaw's character and outlook. It will be seen that many of them say "No" to the correspondents' wishes, but it should be emphasised that, as Mrs Laden and other members of Shaw's household staff have testified, 'printed postcard' replies of a negative kind (refusals) certainly did not go to all who wrote to Shaw about the subjects with which they were concerned. There is no doubt that (according to testimony from other quarters also) Shaw sent gifts of money and donations to many private individuals, whether he knew them personally or not, and to some institutions, and was constantly giving way to requests of every kind (including, even at the great age of 94, that of a certain persistent young photographer and admirer!). Shaw received a huge mail every day, and invariably had the courtesy to read every communication and acknowledge all those which he felt merited an answer: sometimes by complying with requests, sometimes by replying at length (often in his own hand or typed and corrected by himself), but—understandably—more often by using one of the following printed replies. However, even when these were sent, Shaw often wrote the addresses himself, and not infrequently added some lines of personal message on them.

The following collection of 'printed postcards' (culled from various sources) is, to the best of my knowledge, a complete, or virtually complete one. The cards are of normal postcard size (except for a few on subjects such as Temperance, Capital Punishment, and Phonetic Reform, which are about $6\frac{1}{2} \times 4\frac{1}{2}$ inches). Some are white, but most of them are coloured red, green, blue, or yellow—as also are the 'stock reply' *letters* (on sheets of paper of varying size) which are also given here—following the postcards. In some instances Shaw altered the wording when ordering new supplies of a particular item, and such variations are given when they are of interest, but not in cases where only a word or two is changed.

PRINTED POSTCARDS.   (Early ones are given first):—

Until the end of October Mr and Mrs Bernard Shaw's address will be Pitfold, Haslemere, Surrey. Telegraph Office, Shottermill. Railway Station, Haslemere (Waterloo line), 1½ miles. Permanent London addresses as usual: Mrs Shaw at 10 Adelphi Terrace, W.C., and Mr Shaw at 29 Fitzroy Square, W. (Telegrams: 'Socialist, London.')

I am not a professional lecturer; and my work in London does not admit of frequent visits to the provinces. Except on special occasions, or when a course of Fabian lectures has been arranged through the Fabian Society, (through the Secretary, Mr Edward R. Pease, 3 Clement's Inn, London, W.C.). I seldom speak far from London.

I have received so many letters upon Common Sense About The War* that I have had to give up all hope of dealing with them separately. Even the very kind and entirely reassuring letters elicited by my protest in the *Daily Citizen†* must go unanswered. Many branches of the Independent Labor Party and other Liberal and Socialist organizations have passed resolutions which have been of the timeliest service to me publicly, and which have given me sincere personal gratification. In the hope of being able to write a separate letter in every case I have deferred my acknowledgements until it has become plain that I must make them in this fashion or not at all. It is the best I can do; and I rely on the same kindness that prompted the letters and resolutions to accept my thanks in this indiscriminate but very earnest form.

10 Adelphi Terrace,
   London, W.C.

---

*† The sensational pamphlet published in 1914 as a supplement to the *New Statesman*, and referred to by C. B. Purdom on page 197 of *Shaw the Villager*. Accounts of the substance of this pamphlet, and Shaw's protest in the *Daily Citizen*, appear later in the present volume when Shaw's views on war are given.

Please do not ask Mr Bernard Shaw for money. He has not enough to help the large number of his readers who are in urgent need of it. He can write for you: he cannot finance you.

4 Whitehall Court,
    London, S.W.1.

Mr Bernard Shaw regrets that he is unable to undertake any extra literary work at present. His time is filled up for months to come.

4 WHITEHALL COURT, LONDON, S.W.1.
Phone: WHITEHALL 3160.
Telegrams: SOCIALIST, PARL-LONDON.

Mr Bernard Shaw is engaged in heavy literary tasks which he cannot hope to finish in time (or at all) unless he resolutely abstains from private correspondence in the meantime. He is always glad to receive interesting letters; but he must not answer them. He therefore begs you to forgive him if any communication of yours has elicited no response: the sole reason is that given above.

4 Whitehall Court (130)
    London, S.W.1.

Mr Bernard Shaw is frequently asked to read literary manuscripts or unperformed plays and pass judgement on them. As he is not and never has been employed by publishers or theatre managers to do this, his opinion could be of no service to authors, and, even if favorable, might prejudice their chances seriously. He is there-fore obliged, in their interests no less than his own, to rule out all such activities.* They are no part of his business; and he has no leisure to spare for them.

Ayot Saint Lawrence,
    Welwyn, Herts.

Mr Bernard Shaw is often asked to contribute prefaces to unpublished works. Sometimes the applicants add that a few words will be sufficient. This obliges him to call attention to the fact that his prefaces owe their value in the literary market to the established

---

* Another version reads: 'obliged . . . to make it a rule to read published books only.'

expectation of book purchasers that they will prove substantial and important works in themselves. The disappointment of this expectation in a single instance would destroy that value. A request for a preface by him is therefore a request for a gift of some months of hard professional work. When this is appreciated it will be seen that even with the best disposition towards his correspondents it is not possible for Mr. Shaw to oblige them in this particular manner.

4 Whitehall Court (130)
    London, S.W.1.

It is impossible for Mr Bernard Shaw to relieve individual cases of hardship. Nor can he finance elementary schools and churches. There are too many of them. His donations go to undenominational Public Bodies.

Ayot Saint Lawrence
    Welwyn, Herts.

Mr Bernard Shaw receives daily a mass of appeals from charitable institutions, religious sects and Churches, inventors, Utopian writers desirous of establishing international millennial leagues, parents unable to afford secondary education for their children: in short, everybody and every enterprise in financial straits of any sort.

All these appeals are founded on the notion that Mr Shaw is a multi-millionaire. The writers apparently do not know that all his income except hardly enough to meet his permanent engagements is confiscated by the Exchequer and redistributed to those with smaller taxfree incomes or applied to general purposes by which everyone benefits.

Clearly Mr. Shaw's correspondents cannot have his income both ways: in cash from himself and in services from the State. He does not complain of this system, having advocated it for more than half a century, and nationalized all his landed property; but now that it is in active and increasing operation it is useless to ask him for money: he has none to spare.

He begs to be excused accordingly. No other reply to appeals is possible.

Ayot Saint Lawrence,
    Welwyn, Herts.

Mr Bernard Shaw is often requested by correspondents not personally known to him to inscribe his name in copies of his books which they offer to send for that purpose. No doubt many of the requests are made in good faith and appreciated by him as such. But if he were to comply he would be immediately overwhelmed by applications from speculators anxious to get rich quickly by purchasing his books at shop prices and selling them at the fancy prices which autographed copies command. He is therefore obliged to reserve his autograph for volumes which are his spontaneous personal gift, and begs you to excuse him accordingly.

Ayot Saint Lawrence,
    Welwyn, Herts.

It may interest collectors of autographs to know that Mr Bernard Shaw does not regard requests by strangers for his signature as legitimate collecting. He signs enough genuine documents every day to give collectors ample material for the proper exercise of their peculiar industry.* His secretary has instructions to return all albums and refuse all applications which ignore this distinction.†‡

4 Whitehall Court (130),
    London, S.W.1.

Bernard Shaw's books and plays, being on sale in his own editions and subject to various publishing contracts, are not available for anthologies or school editions.

Forthcoming works of his are never serialized, nor extracts from them communicated to the Press in advance of their publication.

---

* Another version reads: ". . . Mr Bernard Shaw does not regard unsportsmanlike requests by strangers to forge his own signature for their benefit legitimate collecting. . ."

† Shaw once replied to a youthful autograph hunting admirer : "Don't waste your time in collecting other people's autographs, my boy. Devote it to making your *own* autograph worth collecting!"

‡ The *Yorkshire Evening Post* of 18th August, 1915, reports how a postcard from G.B.S. was found on the battlefield at the Dardanelles after a charge. It read: "A man who goes on calmly hunting autographs with all civilization crumbling around him, and the Turkish enemy not far below the horizon, really deserves to succeed. So here goes. G. Bernard Shaw."

His plays may not be broadcast nor televised until many stage performances of them in their original form have made them familiar to playgoers.

Ayot Saint Lawrence,
   Welwyn, Herts.

The Copyright Act, 1911.

Clause 2. Copyright in a work shall be deemed to be infringed by any person who without consent of the owner of the copyright does anything the sole right to do which is by this Act conferred on the owner of the copyright.

PROVIDED that the following shall not constitute an infringement of copyright.

(i) Any fair dealing with any work for the purpose of private study, research, criticism, review, or newspaper summary.

(iv) The publication in a collection, mainly composed of non-copyright matter bona fide intended for the use of schools. . . . Provided that not more than two of such passages from works by the same author are published by the same publisher within five years.

(v) The publication in a newspaper of a report of a lecture delivered in public.

Private domestic and school class performances of plays are also privileged; but if numerous spectators are invited to witness them in large buildings they may damage the Author. Admission without payment is not a valid defence in such legal action as may ensue.

Mr Bernard Shaw has neither power nor desire to restrain the fullest exercise of these statutory privileges; therefore he begs writers, publishers, managers and others not to ask him for unnecessary authorizations. His contracts with his publishers, existing and potential, prevent him from extending them.

AYOT SAINT LAWRENCE,
   WELWYN, HERTS.

Mr Bernard Shaw, though he is always glad to receive interesting letters or books, seldom has time to acknowledge them; for his correspondence has increased to such an extent that he must either give up writing private letters or give up writing anything else. Under

the circumstances he hopes that writers of unanswered letters and
unthanked friendly donors of books and other presents will forgive
him.
Ayot Saint Lawrence,
    Welwyn, Herts.

Mr Bernard [sic] implores his friends and readers not to celebrate
his birthdays nor even to mention them to him. It is easy to write
one letter or send one birthday cake; but the arrival of hundreds of
them together is a calamity that is not the less dreaded because it
occurs only once a year.
    Acknowledgement of such unwelcome letters and gifts is not
possible.
Ayot Saint Lawrence,
    Welwyn, Herts.

Mr Bernard Shaw has long since been obliged by advancing years
to retire from his committees and his personal activities on the
platform. He therefore begs secretaries of societies to strike his
name from their lists of available speakers. Mr Shaw does not open
exhibitions or bazaars, take the chair, speak at public dinners, give
his name as vice-president or patron, make appeals for money on
behalf of hospitals or "good causes" (however deserving), nor do
any ceremonial public work. Neither can he take part in new
movements nor contribute to the first numbers of new magazines.
He begs his correspondents to excuse him accordingly.*
Ayot Saint Lawrence
    Welwyn, Herts.

Mr Bernard Shaw is obliged to remind correspondents who seek
to interview him for publication that as he is himself a professional
journalist, he naturally prefers to communicate with the public
through the Press at first hand. He is willing, when time permits, to
answer written questions when they happen to be interesting as
current news *and can be answered in twenty words or less.*†

---

* The ending of this card is different from the two other versions of it
given by Mrs Tuke on pages 136 and 137 of *Shaw the Villager.*
    † An earlier version of this card contains no such limit, and Mr Shaw
received personal visits "only on the understanding that his conversation
is not to be reported."

Please do not ask Mr. Bernard Shaw for money. He has not enough to help the large number of his readers who are in urgent need of it. He can write for you : he cannot finance you.

4 Whitehall Court, London, S.W.1.

An early example

Mr. Bernard Shaw's readers, playgoers, and fans number many thousands. The little time remaining to him in his extreme old age is fully occupied with his literary work and the business it involves ; and war taxation has set narrow limits to his financial resources. He has therefore to print the following intimations.

He will not deal with individual grievances nor answer requests for money, autographs, signed photographs, nor sittings for his portrait in any medium.

He will not read long letters in manuscript. Only postcards and brief typewritten letters (not too autobiographical) have any chance of being read by him.

He will not discuss his published views in private letters.

He will not advise literary beginners nor read their unpublished works. They can study the Writers and Artists Year Book. The Society of Authors and the Institute of Journalists are open to them. Several Schools of Journalism are available. Mr. Shaw's time is not.

He no longer receives visitors at his private residence except from his intimate friends.

He will not send Messages for publication.

He begs to be excused accordingly.

Ayot Saint Lawrence,
Welwyn, Herts.

A later one in similar vein

Questions that require answers at greater length should be accompanied by an offer of a fee of not less than three figures.

Inexperienced editors who imagine that their fortunes are made if they can obtain a contribution from a celebrity should consider that as nobody will buy a periodical on the off chance of its containing such a contribution perhaps once a year or so, only a permanent staff of writers capable of ensuring that every number will contain something topical and readable can make a magazine a success.

Ayot Saint Lawrence,
   Welwyn, Herts.

Mr Bernard Shaw's readers, playgoers and fans number many thousands. The little time remaining to him in his extreme old age is fully occupied with his literary work and the business it involves; and war taxation has set narrow limits to his financial resources. He has therefore to print the following intimations.

He will not deal with individual grievances nor answer requests for money, autographs, signed photographs, nor sittings for his portrait in any medium.*

He will not read long letters in manuscript. Only postcards and brief typewritten letters (not too autobiographical) have any chance of being read by him.

He will not discuss his published views in private letters.

He will not advise literary beginners nor read their unpublished works. They can study the Writers and Artists Year Book. The Society of Authors and the Institute of Journalists are open to them. Several Schools of Journalism are available. Mr Shaw's time is not.

He no longer receives visitors† at his private residence except from his intimate friends.

---

* In an earlier version is added, 'He cannot finance schools and churches. His donations go to undenominational public bodies, and his charities to the Royal Society of Literature.' And the word 'age' is not preceded by the word 'extreme' in the second line. Also, one or two lines are omitted.

† I am grateful to Mr Frank Gerrard of Kings Norton, Birmingham, for pointing out what appears to be a rare instance of a grammatical error passing Mr Shaw's vigilance, for 'visits' would appear to have been intended rather than 'visitors' here. On the other hand, Shaw may have had in mind visitors sent by, or introduced by, his intimate friends.

He will not send Messages for publication.

He begs to be excused accordingly.

Ayot Saint Lawrence,
  Welwyn, Herts.

Please note that Bernard Shaw's plays, books and copyrights generally can be dealt with by THE INCORPORATED SOCIETY OF AUTHORS at 84 Drayton Gardens, London, S.W.10 (Telephone Freemantle 6642/3) to which all inquiries and applications for licences to perform may be addressed and performing fees paid. Dates and places of contemplated performances must be precisely specified in all applications. Box office returns showing the receipts at each performance should accompany payments.*

Ayot Saint Lawrence,
  Welwyn, Herts.

VEGETARIAN DIET

Mr Shaw's correspondents are reminded that current vegetarianism does not mean living wholly on vegetables. Vegetarians eat cheese, butter, honey, eggs, and, on occasion, cod liver oil.

On this diet, without tasting fish, flesh, or fowl, Mr Shaw has reached the age of 92 (1948) in as good condition as his meat eating contemporaries. It is beyond question that persons who have never from their birth been fed otherwise than as vegetarians are at no disadvantage, mentally, physically, nor in duration of life, with their carnivorous fellow-citizens.

Nevertheless Mr Shaw is of opinion that his diet included an excess of protein. Until he was seventy he accumulated some poison that exploded every month or six weeks in a headache that blew it off and left him quite well after disabling him for a day. He tried every available treatment to get rid of the headaches: all quite unsuccessful. He now makes uncooked vegetables, chopped or grated, and their juices, with fruit, the staple of his diet, and finds it markedly better than the old high protein diet of beans, lentils and macaroni.

His objection to carnivorous diet is partly aesthetic, partly hygienic, mainly as involving an unnecessary waste of the labor of

* A paragraph referring to Shaw's Australian and South African agents on this card has been omitted as it is no longer applicable and might have been misleading. There was, in fact, another version of this card omitting it.

masses of mankind in the nurture and slaughter of cattle, poultry, and fish for human food.

He has no objection to the slaughter of animals as such. He knows that if we do not kill animals they will kill us. Squirrels, foxes, rabbits, tigers, cobras, locusts, white ants, rats, mosquitoes, fleas, and deer must be continually slain even to extermination by vegetarians as ruthlessly as by meat eaters.* But he urges humane killing and does not enjoy it as a sport.†

Ayot Saint Lawrence,
    Welwyn, Herts.

BERNARD SHAW ON TEMPERANCE

The Temperance question has many sides. As a professional author and playwright I have found by experimenting on myself that a single glass of wine reduces my self-criticism to such a degree that when writing "under the influence" I let several sentences pass as final where when sober I should let perhaps two. I find this out when the proofs come to be corrected and reconsidered. I have known journalists who, beginning by being unable or unwilling to write an article without a drink, have ended by being unable to write a sentence without one, though they at last loathed the habit that enslaved them. I conclude that in literary work only teetotallers can produce the best and sanest of which they are capable.

* The previous year's version of this card continues at this point:—
". . . by meat eaters. So should incorrigible criminals, dangerous lunatics, and idiots. He therefore advocates the exercise and public organization of the powers of life and death necessary to civilization, but never retaliatory punishment, expiatory sacrifice, or deterrent. The operation should never be avoidably cruel.
"As Mr Shaw reached the age of 82 before he experimented with liver injections after 50 years without eating flesh, fish, and fowl, the inference that his diet was insufficient is silly. He had already lived longer than most meat eaters, and is still (1947) alive. He experiments freely with new biochemical foods, whether they are animal, vegetable, or mineral."

† In a letter dated August 15th, 1946, addressed to G. H. Sanders, of South Yarmouth, Mass., and headed 'Not Private. Quote by all means', Shaw adds: "I have not eaten fish, flesh or fowl for 65 years past. I eat eggs very seldom and not much milk; . . . I have my potatoes baked. I do not smoke nor drink tea, alcoholic stimulants and narcotics; but lately I have taken a little mild coffee, at breakfast—I claim nothing for this diet except that it has kept me alive quite as effectively as a meat diet which costs more and involves an enormous slavery of man to animals and much cruelty and suffering, though the animals owe their lives to it."

Now very few workers ever do their best. Their second or third best is good enough for their job. Only the leaders and geniuses need do their utmost; and the necessary proportion of these in the population is no more than five per cent or thereabouts. An army of Napoleons, a fleet of Nelsons, an industry of Carnegies would be as impossible as an army without generals, a fleet without admirals, and an industry without directors. And without a ration of beer or rum a soldier or marine may become a mutineer, and the labourers strike in spite of their trade unions.

Then there is the hard fact that geniuses can overdraw on their vital capital by dosing themselves with brandy. Ataturk saved Turkish civilization in this way whilst the abstemious Hitler wrecked Germany. Edmund Kean, Frederick Robson,* Charles Dickens (on his American tour which killed him) lived on fiery stimulants. It brought them supreme professional fame called Immortality; but they died before they were 60.

Then we have the soakers, who are never drunk nor ever sober, and live mainly on whisky, of which they consume every day enough to keep me comfortably drunk for a week. We need go no farther than the House of Commons to see what eminence can be attained by veteran soakers, the successors of the gout ridden port wine drunkards of the eighteenth century.

Note also the kindly husbands and wives who are jolly and amiable as dipsomaniacs, but so miserable, quarrelsome, and unbearable without their drams that when they are persuaded to take the pledge their spouses have to set them drinking again to endure life with them.

I wrote many years ago that drink is the chloroform that enables the poor to endure the painful operation of living. The failure of Prohibition has since proved that compulsory abstinence is impracticable. We must first get rid of poverty, and make reasonable happiness possible without anaesthetics.

Meanwhile let the Temperance Societies impress on us that the need for stimulants is a symptom of low vitality of which men should be ashamed instead of glorying in its imaginary virility.

---

* The greatest actor of his day in comedy and burlesque (at the old Olympic Theatre and others). He died at the age of 42 as the result of drink and 'irregular living'.

BERNARD SHAW ON CAPITAL PUNISHMENT

In reply to many enquiries as to his views on this subject Bernard Shaw has made the following statement.

There are three questions at issue. (1) Is punishment a necessary or desirable institution? (2) Is the killing of human beings a necessary practice? (3) If it is, what is the best method of execution?

(1) Punishment should be completely discarded on the simple ground that two blacks do not make a white.

(2) If we find a hungry tiger at large or a cobra in the garden, we do not punish it. We kill it because, if we do not, it will kill us. Fleas, lice, locusts, white ants, anophele mosquitos, Australian rabbits, must be exterminated, not punished. Precisely the same necessity arises in the case of incorrigibly dangerous or mischievous human beings, sane or insane, hopeless idiots, and enemy soldiers.

(3) The kindest method so far known is to let criminals go to bed and to sleep as usual, and then turn on an odorless gas to prevent them ever waking. Enemy soldiers we have to kill how we can.

REMARKS TO BEAR IN MIND

If criminals can be reformed, reform them: that is all.

Many persons: for instance, children, soldiers, and well-behaved prisoners, are useful citizens under tutelage, with their food, clothes, and lodging found for them. Set free, they are unable to take care of themselves, and are presently in the dock for some offence, grave or petty. They should be kept under kindly tutelage, guided and provided for as children are, but otherwise living normal and respected lives.

The official theory of punishment is that it is deterrent. The objection to this is that it makes it the first business of the detective police when a crime is committed to make sure that somebody is punished, guilty or innocent, hanging the wrong man being as deterrent as hanging the right one. All police cases are therefore under suspicion of being "frame-ups."

Most objectors to capital punishment are actuated only by aversion to death as such. They sign petitions for the reprieve of every murderer, however villainous; but when the Home Secretary changes the sentence to one of life imprisonment, a horribly cruel alternative, they are quite satisfied, and forget all about it.

Executions should be kindly and apologetic. The knout, the cat, the gallows, the axe, the stake, the wheel, the guillotine, the garotte, the electric chair, are all psychologically mischievous, provoking imitations of them by hysterical adolescents, and making the tenderhearted sympathize with the criminal. Killing should never be made a sport or a spectacle. There is nobody on earth who will not kill a flea; and only vegetarians will not kill for food.

Revenge, officially bowdlerized as Retribution, is natural to us: but it is ruled out as an evil passion by Christian civilization, involving as it does the horror of a State service of merciless tormentors, including warders and wardresses, hardly more free than their prisoners, having their lives wasted in vindictive cruelty.*

AYOT SAINT LAWRENCE, WELWYN, HERTS.

* Bernard Shaw interestingly qualified his views on this important subject, as expressed in the above postcard, in a letter to *The Times* on December 5th, 1947, from which the following quotation is taken.

Had not the ambiguous and confusing terms capital punishment and death penalty better be dropped? The public right and power of civilized States to kill the unprofitable or incorrigibly mischievous in self-defence can never be abrogated. Were it abolished verbally it would be restored or evaded by martial law in the next emergency. Punishment is a different matter. It should be got rid of altogether on the simple ground that two blacks do not make a white, to say nothing of the fact that criminals cannot help their nature and that retaliation is flatly unChristian. Why not call the subject judicial homicide, or, to avoid unpleasant associations, judicial liquidation? It would clear our minds, now so confused that discussion seems hopeless.

As to deterrence, there are insuperable objections to it. It must be cruel or it will not deter. It is effective only when detection is certain. This could be secured only by providing a police officer to watch every citizen, which is impossible. And it involves the very undesirable consequence that when a crime is committed it does not matter who is punished provided somebody is punished. The police are not impartial. They must do everything in their power to obtain a conviction. As one of Dickens's characters put it, 'Much better hang the wrong fellow than no fellow.'

Criminals should be liquidated humanely, not because they are wicked, but because they are mischievous or dangerous. A vitriol thrower should be got rid of as ruthlessly as a cobra or mad dog. A man who lives by promising to marry women and deserting them as soon as he has spent all their money is a social weed to be uprooted no less than if he drowned them in their baths. Dangerous insanity, instead of exempting from liquidation, should be one of the strongest grounds for it.

To simply ostracize liquidation as something that is "not done" is not humane when the alternative is long deterrent imprisonment, involving

[Continued at foot of next two pages

On the subject of phonetic spelling Mr Bernard Shaw is convinced on two points. A. That the only argument strong enough to carry its adoption is its enormous saving of labor in writing, typing, printing, paper making and in wear and tear of machinery. The cost of spelling one sound with two letters is so prodigious that the initial cost of substituting a phonetic alphabet capable of representing every single sound in English Speech by a single letter is negligible in comparison. B. As phonetic spelling with our alphabet is impossible without a very frequent indication of one sound by two letters, all attempts at it must be ruled out on economic grounds alone, to say nothing of the impressions of illiterate misspelling which they make on educated people.

Innumerable schemes for spelling English phonetically with the old ABC, repeating the same stale arguments and proposing the same changes, come from people who imagine them to be epoch making novelties. Such schemes should not be sent to Mr Shaw, who is finally opposed to any tampering with the old alphabet, and is interested only in the introduction of a New English alphabet containing between 40 and 50 new letters, to be used and taught concurrently with the old alphabet until one or the other proves the fitter to survive.

Ayot Saint Lawrence,
    Welwyn, Herts.

FROM

BERNARD SHAW

A FORTY LETTER BRITISH ALFABET

The number of letters in our Johnsonese alfabet, minus *x*, *c*, and *q* (unnecessary) is	23
The following consonants are missing: *sh*, *zh*, *wh*, *ch*, *th*, *dh*, and *ng*	7
Also missing are the vowels and diphthongs *ah*, *aw*, *at*, *et*, *it*, *ot*, *ut*, *oot*, *yoot*, and the neutral second vowel in *colour*, *labour*, *honor*, &c.	10
	40

the waste of man and woman power by staffs of tormentors and maintenance of prisons. At present our death dreaders are quite satisfied when a murderer is reprieved. If they were really humane it would horrify them.

[Continued at foot of next page.

A quite phonetic British alfabet is impossible because the vowels of British speakers differ as their finger prints do; but the 40 sounds listed above will make them as intelligible to one another in writing as they now are in speech. Thus, though Oxford graduates and London costermongers pronounce son and sun as *san* and Ireland as Awlnd, they understand one another in conversation.

In Johnsonese the missing letters are indicated by using two or three letters for a single sound. For instance, *though* has six letters for two sounds. A 40 letter alfabet providing one unambiguous symbol for each sound would save manual labor at the rate of 25 per cent. per minute (131,400 per annum). Multiply this figure by the millions at every moment busy writing English somewhere in the world, and the total saving is so prodigious that the utmost cost of a change is negligible.

Children who now have to master the multiplication and pence tables, could learn a 40 letter alfabet easily. Johnsonese is so full of inconsistencies that the few who can spell it do so not by the sound of the word but by the look of it.

Ayot Saint Lawrence,
    Welwyn, Herts.

Mr Bernard Shaw's Appeal for a British Alphabet

My appeal to existing Government Departments, Colleges, Trusts, Societies, and other relevant agencies to undertake the production of a British alphabet has failed. The need has not been questioned; but the replies are to the same effect: try elsewhere: it is not our job. As, having called attention to its enormous economic importance, and offered to aid its implementation financially, I am far too old and preoccupied to take the work in hand myself, I have finished my part in it by bequeathing to the Public Trustee the means of financing any qualified and responsible body, corporate or individual, which will take certain defined steps in its direction. These steps are, in brief, the designing of an alphabet capable of

---

What is greatly needed is an institution to deal with people who, under tutelage, discipline, and support (like soldiers and "good" prisoners) are well behaved and useful citizens, but when left to their own resources are presently in the dock or helpless on the street as beggars.

representing at least the 42 sounds of English speech, as listed by the late eminent phonetic expert, Henry Sweet, without using more than one letter for each sound, and finally the transliteration and publication of a few English classics, including two of my own plays, in the new characters. Should this bequest have no effect within twenty years following my death, or be made superfluous, as it should be, by government action, my residuary estate will be administered in other public directions.

The matter is now disposed of as far as I am concerned.

G.B.S.

Ayot Saint Lawrence,
   Welwyn,
      Herts.
         13/9/1944.

In addition, here are the texts of two postcard 'stock replies' drafted by Shaw (in his own version of Pitman's shorthand) but never actually printed:—

MODEL POSTCARD—IRELAND

Mr Bernard Shaw takes no sides in Irish party politics. He has repeatedly declared his conviction that Ulster Protestant Capitalism, which will never yield to Southern Republican agitation, will undo Partition when it is outvoted by organized labor, and can fortify itself against Socialism only by an alliance with the agricultural proprietors of Eire.

MODEL POSTCARD ON RUSSIA

Big political changes are never accomplished without coercive atrocities on both sides.

The rule of the foreigner is more impartial than self-government. Liberation from it is more violently dictatorial than any occupying ruler would dare to be.

These are not opinions. They are facts of human nature, no more [nor less] true in Russia than elsewhere, Russians being only men and women, not angels.

You must accept them as you must accept hailstorms, choosing your political principles accordingly, atrocities or no atrocities.

The following message was not issued by Shaw as a postcard but published by him in the 'Personal' column of *The Times*. Its form, however, is comparable to that of his printed postcards, and I therefore include it here.

MR BERNARD SHAW has received such a prodigious mass of letters on the occasion of his wife's death that, though he has read and values them all, any attempt to acknowledge them individually is beyond his powers. He therefore begs his friends and hers to be content with this omnibus reply, and to assure them that a very happy ending to a very long life has left him awaiting his own turn in perfect serenity.

PRINTED LETTERS:—

Finally, where the message was too long to go on a postcard, Shaw sent his 'stock answer' in the form of a printed *letter*:—

ON VACCINATION

[A letter originally sent individually to Charles Gane, a leader of the National Anti-Vaccination League, which Shaw subsequently had printed for general distribution as an 'open letter'.]

10 ADELPHI TERRACE,
W.C.
22nd February, 1906.

Dear Sir,

... I cannot help thinking that the time is not far off when the work of your League will be lightened by the co-operation of the leaders of bacteriological therapeutics. For years past the strain of countenancing a proceeding so grossly reckless, dirty, and dangerous as vaccination from the calf, has been growing unbearable to all genuine bacteriological experts. The utmost that professional pressure has been able to extort from them of late is silence; but their disgust will soon become too intense for silence. Mrs Squeers's method of opening abscesses with an inky penknife is far less repugnant to modern surgeons than the Local Government Board's method of inoculating children with casual dirt moistened with an undefined pathogenic substance obtained from calves is to modern bacteriologists. Nothing but the natural ignorance of the public, countenanced by the inculcated erroneousness of the ordinary medical general practitioner, makes such a barbarism as vaccination possible. The question whether it is practicable to fortify the blood against disease by inoculations is still an open and very interesting one. Its recent developments have shewn that an inoculation made in the usual general practitioner's light-hearted way, without a previous highly skilled examination of the state of the patient's blood, is just as likely to be a simple manslaughter as a cure or preventive. But vaccination is really nothing short of attempted murder. A skilled bacteriologist would as soon think of cutting his child's arm and rubbing the contents of the dustpan into the wound as vaccinating it in the official way. The results would be exactly the same. They *are* exactly the same.*

You cannot urge too insistently that even if the modern serum treatment not only justified itself tomorrow, but could be made practicable on a large scale instead of as a laboratory experiment, the objection to vaccination as a quite infamously careless and ignorant method of inoculation would become more obvious than ever.

Yours faithfully,
G. BERNARD SHAW.

To CHARLES GANE,
   NATIONAL ANTI-VACCINATION LEAGUE,
     S.W.

[ON PUNCTUATION, LITERARY STYLE, AND PUBLIC SPEAKING]

from

BERNARD SHAW

The most profusely punctuated book in the English language is the Bible; but it is not consistently grammatical, and mixes semicolons and colons, and ors and nors in the same verse. The worst punctuator in the world was Sheridan, who had only one stop: a dash. There is no established practice. Few authors get as far as the colon.

---

* They are *not*, Mr Shaw ! The former would infect with disease; the latter has been proved to prevent disease, and most successfully.

In my own practice a semicolon comes before a conjunction when the nominative changes or is repeated, and a comma when it does not. "He was drunk, but not disorderly." "He was drunk; but his brother was sober."

The Bible translators sometimes follow this purely grammatical rule, but often substituted a colon, which I use artistically rather than grammatically. I use the semi-colon not only when the nominative is changed but when it is repeated. "Thou shalt not take the name of the Lord thy God in vain; for the Lord will not hold him guiltless that taketh his name in vain."

Punctuation is mostly idiosyncratic: there are no rules of thumb for children such as "A conjunction is always preceded by any stop or no stop." But it is advisable that a writer's practice should be consistent, so that anyone reading aloud at first sight can foresee how the sentence is going to turn. Playwrights especially must see to this, as their lines are meant to be spoken.*

Ayot Saint Lawrence,

Welwyn, Herts.

---

* It will have been noted that Shaw dropped the apostrophe when writing such words as *cant* and *dont*.

Some other punctuation rules sent by Shaw to a friend in 1919 are quoted by Dr Loewenstein in *John O' London's Weekly*, February 4th, 1949, and may be of interest here. To wit:—

, precedes "and" when the nominative is unchanged.

; precedes "and" when there is a fresh nominative, or the previous nominative is repeated.

; precedes "but", "for", "yet", "still", "only", "hence", when they begin qualifications or explanations or contradictions or contingent statements with a fresh nominative.

: precedes "namely", "that is", "i.e.", or a list. Ex.: There were six brothers: John, James, Jerry, Jabez, Jaffer and Jenkins.

: never precedes "and". When one phrase confirms, repeats, or flatly contradicts another, it is preceded by a colon. Ex.: "Bob was the photographer of the party: all the Pole films were taken by him." "Paul did not make the Antarctic films: he never took a photograph in his life."

Compare the semicolon—"John exposed the plates; and Paul touched up the negatives."

Compare the comma—"Paul touched up the negatives, and faked the prints." This comma is not indispensable; but strictly its absence would imply that Paul touched up the negatives *and* something else.

() make a parenthesis. [ ] make an interpolation by a quoter in a quotation.   [Continued at foot of next two pages.

Shaw published twelve hundred copies in March, 1947, of the following 'open letter' on further aspects of his views on phonetics:

COLOSSAL LABOR SAVING

An open letter

from

BERNARD SHAW

Simplified Spelling has been advocated for 100 years without producing the smallest effect. To waste another moment on it seems to me perverse indifference to hard fact. People will not accept a spelling that looks illiterate. To spell English phonetically within the limits of a 26-letter alphabet is impossible. A British alphabet must have at least 44 letters; and though the addition of 19 new letters to Dr Johnson's stock would distinguish it from illiterate spelling the result would not be Simplified Spelling.

What hinders a change is its apparent enormous cost. Only one answer can overcome this hesitation. In any fair and simple test between two experts copying the same text for a minute in Johnsonese and in phonetic, the times saved by phonetic will come out round about 20% as stated by our phoneticians. Such a figure impresses nobody: we might as well attempt to move Mont Blanc with an egg spoon. But the figure is wrong: it leaves out the time factor. We are used to read per cent. as per cent. per year; but in the

---

On his own literary style Shaw had this to say in an interview in *The Candid Friend* of May 11th, 1901 (as reprinted—slightly modified—in his *Sixteen Self Sketches* in 1949):—

I never felt inclined to write, any more than to breathe. It never occurred to me that my literary sense was exceptional: I gave everyone credit for it; for there is nothing miraculous in a natural faculty to the man who has it. In art the amateur, the collector, the enthusiast, is the man who lacks the faculty for producing it. The Venetian wants to be a cavalry soldier; the Gaucho wants to be a sailor; the fish wants to fly and the bird to swim. I never wanted to write. I know now, of course, the scarcity of literary faculty; but I still dont want it. You cannot want a thing and have it, too.

And no more excellent guidance for others can ever be given than his magnificent statement in the preface to *Man and Superman*:—

Effectiveness of assertion is the alpha and omega of style. He who has nothing to assert has no style and can have none: he who has something

[Continued at foot of next page.

test per cent. is per cent. per minute. Now there are 525,000 minutes in a year; consequently the saving of 20% per minute means a labor saving of two months' working days per scribe every year. Multiply this figure by an estimate of the number of persons who at every moment of the 24 hours are writing the English language in the British Commonwealth and in America, and the total is astronomical. The mere suggestion of it is enough to sweep away the notion that we cannot afford the change. On the contrary, we cannot afford to postpone it for five minutes.

As far as I know, this overwhelming calculation has never before been presented. I arrived at it by considering the saving of manual labor to myself as an author by using Pitman's phonetic alphabet instead of Johnson's. I have done it so for the last fifty years, ever since I could afford a secretary-typist who could read Pitman.

I reflected on the number of plays Shakespear would have had time to write if he had written them in the phonetic alphabets of Pitman, Sweet, or Gregg, and on the staggering fact that Dickens, though a professional verbatim reporter, had to go through the drudgery of writing all his novels in Johnsonese longhand for the printer.

Why could Dickens not have used his shorthand as I used Pitman? Because Pitman, like Sweet and Gregg, corrupted their scripts into codes for vebatim reporting, which is phonetically impossible, as

---

to assert will go as far in power of style as its momentousness and his conviction will carry him. Disprove his assertion after it is made, yet its style remains. Darwin has no more destroyed the style of Job nor of Handel than Martin Luther destroyed the style of Giotto. All the assertions get disproved sooner or later; and so we find the world full of magnificent débris of artistic fossils with the matter-of-fact credibility gone clean out of them, but the form still splendid. And that is why the old masters play the deuce with our mere susceptibilities.

With regard to public speaking, Shaw tells us in *Sixteen Self Sketches*:—

I became acquainted with old Richard Deck, superannuated Alsatian *basso profundo* opera singer, . . . being a pupil of Delsarte, he taught me that to be intelligible in public the speaker must relearn the alphabet with every consonant separately and explosively articulated, and foreign vowels distinguished from British diphthongs. Accordingly I practised the alphabet as a singer practises scales until I was in no danger of saying "Loheeryelentheethisharpointed sword" instead of "Lo here *I l*end *th*ee *th*iss *sh*arp *p*ointed sword".

men speak faster than they can write, and therefore have to be reported
not by phonetic alphabets but by scrawls on paper which the reporter
has come to associate with a few thousand words and phrases after
years of practice. Such scrawls vary enough to be illegible by anyone
but the reporter, and not always by him or her after the speech
fades from memory. You have only to glance at the final chapters of
the manuals of Pitman, Sweet, and Gregg to see that their contractions and grammalogues and "word signs" have abandoned all
pretence of spelling, and cannot be read, or even guessed, by readers
who know thoroughly the alphabets on which they are founded,
and which can be mastered in a month. Sweet, after seven years'
work at his shorthand, came to believe that anyone who could not
guess a word from a single one of its vowels must be mentally
defective. I once received a letter written in it. It took me two months
to decipher it, though I knew every letter in Sweet's alphabet.

Shorthand verbatim reporting must therefore be left out of the
question. My own speed as an author having to think as I write I
estimate at 12 words a minute, year in and year out; but to save the
manual labor of writing such a sentence as *the kneeling knight thought
he knew* with 17 letters instead of 30 I would go to any length.
What a phonetic alphabet must save is manual labor, no matter
whether it is written at 12 words a minute or 200.

Why not solve the problem as I have solved it for myself by using
the existing phonetic alphabets without reporting contractions?
They all have the requisite 40-odd letters. I recommend all authors
to do this; but it has all to be rewritten by the typist for the printer
in Johnsonese. Besides, they are not graphic enough, not handsome
enough, use vertical and horizontal strokes not writeable *currente
calamo*, and have only a pretence of the sixteen indispensable vowels.
A page of the new alphabet should be as handsome as a page set
by Jensen or Morris, or a page of the Chantilly psalter. Ugly books
would damn any alphabet.

As to teaching children writing and spelling, I urged a Minister
of Education to allow and encourage them to spell phonetically,
just as they speak, which would enable teachers to detect their
mispronunciations and correct them. He replied that the slightest
hint at such a heresy would banish him from public life. Freedom
of spelling should be one of our slogans. If we could carry it into
the schools it would at once shew that phonetic spelling is impossible

with our alphabet. We must have at least 44 letters, and could do very well with some more for the double consonants.

The advocates of duodecimal arithmetic (mostly also phoneticians) have never used the labor saving argument which alone could move the world to add two new digits for 10 and 11 to our tables. When Poincaré devalued the French franc from tenpence to twopence, it was as if he made the astronomers give up light hours as units and count distances in centimetres; but nobody said a word against this monstrous addition to their manual labor of French accountancy, though there was plenty of protest against the dishonesty of the transaction. Our advantage through counting in pounds is enormous, and would be increased if we changed to duodecimals, compared to which the existing decimal notations are wasteful and inconvenient·

Phoneticians waste time and quarrel over their different plans for a universal language and for correct spelling. Complete phonetic spelling is impossible: Henry Sweet claimed that he could distinguish 11,000 sounds in spoken English; and I, as ex-chairman of the B.B.C. Committee for Spoken English, can testify that no two speakers have the same vowels any more than they have the same finger prints. But an alphabet of 11,000 letters is not necessary. Though we have as many different accents as there are millions of population, we can understand one another's speech and writing with an alphabet of 44 letters without the least difficulty; and as the sole purpose of speech and writing is to enable us to communicate with one another, 44 letters are enough.

There is still the question of foreign languages. Here we assume that it is necessary to write and speak these grammatically. On the contrary, we must abolish grammar to the least practical point. For example, Spanish would be an easy language to learn but for its irregular verbs. But why not regularize them? When a child says "I thinked you buyed me a doll" it is perfectly intelligible. What more is needed? When an English peasant says "I be, you be, we be, they be" we understand him quite as well as if he said "I am, you are, he is, we are, they are".

Already this simplification is in use in China and Australia as Pidgin, which will probably be the international language of the future. A thousand words of phonetically spelt Basic English, with a positive and negative of Okay and No Can, will make business easy between all nations without declensions, genders, tenses, conjugations, or what we call scholarship. The word pidgin is a Chinese attempt to pronounce our word business; and we owe its spread to the fact that English ousts its over-inflected rivals by its comparative freedom from grammar. What holds it back is the spelling forced on it by a Phenician alphabet with only five vowels instead of sixteen.

However, one thing at a time.

There need be no more discussion about spelling: the required 44 letters are established in all phonetic treatises and scripts. The reform must be conducted by politicians, statisticians, and mathematicians, with as assessors, printing engineers and possibly an author or two. The new alphabet must be designed by artist calligraphers.

As there will be immense benefit for everybody without reference to commercial profit or loss, the alphabet is clearly the business of the British Council at the public expense. The Council is now expressly charged with Basic English; but everything that can be done for this has already been done thoroughly by the Orthological Institute, leaving no further action possible except the provision of an alphabet in which Basic English can be intelligibly and economically spelt.

It is a hundred years since the first phoneticians did all they could for Spelling Reform, without the slightest success. The motive power must now come from the colossal labor saving figures, which are new. I have done what I can to draw attention to them; but this is a whole-time job for a reformer out for a success like that of Rowland Hill; and I, a super-annuated playwright and Victorian Fabian Sociologist, can only suggest. Perhaps it would suit you?

Faithfully,

G.B.S.

BERNARD SHAW'S PLAYS

TERMS AND CONDITIONS FOR PUBLIC PERFORMANCES

Procedure is by licence only and in no case involves any transfer of rights to the performer.

When the receipts exceed £300 (or $1500) the author's fee is 15 per cent. on the gross; when they exceed £100 (or $500) and do not exceed £300 (or $1500) 10 per cent. on the gross; when they exceed £50 (or $250) and do not exceed £100 (or $500) 7½ per cent. on the gross; and when they do not exceed £50 (or $250) 5 per cent. on the gross.   American managers will please note that this does not mean 5 per cent. on the first $250, 7½ per cent. on the next $250, etc., etc. The sliding scale is exactly as stated. It applies equally to repertory productions, to productions for runs and tours, and to all performances, whether amateur or professional, commercial or charitable, educational or artistic alike. Discounts can be arranged for short plays.

The above figures are per performance instead of per week; but the manager may, if he pleases, calculate the percentage on the average of the receipts for the week, provided all the performances are of works by the author.

Prompt copies cannot be supplied. Performances must be rehearsed from the published books, which contain the main stage directions.

Should any members of the audience be admitted in consideration of their attachment to any theatrical club or society, or of periodical subscriptions to the theatre, or of any method of payment other than the ordinary one, their seats must be accounted for as if purchased at the doors at the ordinary prices. Free admission to all comers is barred unless receipts are obtained by collection.

The licence to perform does not empower the licensee to record any performance or rehearsal for reproduction by the cinematograph or any cognate method, nor to broadcast it.

Licences are not exclusive nor negotiable nor transferable by any method and may be withdrawn should any public statement to the contrary be made or inspired by the licensee or should any transaction in the nature of subletting be effected or proposed on the strength of it.

This memorandum is for information only. It is not a contract nor an acceptance of a proposal; and its receipt must not be taken as an authorisation to proceed with any project touching the author's rights. It merely states the minimum conditions of his general practice without binding him in respect of any particular contract or inquiry.

If a manager desires to employ an agent, it must be made clear that the agent is acting for the manager and at his expense, and not for the author.

Business connected with the plays is in the hands of the Incorporated Society of Authors, Playwrights and Composers to which all inquiries and applications for licences to perform must be addressed and performing fees paid, at 84 Drayton Gardens, London, S.W.10. Telephone Freemantle 6642/3. Dates and places of contemplated performances must be precisely specified in all applications. Accounts shewing the receipts at each performance should accompany payments.*

PLAYWRIGHTS AND AMATEURS

Playwrights receive letters asking them to authorise performances of their plays by Societies formed to develop appreciation of dramatic art in their neighbourhood. These Societies are sometimes University, Y.M.C.A., Labour† College, or Polytechnic Clubs; sometimes branches of Drama Leagues; sometimes isolated ventures calling themselves by any title which occurs to them. As a rule they all make the same mistake. They appeal for special consideration on the ground that they are personally disinterested and actuated solely by public spirit; that they are poor; that all work connected with them is unpaid; and that, if they make any money, they give it away to charities, to political organisations of one sort or another, or to some public object unconnected with the theatre. The result is that the playwright is obliged to class them as "amateurs", and refer them to the Collection Bureau of the Society of Authors, which is, in turn, obliged to make them pay five guineas a performance, and to forbid them to give more than two performances consecutively. The next day an ordinary commercial speculator, who has no other purpose than to make money for himself, will receive from the same playwright or from the Society, without question, an authorisation to perform night after night for a shilling in the pound on the takings when these do not exceed £50.

For this the Societies have themselves to thank. If they would organise themselves as continuing bodies building up a capital fund by the profits of their performances; appoint a responsible director; pay everybody a living wage as soon as they have the means; and

---

* *Note:* The terms given in this standardised letter issued by Bernard Shaw during his lifetime do not necessarily still apply in every detail. And when it was sent by Shaw to correspondents, he sometimes qualified its contents with a personal message.

† The particular copy of this 'printed letter' from which the text here is reproduced may have been an uncorrected proof. Shaw probably changed the spelling on it to his usual Lab*or* in due course.

aim at the foundation of a permanent series of performances every season under a standing title (Blanktown Repertory Theatre, or something of the kind) in, if possible, a theatre of their own, they could at once obtain authorisation on professional terms, exactly as the commercial speculators do. It is their own thoughtless protests that they are doing nothing more than the amateur dramatic clubs do, that is, acting for the fun of it, and giving away all the money they make to objects unconnected with the theatre, that forces the playwright, as a matter of professional etiquette, to class them with the amateur clubs and make them pay the same fees.

The remedy is in their own hands. No sane playwright wants to discriminate against *bona fide* attempts to educate the people in dramatic art: on the contrary, he wants to encourage them by every means in his power. Societies devoted to this object are clearly entitled to go into the play market exactly as the trustees of a picture gallery go into the picture market, or a public library into the book market. But they must constitute and describe themselves accordingly and not insist on being idle amateurs.*

G.B.S.

FROM LONDON TO AYOT ST. LAWRENCE BY ROAD

1. Go out by the Finchley Road through Swiss Cottage. Shortly before reaching the cross roads at Golders Green Station turn left along No. A 5092, signposted as leading to Mill Hill, Welwyn, and the North. About twenty miles further on, this joins the main north road A 1 beyond Hatfield. Keep on northward, avoiding a fork

* A former resident of Welwyn Garden City who ran a very successful amateur dramatic company has recounted to me how he wrote to Shaw objecting to paying 5 gns. for each performance, and received one of these 'stock letters' in reply. He then wrote again, saying that although his company was purely an amateur one, it was entirely self-supporting and not subsidised by any outside body (as so many amateur dramatic societies are) and ploughed back all its profits into new equipment and productions. Shaw wrote back: "So long as you *behave* like professionals, and dont give your takings away to the local nursing association, you may certainly produce my plays at professional rates", and then charged them very little—only 2 or 3 per cent.

What Shaw objected to was not amateur dramatic societies as such, but that his plays should be in any way instrumental in assisting *organised charities*—to which Shaw has always objected strongly *on principle* (though a charitable man in himself).

to the left at the Bull Inn, and another to the right to Welwyn Garden City. At the highest point in the road at the top of the long hill which follows, Ayot Green is on the left. Turn left across it at the signpost marked to Wheathampstead, Harpenden, and Luton; and presently bear right. After passing Ayot Station turn right under the railway bridge up a steep pitch. Bear left at the top; and at the church further on bear left again. Follow the lane as it winds about until you come out on a main road. Turn left along it for a short bit; and then turn out of it to the right at a signpost marked Ayot St. Lawrence. The lane twists about and rises and dips and rises again. At the top of the second rise, at a signpost marked to Welwyn, bear left into the village of Ayot St. Lawrence. Drive through it past the ruined church; and at the end, where the road divides, Bernard Shaw's gate is facing you in the angle.

Time from London about an hour and a quarter.

2. To reach Ayot St. Lawrence from St. Albans, leave the town at the north end of the main thoroughfare by a road to the right signposted to Sandridge and Wheathampstead. After passing under the railway bridge in Wheathampstead turn to the right. About a mile further turn left up a lane signposted to Bride Hall. At the top of a lane, after passing a cottage, turn to the right and follow the windings of the lane past a block of two cottages on the right, then through a widened corner and up a short pitch. The hedge on the left of this pitch is Bernard Shaw's hedge; and his gate is at the joining of the roads at the top.

TELEPHONE:
CODICOTE 18 (through Toll from London)

POSTAL ADDRESS:
AYOT ST. LAWRENCE, WELWYN, HERTS.

NEAREST STATION:
WHEATHAMPSTEAD, L. & N.E., 2 MILES

ON HOW TO BECOME A MODEL PARENT

Shaw's advice on how to reach Ayot St. Lawrence was the last of the items under the heading: "Printed Postcards and Stock Letter Replies". Now follow selected statements by Shaw from his writings and speeches, the source of which is given in each case. The following article appeared in the British Shaw Society's journal, *The Shavian*, No. 1, Spring, 1946.

My parents took no moral responsibility for me. I was just something that had happened to them inevitably and had to be put up with and supported. They did not worry themselves uselessly about my character and my future. I suffered nothing from the intolerable meddlesomeness of the conscientious parents who are so busy with their children's characters that they have no time to look after their own. I cannot remember having ever heard a single sentence uttered by my mother in the nature of moral or religious instruction.

My father made an effort or two. When he caught me imitating him by pretending to smoke a toy pipe, he advised me very earnestly never to follow his example in any way; and his sincerity so impressed me that to this day I have never smoked, never shaved, and never used alcoholic stimulants. He taught me to regard him as an unsuccessful man with many undesirable habits, as a warning and not a model. In fact he did himself less than justice lest I should grow up like him; and I now perceive that this anxiety on his part was altogether admirable and lovable, and that he was really just what he so carefully strove not to be: that is, a model father.

Many of us who are parents go through agonies of hypocrisy to win a respect from our children which we do not deserve. In our virtuous resolution to do our duty as parents we become humbugs, and when our children are old enough to find us out, as they do at a very early age, they become cynical and lose the affectionate respect which we have destroyed ourselves morally to gain. Be advised by me: do as my parents did: live your lives frankly in the face of your children according to your own real natures and give your sons a fair chance of becoming Bernard Shaws.

ON EDUCATION, CONDUCT, AND LIFE

This is the text of a B.B.C. broadcast given by Bernard Shaw on 11th June, 1937, under the heading "Talk for Sixth Forms—Modern Education (ii)".

For "Sixth Forms" one can, I think, without change of basic meaning, substitute "Villagers"—or ordinary men and women everywhere. And since this book is a sequel to *Shaw the Villager—and Human Being*, and therefore concerned with the human side of Shaw (as well as with more complex aspects of his personality to be dealt with later), this script seems a fitting inclusion here.

I reproduce it, with grateful acknowledgements to the British Broadcasting Corporation, because it summarises in simple, straightforward language much of Shaw's attitude to education, to conduct, and to life.

[Certain cuts were made when this talk was broadcast in order to comply with the time-limit allowed. This is the full authentic text, without any cuts or sub-editing, as originally written by Bernard Shaw, and it is published here for the first time.]

Hallo, Sixth Forms. I have been asked to speak to you because I have become celebrated through my eminence in the profession of Eschylus,* Sophocles, Euripides, and Shakespeare. Eschylus wrote in school Greek; and Shakespeare is in 'English Literature', which is a school subject. In French Schools I am English literature. Consequently all the sixth forms in France shudder when they hear

* Shaw, as part of his protest against conventional spelling (his views on phonetic reform have already been touched on and will be given in greater detail in due course) used a single vowel in many words where the diphthongs 'æ', 'œ', are usually used. Thus he would write Eschylus, Esop, archeology, ecumenical, in place of Æschylus, Æsop, archæology, œcumenical. But, paradoxically, he *did* use the diphthong when he wrote Cæsar instead of Caesar, or Œdipus in place of Oedipus. His own spelling of lab*or* in place of lab*our* is well known and has already been noted.

36

my name. However, do not be alarmed; I am not going to talk to you about English literature. To me there is nothing in writing a play: anyone can write one if he has the necessary natural turn for it; and if he hasn't he can't: that is all there is to it. Besides, a man may have this natural turn and be an incorrigible blackguard or a hopeless drunkard; so the bare fact that I possess it does not give me any right to address a respectable school.

However, I have another trick for imposing on the young. I am old: over 80 in fact. Also I have a white beard; and these two facts are somehow associated in people's minds with wisdom. That is a mistake. If a person is a born fool, the folly will get worse, not better, by a long life's practice. My having lived four times as long as any of you gives me only one advantage over you, and that is rather a melancholy one. I have carried small boys and girls in my arms, and seen them grow into sixth form scholars, then into young men and women in the flower of youth and beauty, then into brides and bridegrooms who think one another much better and lovelier than they really are, then into middle aged paterfamiliases and anxious mothers with elderly spreads, and finally into grandads and grannies. The Seven Ages of Man is not for me a boring school recitation; it is an actual experience which none of you have had.

Now you may not think much of this; but I assure you there is a good deal more in it than seeing people grow up and flower and wither, as a gardener sees his plants. For a plant very seldom surprises a gardener; but human beings sometimes surprise their friends and enemies very much. Some of your schoolfellows— quite likeable ones perhaps—may surprise you by getting hanged. Others, of whom you may have the lowest opinion, will turn out to be geniuses, and become [among] the great men of your time. Therefore always be nice to young people. You never know how they will turn out. Some little beast who is no good at games and whose head you may possibly have clouted for indulging a sarcastic wit and a sharp tongue at your expense may grow into a tremendous swell, like Rudyard Kipling. The village poacher who has to leave his native town with a bad character may pop up again as William Shakespeare. You never can tell.

You may possibly rise to the pinnacle of fame yourself. In that case do not forget that there are falls from that pinnacle. I have seen brilliant geniuses end in prison. I have seen titled heads of their profession die forgotten.

It is no use reading about such things, or being told about them by your father. You must have known the people personally, as I have. That is what makes a difference between your outlook on the world and mine. When I was as young as you the world seemed to me to be unchangeable; and a year seemed a long time. Now the years fly past before I have time to look round, and the world changes faster than I can change my mind to keep pace with it. I am an old old man before I have quite got out of the habit of thinking of myself as a boy. You have fifty years before you, and therefore must think anxiously about your future. I have no future and need not care what I say or do.

You all think, don't you, that you are nearly grown up. I thought so when I was your age; and now, after 81 years of that expectation I have not grown up yet. It would take me several hundred years—perhaps several thousand—to feel sufficiently grown up to give myself any airs in talking to you; and I shall be dead long before that. The same thing will happen to you. You will escape from school in all the dignity of the sixth form only to discover that the world is only a bigger school, and that you are back again in the first form. Before you can work your way up into the sixth form again you will be as old as I am. The change will be very trying unless you have a lot of money. At present you are safe in an orderly school in which everything is arranged and thought out for you, and you can be as sure of what will happen to-morrow as you are of what happened yesterday. If you obey a set of rules and get through certain allotted tasks, you need not bother about anything else. Both the rules and the tasks may be more or less irksome occasionally; but they are the price you have to pay for regular meals and safety and shelter, and [for] certainty as to your immediate future and for learning enough to civilise yourself: in short, for everything that makes the difference between you and a tramp. If you think it would be jollier to be a tramp it is quite easy to run away from school and try it. Before the week is out you will probably have had quite enough of it.

The hardest part of schooling is fortunately the earliest part when you are a very small kid and have to be turned into a walking ready reckoner. You have to know up to 12 times 12, and how many shillings there are in any number of pence up to 144 without looking at a book. And you must understand a printed page just as you understand people talking to you. All this you must learn before you are old enough to understand the need for it. It is a stupendous feat of sheer learning, much the most difficult I have ever achieved. It must have been a terrible piece of pure schooling; yet I have not the faintest recollection of being put through it. I remember the governess who did it; but I cannot remember any time at which a printed page was unintelligible to me, nor at which I did not know without counting that 56 pence make four and eightpence. This seems so magical to me now that I sometimes regret that she did not teach me the whole table of logarithms and the binomial theorem and all the other mathematical short cuts and ready reckonings as well. Perhaps she would have if she had known them herself. It is strange that if you learn anything when you are young you remember it for ever. Now that I am old I forget everything in a few seconds, and everybody five minutes after they have been introduced to me. That is a great happiness, as I don't want to be bothered with new things and new people; but I still cannot get on without remembering what my governess taught me. So cram in all you can while you are young.

But I am rambling. Let us get back to your escape from your school or your university into the great school of the world; and remember that this time you will not be chased and brought back. You will just be chucked out neck and crop and the door slammed behind you.

You will find the new school a very disorderly one. It is not only that you have to find a paying job and provide your own meals and lodgings and clothes and so on, but that you haven't been taught how to set about it. What makes school life irksome until you get used to it, and easy when you do get used to it, is that it is a routine. A routine is a program you have to go through every day whether you feel disposed or not. You have to get up at a fixed hour, wash and dress, take your meals and do your work all at fixed hours. Now the worst of a routine is that though it is supposed to suit everybody, it really suits nobody. Sixth form scholars are like other people: they are all different. Each of you is what is called an individual case, needing individual attention. But you cannot have it. Nobody has time enough nor money enough to provide each of you with a separate teacher and a special routine carefully fitted to your individual personality, like your clothes and your boots.

I can remember a time when English people going to live in Germany were astonished to find that German boots were not divided into rights and lefts: a boot was a boot and it did not matter which foot you put it on, your foot had to make the best of it. You may think that funny; but let me ask how many of you have your socks knitted as rights and lefts? I have had mine knitted that way for the last fifty years; but I still find that knitters of socks take it as a new and ridiculous idea. Some of them actually refuse my order and say that it can't be done. Just think of that! We are able to make machines that can fly round the world and instruments that can talk round the world; yet we think we cannot knit socks as rights and lefts; and I am considered a queer sort of fellow because I want it done and insist that it can be done. Well, school routines are like the socks and the old German boots: they are neither rights nor lefts, and consequently they don't fit any human being properly. But we have to manage with them somehow. And when we escape from school into the big adult world, we have to choose between a lot of routines: the college routine, the military routine, the naval routine, the court routine, the civil service routine, the legal routine, the clerical routine, the theatrical routine, or the parliamentary routine, which is the worst of the lot.

To get properly stuck into one of those grooves you have to pass examinations; and this you must set about very clear-headedly or you will fail. You must not let yourself get interested in the subjects or be overwhelmed by their magnitude and importance, and by the utter impossibility of any human being mastering them all even at the age of 500, much less 20. The scholar who knows everything is like the little child who is perfectly obedient and perfectly truthful: he or she doesn't exist and never will. Therefore you must go to a crammer. Now what is a crammer? A crammer is a person whose whole life is devoted to doing something you have not time to do for yourself: that is, to study all the old examination papers and find out what are the questions that are actually asked, and what are the answers expected by the examiners and officially recognised as correct. You must be very careful not to suppose that these answers are the true answers. Your examiners will be elderly gentlemen; and their knowledge is sure to be more or less out of date. This is quite natural and inevitable. Always begin by telling yourself this story.

Imagine yourself a young student preparing for your degree or your diploma early in the fifteenth century, and being examined as to your knowledge of the movements of the sun and moon, the planets and stars. Imagine also that your father happens to know Copernicus, and that you have learnt from his conversation that the planets go round not in circles but in ellipses. Imagine that you have met the painter Leonardo da Vinci, and been allowed to peep at his funny note-book, and by holding it up to a mirror, read the words 'the earth is a moon of the sun'. Imagine that on being examined you gave the answers of Copernicus and Leonardo, believing them to be the true answers. Instead of passing at the head of the successful list you would have been burnt alive for heresy. Therefore you would have taken good care to say nothing about Copernicus and Leonardo, and to give your examiners the answers they expected. You would have said that the stars and the sun move in perfect circles, because the circle is a perfect figure and therefore answers to the perfection of the Creator. You would have quoted Plato, and drawn a scheme of the heavens in perfect circles as they did in the school of Ptolemy to prove that Plato was right. You would have known better than to let the learned Churchmen who were examining you find out that you were such a conceited young imp as to think you knew better than Plato or Ptolemy. You would have said that the motion of the sun round the earth was proved by the fact that Joshua saw it move in Gibeon and stopped it until he had finished licking the Amorites. If you suggested that your word was truer than the Book of Joshua, the examiners would have risen up and denounced you as a blasphemous young beast possessed by seventy times seven devils. You would therefore give the wrong answers and be passed and patted on the head as a young marvel of Aristotelian science.

Now the world to-day is just what it was in the days of Copernicus. If you at twenty years of age go up to be examined by an elderly gentleman of fifty, you must find out what people were taught thirty years ago and stuff him with that, and not with what you are taught to-day.

If you happen to be a young George Washington or Jeanie Deans,* determined never to tell anything but the exact and final truth, you will never pass an examination, because neither you nor the

* The heroine of Sir Walter Scott's *The Heart of Midlothian*.

examiners can ever know the exact and final truth about any
examination subject. To pass the examination all you have to do is
to find out what questions the examiners will ask and then find out
what answers will be accepted as the proper answers, and give those
answers, humbly and cheerfully, knowing that the examiners have
a right to their opinions and are as likely to be right as you.

But, you will say, how are you possibly to find out what questions
are to be asked and what answers are expected? Well, you cannot;
but a good crammer can. He cannot get a peep at the papers beforehand; but he can study the old examination papers until he knows
all the questions that the examiners have to keep asking over and
over again; for after all their number is not infinite. If only you will
swot hard enough to learn them all you will pass with flying colors.
Of course you will not be able to learn them all; but your chances
will be good in proportion to the number you can learn. No teacher,
however learned or gifted, can shew you how to pass an examination
unless he has made a special study of the questions and answers and
the chances of their being asked; in short unless he is a professional
crammer.

The danger of being plucked for giving up-to-date answers to
elderly examiners is greatest in the technical professions. If you want
to get into the navy, or practise medicine, you must get specially
trained for some months in practices that are quite out of date.
If you don't you will be turned down by admirals dreaming of the
Nelson touch, and surgical baronets brought up on the infallibility
of Jenner and Lister and Pasteur. But this does not apply to all
examinations. Take the classics for instance. Homer's Greek and
Virgil's Latin, being dead languages, do not change as naval and
medical practice changes. Suppose you want to be a clergyman.
The Greek of the New Testament does not change. The creeds
do not change. The 39 Articles do not change, though they ought
to; for some of them are terribly out of date. You can cram yourself
with these subjects and save your money for lessons in elocution.

In any case you may take it as a safe rule that if you happen to
have any original ideas about examination subjects you must not
air them in your examination papers. You may very possibly know
better than your examiners; but do not let them find out that you
think so.

Once you are safely through your examinations you will begin life

Shaw posing as a statue between Virgil and Homer (who seem less cheerful about life than he).

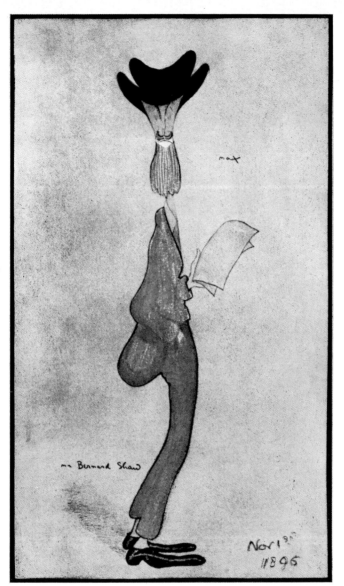

"...You see, I was born with what people call an artistic temperament".

(A rare early cartoon by Sir Max Beerbohm)

A later cartoon —with hat pierced for talking through!

(By "H.A.L.", courtesy the Victoria and Albert Museum.)

CYNIC'S SKETCH OF G.B.S.: Hat (pierced) for talking through

in earnest. You will then discover that your education has been very defective. You will find yourself uninstructed as to eating and drinking and sleeping and breathing. You may not even know how to swim, or row, or sail a boat; and your notions of keeping yourself fit will consist mostly of physical exercises which will shorten your life by twenty years or so. You may accept me as an educated man because I have earned my living for sixty years by work which only an educated man, and even a highly educated one, could do. Yet the subjects that educated me were never taught in my schools. As far as I know my schoolmasters were utterly and barbarously ignorant of them. School was to me a sentence of penal servitude. You see I was born with what people call an artistic temperament, and an insatiable intellectual curiosity. I could read all the masterpieces of English poets, playwrights, historians and scientific pioneers; but I could not read schoolbooks, because they are written by people who do not know how to write. To me a person who knew nothing of all the great musicians from Palestrina to Edward Elgar, nor of the great painters from Giotto to Burne-Jones, was a savage and an ignoramus even if he were hung all over with gold medals for school classics. As to mathematics, to be imprisoned in an ugly room and set to do sums in algebra without ever having had the meaning of mathematics explained to me, or its relation to science, was enough to make me hate mathematics all the rest of my life, as so many literary men do. So do not expect too much from your school achievements. You may win the Ireland scholarship and then find that none of the great business houses will employ a University don on any terms. But if you have lots of money and can ride and shoot and play bridge and have a gentlemanly accent and are a good sportsman you may become a Cabinet Minister with surprising ease.

As to your general conduct and prospects, all I have time to say is that if you do as everyone does and think as everyone thinks you will get on very well with your neighbours; but you will suffer from all their illnesses and stupidities. If you think and act otherwise you must suffer their dislike and persecution. I was taught when I was young that if people would only love one another, all would be well with the world. This seemed simple and very nice, but I found when I tried to put it in practice not only that other people were seldom lovable, but that I was not very lovable myself. I also found that to love anyone is to take a liberty with them which is quite unbearable unless they happen to return your affection, which you have no right to expect. What you have to learn if you are to be a good citizen of the world is that though you will certainly dislike many of your neighbours, and differ from some of them in politics, religion, and personal habits so strongly that you could not possibly live in the same house with them—though, like many great men you may with very good reason feel about the whole human race, including yourself, exactly as the King of Brobdingnag felt when Gulliver told him what a splendid nation we are—that does not give you the smallest right to injure them or even to be personally uncivil to them. It is not a question of doing good to those who hate you: for they do not need your officious services, and would refuse to be under any obligation to you: the question is how to behave to those whom you dislike, and cannot help disliking for no reason whatever, simply because you were born with an antipathy to that sort of person. You must just keep out of their way as much as you can; and when you cannot, deal as honestly and civilly with them as with your best friend. Just think what the world would be like if everyone who disliked you were to punch your head. The oddest thing about it is that you will find yourself making friends with people whose opinions are the very opposite to your own, whilst you cannot bear the sight of others who share all your beliefs. You may love your dog and find your nearest relatives detestable. So don't waste your time arguing whether you *ought* to love all your neighbours. Nothing can make them all lovable. As long as you don't try to punish them for your dislike you may accept it and even nurse it. If you are not a good hater you will be a very dull person.

Suppose, however, that you find yourself completely dissatisfied with all your fellow creatures as they exist at present and with all their laws and institutions. Then there is nothing to be done but to set to work to find out exactly what is wrong with them, and how to set them right. That is perhaps the best fun of all; but perhaps I think so only because I am a little in that line myself. I could tell you a lot more about this; but time is up; and I am warned that I must stop. I hope you are sorry.

ON THE LITERATURE OF THE THEATRE

THE ONLY LECTURE SHAW EVER GAVE ON THIS SUBJECT

On Monday, 3rd November, 1924, Bernard Shaw gave this lecture to the people of Welwyn Garden City, whom he regarded as his neighbours and friends as much as he did the villagers of Ayot St. Lawrence. It was given in the Parkway Hall (under the auspices of the Educational Association) and was a very generous and special concession to them, for he had hitherto refused (and did subsequently refuse) all invitations to talk specifically on the literary aspect of the drama, though repeatedly asked to do so by universities and distinguished societies all over the world. (This unique occasion was mentioned by Sir Frederic Osborn, C. B. Purdom, and other contributors to *Shaw the Villager*.)

For exclusive permission to reproduce this report, which appeared in the *Welwyn Garden City News* (now the *Welwyn Times*) I am extremely grateful to its previous editor, Mr Charles Dalton, and the present editor, Mr William B. Gardner.

THE LITERATURE OF THE THEATRE

Mr Shaw, at the start, announced his intention of being educational. People who did not already know what he was going to say would be bored; only those who knew it already would be interested. If they really wanted to learn about anything, they should never go to lectures about it. If they wanted to learn about literature they should not read books about it; let them read the literature itself, and then afterwards they would be interested in what people said about it.

The subject he had chosen was "Literature of the Theatre." There were many books about the theatre, most of which were worthless. There were many lives of actors and actresses, and there was Jeremy Collier's admirable book on the English Stage, attacking it for being profane and immoral, which it still was, in spite of

45

Jeremy Collier. His subject, however, was not the theatre, but the actual plays of the theatre, the real stuff of the theatre. *

IS FICTION OBJECTIONABLE?

Plays belonged to literature as a branch of fiction, and in a place like Welwyn Garden City, where people had tender consciences— what Ibsen called "sickly consciences"—the first question arising was whether fiction ought to be encouraged. Fiction from a certain point of view was a parcel of lies—stories not true about people who never existed. Many people were troubled about this. He remembered that in the earlier part of his career, when, instead of people wanting to come and hear him, he desired to impart his opinions to other people, he therefore went to all the street corners in London and talked; and as most people in London had nothing whatever to do of any importance they used to stop and listen to him. In those days he often found himself in friendly competition with the Salvation Army.

COMMUNISM AND SALVATION

In those days he was a Communist. He was still a Communist, and intended to remain a Communist. The meetings of the Salvation Army were held to propagate the views of an earlier and more extreme Communist than himself. He used to be struck by the Salvation Army having a certain number of ladies working for it who exhibited great dramatic talent in the singing of a certain type of song, in which they secured an extraordinary effect. The song was usually about an unfortunate woman who was saved, but was married to a terrible scoundrel, who drank terribly and jumped on her with hob-nailed boots, and nothing but the woman's faith sustained her. The climax of the song was when the woman was at home praying, and dreading the husband's return. She heard his hob-nailed boots coming along the corridor, and was expecting to feel them on herself as usual, when the door opened, and she saw his face shining—he had been saved.

Of course, he (Mr Shaw) had made a note of this wonderful and beautiful happy ending. Shortly after this some idiot of a journalist—

* Shaw had spoken on one or two previous occasions on other aspects of the theatre, but not comprehensively on the subject as he defines it here.

the majority of journalists were idiots—had made a remark that some band was almost as bad as a Salvation Army band. He (Mr Shaw) wrote a letter wiping the floor with that man with all the authority of having been a musical critic. He said that the Salvation Army bands were very good. This produced an extraordinary effect on General Booth, who had never received a compliment on his bands before. He was invited to attend the Salvation Army festival, where all the bands played together. There was one item in which 43 trombones played together, and some effects were got by that band which had never been excelled.

Following this he had suggested that, as the young ladies made such an effect with their artistic performances in singing, they should try acting little plays. But they had had trouble with their old people, who were very particular. However, they asked him to write a little play, but they must be able to assure their old people that everything in the play had actually happened. From this he had discovered that the old people really believed that the story of the Prodigal Son and other Bible stories were true; that there was an actual Prodigal Son. In the end they wrote to say that they were much obliged for the suggestion of a play, but would rather have a cheque, which was very sensible of them. The end of it was that he wrote a play called *Major Barbara*, which any number of officers of the Salvation Army came to see.

LITERATURE AND LIES

There were still people who considered that the whole field of literature was a mass of lies. But that was not so. What kept the drama alive was that part of it which is an interpretation of life. Life could not be understood by merely looking at it. A cinema film of the daily activities of Welwyn Garden City would be a picture of life, but for the most part it would be completely meaningless. You could not tell from it what people were doing and thinking. A man would come out of a house looking a little disgusted; another would go into a house looking grim. You could not possibly tell that the first man had just had the sack and that the second was just going to murder his wife.

What the dramatist did was to take out the significant incidents, and put them before you in an intelligible manner, so that you could judge it and learn from it. Such a representation might, of course, be false, but it could be true, and it was its truth that was its final justification.

If they wanted to know about Joan of Arc, they could walk about a long time and learn nothing. The way to find out about her was to go and see his (Mr Shaw's) play. Many of the things did not occur in real life exactly as in that play, but essentially it was true, and when you saw it you learned an interesting piece of history.

The theatre was a most important institution to have. Fiction was valuable, but the man who tells a story on the stage puts it before you in the most striking way.

LITERATURE AND RELIGION

The function of literature as an interpretation of life gave it a religious character. The Greek drama was religious. The drama began by setting before the people various aspects of popular legends, many of which were believed to be true. In the course of doing this it was discovered that it was possible to present a great many other things that were pleasant and interesting, and in this way the drama arose.

The drama also educated our senses. An actress could make herself beautiful. It was not her business to be beautiful, but she ought to be able to make herself appear either ugly or beautiful, more so than any real woman is, and thus to educate the taste of the young men who came to look at her. If young men were in the habit of falling in love with very beautiful women on the stage they were much less likely to fall in love with the less beautiful off the stage. So also it could educate people's sense of colour and the other senses.

A THEATRE FOR WELWYN GARDEN CITY

The sooner they got a theatre for Welwyn Garden City the better. He knew that they had made a start in that direction; he had a vague idea of having received some author's fees from the town. He hoped that the time would come when the Welwyn Garden City theatre [would] be as imposing a building as the Welwyn Garden City Church. They should do all the acting themselves, and make the dresses themselves, and also the scenery. If they found a young lady who thought she could act like Gladys Cooper or a young man who fancied himself an Owen Nares, let them drown the one and shoot the other. Let them find people who were prepared to work at the art of acting. It would be better for them to have a genuine Welwyn Garden City author than to run after *his* plays, which were only Ayot St. Lawrence plays.

FICTION AND DRAMA

Mr Shaw then went on to discuss why dramatic literature had historically separated itself from ordinary literature. The division went back to the period when there were no books. It went back to the street corner, which was the beginning of everything. The story-teller still existed in the East. The best storyteller is the man who could give individuality to the characters, like the boy in Dickens who could read the police news in different voices. This was the beginning of acting, and the next stage was to have a number of people to pretend to be the characters in the story. Then the narrative began to be dropped, and the differentiation of dramatic literature had set in.

Descriptions of scenery had to be omitted. When a novelist could not pad out the story, he described a sunset. When at a loss for dialogue, he put in five or six pages of psychology: "Her mind went back to when she was six years old", etc. Anybody could write a novel; it was a most childish thing. But no such nonsense was possible in a play. A certain sort of narrative existed in the earlier plays; and at one time it was usual for there to be two chairs near the centre of the stage, on which sat two persons who talked to each other and explained the story of the play.

Audiences were extremely patient for the first 20 minutes of a play; they were buoyed up with hope and would stand almost anything, and some exposition was therefore possible. But the author should always bear in mind that what an audience would stand in the first 20 minutes they would not stand in the last 20 minutes.

THE UNITIES

Under primitive conditions, where there was no scenery, and no curtain, the unities of time and place, as they were called by Aristotle, were imposed on the drama by necessity. People at a street corner could pretend to be different people, but they could only pretend to be people at a street corner, that is to say, the unity of place had to be observed. It followed that it was necessary to resort to an extraordinary degree of coincidence. Coincidence had got to occur in a play, because if it did not there was no play. The unity of time had also to be observed at the street corner because no lapse of time could be indicated; the whole action had to comprise events which could occur within an hour or so. Although there were means by which it was possible to some extent to escape from the unities, capable dramatists had discovered that the more closely they could stick to the unities the greater the effect that they could produce. They could take that from him as a professional tip.

The objection to the street corner stage was that people could see it without paying, and the desire to arrange somewhere where people could be shut out if they did not pay had led to the development of magnificent buildings such as those in which the Greek plays were performed. The drama had reached its highest point in the Greek religious tragedies, which were played on a tribune without any curtain or any change of scenery, and in which the unities had to be strictly observed.

Another type of religious plays had come up in the Middle Ages, which were organised by the Christian Church. In these, scenery was introduced as a result of the demand for more realism. At first they had no idea of changing scenery, but all the scenes, from the Garden of Eden and the mouth of Hell, to the house of Pilate and a balcony representing Heaven, were shown side by side at the same time. The characters would pass from one to the others as the play went on, and thus the unities were at the same time preserved and violated.

There followed again another type of play, which reached its height in Shakespeare's time. In this there was no scenery, but only a platform and a few conventional objects to suggest scenes. And then Opera was invented, and the stage as we know it had come in, with painted scenes and the device of dropping the curtain so as to suggest a lapse of time and to allow of the changing of the scenery. Thus it was possible to get a good way away from the unities. The dramatist still had to observe the unities within each individual scene. But as a result of the new freedom the drama began to slop all over the place and had deteriorated very much. If they wanted proof of this, let them see a play of Euripides in Gilbert Murray's admirable translations, and then go and see a 17th century comedy.

THE ŒDIPUS

The Œdipus of Sophocles was a play which had been much praised for its ingenuity of construction. But the necessity of preserving the unities had caused Sophocles to disregard probability in the most amazing manner. The play opened in a time of crisis when people were suffering terribly with the plague. Œdipus recalls that three years ago he sent a man to consult the oracle, and he had not returned. "But see, who is this who comes? If I mistake not," etc.; and the missing man turned up every time. Then by a series of coincidences the story was built up around the innocent man, who is convinced that he has murdered his father and married his mother, and thereupon goes and tears his eyes out. Audiences were always pleased to see the man turn up at the right moment; they never said: This is getting a little thick.

MISALLIANCE

Although he (Mr Shaw) never hesitated to introduce the most out-rageous coincidences, knowing that they would not be noticed, nevertheless, he had found that the unities of time and place are so effective that he had almost always observed them in his plays. In *Misalliance* for instance—which was being played at the Every-man Theatre—the action was a discussion lasting three hours. [That should not] discourage them; it was a most amusing play. They would find that the curtain came down twice during the play, but that was for the sake of the bars. He had achieved the unities in that play. How had he contrived to get so many people together where he wanted them? It was very simple; he simply made the scene a country house; you could get in a lot of assorted people like that. And, as he did not want them to be entirely a family party, it was necessary to introduce a few perfect strangers. So he had done a thing that Sophocles had never thought of. He had caused a man to fall in the garden from an aeroplane—a charming but simple little expedient.

He had done the same thing in *Getting Married* by having it a wedding morning with all sorts of guests in the Bishop's kitchen. Nobody noticed the trick; but every dramatist was tied from beginning to end by necessities of that kind.

Mr Shaw then announced that, as the meeting was under the auspices of the Educational Association, he was now going, for the sake of the general decencies of the occasion, to be more learned than literary.

THE GREEKS AGAIN

He would begin with the old Greek religious dramatists, of whom three had survived. The word for Æschylus* was "sublimity", a word which had gone out of fashion because we had lost the thing itself. A great man never had precisely the religion of the common man. The greatness of Æschylus was partly due to the fact that he had thoroughly believed in the truth of the legends on which he had built his plays. Everybody who came to the Greek theatre knew the story already, which was a great help. He would like to see this idea revived. It would be a fine thing if people came to see, not only Shakespeare's Hamlet, but Galsworthy's Hamlet, Granville Barker's Hamlet, Shaw's Hamlet, and so on. It would save many explanations.

SOPHOCLES AND EURIPIDES

He (Mr Shaw) was not very fond of Sophocles, because he took the prejudices and superstitions of the Greeks and shamelessly exploited them. He never threw any new light on them. He makes Œdipus tear out his eyes, because the legend said so. He never asked, "Would a man really do it? Would he be so very remorseful just because he had found he had killed his father and married his mother?" Marrying his mother would not make him (Mr Shaw) tear his eyes out. The discovery would, on the contrary, give him a certain added tenderness for his wife. Sophocles, on the contrary, was perfectly clear about it; he wallowed in gore. He did not believe that the man had any genuine feelings.

Euripides, on the contrary, did not say anything very unpleasant about them, but he exhibited their pride and inhuman aloofness in such a way as to make the audience question their religion. So he liked Euripides.

THE MEDIAEVAL MYSTERIES

The mediaeval mystery plays were really meant to foster religious belief, and the men who played in them really believed in the truth of their religion. The moment men really believe in a thing they begin to joke about it. In an age when people do not believe in their religion, when it is merely a question of going to Church in their

---

* The spelling here differs from Shaw's written form because this is reported speech.

best clothes, it is considered wrong to say anything funny about religion.

In a mediaeval mystery, Cain would be a funny man, a coarse farmer type, who talked to labourers like Squire Western in Fielding's *Tom Jones*, only more so. Cain then killed Abel, but when God appeared in the play, and talked to him, Cain replied in the same improper vein, and he kept up his comic character to the end. This made the play extraordinarily real and extraordinarily natural, and people believed it.

These plays were taken round the streets on a sort of staging in three storeys, the top one representing Heaven, the middle one the earth, and the lowest, hell. They had no hesitation in representing God on the stage. But in Victorian times this was impossible, and in an opera which he had seen, God was represented by a hole in the ceiling, which was not nearly so realistic. At last, however, Mr W[illia]m Poel had produced the old morality play, *Everyman*, in which God appeared sitting up aloft in his robes, and there was not the slightest difficulty about it.

SHAKESPEARE AND THE RESTORATION

Trouble began because the sensational incidents in the mystery plays became very popular, and the plays began to run to martyrdom, because of the blood and horrors that could be introduced. The theatre became so corrupt that the Church had to drop it, and it only survived through the Strolling Players, from whom the Elizabethan drama had come. This was drama of the sensational type. It had produced Shakespeare, the striking fact about whom was that he had no religion. From that there followed another phase, the Restoration comedy.

Restoration plays were now being revived in their original form. A great deal of nonsense had been written about the Restoration comedy. It ought to horrify people, but it never did. What [was] the matter with it was that it[was]now hopelessly dull, because its principal effects depended upon a sense of humour which we had lost. The Restoration plays were all written round two jokes which were no longer jokes. He had never been able to explain it, but from the middle of the seventeenth century to the end of the eighteenth century it was considered screamingly funny that a man's wife should be unfaithful to him; there was a fanciful idea about such a man having horns growing on his head. It does not occur to us nowadays to laugh at a man whose home was broken up in this way. Venereal disease was also considered excruciatingly funny at that period. The Restoration comedy was all cuckold and pox, and the audiences screamed. Today we sit and stare and say: "Where is the fun?" It was greatly to our shame as a nation that our most witty and literary comedy should centre about such coarse and stupid things. In France Molière had produced a perfectly delightful comedy without any of the English coarseness. From his inspiration a wonderful comedy had grown up and had combined with the new art of music to produce the great operas of Mozart, who had transmuted the story of the coarse and worthless Don Juan to such extraordinary beauty and delicacy that you never thought of it as coarse at all.

THE WELL-MADE PLAY

During these various phases of the drama a great deal had been found out about the technique of the stage. Certain surprises and other tricks were found to be invaluable in bringing down the house. It was found, especially in the nineteenth century, that you could leave out from a play all the spiritual element, and all the character, and yet it would produce a certain effect if these tricks and surprises were kept in. Thus was developed the "well-made play", of which Scribe was the first celebrated exponent. Writing a play of this kind was like playing cats-cradle, or making a mechanical rabbit. Such a play was *Diplomacy* [on show] in London, which he had known 40 years [earlier] under the name of *Dora*—a very ingenious arrangement, but if you anatomised the thing you found it was not real. This type of play only amused the surface of your mind; it gave you no satisfaction for your soul. It was the same with farcical comedy. You might laugh all the evening and think you had been amused, but when you got home you found you were cross and quarrelled with your wife. You had been made the victim of a mechanical joke.

IBSEN, SHAW, WAGNER

Then there came a terrible man from the North, named Ibsen, who suddenly introduced a new element into the well-made play. He retained all the tricks, and was, if anything, too fond of exercising them, but in his *Doll's House*, which made a tremendous sensation all over Europe, instead of ending the play with the catastrophe, the young woman suddenly sat down and began to talk, and the ordinary young husband suddenly turned out to be an extraordinarily mean and selfish character, and the young woman revealed herself as knowing her complete unreality and ignorance, and went out determined to learn to be fit to be the mother of her children.

Everybody was horrified. Henry Arthur Jones re-wrote the play with the proper ending, but it was of no avail. The new feature, the discussion, had come to stay. A little later, another dramatist was writing plays which were discussion from beginning to end. The discussion was all about conduct and morals. Thus the drama began to turn back to its original religious function. In the meantime Wagner suddenly burst into the world of conventional opera with a religious opera, the greatest example of which was the *Ring*, which, like the Greek dramas, put forward a religious theory of society.

MAN AND SUPERMAN

The critics said the new type of discussion play was not a play at all, and quoted Aristotle. In this they were wrong, for Aristotle would have said that they were going back to the real drama at last. At last they got an interesting play called *Man and Superman*, which had in it a statement of what might be called post-evolutionary religion. The revival of the theory of evolution in the middle of the nineteenth century had knocked the old simple ideas of religion on the head, and in the last half of the century most intelligent people had no religion at all. They called themselves agnostics, which was really playing a game with their own intellect. They knew perfectly well that the story of Noah's Ark was not true, yet people really thought that religion depended upon the truth of such stories. It was hardly possible for religion to have fallen to a lower pitch.

But evolution was presented in such an apallingly mechanistic form that people's consciences got into a worse state than ever. Someone had to take up human thought after evolution, and find out its religious significance, and this fell to the lot of the modern playwright.

BACK TO SHAW

The presentation of the religious significance of evolution was begun upon in *Man and Superman*. Later it was done in a series of plays called *Back to Methuselah*.

"Ladies and Gentlemen," concluded Mr Shaw, "I have led it up to this point because I am the author of *Back to Methuselah*."

Warm applause greeted this characteristic conclusion, and Mr Shaw proceeded to answer a number of questions from members of the audience.

To a question about Ibsen, Mr Shaw replied that Ibsen and himself were inspired by the same power. He had found himself driven in the same direction before he had heard that Ibsen existed. As another instance of the same thing, Mr Shaw referred to an early short story he had written called "The Miraculous Revenge", which he had discovered some time ago and read with some curiosity, and found that it was precisely as if he had been caricaturing the autobiographical sketches of Strindberg, although no touch of Strindberg reached him for many years after. The man who did a thing mattered very little. Something had got to be done which was of importance to the universe, and if it did not come out through one pipe it would come out through another.

RABBITS AND NOAH'S ARK

Mr J. W. Sault, who said he believed in Noah's Ark asked whether it was not possible for the ordinary man to be so inspired to see the beauty of a rabbit that he would not need the artist's vision.

Mr Shaw replied that most people when they saw a rabbit were inspired only with the desire to shoot it. Dürer's drawing of a hare had enabled many people to see the beauty of the animal in a new light. The great majority of people were unable to believe in Noah's Ark after the publication of Darwin's *Origin of Species*. Belief, however, was largely a matter of taste. If you wanted to believe in a thing you could believe in it, in spite of all the evidence. People who had given up believing in miracles were found believing in vaccination. People who could not believe in Mrs Eddy could believe in Professor Coué. He did not wish to rob Mr Sault of his belief because he knew that if he did he would believe in something much more mischievous. Probably the reason why he believed in Noah's Ark was that he had read the story in the Bible. He doubted whether he would have believed in it if he had read it in one of his (Mr Shaw's) plays.

Mr W. R. Hughes expressed the thanks of the meeting to Mr Shaw for his lecture. In reply, Mr Shaw said he had not come there to lecture; he had only dropped in as a neighbour. He never lectured on literature, though he had been asked to do so by universities and societies all over the world. So, if anybody asked them if he had done so at Welwyn Garden City, they had better say that he did nothing of the kind.

ON HIS AIMS AS A PLAYWRIGHT

Arising out of the lecture on the literature of the theatre just given, the following definition of Shaw's aims as a playwright is of interest. It is an extract from the Statement by him which was rejected by the Select Committee of both Houses of Parliament which sat in 1908 to enquire into the workings of the official censorship of stage plays—which Shaw and others had complained of as 'imbecile'.

Shaw subsequently published this Statement in 1909 in the preface to his then banned play *The Shewing-Up of Blanco Posnet,* and drew attention to what he regarded as the weak and hypocritical position of the Committee who, on the one hand, had been so shocked as to feel it necessary to turn the public out when discussing a number of low and vicious plays which had already been freely licensed by the Lord Chamberlain and publicly performed on the stage, and on the other hand, had refused to allow him to read his Statement about his own and other plays with themes of social reform—which he regarded as essentially moral plays.

Shaw's complaint was that plays dealing with the 'fashionable' subject of adultery, or of a vulgar or semi-pornographic kind, were freely passed by the Censor—simply because their themes were popular with a large section of the public and (for this reason) regarded by the Censor as in keeping with conventional morality; while conversely, suppression was often the fate of plays like his own which exposed real social evils in the contemporary world, and depicted dissoluteness as no laughing matter. Here is the extract from Shaw's statement:—

I am not an ordinary playwright in general practice. I am a specialist in immoral and heretical plays. My reputation has been gained by my persistent struggle to force the public to reconsider its morals. In particular, I regard much current morality as to economic and sexual relations as disastrously wrong; and I regard certain doctrines of the Christian religion as understood in England today with abhorrence. I write plays with the deliberate object of converting the nation to my opinions in these matters. I have no other effectual incentive to write plays, as I am not dependent on the theatre for my livelihood. If I were prevented from producing immoral and heretical plays I should cease to write for the theatre, and propagate my views from the platform and through books. I mention these facts to shew that I have a special interest in the achievement by my profession of those rights of liberty of speech and conscience which are matters of course in other professions. I object to censorship not merely because the existing form of it grievously injures and hinders me individually, but on public grounds.

Shaw, in this 'rejected Statement', went on to condemn the equating of the word 'moral' with the word 'conventional', pointing out that the doctrines of Mahomet, Galileo, Christ, Tom Paine, and many other historic figures were considered highly 'immoral' according to the *conventional* moral standards of their day. He drew a sharp distinction between this kind of 'immorality'—upon which, he considered, all civilisation and human progress was based—and vice, in the sense of murder, lust, mendacity, adultery, and so on: plays about which were almost invariably passed by the Censor. (The net result being that vice was made entertaining, and virtue banned, by the very institution which was supposed to produce the opposite effect.)

Nevertheless, Shaw was in favour of the *complete* abolition of censorship, because he strongly disapproved of the principle of a single person (whether in conjunction with literary advisers— or possessed of wide literary knowledge himself—or not) having despotic power to make arbitrary decisions on the morality or otherwise of stage shows; and because he did not believe that even some kind of *enlightened* censorship was a practicable possibility. He considered that the good that could be done by licensing all plays with themes of social reform (even if the subjects dealt with were unpleasant or 'shocking' —such as pros-titution, in his *Mrs Warren's Profession*) would far outweigh the harm that would be done by allowing the performance of all plays of every kind—including those of a truly vicious and vulgar kind—the debased character of which he deplored no less than the Church and many others did. He believed in liberty and toleration, and like Voltaire, in the right of everyone to express themselves, even if he and others disagreed with every word they said.

Apart from the question of whether 'vicious' plays should be censored or not, it is not clear from the preface to *Blanco Posnet* exactly where Shaw would have drawn the line as regards the sort of individual play *he* would have considered as falling within the category of 'vice'. (He pointed out, for example, that it was no longer as 'indecent' as it had once been for women to show more of their legs than the ankles, or to ride in the astride position on horseback instead of side-saddle). In so far as Shaw did not consider that the Censor should sit in final judgement, it seems implicit that he did not himself believe there could be *absolute* standards of purity and vice, or of good and evil.

His views on this fundamental moral aspect of life were vigorously and graphically amplified four years later, in 1913 (and two months after the first London production of his play *Androcles and the Lion* had aroused charges of 'immorality', blasphemy, and sacrilege) in the little-known correspondence in the pages of *The Times*—about a contemporary stage show of a different kind from his own—which is given in the next few pages.

ON STAGE MORALS AND CENSORSHIP, RELIGION, ART, AND SPIRITUAL AND PHYSICAL LOVE

The two letters by Bernard Shaw to *The Times* which follow (and the controversy surrounding them) are given because they clarify, in a concise form and in Shaw's own words, his attitude on the above subjects (which have been mentioned by C. B. Purdom, J. W. Sault, James Williams and other contributors to *Shaw the Villager*), and because all these subjects are of the greatest significance in the world of today.*

Although written in 1913, when a prudish attitude to sex and fanatical religious fervour were much more prevalent than today, the basic philosophy behind Shaw's arguments in these letters did not change during his lifetime (any more than the subjects themselves changed fundamentally). In particular, Shaw's attitude towards the question of censorship would not, I think, have been any different had he been alive at the present time (when the question is at least as topical and controversially important as it was in 1913).†

The occasion giving rise to Shaw's spirited attack on stage censorship and on religious intolerance was a show at the Palace Theatre called *A la Carte*, in which the French actress, Mlle Gaby Deslys, introduced her famous 'Gaby Glide' (a hilarious descent of the stairs, not excessively clothed),‡ which aroused complaints by the clergy of indecency and suggestiveness.

* My attention was first drawn to these letters by Mr Warren S. Smith, writing in the American *Shaw Review* in January 1960. The form in which I have edited the correspondence from its original source in *The Times* is my own; but my conclusions are broadly in agreement with his, and I gratefully acknowledge my debt to him.

† There are, for example, many parallels with the arguments involved in the *Lady Chatterley's Lover* trials, in London in 1960, and earlier in the United States.

‡ A popular ballroom dance step was subsequently named *The Gaby Glide*, but this was, of course, a considerable modification of the original act from which it took its name.

The Church of England, after ordering all its clergy to boycott the show, sent one of them, the Rev. Dr W. S. MacGowan, of St. Anne's, Soho, to make a detailed eye-witness report of it. His report was sent to the Lord Chamberlain above the signature of the then Bishop of Kensington. The Lord Chamberlain replied, through an officer, that the manager of the theatre concerned had been given to understand that so long as *A la Carte* was produced at his theatre, the Lord Chamberlain would be represented on each occasion, and that if the public morality was outraged any further in the Palace Theatre, the piece in question would be immediately forbidden, and the manager's licence for stage plays cancelled.

Mr Alfred Butt, then managing director of the Palace Theatre, denied the charges most strongly, adding that in his opinion the National Vigilance Association and the clergy had complained not of the performance *qua* performance, but because it was given by Mlle Gaby Deslys, and that had the same performance been given elsewhere by an unknown artiste, no criticism whatever would have been made. He did not think it fair to him that, merely upon representations made by people undoubtedly biased, after the sketch had been playing seven weeks, he should be expected either to make drastic changes or risk losing his licence immediately.

Miss Gaby Deslys herself also issued a 'reply to the clergy', part of which was quoted in *The Times*. She said: "I know the admirable work that clergymen do. I know how they go into slums and do their duty in the squalor of wretched hovels, in the midst of revolting scenes and surroundings. Couldn't they in the same spirit have braved the loathsome effect of my performance? Couldn't they have come to judge for themselves? Or, if that is too much to expect, couldn't the clergy have inquired from people as they left the theatre?—I would have been satisfied to leave my fate to their verdict. Or couldn't they have come to me with their complaint and discussed it? Or I could have come to them. None of these things has been done. Those gentlemen who signed that letter, heedless of its consequences to me, choose to condemn me unseen and unheard by my judges.

"People come to the Palace [she went on] whose names are household words. Many write to me letters of appreciation of what is, I can assure you, very hard work. How is it that they come and come again? There isn't a line in my part that could not be read aloud anywhere. My dancing is acrobatic dancing; the same twists and turns occur in it as acrobats use in their tricks. Certainly the same as done by hundreds of other dancers. If I do them with more brio than most, it is because I am enjoying the fun of it as well as the audience."

Some slight adjustments in the show were made which apparently satisfied the Bishop, who then attempted to justify his action in the columns of *The Times*. He claimed that he had no personal quarrel with the actress whose performance he criticised: he was only concerned to safeguard public morals, and the chief danger of the sketch lay not so much in its dialogue or acrobatic dancing as in the atmosphere of immorality and the suggestion of vice with which it was pervaded. It was to verify the facts that he had requested the Rev. Dr MacGowan to visit the theatre—"in the company of a layman whose long experience and tried judgement in such matters entitles him to the greatest respect" [!]—and he had accepted their report that the "most objectionable" parts of *A la Carte* had been modified or eliminated. The danger, he said, was that additions and 'improvements' could be, and constantly were introduced after a show had been licensed, "until a once harmless incident is transformed by suggestive representations which make their appeal to the sensual and passionate instincts."

The matter in all its ramifications now became an open controversy in the correspondence columns of *The Times*. Henry Arthur Jones supported the Bishop's position, but asked how it was to be enforced. Was it the Lord Chamberlain's department's intention henceforth to send a censor to watch every performance at every place of entertainment under its control? A couple of days later, in the issue of November 8th, his fellow-playwright, G. Bernard Shaw, entered the centre of the arena with the following letter:—

Sir,—May I, as a working playwright, ask the Bishop of Kensington to state his fundamental position clearly? So far, he has begged the question he is dealing with: that is, he has assumed that there can be no possible difference of opinion among good citizens concerning it. He has used the word "suggestive" without any apparent sense of the fact that the common thoughtless use of it by vulgar people has made it intolerably offensive. And he uses the word "objectionable" as if there were a general agreement as to what is objectionable and what is not, in spite of the fact that the very entertainment to which he himself objected had proved highly attractive to large numbers of people whose taste is entitled to the same consideration as his own.

On the face of it the Bishop of Kensington is demanding that the plays that he happens to like shall be tolerated and those which he happens not to like shall be banned. He is assuming that what he approves of is right, and what he disapproves of, wrong. Now, I have not seen the particular play which he so much dislikes; but suppose I go to see it tonight, and write a letter to you to-morrow to say that I approve of it, what will the Bishop have to say? He will have either to admit that his epithet of objectionable means simply disliked by the Bishop of Kensington, or he will have to declare boldly that he and I stand in the relation of God and the Devil. And, however his courtesy and his modesty may recoil from this extremity, when it is stated in plain English, I think he has got there without noticing it. At all events, he is clearly proceeding on the assumption that his conscience is more enlightened than that of the people who go to the Palace Theatre and enjoy what they see there. If the Bishop may shut up the Palace Theatre on this assumption, then the Nonconformist patrons of the Palace Theatre (and it has many of them) may shut up the Church of England by turning the assumption inside out. The sword of persecution always has two edges.

By "suggestive" the Bishop means suggestive of sexual emotion. Now a Bishop who goes into a theatre and declares that the performances there must not suggest sexual emotion is in the position of a playwright going into a church and declaring that the services there must not suggest religious emotion. The suggestion, gratification, and education of sexual emotion is one of the main uses and

THE STERN MORALIST

*The Bishop of
Kensington in* 1913

THE BEAUTIFUL ACTRESS

*Mlle Gaby Deslys
c.* 1913

THE VOLUPTUOUS "TOAST OF LONDON"

Mlle Gaby Deslys c. 1913

"CHINAMAN'S DRESS"

Bernard Shaw in Hongkong with the noted writers Lu Hsun and Ts'ai Yuan p'ei

glories of the theatre. It shares that function with all the fine arts. The sculpture courts of the Victoria and Albert Museum in the Bishop's diocese are crowded with naked figures of extraordinary beauty, placed there expressly that they may associate the appeal of the body with such beauty, refinement, and expression of the higher human qualities that our young people, contemplating them, will find baser objects of desire repulsive. In the National Gallery body and soul are impartially catered for: men have worshipped Venuses and fallen in love with Virgins. There is a voluptuous side to religious ecstasy and a religious side to voluptuous ecstasy; and the notion that one is less sacred than the other is the opportunity of the psychiatrist who seeks to discredit the saints by showing that the passion which exalted them was in its abuse capable also of degrading sinners. The so-called Song of Solomon, which we now know to be an erotic poem, was mistaken by the translators of the 17th century for a canticle of Christ to His Church, and is to this day so labelled in our Bibles.

Now let us turn to the results of cutting off young people—not to mention old ones—from voluptuous art. We have families who bring up their children in the belief that an undraped statue is an abomination; that a girl or a youth who looks at a picture by Paul Veronese is corrupted for ever; that the theatre in which *Tristan and Isolde* or *Romeo and Juliet* is performed is the gate of hell; and that the contemplation of a figure attractively dressed or revealing more of its outline than a Chinaman's dress does is an act of the most profligate indecency. Of Chinese sex morality I must not write in the pages of *The Times*. Of the English and Scottish sex morality that is produced by this starvation and blasphemous vilification of vital emotions I will say only this: that it is so morbid and abominable, so hatefully obsessed by the things that tempt it, so merciless in its persecution of all the divine grace which grows in the soil of our sex instincts when they are not deliberately perverted and poisoned, that if it could be imposed, as some people would impose it if they could, on the whole community for a single generation, the Bishop, even at the risk of martyrdom, would reopen the Palace Theatre with his episcopal benediction, and implore the lady to whose performances he now objects to return to the stage even at the sacrifice of the last rag of her clothing.

I venture to suggest that when the Bishop heard that there was an objectionable (to him) entertainment at the Palace Theatre, the simple and natural course for him was not to have gone there. That is how sensible people act. And the result is that if a manager offers a widely objectionable entertainment to the public he very soon finds out his mistake and withdraws it. It is my own custom as a playwright to make my plays "suggestive" of religious emotion. This makes them extremely objectionable to irreligious people. But they have the remedy in their own hands. They stay away. The Bishop will be glad to hear that there are not many of them; but it is a significant fact that they frequently express a wish that the Censor would suppress religious plays, and that he occasionally complies. In short, the Bishop and his friends are not alone in proposing their own tastes and convictions as the measure of what is permissible in the theatre. But if such individual and sectarian standards were tolerated we should have no plays at all, for there never yet was a play that did not offend somebody's taste.

I must remind the Bishop that if the taste for voluptuous entertainment is sometimes morbid, the taste for religious edification is open to precisely the same objection. If I had a neurotic daughter I would much rather risk taking her to the Palace Theatre than to a revival meeting. Nobody has yet counted the homes and characters wrecked by intemperance in religious emotion. When we begin to keep such statistics the chapel may find its attitude of moral superiority to the theatre, and even to the publichouse, hard to maintain, and may learn a little needed charity. We all need to be reminded of the need for temperance and toleration in religious emotion and in political emotion, as well as in sexual emotion. But the Bishop must not conclude that I want to close up all places of worship: on the contrary, I preach in them. I do not even clamour for the suppression of political party meetings, though nothing more foolish and demoralizing exists in England to-day. I live and let live. As long as I am not compelled to attend revival meetings, or party meetings, or theatres at which the sexual emotions are ignored or reviled, I am prepared to tolerate them on reciprocal terms; for though I am unable to conceive any good coming to any human being as a set-off to their hysteria, their rancorous bigotry, and their dullness and falsehood, I know that those who like them are equally unable to conceive any good coming of the sort of assemblies I frequent; so I mind my own business and obey the old precept—

"He that is unrighteous, let him do unrighteousness still; and he that is filthy let him be made filthy still; and he that is righteous let him do righteousness still; and he that is holy let him be made holy still." For none of us can feel quite sure in which category the final judgment may place us; and in the meantime Miss Gaby Deslys is as much entitled to the benefit of the doubt as the Bishop of Kensington.

Yours truly,

G. Bernard Shaw.

To this the Bishop of Kensington replied (on November 10th) that he had already stated his fundamental position clearly. He added:—

... I do not wish to obscure that position by yielding to Mr Shaw's invitation to follow him in a discussion of those paradoxes which to any normally thinking man carry their refutation on the surface.

I make no such demand as he puts into my mouth, as that the plays that the Bishop of Kensington "happens to like shall be tolerated, and those which he happens not to like shall be banned." My demand was as stated, that "the dialogue and official visit should form the absolute legal basis of the licence to perform any piece, and that any alteration should be subject to the Lord Chamberlain's written permit." That is a very different issue from the one he wishes to raise.

He takes exception to my use of the words "suggestive" and "objectionable," and states that by "suggestive" the Bishop means "suggestive of sexual emotion." So I do—of a certain kind of sexual emotion. For since Mr Shaw appears to admit that sexual emotion is susceptible of education, he will grant that it may be wrongly educated as well as highly educated.

It is possible to suggest evil as well as good, and because sexual emotion is capable of being educated by the fine arts to the enjoyment of "such beauty, refinement, and expression of the higher human qualities that our young people contemplating" the products of the highest art "will find baser objects of desire repulsive," precisely for that reason there exists the possibility of so perverting it by the suggestion of evil that those baser objects of desire will no longer repel, but attract. This is a possible result which I gather that Mr Shaw would join me in deploring.

The Bishop then quoted, in support of his position, passages such as the following from *Das Programm*, the recognised organ of the music-hall profession on the Continent:—

The contortions of the various shades of "Salome" dancers pales into utter insignificance beside the present day mode of animal posturing and passionate exuberance. And finally the up-to-the-minute vogue of the so-called *revues* leaves nothing to be imagined in the mind of the most ignorant, so ambitious are the music-hall proprietors to cater to the risible faculties of anaemic men and women.

and he commented:—

From these quotations Mr Shaw will, perhaps, understand that there is a kind of "suggestion" which I venture to call "objectionable." I am far from desiring to propose my own tastes and convictions as the measure of what is permissible in the theatre, but I can confidently claim that my contention is backed by a great body of the public that performances are taking place which are a disgrace; I think, further, that I can assert that had Mr Shaw himself seen the incidents in the performance at the Palace Theatre to which we directed protest,* and which were promptly eliminated and altered, even he would have found a difficulty in discovering there the suggestion of that kind of "sexual emotion" which he described as "one of the main uses and glories of the theatre."

A crop of letters from others appeared in the issues of November 11th and 12th. Mr H. B. Irving supported the Bishop, saying that the National Gallery possessed "some works of undoubted art, which never can and never will be placed on its walls." Was it not, he asked, the same with the theatre? He admitted that he had not seen the show which had raised the issue of public morals.

The Prebendary of St. Paul's Cathedral considered that Shaw's concluding quotation proved him to be "a mere cynic, with no real desire to uplift his fellows." Purity of thought, he averred, was the basis of all morality, while impure thoughts led to impure action.

* The Bishop had not seen them himself.

Alfred Butt again emphatically denied that anything vulgar or indecent whatever had been added to *A la Carte* since it had originally been passed by the Censor, and thought it "intolerable" that individual or sectarian views should be allowed to prevail, and stated that if the clergy repeated their accusations they would be made to justify them.

Then a Mr Ronald Campbell McFie, M.A., Ll.D., challenged Shaw's comparison of the Church and the Theatre as mutual rivals. He wrote (I have abbreviated his reply slightly):—

I am neither a working playwright nor a working Bishop; I am a professional educator neither of the sexual nor of the religious emotions; but I do profess to have a little logic . . .

Does Mr Bernard Shaw really mean to assert that among "good citizens" there are no general standards of good taste, decency, and morality? . . . And if he maintains that Miss Gaby Deslys is as good a judge in a moral matter as a Bishop, does he also maintain that she is as good a judge of diamonds as Streeter or as good a judge of Shakespeare as Bernard Shaw? . . . I thought Mr Bernard Shaw was a Socialist; has he suddenly become an Anarchist? Does he draw the line nowhere? Does he hold that nothing objectionable is to be suppressed so long as some people enjoy it? Does he dispute the right and duty of any man—even a man without the duties and privileges of a Bishop—to endeavour to put a stop to any proceeding that, rightly or wrongly, he considers immoral, whether it be "rancorous bigotry", or paralytic tolerance—whether it be pandering to perverted sexual emotions or a pandering to perverted religious emotions. To what anarchical extremes does our Socialistic Mr Shaw intend to carry his *laissez-faire* principles, and how does he reconcile such principles with his own intolerant, combative, and caustic pen? Is not the pen mightier than the sword?

Mr McFie admitted that revival meetings and religious extravagances that seemed pernicious to most sane and good citizens, as well as to Mr Shaw, were tolerated, but averred that religious toleration and moral toleration were very different things. Bishops had a duty to combat the spread of "moral infection" in the community. He also admitted that he had not seen Miss Deslys's dance: "But even if I had seen her dance and considered her dancing most edifying, I am tolerant enough to allow Bishops to hold another opinion and act according to their convictions."

In the same issue (November 12th), Mr C. Craies wrote: "After reading Mr Bernard Shaw's weighty criticism of the Bishop of Kensington, I was almost persuaded that the same emotion is stimulated by the Venus de Milo as by a pornographic photo; by *Romeo and Juliet* as by an indecent music-hall sketch. I said to myself, 'Is there really no difference between the celestial and the common Aphrodite? . . .' The objection alleged against Mlle Deslys's performance was that it is suggestive, not of sexual emotion, but of vice, or the corruption of sexual emotion. . . . Surely Mr Shaw will acknowledge the distinction?"

Also in this issue was a letter from "C.K.C.", who supported Shaw, pointing out that a new philosophy cannot, on the face of it, submit to be tried by ethical standards which it entirely repudiates, and intends to supersede. But voluptuousness, he considered, stood condemned on any ground, and "Mr. Shaw will have to confute the philosophy of the farmyard as well as Christianity before it can be removed from the category of vice. Vergil," he said, "is confirmed by all experience":—

> Sed non ulla magis vires industria firmat
> Quam Venerem et caeci stimulos avertere amoris.*

On November 13th Oliver Lodge, Jun., condemned H. B. Irving's jubilation that works of art [of any kind] should be banished from public view, quoting the passages from Samuel Butler's *Erewhon* which end, repeatedly: "O God! O Montreal."

In the same issue "E.A.B." wrote that Shaw viewed morality subjectively, as a subject for dialectics, and the Bishop objectively, as a factor in conduct. To him ("E.A.B."), the whole discussion was centred round the question of "What is Evil?"

---

* But no self-discipline more fortifies the natural powers
  Than to turn away from Venus and the stimulation of blind passion.

If the sexual impulse was evil, then life itself was evil. The battle between body and soul is the subject matter of all religions, he pointed out. Christian ethics looked upon the body as evil, which he regarded as the negation of life. Mr Shaw, he considered, was an *ultra*-Christian in that respect, for all his plays, especially *Man and Superman*, had depicted his "Superior Man" as struggling—always hopelessly—against the life force of sex. In representing the sexual impulse as an evil tyrant he was a most moral author according to mediaeval ethics, but a most immoral one "in the light of the broader wisdom which glorifies all life as a manifestation of the Omnipotent's Will."

"E.A.B." supported Shaw in considering it quite impossible to formulate a fixed standard of good and evil: "Gaby Deslys's dances and posturing might be a salutary discipline for a race dying from the gradual paralysis of sexual impulse", while conversely, "the Church tacitly upholds warfare." What *is* vice? he asked. Certainly not sexual impulse, unless one held that existence itself was a vice, and the sooner ended the better. He (Mr "E.A.B.") defined sexual vice as "the conscious glorification of a means to an end"—and thus any play, or dance, which sought to traffic on sexual attraction as a conscious end in itself was, according to this definition, immoral. But who had the right to apply such a definition? he asked. Both the Church and the Censor had made ludicrous and ridiculous mistakes in the past when judging morals in art and in plays.

On November 14th, the Rev. T. A. Lacey began his letter by saying that "E.A.B." was a good example of the *anima naturaliter Christiana** which is not aware of its own Christianity. St. Augustine had taught that the sexual impulse was natural, and therefore a good thing, and quoted his famous saying: *Natura diaboli, in quantum natura est, bonum est, sed perversitas eam malam facit.*† If the sexual impulse was perverted, the

---

* The soul which is a 'natural' Christian one, irrespective of training or intellectual belief.
  † The nature of the devil, in so far as he has a nature, is (fundamentally) good, but depravity (*i.e.* the fall from Grace) makes it bad.

impulse remained good, though the perversion was evil. In support of "E.A.B."'s definition of sexual vice as the conscious glorification of a means to an end, he quoted St. Augustine's definition of perversity as *uti fruendis et frui utendis**—a definition which was taken up later by St. Thomas Aquinas. "E.A.B.", he concluded, was "more Christian, more Augustinian, more mediaeval" than he knew.

On November 15th *The Times* published the second letter from Bernard Shaw:—

Sir,—I note the Bishop of Kensington's explanation that in his recent agitation against the Palace Theatre he has been concerned not with public morals but solely with a technical infraction of the Lord Chamberlain's regulations. In that case I have nothing more to say, partly because the management of the Palace Theatre strenuously and indignantly denies that the infraction has occurred, partly because Lord Sandhurst is quite well able to take care of himself, but mainly because this astonishing episcopal reply to an earnest demand for a statement of principle sends me reeling into a dumb despair of making any Englishman understand what political principle means or even persuading him that such a thing exists.

It is useless for me to repeat what I said in my former communication. If the Bishop was unable to grapple with it yesterday, there is no reason to expect that he will be able to do so to-morrow. But lest I should seem to fail in patience, I will comment on one or two points of his letter. I am very glad he has pointed out that the Lord Chamberlain has no real control over performances, and that the guarantee of decency which the Censor's licence is supposed to carry is illusory. I have pointed that out so often that I cannot but feel encouraged when a Bishop repeats it. I am glad that he agrees with me also that the power of influencing people for good is inextricably involved with the power to influence them for evil. But if this is so, why does the Bishop still imagine that he can suppress and destroy the power for evil without also suppressing and destroying the power for good? An evil sermon—and there are many more evil sermons than evil plays—may do frightful harm; but is

---

* To make use of (*i.e.* a business or toil of) things intended primarily for enjoyment, and to make enjoyment or pleasure the end of things intended (primarily) for a specific use or function.

the Bishop ready to put on the chains he would fasten on the play-wright, and agree that no sermon shall be preached unless it is first read and licensed by the Lord Chamberlain? No doubt it is easier to go to sleep than to watch and pray; that is why everyone is in favour of securing purity and virtue and decorum by paying an official to look after them. But the result is that your official, who is equally indisposed to watch and pray, takes the simple course of forbidding everything that is not customary; and, as nothing is customary except vulgarity, the result is that he kills the thing he was employed to purify and leaves the nation to get what amusement they can out of its putrefaction. Our souls are to have no adventures because adventures are dangerous. Carry that an obvious step farther and the Bishop of Kensington will be gagged because he might at any moment utter false doctrines. He will be handcuffed because he might smite me with his pastoral staff. The dog-muzzling order will be extended to the muzzling of all priests and prophets and politicians. The coward in all of us will seek security at any price.

But this does not touch the present issue. I repeat that there is no consensus of opinion as to what is objectionable and what is desirable in theatrical entertainments. Mr. Butt's audiences are as big as the Bishop's congregations, and they pay him more than they pay the Bishop. If the Bishop may say to these people, "You shall not go to the Palace Theatre, or, if you go you shall not see what you like there, because I do not consider it good for you," then these people may say to the Bishop, "You shall not preach the doctrine of the Atonement; for in our opinion it destroys all sense of moral responsibility."

I need not again elaborate the point; but I will point out something that the Bishop may not have thought of in this connexion. Not only is art, or religion, a power for evil as well as for good; but the self-same exhibition or sermon that effects one man's salvation may effect another man's damnation. The placing of the Bible in the hands of the laity by the Protestant Catholics produced great results; but it also produced all the horrors that were predicted by the Roman Catholics as their reason for withholding it, from an epidemic of witch-burning to the political excesses of the Anabaptists and Puritans, and the sour misery of 16th century Scotland. The case against the freedom of the Palace Theatre is as dust in the balance compared with the case against the freedom of the Bible

Society. Is the Bishop, having attacked the Palace Theatre, going to attack the Bible Society *a fortiori*? Of course not, because he can see the overwhelming argument in favour of scriptural freedom which he is unable to see in the case of the theatre, because the theatre is the Church's most formidable rival in forming the minds and guiding the souls of the people. Well, he must compete with fair weapons, not with the bludgeons of official tyranny. He cannot dissect out the evil of the theatre and strike at that alone. One man seeing a beautiful actress will feel that she has made all common debaucheries impossible to him; another, seeing the same actress in the same part, will plunge straight into those debaucheries because he has seen her body without being able to see her soul. Destroy the actress and you rob the first man of his salvation without saving the second from the first woman he meets on the pavement.

It is reported that the Bishop of London, preaching on Sunday in the church of St. Mary Magdalen, Paddington, dealt with this subject. Far be it from me to accuse any man of the fantastic things our reporters put into all our mouths; but I can believe that he proposed "a vigorous campaign for a clean, pure life." If by this he means, as I may without offence assume that he does, life according to the highest conception his lights can show him, then he is on the right tack, though, if his conceptions are at all lofty, he will get more kicks than halfpence for his pains. As long as he sticks to the propagation of noble impulses and aspirations he cannot go far wrong. But if once he turns aside from that honourable work to the cheap and rancorous course of persecuting the people who do not share his tastes under pretext of weeding out evil, he will become a public nuisance. He is reported to have declared that, "It has been said that no Christian Church has any right to criticize any play in London." It may be that there exists some abysmal fool who said this. If so, he was hardly worth the Bishop of London's notice. The Christian Church ought to criticize every play in London; and it is on that right and duty of criticism, and not on the unfortunate Lord Chamberlain, that the Christian Church ought to rely, and, indeed, would rely without my prompting if it were really a Christian Church.

Finally, may I thank the Bishop of Kensington for alleging as a reason for persecuting the Palace Theatre (for he does not, after all, combat my demonstration that his action was persecution) that I should probably disapprove of the entertainment myself? As to that, I can only say that, if the Bishop sets out to suppress all the institutions of which I disapprove, he will soon have not one single supporter, not even

Yours truly,

G. Bernard Shaw.

This letter concluded the public correspondence, but Shaw had not had quite the last word. On November 19th *The Times* carried a brief report that:—

A mass meeting of men, organized by the Men's Committee of the London Diocesan Council for Preventative and Rescue Work, was held at the People's Palace, Mile End,* last evening. . . .

The Bishop of London took the chair, and, in the course of his address, said the Bishop of Kensington and he had figured a good deal in the Press of late, and to judge from what was written in some quarters, it was thought they were trying to crush out all the happiness and spirits from London. Some of the plays which had been produced, and some of the books which had been written, had exalted sexual impulse out of all proportion. The public opinion of men when they met was still rotten on this question. It was better than it had been, and one result of the improvement was the passing of the White Slave Traffic Bill. . . . There were still hundreds of girls going down into degradation, and until men rose, with what he called the shepherd instinct, they would never be able to crush out that great evil. . . .

The Bishop of Kensington said that there were no people more grateful to those who were fighting the battle of purity than those who were in the music-hall business.†

Finally, on November 27th, it was reported in *The Times* that The Bishop of London, in an address in the Guildhall the previous day, had said that the connection between religion and

---

* Then solely a technical college, at which concerts and other entertainments were occasionally given. The present People's Palace theatre (an extension of the college's activities) was not opened until 1936.

† An opinion probably shared by fewer of them than he would have wished, and certainly not by Mr Butt, who was obliged by the unfortunate publicity to close down *A la Carte*, or by Miss Deslys, who returned to France.

morality had been denied. The line taken by the public, he said, was that if the Bishop of Kensington did not like those plays, he need not go to them.

The public's line was: "nothing is objectionable in itself, but only to you. If I like a thing, then it is all right, and if I do not like it, then it is wrong to me." Such opposition took them down below the morality of some of the wild tribes, the Bishop said. Yet he denied that the Church attacked mere vulgarity. [!]— ". . . A good laugh did a busy City man a good deal of good". The Church's was no Puritan narrow-minded line. They could have all the farces in the world, so long as there was nothing in them that would "bring a blush to a girl's face, or make a boy turn his head another way, when they were taken to the theatre".

The Church of England's campaign gained its objective in so far as the act by Miss Gaby Deslys was withdrawn. As regards Bernard Shaw's standpoint in the matter, in my view a careful reading of the foregoing letters reveals Shaw as no hedonist, but on the contrary, as the strictest of moralists. It is, I think, quite clear that Shaw did not deny the existence of evil, but believed in what has by some been termed 'essential' morality—that is to say morality based on self-discipline according to one's own 'inner light', and on a sensitive regard for the possible effects of one's actions on all others concerned; and that he regarded dependence upon the censor, or upon arbitrary religious or moral edicts, as the negation of this—since it merely equates morality with convention, and obviates personal responsibility and moral choice. Shaw believed that both art and religion—like life itself—are powers for good or evil, and that people must work out their own salvation, according to reason and their own individual consciences.

[*Editorial Note:* re the *Lady Chatterley's Lover* trials in America in 1959 and in England in 1960:—

The foregoing correspondence leaves little doubt that Shaw would have approved the verdicts lifting the ban on the unexpurgated editions of Lawrence's novel, and, indeed, it is undoubtedly largely due to Shaw's pioneer efforts that dramatic and literary censorship is so much more enlightened today—even if the principle of *complete* abolition of all forms of censorship at which he aimed has not yet been achieved. However, the appointment of a Government Commission on theatre censorship in 1966 took the battle a considerable stage further. Indeed, in October, 1968, a Bill embodying this Committee's recommendations (which included complete abolition of *stage* censorship at any rate, and therefore the demise of the Lord Chamberlain's office) became law.

It may be of interest to add that, while Shaw would have approved these decisions and the principle of artistic freedom of expression for which they were a victory, he had little contact with D. H. Lawrence during his life, or interest in the latter's work and outlook—which, elevating instinct, Shaw the puritan and intellectual regarded as 'earthy' and which was undoubtedly of an entirely different kind from his own. Of the two, Shaw was by far the more tolerant of the other's point of view.]

ON LOVE, MARRIAGE,
THE NATURE OF SEX,
AND SEX ETHICS

The following letters throw further light on the human side of Shaw. The attitude of individuals to love, marriage, and sex is inextricably and fundamentally bound up with their characters as human beings. It also has a profound effect on their work.

Shaw has often been criticised—both by contributors to *Shaw the Villager* and by others—as being 'all intellect and no feeling', and for being 'not a full man'. In his plays, his female characters especially have been regarded by many as unreal; as puppets or 'mouthpieces' for his scintillating dialogue, but lacking in warmth, femininity, or even a moderate degree of sex appeal. These generalisations (which in the present writer's view are in any case too broad and sweeping) have been connected by some with the fact that Shaw married comparatively late in life (at the age of 42) and that (on the insistence of his wife) the marriage was never consummated, and was in this sense not a 'real' or full marriage.

There are several things which can be said immediately about this. In the first place, Shaw is known to have had several love affairs prior to his marriage, some of which were undoubtedly consummated. Secondly, there can be little dispute that Shaw was a man of genius; and, whilst there have been geniuses of different kinds, it is certainly true of most of them that normal marriage, home life, and sex relations have taken a subordinate position to their work—often, indeed, playing a very insignificant part (or even no part at all) in their lives. Their work *is* their life. To use psychological terms now part of our everyday language they *sublimate* their sexual energy or *libido* more or less completely in creative artistic work (or social reform, or

78

scientific enquiry). That this was so in Shaw's case is abundantly clear from his own *Sixteen Self Sketches*, where he writes:—

. . . no man who has any real work in the world has time or money for a pursuit so long and expensive as the pursuit of women . . . intellect is a passion, and . . . the modern notion that passion means only sex is as crude and barbarous as the ploughman's idea that art is simply bawdiness . . . art can flourish splendidly when sex is absolutely barred, as it was, for example, in the Victorian literature which produced Dickens.

Shaw also explained :—

I was never duped by sex as a basis for permanent relations, nor dreamt of marriage in connection with it. I put everything else before it, and never refused or broke an engagement to speak on Socialism to pass a gallant evening. . . . Do not forget that all marriages are different, and that marriages between young people, followed by parentage, must not be lumped in with childless partnerships between middle-aged people who have passed the age at which the bride can safely bear a first child.

He added :—

. . . Not until I was past 40 did I earn enough to marry without seeming to marry for money, nor my wife at the same age without suspicion of being driven by sex starvation. As man and wife we found a new relation in which sex had no part. It ended the old gallantries, flirtations and philanderings for both of us. . . .

But did it? On the same page Shaw wrote: "As soon as I could afford to dress presentably I became accustomed to women falling in love with me. I did not pursue women. I was pursued by them."

Did this process continue after his marriage? The following correspondence reveals that it did, and shows clearly (*a*) that Shaw was quite as normally virile, susceptible, and capable of tender feeling as most men, and (*b*) that his affection for his wife, and his respect for the sanctity of marriage, completely over-ruled questions of extra-marital attractions on a more instinctual and sensual level. In this attitude—in his abhorrence of 'triangle' situations—Shaw, the great iconoclast, is, surprisingly, shown to have been entirely normal and conventional in his moral outlook (one might almost say *ultra* normal and conventional, in this era of moral confusion.)

The woman in question was a young girl in her twenties, and living in the country, who had developed an overwhelming passion (or 'crush' as some would call it) for Shaw, regardless of the fact that he was a married man, and an extremely busy person. It was not the first time that Shaw was faced with this particular problem (as many authors, film and stage stars, and other public idols are), nor was it to be the last. Shaw obviously could not have "printed postcards" for dealing with such infatuated admirers. How, then, *did* he deal with them?

Of the letters which follow, Dame Sybil Thorndike wrote when they were first brought to light* : "The letters are extremely interesting—and what good advice he gives to all young women who fall in love with famous gentlemen! They throw another sidelight upon Shaw. He gives the young woman excellent domestic advice—the marvel is that he took the trouble to write so fully to someone who must have exhausted him with her impassioned letters."

Here is Shaw's first reply to her:—

10 Adelphi-terrace, W.C.
5th April, 1906.

My dear lady—Why don't you join some Socialist Society and get some work to do? There are always envelopes to be directed and tracts to be distributed.

What is the use of thinking about yourself and writing long letters (three full stops in 8 pages!) to an elderly gentleman—letters which he always tears up the moment they threaten to be the kind that the writer wants to get back an hour after they are posted.

If you don't find some business to do that is not specially your own business you will go quite cracked.

Yours faithfully,
G. Bernard Shaw.

P.S.—The poems are too careless in form to be satisfactory.

* In the *Daily Herald*, in May, 1951.

The Happy Marriage. Mr & Mrs Bernard Shaw

*The Passionate Pursuer. Shaw's "luxurious young
devil", Miss Erica Cotterill*

Shaw warns of the dangers of falling in love with a god.

(Extract from his letter to Erica Cotterill of April 29th, 1908)

Shaw's telegram. The flirtation with Miss Cotterill begins

The girl, however (her name was Erica Cotterill), was determined to pursue her idol, and the following year the first actual meeting between Shaw and her took place, after she had received from him this telegram:—

REPLY PAID, MISS ERICA COTTERILL
GODALMING   AM   OUT   OF   TOWN
TELEGRAPH ME YOUR ADDRESS IN
LONDON AND I WILL ASK YOU TO
LUNCH SOME DAY THIS WEEK SHAW
CODICOTE.

A few months later an embarrassing situation had developed in her home (though not, as yet, in Shaw's). She had tried—evidently without complete success—to keep her developing passion secret. Shaw wrote at length, devoting (according to the date of his letter) three days' thought to the matter, and giving her much sound domestic advice.

Ayot St. Lawrence,
Welwyn, Herts.
Saturday to Monday,
14th-16th December, 1907.

Oh, you are young, Miss Cotterill, very VERY young.

You duffer, why didn't you tell your father and mother that you are in love with me and that you write to me whenever you have nothing better to do, and that what you couldn't stand was to have your father's trash [*he wrote works on education*] set up as superior to my inspired scriptures? How can you expect to get on with your parents if you never tell them anything about yourself?

That would explain everything in a perfectly inoffensive and highly amusing way.

Instead of which you go on nagging at the poor man and pretending to criticise, when you are really in a condition of delightful infatuation and furious jealousy.

He wouldn't mind the truth; it is human, natural, sympathetic. But this arguing—this saying things—this—yah!

Do stop talking about whether this is wrong or that right. Have you read my works in vain that you are still irritating yourself and everybody else with this artificial academic illnatured stuff about guilt and innocence?

You talk of your father and mother and of yourself as if you were three clocks always arguing about the correct time and accusing each other of being slow or fast.

Can't you take your parents as they are, and let them know you as you are instead of stalking them from a perpetual ambush and shooting little arrows at them?

Your priest seems to be a sensible man. But why not marry somebody with a short temper and a heavy fist, who would knock you down the moment you began to say that much of what he said was true but that some of it was wrong?

Oh, you want work, regular work. And babies. You are at present living on yourself, consuming your own spirit. You are consequently a nagging prig.

My blood runs cold when I think of those poor parents of yours. And Mr Cotterill's works on Education! "How to Keep in Perfect Health," by a Doctor with a Sick Family.

It's no use; nothing that I can say will be of any use to you. You must fight your own way out. Only try a little courage, as you did in telling me.

Take people—even your parents—as they are, not as they ought to be on some academic system of yours. But also, carry out your side of the bargain. Plank yourself down as what you are, and not as what you ought to be.

What's the use of telling me that you are in love with me and then hiding that dominant factor in your sentiments from everybody else. How are they to understand you otherwise? I must break-off—post hour.   *G.B.S.*

A month later the young woman announced her intention of writing a book. This evoked much more interest in Shaw than her appeals to his emotions:—

10 Adelphi-terrace, W.C.
31st Jan., 1908.

What is all this about publishing a book? How are you doing it? Where are you doing it? Who is doing it?

Why don't you consult me about it instead of writing endless hypochondria without any stops and "sort of" in every second line (a maddening expression—do you call yourself a lady?)?

You will be fleeced like a sheep, humbugged, swindled, robbed of your copyright, overcharged.

If it is a play, you may lose thousands of pounds by publishing without a preliminary performance to protect your rights in America.

What a household—stewing, nursing, hypochondria, hypochondria, moral and physical hypochondria! And you talk of a Convalescent Home. Your family habit would make valetudinarians of a gang of navvies or a regiment of Amazons.

Yes: I will try to fix up a lunch for you—perhaps when Barker* comes back from America (he talks of going for six weeks), perhaps before. But I shall give you about two hours notice; and it won't be very soon; so don't bother.

Your criticisms of the performances are rather useful in a way. If only you would tell me what you are *doing* and *seeing* and not be so fearfully pre-occupied by your soul and your stomach and, generally speaking, the complaints that all young women have, I might be of some use to you, if I had time.

Anyhow, let me know about that publishing business before you do something irretrievable. *G.B.S.*

Correspondence continued for a further year, until the girl pressed for an opportunity of visiting Shaw in his own home. Shaw had become sufficiently fond of her, and interested in her literary work, and was too kind, to refuse her appeal; but he made it very clear that though he regarded her as a *luxurious young devil*, there was no possibility whatever of an 'eternal triangle' so far as he was concerned. He gave her a lecture on the Sanctity of Marriage and the proprieties.

10 Adelphi-terrace, W.C.
22nd April, 1908.

My dear Emerica,† I should have attended to the enclosed for you sooner but for a very bad bout of influenza. In sending it to the New Age, you need not put it forward as your own device.

---

* Granville Barker, the brilliant stage director and producer.
† Shaw, curiously, called her Emerica instead of Erica.

Anybody else in the world but you would have either paid a guinea subscription to the Authors' Society and got the help of the secretary, or else got your solicitor to negotiate for you.

You understand, of course, that this is only a draft, and that it would be well to keep a copy when you send it to them for their approval. When you have agreed upon it, then two fair copies can be made. Each party signs one and sends it to the other; and that finishes the job.

Now that I have taught you some respect for business and the law, let me assure you that marriage is more sacred than either, and that unless you are prepared to treat my wife with absolute loyalty, you will be hurled into outer darkness for ever.

The privilege of pawing me, such as it is, is hers exclusively.

She has to tolerate worshipping females whose efforts to conceal the fact that they take no interest in her are perfunctory, and who bore her to distraction with their adoration of me; but it is my business to see that her patience is not abused.

You are a luxurious young devil, with the ethics, and something of the figure, of an anteater; and I have no doubt you can coax your mother and your Rupert* by crawling all over them; but if you dare to try those tactics with me in my wife's home you will be very startlingly awakened to the iron laws of domestic honor.

Also, it is not sensible nor decent to write about such demonstrations except to men of your own time of life, and with some assurance that they are equally infatuated, and will read it all as touching poetry.

Whenever I get anything in the nature of a loveletter, I hand it straight to Charlotte, and I am not at all sure that this may not be the explanation of the fact that the lunch here and the meeting with Mr G. B. did not come off.

Remember that your best behaviour will not be too good for me, as you hardly yet know how to behave yourself at all, being the very worst brought-up young woman I have ever met in the course of my half century of "taking notice".

G.B.S.

This letter obviously aroused considerable pique in the girl, who felt (rightly or wrongly) that she had been misunderstood. Shaw then wrote, not unkindly, but very firmly and in detail,

* Erica Cotterill was a first cousin of Rupert Brooke.

Part of Shaw's letter to Erica Cotterill of April 22nd, 1908.

again urging the importance of sex ethics. He warned her of the perils of sex in society, setting forth his views on the nature of sex, and on its relationship to his own Life Force theory:—

> 10 Adelphi-terrace, W.C.2.
> 27th April, 1908.

My dear Emerica, I am so hard pressed for time by my rehearsals that I can write only in the curtest and baldest fashion.

I do not accuse you of proposing to act "wrongly and indecently": I tell you that your proposal was unlawful.

It is entirely natural for a hungry man to take a loaf of bread and eat it. It is entirely natural for an adult woman to kiss a man she likes. People who do these natural things are socially impossible.

There is no more intolerable nuisance than the man who makes love to other men's wives and the woman who makes love to other women's husbands.

Unless when you walk into the house of a married woman you accept the obligation (a highly unnatural one) to consider her husband's person as sacred, you break the covenant of bread and salt, and are a thief, a libertine and a betrayer.

If you say that you mean no harm, you are a fool as well.

The reason is very simple. When an adult woman and an adult man caress one another, the result is entirely different from the result of your kissing your mother.

The whole creative force of the universe suddenly leaps into activity in their bodies. They lose all power of acting otherwise than instinctively.

They act instinctively; and the consequence is that the adult man wakes from his dream exceedingly ashamed of himself; and the adult woman has a baby.

That is what will happen to you the very first time you act in that perfectly natural and beautiful and happy and innocent way which you imagine you can trifle with as a woman because you have trifled with it as a child. And until you understand this danger, you will be a mischievous and silly girl, quite unfit to be trusted by yourself in London or anywhere else.

You have a box of matches and you propose to go about striking them and throwing them into barrels of gunpowder, because you are quite sure you don't mean anything to happen.

When it does happen, the Life Force will make very short work of your intentions.

In brief, if you enter my wife's house, you enter it on the understanding that you don't make love to her husband. If I introduce you to Mrs. Barker,* I shall do so on the understanding that you don't make love to *her* husband.

You may admire and dream and worship and adore until you are black in the face; but you are not to sit and hold their hands, nor kiss them, nor cuddle them, nor nestle in their manly bosoms—oh, so sweetly, so innocently, so heavenlikely—because if you do the Life Force will suddenly leap out and gobble you up.

All these exquisite visions and reveries are only the bait in the trap the Life Force is setting for you.

The reason everybody tells you to get married and have children is that they thoroughly understand the wiles of the Life Force, and wish heartily that you would come to understand it too, and become a reasonable and sympathetic human being through that experience.

That is all I have time to say. That it should have been left to me to say it to you shows the utter uselessness of parents in this matter.

Remember, in entering the world now as an adult woman, you must take on yourself the Laws of Honor.   *G.B.S.*

The girl was inevitably upset and disappointed, and must have made some reply almost immediately, for Shaw sent her another letter only two days later. He was adamant in his attitude that there could be no physical side to the affair, and told her that if she *dared to fall in love with a god, she must be prepared for thunderbolts.*

10 Adelphi Terrace, W.C.
29th April, 1908.

My dear Emerica, It is all very terrible and agonizing and glorious and tragic and unbearable, isn't it.

You are certainly enjoying it enormously and rising to it with great literary power. Only, you might let your poor mother alone.

---

* Granville Barker's first wife, Lillah McCarthy, the famous actress who appeared in many first productions of Shaw's plays.

10 ADELPHI TERRACE W.C.
29th April 1908.

My dear Florence

I am so hard pressed for time by my rehearsals that I can write only in the curtest & rudest fashion.

I do not accuse you of proposing to act "wrongly & inhumanly": I tell you that your proposal was unlawful.

It is entirely natural for a hungry man to take a loaf of bread & eat it. It is entirely natural for an adult woman to kiss a man she likes. People who do these natural things are socially impossible.

There is no more unutterable nuisance than the man who makes love to other men's wives and the woman who makes love to other men's husbands. Unless when you will it the house of a married woman you accept the obligation (a highly unnatural one) to consider her husband's home as sacred, you break the covenant of bread & salt, and are a thief, a libertine, & a betrayer.

If you say that you mean no harm, you are a fool as well. The reason is very simple. When an adult woman and an adult man carry one one another, the result is actually different from the result of your kissing your mother. The whole erotic poetry of the universe suddenly begins to act actively in their bodies. They lose all power of acting otherwise than instinctively. They act unconsciously; and the

I don't matter: writing letters to me is like giving tracts to a missionary: I just cock my eye at all this beautiful, eloquent, child-like-sincere-selfish squirming and bang it goes into the fire lest it should fall into somebody else's hands; and if you suppose you need explain things to me that I understand better than you, then you are very youthfully mistaken.

It is, I suppose, rather brutal of me to tell you things that few people can bear to be told until they are forty. But just as I have to take care of you in literary and dramatic copyright business, I have to take care of you in more personal matters; and some of these matters are so delicate that delicacy in dealing with them is intolerable.

Jupiter could not help shrivelling up Semele; if you dare to fall in love with a god, you must be prepared for thunderbolts.

Now once and for all and finally, when you come to London to begin the world there, you must do so as an adult woman, and accept all the obligations and limitations I have so bluntly described to you.

I am speaking quite impersonally, as I—an old gentleman of 52 —would speak to any young woman who innocently proposed to behave like a child and expect the privileges of a child.

Stop thinking about yourself and read my last letter as if it were a letter you had found from an old man you did not know to a young woman you did not know, and consider whether any other course of conduct is possible.

Anyhow, that is my ultimatum: those are my *orders*, if you have not sense enough to take them in any other way.

And now you must fight it out with yourself to the end. It is exceedingly difficult for me to educate you in this matter—impossible, in fact. I beg you to spare me as much as you can. Would you mind not writing again until you have taken a few weeks to think it over?   *G.B.S.*

G.B.S. ignored her further appeals until, a year later, her emotions still violently inflamed, she threatened to call on him.

10 Adephi Terrace, W.C.
22nd June, 1909.
My dear Emerica, It is no use calling on me: I am engaged up to the last minute every afternoon this week after my return to town; and I am rehearsing in the mornings.

Do write a separate short letter or postcard when you make any practical proposal of this kind. I never now dream of attempting to read your long letters when they come. They have to be left for spare moments; and they often don't get read at all.

You write them to relieve yourself, without the slightest consideration for me; and as they are all the same, they meet the fate they deserve.

I have read the play. It shews, of course, remarkable literary power and dramatic talent; but it is made impossible by your nymphomania. There are two men in it (so-called), one a satyromaniac,* the other a mere imaginary male figment to focus the nymphomania of all the women.

The thing has a certain value as a document, and would no doubt interest young people. It bores old people, and rather disgusts them. I am an old person; and you have got nearly to the end of my patience.

I am not preaching or striking moral attitudes for your good: I am telling you quite frankly as one unaffected human being to another that if you can write and think about nothing but your adolescence I will neither read your letters nor meet you if I can possibly avoid it.

These letters contain perhaps one single sentence which mentions an amusing or interesting fact: all the rest is a slovenly muddle of oh dears and oh please and sort of and you know which is quite maddening and which generally ends in a proposal to come to London and paw me which simply curdles my blood.

I would not stand it from Cleopatra herself.

All this is transfigured by your adolescence into something very touching and beautiful; but I am not adolescing but senescing, and it is intolerably disagreeable to me. So drop it or you will drop me. Keep it for young people who idealize you. To me you are only a quite disgustingly ill-behaved young devil, grossly abusing the privilege of my aquaintance.   *G.B.S.*

The young woman had the sense not to call, but, of course, she did write again, and Shaw replied:—

---

*The Oxford English Dictionary defines nymphomania as "morbid and uncontrollable sexual desire in women" —and satyromania as a similar state in men.

10 Adelphi Terrace, W.C.
9th July, 1909

Dear Emerica, You must get a typewriter if you wish me to read your letters. And you must not tell me lies if you wish to catch me more than once.

You sent me a card to say that the last letter but one was important and not the usual thing. I took the trouble (you forget the strain on an elderly man's eyesight of that terrible tiny pencilling of yours) to decipher a couple of sentences taken at random.

They *were* the usual thing. So I tore it up as I have just torn up this one, unread.

In future, ten lines of typewriting, please, widely spaced, and no more.

Yours to that extent,

G.B.S.

The indefatigable girl bought a typewriter and sent further epistles. But Shaw now found it necessary to point out to her that her infatuation followed the pattern of many others of his experience, and that it must end. On October 13th, 1909, he wrote:—

. . . I am greatly indebted to you for typewriting your letters; but I can't answer them, partly because I haven't time, and also because they never tell me anything.

It is just as if a strange girl stopped me on the road and said, "Oh please you mustn't think I really meant to go there and oh dear if you would only not take that view of my wanting to get there because of what the doctor said; for I really meant the other whenever I meant anything, etc., etc., etc."

Imagine me replying, "Madam: what the devil is the matter?" and the answer coming "They have told me this time that it is impossible for me to go on much longer like this."

Like *what? Who* told you?

But don't answer me: I am too busy to want to know. As you have nothing to do, and are accordingly in an appalling state of hypochondriasis, you are a little insane; and insane people are frightful *bores.* They write to me reams and reams about their symptoms.

I get letters from other women which are almost word for word *your* letters. I glance at them; recognize the old song; and away they go—five or six sheets of tears and blood and confessions—into the waste paper basket.

I used to bear a great deal of it from you because you occasionally got some little thing worth saying, or some definite bit of amusing news into it; but the strain was too great: you have no idea when you are writing what is worth reading, and when you are going on like the telephone girls and typists and school teachers who write endless and absurd letters (poor things!) to public men who have struck their imagination.

They all want to make the victim their priest; and when he takes pity on them and hears their confessions and helps them they promptly abuse the relationship, which is horribly dishonourable and indelicate.

I allow one page, typed, in answer, and no more, and I shall not answer the answer if it is not healthy and amusing.

G.B.S.

The sequel to this was that in the following year the girl rented a cottage in Ayot St. Lawrence in order to be near Shaw, and called at his home soon after her arrival. Mrs Shaw—who had been fully acquainted with the situation by her husband— told the girl in the strongest terms never to call again, confirming this by a subsequent letter—which, she made clear, admitted of absolutely no argument or reply.

The girl wrote many, many more letters to Bernard Shaw during the ensuing years, and received others from him which she eventually burnt after a long lapse of time. This, however, does not affect the interest and value of these letters which *have* come down to us, giving Bernard Shaw's views on so many vitally and fundamentally important aspects of life.

[*Editorial Note:* Since writing the above I have had the sight of certain extensive writings by the girl concerned, which leave me in no doubt that, considering his position, Shaw treated her with far greater kindness and forbearance than many other normal and reasonable people might have done.

Her writings are passionately sincere, but extremely obscure and tedious in their content, and usually lacking in literary style or even correct grammar and punctuation. Almost every paragraph begins either: "And I thought . . .", or "Then it came . . .", or "Then I bent down what was in me to see and understand this with my mind. . .", whilst the words "a consciousness of" appear continually. By way of illustration I quote a few passages:—

"Then it came that I would tell and write down all that I held power to tell by writing it—and with this there came feelings of peace and happiness and I began to write. . . .

". . . and suddenly it came that I would go to whom I loved and that I would ask till this was answered, from what it was wished before all else by who wrote what had been written, to hold me back from whom I loved—and there came again that fear and shrinking which had come before for this lest there should come again what had been before when I had yielded to what seemed pain. . . .

". . . then it came that I would write what was in me with all these words left, and that when this was done I would take this to whom I loved. And it came that it might be that when this was done, what had not been understood would be understood. . . .

"I am a wanderer where there is no way. I am a seeker with nothing to find, I am a dreamer who can never wake. I am a devouring body. . . . What am I bowed down before you? I do not know. I am in a great light and fear has left me and I know my way."

Even though these writings belong to a later period than the Shaw letters to her given in the preceding pages (and to a time when the girl must have been in her thirties) their character is entirely that of adolescent youth—a phase of psychological development she clearly had not yet outgrown.

The feelings at first aroused by these writings (of which I have given only a very few brief examples) is of compassion and the deep need of the girl for a great deal of patient understanding and sympathy to help her towards a more mature and realistic approach to life. But the outpourings are so voluminous, so mystically obscure and abstruse, so endlessly repetitious—in short, so boring—that the inevitable effect, sooner or later, upon almost anyone to whom similar writing was addressed, would be ennui and a desire to terminate the association, coupled with the pious hope that the girl would meet other kindly-disposed people who would listen to her for a time and that she would eventually be fortunate enough to grow up into a more sensible frame of mind.

As Dame Sybil Thorndike has said, "Shaw gave her excellent advice—the marvel is that he took the trouble to write so fully."

I would like to add that when I was originally shown the text of the foregoing letters the name of the recipient had been covered, and it was only subsequently revealed to me. It had been my intention to preserve anonymity, but since Miss Cotterill's name has now been mentioned—albeit only briefly—in other quarters, there seems no longer any point in my not identifying this correspondence.

I have given these letters because of their interest and value as a contribution to a better understanding of the human side of Shaw. The particular girl concerned was not in every sense unique, but rather symbolic of the effusively worshipping attitude of many young women towards Bernard Shaw—who, as he says himself in his letter given on page 80, treated them all in a similar manner.

It should be stressed that the correspondence reproduced here occurred more than fifty years ago. It is not the place here to discuss the development of the girl's subsequent life towards increased maturity and happiness, except to record that she died a short while before Shaw's own death in 1950.]

ON SEXUAL REFORM

Extracts from a verbatim report of a speech delivered by Mr Bernard Shaw at the Third International Congress of the World League for Sexual Reform.

[This report is published by kind permission of the Editor of *Time and Tide*, in the pages of which it appeared in September, 1929. The reporting has been well done, and I feel captures the spontaneity of Shaw's platform personality and lively manner of speech more successfully than a carefully composed or edited 'literary' version of the same material could be expected to do. It appears here in book form for the first time.]

I am not going to-night to beg the question of what sexual reform means. Everybody is a sexual reformer, that is to say everybody who has any ideas on the subject at all. The Pope, for instance, is a prominent sexual reformer, and the Austrian Nudists—if I may call them so—they are sexual reformers. The consequence is that if you had a general congress of all the sexual reformers, not merely the members of a particular society, but all the people who are demanding sexual reform—the Nudists, the Catholics, the birth controllers and the anti-birth controllers, and the hetero-sexualists, and the polygamists, and all of them—if you got them together, there would be a curious cross-party organisation. Probably the Pope would find that on nine points out of ten he was warmly in sympathy with Dr Marie Stopes. And it is quite possible that the most fanatical Nudist or the most fanatical homosexualist, might have the strongest objections, for instance, to polygamy, might have the strongest objection to divorce, and all of them would probably disagree on such a question as the age of consent.

My point really is this, that no matter what people's views are on sexual reform, it is desirable that they should take expert opinion as to the practicability and the probable practical effect of the particular measures that they are advocating. I am not going to discuss the measures for or against. I am simply going to put that down as a general proposition, that instead of following the usual human practice of inventing your science according to what you happen to desire yourself, and inventing your facts in the same way, you should make some attempt to go to the people who have practical experience, who are experts in the matter, and find out what they think would happen if your measures, the particular measures you are advocating, were carried into effect.

There are two effects to be considered of any definite measure of sexual reform. There is the psychological effect, and there is the political effect. Now it is on the psychological side that I wish to speak to-night, because I am speaking, of course, as an expert. (Laughter.) I do not in the least know why that remark of mine has elicited laughter, but as a matter of fact I am an expert in sex appeal. (Laughter and applause.) I do not in the least, I repeat, know what you mean by that laughter, but what I mean is that I am a playwright. I am connected with the theatre. The theatre is continually occupied with sex appeal. It has to deal in sex appeal exactly as a costermonger has to deal in turnips, and a costermonger's opinion on turnips is worth having. He is an expert, and in the same way the opinion of a playwright is worth having, or people connected with the theatre, because they know how the thing is done and they have to do it.

One very important function of the theatre in society is to educate the people in matters of sex. It is not only the people in the theatre who have that idea and wish really to educate the people, but also the other people who simply want to exploit sex appeal—they all have to know how to do it, because if their sex appeal fails, they lose a very great deal of money; and you can hardly call any man a real expert unless he loses a great deal of money if his practice happens to be wrong.

The curious thing is that, in the matter of sex appeal, nobody ever calls in the playwright. Although he is a very obvious person to call in on the subject, they never think of doing it. On the other hand, the priest always rushes in and demands to be accepted as an authority on this subject. Well, if he went into a theatre, behind the scenes of a theatre and made such a claim, we should say, "Mind your own business. This evidently is the one subject about which you as a celibate know nothing." (Applause.) "And if you attempt to meddle with it you will probably make literally an unholy mess of it!"

The Pope represents the priest in this matter. The Pope is the Chief Priest of Europe, and he speaks very strongly on the subject of sex appeal. I, of course, should never dream of appealing to the Chief Priest of Europe, but if there were such a person as the Chief Prostitute of Europe I should go to her immediately. I should say, "Here, clearly, is the person who deals professionally in sex appeal, who will lose her livelihood if her method is wrong, if she is not really scientific in the matter.'

Unfortunately, or fortunately, just as you choose to look at it, there is no such person as the Chief Prostitute of Europe, as there is the Chief Priest, which is perhaps the reason that the priest's opinion gets heard whilst the prostitute's opinion is not heard. Therefore it is that I proffer myself as being the next best thing to the prostitute, that is to say, of course, the playwright.

I find myself up against two sets of people. One of them seeks to minimise sex appeal by a maximum of clothing. The others seek to maximise sex appeal by a minimum of clothing. I come in as an expert and tell them that they are both hopelessly and completely wrong in their methods. They do not understand the matter at all. If you want sex appeal raised to the utmost point, there is only one way of doing it, and that is by clothes.

I remember the nineteenth century. People who remember it are now becoming comparatively scarce. But I remember the nineteenth century, when I was really at a very impressionable age. Being an artist myself I have always been very impressionable in the direction of sex. My first impressions were derived from the Victorian woman. The Victorian woman was a masterpiece of sex appeal. She was sex appeal from the top of her head to the sole of her feet. It was amazing how she did it. She was clothes, of course, from head to foot. Everything about her, except her cheeks and her nose, was a guilty secret, a thing that you had to guess at. All the young men and the boys and so on, the one thing that thrilled them was the idea: if they could only get a glimpse under those clothes. . . .

They did not dress the Victorian woman, they upholstered her. That is the only word. Every single contour, all her contours—to take the principal ones, all four of them, may I say—they were all emphasized. It was not only when the lady herself could not emphasize them sufficiently by her own person. She used artificial aids. She used tiny little pads on her breast which were called palpitators. She had, of course, the bustle and all the rest of it, and there she was. I really think if I exhibited here one of the ordinary portraits or pictures of the woman of the day, you would be rather shocked. But you would stop and think, "What is the woman like?" and you would see that the idea somewhere at the bottom of it all was that you should conceal the fact that she was a human being and make her like a very attractive and luxurious sofa. That was the idea, and it was carried out, of course, by clothing. And every woman knew that. Every actress knew that. The actresses of the French stage, those of them who made a speciality of sex appeal, they did not undress themselves. I do not know how many petticoats they wore, but at any rate instead of exposing their persons, they simply gave you a little glimpse of the fact that they had any amount of pink petticoats round their ankles, and the effect was tremendous.

The result was that the Victorian age was an exceedingly immoral age, an age in which there arose a sort of disease which modern psychiatrists, I think, call exhibitionism. You had a sort of reaction against that. You had a tendency on the part of some ladies to do something dreadful, to show their ankles for instance. Hardly the most desperate or abandoned of them ever dreamed of showing their knees, or anything like that.

You had on the one hand this tremendous sex appeal produced by clothes, and on the other hand the tendency to defy it or exploit it by making a little revelation of some kind.

We have been getting rid of all that. We have had a tremendous spread of Nudism, not carried to the extreme that they carry it in Austria, where you have communities and clubs of people who have the extremely wholesome habit of meeting one another without anything on at all. But the unpopularity of that really depends on the fact that people cling to the sex appeal. They do not want to get rid of it. The Nudist points out that the moment you get to the point when you are perfectly nude, it would be a very delicate situation to be in if you are with only one other person who is nude, but that would not be the case if you were amongst a hundred nude persons; you no longer feel that you are nude, there is nothing in it. But when you tell the ordinary man that there is nothing in it, he at once says, "Then don't let us have any of it. I prefer the sex appeal. I prefer to be in an atmosphere of sex appeal."

I am not going to judge as to whether it is desirable to live as I did in the nineteenth century, where the whole place was saturated with sex appeal, or under existing conditions where the women at least have taken a very large step towards nudity and the sex appeal has vanished to an amazing extent, to an extent which the nineteenth century person can hardly imagine. My business is not to say which is the desirable phenomenon. I simply want to point out to the public and all the rest of them how it is produced. The Pope, at any rate, wants to bring back the old clothing, not intending to bring back the sex appeal, but ignorantly thinking that he would do away with it. If it does come back, the result of it will be to increase sex appeal. There is no doubt about that. Some people will tell themselves that quite frankly. Others will advocate it, but will not tell themselves why they advocate it.

I saw the other day a Jesuit church in Trieste, and I have never been so disgusted as I was in that church. Instead of the usual notices that you see in the Catholic Church in Italy—that women will not be admitted unless they are modestly dressed, a thing quite simply stated, which means that a woman who has bare arms must carry with her a little shawl and put it over her arms as she comes in— there were half-a-dozen notices in different parts of the Church, and they all had been elaborately composed, and every one of them suggested some indecency or other which would never have come into the head of a decent normal person if it had not been put there. Every placard pointed out some particular effect it would have on young men if women were not muffled up so that you could not suspect that they had any flesh and blood at all.

I would like to have the Pope there, as I said before. If I interviewed him on the subject, I can fancy myself saying, "Look here, your Holiness. I propose that for the moment we both throw off any holiness that we have, and we try to imagine ourselves a soldier of the old type, an absolutely licentious abandoned man, who fought for anybody who would pay him and became a soldier because he wanted to live a free life, and because he occasionally wanted to have the glorious experience of sacking a city, because one of the great incidents of the sack of a city is the rapine. Now let you and I honestly and candidly imagine ourselves a soldier, partaking in the sack of a city. We are looking about for women to ravish. There come along two women. One is a nun, in a nun's dress. The other is a harlot, with as little dress on as possible, rouged and painted and all that sort of thing." I would say, "I ask your Holiness quite honestly to tell yourself which of these women you would go for." I have not the slightest doubt the woman I should go for. The harlot would not have a dog's chance against her.

Now I have come to the end of my time. I need not point the moral of what I have been saying. I am simply giving the expert's opinion. If you want sex appeal, clothes. If you want to minimise the sex appeal, get rid of as many clothes as possible.

I hope some other speakers will deal with the political effect, which I have had to omit. The thing which you will have carefully to consider is this. Modern democracy has become associated with ideas on liberty, because it has abolished certain methods of political oppression. And as we all allow ourselves to be actuated far too much by some association of ideas, we are apt to think that what makes for liberty in one thing will make for liberty in all things.

Make no such mistake about modern democracy and popular government. The more the people at large have to do with government, the more we—now I am talking to the members of the Society —will have to fight for our lives, as it were, for our ideals.

I will just take one minute to tell you an anecdote which illustrates the situation. A friend of mine was the late Cecil Sharp, who collected so many songs, especially in Somersetshire where he began. It began in the rectory of the Rev. C. L. Marson,* another old friend of mine. They are both dead. One day they were walking in the garden, and in this garden there was an enclosed fruit garden. Cecil Sharp heard a man on the other side of the wall singing a song, which seemed to him to be a beautiful tune. He immediately wrote it down, and said to Marson, "Who is that man singing?" "He is my gardener," was the reply. Sharp said, "Let us go in and see whether he has any more songs." He went in, full of the enthusiasm of the artist who had discovered something beautiful, and they told the man that they had heard him singing. The man threw down his spade, and he called God to witness that he was an honest and decent man, and that he had never sung a song in his life, and he was not going to be accused of such debauchery and wickedness.

They were amazed, because like many of our cultivated classes they did not understand that to the mass of the people art and beauty are nothing but forms of debauchery. They had the greatest

* The report has Sarson, but this was a misprint.

trouble in persuading that gardener that they were both of them just as great blackguards as he was, and then he told them a lot about songs, and told them where they would find other songs.

Think of the moral of that. That is the sort of thing you have to face. To the mass of people, brought up as they have been, they have no idea of liberty in this direction. On the contrary, they are the most ferocious opponents of it, and you will have to fight, I will not say for a super-morality, because it will appear to them to be a sub-morality, but in the end we will have to have really class morality. The very name is abhorrent to democracy, but certain circles of people in different degrees of spiritual development will have to have moralities of their own in their own circles, and will have to tolerate the other circles with their particular degrees of morality. That is the utmost you can hope for. Do not think your own particular morality can be imposed on the whole nation, and do not, for Heaven's sake, dream that it can be imposed by democracy; that will be the greatest mistake you can possibly make.

ON SOCIALISM

Some of Shaw's views on Democracy have been given in the last page or two, and more will be adduced later.

Bernard Shaw's social and political views were intricate and covered most aspects of life, and they were—perhaps for this very reason—frequently misunderstood, or only partially understood. For example, in *Shaw the Villager* we have Mrs Laden, his Scottish housekeeper, saying: "I often wondered if Shaw was a Socialist at heart;" Mr W. Farnell, the local Conservative Party agent, considered that: "Shaw called himself a Fabian Socialist but his outlook was largely based on Marx. . . . it was his background that was out of gear;" Captain Ames, who was a neighbour in Ayot St. Lawrence for forty-four years, declared: "Shaw was no Socialist! He was Conservative by temperament and in my opinion consistently unconvincing in his expression of his Socialism. He was Shakespeare's 'Puck' fulfilled to perfection;" and Joseph Sault considered Shaw's outlook "one-eyed".

Numerous other people also have found Shaw's political and social views perplexing, and an attempt will therefore be made in this book to remove some of the confusion involved. The first thing I propose to do is to give Shaw a full and fair opportunity of telling us (or reminding us) in his own words exactly what Socialism meant to him.

I reproduce below, in full, the text of a speech Shaw made in the Industrial Midlands in 1911, as a representative of numerous speeches on Socialism which he made—always without fee, and often without even travelling expenses—in various towns throughout the length and breadth of Britain during the five decades from the 1880's to the 1920's (after which increasing age made his platform appearances rarer). I have selected this speech because it is a down-to-earth, practical statement, directed at an audience composed not primarily of intellectuals or fellow-members of the Fabian Society, but of ordinary men and women of every class (including many members of the working class). Also because it is one of the liveliest and most comprehensive of Shaw's addresses of this sort within my knowledge, and because it was delivered during his middle and most active period as a Fabian orator and publicist.

This speech is a *general* statement of Shaw's Socialist outlook. (I shall deal with more specialised aspects of his political views later.)

I am extremely grateful to Mr J. H. S. Tupholme, a Director and Editor of Staffordshire Sentinel Newspapers Ltd, for exclusive permission to include here this report, which appeared originally in the *Staffordshire Sentinel* of 16th February, 1911. This speech has not been mentioned by any other biographer and the following very full report is reproduced in this book for the first time.*

As was often his practice, Shaw opened in a light-hearted vein to gain the good humour of his listeners, reserving the more serious content of his speech till the receptive atmosphere was at a maximum.

THE IDEALS OF SOCIALISM
The People Who Work and the People Who Idle
PLEA FOR THE MIDDLE CLASS
Amusing Impressions of the Potteries

Mr George Bernard Shaw on Wednesday evening delivered a lecture at the Victoria Hall, Hanley, on the subject of 'Socialism'. The gathering had been arranged under the auspices of the Newcastle Fabian Society, the I.L.P., and the North Staffordshire Labour Party, and the interest evinced throughout North Staffordshire in the visit of Mr Bernard Shaw was indicated by the manner in which the spacious hall was filled, and by the representative character of the audience.

---

*I have made one or two corrections of obvious minor printers' errors, but in all essentials the material as reproduced here follows exactly the *Staffordshire Sentinel's* text.

Prior to the commencement of the meeting, selections were played on the organ by Mr George Barlow, and sandwiched between the Chairman's opening remarks and the speech of Mr Bernard Shaw was a part-song by the Clarion Vocal Union.

Mr Enoch Edwards, M.P., was the chairman, and among others on the platform, in addition to the lecturer, were: Dr A. Rowley Moody, the Rev. W. S. Knowles, the Rev. J. Reay, the Rev. E. S. Kiek, the Rev. G. Pegler, Dr Shufflebotham, Councillor and Mrs Tipping, and others.

Mr George Bernard Shaw, who was given a most enthusiastic reception, said:—

Mr Chairman, Ladies, and Gentlemen,—Hanley is a fearfully ugly place, how do you stand it? (Laughter.) Do you really like it? (Laughter.) I don't think you can, because, if you liked it, I do not think you would like me—(laughter)—and you know you must be uncommonly fond of me, coming away from much pleasanter places and paying for tickets to hear me talk. I ought to be grateful, but I am in a peculiar difficulty. I have only been in the Potteries for a day, but I have seriously begun to suspect that the people of the Potteries are mad. (Laughter.) I walked today to a place—I don't know where it is, because I don't know which town is which. It was somewhere near Stoke, and it was called, I think, Hartshill. I wanted to get into the fresh air, but the more I went up the hill the worse the air got. (Laughter.) I remember when I was young the kitchen chimney caught fire, and for three months after that the house smelt exactly like—Hartshill. (Laughter.)

THE POTTERIES CHIMNEYS

I can't say whether all the chimneys in Stoke were on fire, because I started counting them and gave in when I came to 123. I am not talking of small house chimneys—you know the things I mean. When I got to the top of the hill I came to a board on a gate, and this board announced that the gate was opened at eight o'clock in the morning, and was left open till 5.30. I concluded it must be a nice place; that it must be a public garden provided for the recreation of the people of the Potteries, and I went into that 'recreation' ground. It was an awful place. The only object of art that I could see was a sanitary laundry. (Laughter.) I don't say anything against the sanitary laundry, but we have plenty of sanitary laundries just as nice looking all over the country, but we don't make a public garden in front of them. Or at least we don't put a rail round some gravel, and call it a public garden in order to look at a sanitary laundry. So I went past and looked at all the chimneys, and they were all smoking. If those chimneys were smoking in London somebody would take a photo of them, and the man whose chimney was smoking would be brought before the magistrates. The reason of that is, that in London we don't make the owner of the chimney a magistrate. (Laughter and cheers.) I don't say you do it here. (Renewed laughter and cheers.) But I do say that the consequences are very much what I should expect to find if you did do it here.

POINTING A MORAL

I wondered what was the fun of looking at all the chimneys, and I looked at little children and I saw an enormous graveyard. And then I saw that the object of this place is to draw a moral. If chimneys smoke like that you will have a large graveyard as a consequence! Then I began to understand why the people of Hanley and the Potteries are rather nice people. In the first place if they were not very nice people they would go away by the next train and in the next place it must be so very hard for any infant to live in Hanley and the Potteries, unless it is exceptionally healthy, that I suppose all the people that live here are the people born with an iron constitution. But you know I should not mind all this if there were any real difficulty in making the Potteries a very nice place. It could be done quite easily. I came here—I didn't come in any of your vulgar trains. I am a Socialist and I have a motor-car, consequently. (Laughter and applause.) Until I came to the Potteries I was in exactly the same sort of country, exactly the same kind of hills and valleys, but the country was most beautiful, lovelier country could not exist. I have been in other countries, I have been in places that were not so favoured by Nature, and I have seen most beautiful towns, little towns climbing up the hillsides, places that when you came to you wanted to jump out of your car and take a house and live there the rest of your life. But I didn't feel like that in either Stoke or Hanley. You may take it ill or you may not, but I am going away the first thing tomorrow morning, and I will not come here again until you clean it and make it a better place to live in. (Laughter.)

MR ARNOLD BENNETT AND THE FIVE TOWNS

The Potteries have produced one of the most remarkable literary men of our times—Mr Arnold Bennett. (Applause.) I never used to believe what he told me about the Potteries; I now do believe it, and I understand why he lives most of his time in Paris. (Laughter.) If I was in Paris I could tell them something that would make them sit up if I knew their language; but Mr Arnold Bennett, who has a poetic feeling, does not live in it really. His home ought to be a pleasanter place to live in than in London or Paris, because there he has not the poetic feeling. But he has been trying to stuff these five towns down my throat as containing the best, the real English. I mean to have it out with him, for the people here have no sense at all. (Laughter.) I know I ought to lecture on Socialism here, but I did that 19 years ago; and has anything been done? Not a bit. (Laughter.) I told you then what you ought to do and you have not taken the slightest notice of me. In the words of the chairman, you "appreciate my lecture whilst entirely disagreeing with what I say". (Laughter.) Therefore I am not going to talk about the Socialist tonight; I am going to talk about your towns here and to say what I want done before I consent to honour you by coming back here again. (Laughter.) You know I have been in towns that are much better looking than these towns, but they don't produce half as much wealth. You produce a tremendous lot of money in the Potteries.

"A STRAIN OF MADNESS."

You are always working—a great deal too hard; much harder than I work. (Laughter.) That is the reason I have got a motor car and you have not. (Laughter.) But you have got this extraordinary strain of madness in you that, instead of spending the money on your own town, you, having, as Arnold Bennett tells me, the flower of the English race and having good hearts, say: "Never mind us, we will come in at the back of everything. What we want is that with the money we produce we may pay the rates of the other towns, build beautiful towns in other places we will never see, but we will live here in Stoke and have the satisfaction of thinking that we are helping to build those beautiful places." I have been to some of those beautiful places, and they are very beautiful I can tell you. For instance, to amuse myself when my work gets a little too heavy for

me, I have taken a trip round the Mediterranean. I have gone along
the south coast of France, and I have gone right along to Constantinople and to the Bosphorus and the Black Sea, and I have come
back along the north shores of Africa. And there I have seen a
long string of the most beautiful towns you can imagaine—beautiful
villas, beautiful gardens, beautiful opera houses, beautiful racecourses even—as far as a racecourse can be made beautiful—and
beautiful gambling houses. And you are paying for them to a considerable extent. I wonder, did you know that? You know, you all
sit as if you did, but I believe some of you did not know that. The
majority of you, being intelligent men, probably do, but I will tell
you.

MONTE CARLO

There is one of those towns—perhaps the pleasantest of them all
if you may judge by the rush made for it—Monte Carlo. (Laughter.)
You have heard of it, haven't you? Now, the delightful thing about
Monte Carlo is that there are no rates in Monte Carlo. No one ever
pays any rates.* There are beautiful electric trams, which belong to
the town. They do not belong to private companies like your trams
here. I notice you do not say anything. (Laughter.) I hope you will
take it in. Well, they have beautiful electric tramways there on the
stud system, which has been a good deal talked of lately, and it
seems to work there at any rate. They have lovely wide streets;
they have no smoke; the houses are white and the sky is blue. Did
you ever know that the sky was blue? They have a beautiful blue
sky and a beautiful blue sea, lovely houses, splendid sanitation,
magnificent electric light and electric trams, and not one farthing
of rates do they pay. Now who will start by the next train to live in
this beautiful place and pay no rates? They have an intelligent ruler
there—a Prince of Monaco—and the Prince of Monaco provides all
these lovely things for his people, but he makes this condition. He
says: "You may go everywhere, you may go into the beautiful
gardens, travel in the trams, walk about the streets, but there is one
place my subjects shall not go into, and that place is the gambling
house. I keep that for gentlemen who make a lot of money in the

---

* There is a fairly contemporary ring about this passage in view
of the dispute in the winter of 1962 (half a century later) between France
and Monaco about tariffs.

Potteries and other places in England." They go in there and they gamble with the Prince of Monaco.

THE PRINCE OF MONACO

The Prince of Monaco plays a nearly fair game. I won't say a fair game altogether, but still his tables on the whole are so arranged that occasionally people make a little by gambling, but, taking them altogether and all the year round, they lose enough money to pay for all those electric trams and that electric light and all the beauties of the town. Who provides the money? You do, among other people. I don't mean to say Manchester and Glasgow and other towns may not contribute a bit, but the five towns here contribute a very considerable sum in the way of dividends, rents, and other things you have to pay. And all that money, that has turned that gambling town into such a beautiful place—where every man is a happy lodging-house keeper or hotel keeper—might be spent on your town here and might make it just as good a place to live in. (Hear, hear.) What is the good of saying "Hear, hear"? You know you are not going to do it. (Laughter.) What would you say to me if I behaved in such a silly way? Would not you recommend me to see a doctor? You would probably recommend [me] to see two doctors. I believe that is the number of doctors who see people whose minds are affected in that particular way. Over in London we do better than that. We at any rate run our own trams; and if we complain a good deal of the rates, at any rate the rates would be higher if it were not for the trams.

'BENEVOLENCE' IN THE POTTERIES

Here you are so benevolent—your locomotion in the streets, your lighting, your gas supply, and everything else; instead of taking it in your own hands in an intelligent way, as other towns have done, you make it a benevolent affair and hand it over to a private company whose business is to charge you as much for the accommodation as they possibly can, as much more than it costs as they possibly can, in order that the balance may contribute to the trams and the lighting and embellishments of Monte Carlo and other places. I mention Monte Carlo, but that is not the only place. There are dozens of towns like Monte Carlo. Start with Biarritz and then go right round the whole south of Europe and then come back to Algiers—there are lots of places. But, beautiful as they are, I say again they are not more beautiful, and not as beautiful to us, as these towns here might be made if all the wealth produced in them was devoted to making them the sort of places they ought to be. (Applause.)

SOCIALISM AND UNSOCIALISM

Now I think of it, I am getting on my subject, because this is Socialism. You all know that. But do you know what the other thing is? It is Unsocialism. On the whole, don't you think it pays better to be a Socialist than an Unsocialist? You don't seem to think so. I didn't expect to convert you in five minutes. I will now begin to talk serious politics. I want to talk a good deal to the rate-payers, and particularly to the people called invidiously the middle class.

THE MIDDLE-CLASS MAN

I don't want to call anyone here a middle-class man; I should not like to be called a middle-class man myself: a man is either a gentleman or nothing. (Applause.) But still, other people may politely talk of a middle class, and in a certain economic sense there is a middle class in the country. That middle class is in a very curious position. It stands in the middle between the working classes, on the one hand, and what I may term the non-working class on the other. It is very difficult to know what to say of it; because there is no use in talking today about landlords and capitalists as if there was very much distinction. (Applause.) But there is a large class of people who, being ladies and gentlemen, do not want to work. There is no point in being a lady or a gentleman. Yet you treat this class with consideration; and, in my opinion, you treat them with a great deal too much. (Applause.) But then, you know, I am a revolutionary character. (Laughter.) There is one thing in the situation of these people who practically own the land and capital of this country, and who do not work. There is one thing you have to note particularly about them—that they are practically the most helpless class in the community. They cannot do anything—they don't know how. You say, "They have the land." But the land is no use to them. You say, "They have the capital." But really they have not. They would not know what to do with it. Take a typical case of a large landowner—I will call him a duke. (Laughter.) I do so because the dukes are very few, and you get value for your money to this extent—

you like a duke. (Renewed laughter.) We may ourselves become dukes some day. (Laughter.)

THE DUKE AND HIS LAND

But, now supposing you went to a duke and said, "My lord, you possess a number of acres: you have plenty of land. Well, take your land and live on it." What will the duke say? He will say: "My dear sir, what do you mean? You ask me to live on my land! How can I live on my land? I understand vulgar people, by certain operations of digging and farming, and things of that kind, have in some mysterious manner been able to live on land, but I can't do that sort of thing. I should compromise my social position if I were to dig and to earn money in any way. Therefore there is no use in throwing my land on my own hands and telling me to live on it; I shall be a beggar." That is a serious position for a man to be in, and I seriously invite your sympathy. Here are these people, practically helpless in the community. Unless some of us take their land and capital and do something with it, and make the money for them, they are perfectly unable to live. They are dependent upon us. Do you know, the working classes of this country are to a very large extent almost as helpless as the dukes.

THE TASK OF THE POTTER

If you take a workman in the Potteries—I don't know anything about him, but being a literary man I can always imagine what a person is like—(laughter)—if you take a potter—I will call him a potter because he is a potter in the Bible—his position is this: He says: "Here is something I have learned to do that requires a certain amount of skill, and I am prepared to go on doing it for sixteen hours a day"—or what is it? If it is less, then you have probably been going in for trade unionism, or something of that kind. (Laughter and cheers.) At any rate, I will venture to say that it is more hours a day than I work, and I consider myself a pretty hardworked man, too. (Laughter.) But the potter says: "Here is this particular job which I have learned to do, and which I am prepared to go on doing for a certain number of hours a day. But before I can do that job somebody has to bring me the material. Somebody has to build the pottery, and somebody has to buy the materials. In order to do that he has got to be a man of brains, and to know where to buy in the cheapest market with the object of selling in the dearest. He has to know, too, where the dearest market is. He has got to keep all the accounts, and unless I can get somebody to do this for me I am just as helpless as the duke. It is the only respect in which I resemble a duke, but still, to that extent I do resemble him." (Laughter.)

LAND ESSENTIAL

Now, I think if you have thoroughly taken that in, that you will understand where the middle class come in. They are the people who know how to keep books and write letters, who know how to keep banking accounts and know how to get money. They are prepared to organise bodies of workmen, but before they can do anything they have to get land. No matter how clever they might be they will have to get a bit of land to put their pottery on or they are just as helpless as the workman and the duke. The first thing they do is to go to the landlord—the duke if you like—and say: "My lord duke, you have a bit of land. Your grace can't be expected to work on that land but I am prepared to relieve you of it. I am prepared to relieve you of all anxiety on that point. If you will hand that piece of land over to me I will undertake you shall have no trouble, no vulgar work or anxiety, nothing to do but enjoy yourself, and every quarter or every half-year I will pay you so much for the use of that piece of land." And the duke says, "This is an intelligent man. (Laughter.) This is just the sort of man I was looking out for. Will you tell me, sir, how much you said you would pay?" The middle-class man names a figure, and the duke says, "Will any other middle-class gentleman offer me any more?" (Laughter.) When he has found out the top price he can get, all the middle-class competing a little against one another, he strikes his bargain, and he gives the middle-class man a lease. Then the middle-class man has got his land. That is the first step.

THE SECRET OF THRIFT

The next thing he wants is money. He may have a little, but middle-class men nowadays very seldom have. I know, because my father was what was called a middle-class man, and he had none, although he carried on a business. And just as there are dukes who offer to let the land which they cannot employ, there are a great many people who have got money. In the first place there are the younger sons of dukes, and all the relatives of dukes, and all the people who through being landlords in the past have received very much larger sums of money than they have wanted to spend. That is the great secret of what you call thrift and saving. (Laughter and cheers.) If you get more money than you can possibly spend, then you become a thrifty man—(laughter and cheers)—and everybody compliments you upon your thrift. (Renewed applause.)

£1,500 A DAY!

I know people who have got an income of about £1,500 a day! They could not spend it if they tried. There are a good many people like that—not perhaps in comparison with all the millions of the community—but still there is a good deal of money going about. I may mention just in passing that in this country we pay the people who don't work at all, every year, somewhere about £600,000,000. I don't know whether you knew that. I didn't invent the figure. I got it from the income-tax returns. They confess to that. (Laughter.) You quite understand? That is what they pay income-tax on. Where a man makes a return of his income for the purpose of paying income-tax on it, he doesn't overstate it. He very often overstates it to his neighbour, but whenever an Englishman, even when he has been pretending to his neighbour all his life that he is a richer man than he really is, the moment he comes to the income-tax, he repents and he pretends that he is a poorer man than he really is. And so I am entitled to believe that if there is any difference between what they say they have, and what they really have, the difference is that they get a little more and not a little less. There is a good deal of spending in £600,000,000, and there is a good deal over. You are told by statisticians that there is saved up in this country every year over £200,000,000. The people who are rich have got £200,000,000 more than they want to spend. I suppose a good many of you have not saved any of that £200,000,000?

A COMPARISON

If you like you can see what the poor men have saved. If you take the Post Office Savings Bank, the Co-operative Societies, the Building Societies, everything that by hook or by crook you can imagine was saved by a working man, you will find you have not made very much of a hole in this £200,000,000. In fact, since the working classes began co-operation, about 1844 I think it was, when the saving really began for the first time, in all those years from 1844 up to the present time, they have only saved about £200,000,000. That is to say that in all those years the working classes, although there are so many more of them, all together, have only been able to save what is saved every year by the rich classes.

A FINANCIAL TRANSACTION

I will come back to the middle-class man to show that there is a good deal to put the fingers on. He goes to the rich people, and finds a great many are women and children. He does not go to these latter perhaps, but probably to their stockbrokers, and what he says is this: "You have a lot of money there and you are not able to do anything with it. You cannot make railways, or work Potteries, or cotton factories, or build houses. You don't know how to do these things because you are a lady or a gentleman." And the middle-class man goes on to say: "I understand how to do this, and if you will lend me your money you need have no trouble, but will find, at the close of each half-year, there will be a certain amount paid into your account. It will give you no trouble whatever." I am talking about what I know; I have my own bank book, and that is what happens to me. I don't know where it comes from. It is from the San Paulo Railway, but I do not know sufficient of geography to locate it. I never did a stroke of work on that railway in my life; neither did any of my family. But I take my share of every ticket sold on that railway. I take my bit; do you expect me to refuse it? That is how your middle-class man gets rich. You see that if his credit is good and he can get a rich man to trust him, and no other middle-class man offers a higher rate, he has the Duke's land on the one hand and the borrowed capital on the other. He then becomes an employer.

THE MIDDLE-CLASS MAN AND THE WORKER

Your middle-class man is now in a strong position, with his borrowed land and capital, and he turns round to the working-class man and says: "Have you any capital? Ah! I thought not—drink!" (Laughter and applause.) Well, the middle-class man then says: "Now, you have not saved anything, but have spent it all. Here am I with land and capital, and I don't drink or bet—except a little.

(Laughter.) And although you have none of these provisions, and are destitute, you may come into my factory and I will give you enough to live on. (Laughter.) I will give you enough for the children to grow up on, because I want them when they are grown up. I will give you enough to keep a wife to look after them." Well, of course, the working man ought to be full of gratitude, don't you think, for this particular offer?

MIDDLE-CLASS MAN'S STRUGGLE

But then you see the middle-class man, when he has got his land and his capital, his factories and his workmen, sets to work. He buys the raw material, he uses the labour of the working man, he sells the finished product, and then, out of what he gets, he pays the Duke his rent, he pays the capitalist his interest, he pays the working man his wages, and what he has got left for himself, is his profit. Now, you know, I don't altogether grudge it him. He is a very necessary part of society. I don't say that that particular system leads to a man being paid altogether as fairly as he should be paid, but let me tell you that at the present time there are multitudes of middle-class men whose lives are just as great a struggle as that of many of the better-paid working men. (Hear, hear.) This game used to be a very nice game when businesses were carried on in a small way. In my father's time there would be a couple of middle-class men; one of them would have £800 and another of them would have £600. No one would look at such a man of money then. But in those days they went into partnership, and with that little bit of money they called themselves Messrs Smith and Jones, and there were a number of little firms of that kind in the industries of the country. The business was very largely worked by little firms like that. And there was great distinction in those days between the middle class and the working class.

A MATTER OF EDUCATION

The one could read and write—could find out how to buy and sell. But the working classes were cut off from that, because their prudent country took very great care that they should never learn either to read or write, and to this day they would never have been taught to read or write except that the Germans taught their workmen to read and write and the consequence was that, through being able to read and write, they began to do better work, and the result was that their work began to drive the work of our men out of the market. And so our middle class had to turn round and say: "We must educate the working classes," and by this time the elementary school, at which the son of the working man is educated, is a better school than the little private adventure school at which the middle-class man used to have his son educated. And the consequence is that the cleverest sons of working men, provided with better education, are winning scholarships and taking away the prizes from the sons of the middle-class men. And the middle-class men are beginning to grumble at it a great deal. Nevertheless, that sort of thing is going to go on. The middle-class man is finding two things happening to him. In the first place, first as his superior commanding [sic] of money and of a little knowledge enabled him to keep the working class in subjection and take a very considerable advantage of their ignorance —their want of knowledge of business—that very same game is being played on him now to an extent he never dreamt could possibly happen.

SWEPT OUT OF EXISTENCE

The little firms with a capital of a thousand or a couple of thousands are being swept out of existence by the big companies, that have sometimes millions at their disposal and generally hundreds of thousands.* You find in every direction that there are men who used to conduct small businesses and keep small shops, and these men are being squeezed out of business by the competition of big capitalists, big companies of capitalists, big joint stock companies, worked on the American system; and they are extremely glad now, having been made bankrupt and driven out of their business, to go hat in hand to the men who have ruined them and ask for posts as shopmen, as managers and employees of all sorts. And this is beginning to change their point of view a little. When a man changes from being an employer to being an employee, it very often not only changes his commercial position, but it changes his politics and it sometimes changes his religion. (Cheers.) Now what I am here to suggest to you tonight is that the middle classes and the working classes being both persons doing necessary work for society, and

*There is a curiously contemporary note about this passage in these days (more than fifty years later) of chain stores and take-over bids.

being both now fleeced to a prodigious extent by the plutocratic
classes—by the classes who do not work and do not intend to work;
and even those among them who do work, do not intend that their
sons and daughters shall work—I suggest the time has come for a
new division in society.

A NEW DIVISION OF SOCIETY

No longer a division between middle class and lower class and
upper class; no longer a division between Liberal and Tory and
Labour; but a new division between the people who work and the
people who idle. And if you want to know why it is that some
people speak ill of Socialism, it is because they know perfectly well
that Socialism is, in the main, a campaign against idleness. Our
conception is that, in the future, not a single person shall live in the
country unless they earn their living. (Applause.) And although we
are accused of a great many other things of which we are entirely
innocent; and although you see [in] silly newspapers—which are the
property of the wealthy classes, for it takes a quarter of a million to
start a paper—you see it stated that Socialism is an attack on the
family and religion; yet Socialism might attack the family and
religion until it was black in the face, and not a single word be said
against it.

WHY SOCIALISTS ARE ATTACKED

But it is because it has attacked idleness, and begun to insist that
the enormous wealth produced by England shall be devoted to
making England a better place for the people who live in it and
work in it. That is the reason we are attacked, and they are very
wise to attack us in this way. None of the papers can argue with me,
but they can only say that I have six wives, and if I deny it, they do
not print my denial. (Applause.) From Mr Keir Hardie, down to the
humblest member of the Labour Party, you find almost every day
that somebody in this country delivers a mass of argument, a mass
of figures, and puts them very eloquently to public audiences in
this country, who are convinced of the justice and right of what they
say. But do you ever see these speeches reported in the newspapers?
(Voices: "No.") No. Never one! But when you see some representative of the upper classes talking some ghastly nonsense about the
Empire—(laughter)—somebody going into fits about the House of
Lords or the Welsh Church, you get it all at full length. (Laughter.)

THE BREAD AND BUTTER QUESTION

But when you come down to business and the bread and butter question, there is a conspiracy of silence. (Applause.) You find it very hard, even if you have published a little paper of your own, to get it sold on a bookstall; and, accordingly, you have to talk [in] private, as I am doing now. In Parliament, today, the plutocrats, the rich, are represented, and very considerably over-represented, and very powerfully represented. In fact, they very nearly fill the whole place. But, fortunately, the working classes are also represented, and they are going to be more represented. At last, you have got a Labour Party, with its own chairman and its own whips, entirely independent either of [the] Liberal Party or Unionist Party. They have increased from election to election, and they are going to increase from election to election.

THE KING AND MR KEIR HARDIE

In future days it is not going to be a case of thirty or thirty-five Labour members, it will go up to fifty, up to seventy; it will go on and on; and it is quite within the bounds of possibility that, within the experience of men and women who are actually listening to me, there may come a General Election in this country, and after that General Election the King might send for Mr Balfour and might say: "Mr Balfour, may I depend on you to form a Government?" Mr Balfour [might] say: "I am sorry, sir, but I do not command the confidence of the majority of the House of Commons, and therefore I cannot form a Government." The King will say: "Oh, well, I suppose that means calling for Mr Asquith." Mr Balfour shrugs his shoulders and politely retires. The King will send for Mr Asquith then, and he will probably say: "Mr Asquith, may I depend on you to form a Government in the House of Commons?" Mr Asquith will say: "I am very sorry, sir, but I do not command a majority in the House of Commons, and I am unable to form a Government." The King will reply: "Do you mean to say I have got to send for Mr Redmond?" (Laughter.) Mr Asquith: "No, no, sir, not Mr Redmond!" The King will then say: "Mr Balfour says he can't do it," and Mr Asquith will reply: "I believe that is so, sir— (laughter)—Mr Balfour does not command a majority in the House of Commons." Then the King will say: "Who does?" Mr Asquith will reply, "Sir, I should apply to Mr Keir Hardie." (Cheers and laughter.) I suppose then that the King will faint—(laughter)—possibly—but I don't know. I think it is possible that after all, as we have no reason to doubt that he is a very sensible and experienced man, he will send for Mr Keir Hardie and say: "Well, Mr Keir Hardie, I have not any experience of your abilities as a leader of the House of Commons, but I honestly do not think you can make a worse fist of it than a great many of the other chaps have done." (Laughter.)

THE ADVANCE OF LABOUR

Now that is what every workman in this room, and outside it, ought to look forward to. As I say, you are on the way to it. You have got your Labour members and you will find your work easier when you have payment of your representatives. But I have not come here to talk about the working classes; they are able to take care of themselves, if only they will set to work. I stand here on behalf of the distressed and neglected middle classes*—(laughter)—and I want to point out that whereas the upper classes and working classes are respresented in the House of Commons, the middle classes are not. And what is the consequence of that? Here, on the one hand, you have the working classes using their political power more and more to make the Government do greater things for the people.

OLD-AGE PENSIONS

Only the other day they secured old-age pensions. I don't remember the exact figures, but my impression is that when you are 110 years of age you get 2s. 6d. a week. (Laughter.) I don't give you that as the accurate figure, but it is something like it. In New Zealand, which is a small, insignificant, and relatively poor part of this Empire, there is an old-age pension of 10s. a week, and at a very much earlier age. Are the working classes in this country going to be content with 5s. a week, which is the sum, now I come to think of it? Yes, it is 5s. at the age of seventy in England, and at 85 in Ireland. (Laughter.) Well, the working classes are not going to be content with that. They will get the New Zealand 10s., and the time will come when they may demand a much larger pension—almost as much as a gentleman would expect if he had done as much work. They will also demand more expenditure on education, more

* This has a topical enough touch about it still, in the 1960's.

expenditure on the housing of the working classes. That is to say, that since education is levied out of the local education rate—a good deal of it—since houses are built by municipalities out of the local rates, more and more money will be wanted, more and more public money. The working classes will keep constantly pressing for it, and the upper classes, as in the past, will have to keep constantly yielding to the pressure of the working classes. But there will be one point on which they will agree. I don't say those two parties, the upper class party, and the working class party, will be agreed upon all points. That would be a little too much. But there is one point on which they will be thoroughly agreed, and that is that whoever is going to pay for it, they won't pay for it. (Laughter and applause.) Well, who will pay for it? Who pays for it now? (Hear, hear.) Naturally the Party that is not represented in Parliament, the middle-class ratepayer. It will go on to him. More and more on the rates.

INCREASING RATES

The rates are not coming down. They are going up and up and up. The middle class[es] vote at municipal elections for everybody who tells them that he is going to pull the rates down, and who never pulls the rates down, and who has not the slightest chance of doing so. Any rascal, any municipal jobber can get their votes by pretending he is going to get the rates down, but the rates are going to go up and up and up. I rub that into you ratepayers. You will never get the rates down. It would be a very bad thing for the country if you did. I will tell you why. The rates are supposed to be pretty high in Birmingham, although it is by no means a place where they are of the highest. Well, you try the experiment of doing away with rates in Hanley. Fulfil the ideal of the middle class—cut away rates altogether. What will happen? You will all go to Birmingham, because if you did not, there would not be a single person left alive. Unless you keep up sanitation, inspection, and all those public services on which the rates are spent, your town will become a plague spot worse than any in Manchuria. You know it very well. There is no use complaining of the rates. You have to pay rates, and it is a fact that they are likely to go up. It is a cheerful prospect, isn't it? It is so cheerful that at the present time if you go to any Englishman and say, "Are you in favour of the millennium? Do you want to see the Kingdom of Heaven established on earth?"

he will say, "Yes." But if you say, "Will you pay another penny in the pound for it?" he would shout, "No." (Laughter and cheers.) And, ladies and gentlemen, I don't wonder at it, and under existing circumstances I don't blame the ratepayer.

EARNED AND UNEARNED

But is there any way out of this difficulty? In the first place the middle classes won't take the trouble to get themselves represented in the House of Commons, but leave themselves to be represented by the members of the upper classes. It would be better if they would only trust to the Labour Party, at any rate, they would be trusting to the party that has already relieved their taxation, if it has not relieved their rates. Remember that the very first effect of getting the Labour Party in the House of Commons was that something was mentioned in the House of Commons that had never been mentioned there before. For the first time, a Chancellor of the Exchequer had to get up in the House of Commons and mention the terrible fact, the ungentlemanly fact, that some incomes in this country were earned and some were unearned. He did not tell us how much was unearned and how much was earned, but if you will buy a penny tract called *Facts for Socialists* published by the Newcastle Fabian Society, you will be able to see. We call it *Facts for Socialists*, but it is nothing of the kind, because Socialists know all the facts already. They are facts for you. There is not a single one of them given to you on the authority of a Socialist. They are all taken from official returns; made by people whom you consider respectable, but who probably do not consider Socialists respectable. It is the vote which counts, and Parliament had to say that a man who earned his income should only pay 9d. in the pound, while the one who did not earn his income must pay 1s. in the pound. It would never have got to that point but for the Labour Party. But you know that if things were looked at from your point of view in the House of Commons, instead of from the upper-class point of view, it would not be a question of 9d. on earned income and 1s. on unearned income, but a question only of a penny in the pound for earned income and, I won't say anything so rash as 20s. on unearned income—I don't think it would be reasonable* to go far beyond, say, 19s. 6d. in the pound. (Laughter.)

* The report has '*un*reasonable', but this must surely be a misprint for 'reasonable'.

TAXATION AND UNEMPLOYMENT

And when money is wanted and Parliament is trying to raise money, which is wanted for such purposes as giving work to the unemployed—not only the working man, but also the middle-class man—I say that when that money is wanted it ought to be raised by taxation if a single person is out of employment, instead of the money being sent abroad, and invested. For, as you know, millions of money is leaving this country and going out to other countries, and a newspaper, like the London *Times*, which reproaches Socialists for driving capital out of this country, and is publishing a double-page showing the splendid openings and opportunities for capital abroad and in every blessed place on earth except in the Potteries. (Applause.) And here again, with this money constantly going out of the country, the fact that they can get a higher rate for it in those countries makes it more difficult for the middle-class man to borrow, and, therefore, harder for him to give employment. Therefore, the middle class and the working class have to suffer for the lack of that money, which is either wasted in luxury or is to a great extent sent abroad; and you have nothing to do to prevent this but to use your political power.

THE POTTERIES PROBLEM

If you are going to make the Potteries towns decent, the first thing you must do is to see that the Pottery town belongs to yourself —because if you made it the most beautiful place in the world, and it did not belong to you, the only result is that you would have to pay for the beauty you had created in increased rents, and those rents would go out of the country, or be spent in luxuries, just in the same way as now. Therefore, just as the business man acquires his land on freehold before he invests his capital on it, so you ought to acquire the land of the Potteries towns and then set to work to make decent towns of them. You should acquire the land perfectly honestly in the open market; buy the land from its present holders.

TREATING THE LANDLORD GENEROUSLY

Now I would even go further. You will be taking the land from a large number of men who have been accustomed to call themselves the landowners of this country—you will buy the land from them and probably have to get an Act of Parliament first, as you do now when you make a railway and get an Act of Parliament to compel the landlord to sell his land because it is for the public good. So you would have to get an Act of Parliament to enable you to buy the land of your towns here, and such an Act of Parliament would, of course, provide that something extra should be paid because the purchase was compulsory: because the landlord would have to sell whether he liked it or not. And I think you should treat the landlord generously. I think you would pay him not only the market value, but 10 per cent. over the market value. I think perhaps you should even pay him 20 per cent. over the market value, and if he said you should pay him 50 per cent. over the market value, well, be generous and give him 50 per cent. over the market value. And raise the money by a tax on landlords' incomes generally. (Loud laughter and cheers!)

PERFECTLY CONSTITUTIONAL

It is perfectly constitutional. (Loud laughter.) You, of course, would pay the price; you would pay proper compensation for the land. Has the income-tax collector ever paid you compensation? Any of you who ever paid income-tax, did you ever ask the income-tax collector for compensation? I think I will do it next time the income-tax collector comes round. That is where it comes in; you won't take the land without compensation, but the Government will take the income-tax without compensation. Mind you, I don't defend the Government. They take income-tax from me without compensation, and they charge me on the highest scale, too. Consequently, I feel sometimes very bitterly about it. But still they do it, and I don't want to upset good old customs. I am so far a Conservative that I think they had better go on doing it. But I have now shown that it needs nothing but your own determination gradually for the Potteries towns to be acquired for the people of the Potteries, and not only the Potteries towns, but every other town could do the same thing.

MUNICIPAL TRADING

And, remember, you could then, through your municipality, go into the building business. Now, you have heard that next Friday week there is an anti-Socialist gentleman coming down to Newcastle, and he is going to dispute with a Socialist gentleman, the Rev. Mr Kiek. They want to find out whether Unsocialism is more Christian than Socialism. Now that is a very nice point, but if I know anything about these anti-Socialist gentlemen, I would venture to prophesy that one of the things they will say is that municipal building does not pay and never has paid. It is perfectly true, municipal enterprise never does pay in the commercial sense, and you would be very great fools if you ever let it pay. Now, mind, I am talking of what I know. I have been a member of a municipal body for six years, and I worked very hard at it. They were sensible people in my part of London. For instance, we had nearly a quarter of a million inhabitants and we had our own electric light. We did not run to a company for it. We had our own electric light.

NO DIVIDEND!

And in other parts of London they got their electric lighting from companies, and what did the anti-Socialists say? "Ah!" they said: "this municipal electric lighting never paid a dividend, and the others—the private companies lighting the other parts of London—have always paid a dividend." Yes, I should rather think they did, because they always charged more for the electric light than it cost, and that is the way they got their dividend. All the people who bought their electric light paid more for it than it cost, but we, not having to make any profits, but representing the people, charged the people for the electric light exactly what it cost, and there were no profits. If there had been any profits, we should have heard about it from the people. We could have made profits just as easily as the private companies did. We could have stuck on 5 per cent., or 10 per cent., or 15 per cent. to the price of the electric light, but then the man who consumed the electric light, what would he have said? He would have said, "What are you doing with that money that you have overcharged me?" We would have said, "We are reducing the rates with it." But the man would have said, "What is your right to reduce the rates of my neighbour who is not using electric light, while you make me, who use the electric light, pay more than it costs? What right have you to rob Peter to pay Paul?" (Applause.) It is the business of a private company to charge more for a thing than it costs. It is the business of a municipal enterprise to give you a thing at cost price, to have no difference in it. That is the whole point of it. We want to relieve you of this burden of over-charge which you get from the private trader. But when you come to the municipal building and housing, you come to something infinitely worse.

MUNICIPAL BUILDING

In London we built a good many workmen's dwellings, we knocked down insanitary slums, and built comparatively wholesome dwellings . I sincerely hope that before another fifteen years, those buildings we put up will be classed as slums. They are not called slums today, for they are very much better than the buildings they replaced. But you may knock down slum areas, you may buy land for that purpose, and you will have to pay the full market price for it. But we will allow you to buy at the full market value. We will also permit you to admit a lie into your account; and allow you to charge, not what it actually cost, but what you thought it was worth, for the purpose of housing the working classes. We will allow you to put fictitious figures into the accounts in order to show that it pays. With all these concessions, one could not make a profit even on these fictitious figures. How could you make a profit on rent from people, many of whom should not have been paying rent at all, but buying food for their children? (Applause.) We were allowed to do just the part of the business that the private builder could not make pay; and that part which would pay was left to the private builder. Supposing any town or municipality had power, not only to demolish slums, but to erect the better buildings. Supposing it was able to take the plums as well as the stones, to build your churches and cathedrals, your big insurance offices and factories. Supposing the whole of the building was done by the town under proper Building Acts, so as to prevent slums and over-building, and keep light and air. Supposing all your buildings were built as they ought to be!

A CONFESSION

I am going to tell you a little story. My teeth are not all real. (Laughter.) Some of them are real, but they are damaged. Now, I am very vain on the subject of my personal appearance, and the other day when I went to my dentist, and he wanted to put a little gold on the front of my teeth, I said: "If you stand up in front of an audience, it does not look well to see half-sovereigns flashing from your mouth. (Laughter.) Cannot you make me something that will look more like the natural teeth?" "Certainly," he said, "I can put in pottery that will look like a natural tooth." So he made a little mould and put it in the oven.

OVENS WITHOUT SMOKE

He did not make any filthy smoke; he did not dirty his hands, his cuffs and collars; but simply put on an electric switch, and very soon his oven was very much hotter than yours. In these towns I am quite convinced you ought to have a big municipal centre for the production of electrical power. I believe all your ovens should be heated by electrical power, the same as crucibles. I believe you could get rid of all your smoke. It would have to be done by municipal enterprise. Today you have working men working for private employers, and those private employers can throw those employees into the street without thinking of their wives and children, and merely if the employer thinks the man has spoken to him more disrespectfully than he should. There are many men, clerks and managers, who do not know from one year's end to another whether they will retain their berths or not. It is becoming harder and harder for a man of my age to get employment of any sort, even though he is still as able to work as I am able to talk at this present moment. But the more you get your industries into your own hands, and your land into your own hands, the more you will be in the employment of public, responsible bodies, controlled by your own votes. Public employment is the very best possible employment. You will notice that the middle classes spend a great deal of money in trying to get their sons into the Civil Service. They denounce Socialism for you, but are glad to avail themselves of it. They know the man in public employment has an absolutely safe berth, with a pension at the end of his service. He has no anxiety, and he is able to marry when twenty-three or twenty-four years of age, whereas the man in the Potteries cannot marry till forty, and very often not then.

THE UNEMPLOYED PROBLEM

There is also that question which I have not been able to touch on tonight, because I could take up a whole evening with it—the question of unemployment. I dare say all of you at this meeting have got a job, or you could not have paid to come into this room. Nevertheless, there is not a single one of you who may not be unemployed sooner than you think. The thing you have got to understand is this: That the man who is waiting for a job, and is willing to do it, has as good a right to be maintained and kept in good health and training as the man who is doing the job. (Cheers.) Look at your

Army and your Navy. Supposing here, in England, we said: "We will run our Navy in the same way that we run our ordinary affairs. We don't want to keep paying soldiers and feeding soldiers, and clothing soldiers, who have nothing to do but to eat their heads off. Throw them out into the streets." Then when the Germans land next Tuesday, as the *Daily Mail* says, or some other paper which has taken up the cry—(laughter)—we can pay men from the streets sixpence an hour to go out armed to meet them. When the battle is over they can go back to the streets again. What chance would a country have that entrusted its national defence to such a silly system as that? You recognise, so far as your soldiers and police constables are concerned, that you have to keep them in good health and training, ready for the job which you only hope will never come. (Cheers and laughter.)

THE INDUSTRIAL ARMY

Will you ever realise that what you do with the military army you ought to do with the industrial army. (Renewed cheers.) When will you ratepayers realise that it does not pay you, to do what you do now? When you throw a man on the streets looking for a job, and leave him there for months, you have struck a mortal blow at that man's character. (Cheers.) It is from your unemployables that you get your criminals and your feeble-minded, and, as a result of your refraining from timely expenditure, you have in the long run to pay for police, for hospitals, and for all those things which ought not to exist in a properly conducted community. (Hear, hear.) It is not good commercial sense to do as you are now doing. (Cheers.)

THE FABIAN SOCIETY

Now, ladies and gentlemen, I have kept you an intolerable time. (Cries of "No, no," and "Go on.") It is very nice of you to say "Go on," but you ought to be very careful in saying that to an experienced lecturer, because that is exactly the point at which the lecturer sits down. Better leave off your dinner while you are still a little hungry than go on further. I want quite frankly to put before you the ideal of the Fabian Society here—the Newcastle Fabian Society which got up this meeting. We don't want you to join the Newcastle Fabian Society. The Fabian Society is a very superior society indeed. It is only people of very exceptional brains, and public

spirit, and accomplishments, that are allowed to come into the
Fabian Society, and we have got all the people with these qualifications that are in the neighbourhood already. (Laughter.) Our
business is not to get people into our Society; it is to send our people
into the general mass of the people and get them to act intelligently in
their different societies. We don't want to convert you from being
Unionist to being a Fabian. We want to send Fabians into the
Unionist Party to make the Unionists intelligent. (Laughter and
cheers.) Oh, ladies and gentlemen, the Liberals want it just as badly
—(renewed laughter and cheers)—and when we have done it to all
the parties, then there will be only one party in this country on the
main points, and then we shall have something like a healthy and
a happy and great country.

THE GREAT IDEAL

And let me tell you, whatever people may tell you about our
ideals, about the mischief we want to do, our ideal is a very simple
one. It is simply this. We want every man to be able to say: "I have
by the labour of my prime and the prime of my life, paid back the
debt to society which was incurred by my education." I hope in the
future it will be a large debt. I hope every child will have a splendid
upbringing and a splendid education, and that there will be plenty
to pay back. Remember that with labour properly organised, a man
could pay back everything he gets in his childhood handsomely,
and he could provide for his old age handsomely at the same time.
We want a man to say to this country, "I don't want to make more
money than anybody else; I don't want to have everything. My
intelligence and my invention adds to the general stock, because,
even if I were a man of great inventive power, and I nevertheless
took all that those powers had produced and put it into my own
selfish pocket, the world would be none the better. My only reason
why the community should esteem and honour me is not because
I have done something for myself but because I have done something
for them."

THE LIFE BEYOND

And I finish this ideal with the religious ideal. A man should be
able to say: "By the labour of my prime I have paid back the debt
of my education. I have supported myself in a handsome and
dignified way while I was working, and have provided for my old

age in a handsome and dignified way, and I have done something more than that. I shall die, not in my country's debt, but when I die my country shall be in my debt. I shall have produced more than I have consumed." He shall be able to say "England is a better place because I, John Smith (or whatever his name might be) have been there, and yet John Smith has had a good life of it." And there is something beyond that. If there is another life to come, if any man conceives that when this life is at an end that he will then go into the presence of God, who will ask him to give an account of his life, then he would not approach that God crawling, and asking for forgiveness for sins, and admitting he had lived in a wicked and horrible way. He would hold up his head even before his God and say: "When I was in your world I did your work in the world. I did more than your work in the world; I left the world in my debt. You are in my debt. Now give me my reward!" (Loud cheers.)

VOTE OF THANKS

The Rev. E. S. Kiek moved a resolution of gratitude and appreciation to the lecturer for his address. Mr Shaw, he said, had drawn together a wonderful audience, and had shown that Socialism as a practical business ought to commend itself to the business men in that neighbourhood.

ON CHRISTIAN ECONOMICS

Of a quite different kind to that just given is the following speech, which may be said to begin in its scope where the last one left off, and to be complementary to it. It is, in fact, more in the nature of a sermon, and in it Shaw, with exceptional passion and clarity, reveals the fundamentally religious—rather than Marxist or secular—basis of his Socialism and political views generally.

Many of those still living who were present among the audience on this occasion consider this address to be the finest by Shaw they ever heard. As was almost invariably his custom, Shaw spoke extempore throughout. Notwithstanding the great interest aroused at the time, reports in newspapers were, owing to the comprehensive nature of the speech, very inadequate, and to the best of my knowledge, a complete account appears here for the first time.

For exclusive permission to include here the following report, I express my deepest gratitude to Mr C. H. Norman, who made it. Mr Norman was a close friend and Socialist colleague of Bernard Shaw's for half a century, and a prominent figure, particularly before and during the First World War, in many left-wing and radical movements. He was not a Fabian, but active in British Socialist Party and Independent Labour Party circles, and he was also one of the three leaders from its inception of the No Conscription Fellowship (the others were Clifford Allen—later Lord Allen of Hurtwood, and Fenner Brockway—now Lord Brockway). He organised, financed entirely out of his own pocket, and conducted all the negotiations connected with, the Petition he drafted (with Shaw) protesting to the Government over the Denshawai incident referred to by Shaw towards the end of this speech, and he has also been the author of many articles and books on Socialism, Peace, and allied subjects.

130

This address was delivered on 30th October, 1913, at a meeting of the City Temple Literary and Debating Society in Holborn, under the Chairmanship of the Rev. R. J. Campbell. The City Temple was at the height of its fame at this time as a forum for unconventional, radical, and stimulating interpretations of subjects of wide human appeal.

After the Chairman had formally opened the meeting Bernard Shaw rose and was greeted with loud and continued applause. He said:—

Ladies and gentlemen, I must warn you at the outset that though I am going to lecture on "Christian Economics", I do not profess to be a Christian. (Applause.) I notice that two members of the audience applaud that with restrained enthusiasm. (Laughter.)

Now I am quite aware that this announcement is an extremely unusual one. It has always struck me as being rather a curious thing that if you stop an ordinary Englishman, say the first man you meet in the street as you go home, and say: "I beg your pardon, sir; are you a great philosopher?" he would probably say: "Oh no". If you said: "Are you a poet?", well, he would give a modest cough, and admit that he has written some little things, but he does not profess to be a great poet. If you then ask him: Is he a very capable man of business, he will say: "Well, I do my best." If you ask him: "Are you a good oarsman?", "Are you a good boxer?", well, he doesn't like to boast, but perhaps he would go so far as to say that on his day he is not so bad. But if, instead of those questions, you simply asked him: "Are you a Christian?" he would say: "Certainly I am a Christian. How dare you ask me such a question?" He has not the slightest hesitation in making that monstrous assertion. Although, as has already been hinted, I am not altogether lacking in a due proportion of self-conceit, I have never professed to be a Christian. That is rather too large an order for me.

There is also another thing which affects my attitude here tonight. I am by profession mainly a dramatist or playwright. Now a dramatist or playwright is in the position of the King or the Prime Minister of a great modern empire. He may not have any religion whatever, in the sectarian sense. He is face to face with a large mass of people, a small minority of whom call themselves Christians, and the others are

Mohammedans and Buddhists and Brahmins, belonging to all manner of branches of religion. Accordingly, he has to divest his mind of any prejudice in favour of one or other of these great sects: and get into the position which is very often described as having no religion at all. This is a position which is curiously like that, as far as one can see, of Jesus himself: who seems to have been regarded by all sects as a person of no religion, because you do not find that he expressed any very strong preference between them. In fact, the outstanding thing is that whereas they all seem to have classed each other as heretics or Gentiles generally, he was perfectly willing to talk of a Gentile and talk of a heretic. Therefore, my attitude in this matter, although perhaps an unusually impartial one, is not perhaps in theory an altogether un-Christian one. Therefore what I have to put before you tonight, I put with perhaps as much impartiality as is possible to a human being; which is not saying very much.

Now Christian Economics do not really concern you until you begin to make up your mind to introduce Christianity into the world, and into this country. You see, all our existing civilisations are elaborate organisations for the prevention of Christianity. (Hear, hear.) Our police and our soldiers, and all the coercive forces that we have at our disposal, profess to suppress murder and theft: but they do not. They do not profess to prevent Christianity: but they do. Now I must—having made that beginning, and warned you that I am going, as a sensible man, to deal with the world as it exists at present, as a world in which Christianity, however it may be existing in the hearts of some persons, is nevertheless a thing which is not established, [and as one who believes], in fact, that the entire social order as we have it at present is anti-Christian—(Hear, hear)—deal to some extent with the question of what Christianity is.

I should like, although I am rather reluctant to do it, because our Chairman must be extremely tired of it, to deal for a moment with our Chairman's contribution to our consciousness of Christianity. I am not speaking as one of his congregation. I am not making allowances for a great deal that he has said on the subject that I have not heard. I want merely to deal with his contribution to the subject as it reached me, and as it has struck me in the order of its importance. First, shortly, what I think he has done is, he has restored Jesus. He has rescued him from the region of fable and legend; and he has restored him to the sphere of history. He has presented him in such a way that he becomes a credible historical character; which is a very remarkable advance towards the belief that Christianity may turn out to be humanly practicable. But the other thing which he has done, which is, perhaps, a little more startling, is that he has made us conscious, in the face of our previous general conviction that Christ was the first Christian, of the fact that he is the last Christian; that Christianity was a thing that had been growing, and was finally suppressed by the Crucifixion.

I want to lay particular stress on that. I want to point out to you that the Crucifixion was a great political success. It seems to have absolutely destroyed Christianity. It was meant to do so; it was meant to do so by the Jews, with the assistance of the Romans. Probably Pontius Pilate did not mean anything very particular about it; and did not care about it: but at any rate, with his assistance the Crucifixion took place; and Christianity thereupon practically disappeared from the world.

That is a thing which you must get very carefully into your heads; because many people are under the monstrous idea that Christianity has been flourishing ever since.

It is quite true that people since that time, after a brief interval, began to call themselves Christians. That we are all aware of, of course: but as a matter of fact, if you go to the Early Church, you discover as to the religion which called itself Christianity, as it grew up it was in no sense peculiarly Christian at all; that is to say, it dealt with beliefs which were really superstition: it embodied beliefs which are superstitions. It embodied the old doctrine of the Atonement, the old idea that in some way or other you could always get rid of your guilt and your responsibility by seizing on some innocent victim and destroying it—sacrificing it, as it was said. Whether that victim was a goat, as in the sacrifice which Abraham substituted for the sacrifice of his own son, or whether, as it afterwards came to be, it was the sacrifice of a man, still the idea was the same—the notion that in some way or other you could get rid of your guilt or your sin by shifting it on to innocent shoulders.

That clearly is not a doctrine which is in any way specially characteristic of Christianity. I do not find anywhere, in any record or any tradition of the sayings of Jesus, that He ever turned round to the Jews and said: "You need not be concerned about your personal conduct; you must do just anything you like, and put it on Me. My shoulders are broad enough to bear it all". Mind, it is an extremely comforting belief. If you have a lot of guilt on your conscience which you find you cannot get rid of, your Atonement theory comes in very well: but I am not going to deal with that. I am not going to consider that as Christianity; because it does not seem to me to be distinctively Christian.

I go further, and say that it seems to me that we are bound to get rid of that belief, in order to make people shoulder their full share of moral responsibility. (Hear, hear.) I want to destroy every hope, as far as I can, in every human soul, that they can possibly shift responsibility by any sacrifice whatever. (Applause.)

Now when you come to the Middle Ages, you had a religion which also called itself Christianity. It was a very fine thing in a way: it was a very inspiring thing. It produced some of the most magnificent works of art that exist in the world. It proved, in fact, that you can only get the greatest art through religion; and as the expression of a religion of some kind. It was the religion at its best of Chivalry. It was the religion of Don Quixote. It was the religion of attacking evil, fighting it and destroying it. That meant, of course, putting a certain number of the members of the human race in acute antagonism to the religion, and destroying them; and it was a little tainted, I think, by the old notion of the sacrifice. It may not have been any longer the idea that you could concentrate all the guilt of the world on one particular individual, and kill it in his person: but there was always a great deal of burning and slaughter, and making war on the Saracens, or somebody else. There was a tremendous lot of fighting about that religion. The Middle Ages was a tremendous fighting time—fighting for their religion which they called Christianity. Mediaeval Christianity undoubtedly did a great deal of work in the world. It accustomed men to do a great many things which they could not have done without religion; some of them very necessary and very fine things. I submit to you, however, that it was not Christianity.

One of the things that it never did was, it never overcame the fear of death. You may remember that it has been said that Death is the last enemy to be overcome. We have not quite overcome that yet. Always you have had round this early Christian religion, round this mediaeval religion, not only that great fringe of legend, stories of miracles, and so on; but you have had intimidation in the shape of a hell, and you have had a refuge from death in the shape of a heaven, promising you personal immortality. It seems to me that those things were relics of the old Atonement theory. I do not say that the religion was not a useful one and a fine one: but I submit that it was not one characteristically and peculiarly Christian. It was not the thing that separates Christianity in history from all other faiths and religions.

Then, of course, those religions were finally wiped out by modern commerce; which destroyed all pretence even of religion. I think it is something to have come to the point at which we are at present, where even the practice is gone—when it is hardly worth people's while any longer to be hypocritical. In the old mediaeval times, you had a period when no man spoke about business, and no man spoke about politics, without constant reference to his religion, without constant reference to God as an active force in the universe. But the only place where that occurs at the present time is in the wilds of Africa, among the Boganda and other people who have very recently been converted to Christianity. If you read the letters they write to the missionaries and travellers who have converted them, you find they use the old mediaeval language. You will find that they, in almost every second or third line, refer to God as actively interfering in their affairs.

It is a rather curious reflection, because this has often occurred to me: I remember asking a very famous traveller, the late Sir Henry Stanley: "Can these people use modern firearms?" He said: "Of course they can, just as well as you can." I said: "That is a very lively thing. It is evident from the letters you have shown me that these people really believe in their religion exactly as the mediaeval Christian believed in his religion. Now," I said, "supposing they learned to use firearms, and supposing they found out the real state of things in Europe, supposing they discovered that we do not believe in Europe in the way that they believe, may it not be possible that they may start a Crusade with the object of wiping out practically the modern European, on the ground that he is a blasphemer, a thief, and an enemy of God?"

I just throw that out as one of the dreadful suggestions which modern civilisation is almost always making. However, I think you will admit that from the moment that commercialism got into full swing, really from the reign of Henry VII, from the sixteenth century onwards, you find that any sort of pretence at anything like a genuine Christian religion practically vanishes. After that time war, for instance, is no longer even generous. You find from the Thirty Years' War to the war the other day in the Balkans, you have war in its utmost horror—about the worst you can get out of war—a sort of war compared to which Crécy and Poitiers were almost exchanges of gentlemanly courtesies. (Laughter.)

Since we must have a really clean slate for Christianity, shall we attempt to begin Christianity? Shall we try to found Christianity in this country? Is it worth doing? Is it worth undoing the work of the Crucifixion, after this lapse of 2,000 years, during which Christianity has been suppressed—and suppressed by organised and armed force; and during which all the religions calling themselves Christian will really not bear examination from a Christian point of view? Shall we make an attempt really to take up the traditions of Christ, and see what we can do?

Well, many of my friends will say: "Do nothing of the sort." My friend Mr Foote, the Editor of the *Freethinker*, will tell you unhesitatingly [that] all you can do if you attempt anything of the kind, if you cling to this name, will be to continue historical Christianity: and he will tell you a number of terrible things about historical Christianity. He will bring a terrific indictment, an indictment that no human institution ought to be able to survive; and every word of that indictment will be entirely and perfectly true.

I emphasise that because I warn you that, as I believe, if you attempt to go on as Christians with a continuation of historical Christianity, then I think you will fail; then I think you will be beaten out of the field by other forces, some of them intensely hostile to Christian ideas. I think, in short, that we have to make a new beginning.

Supposing thus you say: "Yes, we will make a beginning, as soon as we see our way to it": what does that affirmative answer involve? What will you stand committed to, if you begin to be Christians? In other words, what are the characteristic doctrines of Christianity? If you reject the theory of the Atonement, the miracles, and all the rest of it, all those things which have so often been called Christianity, what is the thing which I am prepared to call Christianity?

Well, I recognise three main things. In the first place, you will have to give up revenge, and you will have to give up punishment completely and entirely: that is to say, you will have to scrap your entire criminal and juridical system. You will have to: "Judge not, that ye be not judged." (Applause.) You will have to stop putting people in prison who rob you. You will have to stop hanging people who murder you. (Applause.) You will have to give up the whole thing. You will have to stop scolding and complaining and writing to *The Times*. (Laughter.)

Well, I am glad you take it in such a light-hearted way. Then you will have to take, in a sense, no thought for the morrow: that is to say, you will have to go in for Communism. (Hear, hear.) You will have to take no thought for the morrow as to what you shall eat or what you shall drink: and that means Communism; because there is no other way in which you could possibly place yourself in the position of not having to think of what you will eat and drink tomorrow, except through Communism. Under our present system, which as you know is the very reverse of communistic, we have brought the necessity for taking thought for the morrow as to what you shall eat and drink to such a tremendous pitch, that very few of us are able to think of anything else. (Laughter.)

Then you will have to adopt the great Christian doctrine which has recently been called the Immanence of God. You will have to begin to understand the meaning of such phrases as "The divine spark in man". You will have to understand that "the Kingdom of Heaven is within you".

That, also, is rather a difficult thing to face; because, you see, God is in rather a peculiar position. God is a person who cannot be insured. What I mean by that is that He has got to stand by His mistakes. If you make a mistake, you to some extent can get out of the consequences of that mistake by insurance. You can join, as it were, with one another. If your house is burnt, we can agree all to club together in an Insurance Company, to build your house again, with only a small sacrifice to yourself. If you have an accident, we can all agree in the same way to compensate you. All these things can be done. We can help each other over the consequences of our mistakes; but the mistakes of God cannot be insured against, if he makes mistakes, and he evidently makes a great many. Those mistakes are absolutely irremediable. Therefore, if you can see God as acting through a conscious agent, that conscious agent has on him the most terrible responsibility, which he cannot shift off to anybody else.

If you once adopt this doctrine that "God is within you",

and that practically, that is what you are here for, to try and give
some executive force to God, that you are the instrument through
which God works, then every mistake which you make becomes
practically in magnitude like a mistake of God.

I remember once being told a story by a very light-hearted gentleman; and it was a very amusing story in its way. I remember that he
told it to me in a tramcar at Florence. He said: There was a
very pious man who had lived very humbly all his life, sustained in a
life of virtue and good works by the belief that at last when he died
he would see God face to face. In the course of time he died; and he
presented himself at the gate of Heaven full of expectation. He
found St. Peter, who admitted him, very much pre-occupied and
apparently very much troubled, and very short in his manner of
conversation. St. Peter, having admitted him, evidently wanted to
get rid of him; but this man clung to St. Peter, and explained what
it was he was looking forward to. St. Peter remonstrated and said:
"You are all right; you are in Heaven; what more do you want?"

No, this man was not satisfied. To be in Heaven was a small
thing to him. He wanted to look on the face of God, and be face to
face with Him, and speak to Him. Nothing that St. Peter could say
would turn him from that determination. At last St. Peter called
St. Paul, Moses, and Elijah; he had a consultation, and said virtually:
"This man insists," and they had to agree that in some way he was
within his rights. Accordingly they told him that he must be very
careful. They led him to a magnificent cathedral. In that cathedral
he saw a wonderful Presence: an old man sitting on a throne in the
choir of that cathedral. He was about to rush forward to throw
himself before the figure on his knees, when St. Peter and St. Paul
held him back. They said: "You must not go; you must not say
anything; and you must not tell this because it is a very awful thing,
but the fact of the matter is, God has gone mad."

Now, ladies and gentlemen, that is a most instructive story;
because if you can once realise what it would mean if the director of
the whole universe went mad, or if, to put it in another way, he went
wicked, perhaps you would begin to have some sort of idea of what is
the matter with the world at the present time. The matter is that God
in you, and in most of us, is mad and wicked; that is just what it
comes to. In some way, to reach the genuine Christian doctrine, the
God that is within you will have to be a sane God, and will have to

be a more intelligent God: you will have to bear all the consequences, and know that you are responsible for the consequences of all His mistakes.

If you say: "We will establish Christianity", you must say: "We will shoulder this responsibility": and I leave you simply to ponder on that, and to think what it would be. The weight and terror of it is very considerable; and it explains the tremendous reluctance of people to accept this very great and central doctrine of Christianity. If you will read St. John's gospel carefully, you will find that according to it, Jesus in his teaching was always coming back to this point. He was always coming back to the fact that the Son of Man was the Son of God; trying to make people realise that God was within them, and their own godhead.

If you read carefully, you will find that although he was allowed to teach many other things, and do many other things, the moment he got on to that point, the Jews generally stoned him. It is curious to know why it was; and I can only suppose that it was some dim glimpse of what it would mean for them—the fact that it would bring every man face to face, as it were, with his own conscience. He would have to shoulder the whole responsibility of the universe, if that were brought home to him: and I suppose that is what made the Jews take to stones, and made them finally crucify Jesus.

My subject tonight really deals with the second point of Christianity. I am not going to deal any further with the Immanence of God; although I tell you, you do commit yourself to God, if you say you will try the experiment of establishing Christianity. I do not propose to deal largely with the question of the entire disuse of revenge and punishment. I am inclined to think that the disuse of revenge and punishment would make matters rather more terrible for evil-doers: because if you ever get rid of the idea of expiation again you make people uncomfortable. At present, if you punish a man, you wipe his offence off the slate. There is no man who has ever been punished for some wrong act—who has had a malicious injury perpetrated on him purposely at the instance of society, because he did something malicious, and who has really done something malicious—who does not believe that the two wrongs cancel one another, and that two blacks make a white. If you give up punishing one another for wrong acts, and if you give up revenging yourself, wrong-doers will go round the world seeking in vain for punishment. They will go about with their guilt round their neck; and every man will know to the end of time: If I have stolen a thing once, I am a thief, and I will never be able to get out of it; but at the present time you can steal, and at the end of three months you are honest men. (Laughter and applause.)

But my subject here tonight, of course, is the economic subject: "Take no thought for the morrow." I am now going to deal with that in a quiet sort of way, and make an unexciting middle part of my speech which will give you an opportunity of going to sleep, as most people do when economics are mentioned. It goes without saying that you are committed to Communism.

You see, one of the consequences of the Immanence of God is, once we have realised that, that we immediately recognise [that] we are members one of another; and when we are members one of another, there is no further question of personal and private property. The welfare of one becomes the welfare of all the rest. You would not have people starving, and you could not possibly have people starving, in a Christian country, unless everybody is starving. As long as there is food, the food has got to go round.

The practical conditions of Communism are not the provision by public authority of a great mass of things to be shared without any ceremony by all the people. That is done largely amongst us at the present time, because it would be quite impossible to organise a large community in any other way. With reference to locomotion, for instance, at any rate walking locomotion, roads, lighting, and things of that kind are all communistic. Holborn outside is a place which is perfectly free to everybody. If a man walks down Holborn, he is not weighed when he goes in at one end, and charged so much a foot as he walks along Holborn for the amount of wear and tear that his walking has made on the pavement. You do not even have turnpikes. You have a great amount of lighting, and water, and things of that sort—all those things are at present communised.

There is no doubt, even under the existing commercial civilisation, [that] events will press the definite provision of Communism a little further. But the weak point of Communism, in that particular method, is that it does not give the consumer any control over production. If all the things that are produced are thrown into the common stock, and everybody comes and takes what he wants, a very large number of people will not find what they want. The only way in which you can secure to each man some sort of power of dictating what he wants in England, is by making use of that wonderfully beneficent invention, money.

One of the greatest blessings which has ever been conferred on the human race was the invention of money as an instrument of exchange. It has been turned into the root of all evil: but that is not necessarily a permanent condition of affairs. When you call money the root of all evil, if you use the expression with regard to another person, you mean that he has got too much. If you use it with regard to yourself, you mean you have got too little. But what I want is to have an income and spend that income; because in no other way can I go into the market and pay my due to the actual controller of production and say: "I want such and such a thing; and I will not pay until I get that simple thing."

Communism, in a word, is supply without demand; and when you have supply without demand, you have no control of supply. It is a mere guess in the dark as to whether you are supplying things that anybody wants. If, for instance, you had general Communism in the hands of such Governments as we have today, those Governments would produce what people wanted say 200 or 300 years ago and nothing that they wanted today. (Applause.) Well, then, your Communism will mean that everybody will have an income: and the communistic part of it will mean that everybody will have an exactly equal income.

Also, the income will not be the price of a man. In a Christian State, a man being a part of God, is infinitely valuable. You cannot buy him; and you cannot sell him. Once you realise, for instance, that God is immanent in man, you cannot take that little instrument of God, that little organisation in which there is a spark of God, and say: "I will have 18s. worth of God; and I will make use of that 18s. worth for my own purposes, to make myself rich without regard to anything else." There is an end of that: the thing becomes inconceivable. The value is infinite: and when you come to infinite values you are done, so far as regular incomes are concerned. It is not conceivable that you could say under those circumstances: "This particular aspect of God which you call the Duke of Somebody is worth £1,000 a day; and this other person is worth a shilling a day." All that goes completely, and it is driven out of your head.

Whilst the idea of this horrible prostitution of humanity, this buying and selling of people goes on, the best way to drive it out is by such a simple question as I have often asked people. A man gets up and says: "Equal incomes are nonsense." I always say: "How much do you want? Do you want more than I do?" He really feels in his innermost feelings that I am a great man, because I have written plays, which is, perhaps, the surest way to be considered a great man in these days; and he does not like to say that he ought to get more than me. Then I say: "Do you think you ought to have less than me?" He is then perfectly clear that any person who is disreputable enough to be connected with the theatre ought not to have more than he should have.

The moment people begin to argue in the abstract about equality of income, do not answer the people in the abstract; but say at once: "How much are you earning? You have a sort of idea that people should have unequal incomes. Give us an idea of what your income ought to be, and what somebody else's income ought to be. How much should Mr Campbell have? How much should Mr Jack Johnson, the prizefighter, have? How much should the Archbishop of Canterbury have; and how much should everybody in this room have?" Let all this congregation here—I suppose I must call it a congregation, although we are in a Debating Society—let each person of this congregation walk away with another person, and before they get home settle exactly how much [each] they are worth. They will find that that simple test will reduce our whole system of inequality of income, and buying and selling of people, to absolute nonsense. It is and always has been nonsense: and what you have now is not a distribution of income on any plan; but simply plunder. (Hear, hear.)

At the same time, although the case for this Communism and for equality is all very well, still I began at the outset by very fully facing the fact that probably this is not an audience of Christians: I am trying to make them consider Christianity, at any rate. Our Chairman is very largely engaged in that arduous task also: but I dare say all of you would be rather more consoled if I could establish any sort of secular case for equality of income.

I can assure you, ladies and gentlemen, that the secular case for equality of income is absolutely overwhelming. In every single department of life it is overwhelming. I purposely do not wish to give you the case, because that is a lecture all by itself, and it is one furthermore which I have delivered several times; but I must just put it shortly in this way. There is a tremendous economic case for it for this reason: that the economic prosperity of a nation depends on its using its resources to produce wealth; and to produce things in the order of the importance of those things. If you meet a man in the street who is starving, we will suppose that you, as a sympathetic human being, are roused to sympathy, and you say: "This man is my brother," and you give him sixpence. We will suppose that the man is really actually on the verge of starvation. Supposing that man, having got the sixpence, says: "Bless you, sir"; and immediately goes into a perfumer's shop and buys a bottle of scent to put on his handkerchief, what would you say about that man? To say that he is a bad economist is putting it very mildly. He is a lunatic. Well, has it ever occurred to you, ladies and gentlemen, that that is just exactly and precisely what we are doing in this country every day of our lives? (Applause.) We have the mass of our people practically starving. We have 13 millions of people, so we are told by our Prime Ministers, always on the verge of starvation: and yet we are buying in large quantities 80-horsepower motor cars, and establishing racecourses, and spending the money in all sorts of luxuries. That is just as bad economy for a nation as it is for an individual. The result is just the same.

The reason that that takes place is inequality of income. One man has £20,000, and another man has nothing. The man who has nothing wants clothes for his children; he wants a decent house for his children; he wants food for his children and himself: but he is unable to get it because he has no money. The man of £20,000 has got more bread and more clothes and shelter than he wants. He does not want anything more. He goes on to obtain his superfluities and luxuries. Having the money, his demand regulates the supply: and, accordingly, you have this terrible phenomenon, which some of us appear to be so proud of, of masses of starvation, squalor, and degradation of character, side by side with ridiculous expenditure in luxury of the most senseless kind—which does not even bring happiness to its possessors.

Now, ladies and gentlemen, that is all because you have inequality of income. (Applause.) Get everybody's income level, and you will find that everybody will have bread enough first; clothes enough second; and decent housing third; and then they will go on to luxuries practically in the same degree and at the same time. You will find there will not be any luxuries produced until there is bread enough for the children; you will find there will not be any superfluities produced until there are decent houses for everybody put up. You will get everything in its order: and if you will only spend a few hours in reflecting on the magnitude of our industrial anarchy, of our wrong production of today, you will find that that single argument will sweep away all the feeble, silly, objections which have been urged against the equality of income. That is the economic argument.

When you come to the region of the administration of justice, it is scarcely necessary to dwell on the subject: the inequality is so obvious. We have recently had the spectacle of our friend Mr Larkin—(loud applause)—in Dublin, tried by a jury of his peers, and also tried by a Judge—who has probably often said that all are equal before the law. If those twelve jurymen and Mr Larkin and the Judge had had exactly the same income, and that was the same as everybody's income, Mr Larkin would be walking about today a free man. I will just give you a last illustration. On every day there are cases of injustice in all your magistrates' courts, and in all your criminal courts. Not a single day passes that there are not a dozen cases far worse than Mr Larkin's, who probably will not be very greatly harmed by the sentence.

When you come into politics, I need hardly say very much about that. Is there any pretence that our governing classes, representing rich people, are capable, whatever their good-will may be, of ruling in the interests of the mass of the people? They have no sort of conception of what the lives of poor people like us may happen to be. It is not that there is any ill-will on their part: but if you are brought up on an income of £30,000 a year, you simply cannot understand the wants and needs of a man who is brought up on an income of £300 a year; to say nothing of the people who are brought up on an income of £30 a year; and not to mention the people who are brought up on no income at all. The whole thing is impossible.* You may introduce as much democracy as you like,

---

* A similar charge was levelled in some quarters half a century later—against the Conservative Cabinet of the 1959-64 period, most of whom were wealthy (in several cases millionaires), educated at Harrow or Eton, and whose chief recreations included grouse-shooting—individuals in short, whose upbringing made them inevitably to some extent remote from the problems of the ordinary British people (such as paying the weekly rent, the rising cost of food, and so on).

but there will be no democracy possible until you have a democracy of income to begin with—something like equality of income.

Then the last point (I am running over them very rapidly) is a physiological point—the point which has been brought forward under the general name of Eugenics. We are waking up to the fact that we are a very poor lot of people: we are not good-looking; I am sorry to be personal, but we are not. We are not good-looking; we are not healthy; we are not strong. A great deal of the apparent increase in the length of life seems to me to be due to taking a great deal of extra care of lives which one is almost tempted to say were hardly worth taking much trouble about. But there is the fact that we have found ourselves out.

We talk about the superman. The mere word "superman" shows that we are realising that at present we are only the super-monkey, and rather a poor sort of monkey at that. Everybody feels instinctively that we want a better sort of man. That is all very well. We are willing, no doubt, to make any sacrifice, and make every effort, to attain that better type of man. That instinctive adoration of life which is in all of us I believe will overcome almost every objection, in so far as there is an upward path before us in the development of the evolution of the highest forms of life, if only we knew exactly how to go forward.

But, you see, the moment you begin to talk about getting a better sort of man, that means breeding a better sort of man. The moment you begin to breed any sort of animal, you have to ask yourself quite definitely: What sort of animal do you want? It is perfectly easy when you are breeding a racehorse. You know quite well what you want. When you want to breed a racehorse which is able to run better than another horse, you do not care much about his temper and character. What you want is a horse that will go faster than any other horse in running a particular race. That is what you want. You want swiftness above everything: and you go forward and you breed swiftness. Many people imagine you can always get it: but I may tell you privately, if you consult a horse-breeder, he will tell you that nineteen times out of twenty you do not get it; but at any rate, you do get it to this extent: that out of the same rough type of horse that men used to mount in the old days of chivalry, you have bred two different sorts of horses. You have bred the great draught horse which we have; and you have bred the racehorse. You did that quite simply, because you knew what you wanted. You wanted a swift animal on the one hand; and you wanted an animal of great draught power on the other hand. That is quite simple: but when you start to breed human beings, what do you want? Can anybody tell me that? Not one of you knows where to begin.

You will say you want a good man: but you do not know what a good man is. You will say you want a healthy man: but you do not know what a healthy man is—you do not even begin to know that. Everybody is trying some particular line for making you healthy, and making you strong. If you consult the advertising pages of the *Strand Magazine*, you will read that a very small expenditure of money will make you presently into a magnificent athlete; and that you will live for ever. Well, we are not magnificent athletes; and we do not live for ever. The terrible thing is that we do not know, and there is nothing for us to trust to except the divine spark within us; there is nothing to trust to but that driving force which has brought us where we are: and we have to see whether it will bring us any further.

The only thing we do know positively is, that very curiously when you walk down a street in London, and sometimes even when you come to the City Temple, you are not much impressed with the people you see. You pass multitudes of women—I am talking of women for convenience, but the same thing applies to men—with regard to whom, if anybody suggested that you should marry them, the idea would be grotesque to you; you could not think of it. Then suddenly, quite unexpectedly, in an extraordinary way, you see somebody who interests you; and if it happens here, you do not listen to the rest of Mr Campbell's sermon. In others words, you fall in love.

Now that is a solid fact. People do fall in love; and it seems to me that that is the only mortal thing that you have got to trust to in the breeding of the human race. You must see, if you have any sort of logic, how remarkable is that curious instinct, that singular preference, that exception from the rule of general indifference; because nothing is more infamously false than the common and vulgar assumption that love is an indiscriminate thing. It is not an indiscriminate thing. The people to whom it is indiscriminate have been brought into a thoroughly unhealthy state. It is a most fastidious thing; it is a most discriminative thing. You may go half through your

life and never fall in love. Some people do not do it at all; but when
it does come, it has some meaning in it.

It is a thing which has governed marriage from the time marriage
began to exist: and if it had been a destructive thing, it would have
destroyed the human race before this. You are bound to believe in it.
You are getting some prompting from Providence. Love is really
prompting you to do the right thing; and it is the only hope for
improving the human race.

Whatever these Eugenic Societies may say, there is only one way
of doing it; and that is by widening what they call the "area of sexual
selection" to the very widest extent. Now what is the existing state
of things? I do not know how many married people there are here.
Probably you are all either married or going to get married; or else
you have determined that nothing whatever would induce you to get
married, though let me tell you, that will not save you; but the
probability is that among the many people within your reach, you
have probably had the choice of two or three; and none of those two
or three perhaps was absolutely your ideal. I go out into the street:
I see somebody, or at least this used to occur to me before I was
married. I am an imaginative person: I am a romantic person. It is
my profession to be romantic. I went and saw some person who
attracted me enormously. She was a duchess; so she would not look
at me. I went on and saw somebody else who attracted me. She was
a charwoman, and I would not look at her, in spite of my socialistic
instincts. I knew perfectly well that it would be quite impossible for
us to live together happily. All the world over you have the same
thing.

Do not suppose you can get down to any section of the community where you do not find that you are working in a little narrow
circle everywhere, instead of having what you ought to have in this
country: that every young man and young woman would be able to
go all over the range of society through the land, and, if they fell
in love with one another, have no fear of any obstacle; that any
young man might go up to any young lady in the street and say:
"I beg your pardon, but are you unmarried?" If the young lady said:
"I am very sorry, I am engaged", then the gentleman would say:
"I am sorry, too"; and he would walk off. If not, then the gentleman
might say: "Would you mind," to use the popular phrase, "walking
out with me?"

I believe the true eugenic idea is to make that possible as between every young man and every young woman in the country: and in that way you would no longer have marriage hemmed in and distorted, and governed, by cash considerations. You would probably have an enormous mass of people who were marrying for love in the widest sense, without regard to any other considerations. I am prepared to back that as an eugenic expedient against everything. I am further prepared to challenge any eugenist in existence to show any other possible way of breeding a good human race. Ladies and gentlemen, that means equality of income.

What stops people from doing that is inequality of income. You cannot marry a £100 a year person to a £200 a year person, or a £500 a year person to a £5,000 a year person. It is no use; it cannot be done, no matter what you think. In the few cases where it does happen, it gets into the newspapers; and is usually connected with something very unpleasant.

So you see, I have been able, roughly and quite shortly, to show you on economic lines, on legal lines, on political lines, on physiological and biological lines, that there is an overwhelming case for the equality of income. So that you need not be bothered about that. You may look forward to the fact that more and more people who are not Christians will be driven by these respective arguments, in spite of all their kicking against it, to see more and more that it is the only way under which a permanently sane society can be constituted . . . .

I want to ask you this. Supposing you say you will not try Christianity, supposing you say, with Mr Foote: "We have had enough of Christianity: that has been tried; and that is done with", of course you may offer me an alternative plan; but supposing you go on as you are at the present time, and trust to democracy, because that is what many very intelligent people are doing at the present day, what is the position then?

Many people think democracy will cure everything: giving the vote. Ladies and gentlemen, it will cure nothing. Giving the vote to a man does not make him any the better a man: sometimes it makes him distinctly worse. I should imagine that the giving of the vote to the American nation has, on the whole, made Americans rather worse than they probably would have been without it. A vote is not something to sell. To sell a vote is like selling a portion of your godhead. It is essentially that: and you had better not do it. The people who buy votes are also doing a dangerous thing. They are like the people who, in the Old Testament, stole the fire from the altar; and got very severely dealt with. We are always stealing the fire from the altar. We burn our fingers with it; and then we blame somebody else.

You must not suppose that enlightenment and Democracy are the same thing. A very remarkable book has just been published by my friend Professor Gilbert Murray. He ought to have called it the Quintessence of Euripides; but it is called simply *Euripides*. It is published in the Home University Library, and you can get it for 1s.: and I advise you to get it for 1s.* Professor Gilbert Murray, in that book, shows you very clearly what happened in ancient Greece.

In ancient Greece, Christianity in the sense that I have been explaining it tonight, was a live force. There were men who saw what we are beginning to see; and what Jesus saw. There was a body of men who established Democracy in Athens as a matter of justice. They were men who represented enlightenment: and they practically, if I may put it that way, realised the godhead in themselves; and saw that the thing they had to do was largely to bring justice to Athens—to try and raise up their fellows.

They established Democracy in Athens: and what was the result? Having by Democracy established the rule of all the people, and made Democracy practically a great mass of persons with equal political power, the people so enfranchised, the Democracy, destroyed enlightenment. They indulged in the most unjust and tyrannical wars. They engaged in the task of building up a great empire; which simply meant stealing other people's countries, and trying to add them to theirs. They plunged into wars; and when they got into trouble with their wars, when they provoked other people to repel them, then they said: If they were attacked by other people, their honour obliged them to go on fighting, and to subdue their enemies.

The consequence was, they began to build up an empire which consisted of a number of persons enslaved. Not only were the people whom they forced into that empire enslaved; but they had to enslave themselves, in order to make the enslavement of the others effective. Then they laid the whole thing in ruins. It was destroyed and

* At present (1971) in print as Oxford Paperback No. 99, entitled *Euripides and his Age*, with a new Introduction by H. D. F. Kitto, price 7/6d.

smashed: and that wonderful thing, the empire which came out of Democracy, is now a dream of faded splendour; and it would not be remembered, if it were not for the great men who came before and practically established the democracy which for one moment, before Democracy wreaked its will on enlightenment, really made Athens practically the saviour of the world, as they said, and were proud to say.

Ladies and gentlemen, that is a thing which may possibly happen here. The other day the Prime Minister of this country [Mr Asquith], at Ladybank put before us a very striking list of the achievements of his Party, which has been in office since 1906. He pointed to a very instructive series of measures of social reform. He said: "This is what we have done": and, curiously enough, in some ways it was really a fine programme. I admired some of it because I suggested a good deal of it [laughter]. Remember that that programme was made possible to a very considerable extent by the fact that in 1906 Labour became organised in Parliament; and Democracy, in the sense of the political organisation of the whole working classes, got into much more direct and pressing contact with the government of the country.

But Mr Asquith, in giving you the programme of what he had done, left out a good many of the things which his Government has done: and I am going to supply that remarkable omission on Mr Asquith's part. It began in 1907 by one of the most horrible and brutal massacres that have ever disgraced civilisation. (Hear, hear.) They began by that horrible affair at Denshawai. In that affair, they got into that sort of terror that only imperialists, apparently, can get into—an ecstasy of terror—that somehow or other the empire was going to be overthrown. They flogged and they hanged innocent men with every circumstance of brutality. They tried them by a mock trial; and they hanged them: and were not content to hang them, but hanged them before their own houses, so that their families could see them hanging; and those they did not hang they flogged.

The whole accusation was so utterly baseless, the charge was so utterly false, that before a year was out, they had to release the survivors. When men had been condemned to imprisonment for life for making a feeble attempt to defend their wives' lives, many people felt: "After all, England is just: we have let them out."

But you did not let out the men you had hanged. If you can conceive those men as in Heaven, and being present at the day of final judgement against you, and some people believe that something like that may happen, you will be very sorry about it.

Then you have had in India a system of repression of public opinion by the most violently anti-liberal press laws; and accompanied by injustice, imprisonments, and torture; testimony obtained by torture; and confessions obtained by torture. You have had all the worst descriptions of tyranny, all perfectly well-known to our Government, and upheld by it, because otherwise the empire would fall to pieces.

Well, let us leave the Egyptians and the Indians out of account; because I am afraid, really whatever we may say, we have not realised that they are fellow creatures like ourselves. I think that even some of the people who are beginning to adopt the theory of the Immanence of God, have the idea that it does not quite apply to persons of another colour.

So let us come a little nearer home, and see what has happened nearer home. We have gone back recently, and gone back at the frantic demands of the Archbishop of Canterbury—who probably quite seriously imagines he is a Christian: and who is less like being a Christian than the most benighted Hottentot that has existed on the face of the earth [loud cheers]—to barbarism. At the demands of that Archbishop, this Government has passed an Act by which an English Judge can order a man to be flogged to death by any instrument that he chooses, that his most fantastic imagination can lead him to invent. We have re-introduced the sentence of flogging with no limit. If you go back to the times of Moses, when they did believe in something divine, they did permit flogging to the extent of forty strokes save one—they would not even give the fortieth stroke. The Act under which that was done, under the false pretence of curing a social evil, which it will not cure in the least, and which it has already made worse, was deliberately put on the Statute book. That is a frightful thing: and that was one of the deeds of the present Government.

Then we have had in connection with the movement for the emancipation of women a definite statement from the Prime

Minister of this country, denying that women have souls. Mr Asquith explained, in the most careful and unmistakable language in the House of Commons, that the reason for not giving the vote to women was that they belonged to an inferior and different species from men. He was perfectly right to say it, if he believed it: but there is not much hope in the spirit of statesmanship that you get from a man who really holds that belief. (Applause.)

Further on you get the forcible feeding of women in prison. (Shame.) You get a Minister who first pledged himself repeatedly and indignantly that forcible feeding did not involve any pain, or any serious discomfort, to the person forcibly fed. He pledged himself up to the hilt over and over again: and then afterwards introduced a Bill to legalise his forcible feeding; and deliberately, in face of his previous statements, retained forcible feeding as an express means of torturing certain persons whom he considered in the movement as specially worthy of it. He absolutely retained it on the ground that it was a horribly painful thing; and there must be some people dealt with in that way.

You have also had the very worst expedients of tyranny. You have had prosecutions, one under the Mutiny Act, under which any person could be imprisoned; and now under an Act in general terms for sedition. If you have not read the legal text books on sedition, which I have, you may not know this: but I can assure you that there is no human being who could live for one day without rendering himself liable, if it were worth the while of any Government to attack him, or any class to attack him, to be convicted of sedition—the terms are so general. It is one of those tyrannical expedients that no Government which is not saturated with the spirit of class tyranny, could for a moment resort to.

Well, those are some of the things that Mr Asquith did not mention that the Government had done. Just think of the significance of them! If on the other hand, he could have shown a constant reaction in social reform on the question of Land and Insurance, if on all those things he had been steadily reactionary, then you might have said: "Here are forces of evil that we understand. Here is the Russian Government tyranny come over here." But now we have this terrible phenomenon, that on the one hand there is this social reorganisation, this walking bit by bit towards Socialism and towards Collectivism; and yet the very same Government that is going ahead with the mechanical part of Collectivism, is going back on the moral part—is going back to the blackest tyranny; and so far from being restrained by Democracy, there is far less protest against these things than there would have been before 1867, when the working classes got the vote first.

Ladies and gentlemen, that is a terrible reflection. There is no use, in face of those facts, imagining that simple Democracy is going to work out our problems for us. I tell you, as an old Socialist who has studied thoroughly, as far as it can be studied, the organisation of society and industry that will be necessary under Socialism, and as one who believes that we are coming to that, that you might have the most complete Collectivism in this country; and you might have at the same time the most completely organised tyranny, the most complete suppression of all freedoms, liberties, and aspirations that make life worth living, the most complete bar to progress, far more complete than could ever have been achieved by the tyrannies of the past, under which some small sections of kings, and small aristocracies, in spite of all their will to be tyrannical, were able to inflict injury on a very small part only of the community they came into contact with. Remember that a king can only strike people that are within reach of his hand: but every one of us is within reach of the hand of democracy.*

When you have got Democracy you have the instrument of the most terrible tyranny, unless you have got enlightenment at the same time. (Hear, hear.) A democracy without enlightenment, without religion, without those things which I have shown you are the real essence of Christianity, is a thing so terrible to contemplate, that really one has to run away from the temptation to be mechanically optimistic and try and persuade oneself that it will be all right: but it will not be all right unless we work very hard to prevent it. I do not know what is going to be the end of it.

* By 'Collectivism', a few lines above, Shaw would seem to mean government based *solely* on the will and wishes of the majority of the electorate—regardless of whether such a government would, in fact be *ultimately* in their best interests or not, or whether it would achieve the aims for which it was elected in a moral manner [these being matters on which skilled political philosophers and sociologists—such as himself—were better equipped to form proper judgements than the majority of the (relatively ignorant) electorate]. He is also preaching, however, that everyone has the possibility of becoming more enlightened by opening their hearts to the spirit of God within them, and that this is the way towards a just society.

I have put the case to you as strongly as I possibly can. I tell you that if you are going to realise that the Kingdom of God is within you, unless you set to work to make the Kingdom of God exist outside of you individually, unless you really make the whole country collectively the Kingdom of God, you will be able to do nothing whatever.

There is no hope for you in Democracy; there is no hope for you in economic reform; there is no hope for you in mere economic Socialism, or mere economic anything else. You must develop your spiritual life, and your spiritual determination. You must go ahead on that. You must put certain things that you are aspiring to first; and you must put political theories and political parties next. That is what you have got to do: and if you do not do it, it will be a very bad thing for this country; and it will be a very bad thing for you. It will mean the wrecking of another civilisation.

It may mean this, and this is my last word. We talk about the superman; and we think that perhaps by some means humanity will improve; and a better sort of man will come. You do not know whether that will be so or not.

Remember, that power that is behind evolution, this wonderful power of life, has scrapped and scrapped and discarded, as being a failure, a great many forms of life. There was a time when it seemed as if to make a black-beetle was a promising experiment; as though making the bacillus of typhoid fever was a necessary bit of the organisation of life. That had to go. The aspiration of life, the thing you call God, could not be satisfied with what black-beetles and typhoid bacilli could do: and then it went on one day and it made more wonderful things. It made reptiles; and then it made animals and mammals as we know them. It made birds, which are very beautiful things; and finally it made monkeys; and then it made men. But, remember, that when the time came that it was evident that these things were not going to achieve the great thing, were not going to achieve the Kingdom of God, were not going to realise God, they were thrown aside; and something else was made. Some new thing was made which devoted itself very largely to their destruction.

Ladies and gentlemen, it is not an impossible thing that some day or other, there may walk out of a bush somewhere a new being of which you have no conception, not a man at all, or a woman at all; something new that has never occurred before: and the work of God may be handed over to that new thing; and it may be said of us: "These people have failed; they are scrapped; they are gone." Part of the mission of the new thing would be to destroy these people as part of the mission of man was to destroy the tiger. Think of that possibility, ladies and gentlemen; and make up your minds to work pretty hard.

Repeated and long continued applause marked the conclusion of Bernard Shaw's address. But there was more to come. The Chairman, the Rev. R. J. Campbell, rose and said:—

Although after that magnificent address Mr Shaw might very well be excused from answering questions, I do not suppose it is your intention to let him off altogether: so that, after the collection has been taken—if he will preach a sermon, he must expect a collection—Mr Shaw will answer questions.

Will you permit me to say a word before these questions are put? We have been listening tonight to probably the greatest master of challenging ideas in the world. I think I have never known him more stimulating, nor quite so magnificent as he was tonight. (Hear, hear.) Of course, one cannot pretend to agree with it all. I confess I listened with considerable trepidation, at the commencement of the address, to know exactly what was one's specific contribution to the subject of Christianity. I agree on the whole with Mr Shaw's interpretation of what it was: but what he said about the Atonement and about miracles, did not form part of that contribution. Miracles are happening round us every day—(hear, hear)—quite as wonderful as any recorded in the New Testament: and, if 'miracle' be not a misnomer, it will probably not be so very long—things are pointing that way, I think—that we shall find that science is giving us a rehabilitation of the credibility of what were once called "miracles". Further, when Mr Shaw tells you that you cannot get rid of any responsibility that is your own, by the sacrifice of anybody else, I noticed you applauded very enthusiastically. Well, there is not a person in this building who is not a constant proof to the force of that theory. (Applause.)

What Mr Shaw said was a grand tonic. There has been a mean way of preaching the doctrine of Atonement; and there is a great way; and there is no greater preacher of it than Mr Shaw himself. I would undertake to prove to him that there is a grand and glorious truth in the Christian doctrine of the Atonement, which in some of its aspects is pre-Christian, too—it ought to be—and that in such a play as *The Devil's Disciple* Mr Shaw shows what it is; and shows that he knows it. No action that any human being ever performs, no evil that any man or woman ever does can in its consequences, in its full responsibility, be borne by himself or herself; for those consequences are universal; and it is the universal that atones—in other words, God. But when Mr Shaw came to economics, he preached Christianity with no uncertain sound (hear, hear), and as very few preachers could preach it today; and this pulpit has been honoured by the sermon. (Cheers.)

I see I have three questions here. The first is: "If Jesus was God in the human flesh, how do you think His Crucifixion immortal?"—well, I do not think that is exactly for Mr Shaw at all. That does not touch the point of his address. The next question is: "How could equality of income be brought about?" That is a very practical question.

Bernard Shaw, replying, said:

Equality of income is not a thing to be brought about as a novelty. Equality of income is the rule at the present moment; and has always been the rule: and every attempt to introduce anything else as a general system has always been a complete and utter failure. I do not think there is anything more astonishing than the fact that men do not see this equality of income staring them in the face all round, with their knowledge that out of 16,000 or 17,000 police constables in London, men of the greatest variety of character, every man gets exactly the same, the soldiers in our army get exactly the same, the majors get the same, colonels get the same, judges get the same. All over, masses of people with all sorts of variations of talents, of character, of energy, and so on, it is utterly impossible to vary their incomes.

Of course, there are differences between the income in the one class and the income in another. It is quite true that the judges all get £5,000; and that the police all get 24s. a week: but I contend that if it is possible to give two policemen 24s. a week each, and you find that works perfectly well, and if it is possible to get two judges—and our judges vary very greatly in character and intelligence—and give them £5,000 a year each, and that works perfectly well, then I believe it is entirely possible to give a judge and a policeman something between £5,000 and 24s. There is no difficulty whatever.

As to the way to bring it about, it does not need to be brought about. You can do it by giving one man 2s. 6d. and the other man half a crown, and the thing is done. That is an extraordinary thing to do; it is a fantastic thing to do; it is a ridiculous thing to do; it is a disastrous thing to do. It is a thing which, if it had never been done before, would stamp the man who proposed it as a lunatic. Well you manage to do it. If you can do this extraordinary and difficult thing, surely you can do this easy thing, which you have been doing every day and all day long. (Applause.)

THE CHAIRMAN: Here is a question which seems to be on the point: "How are we to get people to undertake difficult, dangerous, unhealthy, and disgusting tasks of the community, when they are not forced to do so by pressure of poverty, or bribed to do so by extra income?"

MR G. BERNARD SHAW: Well, it is a curious thing that these things at the present time are all done by people who get worse paid than anybody else. You clearly must not pay them more than anybody else: but there are plenty of ways in which you can level work a little. Men with exactly the same income may work for different hours. They may be doing certain distinguished work and get a great deal of honour, and a great deal of distinction.

It is a very funny thing that people are so full of the difficulties of getting dangerous work and difficult work and arduous work done, when, as a matter of fact, there never is any practical difficulty in getting these things done. The men, for instance, who have been showing it is possible for human beings to fly, have been for the most part doing it at the risk of their own necks; and have been called fools for their pains: but there is an attraction in the thing itself.

You must not face, as I have called it, the Christian order of society, and then begin to ask what would happen if the Christianity were left out. Of course, if everybody were merely moved by external inducements of that kind, no dangerous or difficult work would ever be done at all. Mind you, the people who do these things at present, have the alternative of doing other things. When Captain Scott went to discover the Pole, there was nothing but water to prevent his staying at home, and getting just as well paid at home. Nevertheless, he went to the Pole; and he died there. Other people are doing similar things. Though that is an extreme instance which I have given, there are many other acts, in all classes of society, which represent, even though they be small things, great sacrifices in daily life.

The real truth is that risky and arduous enterprises are dangerously attractive to people. You can see that, if you look around you, in the fact that we are constantly entering on wars. We are creating dangers unnecessarily, both in athletics and in sport, and in war, which is very largely a sport as well. We are actually courting dangers, sometimes of a horrible kind: and we are not doing that from the notion that the multitudes of men engaged in them will become well known. As a matter of fact, many of them hardly get as much as a medal to paw for their pains.

You need not be afraid—things which are needed to be done in this world will be done by men because they are needed to be done. Just think of the enormous effort that it costs men merely to live! You think because you go on doing it that it costs nothing; but as a matter of fact, to keep a human organism together must need a tremendous effort, and an effort that nobody ever thinks of as being an effort that is paid for. You sometimes discover this effort, the effort that it takes to keep up a high standard, a high class of life, by the terrible thing that occasionally occurs that your energy fails; and instead of working on the lines of high organisation, it slips down to the lower type of organisation; and the man who before was maintaining himself as a man, with human flesh organised as human flesh, suddenly finds to his horror that he is slipping down to a less effort; and finds a hideous proliferation of a lower type of cell beginning; and finds that he is the victim of a process in which a lower form of life is destroying a higher form of life. If you once begin to understand these things and to understand this tremendous energy which is constantly going on within you, you will not be stopped by these little weak considerations and be afraid, as to anything which has got to be done, that there will not be people to do it

If it only must be done, remember that the highest form of work, and the lowest form of work, is done, and always has been done, in a society like ours, not with the prospect of reward. You might as well ask me: "Supposing you gave women votes, where would you get suffragettes?" Well, in that case, you very fortunately would not want them: and I hope the necessity for them would be superseded. How any man, looking on what women are doing today, can take the view that people need rewards for doing things which are useful, I cannot understand. (Loud applause.)

THE CHAIRMAN: The next question must be the last. It bears on the preceding question. It is this. "Mr Shaw has been re-affirming tonight certain aspects of the teaching of Christ. Does he think there is any probability that the world will listen to that message now any more readily than it listened to Christ?"

MR G. BERNARD SHAW: Well, I do not know. How can I know? We must assume that the thing is possible. We must assume that although the human race has made attempt after attempt at civilisation, and has always fallen back to a more simple means of life, still, one must remember with regard to the mere willing of creative energy, that everything almost that exists is created by the mere desire that it should exist. One must remember that the mere will on the part of man to do a certain thing will finally, if he goes on trying long enough, give him the power of doing it. Almost all the things that we are learning to do, we are in the habit of saying we learn to do by practice. We do not learn to do them by practice. What is meant by practice is that you keep on trying to do a thing, and trying to do a thing; and quite suddenly a miracle occurs, and you find you can do it.

Any man who has intelligently learned anything, knows that that is the way in which you do learn. Take such a simple thing as learning to ride a bicycle. Do you find, when you practise bicycling, that you ride better every time? Not a bit of it. You try time after time; and you fall off time after time; and you are horribly discouraged by the fact. Sometimes when you thought you were getting on well, the next time you try, you tumble off, and you are worse than before. Then suddenly a miracle occurs; and you ride off on the bicycle: and you can keep on riding ever after. It is the same thing with swimming.

Remember that by merely willing to do something, you have actually created the cellular tissue, and you have created powers which you had not before: there is nothing else which is creative in the universe. That is what you have got to believe in. You have to believe, if once you could get the will—and that is the real difficulty— [that] you will do the thing. If you can only get men inspired by the will, then the old saying is true: "Where there is a will, there is a way."

Of course, it is true that the reason Christ failed was that although he showed the way, the people had not the will; and many of the people who fancied they understood him did not understand him, and so we have come to grief. But, after all, somehow or other you see this will towards the thing that he taught is not a thing that has ever been destroyed. It comes cropping up in all directions. You find that men preach it, and although their preaching is entirely against the interests very often of government, although governments often take them and treat them cruelly, still, there is a sort of tolerance for it. There is a sort of response in people to them. There is some sort of notion that everybody, after all, is striving onwards to some goal in the future—even the most degraded sort of people. A great deal can be done by social organisation to remove material obstacles to improvement.

However, I must not go on trying to be optimistic, but I must answer the question, and say that I do not know; and that nobody knows. Any man who gets up and tells you that all human experience teaches you that any such success as the success of really establishing Christianity is extremely improbable, is putting forward a view that is quite possible: but nevertheless, you have got to go on working as if the thing were a thing that would come to pass. Nobody ever does any good in this world unless he fights for every farthing as hard as he would fight for £100. In fact, you have to fight harder for your farthing than you have for your £100. There is no use in putting conundrums to me; because if you say it is no good, and nothing will come of it, then there is the Thames for you to jump into. (Applause.) That means despair.

The truth is that you cannot really face the negative answer yourself, because the fact that you go on living is the proof that really you do not believe [in] the negative answer. There is a sort of faith in the possibility. It may come slowly or it may come fast; but at any rate your business is to keep on pressing on for it; and then you will see what will happen, without asking me questions. (Applause.)

THE CHAIRMAN: You would not be so impolite as to leave this building without expressing your gratitude to Mr Shaw for what he has given us this evening. (Loud and continued applause.) I feel impelled to tell you what has been the greatest impression made upon me by his address, because I believe the same must be true of you. His address has solemnised me; it has impressed me by its tremendous moral earnestness—not that one is surprised by that. (Hear, hear.) I always resent imputations of the opposite character applied to the teachings of Mr Shaw. I think it is true that our feelings tonight have been elevated as well as solemnised; and if the appeal in his closing words bears any effect, these feelings will not be allowed to evaporate without becoming something definite and concrete in action. In other words, the will has to be put in operation, if this sermon of Mr Shaw's is to have its due effect. I wish him to accept this expression of gratitude from this great assembly for the obligation under which he has placed us tonight. (Loud cheers.)

MR G. BERNARD SHAW: Ladies and gentlemen, it is always such a pleasant experience to speak in the City Temple, and to meet your Chairman, that I assure you that no speaker that you have here deserves any thanks: and I believe you will find that all the speakers who come after me will speak here better than they speak anywhere else; and you deserve a great deal of the credit for that, as well as the speaker.

[*Editorial note.*—As mentioned briefly in the introductory note, this address was, in the opinion of many who heard it, the finest by Shaw they ever heard; they felt it to be the most impassioned, inspired, and brilliantly delivered. A correspondent, Dr Bernard Lytton-Bernard, D.Sc., D.O., M.D., who was among the audience, writing to me in January, 1963, even went so far as to say: "I thought it was the best, noblest, and most powerful, yet clearest and simplest, sermon ever given anywhere—with the exception of the one on the Mount by the One whom Shaw referred to then as the one and only Christian who ever lived."]

ON DEMOCRACY AND DICTATORS,
COMMUNISM, SOCIALISM, CAPITALISM, AND
FASCISM,
REVOLUTION, SEDITION, WOMEN IN POLITICS,
THE BRITISH LABOUR PARTY,
TRADE UNIONISM AND THE WORKING CLASS,
AND THE EQUALISATION OF INCOMES

In his address on *Christian Economics*, Shaw most lucidly explained the fundamental religious factors at the root of his views on Socialism and the Equalisation of Incomes.

On a later occasion however, at the end of his speech on Sexual Reform, Shaw—perhaps surprisingly in view of his profession of Socialism—stated his belief (on p. 102) that people of different degrees of spiritual development form themselves naturally into different circles, each having its own moral outlook, which, he considered, could not be imposed on any of the other circles—least of all in a democracy (which he thus appeared to regard as essentially a class, not a classless, system of society).

How does this latter viewpoint tie up with his belief that a much-to-be-desired classless society would result if equal incomes and complete intermarriageability of people from all sections of the community could be established?

Did Shaw modify or elaborate his ideas on these matters in later years?

Poverty as the most basic evil, was emphasised by Shaw from his earliest days. Thus in a speech on "The Ideal Citizen" on 9th November, 1901, he declared that, in answer to the great question: "What is the matter with the poor?", philanthropists said the drink curse; others said the housing question; others the need for education. But they were wrong. The matter with

162

the poor was poverty, and nothing else. Let the poor man have money and he would not be badly clothed, or fed, or housed; and his children would not go uninstructed. The need was to give a man work, and see that he got the proper value of the money he earned. Take off from his shoulders the intolerable burden of the idle rich and he would get on very well and not be a parasite of the idler. Till matters had been arranged in this manner—or something approaching it—we should not have the ideal citizen.

Apart from a change in the spirit of man to man, what practical and legislative steps did Shaw think would be necessary for the abolition of poverty and the realisation of Socialism and Equality?

Let us investigate some of his pronouncements at other times in his career, including his final statements, about these human ideals—which were undoubtedly of central importance in his attitude to life and his fellows.

Before proceeding, I would like to draw the reader's attention to the fact that Shaw's views on the subjects forming the title to this chapter (and on a number of other political topics which are dealt with also), while most significant and in my view essential to an understanding of him, are also at times complex and paradoxical. Therefore, in view of the concentrated and varied nature of this material, and for the benefit especially of readers who may not wish to read the chapter all through at one go, I have provided 'running half-titles', *i.e.* defining briefly the subject matter at that particular point, at the head of each right-hand page.

To begin with, what exactly did Shaw mean by the word 'Democracy'?

At the beginning of a pamphlet (now among his papers in the British Museum) which had been sent to him, entitled *The New Democratic Freedom and the Democratic Free-domain*, the American Declaration of Independence was printed. Bernard Shaw obviously disagreed strongly with Abraham Lincoln, for he had annotated it in red ink as follows (I give Shaw's words in italic):

THE GENESIS OF MODERN DEMOCRACY

"We hold these Truths to be self evident:

that all Men are created Equal; *They are not.*

that they are endowed by their Creator with inalien Rights; *They are not.*

that among these Rights are Life, Liberty and the Pursuit of Happiness *(which is the surest way to unhappiness*

that to secure these Rights, Governments are instituted among Men, deriving their Just Rights from the Consent of the Governed."

"*The American Declaration of Independence, July 4th, 1776.*"

Why need Governments secure these rights if they are readymade by the Creator?

The present difficulty is that people will not consent to be governed. They prefer Liberty, and are consequently abject slaves.

Democratic-Freedom in the wider sphere is based on the unalterable principle won by the Democratic Peoples of the World, as they have been laid down in Magna Carta, the Bill of Rights, the Declaration of the Rights of Man, the Act of Habeas Corpus and as exemplified in the Gettysburg speech of Abraham Lincoln. i.e., "and that government of the People, by the People, for the People shall not perish from the earth."

Bernard Shaw disagrees with Abraham Lincoln.
His comments on the American Declaration of Independence.

We hold these Truths to be self-evident:
that all Men are created Equal;   *They are not.*
   that they are endowed by their Creator with inalien [*sic*] Rights;
     They are <u>not</u>.
   that among these Rights are Life, Liberty and
   <u>the Pursuit of Happiness,</u>   (*which is the surest*
                            way to unhappiness),
   that to secure these Rights, Governments are instituted
   among Men, deriving their Just Rights
   from the Consent of the Governed.
     Why need Governments secure these rights if they
are readymade by the Creator?
     The present difficulty is that people will not consent to
be governed. They prefer Liberty, and are consequently
abject slaves.

In addition, Shaw had placed a red asterisk against a further quotation from Lincoln's Gettysburg speech on the following page—". . . and government of the People by the People"— and had underlined the last three words <u>by the People</u>, without adding any words of comment.

He did, however, explain his meaning further in the syllabus of a lecture entitled "Democracy as a Delusion" he was to give at the Kingsway Hall, London, on 23rd November, 1927:—

A country governed by its people is as impossible as a theatre managed by its audience . . . Democracy is not a delusion when it means the provision of some means by which a dissatisfied people can change its rulers. It *is* a delusion, and a very mischievous one, when it means that the people must govern themselves . . . government is a fine art requiring for its exercise not only certain specific talents and a taste for the business but a mental comprehensiveness and an energy which only a small percentage of people possess in the degree necessary for leadership. Of this percentage not all are willing to acquire the art for its own sake or that of the community. Normally it is left to ambitious or merely domineering people . . . the problem is how to secure the services of competent rulers without delivering ourselves into the hands of tyrants and talented black-guards, as we have done in the case of industry.

During the lecture itself Shaw declared that basic to the theory of Democracy was the concept of the Citizen as a Microcosm of the Perfect State; nothing could be done without the assent of the whole body of "infinitely sagacious" citizens. The pure and perfect Democrat would wait for complete unanimity before carrying out any reform. That was why Democracy was so invaluable to lazy people and cowards as an excuse for doing nothing.

For, in practice, two hard facts had to be dealt with: (1) Unanimity is a psychological impossibility, (2) Majorities could and would coerce minorities, democracy or no democracy, deeming it a greater evil that one man should prevent ten from having their way than that ten should prevent one. Hence Democracy in effect becomes Majorocracy, and ceases, so far, to be democratic.

Majorocracy, when it began, came up against a physical impossibility. The number of citizens who could be assembled for a discussion and a vote was limited to a roomful. The range of Majorocratic Democracy was the range of a man's voice. A new device called Representation had to be invented. As laws could not be made by an assembly of all the citizens, they had to be made by Ideal Representatives of batches of thousands of citizens—supposed to be of the same mind as the majorities of the batches (called constituencies).

This left so little of pure democracy, that the thing began to work because it substituted the election of men for the initiation and determination of measures.

There were certain questions on which unanimity was possible; and there were communities small enough to assemble and arrive at it at once by acclamation. Families, tribes, ships' crews, and Fabian Societies, for instance. It was in such assemblies that government began; and it was there that the democratic man had his chance of perpetrating democracy. But he never turned up, because he does not exist.

The actual man is not a microcosm of the Perfect State, said Shaw. Not only is he not a diplomatist, not a financier, economist, or thought-reader, but he is not a democrat; because he is conscious of his own deficiencies and mistrustful of the competence of his neighbours.

To escape a terrifying responsibility and an impossible task, he votes for an ideal omniscient and omnipotent despot, the image of his omniscient and omnipotent God.

There are all sorts of gods except one; and that is a Democratic God.

The vote was unanimous against democracy, Shaw went on. There might be differences as to who was to be the Despot, and as to whether he was to be called Chief, Emperor, Pope, King, President, Dictator, Leader, or simply Member of Parliament; but the vote was for Men, not Measures, instead of for measures, not men, as democracy demands.

Hence the paradox, advanced by all despots, that despotism is the most democratic form of government in the world.

The rock on which it stands is consciousness of consent; and its trump card is the plebiscite.

The Napoleons had played that trump; and Mussolini would have played it if put to it. Queen Elizabeth the First's form of plebiscite was the Royal Progress.

Consciousness of consent was revocable. It must be continuous, Shaw declared. The electors being ignorant, their expectations were unreasonable. The first visit of the tax collector or the policeman was resented as tyranny and extortion.

The question arose: "How much did the people consent to be governed?" The answer was: Not at all; they only wanted to be protected and saved the trouble of thinking for themselves.

They became a negative force, an anarchist force, a weapon for revolutionary demagogues. Meanwile, what happened to the despot?

If ill chosen, he would succumb to Caesarian madness —Henry Ford's experience. If well chosen, he rules as well as the people will let him, and chooses his numerous deputies well. But as the consent to which he owes his position is soon withdrawn, he has to upset the basis of majorocracy by disciplining coercive minorities of police.

There are physical limits to this. Besides, dictators die. What then? The continuity of the despotism could be effected by Adoption, Heredity, or Election, said Shaw.

In the case of Adoption, there was the precedent of the Antonines.

As examples of Hereditary Despots, there were Edward II, Richard II, James II, the Tsars, Marcus Aurelius, Cromwell, and Napoleon.

But election might be all too easily by the incompetent, whose choice of despotism was a confession of incompetence.

The general result was a running struggle between the government and the people, the government trying to maintain order and to enlarge its powers, and the people trying to limit its powers and asserting individual liberty against State omnipotence. Thus we produced laws to restrain the government as well as laws to subordinate the people.

As examples, Shaw referred to the Great Charter, Parliament, the Habeas Corpus Act, and the King in Council being replaced by a Prime Minister in a Cabinet, or a President and so on, and said that all movements in restraint of government came to be called Democratic or Liberal.

Then came the question: Which side in this continual struggle between Democracy or Liberalism, and State Organisation, were Socialists on?

Quite clearly, on the State side, Shaw declared. They were proposing a gigantic extension of State organisation, involving a startling curtailment of individual liberty. They believed, like the Fascists, that the State comes first.

But were they to consult the people first? Mr Sidney Webb said 'Certainly not': the people must judge, not the measures, but the results. This (said Shaw) was real democracy.

The question then, was: How were they to be allowed to try the experiment? It *needed* a Dictatorship. There was no difficulty about the principle: all our Cabinets were five-year Dictatorships.

The real issue was, were they to humbug the electorate or coerce it?

There was a new and stupendous alternative. Real democracy was possible at last—through the mass-communication medium of the wireless. There could be speeches by wireless, and votes by wireless.

There was no need for Proportional Representation; both the Initiative and the Referendum could be by means of the wireless.

But, wireless or no wireless, would the Capitalist Party accept the decision if it went against them? Would the Socialist Party?

However, there would be no decision on the issue of Capitalism and Socialism. There would be a series of decisions on surtax, coal, railways, banking, strikes, India, and the House of Lords.

There would be State Control of Press and Wireless, and a battle between Religious Fundamentalism, and Freethought, in schools. Wireless might prove the final reduction to absurdity of Majorocracy. Civilisation might crumble whilst the Socialists were waiting for a majority.

If the Socialists concluded that to convert the majority was impossible, but to convert a Dictator or an oligarchy is possible, then they should throw their weight against democracy, and for oligarchy and dictatorship.

The final truth it would then be necessary to accept, said Shaw, was that they were not democrats but aristocrats; for they were advocating a system which required government by the best of the capable.

How were they to select them? No other method being available, they would be driven to accept the task of selecting themselves and imposing themselves like Mussolini, like Napoleon, like Cromwell.

Although Socialists did not like such people, they must be opportunists like other politicians—but must, none the less, also stand by the Vote, and by Criticism with Good Manners.

What they required, above all, was boundless daring, cruelty in removing obstacles, and tenacity in seizing power. This would bring victory.

This concluded the views Shaw expressed in his lecture to Fabians and other Socialists on 23rd November, 1927.

It is usually accepted that a synonym for 'despotism' or 'dictatorship' is 'autocracy'. A decade earlier in 1917, Shaw, in a lecture in King's Hall, Covent Garden, on 9th November, had proclaimed his view that autocracy has something to be said for it, but had certainly not revealed himself as a *complete* supporter of it.

Autocracy appeals to laziness and idolatry, he said. It involves no other reform; it gets rid of elections and the governing bodies they produce, and sets up a highly spectacular earthly providence to which the citizen can trust everything except his own private business. Its historical record is by no means wholly discreditable, partly because it does not allow anything discreditable to be recorded, but partly also because it has genuine achievements to record, besides taking the credit for all the reforms it fails to checkmate. By way of historical illustrations, Shaw considered that the Hohenzollern régime in Germany had a good deal to boast of; and that if Napoleon III had not been boycotted by the aristocracy and the honest intelligentsia, he might have re-established the Bonapartist régime on the strength of his "benevolent, quite good-natured Caesarism". Shaw pointed out that the Antonines ranked as the most successful rulers in history, and that Venice became great under an autocracy. All autocracies, he said, have an element of reality in them which is absent in our pseudo-democracy—they assume the political incompetence of the man-in-the-street. On the other hand, they also assume the political competence of the autocratic or oligarchic ruler; and although this assumption may occasionally have the good luck to be justified by the facts, no means of securing it as a permanent condition have yet been discovered.

Shaw thus admitted that a great difficulty with autocracy was how to obtain despotic rulers who would remain just and never misuse their power. He criticised both autocracy and democracy simultaneously in the following typically 'Shavian' epigram:—

Democracy substitutes election by the incompetent many for appointment by the corrupt few.

and his printed syllabus for the afore-mentioned lecture (9th November, 1917) had begun, equally characteristically:—

Democratic delusions. Government of the people, by the people, for the people. Suggested parallels: dental treatment of the people, by the people, for the people. Symbolic statue of the people, modelled by the people, for the people. Evidently the weak point is "by the people". Government is an art, and politics a science. Modified formula: government by consent of the governed? How if the people will not consent to be governed? Such consent at present universally unobtainable, owing to the general neglect or perversion of political education.

Shaw rejected out of hand the third alternative idea of no government at all (anarchism), and considered the only practicable alternative to lie in coercion. Did coercion necessarily abolish liberty? Not completely, in his view: the people could be allowed to choose the persons who were to exercise the coercion. This was what was currently being called democracy, to distinguish it from the autocratic or oligarchic system in which the people had no such choice. Contemporary democracy, therefore (in Shaw's view) enabled the people to be governed by those who were most successful in flattering the political ignorance of the poor—and in persuading the rich that they would be governed either not at all, or as little as possible, whilst they would have the widest possible powers of governing other people. Under such circumstances, the more thoroughgoing an attempt to establish democracy was, the greater the likelihood was of its rulers becoming "thieves and assassins" and declaring war at any cost on anybody and everybody in order to keep themselves in power—though they would inevitably be discarded in the end as impossible rulers, and replaced by a dictatorship of some sort.

The central problem was how to substitute "a genuine democracy" for the historically discredited sham. The latter's oppressive influence was maintained, said Shaw, by the plutocrat who wields the Press, by the Press which wields the demagogue, and by the demagogue who wields the coercive machinery of government at the dictation of the Press for the benefit of the plutocrat. Shaw added: "We must choose between an ignorant and obedient people despotically governed, and a people sufficiently instructed in political science to consent to be governed, and, indeed, to insist on it, and to be intelligently critical of the government they get in response to their demand."

Shaw thus saw the answer to the problem partly in terms of increased education and enlightenment of the electorate. From some lecture notes among the Shaw papers in the British Museum (undated, but estimated at between 1917 and 1920) I gleaned the following views expressed by Shaw on the subject of Political Education.

He said that the assumption at the root of modern democratic institutions was that every man is a born political critic. This, he considered, was idolatry at its very worst. There was something to be said for the idolatry of kings and priests, but absolutely nothing for idolising the voters.

What could be said for them? They knew where the shoe pinched. But the worst shoe, for example, the shoe with the highest heels which women liked best, did not 'pinch'. It might disable and deform; but the wearer likes it and chooses it voluntarily, and would reject as unbearable tyranny a law impelling her to wear healthy brogues.

The solution, Shaw averred—admitting it to be a controversial one—was liberal education of the electorate, coupled with a stripping of the profession of government of every advantage over private work.

Shaw then asked: "Why do our wonderful Fabian schemes come to nothing?" (He was, of course, exaggerating, for even though none of the Fabian Society's ultimate aims had achieved full realisation at that time, the Society had grown substantially in size since its foundation, and had already exercised a considerable influence on the growth of the Labour movement in Britain.) Shaw drew a contrast between "the Webb world and the real world" and queried, "was it because the police, wouldn't let them?"

Not at all, he reassured his audience. The Fabian schemes were all constitutional and congenial to the bureaucratic temperament. Who were their opponents? Shaw instanced *The New Witness* and *The New Age* (left-wing journals of I.L.P. or non-Fabian leanings), the Labour Party (predominantly working-class and Trade Union dominated, and not truly Socialistic in Shaw's view—I shall explain this further in due course), Lord Northcliffe and Mr Chesterton, Mr Lloyd George, and Mr Orage (Editor of *The New Age*). The ultra-ambitious and the utterly disinterested alike.

In Ireland there was the same phenomenon, Shaw went on. Horace Plunkett and Mr George Russell were as full of plans for making a paradise of Ireland as Webb and he himself were in England. But the people ran after Mr de Valera, Carson and Redmond, none of whom had a constructive idea in his head.

Whenever the police were abolished, and ideas set completely loose—what happened? In the French Revolution the only man who had understood it was Louis XVI—and they had cut his head off. The idealists became assassins, and when assassins have assassinated one another, their successors are not only assassins, but thieves and hypocrites.

In the Russian Revolution, the same thing was happening, Shaw went on. Why did people turn from revolutionists to dictators? Not because they necessarily idealised the dictators: on the contrary, people idealise a dictator because they want him. What they desire is a settled government and as little of it as possible. They want to know where they are, and to have some security for their debts and their capital and their enterprises. For that they are prepared to pay in money, and homage, and toleration of scandals in the life of the dictator and his parasites. They will even put up with austerity and asceticism and submit to be ruled by Calvin in the Perfect City of God, provided it is a City in the Lombard Street sense, in which you can make money and keep it in peace. Between the French Revolution and the French Empire, the Bourbons could have come back at any moment as triumphantly as Charles II if only they had accepted redistribution of property and not threatened to expropriate the expropriators.

The Revolutions had made no difference. William IV—'Silly Billy'—had had more personal power than the glorious, pious, and immortal William III; and after the Reform Bill, Queen Victoria had much more power than Queen Elizabeth had. The Suffrage made no difference: the Reform Bill of 1867 began a reaction towards what we had come to call Prussianism, which was consecrated by the establishment of Manhood Suffrage in 1880. The republics were as bad as the monarchies, and seemed worse, because they did not hush up their scandals.

'Liberty of the Press', Shaw continued, meant in practice the tyranny of Lord Northcliffe and Mr Blumenfeld, and of Mr Murphy and Mr Hearst. (These four gentlemen all owned or edited newspapers of strongly Conservative outlook; in addition, Blumenfeld, Editor of the *Daily Express*, was founder of The Anti-Socialist League.) The limit was not the resistance of the people, said Shaw, but the incompetence and modesty of the tyrants. When a competent and shameless tyrant like Peter the Great happened, he eclipsed Nero in cruelty and Ivan the Terrible in arbitrary domineering, and yet died of natural causes, without being assassinated, and while still on the throne.

It was doubtless true that the successful tyrants had been those who liked to see their country commercially prosperous and worked hard to make it so: but the commercial prosperity had always been founded on the slavery of the poor. Whenever amiable people had left the proletariat poor without making the business man rich, they had lost their heads.

On 23rd September, 1933, Shaw made a speech in connection

with the Centenary of Charles Bradlaugh,* and defined the kind of benevolent despot he had in mind as the ideal type of ruler:—

... What really made Charles Bradlaugh the great man that he was was not so much those extraordinary heroic personal qualities which made him an almost superhuman figure for his contemporaries as well as a great platform artist, but that he saw that the religious question was *the* question.

Shaw pointed out that there were many men who in their early days were intellectually honest, and, like Bradlaugh, told the truth and fought for the truth; but they ended by going into Parliament. They were classed as eminent statesmen when they "learned how to give the public what it wants, and that is bunk". . . . The British Parliament, said Shaw, was "the most effective engine for preventing progress of any kind that has ever been devised by the wit of man". The sort of men we wanted were men like Bradlaugh, who would risk their liberty for the sake of progress. There were those who shrieked out 'Dictator, dictator' if you suggested a revolt against the British Parliamentary system. The less liberty they had, the more they were afraid of losing it; and when they were dictated to by the boss in all their homes, and had all their opinions dictated to them by the millionaires' newspapers until they could not call their souls their own, they thanked God that they were free. What these people needed to make them capable of real freedom was the right sort of dictator. Bradlaugh, Shaw declared, would have made a very good dictator of that kind.

Shaw wrote in his introduction to Charles Dickens's *Great Expectations* (Hamish Hamilton and Co.'s Novel Library, 1947):—

... Liberty under the British parliamentary system means slavery for nine-tenths of the people, and slave exploitation or parasitic idolatry and snobbery for the rest . . .

* The meeting was at Friends House, Euston, and reports of the various speeches (including Shaw's) were subsequently published as a commemorative booklet.

This fundamental belief lay at the core of Shaw's Socialist outlook throughout his life. The following details are taken from one of his earliest political speeches—delivered to The Liberal and Social Union at the rooms of The Society of British Artists, and reported in *The Christian Socialist* for April, 1885.

Shaw began by saying that he felt in an invidious position addressing the Union, for, although they had invited him to address them on Socialism from the point of view of a Socialist, from that point of view, unhappily, despite their hospitality, he regarded them, and indeed the human race generally, as cannibals of the most dangerous description, whose power "must be completely neutralised before they will cease to retard the evolution of the social instincts of the race by perpetually preying on one another".

In order to live, he continued, mankind must have access to the earth and the fullness thereof. Hence, if one could imagine the earth as owned by a private person, that person could cause his fellow creatures to die by refusing them access to the land. This power made them his slaves. He had only to say: "I will grant you access to the land on condition that you do for me whatever I choose to dictate" and they would be compelled, on pain of death, to accept that hard condition. All his audience knew, said Shaw, that the land of England in 1885—apart from the high roads and "a few patches of common which have accidentally not been stolen"—was owned by private persons. The rest of the community were therefore slaves of these private persons, or of the capitalists to whom such private persons had sub-let their powers in order that they might ultimately resume them in a more effective stage of development. The population was then divided into two great sections, proprietors and slaves, and the 'class' formed by say, shepherds, could be little better than the sheep they tended. Shaw added:—

Between the shepherd and the physician come many grades of slaves. There is the workman, the foreman, the clerk, the manager, and the secretary. Each of these grades has its lawyer, its doctor, and its divine. Then there is the soldier, sometimes a cheap article who has but to obey orders, charge with the bayonet at men with whom he has no quarrel, shoot and be shot at, and give three cheers when titled persons inspect his buttons; . . . With all these varieties of servitude, the slave section gets minutely stratified into classes. Ignorant of the causes that have produced the stratification, each stratum despises or envies the others . . . The unskilled labourer is allowed 2/6d., thirty pence a day. The eminent barrister is allowed fifty guineas, or 12,600 pence a day. . .—420 times as much . . .

Shaw pointed out that it was improbable that any man had 420 times as much ability as another, or even four times, and that if sobriety were the condition of social advance the labourer would be consuming 420 bottles of wine a day to the sober barrister's *one*! Nor could it possibly be argued that the barrister was 420 times as thrifty as the labourer. Yet neither sobriety, nor thrift, nor any ordinary quality could induce the proprietors to raise the labourer to the same class as their most favoured slaves. In either case, said Shaw, he would still be a slave, receiving out of the full exchange value of his services just what was sufficient to maintain him and enable him to reproduce himself with such culture and habits as might be necessary to make him an efficient servant, and—if his services brought him into personal contact with his employers— an agreeable associate. He had no alternative to surrendering all the rest as rent or interest to his masters . . . . This system was made automatic by the action of competition . . . .

Competition was the force that made our industrial system self-operating, Shaw went on. It produced the effects which he had described, without the conscious contrivance of either master on the one hand or slave on the other. It might be described as a see-saw or lever of the first order, having the fulcrum between the power and the weight. The power was the labour force of the slaves; the weight was the body of proprietors who had to be raised above the level of the slaves and maintained there. Hence the more numerous the slaves were, the lower they sank, and the higher they raised the proprietors.

Socialists, Shaw declared, insisted that people should stand on the firm earth, and not on a see-saw, much less on a lever which was "always at see, and never at saw". Socialists sought to disable the lever. The way to disable a lever was to remove the fulcrum. What was the fulcrum of this lever of competition? Clearly it was private property in the raw material and machinery indispensable to subsistence. The slave submitted to the master solely because the master had the power to withhold from him the means of subsistence if he rebelled. The master of the land said, after St. Paul, "If a man will not work for all, neither shall he live." Deprive him of this power of condemning his fellow-men to death, and the fellow-man could snap his fingers at him and quote St. Paul more accurately in his favour. To deprive the proprietor of this power, it was necessary to deprive him of his private property in the land and capital of the nation, which was just what the Socialists proposed. That was why the masters raised so loud an alarm when an attack on private property was proposed.

By way of illustration, Shaw said: "One man enters a farm-house secretly, helps himself to a share of the farm produce, and leaves without giving the farmer an equivalent. We call him a burglar, and send him to penal servitude. Another man does precisely the same thing openly, has the impudence even to send a note to say when he is coming, and repeats his foray twice a year, breaking forcibly into the premises if his demand is not complied with. We call him a landlord, respect him, and, if his freebooting extends over a large district, make him deputy-lieutenant of the country [sic] or send him to Parliament, to make laws to license his predatory habits."

Shaw later in his address said that many members of the proprietor class were willing to give alms and organise charities, concerts, etc., for the poor, and, indeed, had got to the point of being "willing to sacrifice almost anything for the poor, except the power and practice of robbing them". Nevertheless, Shaw observed, that was just what they must sacrifice, if they wanted to avert another failure of human society. The human race had never succeeded in establishing a permanent social State. They had tried on a large scale in Egypt; but the experiment, after progressing hopefully for centuries, had collapsed. They had tried again in Greece with some valuable results, but with the same end. Then Rome tried her hand, and made a tremendous mess of it. Shaw exclaimed: "Now we are trying and, so far, are doing worse even than the Romans. Every reformer has his pet reason for the decay of these civilizations; and I will not assert that luxury and slavery rotted away the foundations of them all. But I may at least claim that luxury and slavery did not prove so beneficial that we need apprehend much danger from ridding ourselves of them."

The Socialists' remedy was to abolish private property in land, and prevent the employment of the means of production as capital. When a Socialist was asked how he was going to do it, said Shaw, the Socialist might lose his temper and retort: "*I* am not going to do it. *We* are going to do it; and the ways and means must be settled by us in council when we have made up our minds on what we have to do." Shaw went on:—

... This alleged right of a man to do what he likes with his own is the private property principle which the Socialist attacks. It is already obsolete except in the case of land and the means of production. Property in other things is subject to the condition that it shall not be used to injure or oppress. A landlord, for example, if he wishes to turn his arable land into pasture, or his pasture into a deer forest, is permitted to drive hardworking husbandmen or shepherds off his property into overcrowded towns, or, for the matter of that, into the sea, with impunity, because he claims a right to do what he likes with his own. But the landlord owns other things besides land. He owns guns and sticks. If he were to take the stick and give one of the husbandmen or shepherds a thrashing with it, the plea that the stick was his own and that he had a right to use it as he pleased would not save him from punishment. Still less do we allow him to present his gun at a tenant, and, by threatening him with death, compel him to give up what he has gained from the soil by his labour. Yet what he may not do with a gun, he may do, and does, with a writ of ejectment . . . the landlord, by studiously confusing private property outside and independent of the law and the commonweal, with the public right of every man to possess and enjoy what he produces, succeeds in persuading careless reasoners that to attack private property is to attack the commonweal. He says in effect "If you abolish my right to wear another man's coat, what becomes of my right to wear my own? The right to wear coats is sacred; and if you violate it, society will be impossible."

Shaw went on to say that one could understand a landlord using this argument; but it was not so easy to understand many tenants also subscribing to it. He declared: "The inability to comprehend economic problems indicated by such suicidal utterances on the part of the slave class is a serious matter." For this reason, he added, the abolition of private property, the equitable distribution of labour and of the products of labour among the community, and the nationalisation of rent, would have to be accomplished by an enlightened majority. They would have to overcome the active resistance of the proprietors, and the inertia of the masses.

But, Shaw warned, the proprietors would fight. Lord Bramwell had made that very clear. They were scaring many people off Socialism by the picture they painted of bloodshed. Yet, said Shaw, there was nothing to which men "so rapidly grow habituated; they even develop a taste for it". Shaw then declared:—

. . . When we have had a little more practice in fighting for our bondholders abroad, we will think little of fighting against them at home, should occasion arise. Civil war is horrible; but we have supped full of horrors in our city slums: and an open, well ventilated battle-field, with wounded men instead of rickety children and starving women, would be an absolute improvement. The proportion of corpses would be about the same, and the suffering would be less prolonged; whilst excitement and hope would take the place of dulness and despair. These human considerations constantly tempt the poor to violence, and weaken the influence of those who would restrain them. . . .

Now if Socialism be not made respectable and formidable by the support of *our* class—if it be left entirely to the poor, then the proprietors will attempt to suppress it by such measures as they have already taken in Austria and Ireland. Dynamite will follow. Terror will follow dynamite. Cruelty will follow terror. More dynamite will follow cruelty. Both sides will thus drive one another from atrocity to atrocity solely because we, the middle class, instead of interfering on behalf of justice, sit quaking and complying with ignorant and cowardly journalists who devote the first half of an article to calling the dynamitards "dastardly wretches", and the second half to clamouring for more dynamite in the shape of further restriction of our liberty and further licence to our oppressors. If, on the other hand, the middle class will educate themselves to understand this question, they will be able to fortify whatever is just in Socialism, and to crush whatever is dangerous in it. No English government dare enact a Coercion Law or declare a Minor State of Siege against the Radical party. The result is that the Radical party never makes us shake in our shoes as the dynamitards do. I trust then that the middle class will raise the Socialists above the danger of Coercion, Minor Siege, and consequent Dynamite, by joining them in large numbers. . . . A party informed at all points by men of gentle habits and trained reasoning powers may achieve a complete Revolution without a single act of violence. A mob of desperate sufferers abandoned to the leadership of exasperated sentimentalists and fanatic theorists may, at a vast cost of bloodshed and misery, succeed in removing no single evil, except perhaps the existence of the human race.

In a later article entitled "The Dictatorship of the Proletariat" in the *Labour Monthly* (October, 1921) Shaw exclaimed that the Capitalist system admitted of so much apparent progress that superficial thinkers could easily persuade themselves that it would eventually progress into Socialism; but it could never really do so without making a complete *volte-face*. Slavery was always improving itself as a system. It began

by working its slaves to premature death. Then it found
out that badly-treated slaves did not—except when they were
so plentiful that they could be replaced very cheaply—produce
so much booty for their masters as well-treated ones. Accordingly, much 'humanitarian' progress was effected. Later, when
modern industrial methods of exploitation were discovered
and developed competitively, it was found that continuous
employment under the same master could not be provided
for the slave. When this point was reached the master wanted
to be free to get rid of the slave when he had no work for him
to do, and to pick him up again when trade revived, and to
have no responsibility for him when he was old and not
worth employing. Immediately a fervent enthusiasm for liberty
pervaded the Capitalist State; and after an agitation consecrated by the loftiest strains of poetry and the most splendid
eloquence of rhetoric, the slave was set free to hire himself
out to anyone who wanted him; to starve when nobody wanted
him; to die in the workhouse; and to be told that it was all
his own fault.

In a B.B.C. talk on 18th June, 1935 (published in the *Listener*
of 26th June), Shaw said:—

. . Naturally the master class, through its parliaments and schools
and newspapers, makes the most desperate efforts to prevent us
from realising our slavery. From our earliest years we are taught
that our country is the land of the free, and that our freedom was
won for us for ever by our forefathers when they made King John
sign Magna Charta [*sic*]—when they defeated the Spanish Armada—
when they cut off King Charles' head—when they issued and made
good the American Declaration of Independence—when they won the
battles of Waterloo and Trafalgar on the playing-fields of Eton—
and when, only the other day, they quite unintentionally changed the
German, Austrian, Russian, and Ottoman Empires into republics.

When we grumble, we are told that all our miseries are our own
doing because we have the vote. When we say, 'What good is the
vote?' we are told that we have the Factory Acts, and the Wages
Boards, and free education, and the New Deal, and the dole; and

what more could any reasonable man ask for? We are reminded that the rich are taxed a quarter, a third, or even a half and more of their incomes; but the poor are never reminded that they have to pay that much of their wages as rent in addition to having to work twice as long every day as they would need to if they were free.

On a different occasion Shaw said of Dickens that he had:—

a complete disbelief in government *by* the people, and an equally complete hostility to government in any other interest than theirs,

and his own outlook would appear to have been the same. He also pointed out (in the preface to *Man and Superman*) that

. . . Liberty means responsibility. That is why most men fear it.

And in the same preface he declared:—

Nothing can be unconditional: consequently nothing can be free.

Freedom was further defined by Shaw in an early undated Ms.:*

. . . 'Freedom.' Is there a sane man alive who still pursues that shadow? Liberty, Freedom: these are the baits that mankind has been snapping at since the words were invented, and the only result is that the hook is faster in its gills than it was before. Our struggle to free ourselves from death resulted in the invention of heaven and hell. Our struggle to free ourselves from the need to labour resulted in the invention of slavery. Nature, like the ideal collectivist state which anarchists fear, lays down for every man an iron line of conduct which will secure him the maximum happiness possible to him. He is free to depart from that line only in the sense in which I am free to shoot the Prime Minister: i.e. on condition that he bears the pre-appointed penalty. I seek such Justice as is possible: Freedom is wholly a dream.

In a statement in 1937† Shaw emphasised his view that there

* Shaw papers, B.M.
† *The New Republic* (U.S.A.), 14th April, 1937 (reprinted in issue of 22nd November, 1954).

was no antithesis between authoritarian government and democracy. All government, he averred, is authoritarian; and the more democratic a government is the more authoritative it is, "for with the people behind it it can push its authority farther than any Tsar or foreign despot dare do." Leisure was the real yardstick of freedom, he considered, and such freedom the yardstick of true democracy.

He pointed out that leisure was not possessed by, for example, farmers who had to work sixteen hours a day to pay rent and interest on mortgages, in addition to buying necessities for their families. They were abject slaves. But although they had neither freedom nor security, they had votes, and lived under the illusion that the right to vote made them free, and that a crowd of voters constituted a democracy. Shaw said he agreed with Adolf Hitler's view of our political democracy as 'a lie', and he declared: "It is the exposure of that lie that Benito Mussolini described as the putrefaction of the corpse of liberty."

Shaw has been much criticised on the grounds that he was sympathetic to Fascism—as seen in his support of Mussolini and Hitler in the 1930's, and his half-sympathetic satire of them in his play *Geneva*, written in 1938. To give another example of the sort of view which made him unpopular: in a lecture on 23rd November, 1933, entitled "The Politics of Unpolitical Animals", under the chairmanship of Lord Passfield (Sidney Webb), he referred to "the unaccountable statement by Aristotle that Man is a Political Animal," and said that the testimony of Aristophanes was conclusive as to the incapacity of Athens in public affairs, and its unfortunate resemblance to our governing classes. Towards the end of the same lecture[*] Shaw referred to Hitler as:—

. . . a very remarkable, very able man. There is one thing about Hitler which recommended him to me from the very first, and that is his face—it has an expression of intense resentment. That is the expression that every statesman in the world ought to have.

[*] Reported in *The Lecture Recorder*, December, 1933.

But, said Shaw, he could not agree with Hitler on every point; Hitler was the victim of spurious biology and bogus ethnology. He seemed to believe in the division of mankind into an Aryan race and a Latin race. That was all nonsense. We were an extraordinarily mixed lot . . . the evidence was irresistible that, unless a stock was crossed, and that pretty frequently, it degenerated. "Look at the English," Shaw said; "In our older hereditary classes, the people who have kept themselves handsome, they are very pleasant to meet, often skilled in all sorts of sports, but it is the beauty of a Borzoi dog. Those who have Borzoi dogs know that although they are irresistibly attractive, they have absolutely no brain, and that is the kind of Englishman we have got from inbreeding."

It was really only a particular aspect of Fascism that attracted Shaw—the capacity to *get things done*, speedily and efficiently, under autocratic control, as against the muddling and prevarication and delays inevitable under democracy,* in which any leadership wishing to effect certain social changes could not simply go ahead with them, but had first to reckon with the arguments and objections of other political parties and individuals—many of whom owed their position to hereditary chance rather than to brains or real political knowledge. There is no doubt that it was autocracy rather than Fascism that Shaw was in favour of; analysis of his beliefs beyond that point makes it quite clear that although he admired the autocratic *elements* in Fascism, he did not agree with Fascism as a basic doctrine: his sympathies were far more with the no less autocratic, but politically diametrically opposed, doctrine of Communism (to which his own brand of Fabian Socialism was allied).

Shaw complained in *G.K.'s Weekly*, 21st March, 1935, that some of the misunderstanding about his views on Fascism had come about as a result of his "analytical method":—

. . . It is this confounded association of ideas as opposed to my analytical method that gets me into trouble in England. If I say

---

* In the conventional British sense of the term.

(as I did) that the Fascist government of Italy really governed, and in some respects governed very efficiently, where the Italian parliament had governed either very inefficiently or not at all, and that the conception of the corporate state is an evident advance towards Socialism and away from *Laissez-faire*, I am immediately accused of having, in effect, murdered Matteotti and exiled Salvemini. When I said that on the question of the Versailles Treaty versus Hitler every German Jew, Social Democrat, or Communist, must vote for Hitler, it was obvious to the English mind that I was advocating the total suppression of any and every sort of liberty; that I am an anti-Semite; that I have repudiated Socialism and Democracy; and that I am a dupe of the bogus Nordic ethnology of Houston Chamberlain. ... When I demonstrate that an Inquisition, with powers of life and death, is a necessity in every organized community where its functions are not performed arbitrarily, amateurishly, and often disastrously by every employer, I am accused of trying to relight the fires of Smithfield and justifying the atrocities of the pious anti-Semite maniac Torquemada.

A few years earlier, a letter to 'a friend' on 7th January, 1927, appeared as part of a report in the *Daily News* on 13th October, under the heading:—

SHAW, FASCISM, AND THE "DAILY NEWS"

REVOLUTION BY CASTOR OIL

G.B.S. Prefers it to the Gun and Bomb

Shaw had written to the effect that some of the things Mussolini had done, and some that he was threatening to do, would go further in the direction of Socialism than the English Labour Party could have ventured at that time had it been in power. They would bring Mussolini shortly into serious conflict with capitalism; and it was certainly not his own business, nor that of any Socialist, to weaken him in view of such a conflict. Shaw added that all the 'tyranny' he saw in Italy was of the kind which our Capitalist Press denounced as characteristic of Socialism; and he did not "boil with indignation at it as the Liberals do". His point, he said, was that the campaign of abuse against the Mussolini dictatorship was just as stupid as the campaign against the Soviet dictatorship in Russia. He pointed out that his 'friend' was not the only one who had jumped to the conclusion that he, Shaw, must have been unaware of the Matteotti affair, and of "the other revolting incidents of the Fascist terror", and explained:—

. . . This is quite a mistake. I knew about them.

But you cannot dispose of Mussolini by simply repeating in a tone of virtuous indignation the admitted and even vaunted fact that he owes his power to a coup d'état.

Since Augustus founded the Roman Empire with himself as Emperor, by a coup d'état which began with the assassination of Caesar, until Lenin became Dictator of Russia by a violent overthrow of Kerenskyist Liberal democracy involving the very unpleasant operations of the Tcheka, there have been dozens of great usurpations effected by coups d'état; and every one of the coups has been a filthy business, in which honest and loyal men have been shouted down in court by perjured witnesses and timeserving magistrates, and have been beaten, tortured, and murdered out of it by gangs of infernal blackguards.

The only novelty of the Italian case was the castor oil; and most men would rather be dosed with castor oil than be tarred and feathered.*

Shaw went on to contend that our attitude towards a new régime should not be determined by the means employed to establish it. It was no use fighting Augustus or provoking him to fight you "merely because Antony points eloquently to the gashes of Caesar's body". It was silly, he thought, to refuse to trade with Russia because the Soviet régime connived at regicide, and silly also to pretend that the Kaiser was still

* A very callous statement. Most men would rather not be subjected to either treatment. The castor oil torture could be as cruel as almost any ever invented (although this naturally depended on the dosage and over what length of time, and how frequently it was repeated). Some subjected to it died from weakness and exhaustion. Those who survived were often invalids for the rest of their lives, the mucus membranes lining the intestines having been partially or wholly destroyed.

the rightful ruler of Germany because the substitution of a republic was accompanied by the murder of Rathenau as well as Liebknecht junior and Rosa Luxemburg. It was equally irrelevant and silly to refuse to acknowledge the dictatorship of il Duce because it was not achieved without "all the usual villainies". The only question to be considered was whether he was doing his job well enough to induce the Italian nation to accept him *faute de mieux*. They did accept him—some of them with enthusiasm. His enemies—his victims if one liked to call them that—could not pretend that they had not had as good a chance as he. Shaw concluded: "I am sorry my fellow Socialists in Italy were totally unable to take command after the war; and I loathe the savageries which attended the establishment of Fascism. But I shall not waste any energies and compromise my reputation for good sense by refusing to accept an accomplished fact. If I did I should lose the right to criticise Mussolini's rule, which I am quite ready to do whenever I think I can do any good by it".

A copy of the foregoing letter to 'a friend' had found its way after a month to the then leader of the Austrian Labour Party and Secretary of the Labour and Socialist International, Dr Friedrich Adler. The correspondence between him and Shaw which came about (as summarised in the following paragraphs) was made public at the same time as Shaw's letter to 'a friend'— in the *Daily News* on 13th October, 1927, and in a slightly fuller version in the *Manchester Guardian* of the same date. (The extracts which follow are taken from the latter's account.) Shaw's letter to 'a friend' had been forwarded to Dr Adler by Mr Gillies, the Secretary of the International Department of the British Labour Party. The Adler-Shaw controversy which ensued also had its origins in an article by Shaw which had appeared in the *Daily News* of 24th January, under the title "A Defence". This was not written by Shaw on his own initiative, but specifically in response to a request by the Editor for his comments on a series of articles written by Mussolini which the *Daily News* had published in this country (syndicated from the Italian press) in the first week or two of January.

This favourable article by Shaw provoked numerous protests from Italians in exile, and Shaw later asked Dr Adler to publish the correspondence which arose between them so that his justification of his sympathy for Mussolini should be made more widely known. Dr Adler, in complying and issuing the correspondence to the press, stated:—

It is perfectly plain to us that this publication will be richly exploited by the Fascists in all countries. However, since G. Bernard Shaw obstinately insists on covering with his renowned shield the régime of criminals in Italy, we hold it to be incompatible with the dignity of the Italian people in its struggle towards freedom to hinder him from doing so by methods such as those which he appears to admire in the régime of Mussolini.

In his article "A Defence" Shaw expressed his view that "the clear self-consciousness and unaffected self-judgement of Signor Mussolini" certainly made "an amusing contrast with the self-delusion and mock-modesty" with which we lectured him for doing in Italy what we had never hesitated to do in England and Ireland on half the provocation he had had. One would think, Shaw wrote, that our "Cabinets of Oligarchs" had never suspended the Habeas Corpus Act, suppressed a newspaper, or persecuted a Cobbett or a Kirkwood. The British oligarch, it seemed, "might steal a horse where the Italian dictator might not look over a hedge". Yet the only essential difference, Shaw considered, was that "the British oligarch kicks constitutional rights out of his way to secure the ascendancy of his class, whereas the Italian dictator does it to get public business done diligently for the public benefit". Shaw concluded by observing that it had not paid to be uncivil to Cromwell while he had lasted, and as the British had not dared to call Signor Mussolini's bluff at Corfu, and were "clearly afraid of him", they "had better treat him with distinguished consideration as a matter of policy, no less than of good manners".

Dr Adler considered Shaw's attitude "very adequate to a Buddha sitting with a fixed stare", but "a really astonishing one for a militant Socialist". He added: "You come dangerously near to the point of view of the British ruling class, for whom their own freedom and its assertion are matters of course, but which considers it quite possible to expect from the "natives" an acceptance of Fascist oppression *faute de mieux*."

Dr Adler considered that the idea that a people should accept absolutism *faute de mieux* could only be put forward by someone for whom absolutism was merely a mental exercise in history, but not a real experience. His view was that the inhabitants of countries who had experienced dictatorship would always feel for and give sympathy with all their strength to the fight against Fascism in any form or any country, and for the restoration of democracy in Italy no less than in Russia.

In the course of a reply to Dr Adler after a delay of six months, on 2nd October, 1927, Shaw wrote that his 24th January article in the *Daily News* had been directed partly as a protest against that newspaper's editorial attitude in writing contemptuously of Mussolini, as if the whole situation in Italy could be disposed of by representing the country as writhing in the grip of a brutal egotist (which he regarded as a gross over-simplification). Shaw added:—

. . . To tell us that this [Mussolini's] extraordinary success was achieved by murdering one hostile deputy and administering castor oil to his supporters is childish. The obvious retort to it is, "If dictatorships can be established in Italy so easily why did not the Communists establish the dictatorship of the proletariat by the same simple means?" They have as much castor oil at their disposal as the Fascisti; and they have not hesitated to shoot and throw bombs.

In your letter you speak of the *restoration* of democracy in Russia and Italy, but do you seriously attach any value to the *status quo ante* in Russia and Italy? I take it that after the war Italy was left in a condition not unlike that in which Napoleon found France under the Directory when he returned from his Egyptian campaign. The Directory, nominally revolutionary and popular, really doctrinaire, incompetent, and corrupt, could not govern. Napoleon turned the Directory out, put the most capable men he could find at the head of the departments, codified the law and brought it up to date, stabilised the currency, disciplined the public services, forced the press to support him, and incidentally kidnapped the Bourbonnist Duc d'Enghien on foreign territory and shot him.

The benefit to the ordinary French citizens was so great that they would have allowed Napoleon to shoot fifty Bourbon dukes, and suppress a hundred anti-Napoleonic newspapers. The Sieyès Liberal doctrinaires and the foreign governments who hated the Revolution and dreaded Napoleon's military genius immediately set up a prolonged howling against the tyrant, the suppressor of popular liberties, the murderer of d'Enghien, insisting that France was groaning under a ruthless despotism when she was in fact enjoying some of the realities of settled liberty after a long stretch of harassing uncertainty.

Are the Italian Liberals going to persist in the same mistake? . . . Mussolini without any of Napoleon's prestige has done for Italy what Napoleon did for France, except that for the Duc d'Enghien you must read Matteotti.

Shaw insisted that the *status quo ante* was the opposite of the Socialist idea, and asked:—

Are we to give him [Mussolini] credit for his work and admit its necessity and the hopeless failure of our *soi-disant* Socialists, Syndicalists, Communists, Anarchists, &c., to achieve it or even to understand it, or are we to go on shrieking that the murderer of liberty and Matteotti is trampling Italy underfoot? You say that "we" can never accept the situation, never submit spiritually. But what exactly is it that "we" cannot accept and will not submit to? Is it that Italy is governed by a man of the people, whilst France, libertarian, egalitarian, and fraternian, is governed by Monsieur Poincaré? . . . Of course, if you compare Italy with a Mazzinian Utopia, it is full of abuses and tyrannies. So is America, so is France, so is England, and so is Russia . . . are you not delighted to find at last a Socialist who speaks and thinks as responsible rulers do and not as resentful slaves do? . . . Of what use are Socialists who can neither rule nor understand what ruling means? Do you expect

me to lecture Mussolini as Kautsky lectured Lenin, as Marx lectured
Thiers, as Victor Hugo lectured Napoleon III and Pius IX, as all
the Socialists who have never had to administer a farthing of public
expenditure or employ a single workman (to say nothing of signing
a death warrant) lecture the cabinets of Europe, especially the
Socialist ones?

Shaw went on to say that he hardly expected his critics to
believe that the brutalities and retaliations, the assassinations
and counter-assassinations which accompany the eternal
struggle of government with anarchy did not disgust him as
much as they disgusted them. But if they were an argument
against Fascism, then the murder of St. Thomas à Becket was
an argument against Feudalism.

In Ireland the new Free State had found itself obliged to hang
many of its old ultra-patriotic comrades for this sort of thing
and the Minister who ordered the executions was assassinated by
their sympathisers. . . .

Mussolini might have to hang some of the cruder Fascists for
trop de zèle before order was completely restored in Italy.
Meanwhile nothing was to be gained by pretending that any
indictment could be brought against him by Britain or any one
else that he could not meet by a crushing *tu quoque*. The blots
on his rule were neither specifically Fascist nor specifically
Italian. They were blots on human nature.

To this Friedrich Adler* replied (on 7th October, 1927):
"After your letter of 2nd inst. I regard it as hopeless that we
should come to any understanding as to an attitude towards
Fascism. Accordingly there would be no point in my re-stating
the general views developed in my letter of March 4th."

---

* Dr Friedrich Adler, who was the son of the veteran Socialist leader,
Dr Victor Adler, had been sentenced to death for assassinating the
reactionary Austrian Premier, Count Karl von Stürgkh (who had helped
to draw up the ultimatum to Serbia in July, 1914, and refused later to
convoke the Austrian parliament) on 21st October, 1916. His death
sentence had subsequently been commuted to imprisonment, and when the
revolution came at the end of the war he had been liberated.

The draft of Adler's letter nevertheless contained further pertinent observations which appeared in the fuller *Manchester Guardian's* report, though not in the *Daily News*'s. Dr Adler pointed out that between March and October, 1917, there had been the beginnings of a democratic government in Russia, and said that for his part, he would certainly have preferred a development of this to either Czarism or Communism.

He objected particularly strongly to Shaw's statements: "Of what use are Socialists who can neither rule nor understand what ruling means?. . . All the Socialists who have never had to administer a farthing of public expenditure or employ a single workman, to say nothing of signing a death warrant . . ." and criticised them in the following terms:—

. . . I believe that on this point you are no longer serious. . . . According to my experience, Socialists are perfectly capable of conducting the business of government with just as much understanding, and indeed success, as any aristocrat or bourgeois, provided only they possess the foundation for all true government—i.e., the assured support of the majority of the people. Whenever that stipulation is not fulfilled those in power either break down or else are driven into the employment of violence. This latter feature may be observed not only in countries of Fascism, but likewise in Russia . . . if you would see how Socialists can administer public money and direct the work of tens of thousands of municipal employees, then I can only advise you to study some day the municipal administration of Vienna.

Dr Adler concluded by expressing the hope that the Italian Socialists would soon drive Mussolini from the government of "that Italy which Nature certainly intended to be a paradise, but in which at present the sons of hell have secured the upper hand".

The final episode of this important controversy was that Professor Gaetano Salvemini, the famous Italian historian, entered the fray with a letter which appeared in the *Manchester Guardian* on 19th October, 1927. He considered that Shaw had found his real hero in Mussolini—"Kate has at long last met her Petruchio. " He felt that Shaw placed too much emphasis on the end, and not nearly enough on the means, and disputed that Mussolini had risen "without a single advantage—social, official, or academic", for he had been substantially assisted in the Civil War of 1921-22—by finance from the banks, the big industrialists, and the land-owners; by guns, bombs, and transport for his Blackshirts from the military authorities; and also by the protection of his Blackshirts' actions by the police and the law. Hence it was untrue also to say that Mussolini's enemies had had "as good a chance as he". Furthermore, in addition to Matteotti, two other Deputies had been assassinated by the Fascists, and Shaw had under-emphasised the large proportion of the Italian nation which did *not* accept Mussolini. Hundreds of people were being arrested daily and imprisoned without trial—in the previous six months a total of 753 years of sentences had been passed. Professor Salvemini disagreed with various other of Shaw's statements, and added:—

. . . I do not reproach Mr Shaw with his ignorance of Italian affairs. I only intend to point out his levity in delivering judgement about matters of which he is wholly ignorant, and his callous ridicule of hardships and sufferings which his intelligence ought to understand even if his moral sensitiveness is unequal to appreciating them.

The Editor of the *Manchester Guardian* in his 'leader' of the same date considered Shaw to be "out of touch with the times" and commented: "Does he think that there is still something original or striking in declaring that 'the democratic idealism of the nineteenth century is as dead as a door-nail'? This is merely the vulgar talk of every complacent clubman and the triumphant vulgarity of every yellow newspaper. The work of thoughtful men today is to find what is good in our method of government, to attempt to build a form of government which may have a securer basis than that of the nineteenth century." Mr Shaw, he averred, was advocating in a singularly brutal form the militaristic nationalism of Prussia, even if he was not a mere "crude believer in the romantic Hegelianism" which had found a new home in Italy.

In another editorial a week later, on 28th October, the Editor agreed that nineteenth-century *laissez-faire* politics were indeed an anachronism, and that the lesson to be learnt from the nineteenth century was that uncontrolled and irresponsible property ownership was incompatible with any real liberty for most people. But, he argued, the rights of property had for some time yielded at almost all points to some form of public control. What was necessary was to ensure that the service was so managed as best to benefit the community. Sensible Socialists admitted that in many cases private enterprise had its place—which came near to the Liberal belief (held by the *Manchester Guardian*) that the crude antithesis commonly drawn between Socialism and Capitalism was altogether out of date in a society which in numerous fields already combined a measure of private enterprise with an enforced responsibility to the public. The Editor's leader concluded: "What is odd to us is that he [Shaw] should seem to make light of the destruction of free speech, of perjury and illegality in the law courts, of personal violence and unchecked cruelty. One may readily concede the need of controlling the right of private property in the interests of the community and still regard it as a high duty to safeguard those personal rights for which men of many parties and many nationalities have struggled in the past and still must struggle today."

Shaw, in his reply on 28th October to Salvemini's letter, and to the Editor of the *Manchester Guardian's* leader of 19th, referred to Dr Adler as the type of politician who "in theory never acts until he has secured a democratic mandate of the people, and in practice shoots first and takes the vote after".* He claimed that Matteotti's and the Duc d'Enghien's deaths were not strictly comparable (though it was he who had made the comparison) because, while d'Enghien had been executed on Napoleon's direct initiative, Matteotti had not been executed as a result of any "deliberate and officially given" order by

* See footnote on page 192.

Mussolini, but murdered—in a manner more comparable to Thomas à Becket's demise—by some of Mussolini's "over-zealous" followers, who had been intended only to kidnap him in order to check his public criticisms of Mussolini, and had killed him only when he had offered physical resistance to them(!). Shaw added that Mussolini, "not being an Englishman", never "pretended to regret the deaths of his enemies," and had been compromised in this and other "excesses", even though he had not dictated them.

Shaw also pointed out that the reason Mussolini had spoken of "the putrefying corpse of Liberty" was that those who took no hand in industrial production or in service to the community were sponging on those who did; and that although liberty was very important to those who took all the leisure and left others to do all the work, it had no meaning for the people who had to work eight to ten hours every day so that others might not work at all. Of course the capitalist *rentier* always declared that liberty was everything to him, since without it his leisure was of no use to him.

Shaw also felt that Mussolini's power owed itself to the public support he was freely given in 1921-22, when he appeared on the political scene as a man of action who, it seemed, would get Italy on her feet after the war. But, Shaw added, since Mussolini could not do everything for himself and could not live for ever, or even feel sure that he might not have to end his days in St. Helena, provision for a succession of leadership after his death would have to be made to prevent "the liability of Fascism to putrefaction when the Mussolini heart ceases to beat".

Somebody would have to elect the future Mussolinis and it had better not be "a sham Pretorian Guard". Shaw admitted: "Caesarian theocracies will not wash nowadays: they all come to some sort of parliamentary complexion at last." (Shaw's use of the word 'parliamentary' here is significant as betokening a grudging acknowledgement, in this letter at least, that the democratic (parliamentary) system is more lasting than oligarchy (dictatorship by a chosen few).

In a letter to Sylvia Pankhurst, published in a newspaper in 1935, Shaw wrote: "I am not a Fascist; I am, and have been all through my political life,a Communist." And apropos of the attitude he shared with Mussolini that the conception of individual liberty under British Parliamentary democracy was a sham, he explained: "... Our representative institutions represent nobody except the comfortably-off people who want to stave off political action by endless talking. ..." Thus, although Shaw regarded Fascism (he sometimes referred to it as 'the Corporate State') as "a great improvement on the anarchism of Liberal *laissez-faire*", he did see it also as protecting the interests mainly of the capitalist producers, and not of the consumers— whom he regarded as the true democratic entity.

A year later, in 1936, Shaw put Hitler and Mussolini in the same category as Napoleon, stating that Fascism was a kind of 'post-Marxian Bonapartism'. (He simultaneously recommended drowning at Margate for the British Labour Party because he did not consider that it had an adequate political creed with which to appeal to the imagination of the general population!)

In *Time and Tide*, 26th November, 1938, Shaw wrote:—

... Now in Herr Hitler we have clearly no raging lunatic to deal with. He is a very able ruler, and on most subjects a very sane one. But a man may be very able and yet have a bee in his bonnet. Herr Hitler's bee is a phobia against the Jews . . . We all know private persons who have these hobbies. We laugh at them. But on the part of an autocrat they are no laughing matter. When they take the form of an attempt to exterminate a section of the human race something may have to be done about it by the other States, especially when the autocrat, instead of, like Nero or Diocletian, throwing the objects of his phobia to the lions or otherwise making short work of them, simply robs them of all they possess and dumps them destitute on his neighbours.

... We talk about a Jewish problem. There is no problem: there is only the crude fact that Herr Hitler is plundering the Jews as Henry VIII plundered the Church, and that we are expected to support them. I have almost damned myself politically by defending

the German and Italian leaders against the silly abuse heaped on
them by the spokesmen and journalists of our pseudo-democracy;
but now that they have let me down by condescending to anti-
Semitism, I must really disown all sympathy with that anachronism,
and point out the way to stop it.

Shaw considered the solution to be quite simple: the League
of Nations ought at once to appoint a committee, assisted by
an international staff of expert psychiatrists, to determine
whether the anti-Semite measures taken by Germany and Italy
were legitimate legislation or pathological phobia. If the report
of the committee and the subsequent decision of the League
was for phobia, the Führer and the Duce would have either to
cancel the measures or stand before Europe as certified lunatics,
and that was a position which no leader could afford. . . . The
League might not be able to prevent or stop war, as people
unreasonably expected it to do: but this was something easily
within its powers and precisely appropriate to its purpose.

At the beginning of this article Shaw expostulated that
Britain and America were in one of their periodic fits of
righteous indignation, and that their "own record was
appalling". To go no further back than Cromwell's attempt to
exterminate the Irish, *we* had persecuted Catholics, Protestant
dissenters, Quakers, Welshmen, Highlanders, Irish 'Shinners',*
Chinese, Japanese, Negroes, Indians, Australian blacks, Asiatic
hill tribes—sometimes to the extent of shooting them at sight.
The United States evidently felt strongly on the subject; but it
was difficult for *them* to take a high moral tone with Colonel
Goering in view of the Ku Klux Klan, the lynching of Negroes,
and the anti-Prohibition gangsters of Chicago and other centres
of American civilisation. Shaw added:—

. . . All this bogus ethnology about Aryan and non-Aryan, about
Nordic dominants and Mediterranean recessives, with which
Houston (not Neville) Chamberlain infected Herr Hitler in his youth,
is, in one word, Bosh.

* Sinn Feiners.

Further views of Shaw on Hitler and Fascism were contained in a draft radio talk entitled "The Unavoidable Subject" in 1940.* Pointing out that the British people had always had an instinctive mistrust of journalists, intellectuals, and politicians, he continued:—

What makes it so puzzling is that nine-tenths of what Mr Hitler says is true. Nine-tenths of what Sir Oswald Mosley says is true. Quite often nine-tenths of what our parliamentary favourites say to please us is emotional brag, bunk, and nonsense.

. . . I was a National Socialist before Mr Hitler was born. I hope we shall emulate and surpass his great achievements in that direction. I have no prejudice against him personally: much that he has written and spoken echoes what I myself have written and said. He has adopted even my diet. I am interested in his career as one of the great psychological curiosities of political history; and I fully appreciate his physical and moral courage, his diplomatic sagacity, and his triumphant rescue of his country from the yoke the Allies imposed on her after her defeat in 1918. I am quite aware of the fact that his mind is a twentieth century mind, and that our governing class is mentally in the reign of Edward the Third, six centuries out of date. I can pay him a dozen compliments which I could not honestly pay to any of our present rulers.

My quarrel with him is a very plain one . . . I have a friend who happens to be a Jew. His name is Albert Einstein: and he is a far greater human prodigy than Mr Hitler and myself rolled into one . . . Well, Adolf Hitler would compel me, the Nordic Shaw, to insult Albert Einstein; to claim moral superiority to him and unlimited power over him; to rob him, drive him out of his house, exile him, be punished for miscegenation if I allow a relative of mine to marry a relative of his, and finally to kill him as part of a general duty to exterminate his race . . . Since then he has extended the list of

* This talk was not broadcast in June 1940 as had originally been arranged becaused of Italy's sudden entry into the war and a tightening of Government control thenceforth. It was first published in *Journal of the War Years* by Anthony Weymouth. Weymouth tells how, when the script was shown by the B.B.C. to the then Minister of Information, Duff Cooper shouted: " I wont have that man on the air. " (My quotation is taken from Mr Weymouth's book, which embodies a few minor corrections made by Shaw in passing the text for publication therein.)

reprobates from Semites to Celts and from Poles to Slavs: in short, to all who are not what he calls Nordic. If he conquers these islands he will certainly add the Irish to the list, as several authorities have maintained that the Irish are the lost tribes of Israel.

Now this is not the sort of thing that sane men can afford to argue with. It is on the face of it pernicious nonsense; and the moment any ruler starts imposing it as a political philosophy on his nation or any other nation by physical force there is nothing for it but for the sane men to muster their own physical forces and go for him. We ought to have declared war on Germany the moment his police stole Einstein's violin.

Writing in the *New Leader* of 10th April, 1943, Shaw declared that Hitler was still the victim of the anti-Semitic phobia which had destroyed his chance of heading a solid combination of Western Capitalism against Bolshevism. He could not understand how a man clever enough to write *Mein Kampf*, which contained "much clear-sighted political criticism", could be blind enough to unite Jewish and Gentile Capitalism in a war for his destruction.   Shaw added:—

With such trumps in his hand as Socialized Toryism* and our folly at Versailles in 1919, he threw them both away in an attempt to revive the craze of Peter the Hermit eight hundred years after Peter's death. Whom the Gods would destroy they first make dotty.

Also, in 1943, Shaw condemned the imprisonment of Sir Oswald Mosley because there had been no trial, not because he supported Mosley's political views. He pointed out the absurd fact that short pamphlets by Mosley were banned, while Hitler's *Mein Kampf* could be bought in any bookshop, and re-affirmed: "No; I am a Communist. That is, I advocate national control and ownership of land, capital, and industry for the benefit of the people, not of the landlords, capitalists, and industrialists."

Any conception of Shaw (the author of *The Adventures of*

* A special Shavian term.

the Black Girl in her Search for God) being favourable to racial prejudice is quite absurd. But to leave no shadow of doubt about it, I will quote once more from his letter to Sylvia Pankhurst:—

Nazi anti-Semite ethnology is balderdash and its biology a recipe for degeneration.

And on another occasion he declared:—

. . . this Chosen Race business is not Socialism, but, as my late colleague Charles Dickens expressed it, "So far from it, on the contrary, quite the reverse."

Genuine democracy, Shaw urged (in the 1937 statement already mentioned*), could only exist when the community's productive labour—without which the community would cease to exist—was shared equally among its individual members, and the leisure left after the labour was accomplished also shared equally. Only in this way could a great and fundamental extension of freedom be produced. But he added:

. . . it is impossible without a corresponding extension of public activity and interference and a careful liquidation of people who want to be free all the time.

He also recognised that there are great barriers in many people's minds against social changes of the radical kind he envisaged:—

. . . The notion, still prevalent in America, that government is a tyranny to be minimized at all costs in the name of Liberty, will have to be eradicated by genuine scientific education of the children. American adults are hopeless; but they mean well; and it would be a pity to shoot them.

Shaw concluded this statement by contending that Security was by itself a meaningless word. Security from what? The proletarian wanted security from unemployment, the business

* *The New Republic* (U.S.A.), 14th April, 1937.

man security from bankruptcy, the professional man security from invasion and conquest. The terms, he said, must be defined before discussion could come to anything.

Four years later, in *The Star* of 4th August, 1938, he published this general reply to his critics—including *The Star*'s columnist "The Man in the Street". The latter had in the previous day's paper held up the freedom of speech of Hyde Park orators as the epitome of British democracy—which, among other things, had allowed Shaw to criticise the country of his adoption to his heart's content—this being something only possible in the tolerant spirit of democracy which had been acquired painfully out of a sordid welter of centuries of religious and political persecutions.

G. B. Shaw Replies to "The Man in the Street"

What I want to know is how much is "The Star" being paid by Hitler and Mussolini to say that I am on the side of the dictators. Anyone who has read my work carefully would know that the very opposite is the case.

What I am trying to prove is that democracy, as we know it, is a fraud. The Government is so all-powerful that it can do what it likes with us.

In dictator countries the Press and all channels of opinion are controlled.

Here the Government is quite happy to let everyone say what he likes. It knows that whatever is said will not make the slightest difference, and that it can still go on in its own way.

The Man In The Street can shout from his soap-box, but what influence has he?

What influence have I? It is true that I have a certain reputation, but what I say makes little impression on the Government.

The point is, do we want to get things done or not? I don't really want to see a Hitler in this country, but I am not sure that it would be a bad thing. [*Sic.*]

It might be an improvement on a so called democracy that is not really a democracy at all.

I am not going to say any more on this subject. I am tired of the way in which the newspapers, bribed or persuaded in some other way by the dictators, continue to make it appear that I am an admirer of dictatorship.

All my work shows the truth to be otherwise.

Despite Shaw's contention in the last line, the above passage would seem to be a contradiction in terms, for to write: "I don't really want to see a Hitler in this country, but I am not sure that it would be a bad thing," surely implies an admiration of dictatorship.

In an interview in *Cavalcade* magazine, 1st November, 1941, Shaw declared:—

Mr Churchill and Mr Anthony Eden are for private property and oligarchy. Stalin is for public property and democracy. So am I.

Seven years later we find Shaw complaining that much of the confusion regarding his political and social beliefs was imaginary, and caused by different interpretations of the common political terms and 'labels.' In a letter in *The Times* of 19th August, 1948, headed "Rebuilding Babel", he suggested that what we all lacked was a common political dictionary, and that until we cleared up our political nomenclature, our political oratory and journalism could come to nothing but "the pot calling the kettle black" without either of them knowing what they were talking about. He went on:—

. . . I myself find it impossible to make myself understood, though when I describe myself by this or that adjective I know precisely what I mean. As a citizen and one of the founders of British Fabian policy I am basically a Marxist Communist;* but I cannot say so without being set down as an infantile advocate of catastrophic insurrection, with capitalism in full swing on Monday, revolution on Tuesday, and Socialism in full swing on Wednesday. I do not wish to see private enterprise† made a felony: on the contrary,

---

* Later in this chapter attention is drawn to earlier statements by Shaw— completely contradicted by that above—to the effect that Fabian Society doctrine (of which he was one of the chief architects) at no time contained any element whatsoever of Marxism.

† Shaw here seems to use the term 'private enterprise' in the usual sense of 'private businesses of a capitalistic nature.'

I look to private enterprise* for experiment and invention in industry, art, and science as the proper sphere of individual talent and genius in the leisure which Socialism alone can gain for everybody.

The alternative to private enterprise, he said, was State-aided enterprise, of which Britain already had many successful examples in the public utility schemes and friendly societies, and he could not see why these and similar institutions which in this country we all accepted, and even praised, should be denounced "under their Italian name of Fascism" as "murderous anti-Semitic tyrannies."

Shaw's reasoning on this point is incomprehensible and not supported by the facts, for there was (and is) a considerable difference between our form of State-aided enterprise, and the ruthless Italian form—known as Fascism—which made Trade Unions illegal, persecuted minorities, and indulged in other practices altogether alien to the British spirit.

Communism and private enterprise, Shaw went on, were only different methods of civilisation, *each with its proper sphere* [my italics], and he considered that Communism, like private enterprise, had to take various forms, one of them being Socialism. In his opinion, bread and milk should be communised like street lighting and sewerage, and suburban travelling provided by the State free of charge, because everybody needed them; but he thought it would be silly to provide, say, trombones, microscopes, or ounces of radium and other specialised articles free, because not everyone needed them, or could afford them if they did. Goods of various kinds, he declared, must be provided by "mixed social methods".

The distinction between Socialism and Communism, as

---

* In this second instance he appears to use the word 'enterprise' in its more literal sense of initiative.

His meaning, I think, was that he regarded the second use of individual initiative—i.e. for the benefit of the community—as the correct one, as contrasted to the first, conventional, use of the term as denoting privately owned businesses run primarily from motives of personal monetary profit.

Shaw saw it, had earlier been defined by him in a reply to a questioner at the conclusion of a lecture entitled "The Fabian Basis"* which he gave at the Essex Hall, Strand, on 9th October, 1908. Under Socialism one had to pay something for a nationalised service, just as one already paid for stamps when using the nation's postal service. But under Communism the postal service would be available to all, without any purchase of stamps being necessary, just as the use of Waterloo Bridge was communised when the ½d. toll for its use was abolished. Roughly speaking, things were communised when they were paid for out of *general* rates and taxes, with nothing extra, no special fee to pay.

Shaw, taking the example of bread, described amusingly what the result might be:—

Supposing you communise bread, what you would have to do would be to provide a large store of bread before the day arrived when communism took effect. I will tell you what [would] happen on the first day bread was communised. Crowds of people would come with barrels and sacks. They would come with pantechnicon vans, and they would take enormous heaps of bread. You would have to lay up a store of bread which would feed the population six times over the first day. Then it would be a very glorious thing to watch the people. They would eat some bread, and eat enough, and then they would find they had a lot of bread on hand which nobody could sell because nobody need buy it. You would find men sneaking about and dropping loaves down the areas. You would see men pretending they were posting letters while they were really posting slices of bread, and the day after you would find that no amount of money that you could pay a man could tempt him to take away more bread than he could eat. Then you would find that the reform was an extremely economical reform because you would not have any starving children, and the bread would cost less than it does now instead of it costing more,† and it would be better bread. If you want

* Reported by C. H. Norman.
† Shaw's deduction that 'free' bread would be economical appears somewhat far-fetched when one considers how wasteful people are with commodities such as water which they do not pay for in proportion to the amount consumed.

to find out whether the State makes better bread than the private individual, go to prison. A person who has been in prison, or in the workhouse even, always tells you that the bread he got there was the best bread he ever ate. I merely throw out that illustration just to show you the difference between Socialism and Communism.

Other definitions of Socialism and Communism, and also of Capitalism, were given by Shaw in *The Spectator* of 17th October, 1925. As follows:—

CAPITALISM.—An economic system based on the demonstration by Ricardo that if land be made the private property of a class, and the savings (called capital) which arise from this class having more than enough to live on be also jealously secured to the savers as private property, and if, moreover, everybody behaves quite selfishly, buying in the cheapest market and selling in the dearest without regard to any other consideration than making as much money as possible, the result will be that every worker in the country will be able to earn a living wage and no more, thereby securing a livelihood and incurring a necessity for continuous and strenuous industry, a consummation so desirable that it justifies all the appalling misery and crime, waste and idleness which it must with equal certainty produce. See Ricardo, Malthus, Austin's Lectures on Jurisprudence, Macaulay's prevision of the future of America. De Quincy's Logic of Political Economy, &c. There is no ambiguity or vagueness about the theory: no social theory has ever been so lucidly and precisely worked out and promulgated, or with such unprecedented candour as to the evils it involved.

It has fallen into discredit because it has never kept its promise for a single day, and in any case, is obviously no policy for a gentleman.

Its disastrousness was foreseen by John Bunyan (*Life and Death of Mr. Badman*) and Oliver Goldsmith (*Vicar of Wakefield* and *Deserted Village*); witnessed and denounced by Robert Owen, and overwhelmed with invective by John Ruskin. Nevertheless, it is still taught confusedly and disingenuously in our universities, and has lamed many public men, notably the Earl of Oxford and Dean Inge, in their dealings with industrial questions.

SOCIALISM (pronounced Soashlism by our most elegant speakers) is the theory that the distribution of the national income is a fundamental social activity which should be vigilantly and continually conscientious, and should therefore be the first concern of the Government. As no other distribution than an equal one will bear examination, Socialism means in effect the equal distribution of the national income among all citizens without regard to age, sex, character, industry, or anything but national vitality, with all the consequences which such a distribution implies.

COMMUNISM.—The same as Socialism, but better English. There is, however, a technical use in which, for example, the streets, bridges, lighting, paving, and police are communized, whilst the telegraphs and telephones and postal services are socialized or nationalized. It does not matter, as the people call the communized services "free".

That Shaw continued to call himself a Communist to the end, and regarded England as having arrived at certain features of a Communist society without having recognised them as such or called them by this label, and also that he believed that many Soviet ideas were adaptations of British Fabianism, is clear from a letter of his in *The Times* of 31st August, 1950—which must be taken as his final word, since it was the last literary or political item written by him before the fall in his garden barely a week later which led to his death. In this letter he asked:—

. . . what have we to show for our own Communism? Plenty. But we never show it. We are ashamed and apologetic, as we always are when circumstances force us to take a step forward and broaden the basis of Communism, on which all civilization, all catholicism, and all enterprise,* public or private, stand.

He added that he could remember the social conditions of sixty years previously—terrible slums which had since become respectable thoroughfares, and agricultural wages of 13/- a week as against the £6 a week demanded in 1950,†—and said

* See previous footnotes on Shaw's different uses of this word.

†As at January, 1971, the *minimum* agricultural wage is £14 16s. 0d. per week (of 42 hours), with most workers getting well above the minimum and averaging £21 per week.

that had this progress been the work of the Soviets they would have "blazed it and boasted of it all over Europe". What, he asked, were our young men told of these advances in our national welfare, which were "all the work of British Communism"?—Nothing, except that Communism was a damnable heresy. He continued:—

. . . What was it that saved Russia from ruin after 1917?—her adoption of British Communism, made constitutional and practicable by myself, Sidney Webb, and our fellow Fabians.

He pointed out that Lenin, whom Mr Churchill, as well as he, had recognised as a great statesman in his early career—when most people in Britain had regarded him as a terrorising bandit—had dubbed him (Mr Shaw) "a good man fallen among Fabians"; yet when later Lenin had had to adjust his life from that of a political philosopher to being the ruling head of a State, Lenin had realised that the practical Fabian policy of 'gradualness' had much to commend it, and had even called his New Economic Policy "the first instalment of Russian Fabianism". Then (Shaw went on) Stalin continued the advance of Socialism in the U.S.S.R. and introduced collective farming—"with a sop to the peasant's need for a little private property in the form of British Jesse Collings's prescription of three acres and a cow". Shaw took pride in the fact that

. . . Marxism, a British Museum export,* was set on its feet by Fabianism, another British export. We are the spiritual fathers of

---

* This is an example of the way in which Shaw's rhetorical literary style tends (doubtless unwittingly) to distort the facts. Karl Marx exercised the right of any resident in Britain to use the British Museum Library, and actually wrote much of *Das Kapital* there; but that most certainly does not make Marxism "a British Museum export" in the sense of being something officially backed and propagated abroad by the British Museum! However, it could perhaps be argued that, figuratively, if not literally speaking, Marx's world-wide doctrine had its origins in his research in the British Museum, and thus in a limited way could be regarded as a product of the British Museum—and in view of the international effect, as an 'export' too (albeit an involuntary and not officially backed one).

modern successful Communism, protesting all the time in our ridiculous British way, that we hold it in abhorrence, yet setting up despotic Soviets all over the land disguised as committees and commissions and boards.

Britain, said Shaw, kept up a stream of propaganda for plutocracy—which it called freedom—and private enterprise, but he would like to see this country advertise (what he called) its Communism much more vigorously. (Britain had a Labour Government in power in 1950.)

Three years earlier, in *The Times* of April 28th, 1947, Shaw had written:—

. . . I agree with Stalin on collective farming and with Sir John [Russell] on cooperative farming, just as I call myself a Communist (like William Morris) and am in practice perforce a Capitalist . . . Of all politicians and reformers those whom I find the greatest nuisances are the boys of the Everything-or-Nothing-All-at-Once Brigade.

When Shaw said that in practice he was perforce a Capitalist, he meant, of course, that, living in England as it actually was, and not as he would ideally like it to be, he had necessarily to conform to some extent to its predominantly Capitalistic contemporary structure. But more than this, he appears like Marxists to have believed in Capitalism as an indispensable political stage in the development towards Socialism, just as he regarded Socialism as a preliminary stage in the path towards Communism; for forty years earlier, in an article on America in *Everybody's Magazine* (New York), December, 1907, and entitled "A Nation of Villagers", he had written:—

. . . Socialism is only possible as the consummation of successful Capitalism, which, with all its horrors, will be adored by history as the pathfinder of Socialism . . . things in America will have to get worse before they get better. Socialism is the remedy; but Socialism is only possible where Individualism is developed to the point at which the individual can see beyond himself, and works to perfect his city and his nation instead of to furnish his own house better than his neighbors. Short of that point Individualism is not Individualism, but Idiocy (a word which idiots cannot understand) and Idiocy and nothing else is just what is the matter with America today.

Shaw went even further by in some respects actually equating 'true' Capitalism with Communism. In an article written in about 1948* for the Soviet Press and entitled" Bernard Shaw on Peace", he declared:—

. . . Communism is Capitalism *in excelsis*. What we Communists call Capitalism is not Capitalism. It is Plutocracy, and should always be called so. It is anti-State. Communism is pro-State. Communism is neither a melodrama in which every Communist is a hero and every Plutocrat a villain, nor a Utopia in which everything is done by the State and nothing by private enterprise. There is more private enterprise in Russia than in England. Only when it is financed by the State and exploited by plutocratic private owners does it call itself The Corporate State or National Socialism. Its popular name is Fascism. Though it is associated in our minds with the anti-Semite mania of Hitler and the imperialism of Mussolini, it has no logical connexion with either. Many activities may be quite wisely left to controlled petty Fascism. Criticism, Art, and Science had better be free from all control except that of the common law.

Shaw's use of the word 'Communism' is clearly his own particular one, and not by any means in accordance with the usual meaning imputed to the term. Shaw was never a member of the British Communist Party, but he did subscribe to the *Daily Worker* till the day of his death, and was also a large shareholder in it. He nevertheless shocked the 'orthodox' Communists by describing their famous theme song, *The Red Flag*, as "The Funeral March of a Fried Eel", and freely admitted that he had "never had any feelings about the English

* My extract is taken from the typescript (probably unpublished) among the Shaw papers in the British Museum—on which no date is given, though it is estimated by the cataloguing officials to be approximately 1948-9.

working classes, except a desire to abolish them and replace them by sensible people." And although Communism and Capitalism are usually regarded as opposed, Shaw sided with the Capitalists in opposing, with considerable vehemence, all forms of taxation of Capital. He would undoubtedly have been strongly against the six-months Capital Gains Tax introduced in Britain in 1962, and even more strongly against the long-term Gains Tax introduced by the Labour Government in 1965—especially as the short-term speculative dealing in shares and other commodities which the 1962 tax was intended to combat was not practised at all by him—his comprehensive holdings in stocks and shares being all long-term investments.

Shaw, nevertheless, in the article for the Soviet press (c. 1948) already referred to, declared himself even more extreme in his Communism than the Communist Party:—

. . . As to the little group which calls itself the Communist Party without knowing what Communism means in practice (Lenin dismissed their dreams as measles) it is assumed that everything they do is dictated by Stalin; and when I say that I heartily wish it were, as they could have no better leader, this simple matter of fact is received as a monstrous paradox.

Shaw had vigorously denied that Stalin was a dictator (while accepting that Mussolini *was* one) in a lecture reported in *The Lecture Recorder*, 1933. Referring to Stalin as an interesting gentleman whose personal acquaintance he had had the pleasure of making, he compared him to the Pope:—

. . . Mussolini, particularly by virtue of his taking all the Cabinet posts, may not unfairly be described as a dictator, but when you turn to Stalin, you get something else. Stalin is not a dictator. The nearest comparison you can get to Stalin is the Pope. Their positions are very much the same. The Roman Catholic Church grew out of a number of men, who were not elected by anybody, but they themselves decided to be priests and joined together in a priesthood and finally elected their own hierarchy. They depended, of course, on the fact that most of the people looked to them and accepted them because of this particular religious conviction. Now, exactly the same position prevails in Russia, where a number of persons had a political conviction and, in the old days, these men faced all sorts of martyrdoms and imprisonments, and they gradually formed what is now called the Communist Party. The Communist Party is more democratic than the Catholic Church is now because, in the latter, the people do not elect their priests, and in the Russian system, *the men at the top are selected from below and the election is a real thing.*

The last sentence (my italics) is controversial, to say the very least.

Writing in the *Daily Worker* on 2nd November, 1948, Shaw complained that all other newspapers and statesmen kept shouting that Communism was devil's doctrine, and Russia the universal enemy of mankind. He went on:—

. . . They simply do not know what the word Communism means, and are throwing it at their party opponents as quarrelsome suburbans throw dead cats back and forward at one another over the garden wall. People who are not fundamentally Communist are not civilised. For a genuine workers' newspaper the present struggle is between Plutocracy and Democracy, disguised for electioneering purposes as between Freedom and Bureaucracy.

One of the dead cats is called Totalitarianism, another the Police State, another Defence against Russian aggression. But the hard fact is that these dead cats all start from our own side of the wall. The practices of which we accuse Communism are all in full swing in the Commonwealth. A law that is not totalitarian is no law at all. What we revile as a Gestapo is nothing but our own C.I.D.

Earlier, in 1941, Shaw had written that we "nursed a blind hatred of Russia, because private property, with its sequel of idle parasitism and poverty, has been abolished there, all property being held subject to the public welfare, whilst trade unionism, though enormously more general and powerful than in England or America, is part of the State machinery and admits of no dictatorship so absolute as that of an English trade union secretary."

Shaw considered that instead of the *Daily Worker*, which was about to be suppressed at that time, it would have been far more sensible to have suppressed *The Times* and all the other papers which had "for years carried on, and were still carrying on, a campaign of insult, calumny, and clamour for a capitalist united front against Bolshevism."

In a review of a book *Fabian Socialism* by G. D. H. Cole, in *Tribune*, 28th May, 1943, Shaw declared:—

Now if Mr. Cole is not a Communist he is not a Socialist. Socialism without Communism is Fascism, which is the enemy the Fabian Society has to overthrow now that its old adversary Cobdenism* is prostrate. And it is precisely those freedoms which the Soviet Government has had to abolish that the Fabians must disclaim also, because they are the most potent weapons of Capitalism, being in fact the right to be idle and do what you like, which Mr. Winston Churchill has explicitly given up. The Russians are the freest civilised people in the world at present; and the English [are] so busy bawling that they never, never, never will be slaves that they do not notice that they have never been anything else.
. . . Mr. Webb's way is the way of Stalin, who saw the other ways tried; and the U.S.S.R. can now be quite properly called in this country the U.S.F.S.R.

By "U.S.F.S.R." Shaw clearly meant to imply "Union of Soviet Fabian Socialist Republics". It is relevant here to include also the following paragraph which was in Shaw's typescript† but cut by the Editor in the version as published:—

. . . The Fabians are not Trade Unionists: they are critics of Trade Unionism, helping it as they do only to permeate it with Socialism and educate it to accept its destiny as part of the State instead of being the personal tyranny, however salutary, it is at present.

It would appear that, etymologically speaking, Shaw would be entitled to call any communal, nationalised activity

* I.e. old-fashioned capitalistic Liberalism based on Free Trade, and reaching its epitome in Gladstone and Cobden.
† Now in the British Museum.

organised for the benefit of the community as a whole communistic, but Russian Communism—whatever its origins or 'spiritual' inspiration may or may not have been—had developed by 1950 into something very different from British Socialism of the same year: particularly in so far as it depended very largely on its arbitrary use of centralised power. (The reader who wishes to pursue further this aspect of Russian Communism will find it well dealt with in Bertrand Russell's book, *Power*.)

It is important to note at this juncture that although Shaw so often described himself as a Communist (and was frequently regarded by others as a Marxist) he once admitted that "there are just as great fools among Communists as among other bodies", and his membership of the Fabian Society instead of H. M. Hyndman's Marxist "Social Democratic Federation" (influential before the first world war, but not now in existence) or of the Communist Party of Great Britain, proves that he never accepted all Karl Marx's ideas. He acknowledged that his interest in Socialism as an intellectual belief received its first impetus from reading Marx's works—"Marx opened my eyes to the facts of civilizations, gave me an entirely fresh conception of the Universe, provided me with a purpose and a mission in life"—but as early as 1887 his admiration had become decidedly "this side idolatry". Thus in a favourable but not uncritical review of Moore and Aveling's translation of Book I of Marx's *Capital* in *The National Reformer* for 21st August, 1887, he gave his opinion that Karl Marx: "treats of labor without reference to variations of skill between its parts; of raw material without reference to variations of fertility; and of the difference between the product of labor and the price [wage] of labor power, as 'surplus value' without reference to its subdivision into rent, interest, and profits". Nevertheless, he also declared:—

. . . I never took up a book that proved better worth reading than "Capital". . . . In pointing out . . . errors, and so implying that Marx was fallible, I have incurred the risk of being accused ... of attempting to pooh-pooh Marx as an idiot ... I have taken a course somewhere between that and worshipping him as a God. To me it seems that his errors arose from several causes. He was a born materialist; and when he attempted to carve a theory, with the tools of the born metaphysician, he cut his fingers. In his time, too, the germ of the truth about value lay in the old supply and demand theory, which was historically anti-popular, whereas the labor theory of Ricardo had a delusive air of being the reverse. Again, the question of the value of labor force was inseparable from the population question; and that, too, he disliked as a recognized staple of capitalist apologetics. This was prejudice, doubtless; and it cost him the coveted secret of value; but he knew the condition of the people; and his sympathies were too wide and his imagination too active to permit him to investigate economic subjects in the purely scientific spirit of Jevons. He would have been more or less than human if he could have written the history of capital with academic coolness. The Marxites who cannot bear to admit that a person named Jevons was right where Marx was wrong, may console themselves with the reflexion [sic] that a person named Young was right where Newton was wrong, and that Newton's reputation stands nevertheless.

I am strongly tempted to launch into a description of the extra-ordinary picture of modern industrialism which gives the book its main force and fascination; but ... My last word for the present is— Read Jevons and the rest for your economics; and read Marx for the history of their working in the past, and the conditions of their application in the present. And never mind the metaphysics.

In the course of time Shaw's views on Marx sharpened and deepened. He came to disagree much more strongly on certain basic precepts, and to be very critical of Marx's character and background, also—while retaining an appreciation of what he felt to be Marx's merits.

On the credit side, Shaw expressed his view in *Everybody's Political What's What* (1944) that Marx's main achievement was that he:—

... proved up to the hilt that capital in its pursuit of what he called Mehrwerth, which we translate as Surplus Value (it includes rent, interest, and commercial profit), is ruthless, and will stop at nothing, not even at mutilation and massacre, white and black slavery, drugging and drinking, if they promise a shilling per cent more than the dividends of philanthropy. Before Marx there had been plenty of Pessimism. The Book of Ecclesiastes in the Bible is full of it. Shakespear in King Lear, in Timon of Athens, in Coriolanus, got to it and stuck there. So did Swift and Goldsmith. But none of them could document the case from official sources as Marx did. He thereby created that demand for "a new world" which not only inspires modern Communism and Socialism but in 1941 became the platform catchword of zealous Conservatives and Churchmen.

On the more critical side, Shaw's far more numerous comments at various times in his life included one of his replies in an interview conducted by *The Candid Friend* magazine and published on 11th May, 1901. Shaw described his evolution to Fabian Socialism from his first Socialist inspirations— hearing Henry George speaking during the great Single Tax campaign of 1882 and then reading Karl Marx's *Das Kapital*— in the following terms:—

. . . the real secret of Marx's fascination was his appeal to an un-named, unrecognised passion . . . the passion of hatred in the more generous souls among the respectable and educated sections for the accursed middle-class institutions that had starved, thwarted, misled, and corrupted them from their cradles. Marx's 'Capital' is not a treatise on Socialism; it is a jeremiad against the bourgeoisie, supported by such a mass of evidence and such a relentless Jewish genius for denunciation as had never been brought to bear before. It was supposed to be written for the working classes; but the working man respects the bourgeoisie, and wants to be a bourgeois; Marx never got hold of him for a moment. It was the revolting sons of the bourgeoisie itself—Lassalle, Marx, Liebknecht, Morris, Hyndman, Bax, all, like myself, bourgeois crossed with squirearchy— that painted the flag red. Bakunin and Kropotkin, of the military and noble caste (like Napoleon), were our extreme left. The middle and upper classes are the revolutionary element in society: the proletariat is the Conservative element, as Disraeli well knew. Hyndman and his Marxists, Bakunin and his Anarchists, would not accept this situation; they persisted in believing that this proletariat was an irresistible mass of unawakened Felix Pyats and Ouidas. I did accept the situation, helped, perhaps, by my inherited instinct for anti-climax. I threw Hyndman over, and got to work with Sidney Webb and the rest to place Socialism on a respectable footing; hence Fabianism.

Shaw further emphasised the middle-class—not working class—origins of Socialist revolt in the *Daily Citizen,* 19th October, 1912:—

. . . Our more prosperous working men hanker thoughtlessly after middle-class respectability, and are as convinced as anyone that Ruskin and Morris were fantastic dreamers. It is in the middle class itself that the revolt against middle-class ideals breaks out: that is why the revolt of Labor has taken place at the call of middle-class revolutionists. Neither peer nor laborer has ever hated the bourgeoisie as Marx hated it, nor despised its ideals as Swift, Ibsen, and Strindberg despised them, nor exposed its essential infidelity and its degradation and subornation of Christianity as Rousseau and Butler did. I defy any navvy, or any duke, to maul the middle class as Dickens mauled it, or as it is mauled today by Wells, Chesterton, Belloc, Pinero, Granville Barker, Galsworthy, Bennett, the young lions of the provincial repertory theatres, or

G. BERNARD SHAW.

In an earlier draft letter,* believed to be intended for the *Clarion* newspaper around 1904 but unpublished, Shaw further described Karl Marx as an aristocratic German Jew completely isolated from the recognised aristocracy of his country, and thrust back into the narrow life of the commercial, middle-class ghetto, and added that he was also "a genius of the imaginative, speculative, literary sort, hating 'business', contemptuous of mere money, and consequently at war from his cradle with the Philistine bourgeoisie into which he was born". Such a man, said Shaw, is driven by all his instincts to aim at the overthrow of the existing commercial order, and to dream

* Shaw papers, B.M.

of a republican democracy foreign to the habits, character, morals, and ideals of his own class, which he loathes. Shaw continued:—

I fancy a good many of us are in the same boat with Marx in this respect. I certainly am; so is Belfort Bax; so was Morris; so is Hyndman; so is Walter Crane· so is Blatchford; so is Kropotkin; so is Edward Carpenter; so is Henry Salt; so is Charles Rowley of Ancoats; so, in short, are all the middle class men and nobles and all the literary geniuses in the movement. We have not, like Marx, the special grievance of belonging to a legally persecuted and excluded race; but after all, our opinions, our sympathies, our disregard of fashionable conventions, cut us off from the Philistine world as effectually as racial and religious prejudice cut off Marx and Lassalle.

Shaw emphasised vigorously, however, that in some cases this anti-conventional attitude, though revolutionary, was not Socialism. It seized upon Socialism, just as it seized upon Anarchism, or Atheism, or Positivism, upon all the revolutionary 'isms', simply because they were revolutionary; and it very seldom demanded more from any 'ism' than that it should be a good stick to beat the bourgeois dog with. Thus all the 'isms' in their early persecuted stages got adherents who only imagined themselves to be genuine 'ists'. From the moment when the 'isms' began to work themselves out in practice, their revolutionary adherents, middle-class, noble and literary, began to cool off, and even to oppose what they formerly supported . . . . In short, as the 'isms' gradually got incorporated with ordinary everyday politics, they incurred the hostility of the men who only supported them in their negative stages because they threatened to "blow ordinary everyday politics into smithereens". Shaw then complained:—

Why is it that I, a hardworking, plodding, straightforward, sober, honest, industrious creature as ever lived, am mistrusted as a sort of Socialist Mephistopheles, delighting in nothing but mischief and misunderstanding? Just because the revolutionary Socialists from the Capitalist class are aiming, not finally at the betterment of the working class, but at the destruction of the existing social order and the ideas of morality and life on which it is based. The only instrument big enough for that job that lies to their hand is the proletariat; and they try to capture it for their purpose by working on the poverty and injustice of the present system to the proletariat, exactly as Mr Chamberlain works on it for Tariff Reform. The moment Socialism loses its revolutionary character, as in Battersea or in the Fabian propaganda, or in the right wing of the Independent Labor Party, they attack it more bitterly than they attack Capitalism itself. Not that they are consciously insincere in their profession of Socialism.

In another undated early draft article Shaw added: "We [Fabians] are essentially State-Socialists, aiming at the rescue of State Socialism from its present exploitation and restriction by Capitalism; and if we lose sight of that fact for a moment we relapse at once into the old revolutionary insurrectionism in which we can be nothing but the catspaws of republican liberalism".

In the draft letter quoted prior to the last paragraph and believed dated about 1904 and intended for the *Clarion*, Shaw further described Karl Marx as a middle-class revolutionist, and a town-bred literary bourgeois, with nothing but a German University Course and his own brains to save him from the narrowness of his class. If one wished to understand Marx, Shaw said, the first thing to realise was that though, like all geniuses of his type, he possessed a brilliant intellect and had read a great deal, throughout his life he never knew the working classes as any trade union organiser knows them, and never knew the governing class as a gamekeeper or Foreign Office clerk knows them. In fact he never really knew any class at all, since he spent all his life surrounded by enthusiastic hero-worshippers who were as out of touch with real people as he was himself. His books were academic and unrealistic. He gave you nothing but two imaginary armies, the one consisting of proletarians, whose sole characteristic was that they were economically exploited, and the other of "burgess gentlemen" who went to church every Sunday, exploited the proletarians,and were conscious hypocrites.

This vision was neither scientific nor impartial, Shaw considered. The mischief done by the acceptance of Marx's incapacities, ignorances, and errors as infallible and authoritative truth, had been continuously increasing to unbearable limits during the previous forty years. His conception of the International was a poetic and inspiring one, but it was founded on the Class War blunder—the fatal notion that the line separating the interests of Socialism from those of Capitalism ran between the property owners and the proletariat, whereas in fact (said Shaw) it ran through the middle of both camps.

The following extract is from an early hand-written draft (undated)* in the British Museum:—

. . . Karl Marx, by his demonstration of the industrial basis of political history, made it impossible for the younger generations to tolerate such superstitions as his melodramatic class war of a heroic proletariat against a villainous bourgeoisie, his childish seventeenth century theory of value, and his brilliantly written but insufferably Pharisaic Jeremiads against Napoleon III, Thiers, etc., etc., etc., who were, according to his own theory, the merest flies on the wheel of capitalist production. In fact, Marx, like his ancestor Moses, brought us up out of the land of Egypt only to leave us wandering for 40 years in the wilderness. To him the whole world consisted of himself and Engels, surrounded by an invisible angelic choir called the proletariat, persecuted by a body of police spies disguised as anarchists and organized by Bakunin, and several million scoundrels, playwrights, and exploiters, including all the Socialists who were turning his own ideas to any practical account in real administration.

Much later, in the *Labour Monthly*, January, 1949, Shaw pointed out that:—

---

* The draft is headed "The Solidarity of Social Democracy" and may have been for a German newspaper. The date is estimated as possibly about 1904. (References in it to Bebel and Pierpoint Morgan—who both died in 1913—as active contemporary figures, confirm this approximate dating.)

. . . Anyone can be a good Christian without believing that Joshua stopped the sun, or Jesus raised Lazarus from the dead. So also is it possible to be a Socialist without, like Engels, making *Das Kapital* 'The Bible of the Working Class', or accepting Marx's version of the exploded capitalist theory of value or his attempt to account for Surplus Value by an analysis of the circulation of commodities that is now tiresome nonsense. He knew nothing of the theory of rent and interest; . . .

In the early draft, quoted prior to the above passage, Shaw (consistent with his later 1949 attitude in the above paragraph) wrote:—

. . . Now, in practical politics, Marx was not a Socialist at all: he was simply an anti-bourgeois humanitarian individualist, whose sole quarrel with the Liberals of 1848 was that they exempted Mehrwerth from their crusade against State Churches, political class privileges, and autocracy. The moment Napoleon III or Bismarck began to meddle with Socialism, he attacked Socialism as bureaucratic "State Socialism" (as if Socialism could ever be anything but a huge bureaucracy) and began pushing his disciples backwards in the direction of anti-State Liberalism, a direction in which they have now retreated so far that the last general election in Germany was fought on a manifesto which the Fabian Society of London would smile at.

Shaw, in his draft letter, possibly for the *Clarion* in 1904 already referred to above, considered Marx's best talent to be in the field of political journalism; he thought Marx would have made an excellent staff man for *The Times*! He admired (while not fully agreeing with) Marx's early pioneering achievements, but was strong in his criticism of the later Marx—the rigid, unadaptable egotist, who, in the end, "acquired all the literary vanity and pretentiousness, the petulance, the jealousy, the pitiful claims to 'originality', the inability to endure any rival philosopher, the spite against all who refused to treat him seriously as a political leader, which are the familiar marks of the suburban panjandrum and the Soho conspirator."

Much later, in 1942,* Shaw referred to Marx's "pitiable"

* *Tribune*, 27th March, 1942.

personal life; how his "first beloved children died of slow starvation, which wrecked his health and shortened his own life," how his two younger daughters committed suicide, and how his wife was driven almost crazy by domestic worry, while he read and studied and eventually produced a book, *Das Kapital*, which, as Shaw wrote the following year,* "blew the golden lid off hell" and changed the entire course of world history.

In the latter article, however, he also emphasised his view that "though Marx could analyse Capitalist policy, bourgeois policy, and proletarian no-policy, like a god, nobody could guess from his writing that he had ever in his life met or spoken to a real natural capitalist, bourgeois proletarian, or living human being of any description".

The following two passages are taken from a paper dated 18th March, 1906,† and intended for reading to the Fabian Society. Shaw subsequently considered incorporating part or all of this paper in his preface to *Back to Methuselah* but in the event did not do so, and these extracts—like most of the preceeding ones giving his views on Marx and Marxism—appear here for the first time:—

. . . To this day Socialism is obstructed by Marxists who are convinced that Capitalism is extinguishing itself automatically. . . . Marx's value theory, his fatalism, his materialism, his atheism, his calm omission of human character, passion, will, or even consciousness as factors in social evolution, his conception of the class war as a discord which will finally resolve itself into the economic concord of Socialism: all these are as early Victorian as they can be; and this is the reason why Marx, when he had once destroyed the moral prestige of Capitalism, was of no further use to the Socialists, and forces them to get rid of Marxism as the first condition of their advance, exactly as Darwin, when he had once destroyed our belief in the book of Genesis, is forcing us all to get rid of him also as the first condition of regaining our spiritual energy.

* *Daily Herald*, 10th March, 1943.
† Shaw Mss., B.M.

Later in the same paper Shaw further condemned as naïve the view cherished by Marxians that Capitalism will collapse of its own accord eventually as a result of its own inner contradictions:—

. . . It is also beyond question that the cognate fatalism of Marx produces hopeless impossibilism in politics. If the forms of production and exchange inexorably dictate all the other social forms, and if Capitalism is inevitably developing by its own immanent laws towards its own downfall and the establishment of the economic harmonies on Socialist lines, why on earth should we trouble ourselves to push an express train? Why not imitate the tramps complained of by Mr John Burns, who accosts the President of the Local Government Board with the remark that the evolution of Capitalism is cruel hard on the likes of us, governor, and can't you spare us a tanner. It is true that there was a middle class practical business side to Marx. He demonstrated that the workers were robbed of fifty per cent. of the product of their labor. He called on the proletarians of all lands to unite for the recovery of that fifty per cent. But somehow men will not unite and make revolutions for fifty per cent. as long as the remaining fifty per cent. is enough to scrape along on. They will fight for their lives, but not for the difference between a cottage piano and a German concertina. Making a revolution is a very serious thing: it means going into the street and blowing your neighbor's brains out with the chance of his anticipating you by blowing your own brains out. A soldier, with the law on his side, will do that for his board and lodging and a few shillings pocket money. That is, he will do it for the difference between, say, fifteen shillings a week and nothing. A man will do anything for the difference between fifteen shillings and nothing. But for the difference between fifteen shillings a week and thirty, he will do astonishingly little. He will certainly not risk his life and liberty, nor think out a social problem. And for the difference between thirty shillings a week and three hundred a year he will do still less, except in the way of petty chicanery and exploitation of his poorer brethren. Consequently all that Capitalism need do to fortify itself against a hunger revolt or an International Socialist League for the recovery of 'surplus value', is to guarantee a subsistence wage to a sufficient majority of the proletariat. This it practically does. And so there is an end of Marxism as a revolutionary force on its economic side as well as on its philosophical side.

There can no longer be any question about it: both Darwinism and Marxism starve and paralyze our energy and devotion instead of rousing them to irresistible activity. . . .

In the *Home Journal* (New York), 28th October, 1896, Shaw expressed his view that the later Marx had himself partly abrogated his earlier views. He criticised Volume I of Marx's *Das Kapital* in the following terms:—

It is hopelessly erroneous and obsolete; it has been thrown over by Marx himself in the third volume of the same work; it would, if it were valid, disprove the existence of "surplus value", instead of proving it; it has been used again and again to discredit Socialism as an economic theory; and the only Socialist who ventured to defend it against the scientific theory which Jevons introduced to England was converted by his opponent.

In a footnote Shaw referred the reader who desired further information on this point to (Earl) Bertrand Russell's book *German Social Democracy* (Longmans, 1896).

In the same article (entitled "The Illusions of Socialism") Shaw went on to explain:—

. . . a Socialist is a Socialist; and whichever theory he adopts, he arrives at the same conclusion—the advocacy of a transfer of "the means of production, distribution, and exchange" from private to collective ownership. If he could be persuaded that the old theory did not support this "principle", as he calls it, he would give up the old theory, even if Jevons were still too hard for him. And thereby comes the cherished illusion that all Socialists are agreed in principle, though they may differ as to tactics. This is perhaps the most laughable of all the illusions of Socialism, so outrageously is it contradicted by the facts. It is quite true that the Socialists are in perfect agreement with one another except on those points on which they happen to differ. They can claim that happy understanding not only among themselves, but with the Liberals and Conservatives as well. But the notion that their differences are at present any less fundamental than their agreements is an illusion.

Shaw said he was convinced that Socialism would not prove worth carrying out in its integrity—that long before it had penetrated to every corner of the political and industrial organisation, it would have so completely relieved the pressure to which it owed its force that it would: "recede before the next great movement in social development, leaving relics of untouched Individualist Liberalism in all directions among the relics of feudalism which Liberalism itself has left". He believed that its dissolution of the petty autocracies and oligarchies of private landlordism and capitalism would enormously stimulate genuine individual enterprise, instead of suppressing it; and that Socialist States would probably connive at highly un-democratic ways of leaving comparatively large resources in the hands of certain persons, who would thereby become obnoxious as a privileged class to the consistent levellers. He added that he thought Socialism at its height would be as different from the ideal of the "Anti-State Communism" of the Socialist League in 1885 as our so-called Christianity was from the ideal of the Apostles and of Tolstoy.

Shaw went on to say that this was not his "principle", but his practical view of the situation; but the fact that he did not think it wrong to take that view, and would unhesitatingly vote for a man who took it as against a man who took what he had called the Calvinist view, appeared to the Calvinist mind to be conclusive evidence that he was no Socialist, or else that he was so cynically indifferent to "principle" in the abstract that he could not properly be said to be anything at all. He con-tinued: "To settle the matter, let us again apply the Jevonian method. Instead of asking 'Are you a Socialist or not?' let us say: 'How much are you a Socialist?', or, more practically still, 'What do you want to Socialize; and how much and when do you propose to Socialize it?' The moment the case is put in this way, all pretence of agreement vanishes."

Later in the same article Shaw declared:—

... By the illusion of the downfall of capitalism we shall turn whole nations into joint stock companies; and our determination to annihilate the 'bourgeoisie' will end in making every workman a 'bourgeois gentilhomme'. By the illusion of democracy, or government by everybody, *we shall establish the most complete bureaucracy ever known on the face of the earth, and finally get rid of popular election, trial by jury, and all the other makeshifts of a system in which no man can be trusted with power.* [*Sic!* My italics.—Ed.]. By the illusion of scientific materialism we shall make life more and more the expression of our thought and feeling, and less and less of our craving for more butter on our bread. But in the meantime we shall continue to make fools of ourselves; to make our journals bywords for slander and vituperation in the name of fraternity; to celebrate the advent of universal peace by the most intemperate quarrelling; to pose as uneducated men of the people whilst advancing claims to scientific infallibility which would make Lord Kelvin ridiculous; to denounce the middle class, to which we ourselves mostly belong; in short, to wallow in all the follies and absurdities of public life with the fullest conviction that we have attained a Pisgah region far above such Amalekitish superstitions. No matter: it has to be done in that way, or not at all. Only, please remember, still in the true Jevonian spirit, that the question is not whether illusions are valuable or not, but exactly how valuable they are.

Having thus warned of the dangers and errors and misunderstandings which Socialists might run into in pursuing their ideals, Shaw declared that, up to a certain point, illusion—or, as it was commonly called by Socialists, "enthusiasm"—was, more or less, precious and indispensable; but beyond that point it gave more trouble than it was worth; in Jevonese language, its utility became disutility. And as the work (of establishing Socialism) required more and more ability and temper, it required more and more freedom from the cruder illusions, especially those which dramatised their opponents as villains and fiends, and more and more of that quality which was the primal republican material—that sense of the sacredness of life which made a man respect his fellows without regard to his social rank or intellectual class, and recognised the fool of Scripture only in those persons who refused to be bound by any relations except the personally luxurious ones of love, admiration, and identity of political opinion and religious creed. Shaw concluded:—

... Perhaps to such a one alone will it be plain that a Socialist may, without offence or arrogance, or the least taint of intentional cynicism, discourse as freely as I have done on the illusions of his own creed.

In a letter to the Press, Shaw wrote:—

... Marx counted on his theory of surplus value to unite all the proletarians of Europe. It utterly failed to do anything of the sort: the International was an absurdly small affair in the light of its magnificent aim.

Shaw would often point out that Marx's name was not even mentioned in *Fabian Essays*, which he first edited in 1889*—and which, basically unaltered, is still (1969) the standard work on the theory of Fabian Socialism. He would emphasise that the latter, far from being based on Marxism, did not contain any elements whatever of Marx's peculiar economic theory and philosophic method, and in a message to the *Labour Monthly* on the occasion of its twentieth anniversary in July, 1941, Shaw linked up his ideas on Fabianism and Marxism with his view of Trade Unionism:—

... Now British Trade Unionism, though Fabianized into calling itself Socialist and adopting parliamentary methods as well as direct action by strikes, is not socialistic: its aim is to exploit the capitalist system so as to secure the lion's share of its product for the proletarian Trade Unionists instead of for the landlords and capitalists ...

Though I am one of Marx's converts I have no use for the Marxist dialectic; my mind does not work in Hegelian grooves, though I had no more difficulty than William Morris had in understanding that private property produces a government of "damned thieves", who cannot help themselves, and must, willy nilly, live by robbing the poor. *Fabian Essays*, which I edited half a century ago, does not

* Not strictly accurate. Marx is mentioned three times:—in a footnote to the article "Historic" by Sidney Webb, and twice by Shaw himself in his article "Transition" (ten and five lines respectively).

mention Marx, nor contain any chain of reasoning on Hegelian lines. It is British from beginning to end, though an Irishman edited it. Later on I had to show that Marx's theory of value was a blunder, and that, like Ruskin, he did not understand the Ricardian law of rent, a grasp of which is fundamental in Socialism.

In a letter to *Plebs* (June, 1943) referring again to Karl Marx's theory of value, Shaw wrote:—

. . . (it) is simple enough to satisfy philosophers who were strong in literary power but, like myself, weak in mathematics.
. . . why bother the British proletarian with abstruse mathematics and Hegelian dialectics? If a baker by working all night makes twelve loaves, and some idler takes eleven and a half of them away from him by organized force, leaving him to console himself with the reflection that half a loaf is better than no bread, is not William Morris's terse definition of the transaction as "robbing the poor", and of the robbers as "damned thieves", good enough? At all events it holds good for Socialism no matter what theory of value may be the fashion.

It should also, however, be borne in mind at this point that Shaw's own views on Socialism, as this chapter continually makes clear, were highly individual ones, and they were often not shared in every respect by his fellow Fabians.

For example, in the *Daily Herald*, 10th March, 1943, Shaw re-stated his controversial view that Marxian tactics broke down ruinously in Russia and gave way to Fabian 'gradualism' under sheer pressure of circumstances:

. . . The revolution in Russia was saved from utter wreck by Lenin's readiness to recognise and remedy his mistakes, and Stalin's sagacious realism and saving sense of humour.[!]. Lenin's New Economic Policy was Sidney Webb's Inevitability of Gradualness under a Russian name.

Shaw added, however—seemingly in direct contradiction to the generally accepted view of Soviet Communism as being based on Marxism, and in contradiction also to his view,

Shaw warmly greeting the Director of the "Underground Press" Section of the Museum of the Revolution in Russia

Karl Marx (for whom Shaw had ambivalent feelings of admiration and condemnation).

One of a set of cards for a lecture by Shaw linking "The Fabian Tradition" with Marx and Stalin

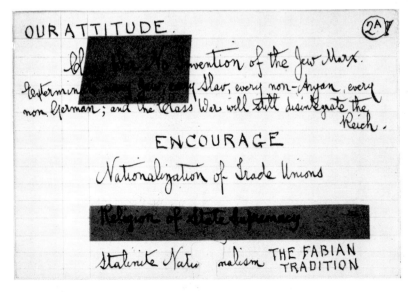

OUR ATTITUDE.   2A

[obscured] ...vention of the Jew Marx.
Exterminate ... Slav, every non-Aryan, every non-German; and the Class War will still disintegrate the Reich.

ENCOURAGE

Nationalization of Trade Unions

Religion of State Supremacy

Stalinite Nationalism   THE FABIAN TRADITION

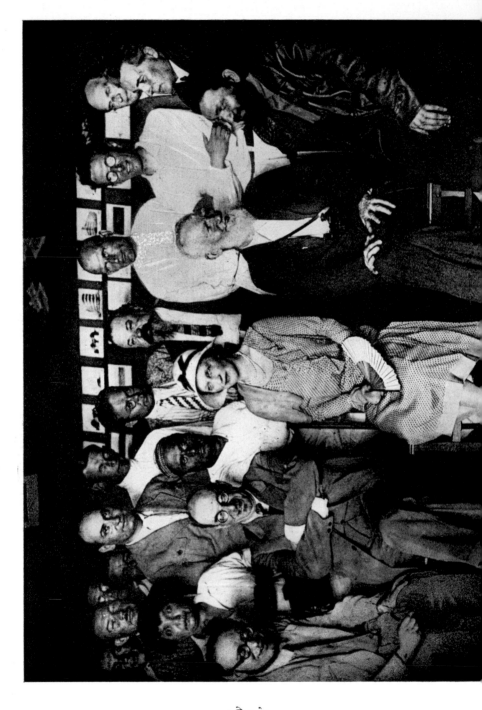

Shaw in Russia with Lunarcharsky and a group of 'hard-core' Bolsheviks

mentioned a little earlier, that the Socialism of the *Fabian Essays* he had edited was entirely non-Marxist in character:—

... Stalin made the supreme change when he declared for Socialism in a Single Country and exiled Trotsky the Internationalist Marxian. Socialism in a Single Country is the Socialism of *Fabian Essays*. And Sidney Webb, the real inventer of Fabian Socialism (for I, had I been left to myself and Marx, might have made most of the mistakes of Lenin) is to-day the leading English exponent of the Russian system, and its most thoroughgoing champion. If ever one man was entitled to say to two hundred millions "I told you so," Webb is that man.

Marxist criticism of Shaw's *Daily Herald* views came from a Mr C. Allen, writing in *The Western Socialist* (Boston, Mass., U.S.A.) of December, 1943. His opinion was that: "Shaw does not know that Socialism means the common ownership of the means of life. This means that private property in the means of life will be abolished in all its forms. There will be no owning class and no working class, no capital and no wages system. Instead, every member of Society will have free access to the means of life."

He charged Shaw with seeking not Socialism, but an improved Capitalist system, and described him as "a bourgeois thinker with a Utopian scheme for the reform of the present system".

Mr Allen also expressed his belief that Socialism in one country was a contradiction in terms: Socialism (by which term he undoubtedly meant what most people call Communism) was by its very nature international in conception. He thought 'Socialism' involved such a complete and fundamental re-orientation of Society that only a revolution could achieve it. (Shaw's view was that Marx had no administrative experience, and dealt with epochs and classes from a theoretical point of view, devoid of practical knowledge of the daily drudgery of government and the immense problems any change from Capitalism to Socialism in a country would involve.)

Allen also considered Shaw wrong in his assertion that "Marxism has produced a new civilisation in Russia", and affirmed that the teachings of Marx were ignored by the Bolsheviks (who made the Russian Revolution). In his view the Bolsheviks, who depended on an illiterate, superstitious peasantry, had not had any chance of gaining power for Socialism, and when they had gained power, they had had no alternative ¡but to carry on the development of Capitalism.

He also thought Shaw quite wrong in imagining that if and when the Socialist Revolution came, it would be accompanied by shooting between different left-wing factions. Socialism, in Mr Allen's view, could only be established by a majority of workers who understood Socialism and organised politically to obtain it. Shaw, he averred, believed that even after the day of the Revolution the working class would still remain as "clay to be moulded by new rulers". Mr Allen's view was that when the working class was ready for Socialism it would not need rulers, for it would be "politically mature" and determined on one single object—Socialism. There would only be elected delegates—and they would take their orders from the workers. Mr Allen thought it something of a joke that Bernard Shaw could possibly imagine that a working class, ripe for Socialism, understanding it and determined to get it, would ever think of electing *him*—Shaw—"or any other anti-Socialist" as one of their delegates.

Mr Allen considered Shaw to have fallen a victim to Bolshevik propaganda, since he was still contending that Socialism existed in Russia, though no longer now attributing its existence to the application of Marxism. But the truth was that Russia (in 1943) was a Capitalist country with great inequality of wealth—the very opposite of Shaw's belief—expressed in *The Intelligent Woman's Guide to Socialism and Capitalism*—that there could be no Socialism where inequality of income existed. Mr Allen added: "However, equality of income is a bourgeois concept that does not apply to Socialism, which is a class-less society where everyone receives according to his needs."

If we go back to Shaw's public statements at the time of the Russian Revolution and shortly after, we find him in 1917, when many Fabian Socialists were wavering in their sympathies, declaring: "We are Socialists. The Russian side is our side". And in a speech at Prior's Field, near Godalming, on 23rd August, 1921, he bitterly criticised other Socialists for their half-heartedness and openly advocated the violent methods of the Bolsheviks if necessary, in order to establish Socialism as he saw it (i.e. a kind of Communism not shared by other Fabians) in Britain. Shaw referred to the "necessities of a Communist system" (in Russia) having turned out to be "of such a character" (i.e. the violent Russian Revolution culminating in the assassination of the Tsar) as to "horrify" most of the Social Democrats of Europe: in short, Socialism was repudiated by the British Socialists the moment it threatened to materialise. Curzon was regarded by them as a superior being, but Lenin was to them "a dirty scoundrel and no gentleman".

Shaw defined "our task" (i.e. British Socialists') as: (1) to change the Nation's mind, and (2) to devise a new constitution and make a new set of laws. He considered that (2) could not be subordinated to (1): because "We may, like the Bolsheviks, be compelled to bring Order out of Chaos" (an ominous phrase!). He regarded the Webb draft constitution as not meeting the case; it suggested the machinery, but not the body of law. What would be the revolutionary factor in the change would be a new body of law, completely reversing the reaction between the Proletariat and the Proprietariat. In his notes he then wrote in Capital letters:—

REVOLUTION INEVITABLE

Coming to the question of "fundamentals", he defined "The Common Morality of Socialism" as "Ruthless extirpation of Parasitic Idleness" and . . . "Compulsory Labour on Pain of Death". The defaulter was a thief, a parasite, a species of social vermin to be exterminated without mercy; and also, by tradition, "a Perfect Gentleman". [!] The "terrible responsi-bility" of the Socialist State he envisaged, after it had been brought into being, was: (1) "Killing", and (2) "Inculcating the State Morality in schools" (i.e. political indoctrination).

This involved the question of "signing death warrants" and "ordering troops to fire". That was easy enough as part of an old and accepted moral code, but there would be a problem raised when the man was to be killed for something that men had never been killed for before—"nay honoured and idolised for", and when the mob was exercising rights which had for centuries been regarded as guarantees of popular liberty. A Socialist government would have to eschew such considera-tions and kill them. Therefore the new public opinion that would be necessary turned out to be "A New Morality" and "A New Religion". (Another decidedly ominous phrase!)

In the *Labour Monthly* of October, 1921, Shaw explained his views further:—

Compulsory labor, with death as the final penalty (as curtly stipulated by St. Paul) is the keystone of Socialism. . . . Socialism . . . like all common moralities, must be founded on religion: that is, on a common belief binding all men together through their instinctive acceptance of the fundamental dogma that we must at all costs not only keep the world going but increase our power and our knowledge in spite of the demonstration (any Rationalist can make it) that the game, as far as the individual is concerned, is not worth the candle except for its own sake.

It was, of course, members of the Capitalist class whom Shaw had in mind when he spoke of "signing death warrants" and "ordering troops to fire". Earlier in his career he had vividly and succinctly described Capitalists in the following terms during an address to the Fabian Society on 19th December, 1890, under the title "Socialism and Human Nature". After observing that "our system of leaving the industry of the country to take its chance in the hands of competing private proprietors" placed a premium on "sordid and unscrupulous

— The Terrible Responsibility —

1. Killing.
2. Inculcating the State morality in Schools.

Signing death warrants
        Ordering troops to fire.

Easy as part of an old routine
        Very difficult when the man is to be
killed for something that men have never
been killed for before — nay, honored & obeyed.
        And when the mob is expressing rights
which have for centuries been regarded as
indispensable guarantees of popular liberty.

        A Socialist Government will have to do both.
Therefore the New Public Opinion turns out to be
                A New Morality and (consequently)
                A New Religion.

ere is
slight
ak in
orig-
l here
→

Shaw always spoke impromptu — helped out by small cards bearing the main topics. The example above was from one of the most violent and seditious speeches he ever gave.

rascality", and "starved out the wider social instincts as if they were criminal", he declared:—

> Our typical successful man is an odious person, vulgar, thick-skinned, pleased by the contrast between his own riches and the poverty of others, unable to see any reason why men should not be degraded into flunkeys in his kitchen or women poisoned by phosphorus* and whitelead in his factory, as long as his pride and his purse are swelled. Need I add that he is religious, charitable, patriotic, and full to the neck of ideals—respectability, true woman-liness, true manliness, duty, virtue, chastity, subdual of the lower nature by the higher, self-sacrifice, abstinence, the constitution, the family, law and order, punctuality, honesty, a good name: he has the whole rogue's rosary at his fingers' ends. How do we contrive to make such a monster as this out of anything so innocent as a man?

Shaw added, however, that if one conversed with "these blackguards" one found them not such fiends as one might expect, but potentially decent enough fellows, who had found that the line of least resistance had led them to unintended enormities, and whose attempt to disguise those enormities from themselves by the clumsy but well meant hypocrisies of idealism showed that they had plenty of good in them— "if only our social arrangements gave it a chance".† It must thus be presumed that Shaw was willing to give Capitalists a chance to change their way of life—reserving only for the most obdurate the sanguinary demise of the firing squad!

Shaw's unusual conception of the apparently contrasting subject of Bolshevism is apposite here. In an article in *The Labour Leader*, 24th April, 1919, headed:—

ARE WE BOLSHEVISTS?

* The reference is to women employed in the 1880's making safety matches, the health of many of whom was undermined as a result of the chemicals involved, and about which there had been a great deal of public feeling, especially among the working class.

† Today there is a much greater sense of social equity and responsibility among people of all political parties in Britain than when Shaw expressed the above sentiments.

he declared:—

Well, of course, we are. What else are we, pray?
Why do we hesitate to call ourselves Bolshevists?
Partly funk, no doubt. But there are other reasons. The name is
ambiguous. Under one definition of the word or another the whole
House of Commons is Bolshevist; and no gentleman could afford
to be mixed up with some of the heroes of the late General Election.

Shaw pointed out that in the mouths of the doctrinaire
democrats a Bolshevist was one who, having given up democracy
as hopeless in view of such events as the afore-mentioned election and the war which had primed it, faced the fact that the
masses are governable only by a mixture of cajolery and
coercion dressed up in fine phrases, and applied by an energetic
minority which knows what it wants and means to have it,
to the majority: "that is, to Carlyle's 'forty millions of people,
mostly fools', formerly known in English as John Bull, Uncle
Sam, or Brother Jonathan, and now rechristened by the more
expressive name of Henry Dubb. This definition ropes in all
our governing classes and their supporters. So we are all
Bolshevists now. Three Cheers for Bolshevism!"
Why then did the British Bolshevist of this second variety
thirst unnaturally for the gore of his brother-Bolshevist of
the primary sort in Russia? Shaw asked. It was true that they
both had the same opinion of Henry Dubb, and acted on it in
the same way, but their aims were different. He explained:—

... Lenin coerces and cajoles in the interests of those whom he coerces
and cajoles, and in the name of the prophet Marx. Our British
Bolshevists (like Fanny Squeers I name no names and say "Let them
as the cap fits, wear it") coerce and cajole in the interests of property,
without bothering about prophets. Profits are good enough for them.
I cannot deny that I am a bit of a Bolshevist myself under the
second definition, though I have called myself a democrat often
enough. One cannot always avoid it when there is a meeting of
Dubbs to be humbugged.

Shaw further stated, in conversation with his American biographer, Archibald Henderson*:—

. . . either the word Bolshevist means nothing at all, or Mussolini and d'Annunzio, Poincaré and Lloyd George and Hamar Greenwood, Mitchell Palmer and the whole Ku Klux Klan, are Bolshevists. All statesmen or adventurers who resort to martial law and suspend constitutional safeguards in an emergency without regard to whether they are in a minority or majority, are Bolshevists. Karl Marx said what was obvious enough: that if there came a revolution, its leaders would have to bridge over the ensuing chaos by assuming a dictatorship. If it were a Socialist Revolution, the dictatorship would proclaim its aims by calling itself the Dictatorship of the Proletariat. That is what happened in Russia, and it got accidentally called Bolshevism. But there is no revolution here; so how can I be a Bolshevist? Now that the chaos has been bridged in Russia, the Bolshevist leaders are sweeping up Bolshevism and sweeping it out. . . . So far, [1924] Fascism is middle-class Bolshevism; and Bolshevism, I repeat, is an emergency policy like martial law.

Shaw was thus far from being always a believer in the Fabian Society's official and specific alternative to violent revolution— i.e. their twin doctrines of 'peaceful permeation' and 'the inevitability of gradualness'. Nor, certainly, was he ever merely an intellectual theoriser on political and social matters! At the beginning of his career as a Socialist, he courted arrest by taking part in the police-prohibited mass meeting in Trafalgar Square in 1887 which came to be known as Bloody Sunday. Even earlier, in 1885, as described on pages 180-1, he spoke of men rapidly growing habituated to and even developing a taste for bloodshed, and countenanced Socialism achieved through Civil War if peaceful means of establishing it should prove ineffectual through lack of adequate middle-class support. And in 1913 he openly preached what at that time was regarded as sedition, and again risked imprisonment.

This occasion was on 1st November, when a great Socialist rally took place at the Albert Hall, London, in connection with

---

* *Fortnightly Review*, June, 1924.

the imprisonment of Jim Larkin, who had campaigned for improvements from the awful squalor and poverty in which the working class of Dublin then lived. The speakers included (besides Shaw) Ben Tillett, George Russell ('A.E.'), F. W. (later Lord) Pethick-Lawrence, George Lansbury, Sylvia Pankhurst, and Mrs Despard. Towards the end of his speech Shaw voiced the following sentiments (as reported in the *Daily Herald*, 3rd November):—

. . . Any Government which will countenance such a thing as the Crown Prosecutor in Dublin charging Larkin with sedition on the ground that he said the employing class lived on profits has reached a cynical depth of absence of all shame which it is hardly possible to characterise without using improper language.

Let me warn the employing class that according to the Attorney-General in Dublin every employer who makes a return that he lives by profits is guilty of sedition. We must make up our minds with regard to working class and industrial questions that we must have law and order.

MAD DOGS IN UNIFORM

What do I mean by law and order? I mean this, that when it comes, as it is inevitable in all civilised communities that it must come—to the employment of physical force, that physical force shall only be applied by responsible men under the direct guidance of an officer responsible to a Minister in Parliament.

If you once let loose your physical force without careful supervision and order you may as well let loose in the streets a parcel of mad dogs as a parcel of policemen. It has been the practice, ever since the modern police were established, in difficulties with the working class to let loose the police and tell them to go and do their worst to the people. Now, if you put the policeman on the footing of a mad dog, it can only end in one way—that all respectable men will have to arm themselves. (Loud cheers. A voice: "What with?").

I should suggest you should arm yourselves with something that would put a decisive stop to the proceedings of the police. I hope that observation will be carefully reported. I should rather like to be prosecuted for sedition and have an opportunity of explaining to the public exactly what I mean by it.

In its leader of 4th November, 1913, the *Daily Herald* commented:—

WHEN DOES G.B.S. GO TO GAOL?

Mr George Bernard Shaw, a man of world-wide reputation, has challenged the Government to prosecute him for sedition, and a section of the Press affects to be awaiting the prosecution with interest . . .

While he was intensely in earnest at the Albert Hall rally, where he threw down the challenge, and while we have no doubt that he would heartily welcome the prosecution, we have a shrewd suspicion that G.B.S. is smiling grimly to himself over the irony of the position.

For the fact is that he is not going to be prosecuted just because he ought to be.

That is to say, as the class-law now stands, or is twisted and distorted, he has very obviously come within the net, within the meaning of the ancient Act. If there was the shadow of a case against Larkin there is palpably the substance of a case against Shaw.

In cold blood, and with the utmost deliberation, he has advised workers to arm themselves so as to be able fitly to deal with the mad-dog tactics of the police—virtually the bosses' police—in times of industrial crisis.

His whole speech was inspired by events in his native City of Dublin, now in the third month of industrial crisis and tragedy. There the memories of police brutality are rankling, and police insolence is an everyday feature of life. Shaw's appeal for the use of arms is likely to meet an immediate response on the part of Irish wage-slaves smarting under their experiences of the Cossacks' savagery . . .

In all the circumstances Mr Shaw's appeal for the resort to arms has come at the dangerously psychological moment. There is nothing theoretical or fanciful or literary about it; it is a frank and forcible incitement to arms and the thorough-going use of them.

All the same, the Government is too cowardly to prosecute him. He is too rich and influential. He is far safer than Carson, because he is far abler and more powerful.

The Government will not venture out of the familar routine of woman-torture* and strike-breaking in its own way. Sending gunboats

* I.e. imprisonment and forcible feeding of suffragettes.

to Leith, unloosing the police savages of Dublin and letting the Lord Lieutenant shirk inquiry into his responsibility, are odious affairs, but they are much simpler in official eyes than tackling a Bernard Shaw or any other rich and world-noted individuality [sic].

And the bosses will encourage the Government to hold its hand. The bosses trust to the efficacy of police barbarians on the one hand and the powers of hunger and cold on the other hand.

G.B.S. has no chance of drawing the Government till he gives up literature, takes a vow of poverty, and starts work as a navvy or a docker.

Shaw's assessment of the differences between Marxism and Fabianism, and his view of Bolshevism, have been given in the preceding pages. It therefore seems appropriate here to include also something of his attitude to the individual brand of English Socialism and Radicalism preached by John Ruskin and his view of the social impact of Dickens.

The following three passages are from a report of an address by Shaw on 21st November, 1919, in commemoration of the centenary of Ruskin's birth.* In it, Shaw *inter alia* coined a new social term—"Tory Communism"—in which he linked the outlook of Ruskin with that of, later, (Sir) Winston Churchill, and again condoned the bloodshed involved in Bolshevist and other violent revolutions as an inevitable necessity for which the instigators could only ask God's forgiveness.

Shaw began by pointing out that Ruskin had been neglected politically by his contemporaries because they had found the plain meaning of his words incredible. If one could imagine him as still alive, was there any political party or activity which he might be expected specially to support? Shaw explained:—

. . . It goes without saying, of course, that he was a Communist. He was quite clear as to that. But now comes the question, What

---

* The report was made by J. Howard Whitehouse, the Hon. Secretary of the Ruskin Centenary Council, which subsequently issued it as a pamphlet in 1921.

was his attitude towards Democracy? Well, it was another example of the law that no really great man is ever a democrat in the vulgar sense, by which I mean that sense in which Democracy is identified with our modern electoral system and our system of voting. Ruskin never gave one moment's quarter to all that. He set no store by it whatever, any more than his famous contemporary, Charles Dickens —in his own particular department the most gifted English writer since Shakespear, and resembling Ruskin in being dominated by a social conscience.

Dickens, said Shaw, was usually regarded as an extremely popular person, always on the side of the people against the ruling class, whereas Ruskin, a comparatively rich man, might have been expected to be on the other side. Yet Dickens gave no more quarter to democracy than Ruskin. He began by unmasking mere superficial abuses like the Court of Chancery and imprisonment for debt, imagining them to be fundamental abuses. Then, suddenly discovering that it was the whole framework of society that was wrong, he wrote *Hard Times*, and after that became a prophet as well as a story teller. Prophets, said Shaw, were not a dead race who died with Habakkuk and Joel: the prophets were always with us (the Dean of St Paul's, Dr Inge, was present). Shaw continued:—

... But Dickens the prophet is never Dickens the Democrat. Take any book of his in which he plays his peculiar trick of putting before you some shameful social abuse, and then asking what is to be done about it! Does he in any single instance say: 'You working men who have the majority of votes: what are you going to do about it?' He never does. He always appeals to the aristocracy. He says: 'Your Majesty, my lords and gentlemen, right honourables and wrong honourables of every degree: what have you to say to this?' When he introduces a working-man, he may make that working-man complain bitterly that society is all wrong: but when the plutocrats turn round on that man and say to him, 'Oh, you think yourself very clever. What could you do? You complain about everything. What could you do to set things right', he makes the working-man say, 'It is not for the like of me to say. It is the business of people who have the power and the knowledge to understand these things, and take it on themselves to right them.' That is the attitude of Dickens, and the attitude of Ruskin; and that really is my attitude as well.

Shaw explained that the individuals who make up a nation's people were each occupied with their own special jobs, but the reconstruction of society was a very special job indeed. To tell 'the people' as a collective entity to make their own laws was a mockery as absurd as to tell them to write their own plays. The people could judge these things, but were (in general) not capable of making them.

Ruskin, like Dickens, had no illusions on this point. Both knew that the reconstruction of society must be "the work of an energetic and conscientious minority", just as government was always "the work of an energetic minority, possibly conscientious, possibly the reverse, and too often a merely predatory minority which produces an illusion of conscientiousness by setting up a convention that what they want for their own advantage is really for the good of society". Shaw continued:—

. . . All our military and governing people who have practical experience of State affairs know that the people, for good or evil, must, whether they will or no, be finally governed by people capable of governing, and that the people themselves know this instinctively, and mistrust all democratic doctrinaires. If you like to call Bolshevism a combination of the Tory oligarchism of Ruskin and Mr Winston Churchill with the Tory Communism of Ruskin alone, you may. So it comes to this, that when we look for a party which could logically claim Ruskin today as one of its prophets, we find it in the Bolshevist party. [Laughter.] You laugh at this. You feel it to be absurd. But I have given you a demonstration; and I want you now to pick a hole in the demonstration if you can. You got out of the difficulty in Ruskin's own time by saying that he was a Tory. He said so himself. But then you did not quite grasp the fact that all Socialists are Tories in that sense. The Tory is a man who believes that those who are qualified by nature and training for public work, and who are naturally a minority, have to govern the mass of the people. That is Toryism. That is also Bolshevism. The Russian masses elected a National Assembly: Lenin and the Bolshevists ruthlessly shoved it out of the way, and indeed shot it out of the way as far as it refused to be shoved.

Some of you, in view of the shooting, repudiate Bolshevism as a blood-stained tyranny, and revolt against the connexion of Ruskin's name with it. But if you are never going to follow any prophet in whose name Governments have been guilty of killing those who resist them, you will have to repudiate your country, your religion, and your humanity. Let us be humble. There is no use in throwing these terms at one another. You cannot repudiate religion because it has been connected with the atrocities of the wars of religion. You cannot, for instance, ask any Roman Catholic to repudiate his Church because of the things that were done in the Inquisition, or any Protestant to admit that Luther must stand or fall by the acts of the soldiers of Gustavus Adolphus. All you can do is to deplore the atrocities. Lenin said the other day, 'Yes: there have been atrocities; and they have not all been inevitable.' I wish every other statesman in Europe had the same candour. Look at all that has been done not only by Bolshevists, but by anti-Bolshevists, by ourselves, and by all the belligerents! There is only one thing that it becomes us to say; and that is, 'God forgive us all.'

Shaw also believed in the Equalisation of Incomes—as the kernel of his 'Communist' faith (and also of his ' Christian' faith, as described in his 1913 Sermon on *Christian Economics*). To *John Bull* magazine on 14th June, 1945, he summed up the ideal State he would like to create and live under as: "A State in which there are neither rich nor poor, but sufficient equality of income to make all the units of population inter-marriageable, as they are now in the section with three or four thousand a year and upward. In short, a basic income sufficient to eliminate ignorance and poverty."

Perhaps no facet of Shaw's political outlook has aroused more misunderstanding than this concept—especially during the last thirty-odd years of his life, when he was himself a fairly rich man. In regard to this aspect, it ought not to be necessary to point out that *believing* in Equalisation of Incomes for society as a whole does not necessarily involve that any pioneer advocating such a doctrine should immediately give away most of his own money as a witness to his faith, prior to the establishment of a new organisation of society in which Equalisation is accepted for everybody. Nor would it be consistent with the Fabian Society's 'gradualness' in which Shaw also believed (at times, at any rate!)—and he was under no illusions that Equal Incomes could be established either easily or quickly.

Equality of Income was, in fact, also central in Shaw's conception of Socialism (which was not, as we have seen, quite identical to his conceptions of Communism or true Christianity —though closely linked therewith). If I may return here temporarily to an early period, in an old Ms. (*c.* January, 1906) in the British Museum, Shaw wrote:—

... by Socialism I mean not only municipal Gas and Water, but the complete acceptance of Equality as the condition of human association, and Communism as the condition of human industry ...

And in a paper on *Advanced Socialism for Intelligent People,* dated 28th May, 1909, on the typescript,* he stated:—

The considerations which lead to Socialism are, in their logical order, as follows:—

1. Unless the distribution of income is regulated by the State, it will, through the operation of natural differences in the productivity of soils and sites and human talent, and of the movement of the population, distribute itself when the primitive stages of civilization are passed, in a disastrous manner, pampering the idle, starving and demoralizing the industrious, misapplying capital to the production of silly luxuries in the midst of a famine of necessities, creating huge and politically powerful vested interests in drunkenness and prostitution, establishing a form of promiscuous slavery in which the

* In the British Museum.

slave's master is not responsible for him, and generally, reproducing all the evils that have destroyed States in the past.

2. That since the State distribution of the national income is thus a matter of life or death, it is necessary to decide the proportions in which it shall be distributed.

3. That the only sane solution of this problem is equal distribution, and that we have now had sufficient experience of the benefits of equality and the mischievousness of inequality to welcome this solution as one of immense promise and encouragement.

Anyone who will subscribe to these three propositions may conveniently and intelligibly be called a Socialist. Anyone who refuses— I had almost said anyone who hesitates—is not a Socialist, and, if he is old enough to have thought much on social questions, probably never will be.

Shaw gave a fuller definition of Socialism as he conceived it during a debate with G. K. Chesterton in the Memorial Hall, Farringdon Street, E.C., on 30th November, 1911.* Hilaire Belloc was in the Chair, and the motion was:

THAT A DEMOCRAT WHO IS NOT ALSO A SOCIALIST IS
NO GENTLEMAN.

(For:— G.B.S. Against:— G. K. Chesterton.) Shaw said:—

. . . By 'Socialist' I mean a person who advocates a state of society which proceeds from one fixed, immutable condition; and that is, that the entire income of the country shall be divided exactly equally between every person in the country, young or old, without regard to their industry, without regard to their character, without regard to anything but the fact that they are live human beings. That is what Socialism means. (Applause; and cries of: "No".) Here we are, we have got the first gentleman who up to this moment has imagined that he was a Socialist and now finds that he is not. (Laughter.) I want to lay particular emphasis upon that definition; because I do not want Mr Chesterton to mistake me as meaning by Socialism

* My extracts are taken from a report made by Mr C. H. Norman, with his kind permission.

Collectivism . . . It is a definition which he will get not from ladies and gentlemen who imagine they are Socialists, or Scientific Socialists, or State Socialists; but it is a definition which he will get from the man in the street, the first person whom he asks. It is the universal, instinctive, real definition of Socialism; it is the correct definition of Socialism. Many people imagine that they are Socialists when they are only Collectivists. The man who really comes at the root of the problem always rushes at the central point of it. He says, "The Socialist is the man who wants to divide up" . . . what distinguishes a Socialist is that a Socialist says that you must divide up equally.

. . . it is a necessity of that, that we must have Collectivism first, because I need hardly tell you that you cannot distribute income until you get hold of the means of production, and [until you] resume that production yourselves you cannot distribute it at all.

. . . I say that if he [the ordinary man] turns round to his fellow-men and says: "I grant you political equality; I grant you religious equality; but I will not grant you cash equality", I say that that man can have no respectable motive for drawing that distinction. I say that practically he is like the officer who should demand 5s. more because he is five minutes more under fire.

G. K. Chesterton began by saying that he did not regard Shaw as a democrat, and had great difficulty in discovering what 'a Socialist' signified in Shaw's mind. He defined a Socialist (differently from Shaw) as: "a person who believes that the present monstrous division of modern property can only be cured by the arm of the Government or the power of the State coming in and coercively claiming all the property and paying it back in wages to the citizens of the State," and added: "I think that most Socialists would agree still that that is the definition of Socialism."

Chesterton flatly disagreed with Shaw's concept of absolutely equal incomes to all human beings without any reference to class, sex, or age (from babyhood upwards), and considered that Socialism and Democracy were distinct ideas, and mutually incompatible if Shaw's definitions were accepted. He believed solely in a more equitable and just re-distribution of incomes than existed at the time between rich and poor. Shaw here countered with one of his old key arguments:—"How can one assess 'justly' what incomes people in different trades, professions, and walks of life should receive?"—Why should the carpenter be paid less than the doctor, since his work is just as essential in society? Or a printer less than a Primate?—and so on.

Shaw gave his definition of a gentleman as a person who could not be bought; who demanded from his country a dignified existence in return for the best service he could give, and felt that any injury to any part of the community was a wound to his own honour. A cad, on the other hand, was someone who would only work for personal monetary gain, not for the benefit of the community as a whole, and Shaw added his conviction that the political government, and the moral and religious education of the country, were largely in the hands of 'cads'; that was why he was a Socialist.*

* Shaw's definitions of A Gentleman and A Cad were given in greater detail in his lecture notes for this debate (now among his papers in the British Museum):

No Gentleman. Definition of Gentleman.

Instinctive objection to be paid for his work—the doctor.	
Final objection to be paid for anything but his work and resolve *to* be paid for that.	His humility.
Continuous attitude of captain of sinking ship.	
Continuous attitude of sharer of short rations.	
His acceptance of social service. Soldier and Servant.	

His objection to prostitution and journalism.	
„ „ „ tipping at his club.	
„ „ „ trade.	His pride.
„ „ „ submit to any will but the will of God.	
„ demand for a handsome, dignified and leisurely subsistence.	

„ pugnacity and courtesy. Resist ye evil and Praise of Virtue.

„ Humanity—a feeling that Inasmuch as ye have done unto the least of these ye have done it unto me.

A Cad. Definition.

Cannot see why he should do anything without being paid for it.
Cannot bear anyone else getting any benefit from what he does.
Will do anything he is paid for if he cannot get paid more for doing something else.
Has no objection to gaining at the expense of others—likes it, in fact.

Chesterton's reply was that he thought the condition of the proletariat under a Socialist State Administration would be little, if any, different in practice from what it was under the existing organisation of industry, although he would like to see property distributed among a far greater *number* of people— i.e. a "peasant proprietary civilisation" such as "already existed in many other parts of the world".

Shaw later in the debate agreed with Chesterton that it was normal and reasonable for people to have *some* personal property—some things which they could call their own. What he (Shaw) was proposing was a *redistribution* of property—and since he had no desire to take away people's right to choose the property they wanted—be it a racehorse or a gramophone— this meant redistribution of money—of personal incomes.

By the term 'property'—which he thought should be distributed equally—Shaw meant not small personal belongings, but *property in general*: that is to say, the Nation's wealth and resources.

Hilaire Belloc, in his summing-up from the Chair, described Shaw as a Communist (rather than a Socialist). Like Chesterton, he considered that Socialism, as normally understood, meant distribution *justly*, not necessarily equally; a *sufficiency* to all.

Fourteen months later Hilaire Belloc was himself involved in direct debate with Shaw.* Shaw enjoyed his debates with these two Catholic friends and coined the term "Chesterbelloquacity" for their discursive arguments. The occasion was at the Queens Hall, London, on 29th January, 1913, under the Chairmanship of Sir John Cockburn. Belloc moved the resolution (diametrically opposed to Shaw's views) that:—

IF WE DO NOT RE-ESTABLISH THE INSTITUTION OF PROPERTY WE SHALL RE-ESTABLISH THE INSTITUTION OF SLAVERY: THERE IS NO THIRD COURSE.

He began by defining the sense in which he used the words 'property' and 'slavery'. He might be asked, he said, why he

* My account is derived from reports made by Central News Ltd., and the *Morning Post.—Ed.*

talked of re-establishing property, and whether the institution of property did not still exist among them. In that great audience he imagined that most persons had heard of it and some few enjoyed it. What he meant by the re-establishment of property was the re-establishment of such a state of affairs as did exist in the main in Christian European Society, under which the means of production—land and the instruments of production other than land—were owned by the greater part and a determining part of the inhabitants of any Christian country. By the institution of slavery he meant that institution in the State whereby a considerable number of human beings were compelled by positive law to produce wealth of which a portion went not to themselves, but to certain privileged persons, and in which so large a proportion of human beings were condemned to such work by positive law as to determine society, and give it its note and character. That was what he called a condition of servitude.

Throughout the whole of history, Belloc continued, from the dawn of civilisation, through the Assyrian and Egyptian eras to our forefathers in the West, it had been taken for granted that a free man must own property and the means of production, and that a man who did not was clearly a slave and compelled by positive law to work for the advantage of others. But Belloc did, nevertheless, agree with Shaw (and also with Chesterton) in opposing the giant financial and industrial organisations, cartels and newspapers, in whose hands, or under whose control, the nation's 'means of production' largely rested—i.e. a very small number of hands who were not representative of the people as a whole.

Belloc then observed that Aristotle was "not without intelligence", and had said of the majority of men that they were born slaves. He (Belloc) did not say he agreed with Aristotle; he thought the crux of the problem was that the means of production was held by only a few in our industrial society, but he felt bound to claim that, despite this fact, everyone, including the vast majority who didn't own, was free.

He argued like Chesterton against Shaw's idea of State-run enterprises on the grounds that there was very little difference in practice between State-supported Capitalistic ownership in the hands of a few State officials, and control in the hands of a few private Capitalists. They were both minorities, and the ordinary man was equally under their thumb.

Belloc continued:—

Mankind, as you will know if you examine yourself, and more so if you will examine your neighbours, is a thing of a multiplex sort. It is organic. You can care for it, admire it, read about it, dream about it, suffer for it, hate it, and love it. It is not an idea, but a thing, and mankind, up against numerous problems, has solved these problems throughout the ages in a fashion consonant to itself. That is what you would expect. A cat does not bark but mews, and man has done human things and not inhuman things . . . There arose the problem of freedom, and he solved it by the organic, complex, and very interesting and human phenomenon of the State. That big problem, the control of the means of production, has been up against him from the beginning, and he has solved it by an institution as complex, as organic, as human as could well be found, and property is its name. Where you find property destroyed, there you find, as in [contemporary] England, misery in human lives.

Hilaire Belloc enjoined the audience to buy his book *The Servile State** if they wanted his further views on the historical aspects and his full logical argument. Belloc, while differing from Chesterton in some respects, agreed with him in being in favour of the *juster* distribution of private property; Shaw said *abolish* it, and *distribute services to the community*, and as a consequence distribute income.

Shaw, when his turn to speak came, pointed out that a man like Mr Cadbury, for example, not only drank and manufactured cocoa, but he had organised the cocoa industry, and thus organised that part of human service which is devoted to the

* Not in print at present (1971) but obtainable second-hand in various editions, or from public libraries.

production of cocoa. He had been thereby enabled financially to become master of a section of the press,* and as a result of that, had obtained control of a large part of the lives of everyone in the community. Shaw considered that private property corrupted every human institution: the reason that the Church lost its hold in the Middle Ages was because it was corrupted by private property. (Belloc disputed this.) Private property made the parson the ally of the squire. Private property bought the Church, bought justice, bought law, corrupted bishops, juries, and judges. . . . A hundred years earlier every man in America could get property for the asking—land without paying a farthing. Everyone knew what had happened. There was no greater home of slavery on the face of the earth than the United States of America. It had grown not from the old historical source of conquest, but from the institution of private property. "I prefer Socialism," Shaw exclaimed.

In reply, Belloc said, amongst other things:—

The normal man is a maker, an artist, and needs freedom, and only property can give freedom. Short of that you don't get production working. That is the whole of my argument. It is an organic and human argument I put forward. I put it forward as a solution because the only other non-human institution corresponding to the complexity and necessity of man is an institution which I don't say I dislike, but which is certainly evident within the modern industrial system, and that is the institution of slavery. That is the argument.

Shaw, returning to the fight, quoted Belloc's statement that Socialism as a conception of service was an unreal thing, and pointed out that Belloc had said again towards the end of his speech that the only security was in property, and thus the poetic part of man demanded property and security. Shaw then said:—

* The Cadbury family owned the politically Liberal and Radical *Daily News*—subsequently called the *News Chronicle* and now defunct. (Incidentally, and paradoxically, the staff were regarded in many quarters as having been treated in a decidedly commercial and ungenerous way when the paper ceased publication.)

I completely deny, I violently deny that. If there is one class of man who is indifferent to property and does not want property, it is the poet —just as a man who is unpoetic, sordid, and away from the poetic standpoint will desire property, cling to property, see nothing else but property. That is what I meant when I contended against Mr Chesterton that if a man is not a Socialist he is not a gentleman . . . Now let us see the actual feeling of mankind. Mankind do not want property; they want service and security, respect and comfort. They don't want exceptional degrees of these things. On the contrary, they want status. They want religion and political direction which they can depend on, and give them that and status, and they are perfectly willing all to take the same income, the same pay for the same service. It is entirely false to conceive of mankind as a number of persons struggling to take advantage of one another . . .

Mr Belloc says that service of the community is not the same thing as service of God. That puts God in a very invidious position. Of course, it is perfectly true that a very large number of people worship in the name of God the thing which is really the Devil—a malign influence. If you talk of a god that is going to set up interests opposed to those of the community, well, that god won't do for me. I really don't think Mr Belloc can be quite serious in that contention . . .

We all know by this time, I hope, that the thing we call Heaven is really a sort of ideal of the thing we want to bring the earth to. I have a very definite conception of Hell as a place where peasants perpetually plod, where peasants continually try to cheat. Heaven is a place where there are no peasants, a highly organised community where very elaborate things are done . . . where what is done is done of co-operation, the willing service together of men working with a high degree of education and noble aims under very high guidance, not the guidance of newspapers which are the property of persons who prey on the community.

Then it was Hilaire Belloc's turn once more. He re-affirmed his belief that the law of God did not necessarily coincide with service to the community, and said that even if it meant that he could make the community happier by breaking the law of God, he would not do it, and conversely, if he would make the community miserable by keeping the law of God, he

would make it so miserable that it would wish it had never
been born. Heaven to him was 'infinite variety', and Hell was
the opposite thing. As to Shaw's contention that Catholicism
was the religious aspect of Collectivism—why, the one force up
against Collectivism in the modern world was Catholicism.
Belloc advised the audience to go and live for three weeks as if
they had no property. He had lived like that for many years,
he said, and considered he knew under which of the two conditions a man was more free.

He added that he was not against all State enterprises or
officials, some of which were essential, but he considered the
State "diseased" when officials acquired "preponderating
power in certain functions of human life which are normal to
the sub-units". He continued: "When you get officials muddling
between men and children, when you get compulsory free
education, you all know what a hash it is, or perhaps you don't
know, but the poor know to what a Hell it is leading. There are
things in which an official is out of place, and as I contend, he
is always out of place in the economic function; certainly in
the productive function." Belloc concluded that he believed in
free proprietors in colleges, in guilds, in families. He maintained
that Collectivism, working through officials producing and
then distributing justly, had no basis in reality, whether in
history—where it was never to be found—or in one's own soul,
if one knew what one's appetites were, and, as the best test of
all, tried to live in accordance with it.

Shaw, in his final rejoinder, said Belloc had allowed his own
arguments to crumble in his hands. He thought everyone,
especially artists, would be happier with the security of fixed
incomes paid by the State instead of having to sell themselves
on the labour market—which he regarded as the inevitable
result and consequences of private property.

He admonished Belloc:

Why do you sit down and despair and say the thing can never be
altered? If we are to believe that, let us go and cut our throats,

Shaw with Hilaire Belloc and G. K. Chesterton

*"Excuses for thieving—requires certain qualities
which ought not to be discouraged . . ."*

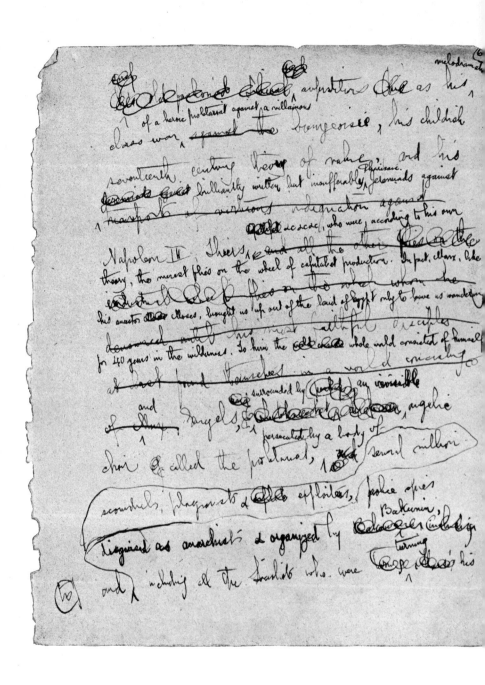

A heavily corrected page from Shaw's article
on Marx quoted on page 220

though I am not sure that we might not do a little more good by beginning to cut other people's throats. I am prepared to go that length if the existing system could be put an end to.*

The Chairman, Sir John Cockburn, in winding up the debate, said the combatants had been true sportsmen and the blows very fair. He concluded: "I suppose that we shall go away with very much the views with which we came. We shall have to fall back upon the old Book, which both debaters seem to take as the great repository of wisdom, and the dictum that the love of money is the root of all evil. At the same time we shall not part with what we have got, and we won't go away sorrowful." [!].

Both Belloc and Shaw had agreed that there was a world of difference between servitude (in the sense of servility) and service, after Shaw, early in this debate, had reminded the audience that "the greatest of all Socialists" had said 'Call no man your master'. Shaw pointed out that no Socialist had ever said 'Call no man your servant', and added: "I was baptised a servant; there is nothing I would rather have said to me at the end of my life than, 'Well done, thou good and faithful servant'." We were all born to servitude (of the social kind); anyone who shirked it was putting the cost of his existence on to someone else, and was therefore a thief or a beggar. Shaw concluded the debate by declaring that contemporary society did indeed consist largely of thieves and beggars.

An illuminating and amusing complement to the last sentence is contained in the course of some notes for a lecture on Socialism given by Shaw at a number of places between 1886 and 1888†:—

EXCUSES FOR THIEVING

Requires certain qualities of mind and body which ought not to be discouraged. Courage, Enterprise, Patience, Calculation, Abstinence, Foresight, Risk, Outlay, Employment to many people.

---

* Another instance of Shaw advocating violent revolution!—in direct contradistinction to the official policy of the Fabian Society.
† Shaw Mss., B.M.

Are you going to discourage these by punishing the thief?

Yes. A Virtue is a quality exercised for the good of mankind.

    A Vice   ,,   ,,   ,,   ,,   harm ,,   ,,

"Whatsoever thy hand findeth to do, do it with thy might."
Ecc. ix. 10.

... A Social System is not good because it encourages or checks any
individual qualities. It must compel them to act for the welfare of
the Community ... We dont punish the Thief for his Courage etc.,
but for consuming what he does not replace.

Shaw went on to pose the question: "But are all Thieves
punished by Law? No. There are two classes of Thieves who
carry out the Laws, and they take good care not to punish
themselves: the Landlord and the Capitalist."

The *religious* case for equality of incomes was given in detail
by Shaw in his "Christian Economics" sermon, and some
readers may wish to refer back to that address, either now or at
the end of this chapter. Shaw on that occasion included also a
brief but vivid résumé of the *secular* (as distinct from the
religious) case—on which, he said, he lectured more often. One
such occasion was at the National Liberal Club on May 1st,
1913, under the title "The Case for Equality". It added certain
points on the secular aspect to what Shaw had included in his
more comprehensive "Christian Economics" speech, and also
expressed some of his main conclusions differently, and, as the
subject of Equal Incomes is a complex one (and was regarded
by Shaw as his most important and original contribution to
Socialist thought) some of the secular arguments Shaw made
at the National Liberal Club will be recapitulated briefly here
with a view to giving as complete an exposition as possible.

To begin with, there was the impossibility of ever formulating
any quantitative comparison between people of different
natural talents and occupations. Human capacity, he averred,
is not a measurable thing. That is to say, a good carpenter is
just as socially necessary and valuable as an Archbishop. Shaw
was fond of illustrating his argument by giving himself as an
example of someone well above his fellows in ability:—

... Taking some person whom we will call X, an average man, you may think ... that I, perhaps, ought to have fifty times as big an income. But if anybody asks you: "Where did you get that numerator of fifty from, and what does your denominator represent?" you will be compelled to give it up. You cannot settle it. The thing is impossible ... the idea that every man could get his value; all that is the vainest Utopian dream; and the most ridiculous, the most impracticable idea that ever came into the head of men ... It would have been far more sensible to go at the question in the old mystic, religious way; when you would have immediately seen that all human souls are of infinite value, and all infinities equal.

Shaw conceded that obedience and subordination are necessary in society. One could not have a civilised society unless tolerably large bodies of men were willing to obey other men, even by executing orders that they did not themselves understand. This, said Shaw, was the foundation of our feudal inequality, and in order to make a common man obey some other man, you had to make that other man uncommon in some way—by making him much richer, differently dressed and housed, and generally considered as of a higher class, whose progeny could not be expected to mix socially with or marry ordinary people. In short, it amounted to the setting up of idolatry to secure subordination in society. But Shaw also believed that the general attitude to idols was fast changing. The popularity of King Edward VII and King George V was due not to a belief in them as extraordinary and supernatural persons, but to the precisely opposite belief in them as rather good fellows much like ourselves. This (according to Shaw) disposed of "the last and only argument in favor of *inequality* of income: absolutely the last one".

Shaw's objections to inequality of income were thus threefold: political, economic, and socio-biological. As regards (*a*) Political objections: if you had inequality of income, you would have— even with universal franchise (women had not gained the vote at this time)—the opposite of real democracy. There would be class government based on plutocracy, and no real representation of the people in Parliament. How could wealthy men like Asquith or Balfour possibly understand or represent poor men with only £50 or £60 a year? Even if they wanted to, public opinion would not let them. Public opinion was controlled by the newspapers, and the newspapers were controlled by their plutocratic owners.* The result was that any genuinely democratic popular government in this country was ruled out.

As regards economic objections (b), inequality of income meant that much of the nation's labour resources were expended in producing luxuries for the relatively small group of people who could afford them, and not nearly enough on the necessities of life, because the poor often could not afford these. Shaw claimed that this argument was backed by Ricardo's law of rent and Jevons's law of value, and that this argument alone was overwhelming against inequality.

Shaw then expatiated on (c), the socio-biological reasons for equality. He told of how his father had forbidden him in his childhood to play with the son of a shopkeeper, because he (Shaw's father) kept a mill, and considered that a wholesaler like himself was in a higher and totally different social class from a retailer. In addition, Shaw described how, as a baptised Irish Protestant, he had been brought up to regard the great bulk of his fellow-Irishmen as condemned to eternal damnation because they were Roman Catholics. There was so much social prejudice of all sorts, Shaw considered, that the answer to the social problems was ultimately a new sort of man. This led him to the question of eugenics.

As to what constituted a good man—only nature could give a right answer. The class structure in society was maintained

---

* Shaw exaggerates a little here. There were a fair number of radical and reformist newspapers and magazines already in existence, though admittedly their circulations were relatively small. Examples are: the *Daily News* (later the *News Chronicle*), the *Labour Leader* (now the *Socialist Leader*), the *New Age*, the *Christian Commonwealth* (later *New Commonwealth*), the *Freethinker*, the *Clarion*, the *Athenaeum*, the *Daily Herald*, started a year or two earlier, and, of course, the *Nation* (now incorporated in the *New Statesman*).

largely by the non-intermarriageability of its members. Only a great widening of the area of possible sexual selection could create a classless society, and this depended on having equality of incomes.

A number of arguments were raised by members of the audience at the National Liberal Club, including the following:—

(1) People are not equal in their capacity to make good use of income.

(2) Big, hefty people need more food than thin, wiry types (and hence need more money); also men need more than women, and adults more than children.

(3) Some people could not appreciate expensive clothes because they have no taste.

(4) Many people in the Independent Labour Party were revolting against the absolute application of arithmetical equality and 'roller-flattening'; they were beginning to see that it was not good for themselves or society that there should be only one level of wages.

(5) Shaw was too sweeping when he said that a wealthy man could not understand or sympathise with a poor man with only £50 or £60 a year.

(6) A wealthy man buying an 80 h.p. car was helping to keep down unemployment, and indirectly helping exports and the nation's prosperity—and hence ultimately increasing the ordinary man's purchasing power.

(7) Sexual attraction is not necessarily a good guide to marriage. It can be mere infatuation, and the offspring then may grow up in an atmosphere of dissension and conflict—even of violence perhaps—which would make their characters far from the eugenic ideal envisaged.

(8) People with the same illness or physical defect are often attracted—consumptives or dwarfs, for example—and their offspring would not be eugenically ideal.

(9) The class into which a person was born under the existing organisation of society was amply wide enough to give all the scope that could be needed for falling in love with another member of it. Each class in Britain included many millions of people.

Supporters of Shaw countered that nothing could change the fact that the adequate feeding, clothing, and housing of starving people should take precedence over the question of building expensive motor-cars; and that Old Age Pensions, and other social services which tended in the direction of equality, were excellent things, even if perfection was seldom, if ever, achieved in life.

Shaw regarded most of the objections as trivial, but dealing with one questioner, he said:

. . . it is quite true that Labor is now getting more and more political power; and the important fact you have to face is that the Labor men are not gentlemen; that is to say, that they have been trained up for generations in the idea and habit of each man selling himself for as much as he can get. The consequence is they are thoroughly against this idea of equal distribution. Every man of them thinks that he should have more than somebody else . . . These are the men into whose hands, by exploiting them, by selling them in the market, you have hammered from their very birth this abominable idea that men should be bought and sold according to what can be got out of them. These are the men who are gradually waking up to the fact that political power is within their reach as soon as they make up their minds to give up idolizing the upper classes. . . . I am trying . . . to show the utter and final impossibility of going on with the plan of every man trying to get as much as he can, and a little more than other people . . .

Shaw claimed that equal incomes were more or less the rule *within* each class, and he did not see why they should not be practicable between people of *all* classes. Shaw's view was that the real gentleman would be primarily concerned with giving his country and his fellow-men the best service of which he was capable, and this would automatically rule out trying to get for himself a more lucrative, handsome, and dignified existence than his fellows—which would mean that equality of income would be perfectly satisfactory to him. He would inevitably wish that his own standard of life should be shared by everyone else, not better than everyone else's, and that the *general level* of life in the country should be raised. What the country needed, said Shaw, was the inculcation of a greater sense of social and religious feeling; that is to say, the creation of a far greater number of 'true gentlemen'. When this had been accomplished, "all other things would be added unto them."

A controversial report of Shaw's lecture appeared a little while after the event, in the *Nation* of 10th May, 1913, and some interesting correspondence ensued. The author of the unsigned report (it may or may not have been the Editor, H. W. Massingham) began by quoting Lloyd George's statement in his Budget speech a year earlier that out of 425,000 men and women who had died during 1912, only 70,000—or one in six—had had any property worth mentioning, while of the aggregate possessions which had come up for Death Duties, two-thirds belonged to 4,000 persons, and one-third to 292 persons. No one, he wrote, could possibly contend that so gross a disproportion had any relation whatever to deserts, talents, productive energy, needs, or any personal considerations whatsoever. Everyone, in fact, admitted the social waste and injustice of the existing inequality of property and income. Thus it was not surprising that Mr Bernard Shaw had had no difficulty in convincing the National Liberal Club members that inequality of income lay at the root of most of our social maladies. All social reformers, whatever party they supported, were in fact committed to levelling processes of one sort or another. But such measures as were already operative, such as Wage Boards and other minimum wage proposals, and progressive taxation of incomes and property (especially the super-tax) were no more than palliatives of the "monstrous" social malady. Democracy was unattainable while wealth remained so unequally divided among the population. The *Nation*'s writer agreed with Shaw that if Britain was to be a worthy and a happy nation, a better ordinary type of man and woman must be reared than most of those they saw around—healthier, better looking, more vigorous in body and in mind, better bred, better mannered, and more public spirited; beings who, in comparison, might well appear as Supermen and Superwomen. Nature had made provision for such evolution by liberty of mating under sexual selection. The worst sin which our inequality of income had committed against humanity was, as Shaw had said, its abridgement of this natural liberty by setting up an elaborate series of social barriers which practically confined choice of mates for each within a narrow section of society. Add to this the absolute economic dependence on men of most women, which limited them still further as regards their free choice for marriage and maternity, and the full enormity of the crime of inequality became apparent. At this point, however, the *Nation*'s writer's sympathy with Shaw ceased. He considered Shaw to have been "driven by an evil genius of combativeness" in pressing a meaning of equality which was impracticable of application. The allotment by society to all its members, men, women, and children, of an exactly equal share of the general income was, he declared, an extreme position, "only irresistible to a wit and logician who wanted to put on to his adversaries the appearance of defending some criterion of inequality".

The difficulties of deciding exactly how much different kinds of worker ought 'justly' to receive might be admitted, but "a fatal fallacy" lurked beneath Shaw's concept of formal equality of income, for it not merely permitted, but ensured, an inequality in the *utilisation* of income. This was not so obvious when one thought of income in terms only of money, but when one thought of *real* income—the stock of food, clothing, etc., that was actually distributed through money— the truth came out. If, for example, the nation's food supply were distributed on an exactly equal basis to men, women, and children, irrespective of age, size, type of employment, health, or even appetite, there would be "a maximum alike of waste and want, and the widest inequality in the amount of good got out of the different units of the food supply". And what applied to food would also apply to clothing, house-room, books, travel, recreation, medicine, and every other form of purchasable goods that went to make up the real income of the nation. Nor was it in the least true that liberty of purchase would redress the balance by enabling persons who needed less food to apply the money they saved on food equally advantageously in some other use. The fact that different persons could not make an equally good use of the same money income in terms of personal satisfaction, meant that an equal distribution of money income would involve inequalities of waste due to the fact that the equal distribution of money income would only substitute one form of inequality for another. He considered that the ordinary Liberal with his formula of 'equality of opportunity' was really on much sounder egalitarian ground than Shaw with his 'equality of money income' conception. Equality of opportunity was, "in accordance with the general law of organic distribution, 'according to needs', the ability of cells, organs, or other co-operative units of an organic whole, to utilise, in healthy vital activities, the food which comes to them". Theoretically, the maximum equality of use obtained from each unit of the social income, and the maximum aggregate utility of the whole income, would require a different rate of income for every person in the community, precisely because no two persons were the same in the amount of their requirements. Though all attempts at such accurate discrimination would be foolish, that was no reason for falling back upon a doctrine of the uniformity of human nature which "had long disappeared from all sober thinking upon politics or economics".

The *Nation*'s writer went on to suggest that an even more vital objection was the danger that such equality might be expressed entirely in a process of levelling *down* to poverty, rather than in a levelling *up* to security and comfort—owing to a shrinkage of the total income available for division on this equal basis. The notion that when the degrading influences of competition were removed, and everyone put on his honour to perform his share of work, the social instincts of common humanity would respond by an adequate amount of willing work, only sounded plausible so long as one ignored the inevitable proportion of useful work which must always retain the repellent character of drudgery. If it were to be replied that society would be ready to insist upon each man doing his share in return for the equal income he received, the difficulties of entrusting the officers of society with the enforcement of this rule would be quite as great as those attending the distribution of income according to merits or needs. Emerson had certainly not been deficient in either humanity or moral idealism, and had merely expressed the fruits of observation when he said: "Mankind is as lazy as it dares to be." Nor had one to provide a sufficient spur only for routine work; it was also necessary for "the intolerable toil of thought" upon which progress in the arts of industrial improvement so largely depends.

In the *Nation*'s writer's opinion, Shaw's views were a "fallacious application of mechanical equality to the solution of an organic problem", at a time when his Fabian colleague Sidney Webb and others were placing all their emphasis on a minimum and not a maximum, and thus, by not placing all upon an equal income basis, envisaging the possibility of "a play of serviceable competition within legitimate limits". The enforcement of *a minimum* standard only, would leave intact the strongest incentives to both workers and employers to do their best work, by giving them some gain over and above that contained in the application of the minimum. Surely it was along these lines that social reformers should move? The writer concluded by urging the necessity of "recognising that large measure of equality which common humanity involves, and which man's inhumanity to man continually violates", but thought "those other elements of inequality which mark one man from another and constitute his individuality" should not be ignored. Equality, he considered, consisted in "treating things that are equal as equal, and things that are unequal as unequal". The doctrine of absolute equality of income violated the latter section of the law.

Shaw replied to these criticisms in the *Nation* of 17th May. He considered that the *Nation*'s writer had misunderstood his arguments in a similar way to the contemporary sociologist Professor L. T. Hobhouse. He, Shaw, had never claimed that Primrose Hill was equal to Mont Blanc, or the scientist Lord Kelvin equal to Oscar Wilde the playwright—or either of them 'equal' to Sir Tatton Sykes, a well-known contemporary horse-breeder. But everyone was agreed as to the enormous evils produced by poverty, by government in the hands of the wealthy and privileged few, and by the control of public opinion by owners of newspapers, etc. It was not to the point to say that different types of people would not enjoy their equal incomes equally—he had never said they would. Equal enjoyment was not the aim of his proposed reform. Shaw explained:—

Daniel may be a Falstaff and Tom a prey to persecution mania. Daniel may be able to digest a flat-iron, and Tom unable to tackle anything beyond a charcoal biscuit and a bottle of Salutaris without agonies of indigestion. Or Tom may revel in Beethoven, Wagner, and Richard Strauss, whilst Daniel may not be able to distinguish the Hallelujah Chorus from "Oh, You Beautiful Doll!" Well, Tom and Daniel must put up with their shortcomings—that is all. If you give Tom ten times Daniel's income to make up for Tom's bad digestion, which, I am afraid, is what the suggestion in your article comes to (at least, if it does not mean that, I cannot see that it means anything), you will not only still fail absurdly to equalise their happiness by improving Tom's digestion tenfold, but you will introduce all the appalling evils of inequality of income as to which there is no dispute.

Let me put the case in terms of the article. "The fact that different persons cannot make an equally good use of the same money income in terms of personal satisfaction means that an equal distribution of money income would involve inequalities of waste, due to the fact that the equal distribution of money income would only [*sic*] substitute one form of inequality for another." Precisely: it would substitute, or rather leave untouched, a form of inequality which does no harm for another form of inequality which, as the writer himself admits, wrecks whole civilisations and makes them wretched while they last. But he is not satisfied: he must have equality of waste as well. Why? What harm does inequality of waste do? Is waste a benefit to be distributed as widely as possible, like wealth? What we want to get rid of is the huge waste of life and welfare caused by inequality of income.

Shaw then expressed his conviction that there could be no equality of opportunity under conditions of inequality of income. The man with a thousand pounds in his pocket had far more opportunity than the man with only three-halfpence in his pocket; the man with an expensive university education behind him (albeit paid for by his parents) had far more opportunity than the working-class man with little education. Shaw continued:—

. . . What other equality can be given them or maintained between them? Can they be given equality of opportunity as mathematicians with Newton and Leibnitz, as classical scholars with Porson and Bentley, as poets with Shelley and Shakespear, as money-hunters with Rhodes and Barnato, as generals with Cæsar and Napoleon? It would have been just as easy to give Johnson and Boswell equal incomes as it was to make Johnson poor and Boswell rich; but that is all the equality that could ever have been established between them, of opportunity or anything else. He who is not in favor of equality of income is not in favor of equality of opportunity; and the positing of the one as an alternative to the other is a mere confusion of thought.

Shaw also thought that the *Nation*'s statement, "Equality consists in treating things that are equal as equal, and things that are unequal as unequal", was utter nonsense. Equality as the carrying out of a political principle by the Government— which was apparently what the writer was referring to— consisted in treating claims which were grotesquely unequal as equal; i.e. claims to justice, to protection of life and property, to votes, to old age pensions, to insurance, and (Shaw contended) to income—no matter how wisely or unwisely, how happily or unhappily, how equally or unequally, these things might be exercised or enjoyed.

Shaw concluded his letter by challenging the sociologist Professor L. T. Hobhouse to explain a statement made by him a few weeks earlier in Manchester, to the effect that the redistribution of incomes—which he had agreed was necessary—should be based on the relative amount of *exertion* put by different individuals into their work. How was the exertion to be measured? And secondly, how was the relative satisfaction from money gained by different individuals to be measured?

A comment by the *Nation*'s writer appeared in the same issue, as an appendage at the foot of Shaw's letter. Its gist was that, although existing inequalities of income caused great evils, it did not follow that inequalities of income which corresponded to the admitted inequalities in the ability to use income beneficially, would be just as bad. And what was the object of the reform if not equal enjoyment in the sense of equal benefit? What was distributed in monetary incomes except benefits? What benefit could there be in giving equal amounts of food to people with different food needs? Various tests of physical or intellectual capacity were possible, e.g. a punching bag, a walking match, a 'general paper' (written examination), or even the output in some standard work test. Though output might not be a thoroughly reliable measure of exertion, or exertion of capacity to use income, it did at least furnish some test and some reasonable presumption of beneficial use. But Shaw's equality of incomes concept would ensure that the money income of the community would be made to yield a smaller *aggregate* amount of enjoyment, benefit, and utility, than any such proposed alternatives, however grotesque they might appear to be.

The eminent Professor L. T. Hobhouse entered the fray in the issue of 24th May. He considered Shaw's method to be "too much that of a prosecuting counsel who said: 'On my theory the prisoner committed the murder. You say he did not. Then tell us who did; or, if you cannot tell us, agree to hang this man'." He denied that he had ever postulated a measure of the gratification different people demanded from money, but as regards exertion, time and piece work were rough measures and better than none. It did not seem to be fair and just that a man should receive the same payment for two hours' work as for one (of the same kind), or for making two pairs of boots as for making one pair—or, for that matter, for making none at all.

Hobhouse said he had never contended that income should be wholly apportioned according to the amount of exertion involved, but he did believe that in a good social order, exertion in directions useful to society might justly be made a condition of obtaining any income at all. But he also thought that it should be open to men and women to increase their incomes by increasing their exertions. Professor Hobhouse's concluding comments were (1) that it was possible to agree in condemning the extravagant inequalities of the day without believing in absolute equality as the remedy, and (2) regarding Shaw's view that equality of opportunity necessarily involved equality of income, it might be true that we could supply a man with the lengthy education of a Newton, but we could not supply him with Newton's brains, and his education would cost money. Furthermore, once educated, why should we supply the man with an income throughout life regardless of whether he worked or idled? This was not to give equal opportunity, but to give equal treatment to the man who used his opportunities and the man who neglected them. As to economic conditions being the only factor in opportunity, there were also such things as colour and sex disqualifications which were important to those who laboured under them.

Shaw wrote again in the issue of 31st May, commenting that Professor Hobhouse had not put forward any proper alternative plan to his, and that some plan was better than none. He also pointed out that equality of income did not imply equality of remuneration—he had never said a word about remuneration. He explained:—

... Remuneration is rubbish—tradesman's rubbish. How are you to remunerate a baby? What are you going to remunerate it for? Yet the baby's share of the national income is of supreme importance, because infancy is the period at which poverty does most harm. How are you to remunerate the unemployed? How are you to remunerate the soldier in time of peace? Remuneration may serve stupid and selfish people as an excuse for leaving others to starve when no profit can be made out of them: it is not a conception that becomes a professor and a gentleman. No matter how you distribute the national income, a good deal of it will have to go otherwise than under the form of remunerating services. It is true that the people who receive it will contract a debt to society. How to make them discharge that debt is another matter. But some of it, in the nature of things, cannot ever be discharged. A share of a child who dies before it is old enough to produce anything but the joy its existence may give to its parents and itself is economically a bad debt that must be written off. Therefore, the confused attempt to make distribution secure the solvency of society by distributing income only under the form of remuneration, is absurd. It reduced itself to absurdity even in the eyes of Parliament under Elizabeth; and the attempt to revive it when commercialism got the upper hand politically in the nineteenth century has led to the hell of poverty and inequity out of which we are now struggling to escape.

As to Hobhouse's concluding statements, Shaw asked: how could the increased exertions of men and women be useful to society unless they increased the income of society: that is, of all the other men and women at the same time? There was one way, and one way only, in which men and women could in any real sense increase their incomes by their own exertions, and that was by effecting an improvement in the arts of life in which everyone shared. No doubt there were people who wished to be richer than their neighbours, not for the sake of making larger purchases, but from sheer uppishness. The remedy for that was simple—snub them.

Shaw pointed out that Hobhouse had admitted that he could not see how reward in terms of income could be measured, but had put forward several possible methods of measuring exertion. Shaw entirely disputed these, considering that a community in which all had to work the same number of hours in order to enjoy the same "remuneration" would find out its mistake in a week. Professor Hobhouse's notion that two hours' work meant twice the exertion of one hour's work was the notion of a bricklayer; and as Professor Hobhouse was not a bricklayer, he (Shaw) could not imagine how he came to entertain it. At some kinds of work men could, and even sometimes did, work sixteen hours a day at routine jobs without holidays and without nervous breakdowns. But an attempt to do original literary, scientific, or artistic work for four hours a day all the year round without holidays would "end in a lunatic asylum, a retreat for dipsomaniacs, or the cremation furnace". Even in the same occupation, the exertion varied from hour to hour as the worker tired. It was quite a mistake to suppose that the fact that a dock labourer was paid twice as much for two hours' work as for one meant that his wage was proportionate to his exertion. His work was measured by the hour because, being bought and sold in the market, it had to be measured somehow; but the recipe was fixed by supply and demand at twopence an hour, and by trade union combination, founded on a conception of a man's needs, at sixpence. A barrister might get, for a day's work which did not exhaust him, five hundred and twenty-five times as much as a dock labourer, who went home from work dog-tired and sub-human. Yet Professor Hobhouse had remarked, in a superior manner, that "time and piece work are measures of exertion which do not belong to Utopia, and however rough, are better than none".

Shaw denied that he had ever said that economic conditions were the only factors in opportunity. He had observed differences of colour, and had heard of differences of sex [!]. He did not believe that any readjustment of economic conditions would enable Professor Hobhouse "to bear twins or to achieve popularity as a Christy Minstrel". If Hobhouse really thought that he was expected, on this account, to get less than his charwoman, or than the nearest Negro with an ear for music, Shaw urged, "let him say so at once and be removed to a lunatic asylum".

As regards Professor Hobhouse's statement about supplying a man with the education of a Newton, but not with his brains, Shaw said he thought it would certainly be necessary to supply the man with an income throughout his life, whether he worked or idled, because it was the social evils arising from economic inequality that he wished to see removed, and this radical change in the social organisation was not dependent on a few individuals who did not pull their weight. Such people should in any event not be allowed to remain poor and ignorant, either relatively or absolutely.

Professor L. T. Hobhouse had the last word in this press controversy, in the *Nation* of 7th June. He observed:—

[Mr Shaw] is out for fun and knows that he can get it. . . . He has only to stand on the platform for the gallery to snigger. When he opens his mouth, it laughs. When he says, "You are a professor and ought to be in a lunatic asylum," it roars at this subtle and delicate wit. . . . Mr Shaw no doubt enjoys himself vastly, but he suffers a much worse penalty than the mere temporary humiliation which he inflicts on his opponent. His power of indiscriminate ridicule is a ring of Gyges, which, by making him invulnerable, ends by making him incapable of self-criticism. Confident of his gallery, he takes his own most whimsical arguments, his fanciful analogies, his strained generalisations, his distortions of his opponents' words, for serious reasoning. He most pitiably deceives himself, and the truth is not in him. In controversy Mr. Shaw wins every battle and loses the campaign. For his methods silence an opponent but convince nobody; even the gallery, when it goes home, is quite aware it has had a good laugh but has learnt nothing.

Hobhouse explained that what he had contended was that, in any system which was likely to work, exertion would have to be a factor in reward, and that for work of the same kind, time and piece rates were rough measures of exertion. Mr Shaw, ignoring the condition "of the same kind", had romped and ramped about at length upon the absurdity of comparing a labourer's work with a barrister's, leaving the reader with the impression that the absurdity was his, Hobhouse's, whereas of course he, Hobhouse, was fully aware that even in the same occupation every hour was not the same as every other. Furthermore, Shaw knew, of course, that even in competitive industry time rates took account of fatigue.

Professor Hobhouse continued:—

Mr Shaw asks how I should remunerate a baby. I should not remunerate a baby. I should feed and clothe him, or, as a member of society, I should see that his parents have the wherewithal to feed and clothe him. Not all that a person receives is "income". Income means a regular supply of money which the recipient can spend as he will, and Mr Shaw's baby, with £40 a year, would not know what to do with it, except to swallow the sovereigns. But the adult and responsible person does need an income. He needs it as a basis for the guidance and direction of his own life, and if he is healthy and fit, he owes society the exertion of his powers in useful ways as a return. On this point Mr Shaw and I are agreed. But Mr. Shaw says that the way to make people discharge their debt is "another matter". That is precisely where we join issue. It is not another matter. It is precisely this very matter of remuneration. Guarantee to everybody a fixed income, entirely irrespective of his work, and you will be reduced with Mr Shaw to admitting that, if he does not work, you will have to kick him, shame him, or even kill him. Precisely so. Give up the principle that work and pay go together, and you will be driven to much rougher, more despotic, and less efficient methods.

Professor Hobhouse concluded:—

... It is no wonder that "Society" takes kindly to Mr Shaw's revolutionary ideas. "Society" is safe so long as Socialism is in Mr Shaw's hands. Nor is there a more convenient armour against a serious assault than a plausible formula which no one intends to apply to things, which has, in fact, no point of contact with things, but serves simply to discredit anyone who makes a serious attempt to deal with things by attacking existing inequality at the point where it is, in fact, most vulnerable.

A more sympathetic attitude was expressed by the Editor of the American *Metropolitan* magazine (who printed "The Case for Equality" in December, 1913, and even offered a prize for the best essay replying to Shaw's case.—Nearly 3,000 were received). The Editor commented in the February, 1914, issue that the ideal of Equality was nothing new: it was embodied in the French Republic's motto "Liberty, Equality, Fraternity", and in the American Constitution: "All Men are born equal . . ." The difficulty was that there was no agreement on what constituted equality. What Shaw had done was to provide one perfectly legitimate definition of it as something based on equality of incomes. And even if it might possibly prove an unattainable ideal, it was well worth aiming at, just as Jowett had said of Plato's Republic that there were many questions which could not be answered, but were nevertheless well worth the asking. . . . The hope of the world was built on ideals.

This Editor* also asked: "Why should great organising power be worthy of a special reward, as against great muscular power?" In his view, what was meant by 'equality' was an equal opportunity for self-development and for the enjoyment of life, and Shaw's contribution was that the means to the accomplishment of that was equality of income.

On another occasion Bernard Shaw observed:—

. . . The fact is that you cannot equalize anything about human beings except their incomes.

In other words, what Shaw really believed in (paradoxical though it might seem) was human *in*equality; it was precisely for this reason that he also believed in equality of income—so

* H. J. Whigham.

that every individual should have an equal opportunity to develop, in his or her unique way, his or her special talents and interests. (More orthodox Socialists than Shaw thought the answer lay not in equal incomes, but entirely in abolishing privileges and 'unearned' incomes, and nationalising or socialising industry. These courses, they held [and some still do], would not increase centralised bureaucratic power, but would give what Shaw wanted—economic democracy. No man could get rich if he had access to no value except that which he produced, and few would want to. The freedom from poverty and power which would be thus established, would free men to pursue other ideals than money or power. They would be free to devote their lives to the work they really wanted to do and were best fitted for, as a result of being freed from the necessity of devoting most of their working life merely to earning a living.)

From the earliest days of his adoption of Equality of Income as the cornerstone of his personal Socialist faith, Shaw had acknowledged that it was open to important criticisms as well as possessing advantages. In a draft article written 1890 approximately, and headed "The Social Danger of Inequality"* he admitted:—

... This doctrine of equality is not at all times a popular one, because, though the majority suffer by inequality, yet the few become rich by it; and until the chances become desperately unfavorable, each individual hopes to become one of the few more than he fears to be one of the many. Lotteries are popular for the same reason. . . . But there is a limit to the popularity of a lottery. . . . Even inveterate gamblers will not run a prodigious risk for an infinitesimal chance. In the same way, inequality, though popular whilst there is chance enough of rising to flatter every man's ambition, excites rebellion when not only specific ambitions, but even vague hopes, are crushed by the improbability of realization. The boy to whom the bells seem to say "Turn again, Whittington, Lord Mayor of London" is

* Shaw Mss., B.M.

content that there should be a master above the apprentice, because he intends to be a master some day, and that there should be a Lord Mayor above the master, because he intends to be Lord Mayor some day. But the boy to whom the bells say "Get up to your day's drudgery, without the slightest prospect of escaping from it until you sink, worn out, into the workhouse" will not be reconciled to that fate by a book narrating how [a few] laboring boys out of millions rose to eminence by "self-help".* He would much prefer the certainty of a modest equality to so slender a chance of fortune.

The above passage refers to inequality of *opportunity*—albeit based on inequality of income. There is, of course, much greater equality of opportunity today than in 1890 or thereabouts when it was written—and this is directly due to the work of Shaw and others.

In the same draft Shaw pointed out that the earnings of even the highest paid hospital nurses and miners were insignificant in comparison to those of prostitutes and jockeys (today this is even more true if one thinks of film stars and pop singers) and emphasised the wrongness of ascribing the sordid condition of the poor of those days to laziness, lack of thrift, and other deficiencies on their part:—

. . . Armies of clever servants, court dressmakers, jewellers, gamekeepers, and the like are organized for the amusement of persons who are already satiated with amusement, and for the care and nurture of their pets, dogs, cats, and birds, whilst the bitterest needs of thousands of hard workers are left unsatisfied. . . . If . . . the line of cleavage between riches and poverty could be shewn to correspond, however roughly, with the line of cleavage between thrift and extravagance, temperance and intemperance, between virtue and vice generally, or between any particular vice and its opposite, the inequality of purchasing power which has led to these anomalies would gain a certain moral sanction. . . . [But] The poor man is coarsened by drudgery: hunger tempts him to pilfer; unhappiness

* The reference is to the book exhorting individual initiative and enterprise entitled *Self-Help*, by Samuel Smiles, which had a great vogue at the time Shaw was writing.

tempts him to drink; the necessity of sharing one comfortless room with his wife and children drives him to keep order by harshness and violence; neatness of apparel he cannot afford; and even personal cleanliness costs an effort of which dwellers in well appointed houses have no conception. More fortunate persons are apt to ascribe his poverty to his coarseness, his ignorance, his untrustworthiness, his intemperance, his incivility and violence, and his disreputable neglect of his appearance, whereas these are, on the contrary, to be ascribed to his poverty.

Shaw stressed that raising the lowest income levels rather than decreasing the higher income levels was the important thing. He succinctly summarised his basic outlook in the same draft article: ". . . the socially important point is that no man should have less than enough. To have the few surfeited and the many in want is an immeasurable social calamity. To have the many satisfied and the few surfeited is hardly even an inconvenience."

Half a century later, in the *Observer* of 13th August, 1944, Shaw, still pursuing his theme of Equality of Income, asked:—

What is the amount of money everyone ought to have to keep civilisation safe and steady? I have had to think this question out, because I am an absentee landlord, a capitalist, a "renter of ability", and by conviction a Communist, which is a combination much more frequent than that of Communist proletarian. In fact, the professed Communists know less about it—if possible—than the rest of our politicians, and, if left to themselves, will attempt to solve it by a plundering match between the rich and the poor, which will end, not in there being no poor but in there being nobody else.

Shaw's contention above that his own brand of Communism was "a combination much more frequent than that of Communist proletarian" is controversial, to say the least. Shaw was again here using a social term—'Communist'—in a highly individualistic and completely different way from that commonly understood by it. (Other differences between Shaw's and 'orthodox' Communists' outlook were given on pages 210-14 *et seq.*, and 229-30.)

Shaw then insisted that the Basic Income must be equal for everybody, because as it applied to newly born babies, centenarians, and families, it could have no regard for differences in personal qualities, talents, and deserts. In this 1944 *Observer* article he summarised twelve key points in his conception:—

(1) The political object of equality of income is the prevention of the ruptures and compound fractures, the internal strains, conflicts, and civil wars, caused by the division of society into financial classes, each struggling for the lion's share of the national income, and nobody being assured of getting any share at all except as a pauper. Every former civilisation known to us (there are half a dozen) has been wrecked by these strains; and ours is going the same way.

(2) This suggests that the best possible distribution of the national income is equal distribution.

(3) It seems to follow that the Basic figure can be ascertained by simply dividing the income figure by the population figure.

(4) It does not follow immediately. The national income provides about four shillings per head per week. A family of two parents and three children would have £1 a week to live on, with no possibility of adding to it by their labour, already absorbed by its production.

(5) The Cabinets, the executive public services, the judiciary, the Bar, the scientific institutions, the cultural institutions, the directors of business and finance, all of them necessary to high civilisation, cannot be recruited from families living on a pound a week.

(6) Nature (sometimes called Providence) produces the necessary percentage of specially capable people; but as this is a percentage, not of any class, but of the entire population, the basic income to be aimed at must be a family income sufficient to put within everyone's reach the cultural home atmosphere and schooling without which natural capacity cannot develop. Four shillings per head per week would mean cultural sterilisation, ending in a relapse into primitive tribalism.

(7) Equality of income must therefore begin with a basic income large enough to produce prime ministers, higher mathematicians, historians and philosophers, authors and artists, as well as ploughmen and dairymaids. They are necessities, not luxuries nor parasites.

(8) Such an income has been estimated by Mr. H. G. Wells at £4,000 a year in present terms. But from eight to twelve hundred would do to begin with. This, in a scientifically organised society, would command a handsomer life than £4,000 does now. Later on, with volcanic blow holes and our British tides harnessed to industry and agriculture,* £800 a year would go farther than our £20,000.

(9) For the present, however, so high a basic income as £800 puts equal division of the national income out of the question for the moment, as the national quotient falls so far short of it. In Communist Russia it has been found that to maintain the indispensable "intellectual proletariat", even with Communist secondary education and "centres of rest and culture" within everyone's reach, it is necessary to distribute income in wages and salaries at rates varying as widely as ten to one.

(10) This means that the basic rate will be enjoyed at first by only 10 per cent. of the population. Only what is left can be distributed among the 90 per cent., who in the factories and mines, the ships and trains and city offices, have only to do what they are told and need not think about it.

(11) From this point progress towards equality of income must depend on increased production. The thinkers and directors being sufficiently paid, and the rank and file underpaid, the increase must be used to raise the family incomes of the rank and file until they, too, can afford the privacy, the leisure, the culture, and all the other

---

* Shaw had the far-sighted idea that one day the pressure and heat of the gases existing beneath the earth's crust, and the inexorable forward and backward movements of the ocean's tides, could be tapped and harnessed, so as to supply unlimited power for industrial and domestic purposes. Shaw's use of the term 'volcanic blow holes' is rather curious, but the ideas are not as absurd as they might at first sight seem, being in the first example something analogous to creating springs of water from subterranean levels, or to the process by which oil is extracted from the earth—when great force and energy are evident in the 'gushers' (quite apart from the qualities of the crude oil itself). And as regards the second, the harnessing of the tides is only an extension of the already widely used water-wheel principle which provides energy not only from streams running alongside farms, but from natural waterfalls or man-made dams for the huge electric power stations situated on them. And others besides Shaw have suggested harnessing the tides—e.g. on the Severn. Indeed, such a scheme has actually been constructed on the French coast at Dinard. Known as *La Rance* Tidal Power Station, it was completed in 1967 and is now fully in operation.

amenities and opportunities which the basic income commands, and which, applied to family life, supply the nurseries from which the thinking and directing functionaries are drawn.

(12) During this process, all attempts and pretensions of the receivers of the basic income to keep their distance above the rest by having their incomes increased must be resisted. Those who have enough must be content with it until those with less than enough are raised to their level.

Shaw then asked, what was to be the test of sufficient equality to make civilisation stable and secure? Would it be achieved when for every two and sixpence allotted to the Astronomer Royal, his housemaid was allotted half-a-crown, both of them being indispensable? Theoretically this might be so, but in practice not, because with the spread of culture there would certainly be competition for the post of Astronomer Royal, and also an increase in the already widespread objection to the drudgeries of housemaiding which could only be countered by adding inducements such as electric fires, vacuum cleaners, luxurious kitchens and servants' bedrooms, bathrooms, and the like, combined with higher wages, shorter hours, and the abandonment by people like the astronomer of all pretence to social superiority.

The test would be intermarriageability. When the astronomer's son could marry the housemaid without the slightest misalliance, the trick would be done.

Shaw added, however, that throughout the whole process of equalisation, certain considerations would have constantly to be borne in mind by the directors, who must not be mere doctrinaire idealists. The road to equality would have to start from inequality—not the haphazard sort of inequality which made millionaires of a few children in arms, and paupers of masses of people worn out by toil that began at school and continued into industrial slavery—but a scientific inequality based on the cost of production of the various grades of human capacity. The greatest geniuses did not need more food, better clothes, a warmer fire, or a more rainproof roof than the ordinary people:

in fact their clothes lasted longer, and they ate less. But they cost
more for Society to produce, and this fact had to be recognised.
They would need not only chairs, tables, beds, and other basic
necessities of life, but plenty of books, pictures, musical
instruments, and other luxuries without which they could not
develop their talents. Moreover, Shaw believed that: "they
must have mothers and fathers to whom such things are
necessities, and whose manners and language differ accordingly
from those of illiterate laborers who are barely kept alive until
they reproduce themselves. Here and there we may come on a
peer who began as a farmer's boy or a millionaire who began as
a bootblack; but there are not enough of these swallows to
make a summer."

Shaw, who thus clearly believed in a differentiated class
structure from the *cultural* point of view, *also* believed that
(at any rate to begin with) Equality of Income should not be so
rigid as not to make *extra* funds available to the superior,
talented, top 5 per cent. of the population. He considered that
neither the industries nor the professions could exist without
from 5 to 10 per cent. of intelligentsia, and that it would be
disastrous to depend on the 0·001 per cent. who might break
their way through from the labouring classes to the top. The
Bolshevik revolution in Russia, beginning with a ruthless persecution of the existing Tsarist education and culture, had soon
found out that it could not organise its army without a majority of
ex-Tsarist officers, nor its industry without bourgeois bosses,
nor its Cabinet without ministers who had never in their
lives handled hammer or sickle to earn their living. Shaw
added:

. . . The U.S.S.R. is really a Fabian Federation, forced into that
mould by sheer pressure of hard facts on Marxian good will towards
men. The same pressure will operate here on Primroses and Reds
impartially. Progressive Conservatives are not lacking in good will.
The struggle will be between the progressive Levellers-up and the
catastrophic Levellers-down; and the Progressives will win if and
when they learn their political business.

A little over a month after Shaw had expressed the foregoing views, another article by him appeared in the *Observer** in which he admitted that no one knew exactly what the national income was, and that he had dramatised it at 4/- per head per week, though this must have been a mistake, as 40/- was what it would be if one accepted the figure often estimated for the national income, of £4,000 million. This, divided by a population of 40 million, gave £100 per head per year, or approximately £2 per head per week.

Shaw added that he thought it would be necessary to give the masses only *half* their 'equal' share of 4/- (or 40/-)—i.e. to give them 2/- (or 20/-) per week only, and to distribute the remainder of the national income among the 'top' 10 per cent. of the population (i.e. giving them approximately 11 times as much each) so as to give them leisure enough to cultivate arts and letters and science, and thus be educated adequately and fitted to conduct the nation's government and finances— including the "direction" of the labour of the masses (the other 90 per cent.) and the "control of their conduct".

To make the arithmetic of this clear: if one takes the strictly *equal* distribution figure as being £2 per head per week, then 100 people would get £200 between them. Under Shaw's somewhat remarkable qualification to the conception of 'equal' incomes, 90 per cent. of the population (i.e. 'the masses') would get half this, £1 per head per week (a total of £90 for 90 out of 100 people), and the "top 10 per cent" would share the remainder of the £200—i.e. £110 between them, thus getting £11 per head per week.

Shaw concluded his letter:—

. . . My point was and is (*a*) that a sane and civilized modern State must determine a basic income sufficient to produce a full social complement of civilized citizens, (*b*) that no family should be too poor for its gifted members (if any) to reach this level, (*c*) that from this point of view distribution of leisure is as important as distribu-

* On 24th September, 1944.

tion of money, and (*d*) that the basic income must have priority and the general level be worked up to it by increased production until culture is within everyone's reach.

I will now add (*e*) that when this level is attained, then and not until then can Liberty and *Laissez-faire* be safely allowed another turn.

In his penultimate statement on Equal Incomes, in the *New Statesman* of 29th January, 1949, Shaw reiterated that he was not "a crude and negligible advocate of 'dividing-up' the national income in equal shares", adding that he believed, on the one hand, that where Capitalism had failed utterly was not in production, but in distribution; and on the other, that without economic equality there could be no democracy, no optimum order of production, no justice, no eugenic breeding: in short, no Socialism. The Webbs, he said, had, after initial hesitation, agreed with him, and from that time onwards Equalisation of Incomes had become an integral part of Fabian policy*—and indeed, "bowdlerised as Equality of Opportunity", in all the party programmes.

How actually to achieve 'Equal Incomes' Shaw admitted to be a difficult problem:

. . . An instantaneous equal division would be catastrophic: it would destroy civilisation, because the national dividend would be at most a few pounds or even shillings per family; and the next generation of proletarians would be left without culture or instructed directors whose cost of production includes not only food and drink, clothing and lodging, costing no more for an Einstein than for a hewer of wood and drawer of water, but a home in a handsome house with pictures, books, and a piano in it, and a school within its means in which all the[ir] children can qualify for a university degree or a profession.

---

* This is inaccurate. The Fabian Society declined to publish Shaw's original lecture "The Case for Equality" in 1913, as they did not, as a body—whatever the views of some leading members may have been—subscribe fully to Shaw's views on this particular matter. (Equality of *opportunity* is, however, a part of Fabian doctrine—as it is, indeed, of the doctrine of most political parties nowadays.)

Shaw obviously would have included himself in the 'instructed director' class. He seems to have had in mind the professional classes in general, and artists, writers, philosophers, and teachers in particular—after the fashion of the 'Guardian Class' in Plato's *Republic*.

Shaw repeated his agreement with H. G. Wells that the ideal figure to which incomes should be levelled-up was £4,000 a year.* The *real* cost of achieving this apparently high figure would, he believed, be much less—in the region of only £800 per annum, if rent and education were socialised. He did not think the precise figures important; his point was the great all-round benefit to be derived from the revolutionary social change of introducing the basic income.

Shaw's meaning appears to have been that if *everyone* was enabled to achieve—as the result of public organisation—the standard of living enjoyed by a person receiving an income of £4,000 under the contemporary state of society (in the 1930's and '40's) the 'real' cost would be reduced to approximately £800 by efficiency and mass production. (An analogy to this would be the high cost of individually produced motor-cars before 1914 and their comparatively low cost under mass production twenty or thirty years later. It was standardisation that enabled the Germans to produce the Volkswagen at an extremely low price within the reach of almost all—and Henry Ford and W. R. Morris [Lord Nuffield] to do the same much earlier in America and Britain respectively).

Shaw again urged that completely successful intermarriageability between people of all trades, professions, and callings in life would be the real test of equality, arguing that people who had been brought up on family incomes of a few pounds a week could not, under the existing social conditions, expect to marry successfully with people in the millionaire incomegroup. But if there was a basic income of £4,000 there would

* This was in the 1930's and '40's. The equivalent figure today (1971) would be considerably greater—around £15,000-£20,000.

no longer be any social barrier, because at this level all the basic human needs would be adequately catered for in everyone. He added that millionaires could not eat fifty dinners a day, or wear a thousand suits of clothes, and he therefore could not see any need for arithmetically equal incomes *above* the basic level of £4000 a year. He declared:—

... When everybody has the basic income it will not matter a rap if one in a hundred thousand or so has ten times as much to play with.

In his article written for the Soviet Press in 1948-9 (already quoted from, in other connections) entitled "Bernard Shaw on Peace", he added (referring to millionaires):—

They can do nothing with their spare cash but endow new social experiments, found new institutions, make great collections of works of art, finance scientific research, or the like, all very desirable activities to be taken over later on, if successful, By [*sic*] the State.

It is pertinent to point out that regarding earlier calculations about Equal Incomes of a somewhat comparable nature to the figures quoted in the last three or four pages Shaw said, when asked about them in a newspaper interview in 1929:* "These calculations are utter nonsense except for the purpose of comparison when the same data are used. All you have to depend on is the flat fact that every worker can produce enough for himself and several others as well. Stick to that and it will not let you down."

And in a letter to the *Daily News* dated December 8th, 1904, Shaw had affirmed:—

... The doctrine I expounded at Chelsea was simply that the evil resulting from the existing unequal distribution of wealth is so enormous, so incalculably greater than any other evil, actual or conceivable, on the face of the earth, that it is our first duty to alter it into an equal distribution. It is no more necessary to fix a maximum

* Interview by Hayden Church in the *Sunday Dispatch*, 6th January, 1929.

than to prevent a man from being honester, if he wishes, than the law compels him to be; but what is necessary is a minimum.

Shaw made the above statement in the course of a reply to critics who thought he was preaching complete equality of all human beings in every respect—which, Shaw agreed on a number of occasions, could never be possible or even desirable.

In this passage, however, and in his two *Observer* articles, Shaw does not seem even to believe strictly in *economic* equality. His view, it would seem, is that it is the *minimum* standard that should be equal—though this may strike some people as a contradiction in terms of the expression 'Equal Incomes'. (One is inevitably reminded of the sentence in George Orwell's satire *Animal Farm* to the effect that all members of the farm community are equal, but some are more equal than others.)

However, in fairness to Shaw, a further quotation from the above-mentioned letter to the *Daily News*, 8th December, 1904, is apposite here. He was replying to criticisms by a correspondent, Mr E. H. Passey, and to a *Daily News* editorial which included the assertion: ". . . we come to this quaint conclusion: that so keen an observer of men and manners as Mr Shaw is utterly blind to the truth that economical [*sic*] equality is as unattainable as physical equality, and that we find him floundering in the quagmire of an impossible ideal, misled by the Will-o'-the-Wisp of a fundamental fallacy". Shaw declared:—

It is the people who write and talk like that whom I would bury in the back garden. . . .

What can you do with such people except, as I suggest, inter them decently in the nearest flower-bed? From the humblest ranks of the Army to the upper division of the Civil Service they see exact economic equality imposed on thousands of men of the most diverse tastes and capacities. In society they see Sir Oliver Lodge and Lord Kelvin dining on terms of perfect equality with sportsmen who do not know the difference between an ion and a logarithm.

They see the criminal law imposing its one crushing level of honesty and forbearance on the thief and the trustee, the ruffian and the Quaker alike. They see the trade union dictating the docker's tanner and the artisan's tenpence without the least regard to the fact that no two of them are alike. They see, in fact—or if they are too unobservant to see anything (as one suspects must be the case) the first Anarchist they meet will point out to them—that the great objection to law is that it ignores individual differences, and is essentially Procrustean in its action. And then, calmly staring all this in the face, they tell you that I am "blind to the truth that economic equality is as unattainable as physical equality".

... I am not bound to keep my temper with an imposture so outrageous, so abjectly sycophantic, as the pretence that existing inequalities of income correspond to and are produced by moral and physical inferiorities and superiorities—that Barnato* was five million times as great and good a man as William Blake, and committed suicide because he lost two-fifths of his superiority; that the life of Lord Anglesey has been on a far higher plane than that of John Ruskin; that Mademoiselle Liane de Pougy has been raised by her successful sugar speculation to moral heights never attained by Florence Nightingale; that the relative personal merits of "The Pall Mall" leader writer, Mr Ernest Passey, and myself are in the precise ratio of our incomes, and that an arrangement to establish economic equality between us by duly adjusted pensions would be impossible. I say that no sane person can be expected to treat such impudent follies with patience, much less with respect.

Shaw—although he regarded himself as a Communist, and was regarded by others as a Fabian Socialist—clearly believed, as part of his unique personal political faith, that there would always be differences among individuals as regards intelligence and mental capacity, and also (as mentioned at the beginning of this chapter) differences in their

* Barnett ('Barney') Barnato, 1852-97, the English financier and multi-millionaire diamond magnate. He was largely responsible for the 'Kaffir boom' in 1895, but when a recession set in he lost two-fifths of his fortune (he had been one of the richest men in the world) and in 1897, aged only 45, he threw himself into the sea during a voyage from South Africa to Britain.

moral outlook. In *Everybody's Political What's What* (published in 1944, five years earlier than the *New Statesman* letter referred to in the previous pages) he proclaimed that:—

... When democratic Socialism has achieved sufficiency of means, equality of opportunity, and national intermarriageability for everybody, with production kept in its natural order from necessities to luxuries, and the courts of justice unbiased by mercenary barristers, its work will be done; for these, and not a mathematical abstraction like equality of income are its real goal. The present stratification of society will be levelled up until the largest possibilities of human nature are no longer starved; but it will still be human nature with all its enterprises, ambitions, and emulations in full swing, and with its pioneering superior persons, conservative average persons, and relatively backward inferiors in their natural places, all fully fed, educated up to the top of their capacity, and intermarriageable. Equality can go no farther.

Shaw's conception of Socialism and a classless society was thus concerned with the removal, mainly, of classes defined by, and primarily caused by, economic factors,—i.e. different income groups. 'Classes' in the sense of different divisions and sections of society arising as a result of the other factors mentioned (i.e. different degrees of intelligence, different trades, professions, interests, and moral outlook) he clearly regarded as inevitable in society. He was concerned with the importance of certain standards of decent material conditions as the only possible basis for the development of the individual, within each individual's natural limitations.

Shaw also urged (in his interview with *John Bull*, dated 14th June, 1945) that all votes for representative authorities should be coupled votes: that is, for a man and a woman simultaneously so that the elected authorities should consist of men and women in equal numbers.

The subject of Women in Politics was dealt with more fully by Shaw in *The Leader* of 25th November, 1944. After admitting that:

. . . In politics I have always worked with women and taken counsel
with them; . . . Yet I have always been in hot water with the
Suffragists. I described Adult Suffrage as the reduction to absurdity
of our pseudo-democracy. . . .

Shaw described how, when Mrs Pankhurst and her daughters
had swept Feminism out of the rut of the parliamentary Liberal
road, and made "Votes for Women" the slogan of a guerilla of
militant saboteuses, he had been the speaker at a Suffragist
meeting, the heroine of which was a rich lady. This lady being
married to a poor man who was legally liable for her surtax,
had refused to pay it herself, and allowed the Crown to take
her husband's body in execution and imprison him for life, in
"the old Pickwickian fashion" which was a royal prerogative.
This action was being held up by the Suffragettes as an outstanding example of self-sacrificing devotion to the Cause on
the lady's part. But Shaw's comment was: ". . . if my wife
treated me so, I would never speak to her again. I was
immediately set down as a bitter anti-Feminist and advocate
of the forceful feeding of Suffragette hunger strikers."

Shaw added that he had given even more serious offence
when he had suggested to the Suffragists that Votes for Women
would probably not secure the return of even one woman to
Parliament, and might do a great deal to prevent it. What was
really necessary, Shaw thought, was a Constitutional Amend-
ment making it obligatory on public authorities to include men
and women in practically equal numbers, whether by election,
nomination, co-option, votes, or no votes. He explained:—

. . . On all questions women, with their feet kept on the ground
by housekeeping and motherhood, are practical, very pugnacious,
want to get things done, and have no patience with men's jocularity,
sentimentality, love of gossiping and of hearing themselves talk, and
lazy dread of having to do anything . . . If public affairs could be
managed by one sex alone, I should vote for leaving them to women.
Having always had to feed and manage men they are trained to
it until it has become an instinct with them, whereas men have

never been able to manage women. Matriarchy is the law of nature; . . . I have been dependent on women all my life, and am quite conscious of it, and keenly aware of the fact that if I do nothing to make me worth their care, they may wake up to the situation like the bees, and kill me when they have no further use for me. The danger in an exclusively female government is that women, who love power more than men do, would jealously disfranchise and dronify men at whatever cost of pampering, dressing-up and glorifying him. I advocate human government by women and men in equal numbers because I want the enormous power at present exercised by women to be made public, responsible, and continually under fire from public criticism.

It may be added that Shaw once declared: "He who confuses political liberty with freedom and political equality with similarity has never thought for five minutes about either."

The Labour Party frequently came under Shaw's fire. In a speech in London on 26th March, 1914,* he declared that it lacked intellectuals and that two Labour bodies were essential: one to do the work of Trade Unionism, and the other to carry out the political work. He criticised the Labour Party as "an unfortunate necessity, but still a necessity", and said he would do, as he had done in the past, everything to help it on in the hope that it would enter into something wider and better. He urged that Socialists must shake off the old idea that they were engaged in a class struggle, and that the movement could ever be a class movement:—

Here am I; I belong to the Capitalist class. I live in an extremely simple way, as you all know, yet there are no fewer than 14 persons directly dependent on my income, and I do not think any one of these fourteen persons, belonging to the working class, is a Socialist. Indeed, I rather suspect, though they do not obtrude the fact upon me, that they are pretty strong Conservatives. Now, these 14 members of the working class are ready to fight in defence of my income.

* Reported in *The Labour Leader* on 2nd April.

The working class was his chief victim on another occasion.* While reaffirming his belief in Socialism, Shaw could not contain his lack of faith in the poor quality of much of the human material forming the working class—though he was careful to blame their laziness and ignorance largely on the social system in which they grew up rather than on any innate and ineducable factors in the people themselves:—

... As to the working classes, I believe neither in their virtue nor their intelligence: on the contrary, my objection to the existing order is precisely that it inevitably produces this wretched, idolatrous, sentimental, servile, anti-Socialist mass of spoiled humanity which we call the proletariat, and which neither understands us, believes in us, nor likes us [i.e. Socialists]. I am not the friend of the working class: I am its enemy to the extent of ardently desiring its extermination; and the one ray of hope it sheds on me is the approval with which it invariably receives these sentiments of mine when I utter them on the platform. It may not understand Socialism; but at least it knows that it is not fit to govern, and despises Democracy accordingly.

Please observe that I, who write all this, am a Socialist, converted to Socialism by reading *Das Kapital* in 1883, and ever since then an active worker for the cause.

But Shaw did not hold the working class entirely blameless for their condition. While regarding them as a product of the Capitalist System and insufficiently educated or socially conscious for real democracy, he had pointed out in the 1892 *Fabian Election Manifesto* that:

[The workers] make greater sacrifices to support legions of publicans and sporting bookmakers than free political institutions would cost them; and there is no escaping the inference that they care more for drinking and gambling than for freedom. The same workman who pleads want of education and opportunity as an excuse for not understanding party politics is at no loss when the subject is football, or

* Ms. in Shaw papers, B.M. (Date believed *c.* 1904.)

racing, or pigeon-flying, or any subject, however complicated, that he really wants to understand. . . . The ordinary working man seemed to take it quite as a matter of course that all this trouble and expense should be incurred for his sake by somebody else. . . .

It would thus clearly be a mistake to regard Shaw's revolutionary Socialistic fervour as directed entirely, or even mainly against "the idle rich", for he saw the opposition to Socialism to lie at least as much in the "parasitic proletariat", who, he considered, not only forced the routine of fashion on to the propertied classes, but forced the parasitic system on to the entire community.

Shaw emphasised the important role played by inverted social snobbery on the part of the lower professional classes (as distinct from, and in addition to, the poverty and ignorance of the working classes) in the following description (in the *New Age*, 7th December, 1907) of the 'parasitic proletariat':—

. . . These are the plutocratic retainers whom Socialism must convert, coerce, or kill, just as Capitalism had to convert, coerce, or kill the retainers of the feudal barons in so far as they did not very obligingly kill one another.

Shaw went on to say that it was these parasites—the West End tradesmen and professional men and hotel keepers, the schoolmasters, the horse-dealers and trainers, the theatre agents, the huntsmen, jockeys, gamekeepers, gardeners, coachmen, and the huge mass of minor shopkeepers and employers who depended upon these, or who, as children, had been brought up with "a little crust of conservative prejudices which they call their politics and morals and religion"—all these were what gave to Parliamentary Conservatism its strength. These people's incomes were bound up with those of the propertied class which Socialism sought to expropriate. And as many of them were better fed, better mannered, better educated, more confident and successful than the productive proletariat, the class war was not (said Shaw) going to be a walk-over for the Socialists.*

Shaw instanced how one of Dickens's characters had been a barber who had refused to shave a coal-heaver, and how the original of his Inspector Bucket was furious when he was once sent to arrest a common pickpocket instead of being reserved for murderers and gentlemanly forgers. Until people realised the happiness of licking a Duke's boots and the shame of 'attending to' a poor person, they could have no conception of the enormous force of snobbery that fortified property and privilege. He added:—

... The rich, then, do something more than employ the poor. They reflect their glory on them. It is not the duke who enjoys his rank: on the contrary, he is the sole person who does not enjoy it. It is his tailor who enjoys it, his outfitter, his bootmaker, his carriage builder, his doctor, his solicitor, his vicar, his valet, down to the very crossing-sweeper who gets a penny from him. Even the executioner who hangs or guillotines him enjoys his importance, and feels that he is demeaning himself when he has to hang a mere commercial traveller the following week.

A few months earlier, Shaw had complained that the recently formed Labour Party was becoming too "Gentlemanly" for his liking, in an article in *The Clarion*, 23rd August, 1907, sub-titled "The Gentle Art of Unpleasantness". He outlined the sort of Socialist Parliamentary Party he would like to see brought into existence. He especially wanted, he said, a party representing his own class—the disinherited poor relations and younger sons progeny of the plutocrats and aristocrats. He explained:—

No Common Working Man need apply: his dissatisfaction with genteel life cannot be sincere, because he has never tried it. Poor

* This last sentence completely contradicts Shaw's attitude in his speech in London on 26th March, 1914 (see page 287), in which he urged that Socialists must shake off the old idea that they were engaged in a class struggle. Shaw seems to have had an ambivalent attitude to the different economic classes, as well as to the concept of a class struggle itself.

people are always objectionable; and no poor person shall be
admitted into my new party unless he can prove that his poverty is
his own fault and that his parents were respectable . . .

I have great hopes of persuading the Fabian Society to adopt
these regulations and to organise A REAL SOCIALIST PARTY, openly
bent on abolishing property; breaking up the family; annihilating
militarism by refusing to renew the Mutiny Act; making our
domesticity decent by stamping out marriage and all other legal
forms of prostitution and chattel slavery; purifying religion from
all forms of idolatry, including the idolatry of saviors, saints,
prophets, prime ministers, playwrights, and pianists; complicating
life until nobody can live on less than several thousand a year, or
earn it without practically continuous activity; abolishing all
pleasures, holidays, and other agents of exhaustion and tedium; and
(incidentally) criticising the Labor Party on all possible occasions
with studied arrogance and without the slightest regard for its
feelings. [*Sic!*].

In the meantime, what is the poor old Labor Party to do? Why,
get a program from the Fabian Society, of course.

Shaw instanced among the reforms requiring immediate
attention (in 1907) the passing of a Minimum Wage Act, the
abolition of the Poor Law, proper provision for widows and
orphans, and for public health and public education, and a complete system of Labour Exchanges. These things would be five
years' work to get on with. What else could a Socialist Party do
if it were in Parliament? Firstly, it could make a desperate
resistance to the annual renewal of the Mutiny Act, and thereby
make it possible for self-respecting free men to form a citizen
army with the ultimate object of conquering their own country,
'now held by genteel brigands'.*

In a letter published in 1913 in *The Twentieth Century
Molière* by his French translator and friend Auguste Hamon,
Shaw defined the Fabian Society's past and future work as:—

---

* Yet another instance of Shaw's advocating violent revolution (i.e.
sedition). Compare to Shaw's other incitements to sedition given on
pages 180, 231-2, and 237.

1. To get rid of the old notion that the Socialist Societies (containing twenty members apiece!) will be able to regenerate the world by merely enlarging the circle of their membership; and to replace it by the notion that it is, on the contrary, the business of Socialists to join all other kinds of organization in order to permeate these with Socialist ideas and to suggest Socialist solutions for their difficulties. This has been termed the Policy of Permeation; and from 1884 to 1892 it was an astonishing novelty for Socialists, who were at that time all split up into little sects, like the Christian sects, each sect expecting all the world to enter its own little Bethel.

2. To reduce Socialism to a series of parliamentary measures making up a constitutional policy (Collectivism), so that a respectable Englishman may just as readily be a Socialist as a Conservative or a Liberal.

3. To detach the working classes from the Liberal Party and to form a parliamentary Labour Party.

All this had been accomplished, wrote Shaw. It still remained:—

5. To constitute in Parliament a Socialist Party independent of all the other political parties, using its ideas and its political science to give a lead to the advanced element of all these other parties.

The Trade Unions, as well as the Labour Party and the working classes, had by 1913 become causes of disillusionment to Shaw, with his middle-class (and to some extent aristocratic) outlook and intellectual approach to social problems—common to the Webbs, Olivier, Bland, and most of the leading Fabians. In Clause 4 of his letter to Auguste Hamon, Shaw urged that the Fabian Society should:—

. . . detached the Socialists from the Labour Party, which is not a Socialist party but a Radical wing of the Trade Unions. The Labour Party is good in that it represents labour, but bad in that it represents poverty and ignorance, and it is anti-Social in that it supports the producer against the consumer and the worker against the employer instead of supporting the workers against the idlers. The Labour

Party is also bad on account of its false democracy, which substitutes the mistrust, fear, and political incapacity of the masses for genuine political talent, and which would make the people legislators instead of leaving them what they are at present, the judges of legislators.

In the *Labour Monthly*, October, 1921, Shaw further explained:—

... The really effective lure is the defiance of Nature in the name of liberty: the apparent freedom to be idle. It is useless to demonstrate that no such freedom is possible for all: that if Adolphus survives in idleness, Bill and Jack and the rest must be doing his share and having their liberty correspondingly curtailed. What does that matter to Adolphus? And who does not hope to be Adolphus, if only for a day or a week occasionally? The moment Socialism comes to the point and hints at compulsory industrial and civil service for all, the difference between Dean Inge and the Labor Party vanishes: they [i.e. the proletariat] will stand anything, even Capitalism at its worst, rather than give up the right to down tools and amuse themselves at any moment. Thus their devotion to liberty keeps them in slavery; and after the most formidable combinations to better their condition they go back to defeat and drudgery under the unofficial but irresistible compulsion of starvation.

Shaw's strong feelings about the Labour Party were further expressed in an Ms. now in the British Museum (undated, but estimated *c.* 1920):—

Wanted.—A public opinion that unproductiveness is dishonorable; that fighting is suicidal and disastrous; that the most sacred obligation of the individual is to pay his way, and his eminence proportion[al] to the extent to which he leaves his country in his debt. Life More Abundant the motto.
              Where is there such a party?
? The Labor Party.
Not at all. It admits all workers by hand or brain, the productive worker and the parasite. Even on its Proletarian side it fiercely resents Compulsory Labor. Its leaders have just declared that they "do not subscribe to the political and social theories on which the

Soviet Government is based". Now these are precisely the desiderated theories.

It is Anti-Clerical and Anarchist. It is Trade Unionist.

On its parasitic side it strenuously supports the Robber Caste and is Anti-Socialist and Clerical.

Intellectually, politically, religiously, socially, it is in utter confusion: a mob of Bolshevists and Tories, Atheists and Methodists, Jingoes and Little Englanders and Conscientious Objectors, Free Traders and Protestants. The R.C. is solider.

In a lecture on the Webb draft Socialist Constitution in King's Hall on 3rd December, 1920, Shaw vigorously opposed Beatrice Webb's view—which he said "took our breath away" —that in a Socialist State the right to strike should be retained. He considered that this involved the right to be idle, and advocated new laws treating idleness as *the* Sin against the Holy Ghost. Striking, he pointed out, was Direct Action; under Socialism it would be Criminal Direct Action. The Socialist State could not withhold wages because under Socialism (as he then conceived it) there would be no wages; there would be, instead, a Distribution of Income, and Communism. The Trade Union as we knew it would pass away by transformation into a Professional Association.

The right of workers to strike (at any rate on a national scale) was again condemned outright by Shaw in his article in *The Labour Monthly* of October, 1921, entitled "The Dictatorship of the Proletariat". He described it as "only a form of the right to commit suicide or to starve on their enemy's doorstep", and declared that a Socialist State (such as he envisaged) would not tolerate such an attack:—

. . . If a Trade Union attempted such a thing, the old Capitalist law against Trade Unions as conspiracies would be re-enacted within twenty-four hours and put ruthlessly into execution. Such a monstrosity as the recent coal strike, during which the coal-miners spent all their savings in damaging their neighbors and wrecking the national industries, would be impossible under Socialism . . . The

— Examples of the New Law —   (8)

B.W. took our breath away by declaring
that the Socialist State would retain

The Right to STRIKE.

But this involves a
        Right to be IDLE.

There will be new laws treating idleness as
the Sin Against the Holy Ghost. (OVER)
                                 COMPULSION.

Striking is Direct Action.
        Under Socialism it will be
            Criminal Direct Action

The Socialist State could not
        WITHOLD WAGES.

F
I There will be No Wages : there will be
N
A DISTRIBUTION OF INCOME
N   &
C   COMMUNISM.
E The Trade Union as we know it will pass away by
   transformation into a Professional Association.

Lecture card: Shaw advocates that striking be made a criminal
offence.

10. W's Plea that Compulsion is impossible applies to all State Compulsion. You cannot make anyone do anything if he will face the penalty of refusal. Passive Resistance, Conscientious Objection, Hunger strike, and Civil War are always possible; but they do not prevent effective compulsory legislation.

Reverse of lecture card depicted overleaf.

"weapon of the strike" must be discarded as the charter of the idle rich, who are on permanent strike, and are the real Weary Willies and able-bodied paupers of our society. The Marxists must cease their intolerable swallowings and regurgitations of Marxian phrases which they do not understand (not having read Marx), and cease boring and disgusting the public with orations . . . calling for that quintessence of anti-Socialism the general strike.

Shaw added, however, that if the coal strike in question had been conducted from the Socialist point of view instead of from the Trade Union point of view (which he regarded as essentially a self-seeking commercial one) the strike might have been worth while. In that event, the leaders of Labour in Parliament would have challenged the Government to stop the strike by introducing compulsory industrial service, and would have promised to vote for it themselves. This, he said, would have at once "put them right with public opinion", and would have effected "an epoch-making advance on Labor policy". And it would have put the Government into a very difficult position, for all the coalitionists of the extreme right, "understanding their own Capitalism as little as they understood Socialism, and having no other idea but to smash these damned Trade Unions and bring the working class to heel", would have rallied to the proposal with enthusiasm. But the Government would have seen, or would soon have been shown, that if the right to strike—that is, the right to be idle—were abolished, the Capitalist system would go with it. Thus the Conservative Party and the Trade Unions were hand in glove, the latter being largely dependent on the former for its existence.

Shaw's contention above that the introduction of compulsory industrial service would have "put the Government right with the public" is, of course, unproven, and not supported by the fact that conscription of any kind has always been unpopular in Britain. Shaw admitted this four years later in a conversation with Professor Archibald Henderson, quoted a little further on.

During a Press exchange between Winston Churchill and Bernard Shaw in the *New York Herald Tribune*, of May 11th,

1924, Shaw agreed with Churchill that the Trade Unions often acted in a selfish way against the interests of the community as a whole:—

. . . Mr Churchill himself breaks into outspoken loathing when he encounters capitalism in his proletarian form of trade unionism. "Feather your own nest; and to hell with the public!" is a game that two can play at. It is an odious game, and finally a ruinous one for the nation that tolerates it; . . . Capitalism was and is the way into this evil. Socialism is the way out of it. Without socialism capitalism and trade unionism between them will destroy us.

Shaw further condemned Trade Unionism in an article on "Socialism: Principles and Outlook" in the 1929 edition of the *Encyclopaedia Britannica*:—

. . . Trade Unionism is itself a phase of Capitalism, inasmuch as it applies to labor as a commodity that principle of selling in the dearest market, and giving as little as possible for the price, which was formerly applied only to land, capital, and merchandise. Its method is that of civil war between labour and capital in which the decisive battles are lock-outs and strikes. . . . Trade Unionism now maintains a Labor Party in the British Parliament. The most popular members and leaders are Socialists in theory; so that there is always a paper programme of nationalization of industries and of banking, taxation of unearned incomes to extinction, and other incidentals of a transition to Socialism; but the trade union driving force aims at nothing more than Capitalism with labor taking the lion's share . . .

Shaw elaborated his views on the relationship of the Trade Unions to the Labour Party in Professor Archibald Henderson's book *Table Talk of G.B.S.* (1925). When asked what he thought about the future of the British Labour Party, Shaw replied:—

It will be complicated by its composite and contradictory character as partly Socialist, partly trade-unionist. Trade-unionism is the capitalism of the working classes; its method is to get as much out of the employer and give him as little in return as possible, precisely as the employer's method is to get as much out of his employees and give them as little in return as he can without killing the goose that lays the golden eggs. Two centuries of capitalism have corrupted the wage worker as deeply as the employer; both, like a certain

American financier now deceased, have been trained to play for
their own hands and damn the public. When trade-unions were little
local or sectional affairs, their strikes were not severely or widely
felt; but now that they enlist millions instead of thousands, and
cover whole industries, the big coal strikes and transport strikes
have become national calamities.

The socialist remedy is compulsory labor; but as it is compulsory
labor for everybody, just like compulsory military service, no
exemption being possible on the score of "independent incomes",
the rich, who want to be free to idle, oppose it as fiercely as the
poor, who want to be free to strike, and have a dread of "slavery"
just because they are as effectively enslaved under so-called "free
contract" as soldiers or chattel slaves. Besides, all governments,
whatever party they represent, are hampered and divided by the
reluctance of men to be governed at all; in short, by natural human
anarchism. But in the Labor party the division is very definite:
there is a socialist centre, a right wing of old trade-unionists, and a
left wing of young anarchists who absurdly call themselves communists, but in action are undisciplined trade-unionists. These
essentially capitalistic individualistic anarchistic wings make for
violent dislocations of social order. The socialist centre has to hold
the fort against them, and will get a good deal of prudent support
as the only remaining bulwark against revolution. This situation is
all that can be foreseen of the future—by which I suppose you mean
the future troubles—of the Labor party.

At the conclusion of some notes for a lecture he was to give
to the Independent Labour Party Summer School at Digswell,
Hertfordshire, on 5th August, 1929, Shaw wrote:—

> Be Ready for Dictatorship if
> Democracy reduces itself to
> Absurdity and remember that
> God
> fulfils himself
> in
> Many Ways

During this lecture he declared that the Labour Party had
totally failed to attempt to organise the working class as

Socialists, and that Trade Unionism was saturated with Capitalism and Opportunism. Shaw instanced among the proposed Socialist measures which he thought would be unpopular: "Compulsory Labor (G. D. H. Cole's *Labor Corps*); the Restriction of Inheritance; Teaching Communism in Public Schools [!]; Disqualifying leaders not so taught; and 'Hohenzollernism'." (i.e. a form of continuing dynastic dictatorship.)

In 1932 Shaw was asked by the Press whether he considered the result of the previous year's General Election a serious setback for Socialism. To an interviewer, Maurice Lewis, he replied:—

No. It was a perfect godsend for Socialism. The Labour Party, held back by Mr MacDonald and Mr Snowden, had become an apparently immovable obstacle to any Socialist advance, and had disappointed all the millennial hopes it held out at the previous election.

Mr MacDonald would do nothing but make speeches which were masterpieces of pure bunk, and burn the national candle at both ends in rents, dividends, and doles.

Lord Passfield and the Fabians urged that indiscriminate outdoor relief was nothing but a return to the Speenhamland system of a hundred years ago, and that the electorate would throw the Labour Party over in disgusted disappointment unless it went to the country next time with a real programme including a great reform of Parliament and some obvious nationalisations, such as coal, transport, and banking.

They might as well have talked to Cleopatra's Needle. MacDonald would do nothing but make imposing but empty speeches, and deride the claim for "Socialism in our own time". The question of how to get rid of him had become serious and pressing.

He solved the problem by transferring himself to the Conservative Party as its leader, which is his proper place.

Shaw added that the last mentioned action was a perfectly honest step which MacDonald must have been contemplating for some time, and it had come as an inexpressible relief to his old

Socialist friends, of whom he himself was one. Actually, of course, Shaw distorts the facts somewhat. Ramsay MacDonald became leader of a *National* Government (albeit composed mainly of Tories) owing to the grave financial crisis in 1931, but he was never at any time leader of the Conservative Party as such.

In the same year, in a lecture he gave during a visit to South Africa (as reported in a Russian Supplement to the *Cape Times* in February), Shaw contrasted the functioning of industry under Capitalism and Communism in the following terms:—

. . . [The Russians] . . . have the enormous advantage of working without that omnipresent friction of conflicting private interests which act like sand in the bearings of our own industrial machinery. The patentee opposing, smothering or buying up and suppressing new inventions; the hugging of trade secrets which robs every manufacturer of the benefit of his competitors' technical experience; the trade union conspiracy to do as little work and get as much for it as possible; the constant menace of strike or lock-out; the destructive handling of buildings and machines by workers who do not own them and feel no interest in them; the struggle over the piece-work rate whenever an improvement in a process is effected; all these applications of the incentive to private profit make up a total of hindering friction which make it a marvel that our industry is able to proceed at all, and explains why it culminates periodically in great strikes which are really civil wars. In Russia the absence of this friction has given an impulse and a volume to production which seems miraculous in the West.

In a manuscript in the B.M. (the date of which is estimated to be 1926-7), Shaw declared that the conventional conception of Socialism as "To each what he produces, and to each what he deserves" was idealistic and impossible. For him, Socialism was specifically equated with Equality of Income, the advantages of which he on *this* occasion summarised thus:—" 1. Familiarity and Practicability (the Impossibility of Inequality of Income outside narrow limits). 2. It secures Economic Order in

THE SOCIALIST PLAN. 4X

Equality of Income.

Its Advantages.   **It is the Established Plan.**

1. Familiarity and Practicability
   (The Impossibility of Inequality
   of Income outside narrow limits)

2. It secures Economic Order in
   Production.

3. It is Eugenic.

4. It does away with the Corruption
of Law, of Administration, of the Church,
the Schools and the Press.

5 It secures Promotion by Capacity.

6 It reserves the Job to the person
who wants to do it because he can, thus
recognising Natural Diversity.

7 It defines the bargain of the
Individual with Society and secures his _Leisure_,
which he calls his freedom.

8 It abolishes Property, Liberty, and with
them Envy and Anxiety.

                              FINIS

Lecture card: "The Socialist Plan".

Production. 3. It is Eugenic. 4. It does away with the Corruption of Law, of Administration, of the Church, the Schools and the Press. 5. It secures Promotion by Capacity. 6. It reserves the Job to the person who wants to do it because he can, thus recognising Natural Diversity. 7. It defines the bargain of the Individual with Society and secures his *Leisure*, which he calls his Freedom. 8. It abolishes Property, Liberty, and with them Envy and Anxiety."

But in advocating the establishment of the basic income as the practical step on which he placed his main emphasis, Shaw later pointed out (in his 1949 *New Statesman* letter) that in the transition period it was to be expected that

... we shall have, among other absurdities, agreement between all parties that increased production is the supreme need of the moment, yet ... with all parties doing their worst to sabotage it— the Capitalist Party denouncing the Socialist half of it as a tyranny, and the Labour Party the other half because it is private enterprise.

Shaw complained in this letter that he had attempted to make his ideas on this matter clear for thirty years, but had always been misunderstood and contradicted, often by critics with whom he was really in agreement.

It may be apposite to mention here that confusion and contention resulting from Shaw's highly individual use of terms had existed for more than twice this period—from his earliest Socialist days in fact. For example, on 22nd May, 1884 (when the Fabian Society had been in existence only four months, and Shaw had attended his first meeting of it only a few days earlier, on 16th May), he declared in a lecture to the Bedford Debating Society on the theme: "That the Socialist Movement is only the Assertion of our Lost Honesty":—

If six hours useful labor exchanges for six hours labor, ten hours for ten hours, and so forth without regard to the degree of skill involved, the result is Socialism. If, on the contrary, a man is fed according to the capacity of his brain instead of that of his stomach, the result is Individualism, founded on the idea that the dog who jumps highest shall get the largest bone. If it be agreed that the greatest among you shall be master of all the rest, as a mother is the ruler of her child, the result is Despotism. If it be clearly perceived that the greatest among you shall be servant to all the rest, as a good mother is the servant and not the tyrant of her child, the result is Christianity, only to be attained, after Socialism has become a matter of course, by the utter denial and rejection of Christ in the common sense of the words. And if you have no discoverable principle whatever, but mere anarchy as of sheep going astray, every one not to his own way, but wherever the rest happen to shove him, the result is the present state of things.

Shaw defined "the standard Socialist day", as he envisaged it, in a later lecture entitled "The Impossibilities of Freedom" in the Kingsway Hall, on 26th November, 1925:—

Work	4 hours
Wash and Eat	4 hours
Sleep	8 hours
	16 hours bond
Leisure	8 ,,
	24 hours

Adjustment to special cases by Leisure, never by money . . . Socialism can give you one third of your life as leisure = one half of your waking life.

In a draft article for *Britanski Soyuznik* (British Ally) dated on the typescript 27th June, 1942,* Shaw, referring to his ideals of Socialism (or Communism) added:—

. . . Millions of us will demand an easy life, a modest income, four hours' work a day, and retirement at 70. Thousands will insist on a

* Shaw Mss., British Museum. I cannot trace in the files of this newspaper at Colindale that it was ever published.

If. The Impossibilities of Freedom. Kingsway Hall
28/11/25 (1)

Possibilities.

Definitions in Previous Lectures.

Saturday morning on Hammersmith
~ afternoon Broadway.

Standard Socialist Day

Work 4 hours
Wash &c 3 at 4 hours
Eat
Sleep 8 hours
———
16 hours bond
Leisure 8 "
———
24 hours.

Adjustment to special cases by
Leisure, never by money.
Art must justify itself by results
(bar decoration art); and so must literature;
but artists would seek exercise as navvies and
foresters &c.
Anyhow, Socialism, can give you one third
of your life as leisure = one half of your
waking life.
For subsequent controversies, see syllabus.
8 hour day really 16.

Lecture card: "The Standard Socialist Day" envisaged by Shaw.

— UNPOPULAR —

Compulsory Labor [Cobs Labr Corps]

Restriction of Inheritance.

Teach Communism in Public Schools

Disqualify teachers not so taught.
Hohenzollernism.

Deliver the Goods or
Hold Your Tongue.

Be Ready for Dictatorship if
Democracy reduces itself to
Absurdity and remember that
God:
fulfils himself
in
Many Ways.

END

*Extracts from two lecture cards from Shaw's address
"The Impossibilities of Freedom" in 1925.*

strenuous life, a big income, work till you drop, and retirement after prodigious exertions at 40. Karl Marx and his dialectic will be no use then.

He enlarged on this aspect in the course of a later draft article headed "The Party System and Socialists" (typescript dated 21st June, 1944*). After praising

. . . the Russian system, in which education is within everyone's reach and there are no classes of rich and poor, productive and parasitic, nor any interests which conflict with the public interests. . . .

he expressed his conviction that when Socialism was established in Britain, and there was "no longer a civil war between a proletariat and a proprietariat, the latter being abolished", we would get "the One Party or Totalitarian State, with Opposition as such disallowed as obstructive and anarchical".

But he also thought many other problems would remain unsolved. There would be more wavering groups within Socialism, including that "between Nationalists and Super-nationalists (Stalin and Trotsky, for example)", and between "the Hardworkers and the Easygoers":—

The Hardworkers will go all out for 8 hours work a day for 5 days in the week, with unlimited overtime and retirement at the age of forty on a Basic Income of £20,000 a year. The Easygoers will prefer three or four hours a day with a three day week and retirement at the age of 60 on £800 a year. The amendments moved will be innumerable. Under Socialism there will be warring groups and parties undreamt of now when so many of us are too preoccupied with the struggle for tomorrow's dinner and money for the week's rent to have any opinions at all.

In his Kingsway Hall lecture on 26th November, 1925, Shaw did not deny that under Socialism as he envisaged it, what the Scots—Sir Walter Scott, for example—called the

* Shaw Mss., British Museum. After a detailed search in many possible media, I think it was probably not published.

Privileged Beggar or 'Gaberlunzie' would be very happy, for
he would receive exactly the same share of the national income
as the 'work glutton'. He also foresaw that the work gluttons
would have more leisure than they would know what to do
with, and this could transfigure the world, for good or evil.
The prospect was really alarming. They would not be able to
take it out in golf, for if they did, nobody could go out of
doors without being hit by a golf ball. Probably golf would
be made a criminal offence, if it did not perish for lack of
caddies!*

Shaw's conclusion was that Leisure was Freedom; that
Socialism would produce an unprecedented quantity of Leisure;
that Satan would find mischief for idle hands to do; and that
He alone knew what would come of it when all our days—
except the whole holidays—were half holidays(!).

As a delicate mental exercise, the reader may care at this point
to meditate on the possible effect of substituting Shaw (with his
'Mephistopheles' eyebrows, etc.) for 'Satan' in the above
passage! Joking apart, however, it must constantly be borne in
mind that one of the factors dominating all Shaw's social and
political beliefs was his fundamental conviction that only
about 5 to 10 per cent. of the population were adequately fitted
by mental endowment and training for the task of governing. In
a letter in the *New Statesman* of 10th June, 1916, headed "The
Case Against Chesterton", Shaw explained:—

. . . Democracy in the sense of government of the people for the
people by the people is only tyranny in (let us hope) its last ditch.
For the poor man there is no freedom; and poverty can be got rid
of only by legislators who not only want to get rid both of poverty
and riches, but who are also very highly qualified as lawyers and
economists, and are, to put it roughly, just the sort of brainy, conscientious, "dry" people the trueborn Englishman loathes from the
bottom of his soul. There is no more dangerous humbug than the

* Shaw did not foresee the modern wheeled contraptions for carrying
golf bags, which do away with the necessity for caddies!

demagogue who declares that the voice of the people is the voice of God, and that "it is for you to decide, gentlemen," knowing full well that the response will be, "Hear, hear, governor: tell us what to decide." If plays were written for the people by the people, nobody would go to the theatre unless they were compelled (as they probably would be); yet it is easier to write a good play than to make a good law, and the penalty of failure is less severe. For playmaking and for law-making you must go to the abnormal people who have the specific talent which these exercises of human faculty require . . .

In *The Times* of 13th August, 1931, Shaw referred to "practical professors of political science like Lenin and Stalin", and extended his earlier definitions by declaring that:—

Russian Communism is neither Anarchism nor Syndicalism, both of which are called, and even call themselves, Communism in England. It is Fabian Socialism.

He added a paragraph or two later:—

Lenin had to shoot the Anarchists and Syndicalists quite as assiduously as Trotsky, with the help of 30,000 officers from the Tsar's Army, shot the White counter-revolutionists . . . The Russian is not trained to regard himself as a Russian: he is a member of the international proletariat, which includes the British proletariat.

Shaw also wrote of Russia as being "led by men of impressive ability and *unprecedented freedom of thought*" (my italics!— the Soviet purges and extreme harshness and repression of individuality were already rife in 1931) and affirmed that Russia had not only political and economic strength, but also religious strength, for its people had a creed in which they passionately believed—a creed which was catholic and international.

It will have been apparent to the reader that Shaw's views were often highly controversial and open to dispute.

Criticism of Shaw's conviction that "Russian Communism is Fabian Socialism" came from the Fabian Society—who, as a body, did not always, especially in the last twenty or thirty years of his life, accept Shaw's personal views as necessarily representing the Society's own standpoint. Criticism also came from various contemporary figures (as indeed it had always done) in the course of speeches they made, or in the course of articles, books, or letters to the Press written by them. An interesting example of the latter was a letter in *The Times* of 14th August, 1931 (commenting on Shaw's letter of 13th August, quoted above) from Ernest (later Sir Ernest) Barker, and the further correspondence which ensued.

Ernest Barker confessed to "a profound and sympathetic interest in the great attempt being made in Russia to try out a new social order", but complained: "... if only [Communism] had some room for diversity, as every true social order must have; if only it left some interstices and breathing-places for liberty, as every true social order should!" He pointed out that the essence of Fabian Socialism was its emphasis on *evol*ution and 'the inevitability of gradualness' (in the Webbs' famous phrase), as opposed to *revol*ution. Thus Shaw's personal 'Fabian' attitude seemed to him a complete paradox—a contradiction in terms.

Ernest Barker concluded: "And now I bow my head. I remember—for I was educated at a college where it was a saying, or a reported saying, of our master—that the paradoxes of one generation became the commonplaces of the next. But that, I am sure, is a fate which will never befall *all* of Mr Shaw's paradoxes. For some of them, I suspect, are not really paradoxes. They are paralogisms."*

The following day there was a letter to *The Times* from a Mr C. H. St. John Hornby, who criticised Shaw's view that Russia "is led by men of impressive ability . . . operating a system from which the disastrous frictions of our continual conflict of private interests and the paralysing delays of our Parliamentary engines of opposition and obstruction, have been ruthlessly eliminated."

* Arguments, the fallaciousness of which the reasoner is not aware.

Mr St. John Hornby thought that although Shaw called himself a democrat, even he could not attempt to maintain that these supermen [i.e. Lenin, Stalin, and other Russian demagogues] had been chosen to govern by the suffrages of the majority of their fellow-countrymen. It must be presumed, therefore, that Shaw was at heart an aristocrat and in favour of an efficient and self-imposed oligarchy.

He pointed out that both Socialism and Fascism are imposed on the mass of the people by a minority, and that both honestly profess to govern for the good of the governed. Was Mr Shaw equally in favour of both systems, or only one—and if so—which? He was inclined to believe that Shaw was only in favour of a self-imposed oligarchy imbued with his own 'Fabian' principles, and pointed out that the opponents of oligarchies always regarded them as tyrannies, and always overthrew them in the end: since no one really believed in such a thing as a benevolent tyranny. So we fell back on democracy, with all its imperfections—which at least gave the semblance of governing ourselves—and most people seemed to prefer governing themselves badly to being governed well by somebody else. He thought Fabian Socialism might be an ideal system if men and women were perfect. But in view of the fact that human nature was imperfect and would probably remain so, and that it preferred adventure to the dullness of a drab uniformity, he believed that individualism (with all its imperfections) made for a higher and in every sense better standard of life, in all classes, than a Socialism under which the great majority of men and women could only be induced to put forth their best efforts by a ruthless system of compulsion.

The Times of 17th August included a letter from a Mr Oliver C. Quick. He pointed out that if the social standard of action became only what the State decreed, then—irrespective of whether the individuals of future generations would or would not be happier as a result—what we were accustomed to call morality would vanish altogether, for any individual whose actions tended to endanger the State would simply be stamped out. He continued:—

If such are the principles on which Communists act, their whole philosophy is a biological pragmatism which destroys not only the economic individualism, which in its extreme form has been challenged by all the best European thought since Plato, but also the whole doctrine of spiritual values by which Platonism and Christianity have moulded the ideals of our Western world. Communism in principle is seeking to convert human society into something which resembles an infinitely more complicated and efficient ants' nest or beehive, where each particular ant or bee is not an individual at all but merely a link in the chain which constitutes a surviving community. Is this really the goal to which Mr Bernard Shaw would have us tread his Fabian way? I cannot believe it.

Shaw's reply to all three appeared on 20th August, 1931. His only attempt to answer Ernest Barker's criticism was to suggest that as Barker could not apparently be happy or feel free unless he had either more or less money than other people, there was nothing more to be said to him. (Barker had, *inter alia*, been sceptical of Shaw's Equal Incomes concept.) As to Mr St. John Hornby, he was wrong in considering that the adventurous life led to civilisation—the Pirate's life was adventurous. . . .

Shaw added that the dullness of a drab uniformity of honesty, security, employment, sanitation, and established expectation of behaviour, was the price that had to be paid for the peaceful conditions necessary for practising such arts as book production (Hornby was a fine art printer).

Shaw then declared:—

As to Democracy in the sense of responsible government in the interests of the governed, and not in those of any class or individual, that is what we all now profess to aim at. As a method of securing it we rely on a routine of adult suffrage and party electioneering. The Russians rely on a system called the Dictatorship of the Proletariat, by which the proletariat is much more effectively dictated to for its own good than under our system. It is a voting system; but the only way to obtain a vote is to show an unselfish interest in public affairs and a competent knowledge of the Communist constitution. . . .

Shaw omits to mention in the above passage that since the Soviet constitution admits of only one political party—the Communist Party—votes can only be cast for that party. His use of the word 'democracy' here is, therefore, the complete opposite of the usual Western use of the term.

However, it may be added—as my friend Michael Beresford, of Manchester University, reminds me—that Article 126 of the Soviet Constitution, while referring to only one party, declares the Communist Party to be the "leading core" of other public organisations, while Article 141 states: "The right to nominate candidates is secured to public organisations and societies of working people: Communist Party organisations, and cultural societies."

It would therefore seem fair to say that a certain number of delegates to the Supreme Soviet are non-party persons, but even so, all candidates, whether Communist or not, are described as forming one *bloc*. The Soviet authorities claim, of course (absurd as it seems to most 'Western' eyes), that their system is more democratic than ours because there are no competing or conflicting economic groups and hence no *need* for more than one political party. This, however, merely serves to emphasise the great diversity of meanings which have been imputed at various times by different nations and individuals (including Shaw) to the term 'democracy'.

Shaw continued the above-mentioned letter to *The Times*:—

... It is found as a matter of experience that any group of associated workers—in a factory or on a collective farm, for example—will naturally secrete one or two exceptional individuals with these qualifications [i.e. for obtaining a vote], easily recognizable by their voluntarily adding public work to their industrial or agricultural tasks, and by their writings or uttered sentiments. ...

Part of their work is to persuade and educate the workers to form factory and farm committees for criticism and complaint, and to give them such powers of control as they are capable of exercising, so that the Government may always know where and when the shoe pinches. The trade unions have quite a large say in the appointment of managers and general ordering of the industries which immediately concern them.

That is Russia's solution of the democratic problem so far. Obviously it does solve it far more effectually than our system. [!]. It excludes from official authority and from the franchise the ignorant, the incompetent, the indifferent, the corrupt, and the pugnacious and politically incapable masses who, though they revel in a party fight or any other sort of fight, can make no intelligent use of their votes, and are the dupes of every interest that can afford the cost of gulling them. Responsibility to such innocents is no responsibility at all. The threat of it kept the oligarchic statesmen of the nineteenth century in order; but the execution of the threat has proved its worthlessness; and now politicians who spend Monday in making promises, Tuesday in breaking them, and Wednesday in being found out are re-elected by enthusiastic majorities on Saturday.

Shaw went on to say that the Soviet Communist Party involved real responsibility: its members knew their business and could not be humbugged; they were all "under skilled criticism" [!] and there was no waste of time "nursing" constituencies. Failures and "recreants" could be "promptly scrapped". Party opposition for the sake of opposition was punished as sabotage; and attempts to paralyse the Government by "constitutional safeguards" against tyrannies that had long lost their powers were not tolerated. He added: "Pious fictions like 'the people's will', 'public opinion' are not admitted as excuses for *fainéant* statesmen. Liberty does not mean liberty to idle and spunge.* The political machinery is built for immediate positive use [an ominous phrase!]; and it is powerful enough to break people who stick ramrods into it. In short, it is much more democratic than Parliament and party." [!].

Shaw, nevertheless, admitted in his next paragraph that "to . . . Unsocialists the Russian system is the Reign of Terror which keeps Mr Churchill awake of nights." He then told a

* Shaw's unorthodox but legitimate spelling.

story about a Russian worker he (in the company of Lord and Lady Astor) had met during his visit to Russia in 1931, who had returned to his native land after spending many years in America, and who gave as his reason for preferring Russia that he had more freedom of speech there. Lady Astor had expostulated: "But surely you are not free to advocate Capitalism here?" "Certainly not," the man replied, "but then I don't want to advocate Capitalism: I want to denounce it." [!]. Shaw drew attention to the fact that the sedition of the West is the constitutionalism of the Communist East, and *vice versa*. He implied that there was little real freedom in the West, for real democratic freedom for employees to speak their minds could not be said to exist if it meant their getting the sack from their capitalistic employers.

Shaw's argument here is surely specious, because Communist and Socialist organisations did exist then in the West (as they do to an even greater extent now)—without, except in rare and special cases, involving any persecution of the holders of such opinions (in accordance with the principles of Democracy as understood in the West). In complete contrast, however, no individual Capitalist opinion of any political sort was then, or is now, tolerated in Russia (with its one-party system).

It seems relevant to add that many people in the West (including the present writer who has visited Russia twice in recent years) regard the contemporary Soviet society as, so far from being Communistic, simply a form of State Capitalism —with, moreover, greater class differentiation than any other country in the world. (For example, on a ship on which I have travelled on the Volga and Don rivers, there were *six* classes of passengers, namely: De Luxe, 1st Class, 2nd Class, 3rd Class, 4th Class, and, in the ship's hold, 'Tourist' Class.)

In an article in *Nash's Magazine* (November, 1933) Shaw praised the Soviet electoral system, in which, he said, the rank and file of the Communist Party did an ordinary day's work with the rest of their fellows and gave only their leisure to the Party.

For their election as representatives of the people they had to depend on the votes of their intimate and equal neighbours and workmates. They had no incentive to seek election except the vocation of public service, for election at first meant no release from their usual and full day's work and the giving up of all of the person's spare time to politics. And if promotion to party ranks involving full-time political work was achieved, it meant a dedicated life and an ascetic discipline, with no pecuniary advantage as compared to their previous job.

On the contrasting subject of Western democracy in the same article, Shaw declared that "the plutocrats" had only "to master the easy art of stampeding elections by their newspapers" to do anything they liked in the name of the people. He added:—

Votes for everybody (called for short, Democracy) ended in government neither of the best nor of the worst, but in an official government which could do nothing but talk, and an actual government of landlords, employers, and financiers at war with an Opposition of trade unionists, strikers, pickets, and—occasionally—rioters. The resultant disorder, indiscipline, and breakdown of distribution, produced a reaction of pure disappointment and distress in which the people looked wildly round for a Saviour, and were ready to give a hopeful trial to anyone bold enough to assume dictatorship and kick aside the impotent official government until he had completely muzzled and subjugated it. [E.g. Hitler or Mussolini.]

The British type of electioneering procedure—"the ballyhoo of the hustings" as he called it—was Shaw's target in the course of an article in the *Political Quarterly* for October-December, 1935:—

. . . No recent reform has delighted me so much as that just announced from Poland, where election meetings and addresses are now made criminal offences [*Sic!*], and such orgies as still disgrace the western States are no longer possible.

Shaw went on to express his view that the rapidly increasing use of the wireless was the best possible medium for giving the people information about policies and politicians. But, of course, for most other people, the term 'Democracy', as normally understood in the West, would lose all meaning if it did not admit of political candidates canvassing their views in any and every manner they might think fit.

Coming to times still nearer to our own we find Shaw in a draft article, "Further Meditations on Shaw's Geneva", (c. 1938)* expostulating about 'the flapper vote' and 'Democracy':—

. . . What is Democracy? Government in the interest of the whole people and not of a privileged class. What are the ideas associated with the word democracy in the English mind? Adult Suffrage, the House of Commons, and the Party System. When I point out the obvious fact that adult suffrage, consummated in England 20 years ago by giving the casting vote to Miss Begonia Brown,† is a guarantee of petty snobbery and parochial ignorance in the choice of rulers, and that the party system in Parliament has made the House of Commons quite useless as a check on plutocratic oligarchy and completely effective in paralyzing the government industrially and reducing all democratic leaders to helpless impotence, it is immediately assumed that I have renounced democracy and socialism and am now a Fascist and adore Messrs Mussolini and Hitler, who, not being reduced to impotence by membership of our House of Commons, have both done a lot of things that badly want doing here, but cannot be done because to do them would infringe British liberty to be governed by Begonia. For what is done or not done these two men are responsible and can be brought to account, whereas in England the political responsibility under adult suffrage is everybody's; and what is everybody's responsibility is nobody's responsibility.

. . . Finally, remember that democracy did great things when it was an ideal. It was its reduction to reality in the idiocy of Begonia Brown that produced the snobocracy of the last twenty years. She and Henry Dubb will not control the destinies of the British Commonwealth for long. If they do there will soon be no British Commonwealth.

The kernel of Shaw's extremely individual view of democracy is perhaps to be found in a draft article entitled "How to Talk Intelligently About the War"‡ in 1940:—

. . . Real Democracy means that the country shall be governed in

*‡ Shaw papers, Brit. Museum.   † A leading character in Shaw's play *Geneva*.

the interest of everybody and not of a privileged class. It does not mean parliaments on the British Party model elected by overwhelming majorities whose political ignorance is discrediting and destroying democracy. *It means government by whatever method will really secure its ends* [My italics]. We should fight, not to save democracy, but to begin it. So take care how you shout the word . . .

Writing in the *Labour Monthly*, July, 1941, Shaw warned the Editor, Mr. Palme Dutt, about a major difficulty to be overcome in converting the British worker to Socialism, namely that:—

. . . men are so constituted that they will work twelve hours a day, and pay monstrous rents out of their sweated wages if only they may think and say what they like in the rest of their time, rather than work eight hours a day for higher wages *under complete State regulation of their lives and thoughts* [My italics]. Their British freedom may be a delusion and an imposture; but if an imposture is successful we must reckon with it even in our efforts to expose it.

I should therefore dwell more on the leisure of the worker under Socialism, and on the fact that leisure is the only real freedom that Nature allows us.

I should always write on the assumption that the English are brain-lazy, fatheaded, and politically ignorant in the lump . . . But I should, I hope, maintain Socialism in its integrity as Mr. Palme Dutt has maintained it.

Shaw could not understand and thought it could not really be the case that men were basically so constituted as to prefer British 'delusive' freedom limited to speech (when really slaves under Capitalism) to 'real' freedom under Socialism, based on the greater leisure which State control would give. He believed this British resistance to Palme Dutt's and his own kind of Socialism could be overcome by reasoning and propaganda exposing it, and ceaselessly hammered away at this view.

It is not clear from the above passage what the position of artists would be in such circumstances—i.e. "under complete State regulation of their lives and thought". They surely need freedom to write what they like, paint what they like, compose what they like, without the odious necessity of rigid conformity to the State's ideas on what constitutes 'good' or 'bad' art based on political considerations (as seen at present in all

Communist countries). Shaw's extremely strong views against censorship of all kinds have been given earlier in this book (pages 58-77) and thus a profound and complete conflict of his views on these subjects would appear to have existed at the time he wrote the foregoing.

Unless, that is, he was referring to the working class only, and had in mind a separate class of intellectuals exempt from such strictures—e.g. his "Instructed Director" class mentioned on pages 280-1. But plenty of writers, composers, and other artists have come from the working class, and if Shaw's "complete State regulation of the lives and thought" were applied even to the working class alone, it would, of course, have prevented any possibility of artists of any sort ever coming again from among the working class—since freedom to control his or her own life and thought (in any or all aspects) is an essential pre-requisite to the possibility of anyone *developing* into an artist, just as suitable soil is a pre-requisite for a seed growing into a flower or tree. However, in fairness to Shaw, it must be remembered that his Equality of Income concept was aimed, *inter alia*, at producing greatly increased leisure for the working class, so that members of it could have a much greater possibility of developing any special individual talents they might latently possess. Even so, if Shaw felt—in his paradoxical way—that it would be feasible to apply "complete State regulation and control of the lives and thoughts" of people to them in their daily jobs, and yet, running side by side with this, to give them complete freedom of thought and action in their leisure time, then his statement is still incomprehensible, for in no true artist can the creative life be wholly dissociated from the everyday working life. Quite to the contrary, Shaw's great friend and hero William Morris specifically believed—as the main tenet of his artistic faith and the social message he preached—that art and work should be combined to the maximum possible degree in the working class—in the form of craftsmanship and pride and joy in work—no less than in any other class.

Further views of Shaw's on the British Parliamentary Party system were given in *Everybody's Political What's What* (1944):—

. . . The British Party system should be scrapped ruthlessly. It was invented two and half centuries ago to nullify the House of Commons by obliging the King to select his ministers from the Party commanding a majority in it, and to dissolve Parliament and inflict a costly election on its members whenever that Party is defeated on a division; so that members never vote on the merits of a measure but always on the question of whether the reigning Party is to remain in office, both sides risking the loss of their seats and incurring heavy expense and trouble if they unseat the Government.

Shaw elaborated this in his 1947 Postscript to *Fabian Essays*:—

. . . the democracy claimed by the British Parliamentary system is a sham, deliberately invented by a clever peer to enable King William the Third of England (a Dutchman) to fight King Louis the Fourteenth of France for the maintenance of the Reformation and the extradition of the Stuart monarchy. Under it we have seen two world wars declared and one abdication of the British throne effected without consulting or informing the House of Commons, whilst (for example) the urgent need for a new bridge across the Severn has been under discussion for a hundred years, and the bridge is still unbuilt.

The part played by the Monarchy in British political life (touched on in the above two quoted paragraphs) had also been described by Shaw in an article in the *Week End Review* of 22nd March, 1930, entitled "Democracy and the Apple Cart":—

. . . the conflict is not really between royalty and democracy. It is between both and plutocracy, which, having destroyed the royal power by frank force under democratic pretexts, has bought and swallowed democracy. Money talks: money prints: money broadcasts: money reigns; and kings and labor leaders alike have to register its decrees, and even, by a staggering paradox, to finance its enterprises and guarantee its profits. Democracy is no longer bought: it is bilked. Ministers who are Socialists to the backbone are as helpless in the grip of Breakages Limited as its acknowledged henchmen: from the moment when they attain to what is with unintentional irony called power (meaning the burden of carrying on for the plutocrats) they no longer dare even to talk of nationalizing any industry, however socially vital, that has a farthing profit for plutocracy still left in it, or that can be made to yield a farthing for it by subsidies.

A little later, in a contribution to a symposium on "The Crisis" in the *Political Quarterly* for October-December, 1931, Shaw exclaimed:—

...the real demand is for a Government without an Opposition. Our plan of setting up one row of front bench notorieties to do our public work, and simultaneously setting up an opposite row to hinder them, defeat them, disgrace them, and talk them out, is admirable for reducing barons, cardinals, kings, and indeed rulers of all sorts to impotence, thus leaving a free hand to irresponsible profiteers and financiers. Unfortunately it is equally effective in reducing government in itself to impotence. That being so, it will have to go.

Shaw added that there was no apparent way out except Marxian Communism (an apparently complete *volte-face* from his earlier denunciation of Marxism in favour of the Fabian "inevitability of gradualness"). He went on to say that we seemed so far from recognising this as a "much more scientific, civilized, and humane system than our own shallow, short-sighted, and historically subversive constitution", that it seemed impossible to induce a body of politically intelligent and studious public men and women to take a stand to the Left of the Labor Party and declare unequivocally for its inevitability.

In an article, "Fabian Successes and Failures", in the *Fabian Quarterly*, April, 1944, Shaw reiterated earlier statements to the effect that the establishment of the Fabian Society had all been done in a thoroughly English way, without a word about Karl Marx or a phrase from his doctrine of dialectical materialism, but he now added, extremely paradoxically: "Socialists who are not essentially Marxist are not Socialists at all." He repeated that the Trade Unions were out to exploit Capitalism, not to abolish it (as the Socialists were), and continued:—

... Though the Society may be officially affiliated to the Labor Party the true Fabian is not, and never can be, a Party man or woman. My Party, right or wrong, is not our slogan. All Fabians have their price, which is always the adoption of Fabian measures no matter by what Party . . . the Beveridge report is quite as likely to be implemented by an Eden Cabinet as by a Stafford Cripps one . . . In that case Mr Eden must have our support even if our own converts on the Left denounce the Fabian Society as Public Enemy No. 1.

State-aided Capitalism was Shaw's subject earlier in this article. Referring to where the Fabian Society had not yet succeeded, he said that they had expected that the Marxian confrontation of classes would produce a definite confrontation of two policies: bourgeois Capitalism and proletarian Communism, but this had proved far too simple a generalisation. What had happened was the rise of State-aided Capitalism, which exactly suited both the dominant Conservative Trade Union leaders, among whom Sir Walter Citrine was conspicuous, and the high-minded and academically cultivated re-discoverers of the Moralised Capitalism of the largely forgotten Positive Philosophy of Auguste Comte (of which Sydney Olivier had been an exponent before joining the Fabian Society). Shaw added, however:—

It may be that State Aided Capitalism, now called neither Comtism nor Trade Unionism, but Fascism in Italy, National Socialism in Germany, and Freedom in England, where we are up to the waist in it, is the best arrangement of which we are capable at present. The case against it is far more difficult for the young Fabians of today

than the simple case of Socialism versus Unsocialism was for the
Old Gang.

The above statement has a distinctly curious ring about it,
for, as I mentioned on page 311, State-aided Capitalism is
exactly what the contemporary *Russian* system (which Shaw so
much admired) seems really to be, according to my own and
many other visitors' impressions.

Elsewhere in this article Shaw repeated that many Trade
Unionists were not Socialists. They were all for State regulation
of employers by means of factory legislation, but they were out
to exploit Capitalism, not to abolish it. They agreed with the
Fabians that private industrialists' profits should be confiscated,
but their object was not Socialisation of the industry but the
appropriation of its profits for themselves (through public
ownership and the general social benefits which they imagined
would accrue).

In his 1947 Postscript to *Fabian Essays*, Shaw wrote of the
need to "eliminate" shirkers who were not contributing
towards the advance of civilisation: "We must weed the
garden." And all "incurably mischievous criminals" who
could not be reformed should, he averred, be "painlessly
liquidated, not caged".

He referred in this essay to the Fabians as "a middle-class
lot" separated by a gulf from "proletarian" Socialists: "They
must remain a minority of cultural snobs and genuinely
scientific Socialist tacticians, few enough to be negligible in the
electoral count of noses, and with no time to spend on the
conversion and elementary Socialist education of illiterates..."
The recurrent cry for fraternisation and unity in the movement,
he added, must have no illusory charm for them, as it had had
for Keir Hardie. When the latter had at last succeeded in
bringing all the Socialist Societies into a fraternal conference,
they had "wrangled until, having expelled each other one by
one, they had left him finally with nobody but himself and a
few personal disciples to face a hopeless fraternal fiasco".

Shaw went on: ". . . when a proletarian joined us he could not work mentally at the same speed and in the same way against the same cultural background as we. He was therefore an obstruction to our work, and finally abandoned us with his class mistrust of us intensified, crying 'Do not trust these men'. As our relations were quite friendly as long as we worked in separate compartments we learnt that cultural segregation is essential in research, and indiscriminate fraternization fatal."

The Fabians, Shaw then urged, must be: "unsentimental scientific pioneers of the next practicable steps, not dreamers of the new Jerusalem and the Second Advent or the Love panacea with justice nowhere . . . they are still, and must remain, missionaries among savages".

Five years earlier, in the *Daily Herald* of 10th March, 1943, Shaw had referred to "the flop of Fabianism in England" and had explained:—

. . . it was meant for the workers and offered to the workers when the Fabians planned the Labour Party in the tract, drafted by Webb and myself, entitled *A Plan of Campaign for Labour*. But we could not publish it for the workers without publishing it for the capitalists as well. And the capitalists, cleverer than the workers, seized it and turned it to their own account by combining the enormous productiveness, power, and scope of State financed enterprise with their private property on its sources, and thus producing the new form of Capitalism called Fascism or Nationalism—Nazi for short in Germany. The Labour Party, dominated by the power of the Trade Union purse, simply missed the bus.

However, it is also worth noting at this juncture that Shaw admitted on a number of occasions that a difficulty about Communism was its being, economically speaking, supply without demand, and this meant that there could be no control of the supply by the people—that is to say, no guarantee that any Communist government will give the people what they really want in the way of goods and services.

A further point of interest is that Shaw the Socialist gave a measure of support to latter-day Liberalism (as distinct from old-fashioned Cobdenism) in the course of an interview (apparently unpublished) with a reporter from the Japanese newspaper *Yomiuri Shimbun* in September, 1941:—

. . . Liberalism must sleep until democracy is made real by the complete substitution of public welfare for private interest in government. Until this is accomplished it will remain true that Western democracy is, as Hitler says, a lie, and Western liberty, as Mussolini says, a stinking corpse. But when this great reform is effected Liberalism will wake up and again become the progressive force [*sic*] in human affairs.

A summarised explanation of some of the other main points of confusion raised in this chapter occur during the course of an article by Shaw in *Time and Tide* magazine on 10th February, 1945:—

. . . By Democracy I mean a social order aiming at the greatest available welfare for the whole population and not for a class. I most emphatically do not mean government by an assembly, at Westminster or elsewhere, which took fifty years to make factory legislation effective in the face of the horrors described by its inspectors and collected by Karl Marx, thirty years to pass (and revoke) a Home Rule Act for Ireland, and was not even consulted when the country was involved in two world wars and its sovereign forced to abdicate. In this I am what is called a Totalitarian as distinguished from, say, the Trinitarian Gladstone, who aimed at preserving the hierarchy of private landlord, farmer, and agricultural labourer, with its necessary retinue of Cobdenist traders, or from the Party politicians whose aim is to keep their leaders in power at Westminster and [who] are not really politicians at all, their business being simply electioneering. In parliament, these Yesmen and Nomen sit in the smoking room or library, and when the division bell rings vote in the lobby to which they are directed by an official called a Whip because his function is that of a whipper-in at a fox hunt. . . . They all now call themselves democrats and applaud the Atlantic Charter (which is Totalitarian); and they all mistrust me because

I am not a partisan but a Totalitarian Democrat,* who will take an instalment of democracy from any party which can be persuaded or frightened or humbugged into achieving it. In short, an old Fabian.

When they talk of the Allies as "the Western democracies," I laugh. There are no democracies in the west: there are only rank pluto-cracies, all of them now Fascist to the finger tips, having thrown over Cobden and Bright, and grasped the enormous economy and lucrativity demonstrated by the Socialists, of State-financed Capitalism, which is English for Fascism. England is in fact at present the leading Fascist power in Europe; and the Fascists who are denouncing Fascism in their speeches on the war do not know what they are talking about. . . .

I believe in government of the people for the people; but I do not believe in Lincoln's Gettysburg addition of government by the people. Division of labour is the law of Nature (*alias* Providence) in this matter. The belief that "the human race is divided into two categories: men and supermen", is not anti-democratic: the fact stares us in the face all through history, past and present . . .

It must not be forgotten that the human race does not consist of democrats and anti-democrats. Both of these are in favour of government as such, and differ only as to its form. But the average citizen has the most intense objection to be governed at all, and rallies always to the cry of liberty, which is the negation of govern-ment. They have never been taught civilization, which should be their first intelligent lesson in school, and be in fact their religion.

In a second letter to the Editor of *Time and Tide*, dated 21st April, 1945, Shaw added:—

. . . The whole business of an executive Government is to dictate and restrict the conduct of its subjects. Without dictation and restriction civilization is impossible. It can be democratic or, as at present, plutocratic. It can be honest or corrupt, excessive, or defec-tive, theocratic or evolutionary, Communist or Capitalist, Cobdenist or Hitlerist: in short, mischievous or salutary, but it is always on its positive side dictatorial and restrictive . . . prosperity depends on the

* Yet another special category in which Shaw placed himself.

wise choice of rulers much more than on the power to dismiss them in anger when they have been chosen unwisely. Government by the politically ignorant, which means by the uneducated or miseducated (at Eton and Harrow and their imitations for instance) is the very devil, as the present crisis gives terrible proof; and unrestricted unguided adult suffrage, supposed to be democratic, is government by the politically ignorant. The question should, therefore, be what are the tests by which citizens can acquire eligibility for election. At present we have none, except the deposit of a modest sum of money to be forfeited if the candidate fails to receive a respectable quota of the votes cast.

My facing of this question does not class me as an anti-democrat. If my aim is the maximum general welfare as against the maintenance of the existing plutocratic oligarchy I am a democrat,* though I am in favour of ruthlessly exterminating the poor in spite of their amiable jollity and charity, and burying the rich along with them in pity for their disablement, demoralization, unhappiness, insecurity, and abject slavery to their servants, their tradesmen, their tailors and dress makers, with restriction of their choice of professions to two or three for which they may have no aptitude and in marriage to three or four partners for whom they may have no great liking . . .

On the platform and in the Press just now it is assumed that we have to choose between "totalitarian" regimentation or totalitarian individual liberty, totalitarian Communism or Capitalism, totalitarian Socialism or Fascism, totalitarian soot or whitewash. That is all baby talk. Modern civilization could not exist for a week without a broad basis of Communism (roads and bridges, water supply, street-lighting, police, civil and military services, etc.) and a superstructure of Socialism (posts, telegraphs, wireless), Fascism (State-financed Capitalism), and Cobdenism, all making what is called private enterprize possible. Only through using them all can we achieve the utmost practicable release from the slavery imposed on us, not by governments, but by Nature, which reduces the whole question of liberty to the calculation of how to organize our necessary

---

* Shaw here is, of course, using the term 'democrat' according to his own special meaning—the uniqueness of which is emphasised in the lines which follow, in which he advocates the 'extermination' of the poor and the rich alike!

labour so as to produce and distribute as much leisure as we can desire or endure. Liberty without leisure is nonsense.

Two years later, in an article in the *New Statesman*, dated 26th April, 1947, Shaw amplified the above:—

Socialists who want to have everything Socialised, Liberals who want to have everything Cobdenised, Conservatives who want to have nothing changed, and people who are unaware that all civilisation is based on a foundation of Communism and a surrender of individual liberty in respect of totalitarian agreements to do or not to do certain fundamental things, should be disfranchised. Some of them should be sent to mental hospitals. Every competent citizen should be Communist in some things, Conservative, Liberal, and even Capitalist in others all at once, before he or she can rank as a competent citizen.

He added:"But the social provision for genius will still be leisure for voluntary experimental apprenticeship." And in an unpublished draft letter dated 27th September, 1949, to the Editor of *The Times* and headed " Election Prospects ", he wrote:—

. . . First, as to the current cant about freedom and slavery. There are two slaveries: the slavery to nature from which none of us can ever be free, except by imposing our share of it on our landless and penniless neighbours. As far as this natural slavery is concerned, I am the Reddest of Red Communists. Outside it I am all for the utmost freedom of contract, *Laisser-faire*, invention, enterprise, criticism, toleration of speech and opinion, and every heterodoxy compatible with civilized conditions.

There is no inconsistency in this: the two policies are complementary. I am not one of those for whom there are no alternatives to complete universal Bohemian and Plutocratic anarchism but a world in which every worker toils with a policeman called a Gestapo standing over him club in hand to batter his head in if he deviates for a moment from the orders of the Cabinet. Such unobservant thoughtlessness would be negligible were it not that it is implicit and often explicit, in every platform speech now being declaimed. .

Shaw's shorthand draft of the letter quoted on the opposite page. Note the neatness and steadiness of Shaw's handwriting in his 94th year.

Even geniuses of the calibre of Rousseau and Herbert Spencer thought that all are born free, and all slavery avoidable . . .

Shaw's statement above, "There is no inconsistency in this", should be viewed in the light not only of the same paragraph, but of various other statements by him given earlier in this chapter. Perhaps the operative word is 'compatible' given in the preceding line; i.e. he is in favour of "every heterodoxy" which he has not elsewhere specifically condemned as *in*compatible with "civilised conditions"!

In a lecture on 7th December, 1917, Shaw declared: "The problem of liberty is a paradox: it is the question of what we must do in order to do what we like." He explained this point more fully in a B.B.C. talk on 18th June, 1935:—

. . . What is a perfectly free person? Evidently a person who can do what he likes, when he likes and where he likes, or do nothing at all if he prefers it. Well, there is no such person; and there never can be any such person. Whether we like it or not, we must all sleep for one-third of our lifetime; wash and dress and undress; we must spend a couple of hours eating and drinking; we must spend nearly as much in getting about from place to place. For half the day we are slaves to necessities which we cannot shirk, whether we are monarchs with a thousand slaves or humble labourers with no servants but their wives. And the wives must undertake the additional heavy slavery of child-bearing, if the world is still to be peopled.

In the *New Statesman*, 3rd July, 1943, Shaw was hammering away at his theme that government by adult suffrage had made democracy impossible; the political ignorance of Everywoman had been enfranchised and added to the political ignorance and folly of Everyman, and government had become "by Anybody chosen by Everybody". And as to equality, he declared that Stalin was as impatient of 'Equality Merchants' as he called them, as of "Trotskyists, World Revolutionists, Currency Cranks, and in general, Lefts who are never right". Shaw added:—

. . . to give everybody an equal share of the national income today would reduce us all to such overcrowded poverty that science, art, and philosophy would be impossible. Civilization would perish, and with it most of the people. In Russia they can maintain their Socialism only by paying their directors and experts ten times as much as they can spare for the rank and file of the laborers. It is the business of the favored ones to work up production until there is enough to afford the tenfold figure for everybody. Then, and then only, can intermarriageable equality become possible; and when that is achieved nobody will bother more about mathematical equality of income than they do now in the rich sections where ten thousand a year can intermarry with fifty thousand without friction. Enough is enough: when there is plenty for everybody nobody will listen to the Exact Equality Merchants; and meanwhile they must be shoved out of the way as Stalin has shoved them.

Shaw here appears to have been preaching the extermination of believers in something very similar to just what he had been the most ardent and leading believer in himself, thirty years previously. It doubtless depends on what you mean by "shoved out of the way" (though Shaw's reference to Stalin does not leave much room for doubt).

Bernard Shaw introduced another unique Shavian term, "Democratic Aristocracy", in his 1947 Postscript to *Fabian Essays*:—

. . . The first step towards equality of income is not the division of the existing national income into equal parts. It is the determination of the basic income needed to abolish poverty and ignorance and make every family a potential breeding place for an aristocracy of talent. Fabianism thus becomes Democratic Aristocracy in strong opposition to Underdog Authority or Government by the Unfittest, which is the bugbear of the cultured classes today.

Shaw's final word about his conviction in Equality of Incomes was in a letter to *The Times* on 1st May, 1950, headed "The Wages Paradox". He wrote that, whilst he believed that the lowest incomes would have to be raised gradually to the basic income level by reducing the higher ones to it, it would be "the blindest mistake to do the same catastrophically with salaries and wages". But since salaries and wages are synonymous with income for the vast majority of mankind, Shaw's argument here appears difficult to follow. He went on to point out that the "suburban professional" man was "fairly comfortable and secure on a fifth of the salary" which kept "the Mayfair one pulling the devil by the tail all the time". Shaw, in the latter part of this sentence, was referring to 'top' executive administrative and professional people (in the existing state of society) with heavy responsibilities and expensive positions to keep up—which, he suggested, might cost ten times as much as those of the average "suburban professional man", although their income might be only five times as much. Shaw's argument could thus be taken to imply that reducing 'top' people's salaries and wages would not reduce their expenses and responsibilities of living to a *proportional* degree. He drew attention to the insecurity, and even the risk of bankruptcy, of the 'top' people—which was averted by the humbler public servant and many of those employed by others, and concluded: "Pardon my depredation on your space. When the basic income and the miseries of the rich are in question, I cannot keep silent. It is very trying to be a Communist in a country where nobody knows what the word means, and every political catchword means the opposite of what it says."

However, it is to be noted that Shaw's belief in equality of incomes has to a considerable extent become reality in Britain during the last decade or two as a result of the Labour Party's 'Fair Shares for All' policy ('Levelling Down' as the Conservatives call it) and taxation scales which increase markedly above professional incomes of around £2,000 a year—while at the same time wages have increased to the point at which factory mechanics, printing operatives, bricklayers, and so on, can regularly earn £20 to £30 per week (£1,000 to £1,500 a year). Indeed, not a few manual workers earn around £40 or more—even up to £100 a week in some cases, especially in certain industries such as the printing industry. I am told that members of the "Natsopa" trade union—whose members are all unskilled—can, and frequently do, earn up to £50 per week (£2,600 per year) for work such as cleaning printing machinery, or tying up parcels for dispatch. This compares favourably with the earnings of many professional and highly skilled men, and more than favourably, certainly, with those of most of the writers on whom their livelihood ultimately depends. (Indeed, the majority of book authors earn only between a tenth and a quarter as much, according to a Society of Authors survey in June, 1966. Even so great an author as Bernard Shaw endured many years of poverty before reaching the equivalent income of an unskilled labourer. His views on this subject are given in a later chapter.)

Moreover, many of the other aims of Socialism have largely been accomplished and are now accepted as a normal part of life by supporters of all our political parties. As Shaw told the Liverpool Fabian Society on 28th October, 1908:— "... remember, Socialism is a very elastic thing; it is a thing which comes on gradually, and you can stop it whenever you like. Whenever a little bit of Socialism is adopted, people cease to call it Socialism."

Nearing the final section of this chapter it seems fitting to quote this statement, made in 1948 approximately, which proves that whatever sympathies Shaw may have had with autocracy (and despite his periodic advocacy of *extermination* for various groups of people!) he did not—at any rate in his last years—support the violent *methods* which were actually employed by Fascism and Communism in attempting to gain their ends:—

... All the coercive systems aim at the establishment of a police system as ubiquitous as gravitation or the need for air to breathe, and the total elimination of conscience as a factor in human conduct and the substitution of terror. As this is as impossible in fact as it is horrible in conception, sensible and decent people will have nothing to do with it, and aim at the cultivation of conscience and responsibility.

It is also apposite here to quote again Shaw's aphorism:—

Democracy substitutes election by the incompetent many for appointment by the corrupt few.

Where Shaw would draw the line between the apparently disparate political systems of democracy (with its humanity, but inherent slowness and inefficiency) and totalitarian dictatorship (with its efficiency, but inherent danger of corruption, megalomania, and harsh coercion) is, as the Americans might say, the $64,000 question.* Shaw, when he described himself as a "Totalitarian Democrat," would appear to have believed in a balance between the two approaches. But how is the balance to be struck? Shaw undoubtedly believed that the ruler should be a dictator—and that the dictator of a country should be a benevolent dictator with, it would seem, John Stuart Mill's "greatest happiness of the greatest number" as his ideal. But how is such a wise and just dictator to be chosen? Not by the vote of the people, in Shaw's view—his statements earlier in this chapter make that quite clear. In addition, in his article "Bernard Shaw On Peace" for the Soviet Press (c. 1948-9. B.M. Mss.) Shaw stressed the fact that a hundred years previously Thomas Carlyle had described the British Nation as "Forty millions of people, mostly fools", adding that as it was impossible to foresee what fools would do, only fools would pretend to be prophets in the matter of peace and war.

Shaw, a paragraph or two later in this statement, generalised it to include all nations:—

And if nations are 'mostly fools,' and are helpless without the leaders and rulers whom Nature produces only at the rate of five per cent of births, questions of peace and war depend on the selection of this gifted five per cent as rulers. Fools do not select them: they instinctively fear them: and fear always breeds hatred.

---

* An expression current at the time of writing signifying the crucial question, *the* question.

Therefore, if all nations are "mostly fools", wise selection of rulers is not compatible with Adult Suffrage. The mob will never vote for the *élite*. Jerusalem slays the prophets . . . Hitler was right when he called Adult Suffrage sham democracy. None the less his election of himself as Allerhöchst for life turned his head. He went the way of Paul I.

Whilst Shaw was clearly more sympathetic, generally speaking, to dictatorship than to democracy (in the conventional sense of the term) parallel statements to his acknowledgement, in the last sentence above, that dictatorship no less than democracy has inherent problems and dangers, can be found throughout his career. Thus in a lecture at the South Place Ethical Chapel on 30th June, 1901, referring particularly to *hereditary* despots as distinct from *elected* despots, he declared:—

. . . the Democratic notion that a million fools can govern better than one hereditary despot not only was not true if the despot happened to be a capable person, but was at best only a choice between two thoroughly bad ways of governing. Nobody can have seriously supposed that the divine right of the majority was any less nonsensical than the divine right of Charles I: all that could be said was that the fewer people under coercion the better; so [reasons the Democrat] let the majority coerce the minority instead of the minority coercing the majority. . . .

In an article in *La France Libre*, October, 1944, entitled "Quelle Sera la France de Demain?" ("What Will be the France of To-morrow?") Shaw expressed his view that mere majorities left to govern themselves do it so badly that they soon lose all faith in Parliament and throw themselves at the feet of any Napoleon or Kaiser or Hitler or Mussolini who cries "This stable must be cleaned out"—an incontinence which had cost the Italian Matteotti his life. Their demand is: "Then clean it out for us: we give you absolute power: you are our father and our mother: you are our Messiah."

The 'Messiah' (i.e. the dictator) always began with the best intentions. His first attempts to clean out the stable were always promising. Trains began to run punctually, even in Italy. Sinecurist civil servants found themselves called upon to work or be sacked even in Spain. Futile local councils (petty parliaments) which did nothing but talk were replaced by active prefects who did in five days what the elected bodies had only wrangled about for fifty years. For a time everybody was hopeful; and compliments were showered on the Messiah by statesmen at home and abroad. In short, everyone was so pleased with what they thought they could understand that the Messiah's head was turned by his success.

But when it came to the more fundamental jobs that only five per cent. of the citizens understood—when the taxpayer who had saved ten francs by the Messiah's inauguration of the kingdom of heaven on earth had to pay for social changes which upset all his arrangements and cost tens of milliards of francs—when he was forbidden to do things he had always done and compelled to do things he had never done, the Messiah found himself resisted and unpopular. He had to buy a bullet-proof waistcoat, and organise an omnipresent Gestapo and delegate his powers to it instead of to his Utopian prefects. His régime of reform became a régime of coercion; and—as coercion is obviously easy and popular with those who coerce, whilst social problems are too difficult to be solved by one turned head—the Messiah is forced to resort to the only political activity that Monsieur Tout le Monde understands and will suffer any extremity of coercion for; and that activity is War. The would-be Saviour becomes an enemy of mankind as arch coercionist and glorymonger; and the nations on whom he makes war combine against him and defeat him. He ends as a fugitive refugee in some neutral country if there is one left for him: if not, in Elba, St. Helena, South America, or on the scaffold as a 'war criminal' at the hands of the jealous rival criminals who have conquered him.

So far, Shaw admitted, this was the story of Germany, Italy, and Iran. But it was not the story of Russia nor of Turkey, where abler but equally despotic revolutionists had succeeded in establishing new and so far stable civilisations. Shaw declared: "France alone has despaired of and revolted against her pseudo-democratic parliamentary system without finding a Messiah. . . ."

France, he said, was again (in 1944) in the same mess she had been in under the Directory when the Revolution of 1789, having beheaded the marquises and substituted poor peasants for rich feudal seigneurs as proprietors of her land and operators of her agriculture, had relapsed into mere bourgeoisie. But it had been rescued then by Messiah Bonaparte; and when the Kings rose up and crucified him, France relapsed again under the restored Bourbons, who were simple anachronisms. Bonaparte's nephew then snatched the vacant Messiahship by a *coup d'Etat*, and kept France going for the usual twenty years "until the Messiah process finished with biochemical inevitability".

Shaw considered that the French Revolution had failed because it was "all for liberty, which is incompatible with equality and fraternity". He concluded:

What are the French to do now? If I refer them to Proudhon, who denounced bourgeois Capitalism for them as Marx did for the Russians, if I refer them to Comte, who elaborated for them a philosophy and a ritual, they will say: "Who the devil are the two authors this old man is talking about? We have never heard of them." The French are waiting for a third Napoleon . . . *Faute de mieux*, General de Gaulle must take charge and carry on.*

Sympathy with autocracy as a personal attitude as well as a political doctrine was not confined to Shaw in the early Fabian Society. In an Introduction dated 22nd September, 1944, to a Memoir by Margaret Olivier published in 1948 of (Lord) Sydney Olivier (one of the Fabian Society's original leaders in 1885, with Sidney Webb, Hubert Bland, and himself) Shaw

* Though written a quarter of a century earlier, this prophetic utterance had a very topical ring until de Gaulle's retirement from politics in 1969 and his death the following year.

described Olivier as a man who though fortunately "of good intent and sensitive humanity" was a law unto himself, and never dreamt of considering other people's feelings . . . a man who had apparently no conscience, "being on the whole too well disposed to need one"; but who when he had a whim that was flatly contrary to convention, gratified it openly and unscrupulously as a matter of course, dealing with any opposing prejudice by the method recommended by the American Mrs Stetson of walking through it as if it wasn't there. Shaw then gave a concrete example of this autocratic and dictatorial attitude; he described how he had visited Olivier when the latter was Governor of Jamaica, and had asked him whether he had tried to rule on a democratic plan (he meant in the conventional sense of the word), and if so, how it had worked. Olivier replied that he had indeed tried it, but found that whenever he proposed a measure intelligible only to people who could see further than the ends of their noses, he was invariably opposed by his democratic councils. "I now" he went on, "do not consult them. I do what is needed. In eighteen months or so they see that I was right, and stop howling about it."

Shaw's comment on this was: "Hitler could say no more; and it is a pity that Hitler had not Olivier's brain and kindly objectivity." [!].

As a corollary to his belief in autocracy (dictatorship), Shaw clearly believed also in a one-party (undemocratic) political system, such as that which has existed in Russia since 1917. In his draft article "The Party System and Socialists" (1944) he expressed the view that a party "made absolute, automatic, and totalitarian" becomes, in fact, a Church, and may revive imperialism by aspiring to be a Catholic or Supernational Church. It would suppress any rival State Church just as the Soviet suppressed the Comintern even in the act of making a Concordat with the ritual clergy. In politics, only one party, that of the Government, would be tolerated; but as every party would pretend to be that party, there would be party elections and party government, though the parties might

call themselves societies or groups or movements or "Actions".
Plenty of aliases would be available. They would combine and
recombine to gain their ends. In fact there would be more
parties than ever when the Party system was discarded and
there were dozens of opinions operating in Parliament instead
of the one opinion, quite irrelevant to the public welfare, which
(Shaw considered) was all that usually operated in our division
lobbies.

He went on:—

I could expatiate for many columns on this theme; for I foresee
that [as] Socialist politics develop, our stalwarts will be crying in
all directions though not in the original French, that "The more
things change the more they remain the same," or worse, for there
will be no new world: we must still put up with the old one, and
make the best of it. And that process will be full of surprises, most
of which to the best of our Utopian stalwarts will present themselves
as bitter disappointments. And I, who will not be surprised by the
surprises, and will work for half a loaf as better than no bread, will
be described, as Sir Harold Webbe lately described me, as "that
fine old Tory, Mister Bernard Shaw".

It is interesting to note that some almost complete contradictions (or at least qualifications) to certain of his views
expressed in the last few pages, and earlier in this chapter, were
contained in an article in *The Irish Statesman* of 11th October,
1919. In it, Shaw proclaimed that no government could govern
without the consent and co-operation of the people, and that
any dictatorship other than a *benevolent* dictatorship which
was fully accepted by the people—whom Shaw on this occasion
apparently regarded as sufficiently intelligent to be capable of
forming valid political judgements—had within it the seeds of
its own destruction: it would be bound to collapse sooner or
later—more or less of its own accord. On this occasion (if
possibly on no other) Shaw in effect supported the conventional
and usual meaning imputed to the term 'democracy', namely

that it was the people, and not the rulers, who were the ultimate political authority and the real wielders of power.

After declaring: "We may agree with the old Unionists with great heartiness in their advocacy of resolute government and plenty of it", Shaw asked: "How is it to be brought to pass?" He continued:—

Everyone who is not an idiot will admit, to begin with, that no government can be strong, or indeed govern at all, without the consent and co-operation of the governed. Laws are enforced, not by the police, but by the citizens who call the police when the law is broken. If the citizens connive at breaches of the law and shield the lawbreaker instead of denouncing him, it is all up with the government. The executive may refuse to admit checkmate for a time. If it has sufficient manpower at its disposal it can bring about a state of things in which out of every five persons in the country one is a spy, one a policeman, and two are soldiers. If it has sufficient money it can put the whole population in prison and support them there. But that is not governing: it is mere coercion, destructive to production, incompatible with prosperity, ruinous alike to the coercer and the coerced. It cannot settle the country, develop the country, secure property and person in the country, satisfy the country, or, in short, achieve any of the ends of government. This is so obvious that the advocacy of such coercion by sane men will be taken as evidence of a design to ruin the country, and a very stupid one when the circumstances are such as to make it impossible for even a Cromwell to go through with the process.

A government, then, can govern just as much as the people will allow it to govern, and not a bit more. . . . When the man who disobeys its orders and slays its officers to avoid arrest can depend on his neighbours not to denounce him . . . the authorities . . . cannot keep the peace . . . such a government is miserably weak, irritable, mischievous, and perpetually at its wits' ends . . . it is never for a moment master of the situation; and the end, however long it may be delayed, is foredoomed.*

* Illustrations in recent history are the governments in various countries against whom 'resistance movements' developed during and after the Second World War. The Vichy government of Pétain and Laval, opposed by the Free French led by General de Gaulle, is a particularly apposite example.

Some further important contradictions and interesting qualifications occurred in a draft article dated about 1911 among the manuscripts now in the British Museum, in which Shaw expressed views diametrically opposed to his later conception of an "instructed director" class of ruling intelligentsia analogous to Plato's 'Guardian Class' (see page 281), and dealt with other facets of his Equality of Incomes concept, together with the subjects of Idolatry, Plutocracy, and Oligarchy, and with the ever-recurring controversial and central question of how precisely to define democracy. On this occasion he wrote:—

. . . What is a democrat? He is one who would have the majority of the people judge their laws and elect and remove their lawgivers according to their favorable or unfavorable judgements of them and their work. Opposed to them you have Aristocrats, Plutocrats, Oligarchs, priests, kings, judges, schoolmasters, and so forth; but at bottom you will find that on this point there are only two systems before you, the system of Democracy and the system of Idolatry, and only two sorts of advocates: the Protestant and the Priest, the Democrat and the Organizer of Idolatry. On the one side it is said that subordination and obedience are necessary to society and that men are so constituted that they will not obey or respect their equals, and that it is therefore necessary to set their rulers apart from them as creatures of another species, decorating them with gorgeous dresses and ornaments, forbidding their children to intermarry with the children of the vulgar, paying them huge sums to maintain palaces and equipages: in short, idolizing them. Against the man who believes this I cannot hurl the reproach that he is no gentleman because he is not a Socialist. I am prepared to tackle him on other grounds, but not on that ground. But the Democrat, the Protestant, lies open to my insult. For the Democrat concedes political equality and religious equality; and if he denies economic equality he can have no other motive than to secure a bigger dividend than his political and religious equals, and to set his own personal welfare before that of his fellow-workers. I am not here to argue the case as between Democracy and Idolatry. We see plainly enough that Democracy without Equality of Income means Plutocracy, and that Idolatry under the same conditions means tyranny and imposture. Demagogues and Republican Presidents have as much to answer for as priests and popes or country gentlemen and kings. But that may be the fault of Inequality. A Church under vows, not of Poverty, which is a damnable sin, but of Equality, might not be the sort of professional conspiracy against the human race which all Churches are now. Democracy with Equality might work quite well, especially as nobody would take the trouble to vote, and unpopular laws would simply be disobeyed. But I am not concerned with that for the moment. Whether Idolatry, or Idolatrism, be right or wrong, it furnishes a motive for Unsocialism which is not necessarily an ungentlemanly one. Whether Democracy be right or wrong, the Democrat who is willing to share everything national with his fellow voter except the national cash seems to me to be, in respect of that exception, a cad.

In the November, 1933, *Nash's Magazine* article quoted on page 311-12, Shaw stated that for many years he had said that what democracy needed was a trustworthy anthropometric machine for the selection of qualified rulers. More recently he had elaborated this by demanding the setting up of panels of tested persons eligible for the different grades in the government hierarchy. Panel A would be for diplomacy and international finance; Panel B for national affairs, and so on. Nobody had disagreed with him, said Shaw, when he had advocated these panels, but when he was challenged to produce an anthropometric machine or endocrine or phrenological tests as a means of selection of the right people, he had been forced to admit that no satisfactory ones had been invented, and that such existing attempts as competitive examinations were so irrelevant and misleading as to be worse than useless as tests of education, let alone of potential ability to govern.

Apropos of such tests of education, endowed ability, and potential fitness to rule over others, Shaw had earlier explained, in the Workers' Educational Association *Education Year Book* (1918):—

. . . some of them are obviously cranky, and none have superseded the experienced college tutor who tells an undergraduate what honors it is worth his while to read for in view of his natural capacity. But tutorial measurement is founded on a degree of intimacy and familiarity which is not practicable for general public purposes. We seem far from the day when persons classed by natural capacity as distinguished from acquirements will be disqualified or conscribed for public work according to their degree; when Class A1 will be compelled on incorruptible evidence to elect representative peers to undertake the highest duties of the State, and Class Z17, however self-assertive and noisily popular, will be absolutely debarred from voting at elections, contesting Parliamentary seats, or running newspapers.

In making this rough suggestion I am not forgetting that one of the uses of democracy is to save people from being intolerably well governed, and, in fact, discouraged out of existence as savages are by civilized men. I would give Class A1 rights of counsel and criticism, but no vote. The mass of men coming between J and K should neither be dragged in the mud by Z nor dragged up to the clouds by A to share the fate of Phaeton; and my old proposal that Parliament should contain 50 aldermen elected by proportional representation under the original Hare scheme, the whole nation voting as one constituency, should be safeguarded by the proviso that their rights of speech in the Assembly should not include access to the voting lobbies. But even with such safeguards, which would not exclude the popular actor of the day and the popular general, however incapable they might be politically, a wise electorate would still ask for some scientific, bias-proof test of capacity, taking capacity in its widest sense to include intellectual integrity and social instinct, and giving no more than its due value to that power of working for 16 hours a day every day for 30 years which at present enables the stupidest routineers to oust from important posts men of much higher faculty, whose real work cannot be sustained except in emergencies for more than two or three hours, and even at that imposes extensive periods of total recreation.

Now secondary education, as we have it today, wholly fails to supply such a test.

Thus the $64 billion billion question remains: Assuming that power in the hands of benevolent dictators is not an impossibility from time to time in the future, how are such rulers to be *kept* wise and just and benevolent, and protected from the tendency to lapse into degradation, lust for world conquest, harshness, and cruelty—which absolute power, history teaches us, has all too often led to in its possessors in the past? (notwithstanding that there have indeed also been a number of dictators whose influence has been mainly good—such as Caesar, the Emperor Augustus, Queen Elizabeth I, Cromwell, Napoleon III, Bismarck, and in more recent times, Kemal Ataturk).

Furthermore, as Shaw himself once admitted in a draft letter dated 8th October, 1939*, intended for the *Manchester Guardian*:—

... an idolized One Man autocracy is never a reality, because the Idolized One cannot be everywhere, and must therefore delegate his autocracy to a host of nobodies whom he is obliged to support no matter what atrocities the worst of them commit.

Shaw's consciousness of the great difficulties of the problem of government even drove him to half-advocate Anarchism (no government at all) in a lecture at the Kingsway Hall, London, on 28th October, 1914. After saying that the paving of hell with good intentions was not peculiar to the private property system, he declared:—

History is mostly a record of the tragedy of politically uneducated citizens giving their loyalty to equally ignorant rulers and politicians for the maintenance of shallow and obvious moralities which defeat their own purpose so completely that at last even professional sociologists are driven to set up Anarchism as a political principle on the ground that nothing worse can possibly come of it than the results of laws and creeds.

However, it is also of considerable interest to note that in a letter to the *New Witness* (8th March, 1917), replying to a criticism of his 'Superman' conception, Shaw declared that what he believed in was not "*a* Superman" but "a democracy of

* Shaw papers, British Museum.

Supermen". He reminded readers that in 1903 in the preface to *Man and Superman* he had written:—

... Until there is an England in which every man is a Cromwell, a France in which every man is a Napoleon, a Rome in which every man is a Caesar, a Germany in which every man is a Luther plus a Goethe, the world will be no more improved by its heroes than a Brixton villa is improved by the pyramid of Cheops. The production of such nations is the only real change possible to us.

On the face of it, any such nation with a population composed entirely of great leaders and no one being led by them, would be an impossibility, but at the end of this letter, Shaw made his meaning clear by re-writing a passage from a book by his 'friendly rival' H. G. Wells called *War and the Future*, which had just been published. As follows:—

The true Superman comes not as the tremendous personal entry of a star, but in the less dramatic form of a general increase of goodwill and skill and common sense. A species rises not by thrusting up peaks but by brimming up as a flood does. The coming of the superman means not an epidemic of personages, but the disappearance of the Personage in the universal ascent! That is the point grasped so superbly by that great anti-Prussian Nietzsche ... Its organ tones boom majestically from the battle axe of Gilbert Chesterton, and fly in stinging spindrift from the Jew's harp of Israel Zangwill.

Pending the invention of any scientific method for the election of rulers, Shaw admitted, in his preface to *The Apple Cart* (1930), that we would have to go along as best we could with the sort of government our present system produced, though several reforms were possible without any new discovery. He explained:—

... Our present parliament is obsolete: it can no more do the work of a modern State than Julius Cæsar's galley could do the work of an Atlantic liner. We need in these islands two or three additional federal legislatures, working on our municipal committee system instead of our parliamentary party system. We need a central authority to co-ordinate the federal work. Our obsolete little internal frontiers must be obliterated, and our units of local government enlarged to dimensions compatible with the recent prodigious advances in facility of communication and co-operation. Commonwealth affairs and supernational activities through the League of Nations or otherwise will have to be provided for, and Cabinet function to be transformed. All the pseudo-democratic obstructive functions of our political machinery must be ruthlessly scrapped, and the general problem of government approached from a positive viewpoint at which mere anarchic national sovereignty as distinguished from self-government will have no meaning.

However, Shaw qualified his views on this topic by a warning that when everything had been done that could be done, civilisation would still be dependent on the consciences of the governors and the governed. Our natural dispositions might be good, he said, but we had been badly brought up, and were full of antisocial personal ambitions and prejudices and snobberies. Had we not better teach our children to be better citizens than ourselves? We were not doing that, said Shaw, but the Russians *were*.

The view that conscience, when freed from such effects of upbringing as prejudice and snobbery, must lead to a Socialistic attitude, had been expressed throughout his career by Shaw. For example, in *The Times* of 5th February, 1909, he declared:—

. . . if all decent men were not nine-tenths Socialists to begin with, whether they know it or not; if there were any possibility of controversy as to the fundamental proposition of Socialism that whoever does not by the work of his prime repay the debt of his nurture and education, support himself in his working days, and provide for his retirement, inflicts on society precisely the same injury as a thief, then indeed the prospect would be black for civilization.

Two final quotations on the theme of Liberty and slavery are apposite here. The first is from *The New Republic*, 9th February, 1918:—

. . . any fool can be a slave: in fact, every fool *is* a slave, though he may be too great a fool to know it. The great aim in life is not to find out how little you *need* do, but how much you *can* do. Liberty is the right to think and choose for oneself. What liberty costs is the trouble of thinking and choosing for oneself. He who thinks liberty worth the trouble, and actually likes the trouble, is the only really free Englishman.

The second is from his draft article in the British Museum dated 28th May, 1909, and headed "Advanced Socialism for Intelligent People":—

Theoretically, since there are no indifferent actions, there is for every man a rigid line of conduct from which he cannot swerve one hair's breadth in the minutest detail without injury to the community; and if the community could ascertain that line it would be justified in compelling him to keep to that line, to the entire abolition of his "freedom". Conscientious educated men seek the guidance of that line throughout their lives, and never for a moment think of themselves as free agents. . . . So much for the theory of "liberty". . . .

Later in the same draft Shaw added:—

The truth is, revolutions are not wholly human affairs. Just as the individual economists and philosophers of the Benthamite school built very much worse than they knew, less able and public spirited men have often built very much better than they knew. You have not only to allow for such moral forces of evolution as are appealed to in the famous communist manifesto of Marx and Engels, but for the driving power which makes . . . men do things quite unrelated to their own individual needs, and which they often call by the name of God.

For the ultimate basis and explanation of Shaw's political and social views (on which he based his hopes for the uplifting of mankind) one must turn, I feel sure, from his intellectual arguments to his fundamentally religious and indeed mystical nature. Shaw once described politics as "essentially a religious vocation". The reader may wish to refer back to his *Christian*

Economics sermon at this juncture, and to be reminded that Communism is not necessarily or basically associated with the harshness and cruelty of the Soviet travesty of it, but on the contrary, specifically equated by Shaw (and he was, and is, not alone in this) with the practical expression of Christianity.

In Shaw's own words—at the conclusion of a speech on Socialism at Coventry, as reported in the *Coventry Herald* 16th March, 1912:—

. . . There is a general ideal towards which I am working. I do not want you to merely call yourselves Socialists. . . The founder of the Christian religion was a communist, but there is an extraordinary number of people who take His name in vain and profess to follow Him. I do not want the word Socialism to be adopted in the same way that the word Christianity has been adopted. I have known too many Christians to attach very much importance to that.

A man should be able to work without anxiety about his own future or his children's future, so long as he is prepared to do his share of work.

And in an address at the City Temple on 11th October, 1909, he told his congregation:—

. . . Don't go about with long faces sympathising with the poor and with ills. Take poverty and illness in extremely bad part; and when you meet a man whose wife is ill or who is poor, and all that sort of thing, don't say to him that it is the will of God, which is a horrible blasphemy. Tell him in solemn scriptural language that it is a damnable thing, and that you have to come to try and put a stop to it because you are the will of God. And then you will have put the man you are talking to on the high road to understand that his will is the will of God too.

I will only add here that Shaw's religious views unquestionably had a profound influence on his attitude to political and social matters, and indeed on every ramification of his life.

From all of the foregoing, it is clear that Shaw felt that a good deal of the misunderstanding of his views was due to misinterpretation of the words he used. Partly this confusion arises because the meaning of these words *is* complex, and therefore inevitably subject to various interpretations. There is, for example, much confusion at the time of writing, 1968-9, within the Labour Party as to the meaning of the word, 'Socialism', and writing in the *New Statesman* on 3rd July, 1943, Shaw himself admitted:—

. . . When Ibsen was invited to assume a Party label he replied that he had both the Left and the Right in him, and was glad to have his ideas adopted by any Party. I find myself very much in the same position, and am sometimes surprised and amused, as I go farther and farther to the Left, to find that the world is round and that the extreme Left is the old Right with its nonsense and corruption cleaned off.

In a variation of the above in *Everybody's Political What's What* (1944) Shaw explained that Ibsen, while pleased to find his views influencing Liberals, Conservatives, and Socialists alike, and especially workmen and women, had at the same time, refused to label himself either Liberal, Conservative, Labour, or Suffragist, declaring that Party rules were not golden rules—there were none. Shaw added:—

. . . I find myself in the position of Ibsen. His objection to adopt a party label is shared by those who have room in their heads for more than one political subject, and who take the trouble to find out how their views would work out in practice.

But can Shaw himself really be said to have done this?
The various extracts given also show that Shaw's challenging, original turn of phrase often tended to divert attention from the sometimes questionable logic upon which his arguments were based, and that he thus—in his inability to resist the rhetorical Shavian *bon mot*—contributed not a little himself, on occasions, to this misunderstanding.*

---

* [It may be of interest to add that, among other believers in the doctrine of Equalisation of Incomes, the late Mr Victor Gollancz, the publisher, was (according to a television interview) probably the best known.—*Ed.*]

ON WAR AND PEACE

Reference was made by C. B. Purdom (in *Shaw the Villager*) to the storm of controversy aroused by Shaw's famous supplement to the *New Statesman* of 14th November, 1914, entitled *Common Sense About the War*; and Shaw's reply of thanks to his supporters at the time was given in the collection of his 'printed postcards and stock letter replies' at the beginning of the present volume.

In *Common Sense About the War*, Shaw's main point was that it takes two to make a quarrel. He considered that just as the British Nation blamed German militarism and 'Junkerism' so the German Nation had some right to blame British militarism and 'Junkerism'. (A Junker being defined as a young nobleman, younker, lording, country-squire ... or squirearch:* i.e. a young—or not so young—member of the ruling class).

Shaw also criticised the British War Office, the Foreign Office, blind patriotism of the 'my country, right or wrong' variety, and what he regarded as British hypocrisy. He considered that Britain and her allies had taken little effectual action to save 'Brave Little Belgium', and that Sir Edward Grey—whom he regarded as the epitome of British Junkerism "from his topmost hair to the tips of his toes"—had gravely misled both the British public and the German nation into thinking that the understanding he had entered into with France would not involve Britain in war if Germany attacked France, whereas in fact it definitely would. Shaw regarded this as dissembling and prevarication, and the cause of the unpreparedness for war which had, in the event, been a tragic and inevitable result of it. Shaw's attitude was not a pacifist one, for he referred to Winston Churchill as "an odd and not disagreeable compound of Junker and Yankee: his frank

---

* The definition is that quoted by Shaw from the *Enzyklopädisches Wörterbuch* of Muret-Sanders.

anti-German pugnacity is enormously more popular than the moral babble (Milton's phrase) of his sanctimonious colleagues", and he admitted in this pamphlet having earlier advocated greatly increased British re-armament. (And in March, 1913, he had expressed himself "very strongly in favour" of compulsory military service). He also affirmed his belief that the Christian Churches should close down during time of war.

In amplification of his views on the Churches Shaw wrote:—

. . . No doubt to many of us the privation thus imposed would be far worse than the privation of small change, of horses and motor-cars, of express trains, and all the other prosaic inconveniences of war. But would it be worse than the privation of faith, and the horror of the soul, wrought by the spectacle of nations praying to their common Father to assist them in sabring and bayoneting and blowing one another to pieces with explosives that are also cor-rosives, and of the Church organizing this monstrous paradox instead of protesting against it? . . . If all the Churches of Europe closed their doors until the drums ceased rolling they would act as a most powerful reminder that though the glory of war is a famous and ancient glory, it is not the final glory of God.

Shaw went on to proclaim that his heart lay with Russia (this was, of course, three years before the Russian Revolution), and he praised Socialism as what he considered to be the only true road to international peace—since it got rid of the 'Junker' class. He wrote:—

. . . Will you now at last believe, O stupid British, German, and French patriots, what the Socialists have been telling you for so many years: that your Union Jacks and tricolors and Imperial Eagles ('where the carcase is, there will the eagles be gathered') are only toys to keep you amused, and that there are only two real flags in the world henceforth: the red flag of Democratic Socialism and the black flag of Capitalism, the flag of God and the flag of Mammon.

Shaw also, a little later, attempted to debunk the 'righteous indignation' of many people regarding the sinking of the

Lusitania and the Zeppelin raids on London, on the ground
that civilians had no real justification for complaining if they
had on a few occasions to face a small part of the danger and
horror which the fighting services were having to put up with
all the time. Then he supported the still highly unpopular cause
of the suffragettes by urging that the vote be given to the wives
and mothers and sisters of the soldiers—many of whom were
increasingly becoming engaged in nursing, munitions, and other
war work. He also pleaded that the Peace must be *inconclusive*—
the only conclusive peace was the Peace of Death whilst war
lasted as an institution. Another of Shaw's aims in writing his
Common Sense pamphlet was to improve American feeling
towards Britain, which was in 1914 very strained owing to the
Americans' criticisms of British hypocrisy.

Actually, Shaw made out a much stronger case against
Germany in *Common Sense About the War* than the official one
put forward by the British Government. But because—in his
typical fashion—he gave both sides of the argument in great
detail, in order to bring the truth the more vividly and effectually
home to people, he was—as he had so often been—completely
misconstrued and misrepresented by narrow, bigoted people.
(And the patriotic fervour and blindness to the views of others
in Britain in 1914 was of a degree which today we would
associate with complete fanaticism. It was epitomised in the
feeling of "My country, right or wrong" and the capacity to
believe, as large numbers of the population came to, that the
Germans—"the Huns"—ate roasted human babies for their
Sunday dinner!)

Shaw's fellow-playwright, Henry Arthur Jones, is said to have
nearly died of apoplexy when Shaw published *Common Sense
About the War*, and he and all the other noted playwrights of the
day (with Pinero and Lonsdale as the sole exceptions) combined
in obtaining Shaw's expulsion from the Dramatists' Club on
account of the views he expressed therein and his 'outrageous'
views on the sinking of the *Lusitania*.

William Archer, a former close friend, wanted Shaw

guillotined in Trafalgar Square, whilst Pinero also was critical, though not to so extreme a degree. Arnold Bennett's opinion was more moderate. He thought *Common Sense About the War* excellent sense on such matters as recruiting, the treatment of soldiers' and sailors' dependants, the closing of Churches in war-time, jingoism, disarmament, etc., but pointed out that "mixed up with the tremendous commonsense of such proposals" there was also, in his view, "the usual percentage of perverseness, waywardness, and harlequinading". Henry Arthur Jones was Shaw's arch enemy. In an open letter he wrote: "The hag Sedition was your mother and Perversity begot you. Mischief was your midwife and Misrule your nurse, and Unreason brought you up at her feet—no other ancestry and rearing had you, you freakish homunculus, germinated outside of lawful procreation." He wanted twenty pairs of stocks put up in Trafalgar Square for use on Shaw "and a lot of Englishmen who hate England, and write nasty things and say nasty things about our country, and do all they can to make our own people hate her and to make other countries hate her".

This was not fair to Shaw, who (apart from being an Irishman, not an Englishman) felt that the war had to be fought, and even showed some sympathy with the general patriotic fervour. A week after the outbreak of war, for example, he had written in the *Daily News* of 11th August, 1914:—

... The wickedness of war is a reason for keeping out of war; but the field once taken, it is not a practicable reason for betraying your allies and your country by throwing down your arms and kneeling down to pray. . . .

It was the historical background and the tragic political mistakes which had led up to the war, and the likelihood of equally tragic blunders after the war was over, that aroused his wrath and impelled him to speak his mind so plainly. A few weeks after his *Common Sense* Supplement, in an article in the *New Statesman* on 12th December entitled "The Last Spring of the Old Lion", Shaw referred to:—

. . . the old British lion, the lion of Waterloo, the lion of Blenheim, the lion of Trafalgar, making his last and most terrible and triumphant spring. You see him with his old craft and his old courage and strength unimpaired, with his old amazing luck, his old singleness of aim, his old deep-lying and subtle instinct that does better without great men at a pinch than his enemies do with them.

For centuries, Shaw continued, the lion had held to his one idea, that none should be greater than England on the land, and none as great on the sea. To him it had been nothing whether a rival to England was better or worse than England. When Waterloo was won, Byron had said: "I'm damned sorry"; and humanitarians and libertarians had looked aghast at "the re-establishment of the Inquisition and the restoration of an effete and mischievous dynasty by English arms on the ruins of Liberty, Equality, and Fraternity". Little recked the lion of that, said Shaw. England's rival was in the dust; England was mistress of the seas; England's general (what matter that he was an Irishman?) was master of Europe, with its kings whispering in his presence like frightened schoolboys; England right or wrong, England complete with her own native corruptions and oppressions no less than her own native greatness and glory. England had emerged from the conflict and continued to hold the balance of power in her hand. And for a hundred years after that, no Englishman was ever to turn pale at the possibility of invasion. For more than two generations of Englishmen the lion lay and basked and smelt no foe that a pat of his paw could not dispose of . . . .

Shaw emphasised both his understanding of Britain's position—her need to fight the war—and his deep concern about the outcome and its various side effects:—

. . . I vibrate to it; I perceive the might and mystery of it; and all sorts of chords in me sound the demand that the lion's last fight shall be the best fight of all, and Germany the last foe overcome. But I am a Socialist, and I know well that the lion's day is gone by, and that the bravest lion gets shot at in the long run. I foresee that his victory will not, like the old victories, lead to a century of security: I know that it will create a situation more dangerous than the situation of six months ago, and that only by each western nation giving up every dream of supremacy can that situation be mastered. . . . In future, we must fight, not alone for England, but for the welfare of the world. But for all that, the lion is a noble old beast; and his past is a splendid past and his breed more valiant than ever—too valiant nowadays, indeed, to be merely Englishmen *contra mundum*. I take off my hat to him as he makes his last charge, and shall not cease to wave it because of the squealing of the terrified chickens.

To most of the numerous criticisms of his *Common Sense* pamphlet, even the most misunderstood and offensively and vitriolically expressed, Shaw remained impervious. He even issued a public request that, to spare his secretary, such critics among his correspondents should mark their envelopes 'obscene'. But strong criticism came from some of his fellow-Socialists as well as from 'Capitalist warmongers' and hysterical jingoes, and these he did feel deeply, as instanced in a letter he sent to the *Daily Citizen* of 26th November, 1914. In this he complained bitterly that this newspaper, representing the voice of Labour and the working class, should have printed a letter from a reader severely criticising him for his *Common Sense About the War* pamphlet. He declared:—

. . . Properly handled, this war can be led to a victory not only for the Allies over Germany, but for democracy over its worst enemies both at home and abroad. And when I say democracy I do not mean Mr Asquith's pseudo-democracy, which uses Mutiny Acts in time of peace to imprison Labour leaders and muzzle the Labour Press, but genuine working-class democracy. . . .

I have shown that there is a tremendous case for pushing this war to a victory over Prussia from the Labour point of view, and that it is being spoiled by the official case, which is a very bad one.

Shaw added:—

. . . I have stood for a brave and straight democratic fighting case, for open democratic diplomacy, full civil rights, and for a fair livelihood for the soldier and his dependants; for clean hands and clean mouths, and the discarding of the dirty lies and rancours that are invented and fomented to take the attention of our people off speculators in shoddy khaki and refreshment contractors, who bribe sergeants to wink at the supply of uneatable food, even to our troops in training at home (with what effect on recruiting can be imagined); and for an energetic pushing of the interests of Labour and democracy now that a formidable emergency has at last given serious men the opportunity of making themselves heard above the din of party twaddle.

In short, I have put my best brains and skill at the service of the Labour cause, with no other defence against the inevitable storm of capitalist and official abuse than the support of those for whom I did the work.

Shaw considered the contributor's objections to be of precisely the same kind as those in the Capitalist (Tory) press— the *Daily Citizen* was showing the same loyalty to the Foreign Office, support of military conscription, and abhorrence of Socialists and Labour agitators, and was thus aligning itself with the *Daily Express*, *The Times*, and other Conservative newspapers. Shaw explained:—

When I am repudiated by the *Daily Citizen* I am repudiated by the Labour Party and the trade union movement, and it becomes open to the anti-Labour papers to declare that I am utterly ignorant of the aims and sympathies of democracy; that the Labour movement is wholeheartedly in favour of Sir Edward Grey and his foreign methods, and of Mr Asquith and his home methods; that Labour makes no claim for representation at the War Office and has no objection to the system, imported from Prussia, under which soldiers are denied all ordinary civilian rights; and that when our men in the trenches have won the victory with their blood and our substance, we shall be perfectly content to have the terms of peace settled behind our backs by Sir Edward Grey, and to go on humbly and obediently until he sends us to the trenches again without consulting us.

Shaw went on to ask whether readers of the *Daily Citizen*

really agreed with this attitude and approved of him "being stabbed by their paper in the back when I am making a stand for them at a crisis when such stands, never very easy to make, are exceptionally difficult and even a little dangerous?"

If this was so, he continued, then at least he knew where he stood and could continue to cry in the wilderness, "without making any pretence that the contemptuous estimate of my aims and opinions expressed by the baser sort of capitalist papers are not thoroughly shared by the working classes and even by the Socialists".

Shaw appealed to readers that if, on the other hand, he still commanded any support in the Labour movement, it was a time for his supporters to protest at the criticisms levelled at him in the *Daily Citizen*.   He concluded:—

> In my thirty years' public work I have seen man after man in the Labour movement sell out because he could not trust his future to the loyalty of the workers; and I should, perhaps, have had to sell out myself long ago if I had not possessed certain powers as a writer which made me a little more independent than others.
>
> I suggest that the treatment I am meeting now from the *Daily Citizen* is not such as to encourage any man with a talent for public life who may be hesitating between the Labour and the Capitalist causes to come down on the right side.

(By "right side" Shaw meant, of course, the Socialist and working class side, not the Right-wing or Conservative-capitalist side—though the previous sentence clearly indicates his half-sympathetic view that Right-wing supporters had plenty of justification for their attitude.)

Nevertheless, remaining undaunted by his other critics, Shaw in an article in the *Boston Sunday Post* (10th January, 1915), entitled "Responsibility for the War", again declared that the British and French had completely failed Belgium at Liège, and that Britain ought to accommodate Belgian refugees so as to relieve pressure on refugees in Holland and France. Shaw thought it utterly hypocritical that the debt to Belgium had been acknowledged in *King Albert's Gift Book* by many of England's most illustrious spokesmen, poets, and composers, but that almost nothing had been done to assist her in the ways she really needed of money, supplies, and help for her refugees:—

... our acknowledgement has stopped just so far short of complete justice as our bias about the war stops short of the utter honest truth about it. And that truth is, as I have said, that of all the belligerents, Belgium and Belgium alone is innocent of all warlike designs; whilst, as to the neutral nations, there is not one of them that will not be a gainer by Belgium's sacrifice.

It is noteworthy that Shaw's commissioned contribution to *King Albert's Gift Book* was cut out by the publishers, the *Daily Telegraph*, on account of the controversial views he had expressed in *Common Sense*. Shaw's attitude was, however, handsomely vindicated by the fact that the Belgian Minister subsequently appealed successfully to Shaw direct to write a special separate article to help the Belgian fund, knowing well that Shaw's power and abilities to raise money for Belgium in America and elsewhere, were probably equal to those of all the contributors to *King Albert's Gift Book* put together.

In November, 1915, Shaw wrote a preface to a proposed reprint of his *Common Sense* pamphlet. This little-known document came to my notice too late to be dealt with here, but I have included the gist of the additional points in his defence Shaw made in it as an APPENDIX, on page 524-6—to which readers may wish to turn either now or later.

Shaw further explained his motives in writing *Common Sense* in the course of a conversation recorded by Professor Archibald Henderson in *The Fortnightly Review*, 1st January, 1925:—

... I made the Germans a handsome present of all the rubbish about our disinterestedness, our unpreparedness, our respect for treaties and for the sacredness of neutral soils, and all the rest of our recruiting propaganda and Jingo tosh, which naturally did not impose on anybody except ourselves. Then I gave the real reason why German

Imperialism had to be smashed. To allow it to triumph would, I said, be "to shut the gates of mercy on mankind".

Henderson next asked whether Shaw felt that subsequent events had justified his standpoint in *Common Sense*. Shaw replied:—

Completely, even where I had been guessing. Within a few months of its publication *The Times* and *The Pall Mall Gazette* were going far beyond anything I had ventured to say. Great offence had been given by my contemptuous dismissal of the pretence that we had not been prepared for the war—that we were innocent lambs suddenly and wantonly attacked by a German wolf who had been preparing for years. The silly people who were spreading this sentimental fairy tale forgot that they were accusing the War Office, the Admiralty, and the Foreign Office of gross blindness and neglect of duty. Lord Haldane hastened to explain that General French had been sent to study the country in Flanders years before the war broke out, and claimed rightly that the War Office had fulfilled to the letter the military arrangements it had made with France and Belgium in view of the war as early as 1906. Mr Winston Churchill claimed that the British Navy had gone into the war with five years' accumulation of ammunition made expressly for it. Lord Fisher's autobiography revealed the pressure put on the British Government to attack and destroy the German Fleet—to "Copenhagen" it—without notice in the days of Edward VII* who had finally to ask Fisher to be good enough to stop shaking his fist in the royal face.

Anyone now reading *Common Sense* will be astonished at the severity of the censorship I imposed on myself when all the hyper-patriotic publicists were raving in utter recklessness of the effect their transports might produce on foreign opinion, especially on American opinion.

Henderson then referred to the particularly violent outburst of popular feeling aroused by one of his speeches following the sinking of the *Lusitania* in 1915. Shaw commented:—

* i.e. before 1910 (when Edward VII died).

The violent outburst was against the sinking of the *Lusitania*, not against me. I did not conceal my contempt for the people who had taken that frightful slaughter of our soldiers in Flanders as if it were a cinema show got up to please their patriotism, but who went stark raving mad when one of their favourite pleasure boats—actually with first-class passengers aboard—was blown up. But they were too mad to mind me. The truth is that the *Lusitania* catastrophe —much too big a word for it, by the way—was the first incident in the war that was small enough for their minds to take in: they suddenly realised at last that the Germans meant to kill them, and that the war was something more serious than reading despatches from correspondents at the front about "our gallant fellows in the trenches". Their frivolity infuriated me; but no newspaper dared rebuke their silly heartlessness as it deserved; and I did not tell them off until the war was over, in the preface to *Heartbreak House*. Besides, I was not troubling much about them, with the prospect suddenly opened up of America having to come in. Like Von Bernhardi, I knew that America held the winning card.

Henderson here pointed out that it had since been more or less proved that the Germans' contention that the *Lusitania* had been carrying munitions of war as well as civilian passengers, had been correct, and Shaw agreed, adding that in his opinion the Germans had a military right and duty to sink every vessel *capable* of carrying munitions and food to the British Isles, irrespective of whether it was actually carrying such a cargo or not. A blockade, to be effective, must be ruthless and have no loopholes.

Henderson, a little later in the interview added:—

One of your bitterest opponents since the war*—a friend of other days—has been calling you a lot of awful names: "most poisonous of all the poisonous haters of England; despiser, distorter, and denier of the plain truths whereby men live; topsy-turvy perverter of all human relationships; menace to ordered social thought and ordered social life; irresponsible braggart, blaring self-trumpeter;

---

* The utterer of these epithets must, presumably, have been Henry Arthur Jones again.

idol of opaque intellectuals and thwarted females; calculus of contrariwise; flibbertigibbert; pope of chaos; portent and epitome of this generation's moral and spiritual disorder"—and then some.[!].

Towards the end of 1915, in the *Daily Sketch* of 2nd September, Shaw was quoted on the subject of soldiers and military service:—

... It seems to me that all Socialists should advocate compulsory national service, both civil and military. But compulsory soldiering is another matter. A soldier is a slave, without rights of any kind.

There is no reason why the work of the Army should not be done by citizens with full civil rights. I have dealt with the question in the preface of *John Bull's Other Island* and in my *Common Sense About the War*.

Human nature breaks down under the strain of war just as it does under the strain of fever. You must regard people at present as more or less delirious. They will come right again when the war is over.

Shaw went on to suggest that soldiers should have full citizen rights and receive the Trade Union rate of wages proper to skilled workers at a dangerous trade. The *Daily Sketch* thought Shaw's views 'perverse' while agreeing that soldiers were 'abominably underpaid'. (Shaw's standpoint seems, however, to have found its ultimate vindication in the vastly improved conditions in the present army of the 1960's.)

Shaw's earlier views on soldiering and military service may be interpolated here. In a draft article entitled "Why Not Abolish the Soldier?", dated "Hindhead, 20 April, 1899", he wrote:—

... I am a timid civilian, detesting war as sincerely as anybody can; but in extremity I should take my part in the defence of the community if I were permitted to do so on honorable terms: that is, if I could do so without becoming a soldier and thereby surrendering all the rights and liberties of a British subject. A soldier is above all things an outlaw and a slave. If he dislikes his trade, he is not free to leave it. If under great provocation he attempts to correct his sergeant's manners and language by hitting him on the nose, an indulgence which would cost a civilian £2 in a police court, he is deprived of trial by jury, and sentenced, by officers, all professionally bound to back the sergeant, to the punishment of a garotter. Once in prison he is flogged frequently and mercilessly. . . . Freedom of speech and of the press do not exist for him; and his fellow-countrymen, very naturally and properly despising him for selling his birthright for the Queen's shilling, demand that soldiers in uniform shall not be admitted to places where gentlemen assemble to drink. All this is said to be indispensable for the maintenace of discipline. . . .

The way to provide for the defence of the country is either to abolish the army, or else retain it only as an organization of brilliantly equipped beadles, for exhibition outside the Horse Guards and other public buildings, and for forming processions and walking out with the nursemaids who so patriotically supply our warriors with pocket money. Also, of course, for keeping our silly War Office harmlessly occupied. In the meantime employ a number of ordinary English civilians to do the actual fighting, subject to no special legislation, and free to leave at a week's notice if they do not think the situation and pension worth having. Let their officers have precisely the same authority over them as a station master has over a railway porter, and no more. Pay them well; treat them honorably; give them cartridges enough to learn shooting; and there will be no difficulty about recruiting: on the contrary, the police will probably have to be called in to regulate the crowd of applicants. The plan is not novel in its essence: Cromwell tried as much of it as was necessary in 1645; and he immediately went over his opponents, hitherto victorious, like a steam roller. The fact is, the British Empire has now come to a pass at which it needs men, not soldiers, to defend it. The military idea is a superstition; and the future, as far as it depends on fighting, belongs to the nation that first abolishes the soldier.

Our present forces could be retained temporarily as an organisation of

Yours truly,

G. Bernard Shaw.

Yet, eight years later in 1907, Shaw was describing disarmament as "pure nonsense" while, nevertheless, still maintaining that soldiers should be civilians with full civil rights. He also advocated the maintenance of peace by means of an international combination of nations backed by force such as several decades later came to exist as the League of Nations, and after that, the United Nations. The following views were reprinted by the *Evening Standard and St. James Gazette* on 25th May, 1907, from the Vienna *Tagblatt* of a few days earlier:—

Disarmament is pure nonsense! The only objection one can raise against national armament is its cost, and this might easily be disposed of by progressive taxation, so adjusted as to fall on the enormous sums which are yearly lavished by wealthy do-nothings on their amusements. England wastes enough in this manner to triple her armaments, and others nations are more or less in the same case. Lastly, why should they disarm under such conditions? Two answers will probably be made to these questions: (1) That we should do away with war; and (2) That we should free ourselves from militarism.

To (1): No nation would try to prevent war by unmanning itself. We do not cut off our arms and put out our eyes in order to make assault with violence impossible. The only way likely to succeed in putting an end to warfare would be an international agreement to guard the whole world by a combination of compulsory methods and Powers, who should incontinently fall upon any State which undertook a breach of the peace. The only effective weapon for the suppression of international aggressiveness would be international aggression. And to (2): Militarism would disappear instanter if one would dispense with the absurd legendary soldier. There is not the slightest reasonable motive for making slaves, deprived of their citizen rights, out of the men who fight their nations' battles. The army of the future will be an army of civilians enjoying their full civic privileges and freedom.

Coming back to Shaw's attitude during the First World War, Shaw became a subscriber to the War Loan in 1915—to the tune of £20,000. In an interview by a Mr W. Orton Tewson in the Hull *Daily Mail* of 21st September, 1915, he replied to questions as follows:—

Q: "What do you think of the War Loan?"

A: "I don't think about it. If a man has to stop to think about so very obvious an affair his opinion is not worth having."

Q: "Is it wise or right for posterity to be burdened with both the interest and principal of this colossal sum, seeing that they have had no voice in the waging of the war?"

A: "Nothing connected with war is either wise or right, except perhaps stopping it. All war affairs are affairs of necessity, not of wisdom or rectitude. Unless the war is as important to posterity as to our own generation, it cannot be justified. And they will have just as much voice in it as the masses of the British, French, Russian, or German people had in starting it—that is, no voice at all."

Further aspects of Shaw's attitude to the First World War, and to war in general, were given vivid expression in a lecture at King's Hall, Covent Garden, on 26th October, 1915, under the title "Some Illusions of the War".* The Hon. Bertrand Russell (now Earl Russell) was in the Chair.

In his introductory remarks Shaw pointed out that he had suggested to the government the adoption of the following slogan as a means to getting the maximum effort from the public:—

IF YOU HAVE ANY BUSINESS, GO AND DO IT.

IF NOT, GET OUT OF THE WAY.   KITCHENER.

He considered that most members of the government were too old, and deplored the fact that they and all officials who had been proved incompetent were not sacked, but promoted. He called for a General Election to clear up the confusion. He then declared that war, like love, created a whole range of *illusions*. As soon as war started there sprang up a tremendous amount of sentimental raving which was really funk and founded on illusions. Our success in the war depended, on the one hand on sticking to *facts* and unveiling the illusions, and on the other, on encouraging in the people pluck, good humour, industry, a light heart, and a serious mind.

* Reported in various London and provincial newspapers.

The first danger that arose in war was looting, said Shaw. When an earthquake or any other great calamity that disjoints the frame of law and order occurred, certain people plunder, burn, murder, and are shot. But there was also such a thing as intellectual looting; there were people who in wartime looted the character and morals of a nation. He declared: "The part I have chosen for myself in this war is that of shooting these looters". War's great danger being looting, its great need was economy. Every man who was using his brain in talking nonsense about subjects he had not carefully studied, or documents he had not read, was guilty of intellectual waste—and intellectual waste might lead to our defeat in the war.

Shaw continued:—

. . . We are in a condition of illusion. We are like the Bacchantes in Euripides' play; and the awakening will be just as terrible.

Truth may seem a prosaic thing, though it is the only really poetic thing; but at all events it has no such awakenings as that.

It is this steadfastness of truth and self possession that gives it the advantage over illusion and romance. Those of us who have kept our commonsense and stuck to the facts since the beginning of the war have been reviled for our self possession by the ecstatics;* but you will notice that our story has never changed, and that every disclosure that time brings confirms us, and that sooner or later the ecstatics themselves are shrieking what they abused us for simply remarking.

They [the ecstatics] on the other hand, never tell the same story for two weeks running. Nay, you cannot find one of their newspapers that does not on the same day and in the same edition contradict itself absurdly, glorifying in one column what it describes as cowardly and murderous in the next one . . .

Shaw's main theme, as summarised in his lecture notes, was as follows:—

(1) The Judgement of God is an Illusion.

(2) The destruction of Germany is an Illusion.

* Shaw's term for those bloodthirsty people more commonly known then as 'jingoes'.

(3) The notion that we can never again be friends with the Germans is an Illusion.

(4) The Conclusive Peace is an Illusion.

(5) The Inviolability of Neutralised Buffer States is an Illusion.

(6) The Sacredness of Treaties is an Illusion.

(7) The War to End War is an Illusion.

In the course of this lecture, Shaw described the psychology of war as the satisfaction of a primitive passion, rooted, like all primitive passions, in crude necessity. When a primitive passion survived its crude utility, and persisted into the age of reason, it became a sport.

When it retained its utility but came into conflict with morality and religion, it became a romance.

Sport and romance maintain themselves in the teeth of reason and morality by raising a protective crop of illusions.

War (Shaw continued), though both a sport and a romance, is something more than either because, although it has lost its subtlety and conflicts violently with morality and religion, it has not lost its necessity.

It can be imposed as a necessity at any moment on the higher organisation which loathes it, by the lower organisation which loves it.

The object of human war is victory, or the triumph of the victor's will: its method is homicide; and when the object is no longer desired or can be better obtained in other ways, the method survives as a habit and an instinct.

The duellist never demanded victory: he demanded satisfaction. War promises endless satisfactions. Hatred, envy, spite, vengeance, pride, chivalry, courage, emulation, cupidity, and mere superfluous energy, all dream of intense satisfactions in victorious combat.

The method of war, Shaw went on, also involved terrors and sacrifices; and when war was a necessity, terrors and sacrifices were also necessities and these imposed themselves on man's imagination as a dreadful urgency without which the community must perish.

This urgency also had become independent of its reasonableness, and found its satisfaction in the sensational horrors and atrocities of war.

Thus we had the original primitive fighting passion first producing an instinctive culture of secondary passions.

These could not obtain their satisfaction until they were directed specifically against living persons.

One could not make war in the abstract: one had to make war on somebody, hate somebody, envy somebody, dread somebody, be killed by somebody, and so forth.

And if one professed religion and morality and regard for justice, one had to have moral, religious, and legal excuses for making war on the somebodies.

Hence the prodigious crop of *illusions* in which war dressed itself, and the extreme difficulty of disentangling the fictitious from the valid in these excuses. It disguised every martial passion as patriotism and some benevolent but unpatriotic ones as well.

Among the illustrations Shaw gave from the 1914 war were:—the dangerous selfishness of the war fever; the absurd contradictions of the attempt to exhibit ourselves simultaneously as a warlike nation, 'Ready, Aye, Ready', and a peaceful people surprised by a treacherous and wholly unexpected attack; the encouragement of the Germans by the thoughtlessness of the agitation for conscription; the columns of derision of German patriotic extravagances side by side with columns of precisely similar English extravagances; dangerous disregard of foreign feeling, especially in Scandinavia and the United States; the fatal effects of the suppression of criticism; the insane assumption that normal causes cease to produce their normal effects in war-time; and the strange relations of the Censorship with martial law.

Shaw considered that the supreme need in war-time was for national self-criticism and self-possession. Passionate criticism of the enemy's morals was not only worthless, but a most dangerous diversion of energy from the urgent business of defeating him in the field. Englishmen were ready to risk everything for their country, even their lives, but not their popularity. Until our national leaders were prepared to make that sacrifice every day, the war would have to be won by the common soldiers in spite of the national leaders.

There was a dramatic illusion resulting from the extraordinary susceptibility of the English people to dramatic rhetoric and its attitude to political oratory. Public orators were often reckless; checking of facts or previous utterances was almost unknown in England. There was a Celtic fervour in our loyalty to our leaders, and a dramatic imagination on its romantic side, that is, its popular side—to the glorification of triumphant violence.

Shaw also pointed out that in wartime the Gentleman is on his best behaviour, the Cad on his worst. The Cad, he said, has no code, but the Gentleman follows 'The Code of Decent Pugnacity'. I.e.:—

—Not to Fight with the Mouth.
—Not to Kick Your Man When He Is Down.
—To be ready to fight him Any Day In the Week.
—Not to Hate him: the Christian ethic.
—To Shake Hands Without Malice After the Fight.

Shaw also proclaimed that he would rather see the Kaiser installed at Buckingham Palace than that anyone should be imprisoned for freedom of speech.

It is perhaps not to be wondered at that this speech of 26th October, 1915, like many of his more provocative statements on a variety of subjects, was grossly misrepresented by most sections of the press.

The *Sheffield Daily Telegraph*'s was one of the few moderate and fair reports—headed: READY TO SHAKE HANDS. MR G. B. SHAW SAYS WAR CAN'T BE TO DEATH. But the *Western Mail*, for example, headlined its report: G.B.S. ON THE WAR. HOPES THAT GERMANY WILL LIVE TO FIGHT ANOTHER DAY;

GOOD HUMOR
INDUSTRY
LIGHT HEARTS
SERIOUS MINDS
} FOUNDED ON FACTS

V.

SENTIMENTAL
RAVINGS
FUNK
} FOUNDED ON ILLUSIONS.

IF YOU HAVE ANY BUSINESS
GO AND DO IT
IF NOT
GET OUT OF THE WAY
KITCHENER.

WAR'S DANGER | WAR'S NEED
LOOTING | ECONOMY
| Economy of BRAINS
(OVER) | (OVER)

Lecture cards:—(i) The Illusions of War (1915).

The Cads.

The Gentleman On his Best Behaviour.
The Cad on his Worst.

— The Code of Decent Pugnacity —

— Not to fight with the Mouth
— Not to kick your man when he is Down.
— To be ready to fight him any day in the Dark.
— Not to hate him — the Bayonet etc.
— To Shake hands without Malice after the fight.

— The Cad Has No Code —
— Pay his debts you shall know him. —

The Macdonald Pontificate
The Great Hill Church (   )
The Submarine Prisoners (the Lusy) .

Is it not time for the Gentleman to take

THE UPPER HAND?

(ii) The Morals of War: The Gentleman's and the Cad's.

whilst the *Yorkshire Telegraph* commented: "Mr Bernard Shaw informs us that we ought to be ready to shake hands with Germany after the war, deducing this doctrine from a false analogy with a fair fight in a ring. That is not the character of the war at all. Germany must be dealt with as convicted outlaws and murderers are treated. In their cases you let bygones be bygones when you have satisfactorily killed them, and not before. It is true that we cannot wipe out Germany, but what we can and must do is completely to paralyse her for war for many years, and afterwards to watch that she is never again in a position to wage it with any chance of victory."

The *Sunday Chronicle*'s line was: THE RETURN OF BERNARD SHAW. IS HIS PURRING MORE DANGEROUS THAN HIS SNARL? and in the course of its report the journalist responsible, a Mr Alex M. Thompson ("Dangle"), averred: ". . . the plain meaning of Mr Shaw's advice is that, in ten or twenty years, the Germans will come again, with submarine transports and improved Zeppelins, to invade Britain, to subject our land to the horrors wreaked last year on French and Belgian Flanders, to burn Oxford as they burned Louvain, to rape our women, to crucify our babies [!], to shoot down our civilians, and to establish finally their tyrannous military lordship over Britain."

A month later, on 23rd November, 1915, Shaw gave another lecture at King's Hall, Covent Garden, his subject this time being

DIPLOMACY AFTER THE WAR.

It seemed to him, he said, that all wars were bound to stimulate militarism. There was no hope in a pacifism that was merely a negation of war. In future pacifism must be militant, and, more than that, it must be constructive. Instead of a Minister of War we wanted a Minister of Peace, and that Minister should be the strongest figure in the Cabinet of any country. And it should be clearly understood that immediately war broke out the Minister of Peace should be shot. [!].

Diplomacy after the war would have two problems which demanded serious thought forthwith. The problem of the terms on which the war was to be ended, and the wider and more important problem of the future of Europe. Until Britain had made up her mind what those terms were to be, her people did not know what they were fighting for. Did one want a strong Germany after the war, or a crushed Germany? . . . . It was entirely possible that they might want a strong Germany after the war. Did they want a Russian hegemony after the war? They would have to carefully consider exactly how strong they wanted Germany to be. . . .

A treaty would never be more than a scrap of paper until we had a supernational court with a Power which would be able to enforce it, he added. Our system of alliances in the future would have to be largely alliances with a view to the balance of power, and there would come on the very important question of the relations between Eastern civilisation and Western civilisation; between the white and yellow races. The current war had given reason to be anxious on this point.

Coming to the question of whose fault the war was, Bernard Shaw replied:—

It was our fault, ours more especially in this room, and similar audiences like this. The war was the fundamental fault of the democrats of this country.

For the prevention of future wars he suggested a League of Western Civilisation. He wanted to see Western civilisation organised on a democratic basis. The only way to prevent war was to make the whole of the West solid against it. . . .

The time might come, he said, when the whole of Western Europe might have to fight for its life against the yellow race. The white races must league themselves against this peril. But if the League was to be effective it was essential to make our democracy a real thing. We would have to establish equality and liberty among ourselves and destroy the sham democracy which was ruining us.

Speaking at Clapham in May, 1916,* Shaw referred to the

* Reported in the *South Western Star*, on 26th May.

government-sponsored Committee for Public Retrenchment's proposal to suspend street watering and some other forms of sanitation for the duration. He said: ". . . Any man who supports that in the name of economy is an enemy to his country." Such a man, he hoped, would be declared by Act of Parliament incapable of sitting on any public body for seven years, and only then if he could prove that he could pass the same kind of examination that a sanitary inspector had to pass. He would suggest that the police, making use of the Defence of the Realm Act, should very carefully examine that man's papers and bank account to discover if he had deposited a cheque for £50 signed 'William Hohenzollern'. [!]. If the Kaiser wanted to invest his money with a view to success in the war, he could not spend it better than by bribing borough councillors, and county councillors, to stop sanitation in the name of economy. He added, in regard to members of the Retrenchment Committee, that: "It would be better for us that these gentlemen . . . should sling a millstone around their necks and jump into the Thames and stay there, rather than that they should continue to give us mischievous advice."

During an interview by the Editor of *Everyman*, reported in the *Liverpool Courier* of 14th July, 1916, Shaw was asked the following questions (among others):—

"What do you think of the present attitude of the British public towards the foreigner and his Governments?"

Shaw replied: "The British public is not really conscious of any other public or any other interests. To it, the universe consists of a great central fact called, according to its size, Peckham, England, or the British Empire. . . ."

"If the British public took up a sensible attitude, what do you think would be the first thing it would demand?"

"It would drop down dead, slain by the novelty of the sensation."

"Can you name any actual instances when an informed British opinion could have been of any practical use in foreign affairs?"

"Yes. This war is due to our insular ignorance of the terrifying dangerousness to the military imagination of the situation of

Germany with France on one frontier and Russia on the other. We should have done either of two things: Guaranteed Germany against an attack from the West in the event of an attack by Russia on the Central Empires, or declared that if Germany attacked France she would have to fight us, too. If we had done the first, the war would have been confined to the Eastern half of Europe. If we had done the second, there would probably have been no war at all. We did neither, and the result has been Armageddon. We simply did not take any interest in the situation of Germany, or any other Continental Power. We were satisfied that as we felt all right they must feel all right if they were reasonable people. And we have not yet recovered from our scandalised surprise at Germany losing her head and making a desperate attempt to break by force the ring that encircled her. All that is the result of pure ignorance of foreign affairs, and, of course, reckless indifference to them . . ."

"Will war cure bellicosity, or ignorance, or anything else?"

"War will cure nothing. The business of war is to inflict wounds, not to heal them."

Despite his view that the Churches should close down in war-time, Shaw gave several religious grounds for Britain prosecuting the war, and also some Republican reasons, in the course of a lecture in King's Hall, Covent Garden, on 1st December, 1916. In his lecture notes* Shaw asked: "What is the case against Germany?" and continued:—

Solely the Republican case; and that could not be stated officially. I, a Republican, stated it, but just because I am a Republican I am officially impossible.

Not Aggression: the Initiative in war is everything. (Churchill.)

Not Treaty breaking: we have broken lots of treaties from Limerick to Berlin and Algeciras.

Not Rheims: we are probably bombarding the Acropolis *now*. . . .

Simply that the Prussian Monarchy could not depend on the West not to attack it in the rear if it were attacked in front by Russia.

The fatal want of political homogeneity in Western civilization.

(1) Under the Victorian tradition, we, as a German monarchy,

* Shaw Mss., British Museum.

are the natural ally of the Prussian monarchy against the French Republic (Salisbury and the Exhibition).

(2) Our alliance and hostility drives France into an unnatural alliance with Russia, which is a Prussian autocracy, now as anti-Prussian as anti-Russian.

(3) We join the Franco-Russian alliance secretly, but make our intentions sufficiently ambiguous to encourage Russia to believe that we will not fight our monarchical cousin on behalf of the Republic.

(4) Germany is left with no ally but Austria face to face with the hostile Russian autocracy, and with no security for her western frontier but the power of democratic sentiment in the West to keep Imperialist tradition and Balance of Power diplomacy in check.

(5) The heir apparent to the idol Emperor of Austria is killed by the Serbians; and in a moment 200 millions of Europeans are tearing one another to pieces in a horrible manner solely because, as they did not know their own minds, and said It Didn't Matter, they did not know one another's minds either, and thought it safer to kill one another.

Such a thing, Shaw declared, would have been impossible if Republicanism had been solid from Switzerland to San Francisco, or even if Britain, holding the balance of power as she did, could have made up her mind religiously as to which side she was on.

But we would not make up our minds as to the Will of God, and consequently made colossal sacrifices "to fulfill the Will of Peter the Great"—which we had been so determined to defeat in the nineteenth century—that we had nursed the Turks to gain over us the victories of Gallipoli and Kut. The issues were frightfully confused. Shaw summarised them:—

We are defending an assassination.

We are strengthening the most formidable autocracy in the world against the western democracy of which we are a part.

We are strengthening the yellow world against the white.

We are madly striving to alienate America because America

cannot trust either the white monarchy on her eastern flank or the yellow one on her western* flank.

We don't want to do any of these things: we want to do the very contrary; but we are doing them all the same.

Why?

Simply because we have lost our Religion.

Nature abhors a Vacuum.

The Fear of God is replaced by the Fear of Germany.

What would the Fear of God have done for us? asked Shaw.

It would have united in the Bond of Republicanism all the civilizations of the West against Idolatry for a common political purpose identified with the purpose of Evolution.

What had the Fear of Germany done for us?

Firstly, it had exaggerated itself into a ridiculous idolatry of German science, foresight, organization, and, in short, invincibility, until at last we had been afraid to say that we should fight her if she attacked France, and equally afraid not—like France itself—to join any combination that was hostile to Germany.

In this way, Shaw explained, it produced "the most incongruous, heterogeneous, apparently impossible alliances known to history: the alliance of Britain, France, Portugal, Italy, Serbia, Rumania, Russia, and Japan, against the central empires". Nothing but the fear of Germany—"that gigantic cowardice of the Godless"—could have produced such a fantastic combination.

What was the danger of that combination? It was that the fear of God endured for ever, but the fear of Germany was at the mercy of a battle. Where was the fear of Germany now that Germany was suing for peace? Why was she doing so?

Shaw did not think it was because she was beaten; on the contrary—she was winning battles at that time and would like to leave it at that. The reason, he considered, was because

* Shaw's script has 'eastern' here, but obviously he meant 'western'.

her royalists were "thoroughly awakened from their operatic dream of a Pax Germanica dictated by a victorious Hohern-zollern striking down Europe as Lohengrin strikes down Tebramund on the stage, and Tebramund is so thoroughly cured of the sorcery that held him terrified that he now shrieks Hands Off when he thinks that President Wilson may interfere between him and his doomed antagonist".

Shaw said he had never observed a cleaner army than the German one, or a dirtier army than the French; but he could see that the French conscripts drilling fiercely on the German frontier with their dirty clothes, their dirty cannons, their dirty hands and faces, their dirty waggons and horses, would be no dirtier than the Germans in the field, and were hard-bitten, hard-worked, tough, sudden men who would fight as mischievously as "the beautiful regiments of Germany swaying down the street to a sentimental German tune without a speck or stain on their clothes or equipment".

We had been at every possible disadvantage with the Germans. We had been outnumbered 10 to 1. Some of our batteries had been so destitute of ammunition that they could promise only one shell a day to frantic demands for support. Our soldiers' lives had been wiped out by the new gas so that a four miles gap opened the way to Calais through them. They had had to run away for days from the Germans at the rate of from five to eight miles an hour. By all the rules we should have been down and out a dozen times; but in spite of all this, said Shaw, the betting was in our favour in the west. No one feared the German army any more. Shaw continued:—

Let us, after giving 3 Cheers for Old England, and one more for those deserving auxiliary troops supplied by *la belle France*, consider the consequence of this experience.

German militarism is found out and shewn up as the ineffective thing it [is]. It has had us down, and could not—again I quote Lloyd George—bring off the Knock Out. But are we quite sure that our militarism and the French militarism can do any better. Suppose that the thing we have found out and shewn up is not the Prussian army, but modern war. When we do all that the Germans did, when we get the Germans on the run, outnumber them, fire ten shells to their one, break gaps of many miles in their lines, capture German towns as big as Lille, shall we be able to bring off the Knock Out any more than they could when they did all this to us, and even the Turks retrieved their old military glory by driving us into the sea in Gallipoli and gathering our expeditionary force like a daisy on the road to Baghdad? Talavera's Plain . . . .

We say, Oh yes, next spring. But it was to have been last spring, and that was when the previous autumn disappointed us. . . .

Wars lasted not only 30 years but 100 years when battles were decisive. Why should they not last longer—nay, for ever—now that war seems to have lost the power to stop itself—the power it was valued for.

Perpetual War is a Perpetual Possibility.

I submit that nothing can stop war now but a Conscientious Objection to it and these objections are now made illegal during war. . . .

Only Religious Men will Stop it.

Are our politicians religious?

Shaw's view on the amazing activities, trial, and execution in 1916 of Sir Roger Casement, the Irish patriot, were succinctly summarised in a draft article supplied to Julius Klein, of the Universal Pictures Corporation, California, on 19th December, 1934. He wrote:—

. . . I did not agree with Casement's policy, because I never believed, after the hold-up of the German advance before Liège, that Germany could win; nor did I want her to win. The suggestion that an independent Ireland could be of any real use to a victorious Germany was not plausible enough for the German general staff, whose feeling evidently was "You have a horse to sell, Sir Roger", though they were always too credulous as to the value to them of the Orange and Nationalist rebellions. I was therefore in no sense a Casementite; but I have no patience with judicial murders in which the infuriated accuser is also the judge, the jury, and the executioner. The crucial issue was whether Casement was or was not a prisoner of war in a struggle for the independence of his country. That issue, in the absence of an international tribunal, should have been tried by a neutral court in a neutral country.

(Casement, of course, had felt that Germany would win the war—hence his vision of Germany as the possible means to gaining a guarantee of independence for Ireland as his reward from a victorious Germany for supplying Irish military help against England.)

Early in 1917 Shaw received an invitation from Earl Haig to visit the front if he wished, in order to gain first-hand impressions. In the third of a series of subsequent articles entitled "Joy Riding at the Front" which appeared in the *Daily Chronicle* of March 8th, Shaw said that he had found talking about the war to soldiers neither depressing nor even revolting, in contrast to his conversations with civilians: "To the civilian the war is often not a war at all; it is a squabble . . . . To him, when a British soldier kills a German soldier, it is a heroic deed: when a German soldier kills a British one, it is a dastardly assassination."

But, Shaw pointed out, the soldiers' morality was quite different. They realised that their single aim was to win victory (i.e. "Not to reason why, but just to do and die"). There were no *just* quarrels in the world, because when people quarrel they cease to be just; if they had been just in the first instance they would not have quarrelled.

War is thus not concerned with the justice of its quarrel. Shaw considered this one of the main objections to war as an institution, and the one that would eventually uproot it from human morality. If a nation was in the wrong and decided to acknowledge it and make amends, it had to achieve victory or its amends could have no value.

The soldiers all damned the party politicians and courtiers, and felt far more strongly against those who smoothly said 'Peace' when there was no peace, and left the nation only half prepared for the possibility of war, than they did against out-and-out Tolstoyan pacifists.

The soldier involved in war had to fight to win whether he was the aggressor or the aggrieved, and whether he loathed war or regarded it as a noble calling. It was not, said Shaw, that a man had to defend himself or perish—many a man would be too proud to fight on those terms. But the soldier had to defend his neighbour or betray him—that was what 'got' him— made him feel honour-bound to fight with every ounce of his strength. That was why, although there were plenty of internationalists and pacifists at the front, there were no political or pacifist agitations there.

Shaw thought some of the devastations of war not altogether to be deplored: they were sometimes a form of slum clearance— perhaps the only way in some districts in which old buildings no longer fit for use would ever be replaced by new and up-to-date ones.

Shaw pointed out that pugnacity was still a part of human nature, and that civilisation was still in its infancy. The popularity of war stories in books, magazines, and the cinema, proved war's appeal. When Garibaldi had offered men "starvation, wounds, and death" they had jumped at it, but when Mazzini offered them the millenium they showed little or no interest. Nothing but the fascination of war could make it bearable to men. And even though they often complained of its boredom, they always found something exciting about it. That something was war itself. War gave colour to the lives of those formerly employed as drab clerks and in other routine jobs. The 'Never Again' of the civilian newspapers, the apology for the war on the ground that it was to end war, found no echo at the front, said Shaw. The soldier might consider war hell, but he did not consider it a crime.

Then there was the financial security of the army. All anxiety about money and commercial competition was obviated and replaced by a comradeship and feeling of disinterested fellowship. Shaw thought it reasonable to hope that many a man who had gone into the army "a commercialised cad" would come out of it "a public spirited gentleman".

Among the disadvantages of war, were that it produced a good many automatons—a type of being even worse than rogues (in Shaw's opinion)—and, more important, that the huge military machines came into their own only in time of war and were absurdities in times of peace. Shaw concluded that for the soldier in the field there was something to be said; for the soldier in barracks, nothing. War should be abolished, as it was, after all, a tremendous calamity. The virtues it brought out in people could find outlets in a re-organised civil life; the necessary reforms could be effected by reason and conscience as well as terror. But neither the Germans nor the British tried to effect such a re-organisation of society (on less commercial, less competitive, more community-conscious lines) and they must therefore accept the war which was the consequence of this, and fight it out. After it was over, their prayer must be not "Give us peace in our time", but "Give us peace in all time."

That a very important and often overlooked defect of war was that its effects are often very different from the aims of those who embark upon it, and that this point should be made more of by pacifists, was urged by Shaw in the course of an Open Letter addressed to Colonel Arthur Lynch, dated September, 1918, and published as a pamphlet* under the title *War Issues for Irishmen* in November, 1918. He explained:—

. . . war has a way of taking very little account of the aims of the individuals who plan it. In 1871 nothing was further from the thoughts either of Bismarck or Napoleon III than to give Monarchy its death blow in France and finally establish Republicanism in its place. Bismarck, when he made France pay what he thought a colossal indemnity, certainly did not intend to produce a ruinous financial crash in Berlin, and provide the peasants of France with a first rate investment for the contents of their old stockings. If the Pacifists, instead of alleging in the teeth of all experience that war produces no results except its own miseries and atrocities, were to

* By Maunsel & Co., Dublin and London.

remind pugnacious statesmen that wars hardly ever produce the results they were intended to produce, and often overthrow the order they were meant to consolidate, they could make a stronger case for themselves. Any fool can make a war if chance places him in command of the army, just as any fool can open the door of a tiger's cage if he happens to inherit the key. But to control it afterwards may be beyond the powers of Alexander, Cæsar, Cromwell, Peter, Catherine, Washington, Lincoln, and Napoleon all rolled into one.

Later in the same article, Shaw described himself as—up to a point—a pacifist, and again emphasised that Christianity was incompatible with war:—

... You will notice that I have said no word about that conscientious objection to war as war which is nevertheless a powerful factor in the situation. I myself, like that very typical Irishman the Duke of Wellington, have a conscientious objection to war so strong and deep that I do a most painful violence to my nature and conscience whenever I am compelled, as I am now, to accept war as a necessity of which we must make the best by acquitting ourselves like brave and astute warriors and statesmen rather than Christians. ... If my own acquaintance with the men now actually fighting is at all typical, I must conclude that at least ninety-nine per cent. of the men agree with the conqueror of Napoleon that war is so dreadful a calamity that only half-witted men would engage in it, or countenance it, if any honorable alternative were possible. I can respect no Christian pope or priest who ceases during war to press the question "Sirs, ye are brothers: wherefore do ye wrong one to another?"

In an article in the *Daily Chronicle*, 12th January, 1918, under the heading, "The Falling Market in War Aims," Shaw referred to "the revolt of the human conscience against war", and added:—

... When everything that can be said for war has been said a thousand times; when to the wretched plea that the distribution of our wealth was so bad, the condition of our people so poor, and our public sloth and carelessness so disastrous that an iron scourge was needed to drive us to do better, we add the less disgraceful claim that pride, honor, courage, and defiance of death flame up in war into a refiner's fire, yet nothing can conceal the blasting folly, the abominable wickedness, the cruelty and slavery with which war wreaks Life's vengeance on those who will respond to no gentler or holier stimulus.

In the same article Shaw also described himself as "a Jusqu'auboutist"* and wrote prophetically about 'the war to end war':—

. . . There is a war to be averted ten times more terrible than that war which we are told to get on with by fools who imagine that we have any choice in the matter, and flick their little whips at the earth to make it go round the sun. Which of us would not stop the war to-morrow if we could? Which of us can?

For my own part I am a Jusqu'auboutist. I do not want this war to be compromised as long as it will be possible for any of the belligerent Powers afterwards to pretend that if it had only gone on for another year it would have won. If we win there will be such a surge of exultation throughout the country that every counsel of moderation or prudence will be swept away as irresistibly as Bismarck and the Socialists were swept away in 1871, when they asked their countrymen to spare Alsace-Lorraine. The same thing will happen in Germany if the Central Empires win. It is our business to see that they do not win. When both sides become convinced that neither of them can both win and survive the effort then it will be time to talk of peace. Until then, I shall not join the ranks of those kindly people who cry peace when there is no peace.

As a contributor to a symposium on "The Ethical Principles of Social Reconstruction" held at the Aristotelian Society on

---

*A term which came into use in France and subsequently in Britain during the First World War to cover all who—from a variety of reasons and standpoints—believed that the war against Germany had to be fought 'right to the end'—with no 'compromise peace'. 'Bitter-enders' was another version of the expression. Shaw describes his own particular *Jusqu'au bout* attitude in the above passage.

23rd April, 1917, details of which were subsequently published in the Society's *Proceedings*, Vol. XVII, 1917, Shaw declared:—

The ethical principles imposed on us by the war are simple enough. War throws us back on the crude ethic of immediate self-preservation. Every contrivance, however diabolical, which saves British and destroys German lives is right; and every contrary word and deed is wrong. It overrides all higher ethics, from the ten commandments to Herbert Spencer's principles. Liberty has become a public danger, and homicide a science and a virtue: we pray that friendly Americans may be drowned; and we deliberately produce artificial famine, earthquake, and thunderbolt, on a scale which makes the most appalling natural catastrophe seem insignificant in comparison. And we take our part, directly or by consent and contribution, with a sense of ethical approval so heightened that manifest fools are seen in all directions almost bursting with their own importance, which nobody ventures to challenge, whilst philosophers are intimidated, or, if they resist the process, suppressed by force. . . There is not much interest in discussing whether, being inevitable, it is also right. The inevitable is practically outside ethics; and the inevitabilities of war drag us back from the forward side of good and evil, to which Nietzsche invited us, to the side we thought, until war broke out, we had long left behind us. . . .

Shaw explained that the ethical situation was, however, not so simple as this, because our ethics of peace were very far from being the ethics of Immanuel Kant or Plato. When we said to Germany: 'Thou shalt starve ere we starve', and she said the same to us, we were both only saying what we had said to our own countrymen and neighbours in the false peace of commercialism. To many men the war had brought "salvation from the most callous selfishness and the most hoggish quarrelsomeness". The war between the patriotic German and the patriotic Briton was an ennobling activity compared to the war between the kitchen and the drawing-room, the farmer and the labourer, the employer and the trade unionist, the landlord and the tenant, the usurer and the borrower, not to mention the competitive war which each man waged with his fellows in

all those hostile camps. The ethics of our trenches were higher
than the ethics of our markets. A man might pass through a
barrage with less damage to his character than through a
squabble with a nagging wife. Many domestic and commercial
experiences left blacker and far more permanent marks on the
soul than thrusting a bayonet through an enemy in a trench
fight. We therefore had the complication that the retrogressive
transition to the primitive morality of war might involve a
progressive transition from a narrow and detestable private
morality to a comparatively broad and elevated public morality.
Shaw added:—

We must also take into account the ethical illusions of the war.
The primitive ethic of war, that they shall take who have the power,
and they shall keep who can, is so revolting to highly civilized men that
they can reconcile themselves to it only by setting up an elaborate
fiction that they are acting in shocked self-defence against an
unprovoked and wicked attack, and that, in defending themselves,
they are defending liberty, humanity, justice, and all the other virtues,
their enemies being consequently human fiends devoted wholly to
the triumph of evil. This is manifest nonsense; but those who believe
it sincerely may be cultivating their character at the expense of
their intellect, just as those who look the truth in the face, and yet
hack their way through, may be cultivating their intellect at the
expense of their character. Those of us who believe that our intellect
is a very important part of our character, and that stupidity and
ignorance are more disastrous than roguery, will derive only a
very doubtful and troubled consolation from the fact that both
Germans and Englishmen believe that they are fighting for something
more than the balance of power; for if sacrifice for an ideal is good
for man, hatred of the enemy and assumption of moral superiority
is very bad for him. Still, the thing exists and has to be taken into
account. It may make the combatants fight more fiercely; but it pre-
cludes all terms of peace except those imposed by force; for none of the
belligerents will agree to a stalemate on a footing of moral equality.

Shaw went on to say that he did not think it conceivable that
a treaty concluding a war should have any higher ethic than

war itself. All the belligerents would take what plunder they could. None of them were pacifist States, they were all steeped in blood, and most of them were empires holding down subject nationalities ruthlessly with all the circumstances of cruelty and oppression which attended such holdings-down. They had all kept treaties when it was in their interests to do so, and broken them on the same basis. All had been guilty of frightful cruelties, and those who were not fighting for a European hegemony were fighting openly to wrest territories from one another. Germany would stay in Lille and Antwerp if she could; France would take Alsace-Lorraine if she could; Austria would keep Serbia and Bosnia if she could; Russia would get Constantinople if she could; Rumania would take Transylvania if she could; and Britain would keep the German colonies if she could; Italy would hold the Trentino if she could. In addition to territory, they would each, if they could, bleed their enemies white in indemnities; and if they had to abandon territory, they would devastate it so as to reduce to the utmost its value to the conqueror. And according to the ethic of war they would be quite right in doing so, and would be guilty of a political crime if they sacrificed the smallest fraction of the fruits of victory. What else was war for?

Shaw explained that even Bismark had not been able to restrain Germany from annexing Alsace-Lorraine in 1871, and that there was no longer any Bismarck to make the attempt. Thus there would be no ethical reconstruction. There would be a division of spoils and shifting of frontiers on the basis of the established military ethic. The proceedings would be governed by the example of England and Germany. Our war ethics had been perfectly expressed at the beginning of the war by Lord Roberts. He had founded himself on the "will to conquer" of the British race, claiming its satisfaction as a good in itself; and he had held out to the rest of the world as its highest interest that it should be governed, as one-fifth of the human race was already governed, by men educated in the public schools of England—meaning thereby Eton, Harrow, Winchester, and Rugby. The Germans, though they might not have phrased this creed quite so bluntly, had adopted it as they had adopted so many other of our institutions, and opposed Pan Germanism to our Pan Anglicanism. There was a great deal to be said for both, Shaw averred, but not relevantly to the symposium to which he was contributing—which pursued newer ethics, or reconstruction in the light of newer ethics. Shaw continued:—

... it may happen that the war will end either in a stalemate, or in a decision manifestly not worth its cost. In that case there will be at least an attempt at a genuine ethical reconstruction. We shall admit that President Wilson is a great philosopher-statesman, and that Lord Roberts was a barbarous romantic schoolboy; and the Germans will agree, substituting Von Bernhardi for Roberts.

The principle of reconstruction is clear enough: we must renounce the Will to Conquer, and assert the rights of civilized communities to be governed according to their own lights and not according to those of English public schoolmen, Prussian Junkers, or any other persons claiming to represent a super-civilization ... the renunciation of the Will to Conquer involves the renunciation of sovereign nationality and the subordination of nationality to a supernational power.

Half a dozen supernational schemes have already been put forward. Those which have been carefully thought out provide for a supernational legislature as well as a supernational tribunal backed by a supernational militia to enforce the laws of the legislature and the decisions of the tribunal.

... I ... [will] point out their psychological superficiality. They assume either that the supernational authority will at once represent the whole human race, thus fulfilling the dream of Anarcharsis Klootz and Tennyson, or at least that because Russia and Japan are among the eight great Powers they must necessarily combine with the western Powers in the new organization. I suggest that such a combination would be wrecked by its psychological heterogeneity, or else, like the old Concert of Europe face to face with the Turk, avert the wreck only by paralysis ...*

---

* What a prophecy of the League of Nations of the 1930's, and after the Second World War, of the United Nations, and the Russian veto!

. . . ethical reconstruction will take the form of a substitution of the ethics of Communism for the ethics of commercialism, and of the ethics of democracy for those of feudalism. Nothing short of these changes will involve any ethical change at all except in the backward direction of crudity and barbarism . . . we shall be able to consider many measures after the war that were not practical politics before it. Yet we shall not have new ethics, nor new politics, nor new economics, nor indeed any new synthesis or dogma. What will happen is that we shall no longer say of any important social reform that it is impossible because it would cost twenty million pounds. And we shall not say that the British people would never stand this or that sacrifice of their personal convenience, much less their lives, to social principles. That is a considerable advance in our executive effectiveness, and enlarges widely the possibilities of applying the principles we have already thought out. Therefore we cannot say that the war will make no difference. It will not, however, make a new heaven and a new earth; for these mean a new philosophy; and the war will certainly not produce that. We shall be fortunate if we recover without excessive effort the ground it has already lost us by throwing us back to the primitive ethic of the battlefield.

The following quotation is from a letter to the *Manchester Guardian*, 3rd February, 1919, entitled "Bury the Hatchet":—

. . . At Versailles the great ceremony of burying the hatchet is drawing the attention of the entire world. But there are two ways of burying the hatchet. One is to bury it in the skull of the prostrate enemy alien. The other is to establish that peace for which nine hundred thousand of our young men went to their graves like beds. Is it not time that we should begin to enjoy the peace they died for. Or is peace to be nothing but the vilest spite and unreason of war without its braveries, its heroisms, its patriotisms, its chivalries, and the dangers that give reality to these noble words? Are the very spoils to be to the camp-followers instead of to the victors?

In the *Daily News and Leader* of 31st June, 1919, Shaw declared that "the whole centre of Europe" having been reduced to starvation and "the blockaders to the verge of bankruptcy", it was evident that the first thing the victors had to do was to set

Europe on its legs again for their own sakes. One would think, he averred, that even a born fool would know that if he kicked a man down, broke his arms and legs, and rifled his pockets, there would not be much sense in declaring that the next step was to "make him pay", and then begin kicking him and refusing him food as a practical step to that end. This was utter childishness.

Shaw elaborated some of the views he had expressed during the First World War in a broadcast on 11th October, 1931. He said:—

In 1914, as some of you remember, I declared that if the soldiers on both sides had any common sense they would have come home and attended to their business instead of shamelessly slaughtering one another because their officers ordered them to. Some of you were very angry with me for taking a commonsense view of war, which is an affair of glory and patriotism and has nothing to do with common sense. Well, the British soldiers had no common sense and kept blazing away. The German and Austrian soldiers were just as foolish. The Italian soldiers joined up; and presently the American soldiers rushed in and were the silliest of the lot.

But in 1917 an astonishing thing happened. The Russian soldiers took my advice. They said "We have had enough of this" and came straight home. They formed bodies of workmen and soldiers called Soviets; and they raised the cry "All power to the Soviets". The government of the Tsar, which was as rotten as it was abominably tyrannical, collapsed like a house of cards, but the Soviets could do nothing without leaders and a plan of Social reconstruction that was the opportunity for Lenin and his friends who had followed his example and educated themselves politically by reading Marx. They had the courage to jump at it. They took command of the Soviets, and established the Union of Socialist Soviet Republics exactly as Washington and Jefferson and Hamilton and Franklin and Tom Paine had established the United States of America 141 years before.

Shaw, as suggested above and in earlier contexts, did not, therefore, regard the First World War as wholly evil in its effects. In the third of a series of articles entitled "The Limitation Conference" in the *Nation and Athenæum*, 26th November, 1921, he added:—

So much for the failures of the war: what about its successes? It has swept the Hapsburgs, the Hohenzollerns, and the Romanoffs into the dustbin of history; scattered the empires into groups of republics which have changed the typical form of modern government from the monarchical to the democratic-republican; and set up in the huge country which straddles across the Eurasian frontier a Communist State with an army which has made mincemeat of the invasions of Koltchak, Wrangel, and Denikin: Trotsky, its Carnot, being a genius whom the British police imprisoned as a dangerous character when he was in England.

In a statement on 13th November, 1925, Shaw exclaimed:—

It was I who proposed the Locarno Pact in 1913, and again on New Year's Day, 1914, when it might have prevented the war.
What use is it now, when all the mischief is done?
However, it is greatly to Mr Chamberlain's credit that he is only 12 years behind me instead of 50.

Contemporary critics of the attitudes expressed in the foregoing few pages and of his 1914 pamphlet *Common Sense About the War* reviled Shaw, as I have earlier described, as distinctly pro-German and traitorous. However, it is generally accepted now that it was indeed the harsh 'crush Germany till the pips squeak' treaty of Versailles, and the humiliation and deep bitterness in the German people aroused by it, which provided the fertile soil for Hitler's mass-appeal and rise to power, and which was thus the main factor in the causation of the Second World War. At half a century's remove we can see how emotional and superficial the views of Shaw's critics were, and how full of shrewd wisdom and prophetic insight into the future many of Shaw's were. For example, his view of collective security and its practical difficulties in the last paragraphs on

p. 367, and also on p. 382, and his advocacy of an armed international police force in 1907 on p. 359, which have been fully
substantiated by subsequent history—the League of Nations
and then the United Nations (with its difficulty of the Russian
veto), and the current Nato Alliance with Germany against
the threat to the Western world from Russia and the so-called
'yellow races' headed by China.

Shaw made the following comment to the Secretary of the
local British Legion group on an Armistice Day Service held
under its auspices in the neighbouring village of Welwyn on
11th November, 1928: "If there is any lightning left in Heaven,
God help you when you go to church to congratulate Him and
one another for four years of murder and devastation. I have
never read anything more wickedly blasphemous than the
Service you have sent me."

To a reporter from the *Welwyn Times* he explained: "I have
just heard Mr M'Cormick, and I heard him say we went to the
war in the spirit of Christ. Have you ever heard such ridiculous
nonsense?"

Shaw annotated the printed Order of Service he had been
sent in the following manner. (I give the words Shaw had
underlined in italics, and the words Shaw added within square
brackets.)

(*a*) The ending of the well-known hymn:—

> *Christ has gone before us*
>   *Christians follow ye*   [to war!]

(*b*) The following extracts are from the prayer:—

> . . . so that their fellow-citizens may not forget
> *the Great Deliverance wrought through Thy help*
> [that is, God was our accomplice in murder and devastation.]

(*c*) . . .   Grant that the courage which was shown them in
repelling the foreign foe *may uphold them in resisting all
attempts in the Empire to undermine Law and Order.* [Cries of
"No politics".]   Grant that *the symbol of loyalty, justice, and*

Caricature by Henry Furness. Shaw as he appeared during the First World War to some of his critics, including Henry Arthur Jones, who described him as "a freakish homunculus".

Lecture card:—
"The Illusions of War" (1915).

liberty [no military flag can symbolise anything but the suspension of justice and liberty] . . . [Note the assumption that our opponents were to God not our fellow-creatures, but the 'foreign foe'.]

(*d*) Dearly beloved of the Lord, forasmuch as men at all times have made for themselves signs and emblems of their allegiance to their rulers, and of their duty to uphold those laws and institutions which *God's Providence has called them to obey* [Has it? Is our Statute Book a Divine revelation? Dora, for instance?]

(*e*) We . . . are met together before God *to ask His blessing on this Colour* [the colour being the rallying point in battle].

(*f*) Let us, therefore, pray . . . to grant that it may never be unfurled save in the cause of justice and righteousness; and that He may make it to be to those who follow it *a sign of His presence with them in their endeavours to promote peace and good will amongst all people* [by murdering them].

(*g*) In the Name of the Father and of the Son and of the Holy Ghost, we dedicate this Standard to the Glory of God, that it *may be a sign to us of the organised service we are called to render those for whom He suffered and died* [that is, the flag of battle is to be substituted for the Cross].

Let us Pray. Lord have mercy upon us. Christ have mercy upon us. Lord have mercy upon us [Good].

(*h*) . . . *Oh God who has caused our Empire to be established on the farthest coasts* [by Drake and other pirates and conquerors].

Shaw added:—

It would have been so easy for the Church to be consolatory without being insincere and foolish. When will it realise that its word should mean something more than Mesopotamia? There were plenty of true things to say that need not have been bitter things.

Shaw's final overall comment, after the National Anthem, was:—

Not a word of penitence and confession, of disillusion and humility. Not a suspicion that God is not a Colonel in the British

Army. Nothing but an unashamed conviction that we are entitled
to God's congratulations on an event in which he had the honour
of being entirely on the British side.

By the nineteen-thirties, concern in Shaw's mind, like most
people's, was increasingly shifting from the First World
War and its aftermath to the possibility of a Second World
War—except in so far as the first one might prove to be a
direct factor in the causation of a second. He gave his views on
disarmament at this time in the course of a broadcast entitled
"Whither Britain", a transcript of which appeared in *The
Listener* of 7th February, 1934:—

Disarmament will not prevent war. Men fought just as fiercely
as they now do before a single one of our modern weapons was
invented; and some of the greatest naval battles were fought
when fleets were moved by oars instead of by turbine engines.

I have no doubt that, in the African tribes, when it was first
proposed to use poisoned arrows instead of plain ones, there was
just the same cry of horror about it as we had in England when the
Germans attacked us with poison gas. Only fiends, we said, would
use such a weapon! But at the end of a fortnight, when Lord
Kitchener told us not to fuss, as we were going to use it ourselves,
we settled down to it just as the African tribes settled down to the
poisoned arrows; and we may as well settle down to the fact that in
the next war all the most diabolical means of spreading death and
destruction will be ready for use. We are at present working hard
at them, and so are all the other Powers; so let us face it. We have
got to, whether we like it or not. . . .

So do not let yourselves be scared into perfectly useless attempts
to keep war on its old Napoleonic footing. . . .

In an interview by a reporter from a Press agency, Raymond
Savage Ltd., on 12th March, 1935, Shaw was asked: "Would
you allow Germany to build twenty more battleships and a
thousand more airplanes?" He replied:—

I could not prevent her, and I would not if I could. A strong
Germany is as important to civilisation as a strong Britain. What is

it that has put Herr Hitler in his present Napoleonic position in Germany? Two things. First, our silly persistence in trying to keep Germany in a state of abject subjugation when it was no longer possible for us to fight for it. Second, Herr Hitler's grasp of the realities of the situation. Knowing that we and France dared not re-open the war to enforce the subjugatory clauses of the Versailles treaty, he tore those clauses up and threw them in our faces, re-arming his country and raising it to its former rank as a European Power. Naturally the Germans not only voted for him: they deified him. When France still clung to the Locarno agreements which demilitarised the Rhineland, he snapped his fingers in France's face and marched 40,000 soldiers right up to the French frontier. And though this was only the logical sequel to the German re-armament it frightened the wits out of the Allies and sent the Führer to the top of the polls again, though there was really nothing in it that a child could not have foreseen. All this was our doing. If the British and French governments had had the gumption to face the situation by tearing up the subjugatory clauses themselves, and inviting Herr Hitler to arm Germany to the teeth and march where he pleased, they would have cut the ground from under his feet and stolen his thunder. But no: they gave him his triumph; and even now they are still yapping about the sacredness of treaties and looking like fools while Herr Hitler is looking like Lohengrin.

Shaw amplified these views on the events which were to culminate in the Second World War in *Time and Tide* magazine on 12th October, 1935. Reiterating that Hitler had had "the gumption to see that the victorious allies would not fight for the treaty", he added:—

They were very sensibly afraid to. So he tore up the subjugatory clauses of the treaty with a gesture which reminded me of the lines of Gabriel Rossetti "the thumb as it goes to the end of the nose conveys one's opinion of"—the League of Nations. There was nothing in that but one schoolboy "daring" another, and getting away with it. We funked it. We had to. It served us right for signing a cowardly, amateurish, and impossible treaty with one hand, and, with the other, an equally impossible Covenant to which the Allies had not given a moment's thought, and never on any important occasion shewed the slightest intention of taking seriously.

In a letter to *Time and Tide*, 26th October, 1935, in reply to some points raised by his friend, the well-known literary critic Desmond MacCarthy, Shaw explained:—

. . . the League of Nations . . . was inaugurated here by that honest gentleman Austen Chamberlain with the memorable words "The British Empire always comes first with me." Since then it has been a whirlpool of the jealousies of rival imperialisms, each of them armed to the teeth, and all playing the game of diplomatic all-in wrestling, manœuvring for the inside grip and the hammer lock on each other . . . when Italy moved to take her share the other day it seemed rather a good opportunity to bilk her by raising the Banner of Peace in the League of Nations. Before we could wink we found ourselves on the verge of a military combination of the British Empire and the French Republic to smash the Italian Empire in the name of Peace, of Abyssinian integrity, of the League of Nations, of the plighted honor of the Powers, of the rest of the ragbag of appropriately fine phrases, and of popular dislike and fear of the resolute man, Mussolini.

Desmond is momentarily taken in by this nonsense, and does not grasp the fact that it means simply another war more infernal than the last one, and a century of bad blood between us and a hitherto friendly Italy. When he does realize it he will rise up and give me the Fascist salute. [!].

The following statement by Shaw is a transcription of a short-wave broadcast in 1937.* It gives Shaw's views on Peace and War at a period of his life fairly near to our own times. The world has indeed been rocked since by a second world war, but the subject, in its fundamentals, has surely at least as much relevance for our world of today as when this script was written by Bernard Shaw. In it he supplements his earlier views and defines in broader terms his general attitude to war, and to the social and political factors involved in the causation of war and the maintenance of peace.

*Broadcast on the B.B.C. Empire programme on 2nd November, 1937.

What about this danger of war which is making us all shake in our shoes at present? I am like yourself, I have an intense objection to having my house demolished by a bomb from an aeroplane and myself killed in a horribly painful way by mustard gas. I have visions of streets heaped with mangled corpses, in which children wander crying for their parents and babies gasp and strangle in the clutches of dead mothers. That is what war means nowadays. It is what is happening in Spain and in China whilst I speak to you, and it may happen to us tomorrow. And the worst of it is that it does not matter two straws to Nature, the mother of us all, how dreadfully we mis-behave ourselves in this way or in what hideous agonies we die. Nature can produce children enough to make good any extremity of slaughter of which we are capable. London may be destroyed, Paris, Rome, Berlin, Vienna, Constantinople may be laid in smoking ruins, and the last shrieks of their women and children may give way to the silence of death. No matter. Nature will replace the dead. She is doing so every day. The new men will replace the old cities, and perhaps come to the same miserable end. To Nature the life of an empire is no more than the life of a swarm of bees, and a thousand years are of less account than half an hour to you and me. Now the moral of that is that we must not depend on any sort of Divine Providence to put a stop to war. Providence says: "Kill one another, my children. Kill one another to your hearts' content. There are plenty more where you came from." Consequently, if we want the war to stop we must all become conscientious objectors.

I dislike war not only for its dangers and inconveniences, but because of the loss of so many young men, any of whom may be a Newton or an Einstein, a Beethoven, a Michael Angelo, a Shakes-pear, or even a Shaw. Or he may be what is of much more immediate importance, a good baker, or a good weaver or builder. If you think of a pair of combatants as a heroic British Saint Michael bringing the wrath of God upon a German Lucifer then you may exult in the victory of Saint Michael if he kills Lucifer, or burn to avenge him if his dastardly adversary mows him down with a machine gun before he can get to grips with him. In that way you can get intense emo-tional experience from war. But suppose you think of the two as they probably are, say two good carpenters taken away from their proper work to kill one another. That is how I see it. And the result is that which ever of them is killed the loss is as great to Europe and to me.

In 1914 I was as sorry for the young Germans who lay slain and mutilated in No Man's Land as for the British lads who lay beside them, so I got no emotional satisfaction out of the war. It was to me a sheer waste of life. I am not forgetting the gratification that war gives to the instinct of pugnacity and admiration of courage that are so strong in women. In the old days when people lived in forests like gorillas or in caves like bears, a woman's life and that of her children depended on the courage and killing capacity of her mate. To this day in Abyssinia a Danakil woman will not marry a man until he proves that he has at least four homicides to his credit. In England on the outbreak of war civilized young women rush about handing white feathers to all young men who are not in uniform. This, like other survivals from savagery, is quite natural, but our women must remember that courage and pugnacity are not much use against machine guns and poison gas.

The pacifist movement against war takes as its charter the ancient document called the Sermon on the Mount, which is almost as often quoted as the speech which Abraham Lincoln is supposed to have delivered on the battlefield of Gettysburg. The sermon is a very moving exhortation, and it gives you one first-rate tip, which is to do good to those who despitefully use you and persecute you. I, who am a much hated man, have been doing that all my life, and I can assure you that there is no better fun, whereas revenge and resentment make life miserable and the avenger hateful. But such a command as "Love one another" as I see it is a stupid refusal to accept the facts of human nature. Why, are we lovable animals? Do you love the rate collector? Do you love Mr Lloyd George, and, if you do, do you love Mr Winston Churchill; have you an all-embracing affection for Messrs Mussolini, Hitler, Franco, Ataturk, and the Mikado? I do not like all these gentlemen, and even if I did, how could I offer myself to them as a delightfully lovable person? I find I cannot like myself without so many reservations that I look forward to my death, which cannot now be far off, as a good riddance. If you tell me to be perfect as my Father in heaven is perfect, I can only say that I wish I could. That would be more polite than telling you to go to the Zoo and advise the monkeys to become men and the cockatoos to become birds of paradise. The lesson we have to learn is that our dislike for certain persons, or even for the whole human race, does not give us any right to injure our fellow creatures, however odious they may be.

As I see it, the social rule must be "Live and let live",* and that people who break this rule persistently must be liquidated. The pacifists and non-resisters must draw a line accordingly. When I was a young man in the latter half of the 19th century, war did not greatly concern me personally because I lived on an island far away from the battlefield, and because the fighting was done by soldiers who had taken up that trade in preference to any other open to them. Now that aeroplanes bring battle to my housetop, and governments take me from my proper work and force me to be a soldier whether I like it or not, I can no longer regard war as something that does not concern me personally. You may say that I am too old to be a soldier. If nations had any sense they would begin a war by sending their oldest men into the trenches. They would not risk the lives of their young men except in the last extremity. In 1914 it was a dreadful thing to see regiments of lads singing Tipperary on their way to the slaughter house, but the spectacle of regiments of octogenarians hobbling to the front waving their walking sticks and piping up to the tune of "We'll never come back no more, boys, We'll never come back no more"—wouldn't you cheer that enthusiastically? I should. But let me not forget that I should be one of them.

It has become a commonplace to say that another great war would destroy civilization. Well, that will depend on what sort of war it will be. If it is to be like the 1914 war, a war of nations, it will certainly not make an end of civilization. It may conceivably knock the British Empire to bits and leave England as primitive as she was when Julius Cæsar landed in Kent. Perhaps we shall be happier then for we are still savages at heart, and wear our thin uniform of civilization very awkwardly. But anyhow there will be two refuges left for civilization. No national attack can seriously hurt the two great federated republics of North America and Soviet Russia. They are too big. The distances are too great. But what could destroy them is civil war—wars like the wars of religion in the 17th century—and this is exactly the sort of war that is threatening us today. It has already begun in Spain, where all the big capitalist powers are taking a hand to support General Franco through an intervention com-

---

* This statement by Shaw is a curious anti-climax to his social and political views expressed in the previous chapter.

mittee which they think it more decent to call a Non-Intervention Committee. This is only a skirmish in the class war, the war between the two religions of capitalism and communism, which is at bottom a war between labor and land owning. We could escape that war by putting our house in order as Russia has done, without any of the fighting and killing and waste and damage that the Russians went through. But we don't seem to want to. I have shown exactly how it can be done, and in fact how it must be done, but nobody takes any notice. Foolish people in easy circumstances flatter themselves that there is no such thing as the class war in the British Empire, where we are all far too respectable and too well protected by our Parliamentary system to have any vulgar unpleasantness of that sort. They deceive themselves. We are up to the neck in class war. What is it that is wrong with our present way of doing things? It is not that we cannot produce enough goods, our machines turn out as much work in an hour as ten thousand hand workers used to. But it is not enough for a country to produce goods. It must distribute them as well, and this is where our system breaks down hopelessly. Everybody ought to be living quite comfortably by working four or five hours a day with two Sundays in the week. Yet millions of laborers die in the workhouse or on the dole after sixty years of hard toil so that a few babies may have hundreds of thousands a year before they are born. As I see it this is not a thing to be argued about or to take sides about. It is stupid and wicked on the face of it, and it will smash us and our civilization if we do not resolutely reform it. Yet we do nothing but keep up a perpetual ballyhoo about Bolshevism, Fascism, Communism, Liberty, Dictators, Democracy, and all the rest of it. The very first lesson of the new history dug up for us by Professor Flinders Petrie during my lifetime is that no civilization, however splendid, illustrious, and like our own, can stand up against the social resentments and class conflicts which follow a silly misdistribution of wealth, labor, and leisure. And it is the one history lesson that is never taught in our schools, thus confirming the saying of the German philosopher Hegel: "We learn from history that men never learn anything from history". Think it over. So long, so long·

In the following year, 1938, in a draft article for the British International Press Ltd., dated 13th August, on the subject of the Anschluss with Austria which had been signed by Hitler and Mussolini, Shaw expressed the view that Britain could not interfere; the only alternative was to send an ultimatum to the effect that unless all German troops were withdrawn immediately from Austria, and Hitler deprived of his dictatorship and exiled from Germany within three hours, Britain and her allies would lay Berlin in ashes immediately. Shaw concluded:—

This being for various reasons inexpedient we may as well accept the Anschluss without grumbling, not only because it is an excellent thing in itself, but because at Versailles we helped to create the situation which has made it inevitable. And so, Heil Hitler!*

After the war had broken out, in a draft for an article headed "How to Talk Intelligently About the War", Shaw wrote:—

Aggression is a word very much in vogue just now; but you had better think twice before you use it. We are not the terrified victims of Mr Hitler's aggression: quite the reverse. He did not declare war on us: we declared it on him, and must live up to that proud position. He has taken up our challenge undauntedly, and won the opening round with so much to spare that if we stop fighting before we have at least got even with him we must go out of business as a first rate power. He, as the attacked party, and so far the victorious one, can without discredit propose an armistice or a peace conference; but the least suggestion of such a thing on our part would be a "Hold! Enough!" for which there would be no excuse, as we are not yet within sight of the end of our resources. There must be no more nonsense about our being certain to win, and God being on our side, as in that case we have nothing to do but sit down in our armchairs and let God win. God helps those who help themselves; and Mr Hitler helps himself so energetically that he will knock us into a cocked hat as he has knocked France unless we put the last ounce of our weight into the fight with him. When we do, God help him!

The Russo-German agreement was the subject of an article by Shaw in the *Daily Herald* of 25th October, 1939, in the course of which he exclaimed:—

* Cf. Shaw's reference to the Fascist salute on page 391.

... Witnesses to the character of British Imperialism, not only from India, Ireland, Waziristan, and North America, but from Jarrow, our distressed areas, and the custodians of our little evacuees, can testify that what we call Hitlerism and Stalinism are not yet old enough to have committed a tenth of the atrocities and criminal negligences through which we have muddled our way to the present complete despotism of Mr Chamberlain's War Cabinet and its innumerable local Gestapos.

In a proposed B.B.C. talk on the war in June, 1940 (which, owing to a tightening of the censorship, was never broadcast but was published later in A. Weymouth's, *Journal of the War Years and One Year Later*, 1948), Shaw wrote:—

... we must not give ourselves moral airs as a peace-loving people. ... Mr Hitler did not begin this war: we did. It is silly to revile him as a treacherous wolf pouncing on a nation of innocent lambs. We are not innocent lambs: we are the most formidable of all the Great European Powers, claiming command of the sea, which is nothing more or less than the power to blockade and starve to death any of our rivals. Having that terrible power we are under the most sacred obligation to use it to defend, not ourselves alone, but common humanity.

A little earlier in the same script, Shaw said:—

... one of the beauties of what we call our democracy is that nobody is responsible for anything. So we must stop squabbling and remember that this reckless habit of ours is a very sensible one, and is in fact what we are fighting for.

Shaw here markedly contradicted his earlier views on British democracy.

In the same script Shaw attempted to clarify—but also to some extent contradicted—his earlier views on Fascism:—

... Remember that the really dangerous Fifth Column consists of the people who believe that Fascism is a better system of government than ours, and that what we call our democracy is a sham.

They are not altogether wrong in this; but the remedy for us is to adopt all the good points of Fascism or Communism or any other Ism, not to allow Mr Hitler and his Chosen Race to impose it on us by his demoralised police. We are fighting him not for his virtues but for his persecutions and dominations, which have no logical connection whatever with Fascism and which we will not put up with, from Mr Hitler or anyone else.

Some years earlier, however, as reported in *Fabian News*, January, 1934, Shaw had defended even Hitler's "persecutions and dominations":—

. . . his efforts had been obscured in this country by the natural indignation and horror at the persecution of the Jews.

But he was no mere Titus Oates, and his violence and brutality were the regrettable but natural retorts to the continual kicking, the exploitation and robbery to which his people had been subjugated since 1919.

In the *Fabian Quarterly* of April, 1944, Shaw put much of the blame for the rise of Hitler and Mussolini on to his pet hobby horse, the extreme inefficiency, prevarication, and slowness of our democratic political system:—

. . . [Hitler and Mussolini] . . . rose to supreme power on the general disgust and disappointment at the performances of the Party Parliaments in which, as I said (meaning exactly what Hitler and Mussolini, Dickens and Oswald Mosley said) that if we persist in governing ourselves by parliaments which take 30 years to do a week's work we shall some day have to do thirty years' work in a week, which will give us an extremely unpleasant rush hour, and most likely a very bloody one.

Right up till the end of his life Shaw held sincere convictions which ran directly counter to almost everyone else's, including his fellow-Socialists'. In some notes for an unpublished letter to *The Times* dated 27th September, 1949, he expressed the following sentiments:—

... As to foreign policy, the Labor Party knows less about it than a pig knows of a holiday, having grown up wholly preoccupied with home industry. It is true that Mr Bevin, being a very able man is at last shewing signs of having some diplomacy knocked into him by hard facts. . . . Were it not for Stalin's commanding ability we should now be at war with the U.S.S.R. He has now reached the traditional span of life. His death would be the direst calamity to be dreaded at present. Mr Churchill, who, to his great credit, was the first to recognise the eminence of Lenin, might well now warn our politicians of all parties, who seldom speak without naming Stalin, and never without insulting him, that Stalin is neither a would-be Napoleon nor a Hitleresque "bloodthirsty guttersnipe", but the mainstay of peace in Europe.

Finally, voters should know that civilization is founded on a broad basis of Communism, without which it could not exist for a week; that a law that is not totalitarian is not a law at all; that our C.I.D. and secret service is a model for all the Gestapos; that the Atlantic Pact is a Superstate police force; and that the despotic regional and local authorities which have been forced on us by the slowness of parliamentary action are Soviets in everything but their names. Citizens for whom all this is Greek had better vote for their Parties right or wrong; for, as Pascal said, when we do not know the truth, we need a common error to keep our heads steady.

The number of people during the First and Second World Wars and at other times, who have regarded Shaw as a pro-German, a Pacifist, a defeatist, and even as an enemy of Britain who should be shot as a traitor, is legion. As I trust the foregoing material has demonstrated, there was much more behind Shaw's admittedly somewhat startling views on war (particularly on the Second World War) than at first might seem to be the case.

Thus in the passages quoted in the last page or two, Shaw really is not so much praising Hitler (as he a little earlier praised Mussolini) as condemning English muddle-headedness and hypocrisy—as he had done all through his life, in whatever shape or form it manifested itself. He is criticising Britain in the 1940's for smugly condemning Hitler and Mussolini for doing the same kind of thing (imperialistic conquest)—albeit more brutally—as Britain had herself done in earlier times, and for trying to cover up for her gross mishandling (with France) of the Versailles Treaty by blaming its end-results—which he had predicted in 1919—entirely onto Germany and Italy and their leaders, instead of onto Britain's own greed, inefficiency, and stupidity. Shaw was also saying, or implying, that in view of the fact that Britain and her allies were 'HAVE' nations, and Germany and Italy 'HAVE NOT' nations, the latter countries' strong drive to expand their territory (to gain *Lebensraum*) was not to be wondered at, and no different in principle from Britain's attitude generations earlier when she overran India and many other foreign countries in building up the British Empire.

Similarly, Shaw could see no difference in principle between the mass bombing of cities indulged in by both sides in the Second World War, and even blamed Britain for taking the initiative, in an article in the *Daily Mail* of January 6th, 1944:—

When this war is over, we must either admit that it has reduced war as an institution to absurdity, folly, and unbearable mischief, and abolish it, or else be ready to fight Germany again not only once every 20 years but "any day of the week". . . .

As to atrocities, we have rained 200,000 tons of bombs on German cities; and some of the biggest of them have no doubt fallen into infant schools and lying-in hospitals.

When it was proposed to rule this method of warfare out, it was we who objected and refused. Can we contend that the worst acts of the Nazis whom our Russian allies have just hanged were more horrible than the bursting of a bomb as big as a London pillar-box in a nursery in Berlin or Bremen?

The *Daily Mail* article from which the above quotation is taken was a commentary, invited by the Editor, on an article published the previous day by a political observer writing under the pen-name "Victory". Some of Shaw's further views in it are of interest and are given below—though I will first give

''Victory's'' Plan For Germany. It was:—1. Complete disarmament. 2. The right to manufacture or import arms to be permanently and completely forbidden. 3. Britain, the U.S.A., and the U.S.S.R. to be jointly responsible for seeing that complete disarmament be carried out, for a period of 75 years. 4. Violation of '1' or '2' by Germany would involve immediate bombing by the three powers named in '3'. 5. The three-power "European Commission" should control the direction of German education for 75 years. 6. Full Army of Occupation for one year. 7. Individual war criminals to be tried and punished, as agreed at the Teheran Conference.

Shaw's comments were:—

All article 1. of "Victory's" Plan, screaming for the permanent disablement of the enemy, is cowardly rubbish, impudent, pretentious, and so deliberately wicked that if it were not, fortunately, quite impossible to put it into practice it would justify a Holy Alliance against any Power giving the slightest countenance to it.

When I was a schoolboy I was expected to conceal my terrors by professing my readiness to fight any other schoolboy on earth. But if I had added that I should, if I got him down, kick him until he was so disabled that he could never fight again, I should have been ostracised as the blackest of foul-playing dastards. I had to add, instead, that I was ready to fight him "any day in the week". And if the fight had come off, and I had knocked him down, I should have had to let him get up and try again until he confessed that he had had enough and that I was the winner.

A disabling blow—the blow below the belt—was strictly forbidden. . . .

War without chivalry (that is, without rules, without laws of war) reduces itself to an absurdity like all-in wrestling, which, as experts know, is a sham. . . .

If there is to be disarmament, all must disarm. And nobody will. We absolutely refused when Russia called on us to do it if we really meant business by our signature of the League of Nations Covenant.

. . . if . . . Germans in responsible positions who influenced and encouraged the initiation of the war are to be exiled to Siberia, why are our own militarist Imperialists to be left at home?

It was we who declared war on Germany in 1914, and again, without consulting the League of Nations, in 1939. The House of Commons was not consulted beforehand on either occasion. Is Mr Churchill to be sent to Siberia also?...

We have a case, and in my opinion a smashing case, against Hitlerised Germany; but the Articles set forth in "Victory's" plan not only do not state it but put us hopelessly and ridiculously in the wrong before the world and drive even the friendliest Germans to set their teeth and resolve to die in their last ditch rather than surrender.

P.S. German papers, please copy. Our enemies had better know that we have not all lost our heads, and that some of us will know how to clean our slate before we face an impartial international court.

Shaw's attitude was basically an anti-emotional one, comprising the attitudes: "Don't gesticulate—you caused it, so put up with it; Why didn't you use your intelligence at the proper time to prevent the developments which have subsequently taken place? As you have made your bed, so you must lie on it. What is the use of blathering moral platitudes about the League of Nations when *all* countries, including Britain, used this organisation for their own Imperial advantage, not for moral purposes?"

However, this is not to excuse Shaw for his specific condonation of Mussolini's overthrow of Abyssinia ("Desmond . . . will rise up and give me the Fascist salute"), or Hitler's Anschluss in Austria ("And so, Heil Hitler!"), or his statement on 12th March, 1935, that if the British and French had torn up the subjugatory Clauses of the Versailles Treaty and invited Hitler to "arm Germany to the teeth and march where he pleased", they would have "cut the ground from under his feet and stolen his thunder" (which view, of course, completely contradicted his earlier attitude).

And regarding the quotation on page 400 about the bombing of cities by both sides, Shaw did not extend his comparison to cover the extermination by the Germans of six million Jews in concentration camps and gas chambers, the like of which finds no parallel in Britain's or any other nation's history. Shaw's naïve inability to imagine or believe in the horrible *realities* of places like Dachau and Belsen was described by Mrs Laden, his housekeeper, in *Shaw the Villager* (p. 30). In theory, at any rate, Shaw frequently expressed himself in sympathy with what he termed "the liquidation of undesirables", and actually claimed that Hitler should have given him the credit for first putting forward the idea of gas chambers.

This topic has been earlier touched on in connection with capital punishment on p. 18 ('Printed Postcards') and is seen also in Shaw's sympathy with Stalin's "liquidation" of five million Ukrainian Kulaks by starvation when collectivising their farms. It is an important and central quirk in Shaw's character. It may, however, be added here that Shaw wanted the gas (when used) to be a painless one (unlike the cyanide gas used by Hitler which often took as long as twenty minutes in one of the most extreme forms of agony known to man to kill its victims). In the course of a reply in 1938 to a newspaper reporter who asked about the new play he was writing called *Geneva*, Shaw replied: "It is no use trying to stop Mussolini by enforcing Sanctions. Why don't you start an agitation for a humane kind of poison gas? Something that will kill you in a gentlemanly way and not poison the grass and cows? Chemical science should be able to invent it."*

Shaw's great ability was not his own infallibility but rather his talent for spotting the fallibility of other people. This can be a constructive and valuable function in society, but it is open to doubt whether Shaw really understood himself how the 'sheep'-like 'masses' should be 'managed' (or ruled or led) any more than the actual political leaders of his day. But being very much of an individual, without any strict ties

---

* In 1968-9, the Americans were using a non-lethal gas causing temporary vomiting, in Vietnam.

to political party or Cabinet, he frequently had far greater freedom than they did to comment on the often very complex problems involved, and perhaps sometimes used this freedom too extravagantly. Shaw after all, despite his leading position in the Fabian Society, his seven years as a Vestryman, and his undoubted brilliance as an orator, had at no time in his life had any actual experience of statecraft, and that perhaps partly explains why he had so little sympathy with those who were failing at it.

Shaw admitted some of mankind's (and hence his own) limitations in his draft article entitled "Further Meditations on Shaw's Geneva" (c. 1939):—

> Man is so far a failure as a political animal: he can manage neither aggregations of millions of his species nor the powers of destruction that chemistry has put into his hands. His big civilizations have broken down again and again. That is a hard fact which I recognize. But it does not follow that I despair of mankind, that I have fallen at the feet of the dictators, that I am no longer a Socialist but a pessimist. . . .

Shaw again and again showed himself blind to the fact that most people do not behave rationally, and that ideas which seem excellent from an intellectual, rational, logical, theoretical point of view, often do not work in practice because of the considerable irrational element in human nature.

The present chapter would not be complete without enlarging on Shaw's views on conscientious objection as quoted on pages 313 and 377-8, The following extract is from *Everybody's Political What's What* (1944):—

> . . . As long as laws are made by people whose proceedings make our more intelligent citizens wonder at the lack of wisdom with which the world is governed, conscientious objection will persist; and authority will have to maintain itself by persecuting it. There is therefore something to be said for the registration of conscientious

and reasonable objection to obey a law, and, on examination of the cases, the considered exemption of individuals from its obligations. I, for instance, am exempt from military conscription on the ground that I am too old to be of any use as a soldier. I am not exempt from war taxation on the ground that my political conscience revolts against most modern wars as senseless and mischievous. I pay partly because I have no power to withhold, and partly because if I were on a ship which had sprung a leak I should take a hand at the pumps even if I knew that the damage to the ship had been caused solely by the incompetence of the captain and his navigating staff. My exemption from first-hand killing is shared in all directions by able-bodied people in reserved occupations. There is no apparent reason why the tribunals which deal with these exemptions and reservations should not deal also with the plea of conscientious objection to fighting and killing as such. There is in fact no serious difference between the improvised tribunals which specialize between combatant and noncombatant cases. When I say that in my private opinion I am better employed in writing books and plays than in forming fours on a barrack square or playing battles as a Home Guard, or stabbing and shooting young persons who may be incipient Goethes or Beethovens, I am on the same footing as any woman who pleads that she is better employed in domestic work than in filling shells, or a man who claims a return of deducted income tax on the ground that he is too poor to afford it. . . . If, as is not impossible, the Western Powers were to declare war on the U.S.S.R., which would mean a war of State Capitalism against Democratic Communism, the number of conscientious objectors might run up to millions and make such a war impossible. The social organization of such conscientious objection is the only method now available of preventing a war. So far, the only preventive recommended is the Trade Union one of a general strike. This has been tried over and over again, and has always broken down, as it always must break down; for it is nothing but the latest form of the ancient plan of bringing the oppressor to reason and justice by starving on his doorstep. It fails because Lazarus dies of starvation before Dives misses a meal, which serves Lazarus right for being such a fool. The way to make a strike successful is to confine it to one trade whilst all the others work full time, and overtime if necessary, to support it. The conscientious objector does not starve himself: he asserts himself in the practical form of a flat refusal to fight; and if he is numerous enough there will be no war.

Compulsory State service, when, as in the fighting branches, it involves State boarding, lodging, and medical treatment, may bring about very serious conflicts between the State and the individual. We are so preoccupied just now with being ordered by the State to fight whether we think it right or not, that we forget that if we submit, we shall be ordered to share our sleeping rooms with scores of other persons, to eat certain foods whether we think them healthy or not, to wear certain clothes whether we like them or not, to take certain drugs when we are ill whether we believe in drugs or not, and, when we are well, to endure certain inoculations, supposed to prevent disease, though we may be convinced that they are dangerously mistaken. . . . There are people like myself who drink neither beer nor even tea, and will eat neither fish, flesh, nor fowl. There are invalids who will take drugs homeopathically but not allopathically, and others who will not take drugs at all. Anti-vaccinationists are now only one of several sects of antis who not only practise their beliefs but propagate and suffer for them with the zeal of martyrs. . . .

In the seventeenth century John Bunyan was imprisoned for twelve years because he conscientiously objected to be a member of the Church of England; but today there are so many who share his objection that our prisons could not contain them; so anyone may now belong to no Church at all with impunity. . . . Now the modern compulsion to be a soldier is immensely worse than the obligation to go to church instead of chapel on Sundays. In Bunyan's day it was bad enough to besiege a city, storm it, and sack it; but to destroy a city by fire and high explosive, incidentally blowing its inhabitants inside out or into fragments without discrimination of age, sex, or combatancy, as has just happened in Stalingrad, Kharkov, Hamburg, Cologne, Naples, Berlin, Bermondsey, Coventry, Plymouth, the old City of London, and elsewhere, is a horror compared to which the worst that Tilly did at Magdeburg and Suvarov at Ismail shines out as merciful. The British frightfulness of 1943 has left the German *Schrecklichkeit* of 1915 far behind, though the use of poison gas has been discontinued because high explosive and incendiary shells are more destructive and lethal. The only plea for frightfulness that can appeal to any humane person is that though its effect in slaughter and demolition may be confined to the enemy it frightens both sides impartially; for what London did to Berlin yesterday (as I write) Berlin may do to London tomorrow.* Bomb weight, which used to be measured in pounds, is now measured in tons;† and the contents explode more violently, wrecking streets where only single houses suffered formerly. Conscientious objection to their use in war grows with their atrocity, and is reinforced by the business objection that whereas when Tilly or Suvarov sacked a city they had the city for their pains when the few days of slaughter and rapine and loot ended, when Stalingrad and Kharkov were recaptured there was nothing left of them for the victors but heaps of rubble, corpses to bury, and enemy prisoners to feed. The use of high explosive does not pay.

. . . As the State becomes more and more Socialized, civil service will be imposed as military service is at present: every ablebodied person will have to work, as every man of military age now has to drill and fight, whether he is a penniless tramp or a millionaire. Can anyone imagine Conscientious Objection being extended to allow Manchester School Individualists to escape national service on the plea of a conscientious objection to Socialism? Everyone could if Socialism were to do the mischief that war does, and become abhorrent to humane people. But as Socialism has so far proved as enormously productive as war is destructive, this is not likely to occur. . . .

The time may come when people who have no conscientious objection to war will be treated as the Conshies are treated now, or worse; for they could not plead, as the Conshy can, that if everybody acted as they do (the Kantian test) the world would be much more comfortably prosperous than it is at present.

With Shaw's views expressed in the last paragraph—or at least with the right of others to hold such views—few, if any, people in Britain today would disagree. There has been widespread sympathy, and in numerous cases direct support—in many foreign countries as well as in Britain—for such recent pacifist movements as the Campaign for Nuclear Disarmament

* The 'deterrent' idea.
† Alas, now, twenty-six years later (1971) explosive power is measured in many megatons.

and the Committee of One Hundred, and for the prominent efforts for peace made by Shaw's old friend (Earl) Bertrand Russell.

But in the preceding paragraph, Shaw, while clearly upholding the right of the individual to conscientiously object to war, vaccination, meat-eating, and certain other activities, does not appear to have held out such a right to people who happened to hold (perfectly sincerely) political views which were different from his own Socialist ones—e.g. to "Manchester School capitalists". This general attitude was an aspect of his enthusiasm for autocracy and dictatorship, and it immediately involves him in complete paradox and inconsistency, for, in contrast to Britain, none of the dictatorships of recent times— German Nazism, Italian Fascism, Soviet Communism, Chinese Communism, Imperial Japan, etc.—have had any legal provision for sincere conscientious objectors to war, all such objectors having been ruthlessly shot or imprisoned.

Indeed, in these countries, the violent suppression and extermination of those who conscientiously objected on religious or political grounds to their régimes (e.g. members of the Jewish faith in Hitler's Germany) by means of "purges", "pogroms", concentration camps, and gas chambers, has been the most marked and worst feature of such dictatorships. In a sense, the entire Conservative electorate may be regarded as political conscientious objectors to Socialism, and Shaw is clearly advocating that any Labour Party in power should conscript all Conservatives (and Liberals) or even exterminate them.

The foregoing remarks are concerned chiefly with Shaw's opinions on the 1939-45 war. He subsequently advocated abolition of the atomic bomb, and, controversial as they may be, there is a good deal of wisdom and shrewd sense in many of his earlier views. His *Common Sense About the War* pamphlet in particular won a wide measure of support among the more discerning section of the community in Britain, America, and other countries.

Before closing this chapter it may be of interest to note that

Shaw remembered reading in the newspapers as a child about the aftermath of the American Civil War and the Crimean War, and he was well in his teens when the Franco-Prussian War of 1870-1 took place. And later still—though before the two world wars with which we have mainly been dealing—he lived through the period of the Boer War.

Shaw's attitude to the latter was typically paradoxical—the opposite of what one would expect: for, while the Socialist movement almost to a man was opposed to British imperialism and therefore sided with the "oppressed" Boers, Shaw supported Britain's attitude. The following extracts giving something of Shaw's view on the Boer War (and on war generally) are taken from a notebook compiled in 1902.* On the first page, preceding Shaw's draft for a letter to *The Times* (hitherto unpublished) was this inscription:—

> For where soever the carcase is, there
> will the eagles be gathered together.
>
> St Matt. xxiv. 28.

In the course of the draft itself, Shaw wrote:—

. . . The Kaiser is now holding in the dogs of war instead of letting them slip on us; so we are free to fight it out with the Boers. And the commonsense of the majority divines that there is no right in the case at all, but that another Power having taken off its coat and hit us squarely in the eye (on what provocation matters not at all) we have got to fight that Power to a finish on penalty, not merely of having our international number taken down, but possibly of losing South Africa as we lost North America.

These facts may not be moral facts. They are not even moralizable. But they are hard ones; and they are there; and it is clear that until the nation is beaten to the point of crying "Hold!—Enough", it will not return to parliament a majority or even a considerable minority which shows the slightest leaning towards a moral view of the situation. . . .

* Shaw Mss., B.M.

I can quite understand the Englishman who says that he hopes the Boers may win; and that if he were a combatant he would fight under the *vierkleur*, even with a rope round his neck. There is so much to be said for that view that I myself should not regard our defeat as an unmixed evil even for us, much less for the world. I am even biassed against loyal England because I am a republican by conviction and by birth an Irishman: that is to say, something much nearer to the insular eighteenth century Englishman than to the modern Stock Exchange British Imperial patriot whose Dutch or German and Syrian origin has taught him to regard the once petted "tight little island" as only "little England". But I am intelligent enough to know that when the striking of a blow removes a dispute from the council chamber to the camp, from the moral platform to the field, the two parties must fight it out with all their might. All these exhortations to the British soldier to pull his trigger gently because Lord Derby said this, or Mr Chamberlain did that, or Lord Milner thought the other—all this stuff about women and children, as if killing were a mere matter of age and sex—all these notions that we can give in on any other terms then accepting defeat, can have no other effect than to secure the tenure of the present government in spite of an unpopularity which would unseat it before next August if the Opposition would only face the situation—the totally unmoral situation—created by the first shot fired in the war, and give up crying for spilt milk.

In the same draft article Shaw explained his partial support of imperialism further:—

. . . Julius Caesar had no "right" to invade Britain; but on the whole we are rather glad that he did. Napoleon had no "right" to propose to invade England; but when our feudal relics become more than usually exasperating, we are occasionally sorry that he did not. There is really no other way in which the possession of territory can be settled between Powers except by war, if they are not sufficiently afraid of one another to go to arbitration. In short, international relations are not moral relations, but competitive ones; and international justice uses the sword and not the scales.

On the face of it, these passages give an impression of Shaw not simply as a realist, but as a cynical supporter of imperialist exploitation—that is to say, of a "grab-and-keep-whatever-you-can" attitude in international politics (e.g. *re* South Africa, North America). But I think it would be nearer the truth to say that he was in favour of the Boer War because, although opposed as a Socialist to many aspects of imperialism, he felt that a British administration in South Africa would be better than a Boer (Dutch) one—it would be the lesser of two evils. A parallel may clearly be drawn with the situation today (1969), when the Afrikaans Government is generally regarded as harsher and more corrupt than a British administration would be—notwithstanding that both would be imperialist.

Perhaps further light on this aspect can be gleaned from the following extract from the *Daily News*, 11th August, 1914, in which Shaw, *inter alia*, draws a distinction between Capitalist- and Socialist-inspired imperialism:—

The difference between the foreign policy of Socialism and the foreign policy of Capital is very simple. Capital sends the flag at the heels of commercial speculation for profit: Socialism would keep the flag at the head of civilisation. Capital, badly wanted at home, is sent abroad after cheap labour into undeveloped countries; and the financiers use the control of our army and fleet, which they obtain through their control of Parliament solely to guard their unpatriotic investments. That is the root of the present mischief.

(This, like most of Shaw's views, is controversial.)

Readers who wish to study Shaw's attitude to war further should consult the volume entitled *What I Wrote About the War* in the Collected Edition of his works. Most of the material comprising this chapter in *Shaw—the "Chucker-Out"* is taken from altogether different sources, but the full text of *Common Sense About the War* is to be found in *What I Wrote About the War*.

Also included in the latter are letters written by Shaw in 1913 advocating the international arrangement that was made too late after the war at Locarno, his "Peace Conference Hints", and articles by him on the Washington Conference and on the League of Nations—forming commentaries on the war which have been compared as literature to Swift's finest political writings—e.g. his classic pamphlets in 1711 on the conduct of the Allies in the war of the Spanish succession.

Not the least remarkable fact about Shaw was that his life, which began in the era of the Crimean War, the American Civil War, and the Indian Mutiny, reached well into the age of the atomic bomb, which he condemned. In *The Times* of August 20th, 1945, he drew an analogy between atomic bomb explosions and the complete disintegration—"leaving nothing but a cloud of dust called a nebula"—of old stars which, having contracted and cooled, can sometimes burst and blow up suddenly, producing: "a temperature at which the whole star has pulverised and evaporated, and its inhabitants, if any, have been cremated with an instantaneous thoroughness impossible at Golders Green".

Characteristically, Shaw added that in view of the human race's contemporary behaviour he could not pretend to deprecate such a possibility. However, at the time of writing this note (1969), when one ponders the colossal technical developments and proliferation of nuclear weapons which have taken place in the intervening twenty-five years, can one not see in this apparently superficial and cynical warning yet another example of Shaw's prophetic insight and fundamental concern for mankind?

ON SHAW'S PROPOSED NEW ENGLISH ALPHABET

Perhaps the most controversial and most misunderstood of all Shaw's ideas was his almost lifelong enthusiasm for the subject of phonetic reform, and the practical expression he gave to it in the form of extensive bequests in his Will for the design and establishment of an entirely new British alphabet.

Criticism has been particularly strong since Shaw's death, when it was revealed that he had left the bulk of his large fortune to this cause—both by contributors to the *Shaw the Villager* symposium (including some of his most ardent admirers and oldest friends, such as Dr Maxwell)—and by the world at large.

Shaw's 'printed postcards' and a 'printed letter' on the subject have already been given (on pp. 20-22 and 26-30). In supplementation of these I now have pleasure in printing two further detailed statements by Shaw about an aspect of his general outlook which some have found intriguing, some exasperating, and concerning which most people, perhaps, would acknowledge themselves as being in the 'Don't Know' class, in regard to having any real conception of what Shaw was getting at.

This article, and the letter appealing for support following it, are reproduced from *The Author* (organ of the Society of Authors), Summer 1944 number, by kind permission of the Society.

THE AUTHOR AS MANUAL LABORER

By Bernard Shaw

One would suppose that authors, as they make their living by writing, would be much more keenly interested in labor-saving devices in their trade than artisans and laborers. The author, owning his raw material (paper), his tool (the pen), and his machinery (the typewriter), gains by every invention that saves time and labor in the production of copy for the printer. And the right to publish it is his absolute monopoly. The artisan, being a hired operative owning neither raw material nor machinery nor product, is threatened by every improvement in process or machinery with reduction to the rank and wages of an unskilled laborer; and the laborer is thrown out of employment altogether by it. The author, if he had any economic sense or mathematical faculty (mostly he has neither, and is nothing but an artist) would be intensely interested in every chance of shortening his working hours or making them more productive. Yet he seldom gives them a thought except when he thinks it funny to deride them, whilst the artisans and laborers, individually and through their unions, are continually agitated about them. Of course there are exceptions: all authors are not lost when they leave their imaginary worlds for the real one; but in the lump it is notable that scriptorial reforms receive hardly any support from authors, and rather too much from Utopian cranks.

The basic difficulty in writing English is that we have no British alphabet in general use. Our ancient Phoenician alphabet has only 26 letters, whereas the least we need are 42. There are only five vowel sounds to represent the speech of millions of Britishers whose vowels are as different as their finger prints. But as the differences are not wide enough to make Yorkshire unintelligible to Somerset, or Trinity College, Dublin, to Oxford University, it is found in practice that a dozen or so of vowel symbols* are quite sufficient to make English writing as intelligible as English speech. There is no need to distinguish between the vowel sounds in *to, too* and *two*, nor between *city* by itself and as it occurs in *publicity*. All British readers will understand without cutting it as fine as that, which reminds me that Robert Bridges would have spelt the last pronoun *thatt*.

But Bridges made this distinction by using two letters for a single sound instead of one; and this meant a colossal addition to the manual drudgery of writing. It seems at first that the time lost by writing *tt* instead of *t* is negligible; but this depends on the number of times you have to write it. Just count the number of *ts* I have had to write since I began this article. Then think of the number of *ts* in this morning's *Times*. Include all the other newspapers in the British

* This word appears as 'syllables' in the original owing to an obvious shorthand mis-transcription.

Commonwealth and the U.S.A. Add the *ts* in all the books, letters, and documents of every sort that are being written during the current 24 hours. The figure becomes monstrous. Multiply it by 313 to arrive at its amount for all the working days in the year. It becomes astronomical. Bridges was proposing, not the expenditure of a fraction of a second of time, but the cost of a war. And *t* is not the letter we have to write oftenest. Substitute *e*, and double it, as we do to spell *keep* or the American *Gee*; and human imagination staggers at the sum.

Yet it is only by doubling letters or writing one sound with two letters and in different order that we can make our Phoenician alphabet spell English. By resorting to these permutations we have tried to do it; but we have not tried consistently. To spell *receive* and *believe* we have to think of the unpleasant word *lice*.* Such consonants as *sh*, *zh*, *th*, *dh* we simply cannot spell at all, and find ourselves calling *Lewis Ham* Louis Sham and *Cars Halton* Car Shallton for want of a symbol to write the first consonant of my name.

As to spelling the very frequent word *though* with six letters instead of two, it is impossible to discuss it, as it is outside the range of common sanity. In comparison such a monstrosity as *phlegm* for flem is merely disgusting.†

No author in his senses, having grasped the figures, would use the Phoenician alphabet if a British phonetic one were available. I wish some person with a mania for arithmetic would count the sounds in Shakespear's plays or Dickens's novels, and then count the letters these unfortunate scribes had to write to make readable manuscripts of them for the players and printers. I would burn all the commentaries and criticisms that have been wasted on their works for such a cast-up. It would prove that they in their short lives (I have lived nearly twenty years longer than either of them) could have written two or three more plays and novels than they had time to get through. Shakespear's signatures shew that he suffered from writer's cramp. How his actors read their parts (unless he dictated them to scriveners) is a wonder.

The case of Dickens is extraordinary. He began as a Parliamentary

* Why? Most people surely do *not* do so in this connection.

† Shaw's comment here is not entirely valid, for although the 'g' is not sounded in *phlegm*, it *is* sounded in the adjective *phlegmatic*. The complete interchangeability (and therefore superfluity) of 'ph' with 'f' is, however, another matter.

reporter, and had learnt and mastered Gurney's shorthand. Yet he had to write all his novels in Phoenician longhand because his shorthand was legible by nobody but himself. Gurney's shorthand can be written legibly and transcribed by specially expert masters of it. But that means many years of practice, beginning with special natural aptitude.

Take my own case. I learnt Pitman's phonetic alphabet in my teens easily in six weeks or thereabouts. Any author can. But I was put off it by the absurd notion that I could not be fully qualified as a shorthand writer until I could report human utterance verbatim, which means writing 150 words a minute. Now this cannot be done by an alphabet. No mortal can *spell* 150 words in 60 seconds, nor even 100. To do this the alphabet must be contracted and contorted and reduced to a code, with all the prepositions and conjunctions and pronouns represented by ticks and dots, and the vowels not represented at all, and seldom even indicated. It ends in each reporter having his own tricks and his own code, illegible to anyone but himself, and not always by himself after his memory of the speech fades. If he has to spell or even to think for a moment he is lost: the speaker has outstripped him.

But what has all this to do with authorship? An author is not a reporter. His writing speed is not 150 words a minute: it is, year in and year out, about 12. He has to think out every sentence, every phrase, before he writes it. Sometimes he has to think about how to spell a word, and, if our ludicrously inconsistent usage baffles him, to write the doubtful letters illegibly and leave the decision to the compositor. Speed of hand is nothing to him: he can make any phonetic alphabet, Pitman or Gregg (now the most generally known in England and America), perfectly legible by writing the words separately at full length with all the necessary vowels and yet beat the Phoenician alphabet by some years of his working life. That is what I have done with Pitman. For over forty years past all my books and plays have been written in Pitman's phonetic alphabet and transcribed into Phoenician by my secretary for the printer. Sometimes, when time presses, I send my shorthand direct to a newspaper, where the typists always transcribe it easily.

The time may be at hand when authors will not write at all. They will speak into a dictaphone, when dictaphones become cheap and portable. The dictaphone may even operate the linotype without the intervention of a compositor. But meanwhile the author who can afford a secretary is wasting much of his life in writing or typing in Phoenician longhand.

The reader will now be able to understand the long letter which I have addressed to the public bodies mentioned in it, and to some others as well.

AYOT ST LAWRENCE
WELWYN, HERTS.

I am at present making my will. As I intend leaving my property, including certain copyrights the value of which may run into six figures, to the nation for a specified purpose which is outside the routine of any existing Government department, including that of the Public Trustee or the Charity Commissioners, but which aims at the achievement of an immense national economy, I am up against the difficulty of ascertaining which public department or committee, or what learned Society, I should nominate as an executant of my scheme instead of attempting to create a private Trust *ad hoc*.

My particular fad is the saving of labor by the establishment of a fit British alphabet containing at least 42 letters, and thereby capable of noting with sufficient accuracy for recognition all the sounds of spoken English without having to use more than one letter for each sound, which is impossible with the ancient 26-letter Phoenician alphabet at present in use.

There are before the public several phonetic alphabets which fulfil this condition, notably those of Pitman in the British Isles and Gregg in the United States of North America. Both have behind them capable business organizations, for lack of which the alphabets of the eminent English phonetician Henry Sweet and others remain practically unknown. But they have been corrupted and spoilt for general use by being taught exclusively as shorthands for verbatim reporting. Phonetic writing can never reach the speed of human utterance; for the contractions, grammalogues, phraseograms and arbitrary dots and dashes and ticks by which verbatim reporters contrive, after years of practice, to report speeches verbatim, are illegible to anyone but the writer, and hardly even to the writer after memory of the utterances has faded. The classical instance is that of Charles Dickens, who, though qualified as a professional reporter by prolonged and irksome study and practice, nevertheless had to write all his novels in the ordinary script to make them legible by the printer. Shorthands as such may be dismissed as useless for general scripture, though their alphabets, if used without contractions, should be examined by all designers of new alphabets.

Besides these shorthands there are in use, in pronouncing dictionaries, and by professional phoneticians and students, ways of making the 26-letter alphabet phonetic. But the notation of our 16 vowels by the five letters *a e i o* and *u* can be done only by using two letters for one sound, and attaching consistent meanings to each permutation. This seems simple and practical because the possible permutations of five letters are far in excess of the number of sounds that need be noted to make a script generally intelligible. Hence we have what is called Simplified Spelling and the spelling of the phonetic textbooks, to say nothing of the attempts of novelists and playwrights to represent the dialects of their characters—of Sam Weller, Caleb Balderstone, Handy Andy, Fluellen and the rest—by grotesque misspellings. My own experience as a playwright in efforts to write modern cockney dialect phonetically with 26 letters has convinced me of its impossibility. Actors who specialize in cockney have had to transcribe my text into conventional spelling before they could study their parts.

My own contribution to the subject, however, has nothing to do with literature as a fine art. On the contrary, I am persuaded that nothing will be done to reform our scripture until its advocates change their ground and admit that the arguments they have been repeating for the last hundred years have produced no considerable result, and are ranked as more or less amusing essays on the curiosities of literature. My special contention is that the matter is one, not for men of letters, professional or dilettanti, but for economists, mathematicians, and statisticians. To any others the inadequacies of our 26-letter alphabet seem trifling, and the cost of a change quite prohibitive. My view is that a change, far from being an economic impossibility, is an economic necessity. The figures in its favor, hitherto uncalculated and unconsidered, are astronomical. That my name, containing two sounds, has to be spelt in our 26-letter alphabet by four letters, or even that the very common word "though", also a two-sound word, should be spelled with six, seems the most negligible of trifles; for what does one name or one word matter? Is the English language, with its established triumphs of "immortal" literature, stored in millions of printed books, and employing a vast machinery of printing presses, and armies of authors compositors, readers, writers, school teachers, and etymologists, to be upset and made obsolete at enormous expense for a fad called phonetic spelling?

When the question is put in this way the answer is No: contemptuously No.

When it is tackled mathematically the No becomes a clamorous Yes; and the objections are seen to be hot air exhaled by aesthetes who have never counted the prodigious cost of using two letters where one would suffice. To spell Shaw with four letters instead of two, and "though" with six, means to them only a fraction of a second in wasted time. But multiply that fraction by the number of "thoughs" that are printed every day in all the English newspapers in the British Commonwealth and the United States of America—in the books, in the business letters and telegrams, in the private letters, in the military orders; and the fractions of a second suddenly swell into integers of years, of decades, of centuries, costing thousands, tens of thousands and millions. The saving of this colossal waste would pay for the cost of a British alphabet in days, hours, and even minutes. Even the literary upholders of the Phoenician alphabet and its fantastic corruption by the etymological craze would begin to see that Shakespear might have written two or three more plays in the time it took to spell his name with eleven letters instead of seven, "bough" in five instead of two, and so on through much of his vocabulary, though he spelt much more phonetically than Dr Johnson.

In my own practice I use the phonetic alphabet of Isaac Pitman, writing without reporters' contractions at my speed of authorship, which averages about 1,500 words *per day*. It has saved me a prodigious quantity of manual labor, and can be transcribed on a typewriter by anyone who has spent six weeks in learning the Pitman alphabet; but the time it saves is lost again by the typist, the compositor or linotypist or mono-typist, the machinist, the paper makers, and the distributing carriers.

In view of this situation I am ready to make a will leaving all my residuary estate to defray the cost of designing and introducing a British alphabet, transliterating the masterpieces of English literature and our school reading books into it and publishing the transliterations, advertizing these publications and propagating their desirability, and, always without tampering with the existing alphabet, launching the other in competition with it until one of the two proves the fitter to survive. Official adoption or compulsion must wait upon prevalence: any attempt to begin with them would only prove the political inexperience and incompetence of their advocates. Nevertheless, appropriate State departments may and should undertake and invent improvements in our national scripture just as they do in weights and measures, coinage, postal operations, traffic machinery, military and naval mechanization, building, sanitation, town planning, &c., &c. The rationalizing of our scripture by a native British alphabet may be added to these activities without any fresh legislation or change of policy; but its adoption for official publications and national records, and its tuition in public schools: in short, its virtual enforcement for general use will not occur until its utility enforces itself. Meanwhile the existing generation must have its literature in the form to which it is accustomed, reading and spelling by visual memory, not by ear. I should strenuously object to have to read, much less write, my own works in a strange script, though I know I should get accustomed to it in a few weeks if I took that trouble.

I must repeat with all possible emphasis that the scheme is purely economic. Its object is to save time and labor, whether in producing books and newspapers or teaching children to read, write, and speak. Its execution must not be directed by a committee of professional literary persons or educational authorities. Such a committee would at once become a conspiracy to defeat the scheme by endless discussions as to whether it should be adopted or not. Only economists as free as possible from literary or pedagogical prejudices, and already convinced of its labor-saving importance, should be given any part in its direction. Artists should be employed only as artist-calligraphers and designers, or consulted as assessors on the aesthetic amenability of the new scripts and types under consideration.

And now comes the difficulty with which I began this letter. I am a citizen desirous of bequeathing my property to the public for the public good. If I do so unconditionally this will be easy enough: the Exchequer will "impetticose the gratillity"* as conscience money, and use it to pay for the war or to reduce the income tax. But if I earmark it for a specific purpose, as I propose, I am faced

* Shaw's spelling. The quotation from *Twelfth Night* appears in most modern Shakespeare texts as "Impeticos thy gratillity".

with the question of what public ministry or agency I can name as willing and competent to include the fulfilment of my purpose among its functions.   The Public Trustee can accept the bequest, collect its revenue, and pay all the personal legacies to relatives and servants and charities with which it must be saddled; but he cannot invent or propagate a new alphabet. What public body can?

The most obvious choice is the British Council. But the British Council has just been charged by the Government with the propagation of Basic English; and though Basic English needs an English alphabet as urgently as any other sort of English its acceptance would be seriously retarded if it were presented in a strange script. The two reforms had better be kept separate. One job at a time is enough for the Council, and one novelty enough for the public. Also the opposition of the thoughtlessly customary people who are the enemies of every change should be divided, not combined.

What public organization then, other than the British Council, can conceivably tackle the alphabet? The Board of Works, which has over thirty divisions with various economic functions? The Imperial Economic Committee of the Home Office? The National Service Department of the Ministry of Labor? The Privy Council? The Paper Economy Committee plus the Scientific Advisers' Division of the Ministry of Production? The Royal Commission for the exhibition of 1851? The National Savings Committee? The Department of Scientific and Industrial Research? The National Council of Social Service? The Service for Economic Action? Or among the private organizations for the public benefit, the Carnegie Trust? The Economic Association? The Orthological Institute? The Pilgrim Trust? The Royal Society of Arts? The Mathematical Society? The Statistical Society?

Among the London City Guilds, the Scriveners and the Stationers and Newspaper Makers might establish their usefulness by providing their country with a British alphabet.

Who speaks first? Or last? I beg the favor of a reply, positive or negative.

[*Editorial Note:* The following letter appeared in *The Author*, Vol. LV, No. 1, Autumn 1944, p. 13, and is also reprinted by permission of The Public Trustee and The Society of Authors.]

My appeal for a new British alphabet has been so far a complete failure. Every Government Department to which I have addressed it has replied that that it is not its job. The colleges, Trusts, and Societies sing the same song, the few who vary not being in a position to take action. None of them question the importance of the matter, nor fail in distinguished consideration for myself as an author. For this I thank them sincerely.

As it is quite impossible for me to undertake the business myself (inventors of phonetic alphabets please note this) I have decided to empower my executors to accumulate a fund from which they may finance any promising scheme for providing a new phonetic alphabet capable of expressing the forty-two sounds listed by the late Henry Sweet, Oxford Reader of Phonetics, and then publishing and depositing in the leading libraries certain English classics trans-literated into the said alphabet.

Failing the achievement of these objects within twenty years from my death (the legal limit of accumulation) the money will go to other public purposes.

G. B. S.

G.B.S. AND THE A.B.C.

By BARBARA SMOKER

Formerly Secretary of the Phonetic Alphabet Association, London, and also of the Shaw Society, England

[*Editorial Note:*—The article and letters by Bernard Shaw in the preceding pages do much to clarify his aims and attitude on the subject of Phonetics, and his reasons for the 'New Alphabet' bequests in his Will. Since this matter has given rise to more popular fallacies than any other aspect of Shaw's work and personality, and in view of its great interest and relative complexity, I am pleased to include also the following article by Barbara Smoker, who is uniquely well qualified on the subject by virtue of being a leading figure both in the Phonetic Reform movement and in the British Shaw Society.

This article is a combination of five written by Miss Smoker which she kindly placed at my disposal, comprising that published in *Modern Drama* (September, 1959) and that in *The Californian Shavian* (January, 1960), with later ones from *The Shavian*. With her permission I have made certain emendations and cuts in the material as a whole—especially of the more technical aspects—while retaining sufficient of the latter to enable the fair-minded reader to gain some real insight into the reasons why Bernard Shaw (and other alphabet reform enthusiasts) feel so strongly on this subject. It is a subject about which surprisingly little is generally known—though proposals originating many years ago for changing our distance, weights, and monetary systems to the metre, gram, and decimal systems (or some other numerical system) have now achieved official recognition].

During 1962 every public library received a new edition of Bernard Shaw's play *Androcles and the Lion*—a special bi-alphabetic edition, for which Shaw left instructions in his Will. In this article I will attempt to demolish some of the many popular misconceptions about Shaw and the alphabet question.

But first, a little demolition on the subject of Shaw's work as a whole. Most people—Shavians and anti-Shavians alike—are erroneously convinced that Shaw was an original thinker. In my opinion he was not. The original thinker gives his original thought—rarely more than one—to the rest of mankind, and bores us stiff with it. Shaw was teeming with ideas—other people's—and scattered them with exuberant vitality.

He was essentially a craftsman. His own description of his job was 'that of a master of language.' He took his ideas, as most thinking people do, from this philosopher and that, from this economist and that, from this biologist and that, selecting all the ideas that fitted in with his own general outlook and rejecting the rest. He himself never claimed that his ideas were original. He said: "I never remember who puts the things into my head: it is the *Zeitgeist*."

But to deny that Shaw was an original thinker is not to belittle him or his contribution to civilisation. How many of us who drink thirstily from Shaw's bubbling decanter of ideas would ever go to the original sources for them? Or, if we did, would find them digestible, let alone palatable?

Since Shaw's profession was that of a master craftsman in the craft of putting ideas on paper, he was in all his other activities an amateur. Not amateurish, but a 'round' man, participating in many different fields for the love of the game, and, without attempting to specialise, acquiring a good general grasp of most of them. What this century is most in need of, perhaps, is the non-specialist with a wide range of interests and a keen mind capable of seizing on essential points in the great mass of knowledge accumulating round every subject, so that one subject can be related to another. Shaw was such a man.

In his plays, speeches and prose writings he took the lid off slum landlordism, prostitution, the medical profession and the Irish question; he denounced hypocritical respectability and romantic idealism; he preached socialism and sex equality; he expounded the philosophy of creative evolution; and he urged social reforms ranging from easier divorce to the foundation of a National Theatre. Few dramatists would have considered these themes promising material for their art, but Shaw wove them into some of the best plays ever written. One amateur interest after another thus provided him with material for his plays, and one hobby-horse after another found a home in the Shavian stables and was ridden round the stages of the world's theatres.

The science of phonetics was one of Shaw's amateur interests, and the introduction of a modern phonetic alphabet for English was one of his hobby-horses. But even Shaw found this subject a difficult one to dramatise. He set out to write *Pygmalion* as an advertisement for phonetics, but it turned out as a Cinderella story about the transformation of a Cockney flower-girl into a duchess and thence into an independent woman, the phonetic theme being very subsidiary indeed to the human situation, so that most of the actual propaganda had to be relegated to the play's preface.

Many people, therefore, knowing Shaw only through the theatre, had no idea how strongly he felt about the inadequacy of the ABC until after his death, when the newspapers published the fact that he had left the bulk of his money for a new English alphabet. The general reaction then was that either the whole thing was simply a posthumous joke of Shaw's, or else a bee that had got into his bonnet in his declining years. Nothing could be further from the truth. If we look at Shaw's writings as a whole, and particularly his letters to the Press, we find a surprising number of letters, articles and prefaces, devoted to the subject of spelling and alphabet reform, and spanning most of his long life.

In fact, Shaw's amateur interest in phonetics, spelling reform, shorthand systems, typography and allied subjects, was first roused as early as 1879, when he was only 23, by his friend James Lecky. And it was through this friend that he got to know the eminent phonetician Henry Sweet—the original of Pro-fessor Henry Higgins in *Pygmalion*, in whom Sweet's irascibility is as faithfully portrayed as his skill in applied phonetics.

Shaw, as a young man, also met the philologist Alexander Ellis, whom he later described as "a London patriarch, with impressive head always covered by a velvet skull cap, for which he would apologise to public meetings in a very courtly manner." Ellis had been steeped in alphabet and spelling reform since 1843, when he collaborated with Isaac Pitman (inventor of Pitman's Shorthand) in designing Phonotypy—an enlarged Latin alphabet which Pitman considered more important than his shorthand. Thus, Ellis and Shaw spanned between them more than a century of attempts to reform English orthography. And before Ellis there was a long unbroken line of enthusiasts for spelling and alphabet reform, going back to the sixteenth century and including such great names in other spheres as Sir John Cheke, John Milton, James Howell, Benjamin Franklin, Herbert Spencer, Mark Twain, Andrew Carnegie, William Dean Howells, Robert Bridges and Nicholas Murray Butler, to name only a few. So much for the popular conviction that the idea of alphabet reform, if no other, originated with Shaw! The idea is one with firm roots, and not, as some newspapers have sneered, just 'a tom-fool idea that only Shaw would put forward.'

In fact, Shaw's contribution to the cause of alphabet reform was not invention but propaganda, plus the indirect publicity gained by it from association with his name, owing to his literary prestige and notoriety, plus his much publicised monetary bequest.

He announced his intention of bequeathing most of his money for a new alphabet in an article entitled "The Author as Manual Laborer", which appeared in the summer of 1944. At the end of the article he gave the text of a letter* he was sending to all the Government Departments, learned societies, com-

* This article and letter are those which have been given unabridged in the preceding pages—*Ed.*

mittees, councils, guilds, trusts, institutes and colleges whose functions seemed even remotely relevant, offering to leave them his money for propagating a new alphabet. But none of the addressees would accept the job, so he had no option but to create a private trust *ad hoc*, though he was well aware that the validity of such a trust would probably be the subject of a Chancery Court action. But even this would, he remarked, provide the cause of alphabet reform with valuable publicity! It was by no means, however, just a posthumous joke.

In the event of the trust being declared invalid (as it was, in 1957—its objects not being accepted as charitable, in the legal sense—but more of that later) Shaw named three ultimate beneficiaries: the British Museum, the National Gallery of Ireland and the Royal Academy of Dramatic Art—representing, respectively, the preservation of books, of paintings and of acting. These three bodies were in any case to receive any income that accrued to the estate after the expiration of the statutory 'perpetuity' period of 21 years, but if the alphabet trust failed they would receive all the earlier residue too.

Since Shaw had been interested in alphabet reform for most of his long life, it is natural to wonder why he himself never selected a particular alphabet of the kind he advocated, for a great number were sent to him by their inventors and sponsors. Part of the answer is that he regarded himself as an agitator, not an executive, and he preferred to leave the actual selection of the alphabet to phoneticians and other relevant experts; but part of the answer is also that he realised the importance of an aura of official sanction for the chosen alphabet, to avoid any conflict of rival alphabets, and he thought that having the Public Trustee for his executor and leaving the selection of the alphabet to him would make it seem more official. At the same time, he was certainly not in favour of compelling people, by law, to adopt the new alphabet. He merely wanted it to be launched in competition with the existing alphabet, in the belief that eventually the better would oust the worse, just as our Arabic numerals have supplanted the clumsy old Roman ones.

Within a few days of Shaw's death, an anonymous defender of English orthography paid the statutory shilling to file a protest in Probate Court against Shaw's Will, petitioning the Court to suspend probate on the ground that it would 'gravely affect the majesty of the English language and would have serious repercussions on English literature.' Such irrational fears are not uncommon, but they did not apparently weigh unduly with the Probate Court, though probate of the Will *was* delayed, for reasons of a more technical kind.

The estate was provisionally valued for probate in 1951 at £301,585, including a provisional estimate of the value of the Shaw copyrights, which Shaw had stipulated were not to be sold. The sum of £180,571 was paid to the Exchequer on account of estate duty and interest, leaving the estate temporarily penniless. But worse was to follow. After $5\frac{1}{2}$ years of negotiation between the Estate Duty Office and the Public Trustee (as Shaw's executor), the final valuation of the copyrights was agreed in April 1956 at £433,500. This, being far in excess of what had been generally expected, prompted Mr I. J. Pitman, M.P. for Bath, to ask the Chancellor of the Exchequer (then Mr Harold Macmillan) how and why the basis adopted for the valuation of Shaw's copyrights had differed from the basis adopted for those of other authors. The official reply was that the statutory basis for the valuation of copyrights was the price they would have fetched if sold in the open market at the time of death,* and that there was no standard formula or rule for applying this basis to particular cases, valuation being made in each case 'by reference to its own facts in the light of expert opinion obtained.' The effect of the new valuation of the copyrights was to increase the value of the estate to more than £700,000 and make it liable to estate duty of about £524,000. This not only swallowed all the liquid assets, including all the royalties that had accrued to the estate since Shaw's death, but actually put the estate in debt again.

* [Section 7 (5) of the Finance Act, 1894.]

Meanwhile, there had been the fiasco of the Shaw Memorial Appeal in 1952, the objects of which were, in addition to endowing Shaw's Corner as a literary shrine, to form a permanent repertory company for the regular presentation of Shaw's plays on tour and to help creative artists.

Lady Astor appealed to the Chancellor of the Exchequer to 'break that ridiculous Will', and others also wanted to see it and the alphabet bequest broken. Had Shaw spent his money on high living, as soon as he had earned it, or had he left it to distant relatives or a home for stray cats, there would presumably have been no hard feelings; but he left it for a new alphabet, and that was unforgivable. It was almost like financing a new decalogue. But since there was no money in the estate, no one knew yet to what extent the bequest would be worth the breaking.

Then something happened that completely changed the situation: the fabulous *My Fair Lady* came on to the scene with a percentage of profits that added over £1,000 a week to the Shaw estate. Even so, among the many popular mistakes about Shaw and the alphabet is the assumption that the Shaw percentage from the enormous profits made by *My Fair Lady* (the musical based, appropriately enough, on Shaw's one play with a phonetic theme) were *all* available to finance an alphabetic revolution. First, Estate Duty took £524,000, and the Shaw estate did not get out of debt to the Estate Duty Office till about the beginning of 1957. The debt would probably not have been cleared yet had it not been for *My Fair Lady* coming to the rescue. Since the last instalment of the Estate Duty was paid, all royalties accruing to the Shaw estate until November 1971 (the end of the statutory 'perpetuity' period) should certainly have gone to swell the alphabet trusts, if Shaw's wishes were carried out—except, of course, that Shaw would certainly never have allowed *My Fair Lady* to be born in the first place, whatever the financial prospects (he actually refused a percentage from *The Chocolate Soldier*, the unauthorised musical version of *Arms and the Man*). In his Will he directed that the Public

Trustee (acting through the Society of Authors) should not, in dealing with the copyrights, "be bound by commercial considerations exclusively it being my desire that he shall give due weight to artistic and public and human considerations to the best of his judgment and counsel." On the other hand, 'artistic and public and human considerations' have less tangible criteria than 'commercial considerations', and the Public Trustee can hardly be blamed if he has concentrated on the latter.

This brings one to the Chancery Court case of 1957 that set the Shaw alphabet trusts aside.

My Fair Lady soon paid off the rest of the estate duty, with the result that the British Museum and the Royal Academy of Dramatic Art were able to challenge the alphabet bequest. The case could not be fought while the estate had no money, since barristers prefer not to represent a penniless client. The National Gallery of Ireland quixotically stood aside, not choosing "to urge anything which would defeat the wishes of a fellow Irishman, and one so distinguished, in a matter which was clearly so dear to his heart." The Attorney-General, as official protector of charities, represented the alphabet trust, maintaining that it came into one or another of the legal categories of charity; while the Public Trustee, as executor of the estate, maintained that even if the trust were not charitable he should be allowed to carry out the provisions of the bequest.

Under English law, no one may make a bequest for an abstract cause—that is, without a personal or organisational beneficiary—unless the object of the bequest is charitable. The reason for this is that a legal bequest must be legally enforceable, and must therefore have a beneficiary to take the executors of the estate to court if necessary. In the case of a charity, this function is fulfilled by the Attorney-General, who officially represents all charities. But the legal definition of a charity depends, believe it or not, on the categories laid down in the Preamble to the Statute of Queen Elizabeth I! Two of the categories were possibilities for Shaw's alphabet trusts—

Education and Public Benefit—but after six days of argument by learned gentlemen in white wigs it was decided by Mr Justice Harman* that the alphabet trust could not come under either of these categories of charity, and did not, therefore, constitute a charity, in the legal sense, at all. So they were held invalid.

Every effort was made by phoneticians and many of Shaw's friends and supporters to persuade the Attorney-General to appeal against this decision, but he refused to do so. There was no one else in a position to appeal on the charity issue, but, on the very last day of the period allowed for appeal, the Public Trustee, as Shaw's executor, lodged an appeal on the issue that, although he could not be forced in law to administer the alphabet trusts, he should be allowed to do so.

Before this appeal was heard, a compromise settlement was reached out of court between the Public Trustee on the one hand and the three ultimate residuary legatees—the British Museum, the Royal Academy of Dramatic Art and the National Gallery of Ireland—on the other, by which the sum of £8,300 was allocated from the estate for the alphabet project outlined in Shaw's Will. This is a paltry sum in comparison with the total amount that can be expected to accrue to the estate before all the Shaw copyrights have expired. But even £8,300 is better than nothing.†

Immediately this settlement was reached, the Public Trustee announced a £500 prize competition for a suitable alphabet of at least 40 letters, enabling the English language to be written without having to represent single sounds by more than one letter. Competitors were given a full year in which to design and polish their alphabets, the closing date of the contest being January 1st, 1959. More than 1,000 applications for details were received, but, as was to be expected, less than half

---

* For reference, *The Times* report of Mr Justice Harman's judgment is given later in this volume, following Shaw's Will (which is given in full).

† The credit for securing this meagre (yet valuable) concession was largely due to Mr I. J. Pitman, M.P., a foremost enthusiast for the phonetic cause and friend of Bernard Shaw's for many years.

of the applicants actually submitted entries. The total number of entries finally sent in was 467 and about 250 of them survived the first sifting, the rest either being based on the present alphabet, which was not required, or else containing far too many symbols. The panel of three experts appointed to assess the entries took almost a year to do so; then, on December 31st, 1959, it was announced that the £500 would be divided equally among four of the entrants, since none of the alphabets submitted was considered to merit final adoption for propagation as a new general alphabet which might eventually supplant the ABC. The four winners were asked to improve their designs in accordance with expert guidance made available to them, after which the final alphabet was to be chosen.

Under the terms of Shaw's Will, there was to be a statistical inquiry into the wastage of time and money caused by the inadequacy of the present alphabet for English, and *Androcles and the Lion* was to be published in the new phonetic alphabet derived from one or more of the four winners' designs, side by side with the traditional version; it was to be distributed free to 13,000 public libraries in the English-speaking world and to national libraries elsewhere, besides being sold over the counter to the public. This volume made its appearance in 1962—of which more anon.

One popular fallacy is that Shaw designed an alphabet of his own and left money for its propagation. It is an indication of his modesty (a trait with which he is rarely credited) that he preferred to leave the phonetic analysis and selection of symbols to experts, though he had prepared a phonetic analysis for his printed postcard on the alphabet question*—one of the famous printed postcards which enabled him to cope with his huge daily correspondence.

Another popular fallacy is that the court case concerning the alphabet trusts was part of Shaw's deliberate intention. It is true that he knew there was likely to be a court case, and he

---

* See pages 20-21.

knew that this would provide valuable publicity for the cause of alphabet reform, well worth the few thousand pounds of lawyers' costs involved. But there can be no doubt that Shaw also wanted the trusts to be upheld, and, fully aware of the legal position as to abstract bequests, he did his utmost, before making his final Will, to find a suitable beneficiary who would accept the task of launching a phonetic alphabet for English. But, as has been mentioned earlier, since none of those to whom he sent his letter broaching the matter in 1944 would accept the job, there was nothing for it but to create a private trust *ad hoc*, and hope that it would be accepted as a charity.

The most fallacious of all the popular fallacies about Shaw and the alphabet are, however, those concerning his ultimate aim. Some people think he wanted mere spelling reform with the traditional letters. Others think he wanted an overnight switch from the old system to a new one, involving the necessity for everyone to start learning to read and write all over again. What he actually wanted was a one-sound-one-letter alphabet comprising simple, shorthand-like signs, to be launched in competition with the existing alphabet for use as an alternative system of writing until one or the other proved the fitter to survive. In that way, the acquired visual memory of the existing adult generation would not be sacrificed, for only young children would have to learn both systems—and for them the easier phonetic system would actually be (as experiments have proved) a helpful stepping-stone to the more difficult traditional one.

Shaw held that, far from having less chance of acceptance than mere simplified spelling, an entirely new alphabet was the only hope of orthographic reform. Tampering with the traditional spelling would be up against the emotional hostility with which we all defend our habitual mental processes, as well as causing confusion between the two orthographies. An entirely new alphabet, on the other hand, could exist side by side with the old one, and gradually take over from it more and more, until, after a century or two, when everyone living has grown up with both notations, the ABC becomes merely an academic subject. That is how our numerical system was changed. Over a period of several centuries, the Arabic numerals (with a symbol for zero, making place value possible) gradually superseded the clumsy old Roman ones. The idea of introducing a symbol for zero existed as early as the sixth century A.D., but most of the people in this part of the world went on using the Roman numerals for another nine hundred years because they had learnt them in childhood and would have found it too troublesome to change! When the change was finally made, it opened the door to mathematics and the machine age. (Just try doing a 'long division' with Roman numerals!)

The only way that a new alphabet can, and eventually must, come in is through the infant school. Appeals to the reasonable nature of the general public are doomed to failure. It is the story of the Arabic numerals all over again: people who have already mastered the old notation will not be bothered with a new one, however much more efficient it may be.

Now, what is wrong with the ABC? Apart from the insufficiency of letters, which is the main drawback of the present alphabet, it has many other defects which could be avoided in a brand new one. For one thing, the shapes of some of the present letters are unnecessarily complex. This is bad enough in reading—it has been demonstrated in tests that reading is slowed down by the complexity of letters—but in writing by hand, the number of strokes used for each letter is, of course, a major factor in the consumption of time. Then, the shapes of some of the letters are unnecessarily complex as far as handwriting is concerned, 'm' and 'w' having as many as six strokes each, and 'x' necessitating the lifting of the pen in the middle. Even more time-wasting is the need to go back on words to dot i's and cross t's.

The fact is that the letters were not scientifically designed, but simply evolved from prehistoric pictographs, with modifications dictated by the different writing tools used at different times. This haphazard development is all too apparent. There is no relation between the shapes of letters representing similar sounds: the 'k' and hard 'g' sounds, for instance, are similar, but the characters we use for them are very different. On the other hand, the capital forms of the vowel letter *E* and consonant letter *F*, though having nothing in common phonetically, are similar to look at.

We have two series of letters—capital and small—to represent one and the same series of sounds, and the capital letters are mostly quite different in shape from the corresponding small ones. In fact, only 8 out of the 26 letters have the same shape in each series. Capital *D* is more like small *b* than like small *d*, which has the curve on the opposite side—an incongruity that gives trouble to many a child. Then the manuscript letters, both capital and small, are sometimes different again from their printed counterparts, and the printed letters may even differ in their Roman and italic forms. (Compare the shapes A, a, *a*.)

The order of the letters in the alphabet is arbitrary: one might at least expect the vowel letters to be grouped together at the beginning or the end. As for the names of the letters, some of them bear no resemblance to the sounds they represent: an adult introduced to the English ABC for the first time might suppose *H* to represent the 'ch' sound, *U* the 'y' sound, and *Y* the 'w' sound, while the name of *W* offers no clue to its sound at all. Benjamin Franklin wrote of a chamber-maid who thought that 'wife' was spelt *yf*!

The main drawback of our alphabet, however, and far more important than anything mentioned so far, is the insufficiency of letters.

The Latin version of the alphabet was never really suitable for Latin, and is far less so for English. Whereas most modern European languages using a form of the Latin alphabet have about thirty distinct sounds (or, more technically, phonemes) to be represented with twenty-one to twenty-seven letters, English has about forty phonemes, and therefore has to pull and stretch its twenty-six-letter alphabet (of which three letters

—*C*, *Q*, and *X*—are completely wasted!) in all directions. Some of the letters have to do duty for two or more sounds, and we also fall back on digraphs—*i.e.* pairs of letters for single sounds—such as *aw*, *oo*, *sh*, *th* and *ng*.

On top of all this, we spell our language with such abandon that it might be supposed we had too many letters instead of too few! This strange state of affairs has come about chiefly because the English vocabulary derives from various languages, each with its own system of spelling, so that several conflicting systems using the same Latin letters exist side by side in the written language. Add to this the fact that our spelling has been more or less fixed for centuries past whilst the pronunciation has been changing all the time, and the chaotic nature of English spelling is no longer a matter for astonishment—nor, surely, for passive acceptance.

Unphonetic spelling not only makes it harder for children to learn to read and spell; it also perverts the natural tendency of children to perceive relationships—a fact deplored by educational psychologists. In addition, it leads to distortion of the spoken language—one of the factors that most weighed with Shaw, who could not bear to hear English maltreated. And it is a brake on English becoming a universal second language for international communication.

Another of Shaw's hates was inefficiency, and particularly the inefficiency of using silent letters and digraphs. "As to spelling the very frequent word 'though' with six letters instead of two," he declared, "it is impossible to discuss it, as it is outside the range of common sanity." Shakespeare and Dickens, he added, might have written two or three more plays and novels "in their short lives" if a phonetic notation had been acceptable to their players and printers.

Most of the inconsistencies of English spelling could be eliminated by mere spelling reform, but it would require a reform of the alphabet itself to eliminate the digraphs. As Shaw has pointed out, one has only to consider the two words 'mishap' and 'bishop' to realise that no more than a partial reform could otherwise be effected. Thorough reform of spelling is not possible with a deficient alphabet.

Much more could be written about the drawbacks of the ABC, but perhaps this brief exposition will suffice to show that when Shaw left the bulk of his fortune for the propagation of a new alphabet, he was neither suffering from senility nor perpetrating a posthumous joke.

Tools and machines have been vastly improved in the last few generations, yet we have been using basically the same alphabet for 3,500 years! When it came into being, it was, admittedly, a wonderful advance on the logographic systems of writing that preceded it, but the science of phonetics has progressed since then. And its formulation took place 3,000 years before the introduction of printing as we know it today. Moreover, the alphabet was originally designed for a particular Semitic language, long since dead, and has suffered in the process of adaptation from one language to another.

What Shaw demanded in his Will was an alphabet of at least 40 letters, of which 16 would be vowels, and the terms of the Public Trustee's competition followed this specification 'to the letter,' though the spirit of it was simply, as Shaw said himself, to enable the English language to be spelt unequivocally without the use of either digraphs or diacritics (additional signs, such as the French accents, the Spanish *tilde* and the German *umlaut*). Many phoneticians put the requisite numbers of letters for this as low as 37 or 38, if sounds like *ch* (t-sh) and *j* (d-zh) are treated logically as double sounds.

As has been pointed out, the order of the letters in the present alphabet is quite arbitrary, and some of the names of the letters bear no resemblance to the sounds they represent. All such defects would be avoided as far as possible in a new system. Also, speech-sound frequency might be taken into consideration, so that the simplest signs were allotted to the most frequent sounds, at least where this was compatible with consistent symbolisation in accordance with phonetic relationships.

Apart from the saving of time and space which would automatically result from phonetic spelling with one letter only for each sound—the word *though*, for instance, being spelt with two letters instead of six—there should be an additional saving of about 60 per cent. if really simple, shorthand-like characters were used, provided they were joinable in handwriting, either directly (as in geometric shorthand systems) or with coupling strokes (as in our present handwriting). The use of coupling strokes for joining is actually the more practical method, as direct joining results in some words protruding awkwardly above or below the line of writing, and also results in an undesirable difference of shape between the handwritten outline of a word and its typographical version, unless advantage is taken of modern developments in printing which make a joined sequence of letters possible. Finally, the ideal script would be not merely technically efficient, but also a schematic reflection of speech itself and, on eurhythmic principles, psychologically satisfying.

The panel of adjudicators set up by the Public Trustee consisted of a professional phonetician, a typographical expert, and Mr I. J. (now Sir James) Pitman, M.P. Of these three, two were eminent members of the simplified spelling movement, which is in a different category altogether from alphabet reform, and one of them stated in print the previous year that he considered a redeployment of the existing 26 letters all that was necessary. (But that, of course, was before the adjudication committee was formed.) There was no expert calligrapher on the panel, and—a more important omission this—no one experienced in teaching children to read and write, let alone qualified in educational psychology. While there was something to be said for keeping the committee small, five would not, surely, have been too many for such a project. An educational psychologist at least might have been added.

For the guidance of competitors, the Public Trustee provided lists of recommended sounds which had been prepared by a phonetic expert, as well as the sheet of rules governing the competition. Though neither of the two lists of sounds given was binding on competitors, they were most helpful, and almost indispensable to anyone with little prior knowledge of phonetics.

List No. I was based (with a few exceptions) on Shaw's own analysis, as set out in his printed blue postcard entitled a FORTY-LETTER BRITISH ALPHABET. The differences between this list and Shaw's analysis are: the addition of the diphthongs in *boy* and *how*, the omission of *wh* which is really *hw* (and being a combination of two sounds is redundant), and of the neutral vowel, as heard at the end of the word *china*. Whether there should or not be a neutral vowel in the ideal alphabet is a very controversial point, which I cannot attempt to go into here. The other two alterations were certainly for the better, I think, but I would have been inclined to go further and leave out the *ch* (*t-sh*), *j* (*d-zh*), and *yoo* sounds, which, like *hw*, are combinations. However, that would have made 37 sounds only, 15 of them being vowels, and Shaw's Will stipulated at least 40 sounds, of which 16 must be vowels.

As I have said, it was a pity, perhaps, that the Public Trustee obeyed this stipulation 'to the letter', for Shaw did not pretend to be an expert phonetician. The spirit of the stipulation was simply that the new alphabet should enable the English language to be spelt unequivocally without the use of either digraphs or diacritics; and I would put the minimum number of letters required for this at 37, not 40.

List No. II provided for a 'narrower' representation of sounds, and therefore exceeded Shaw's minimum, having 21 vowels as against the 16 of the first list. It discarded the *yoo* combination but added the neutral vowel and 5 'R'-coloured vowels.

How did the four co-winning alphabets of the competition measure up to the theoretical ideal? Not very well, it seems to me. It was naturally assumed that competitors would take the opportunity of making the new letter shapes simpler and more scientific than the old ones. The most artistic of the four was definitely the one designed by Mr R. Kingsley Read, which looks like some oriental script; but not all of its symbols could be joined, and this was a serious practical drawback. Its designer had been a professional designer of advertising lettering, and it is difficult to estimate how far the appearance of the other three designs might have been improved with some professional treatment.

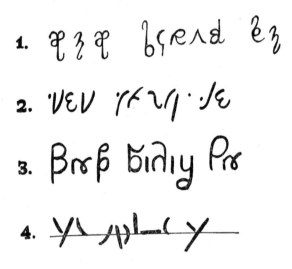

The words 'George Bernard Shaw' written in the prizewinning phonetic British alphabets devised by (1) Mrs Pauline M. Barrett, (2) Mr Kingsley Read, (3) Mr J. F. Magrath, and (4) Dr S. L. Pugmire.

The one with the simplest characters was that designed by Dr S. L. Pugmire, a psychiatrist; and here again the designer's profession had its effect on the result, for Dr Pugmire said that his idea was to devise an alphabet that could be learnt easily by mentally handicapped children who are unable to master the traditional alphabet. The simplicity of the letters, however, was outweighed by the fact that they could not be joined, and also that, since the position of a letter in relation to the line of writing is phonetically significant, lined paper is almost essential, at least for handwriting. Moreover, the slant of a stroke is significant, and this, as Shaw put it, "is drawing, not writing."

Designing the letters so that they can be joined adds considerably to the designer's difficulties, and competitors who took this trouble must have felt a little cheated to find that systems with unjoinable symbols were not only seriously considered but actually awarded half of the prize.

The other two alphabets, designed by Mr J. F. Magrath (who worked for a firm of City brokers) and Mrs Pauline M. Barrett (of Nova Scotia) were more in the style of our present letters, and were suitable for linking together with coupling strokes. Mr Magrath demonstrated a joined as well as a disjoined version of his alphabet, and Mrs Barrett's looks as though it could be joined quite easily with little distortion, although I have seen only a disjoined version of it. Some of the letters in Mrs Barrett's system, however, look as if they would defy being written without lifting the pen. One fault in Mr Magrath's system—but a fault easily rectified—is the unnecessary provision of slightly different letter shapes for use as capitals. Capitalisation, in my opinion, is better indicated, if at all, by the mere size of the letter, or else by means of an external mark, such as the dot placed before the initial letter of a proper name in Mr Kingsley Read's system.

Professor P. A. D. MacCarthy*, the one of the three assessors who had taken on the difficult task of producing a single alphabet derived from features of one or more of the four winning alphabets, when asked about the matter, said that they all had a good deal in common, since they all read from top to bottom and from left to right, could all be handwritten, and all used ascenders and descenders (strokes protruding above or below the height of the smallest letters) which gives words a

* Head of the Department of Phonetics at Leeds University at that time.

more distinctive shape and so makes for greater legibility. But these common features are surely a very inadequate basis for a fusion of the four designs into one—and, indeed, are less fundamental than some other features which are not common to all four designs. Reading from top to bottom and from left to right may seem at first sight absolutely fundamental, but in fact the direction of writing can generally be altered fairly easily. (The traditional alphabet was originally written from right to left, and went through an intermediate phase of boustrophedon* writing, before it settled down to the present left-to-right arrangement which is the most convenient for right-handed people.) What cannot be altered so easily is the basic style of the letter shapes—whether geometric as in Dr Pugmire's design, cursive as in Mr Kingsley Read's, or 'current' (to use Henry Sweet's term, adopted by Shaw) as in the other two winning designs—and this ties up with whether, and how, the symbols can be joined in handwriting.

Before commenting in detail on the new "Shaw Alphabet" finally produced it is pertinent to ask: What are the chances of its ultimate success against its 3,500-year-old rival? In my opinion, Shaw was far too sanguine in his reliance on an appeal to the reason of adults. He was always inclined to over-estimate the rationality and social conscience of the average man and woman. Though many people will no doubt look at the library copies of the transliterated *Androcles* out of curiosity, I do not foresee many bothering to learn the new alphabet from it. Indeed, why should they? Those who have already mastered the traditional letters and spelling are not the people who would benefit from an easier system. It is small children who principally need a simpler alphabet, a more rapid script and logical spelling; and if such a system were taught in the first year at school, as a stepping-stone to the traditional letters, it would automatically oust the present outworn alphabet for most practical purposes within eighty or ninety years. Only when everyone living has grown up with the new as well as the

* Written alternately from left to right and from right to left.

old will a general changeover be possible. With this method of propagation, the only adults who need to bother with a new alphabet are educationists.

A most interesting experiment has taken place in Western Germany, where, since the war, about 20,000 children have learnt a simple phonetic script (invented by Felix von Kunowski thirty years ago) generally before proceeding to the conventional letters. These children are thus growing up knowing a new system of letters as well as the old, and it has been found that, though teaching the conventional letters is postponed for a year, the children who start with the new script not only catch up the time lost to the old one, but actually surpass in ordinary reading and writing the children who begin straight away with that.

When this practice becomes widespread, and the phonetic script used is standardised (with adaptations of the same script made from one language to another), then, within eighty years, everyone will know both systems, and the better will naturally oust the worst for all practicable purposes, just as the Arabic numerals have, after many centuries, finally ousted the Roman ones.

It is a great pity that Shaw did not tie up his alphabet trusts specifically with infant education. Had he done so, not only would the Chancery Court decision of 1957 have undoubtedly gone the other way, so that more than £3,000,000 would now have been available for the project, instead of the paltry £8,300 that was allowed as a 'compromise' by the residuary legatees, but also concentration on the first year of schooling would be far more likely to lead to ultimate success than any amount of irrefutable statistics and bi-alphabetic plays.

Though *Androcles* is one of the most delightful of all Shaw's plays, I am sorry he did not nominate one of Enid Blyton's *Noddy* books instead.

The last debate in the House of Commons before the Christmas recess in 1959 concerned Shaw's money yet again. It was alleged that the normal State subsidy to the British

Museum had been docked because of Shaw's bequest! This was denied by the Financial Secretary to the Treasury, who revealed that the amount received by the British Museum from the Shaw estate was then £163,924, to which there was to be added about £85,000 repayment of income tax, levied on the estate before the invalidation of the alphabet trust. [Multiplying the total by three—since the other two beneficiaries have presumably received like amounts—gives the amount that had accrued to the estate during the three years (from the end of 1956 to the end of 1959) since *My Fair Lady* had rescued it from debt.] During the debate, Mr Emrys Hughes, M.P. for South Ayrshire, who had been a friend of Shaw's, said:—

I am not sure whether I am lost in a maze of legality, but I impress upon the Financial Secretary that the last thing Bernard Shaw would have wished was to relieve the Treasury. I hope that the Minister's speech does not mean that, in some indirect way, Bernard Shaw's literary work will finance the armaments programme, or result in easing the expenditure which might otherwise be incurred by the Government on such things as hydrogen bombs, which would have been a horror to Bernard Shaw.

This debate was soon followed by the news that funds had been allotted to enable the British Museum Reading Room to be kept open in the evening twice a week for the benefit of those who cannot use it by day. Though in no way a result of, or connected with, the Shaw bequest, this would have pleased Shaw, who always admitted his debt to the British Museum Reading Room, where he trained himself to be a writer.

The amount of money shared by Shaw's three residuary legatees has now (1971) long passed the magic figure of three million (£3,000,000), having been considerably boosted by *My Fair Lady* and also by the film based on his play *The Millionairess*. By the time Shaw's copyrights expire at the beginning of the twenty-first century, they will doubtless have made a great deal more. But the alphabet project 'so dear to his heart' has had to make do with less than one per cent. of the sum that, according to his Will, it should already have received.

Now what of the Shaw Alphabet edition of *Androcles and the Lion* which finally emerged in 1962?

Guarding his home during the air-raids of 1940-41, Mr Kingsley Read, an architectural letterer, used to while away the hours designing letters for an entirely new alphabet. In 1942 he wrote to Shaw, who was then known to be interested in promoting a new alphabet, and enclosed a copy of what he had worked out. Shaw replied, "This is far and away the best alphabet with the best head at the back of it that has come my way"—but, despite this encomium, he did not go so far as to nominate Kingsley Read's alphabet when drafting the relevant clauses of his Will some years later, although he was well aware that his creation of an *ad hoc* trust for an unspecified alphabet would probably lead to legal complications; as, in 1957, it did.

In the event, it is an improved version of the alphabet which Kingsley Read sent Shaw in 1942 that was finally chosen by the Public Trustee (acting as Shaw's executor) for the implementation of Shaw's alphabet bequest, and which is now known as 'the Shaw Alphabet'. Had Shaw himself chosen the alphabet before making his Will, the trust fund for its propagation might have comprised all the royalties accruing to the estate (well over a million pounds at the time concerned) instead of the mere £8,300 capital sum paid under the compromise settlement of 1957; but Shaw elected to leave the choice of an alphabet to experts and to give the alphabet an aura of official sanction by leaving its promotion in the hands of the Public Trustee.

However, one of the four designs selected to share the prize could not be joined, either directly or by coupling strokes; two of the others could be adapted to linking by coupling strokes, but had rather complicated letters, which, in both cases, seemed to owe a great deal to the present Russian alphabet; and the fourth, Mr Read's system, allowed only spasmodic linking wherever a natural junction happened to occur. At the press conference where the result of the competition was announced, it was stated that the four winning alphabets would be co-ordinated to produce the final design for use in implementing Shaw's wishes.

The fusion of the four designs was never really practicable, since the basic style of the letter shapes was so different—two of the systems being in a script style, one in a geometric style, and the other (Mr Read's) in a cursive style. It is not surprising, therefore, that any attempt at co-ordinating the alphabets was jettisoned, and the one designed by Mr Read—which was definitely the most pleasing of the four aesthetically—finally chosen, after considerable improvement but with little or no reference to the other three systems.

In the preface which Shaw wrote for R. A. Wilson's book *The Miraculous Birth of Language*, he suggested that the uncontracted 'correspondence' version of Henry Sweet's shorthand system, Current Shorthand, might be used as the basis of the new alphabet, and Mr Read claims that his design has affinities with Sweet's, since both use forms derived from a straight line and an oval. But the main principle underlying Current Shorthand, as its name implies, is that it is written in a flowing hand, while Mr Read's system, as already indicated, involves lifting the pen between letters. This seems a rather serious drawback, particularly in view of Shaw's emphasis on writing speed. But the advocates of disjoined letters point out that illegibility caused by distortion of the letters is more likely to occur when letters are joined; also, the recent return to favour of italic handwriting, which (like the Shaw Alphabet) allows for joining certain letters only, does not apparently result in much loss of writing speed, once the writer is practised in it.

The earlier version of Mr Read's alphabet, called 'Soundwriting', which won him a quarter of the competition prize, differed from this final Shaw Alphabet in several particulars. However, it is immediately recognisable as basically the same alphabet, having mainly the same letter shapes, although these have been redistributed phonetically. As in the earlier version, sounds which differ only in being breathed or voiced (e.g. 'p', 'b', 't', 'd') are represented by signs which differ only in one consistent variation, but, whereas this variation was originally the position of the symbol in relation to the line of writing, in the Shaw Alphabet the voiced sounds are upside-down mirror images of their breathed counterparts. This is a notable improvement, as it means that, even when standing in isolation, any letter remains unambiguous. Apart from the breathed/ voiced figural relationship and a similar pairing of short and long vowels, there is little attempt at any consistent plan of symbolism for phonetic characteristics, as there is, for instance, in Kunowski's *Sprechspur*. This may be merely an academic, not a practical, defect, though there is something psychologically satisfying in complete consistency, and it also has a definite practical value when an alphabet is adapted to different languages. Diphthongs (with the exception of 'centering' diphthongs) are simply treated as long vowels, instead of being represented by contracted ligatures of the signs for their component elements, as is more usual in alphabets of this kind. This seems to me a real, if minor, defect, as there is no clear dividing line between a diphthong and two separate vowels. (For instance, has 'Troilus' two syllables or three?)

On the credit side, there is no additional set of letter shapes for use as capitals. (One of the four original co-winning entries in the alphabet competition actually provided a set of capital letters, for no better reason, as far as I can see, than their traditional existence.) Instead of capital letters, bold type is available for headings and to indicate emphasis, and there is a 'namer' dot to precede proper names where some such indication might be helpful.

One of the means used to achieve economy is the allocation of some of the simplest letter shapes to the most frequently occurring sounds. There are also four standard contractions or word-signs: for the four words 'the', 'of', 'and', 'to', which are abbreviated to their first consonants. These four single-letter word-signs, together with the single-letter word 'a', constitute the five most frequently occurring words in the language, with the result that, on an average, one word in five will be written with a single letter. All this does mean a considerable saving over our present system, on top of the saving effected by any phonetic alphabet through not having to use more than one letter for a single sound. (To quote Shaw on this, "As to spelling the very frequent word 'though' with six letters instead of two, it is impossible to discuss it, as it is outside the range of common sanity"). The saving claimed in the Introduction to this book is up to 50 per cent. for the writer who has acquired automatic fluency. However, far greater economy could obviously have been achieved, with little loss in legibility, if the alphabet had been genuinely based on the graphical principles of Sweet's Current Shorthand.

The choice of Shaw's play *Androcles and the Lion* as the first work to be published in the new alphabet was made by Shaw himself, who nominated it in his will. There are two simultaneous editions of the book—the ordinary Penguin paperback for sale to the public, and the Public Trustee's Edition for free distribution to public libraries as specified in Shaw's will. The original printing order for the paperback was 25,000 copies, but this had to be increased to 40,000 before the publication date; the Public Trustee's Edition comprised 13,000 copies.

Apart from the covers and end-papers and the quality of the paper used, the two editions are identical. The typography is a tribute to Mr Read's artistry and the type-makers' skill. The same size of type (12 point) is used for the orthodox ABC version on the right-hand pages as for the line-for-line Shaw Alphabet version on the left, thus enabling one to see at a glance that one-third of the space is saved with the new alphabet.

Shaw's preface to the play is, naturally enough, omitted. But the book includes: a Foreword by the Public Trustee; an Introduction by Sir James Pitman; Notes on the Spelling by Peter MacCarthy; and Suggestions for Writing by Kingsley Read; as well as two keys to the alphabet—one arranged phonetically (for writers) and the other graphically (for readers).

These two keys are repeated on a card inserted in the book for use as (*a*) a bookmark, (*b*) a reading key, (*c*) a writing key, and (*d*) a guiding edge from the line of 'Shavian' text being deciphered to its orthodox 'crib-line' opposite.

Is the Shaw Alphabet the alphabet of the future? It is just possible that it is. The long overdue adoption of a new alphabet for general use is rapidly becoming more imperative, if only for the sake of electro-mechanical readers and talk-writers. The Shaw Alphabet, though far from ideal in my opinion, is better than most of the other alphabets on the market, and has the advantage of being launched by the Public Trustee on behalf of G.B.S., 'the man of the century'. That it is a vast improvement on the present Roman alphabet almost goes without saying. But before any alphabet can begin to take over from the traditional one, it must be taught in all primary schools—preferably as a stepping-stone to the ABC. Shaw did not stress this sufficiently, in my opinion, either in his articles or in his Will. Indeed, he had such excessive faith in the rationality of human beings, that he placed his reliance mainly on the persuasive results of a statistical inquiry. Even if the remnants of the alphabet fund can be stretched to carry out a vestige of the inquiry that Shaw wanted, I cannot share Shaw's belief that this would break through the wall of prejudice with which people defend their comfortable ruts. Until the battle of the kindergarten has been won, the ABC will never be superseded for general use by human beings, even if it is by robots.

The Shaw Alphabet was offered to the Ministry of Education at three stages—in principle, in draft, and upon completion— and was declined by them each time. Perhaps they felt that the present experimental use of Sir James Pitman's teaching alphabet (which is proving so successful) was quite drastic enough, and as much as could reasonably be expected of a government department in one century. Meanwhile, a few thousand people have bought the Shaw Alphabet Edition of *Androcles and the Lion*; a few hundred have learnt the alphabet

The Shaw Alphabet for Writers

Double lines ⁼ between pairs show the relative height of Talls, Deeps, and Shorts. Wherever possible, finish letters rightwards; those starred * will be written upwards. Also see heading and footnotes overleaf.

Tall	Deep		Short	Short
peep	bib	if		eat
tot	dead	egg		age
kick	gag	ash*		ice
fee	vow	ado*		up
thigh	they	on		oak
so	zoo	wool		ooze
sure	meaSure	out		oil
church	judge	ah*		awe
yea	*woe	are		or
hung	ha-ha	air		err

Short	Short			
loll	roar	array		ear
mime*	nun	Ian	Tall	yew

The Shaw Alphabet Reading Key

The letters are classified as Tall, Deep, Short, and Compound.
Beneath each letter is its full name : its *sound* is shown in **bold** type.

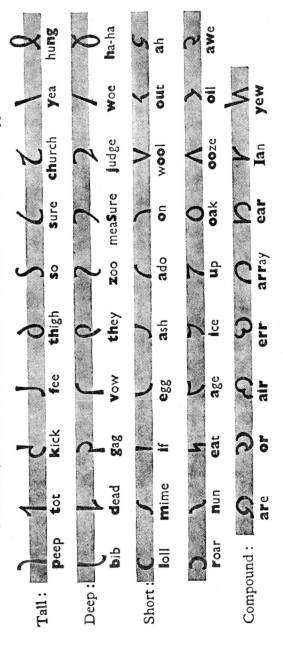

Tall : peep tot kick fee thigh so sure church yea hung

Deep : bib dead gag vow they zoo meaSure judge woe ha-ha

Short : loll mime if egg ash ado on wool out ah

roar nun eat age ice up oak ooze oil awe

Compound : are or air err array ear Ian yew

The four most frequent words are represented by single letters : **the** ɿ, **of** ſ, **and** ∨, **to** ʇ.
Proper names may be distinguished by a preceding 'Namer' dot : e.g. ˙ɔɔſ, Rome.
Punctuation and numerals are unchanged. Learn the alphabet *in pairs*, as listed for Writers overleaf.

from it; a few dozen are actually using it regularly; and a handful, perhaps, are teaching it to their children. Whether this alphabet, or another, will finally prevail, is anybody's guess.

History is certainly on the side of a new alphabet, whether the winner of the Public Trustee's competition or some other system. It is absurd that in the twentieth century we should still be using what is basically the ancient Phoenician alphabet, with its cumbersome letters and its bad phonetics. Far from ideal for any language, it is quite inadequate for English, with its comparatively large number of phonemes. If Shaw's dream comes true—a dream shared by men of vision for nearly five centuries—who knows what miracles of human progress it may bring in its wake? The man who first dreamt up the zero of our numerical system did not forsee the standard of living we enjoy today, but his dream made it possible. When letters are as straightforward as numbers, wisdom may even catch up with science.

Editorial Comment:—

Enthusiastic phonetic reformers like Barbara Smoker will, I trust, forgive me if in the interests of the search for clarity in Shaw's theoretical ideas and their practical applications, I feel that attention should be given to the fact that the size of type used ('12 point') for both the Shaw Alphabet and ordinary alphabet—on the left and right pages respectively of the Shaw Alphabet edition of *Androcles and the Lion*—does not contribute anything towards a precise comparison of the amount of space saved by the Shaw Alphabet, for the reason that—as everyone who has practical experience of the printing industry knows well—different type faces (i.e. artistic designs or styles of type) occupy, according to their designs, relative large, medium, or small amounts of space compared to each other *in the same point size.* This is clearly illustrated in the examples on p. 456 of the same number of letters set in different type faces of the same 'point' size (I have used 12 point) to which I refer further in the next page or two.

In the special edition of *Androcles* it is not made clear—or even mentioned—whether the type of the Shaw Alphabet, as used on the left-hand pages, is large, medium, or small, as compared with the various *ordinary* type faces of the same point size that exist. Ancillary to this is the question whether the particular ordinary type face used on the right-hand pages is a relatively 'large', 'medium', or 'small' one for the same point size. The answer to the latter can be quite simply stated, and is obvious from the examples on p. 456. It is Monotype "Imprint", which is one of the largest type faces for its 'point' size. Per contra, the type of the Shaw Alphabet is comparable to the smallest type faces (such as "Perpetua") *for the same point size.*

If, therefore, as seems undoubtedly to be the case, the design of the Shaw Alphabet is relatively *small* for its point size, and the design of the ordinary type used on the right-hand pages is a 'large' one for its point size, then obviously, although they are both the same 'point' size, this provides no direct standard of comparison for assessing the saving in writing *by hand* which the Shaw Alphabet might produce, and one can only conclude that the saving of space and energy and time which seems so apparent from the two alphabets as *printed* in the book is in fact due partly to reasons of typographical design rather than to intrinsic features of the Shaw Alphabet as— if generally adopted—it would actually be written by the numerous authors, clerks, and "scribes" of various kinds whose saving in work (i.e. in the manual labour of writing) was what Shaw had most specifically in mind.*

In other words, people writing in their normal manner, with their normal arm and wrist movement and size of writing (including the spacing between each letter and between each word) and *not* making any special effort to compress their handwriting when writing in the Shaw Alphabet (but using, as I say, their normal, natural rhythm of writing), would show a much smaller saving than the $33\frac{1}{3}$ per cent. claimed. To be

---

* Furthermore, as elaborated a page or two on, even in the printed form the saving would in practice be much less. (See caption to illustration on page 456.)

sure, there would be *some* saving of space, time, and energy, but this would, I suggest, be mainly related to, and limited by, the smaller *number* of characters (i.e. letters or symbols) which the Shaw Alphabet would involve, rather than due to the design of the Alphabet's *form*. Indeed, if one counts the number of characters used on the left-hand and right-hand pages of the special edition of *Androcles and the Lion* one finds that the number involved in the case of the Shaw Alphabet—for exactly the same matter (I have taken the average of 10 pages)—is almost exactly 20 per cent. less: i.e. a saving of one-fifth—not one-third as claimed.

In this connection, it must be borne in mind that not all words use fewer characters in the Shaw as opposed to the ordinary alphabet. On the contrary, many use the *same* number —as in the words 'Androcles' and 'his'. Following p. 457 I give eleven people's handwritten versions of these two words in both alphabets—which collectively prove that for them (and one can assume for most writers*) there is virtually no saving at all as a result of the form of the alphabet—there would only be as a result of the number of characters used, i.e. at most the saving of 20 per cent., not 33⅓ per cent. mentioned above.

In the illustration following p. 457, the word 'his' in the two alphabets illustrates my arguments particularly vividly. Not only is the same number of characters used in both alphabets, but the form of the Shaw Alphabet characters involved closely resembles that of the letters of the ordinary alphabet. It can hardly be doubted, I think, that anyone writing this word in the two alphabets would take up exactly the same or more space with each. Yet as *printed*, the Shaw Alphabet version takes up considerably less—due largely to the typographical reasons I have given.

Defenders of the Shaw Alphabet would probably claim that with practice the average writer would find it natural to

---

*I tested thirty people in all for handwritten results, but have only illustrated eleven examples.

compress his or her writing more, especially as many of the characters consist of upright or semi-upright lines. But against this, since, as Barbara Smoker has pointed out, most of the characters cannot, by the nature of their abrupt, self-contained design, be joined together in writing, it would actually take longer to write in the Shaw Alphabet for those who normally join characters (letters) in their handwriting into a more or less continuous flow. And this difficulty would, for them, to some extent—often entirely—offset the saving resulting from using a smaller number of characters. There can be little doubt that, generally speaking, people who join their letters into a continuous flow write faster than those who don't, and they probably constitute the majority of writers. Using the Shaw Alphabet would for them, even after a lot of practice, be rather like writing words in capitals—which unquestionably takes most people much longer (up to 50 per cent. or even 100 per cent. longer) than to write in normal longhand. Thus the 20 per cent. saving alluded to above would for most people probably come down to about 10 per cent., and for not a few writers there would probably be no saving at all.

It is also relevant to point out that Shaw's reasoning about the amount of time which the world could save, though often embodying interesting suggestions, was also frequently quite wrong on other scores, including simple arithmetic. Typical of many claims made by Shaw in the press from time to time for the saving which might be effected is the following extract from a B.B.C. broadcast published in *The Listener* of December 1st, 1949:—

... Take the word debt. Spell it det; and write it over and over again for a minute. Then do the same spelling it debt. The difference between the number of times you have written det and debt gives you the difference in time and labor between writing one letter of the alphabet and two.

If, like some of our spelling reformers and phoneticians you are mathematically silly enough to play the old trick of disguising this difference as a percentage, you will get a figure too small to

ANDROCLES AND THE LION

armorer named Ferrovius, of dangerous character and great personal strength, and a Greek tailor reputed to be a sorcerer, by name Androcles. You will add the three to your charge here and march them all to the Coliseum, where you will deliver them into the custody of the master of the gladiators and take his receipt, countersigned by the keeper of the beasts and

Above: Facsimile reproduction of part of the '12-point' bi-alphabetic edition of "Androcles and the Lion".
Below: Other type designs for comparison of relative size and space occupied in the same '12-point' size.

abcdefghijklmnopqrstuvwxyz	Scotch Roman
abcdefghijklmnopqrstuvwxyz	Baskerville (the widest type in common use)
abcdefghijklmnopqrstuvwxyz	Imprint (as used on the right-hand page above)
abcdefghijklmnopqrstuvwxyz	Garamond
abcdefghijklmnopqrstuvwxyz	Bembo
abcdefghijklmnopqrstuvwxyz	Perpetua
abcdefghijklmnopqrstuvwxyz	Walbaum
	The Shaw Alphabet. (A line is drawn after 26 of the

All
are
12-point

It will be seen that the difference above between 12 point Scotch Roman and 12 point Walbaum is very great, and that the difference between 12 point Imprint and 12 point Shaw type is even greater.

Clearly, so far as artistic design and form are concerned, the Shaw Alphabet type is more directly comparable to the narrowest ordinary type faces in the same point size (such as Walbaum or Perpetua) and not to the widest (such as Imprint).

Therefore the Imprint type used on the right-hand page of the bi-alphabetic edition of Androcles gives an exaggerated impression of the saving in space claimed. Had Perpetua, Walbaum, or any other 'narrow' type such as Centaur or Van Dijck been used on the right-hand pages, relatively little saving would have been apparent.

Looked at in another way, 12 point Shaw type would be more comparable to 10 or even 9 point Imprint, and such saving in the printed word as the Shaw Alphabet could produce (if ever adopted for general use in the usual printers' range of sizes from 6 to 14 point) would thus depend mainly on the fewer number of characters required to write the same words, rather than on the design of the Shaw Alphabet characters as such, if Shaw type of a size giving the same visual effect and readability were used. Measurement of the examples above shows that 26 characters of the Shaw Alphabet type occupy only about 10 per cent. less space than 26 characters of Perpetua or Walbaum, in contrast to a 33⅓ per cent. saving compared to Imprint, in the same point size (but not the same visual size).

𐑕𐑮𐑕𐑛𐑝𐑕𐑤𐑙𐑣𐑵𐑳𐑷𐑿𐑰𐑦𐑱𐑲𐑳𐑺𐑻𐑼𐑽𐑾𐑿𐑬𐑭𐑩𐑸𐑹𐑞𐑔𐑖𐑠𐑡𐑗𐑘𐑳𐑢𐑥𐑟𐑙?

The complete 48-letter Shaw Alphabet.

218 his
218 his
218 his
218 his
218 his
218 his
218 his
218 his
219 his
218 his
218 his

Androcles
Androcles
Androcles
Androcles.
Androcles
Androcles.
Androcles
Androcles
Androcles
Androcles
Androcles

their hand freely and naturally in their normal scale and rhythm of handwriting.

Their product was then removed, and a separate sheet of paper placed before them, on which they were asked to write the same word in their normal size and style of English script.

This procedure was then similarly repeated with the word 'his', in both the Shaw and the ordinary English Alphabets. Subjects were tested in complete isolation from each other, and no indication was given of the purpose of the test which might influence their performance.

When the results were later correlated as above, it was clear that in nine of the eleven cases the Shaw Alphabet *as written by hand*—which is what Shaw had chiefly in mind—saved no space at all, and indeed, took up *more* space. One subject took up the same space, and one taking less will be referred to later. (The vertical columns are of identical relative width to facilitate comparison.

Furthermore, all subjects took between *twice* and *seven* times longer in time to write the words in the Shaw Alphabet, although admittedly with practice this would be considerably reduced. When questioned, however, the six adults whose writing appears first above were unanimous in feeling that even with prolonged practice they would never be able to write more quickly using the Shaw instead of the ordinary English alphabet. One thought he would eventually be able to write *as* quickly in it, but the others thought that the Shaw Alphabet would always take them definitely longer.

The reason they gave was that they found it impossible to join most of the Shaw letters into a 'flow', making it necessary to 'print' them individually like a succession of capital letters. One subject added that owing to the relatively simple form of the Shaw letters, their form would tend to be lost if any attempt to join them were made—and hence it would in any case be essential to 'print' them individually. Another (an artist) pointed out that if the 'quaver' thick-and-thin quality of the Shaw characters was to be followed, this also would add to the time taken—ball-point pens having now almost entirely superseded ones with flexible nibs.

It is noteworthy, however, that the two older of the three children tested (Examples 7 and 8) thought that with practice they *would* be able to write more quickly in the Shaw Alphabet. The first, aged 15, gave as her reason that there were "no whole-circle letters—only up-and-down curved lines". Her mother pointed out that children have more pliant minds than adults, and further, that all small children, when first learning to write, 'print' their letters—the joining into a flow being a relatively adult development coming only after years of practice. The second child, aged 11, thought that if she had learnt the Shaw Alphabet *from the beginning* in school she would have been able to write more quickly in it. To her (in contrast to the adults) this was just because it was *not* necessary to join up the letters, as compared to: "the ordinary English alphabet, which is all curly". These comments support Barbara Smoker's contention that to be effectively introduced any new alphabet would have to be taught at the earliest age in schools.

The third from last example is that of a girl of 6 years. She differed (tearfully!) from her older sisters (but unwittingly agreed with the adults) in feeling that she would *never* be able to write more quickly in the Shaw Alphabet.

The penultimate example is that of a Jewish person fluent alike in writing in the disjointed Hebrew alphabet and the joinable English one. His conclusion was that he would expect, with practice, to be able to write as quickly in the Shaw Alphabet as in Hebrew, but he added that he did not write in Hebrew quite as quickly as in the English alphabet, and would expect the same to apply to the Shaw Alphabet. It is interesting to see that (notwithstanding his writing the Shaw Alphabet from right to left like Hebrew) he spontaneously joined the first and second characters of 'Androcles'.

The final example (a woman in her forties) alone shows a decisive saving in space with both words (about $27\frac{1}{2}$ per cent.). In addition, she thought the Shaw Alphabet would eventually be quicker for her. However, she pointed out that she had learnt to write in a school where any natural tendency to join letters "was regarded as a crime", and her result must therefore be regarded as exceptional.

impress anybody. A percentage may mean a halfpenny or a million pounds sterling, a fraction of a second or a thousand eons, a parish council or a world federation. Keep to the facts. The first fact is that the difference you have counted is a difference per minute. It will prove to be twelve seconds. Therefore, as there are 365 days in the year, the difference is 73 days per individual scribe per year.

How many scribes are there? As the English language goes round the earth, the sun never setting on it, it is impossible to ascertain exactly how many people are writing it, not for one minute as an experiment, but all the time incessantly and perpetually. No matter: a big cross section will be just as conclusive. In the British Commonwealth and the United States of North America there are more than 270,000,000 born writers and speakers of English. Of these the proportion of authors, journalists, clerks, accountants, scholars, private correspondents and others writing continually and simultaneously all round the clock may safely be taken as one in every hundred, making 2,700,000. Multiply this figure by the 73 days. The answer is that every year in the cross section alone we are wasting 500,000 years of time and labor which we could save by spelling English phonetically enough for all practical purposes, adding to the Johnsonese alphabet fourteen letters, all of which can be borrowed provisionally from the stocks now held by our printers for setting up foreign and classical grammars, algebras, and the like.

I have left India, Pakistan, and Ceylon out of the calculation with their 400,000,000, whose dozen dialects are giving way to English. They would make the figures too enormous to be credible. One could only laugh. Enough to note that there is no industrial company on earth that would not scrap and replace all its plant, at whatever cost, to save in cost of production a fraction of such magnitudes. In the face of them it is folly to prattle vainly for the thousandth time about universal languages, teaching children to read, standard pronunciation, and the rest of the argy-bargy our phoneticians keep regurgitating.

It is Johnsonese that we cannot afford, not a forty-letter alphabet. For more than seventy years I have written books, plays, articles, and private letters, in legible phonetics, and thereby added at least two months every year to my productive lifetime as compared to Shakespear and Dickens, who had to write their works in longhand, though Dickens was an adept in reporting shorthand, which is unreadable by printers and typists.

I do not pretend to know what language will become international, though I agree with Mr Birley that it will not be an artificial one. The fittest will survive. My guess is Pidgin English, the *lingua franca* of the Chinese coolie, the Australian black boy, and the traders and seafarers who employ them. It gets rid of the incubus of much useless grammar. In commercial Johnsonese we write 'I regret to have to inform you that it is not possible for me to entertain the proposal in your esteemed letter.' In Pidgin this is 'Sorry no can.' Pidgin, whether spoken or phonetically spelt, is a labor saving device which leaves the harvester, the internal combustion engine, and the telephone nowhere.

The case of children learning to read is an over-worked bugbear. Children learn to read and write by sight, not by sound. Those who have deficient visual memory spell phonetically and sign with a mark. Blind children read by touch, deaf ones lip read. I cannot remember any time when a page of print was unintelligible to me; so I can hardly have suffered much when learning.

Children should be taught to spell phonetically, and corrected only when their spelling betrays a mispronunciation, which for the present may be taken to mean a departure from the usage of Mr Hibberd, chief announcer to the British Broadcasting Corporation. His vowels are much more representative and agreeable than those common to the University of Oxford and the Isle of Dogs.

... All teachers should bear in mind that better is the enemy of good enough, and perfection not possible on any terms. Language need not and should not be taught beyond the point at which the speaker is understood. Not five minutes should be wasted in teaching a chauffeur who says 'Them hills is very deceiving' to say 'These mountain gorges are very deceptive.' ... an English child who says 'I thinked' or 'I buyed' is just as intelligible as an adult who says 'I thought' or 'I bought.'*

---

* Another statement by Shaw on the same subject which may be of interest to teachers is from a typescript in the British Museum dating from 1947 and apparently hitherto unpublished, headed "A Modern Spelling Primer":—

"... The experienced teacher knows that our Johnsonese etymological
[Continued at foot of following page.

The first point calling for comment in the foregoing is the statement in the third line—"The difference between the number of times you have written *det* and *debt* gives you the difference between writing one letter of the alphabet and two." This is not at all clear. The difference between writing *det* and *debt* is obviously the difference between writing a three-letter word and a four-letter one. The former will take three-quarters as long as the latter, and the saving will actually be 25 per cent., whereas the difference between writing one letter and writing two, as Shaw rather loosely refers to it, is obviously half as much (i.e. a 50 per cent. saving). The saving if the letter is part of a word obviously depends on the total number of letters in the word, which is not necessarily four, and could be anything from two to fourteen or more.

Secondly, Shaw then argues, with almost unbelievable naïveté and illogicality, that the saving due to writing the particular word *det* instead of *debt*, which he calculates as 12 seconds per minute, or 20 per cent. (actually it is 15 seconds or 25 per cent.) means a saving of "73 days per individual scribe per year". In the previous sentence he says "Keep to the facts!" Yet he is assuming:—(1) that the difference between writing *det* and *debt* is a fair representative of all the words in

alfabet cannot be taught nor learnt phonetically; but in spite of its anomalies and absurdities, it is, nevertheless, easily learnt by many children whilst others, often superior in general ability, are incurably "bad spellers", and remain so to the end of their lives. Quite the worst speller in the world was George Fox, founder of the Society of Friends (Quakers), a prolific author and eloquent preacher. A relatively stupid child may make very few mistakes in spelling. A relatively clever one may be orthographically hopeless.

"The explanation is that the correct spellers spell by sight, having good visual memories. They know the word by the look of it without reference to its sound, and copy such monstrosities as *though, ought, taught, plough,* as if they were drawings. The others write *tho, awt, tawt, plow,* and are most unjustly punished instead of praised for their phonetic intelligence.

"The teacher of any New Spelling must aim at connecting the visible printed letter with its sound, thus learning from the child's spelling how it pronounces, and correcting it accordingly if necessary.

"Above all, the teacher must not regard a New Spelling as a step to the old. The old must be regarded as something to be replaced by the new as standard British orthography. This change of attitude is essential."

the British language, which is totally unwarranted, for many words, as I have already pointed out, would involve *no* saving at all with a phonetic alphabet—in contrast to the special case of words like 'though', and short commonly used words such as 'and' and 'the', which *would*; (2) that "scribes" (a somewhat vague term) never sleep, and work 24 hours per day, for 7 days a week, all through the year of 365 days. The figure of "73 days per individual scribe per year" (i.e. one-fifth, or 20 per cent. of 365) is the result of this assumption, and is obviously absurd. If one took the figure as 8 hours per day instead of 24 (8 hours being a pretty average working day) the saving comes down from 20 per cent. to $6\frac{2}{3}$ per cent. (assuming for the moment that the saving would be 20 per cent.— which as mentioned above I do not concede to be a valid general assumption or an accurate percentage, since it is based on one four-letter word only). And if one takes a 5-day week instead of a 7-day one, and allows also for at least a couple of weeks' holiday in the year, the saving comes down to about $4\frac{1}{2}$ per cent. instead of 20 per cent. (3) The further erroneous assumption is clearly made that "scribes" spend every single minute of their *working time* (reckoned as above as 8 hours per day for 5 days a week, plus holiday) in the active physical process of writing—i.e. committing words to paper. This is also absurd, for—apart from the fact that they stop periodically for tea breaks and lunch (taking say $1\frac{1}{2}$ hours out of the 8-hour working day, leaving $6\frac{1}{2}$ hours *actual* work in a day), all work by "scribes" involves *thinking* about what to write—i.e. mental calculations, cogitations, and pauses, and these take up far more time as a rule than the physical application of pen to paper. Even the most industrious clerk or book-keeper engaged on routine work is unlikely to spend more than, say, $2\frac{1}{2}$ out of the $6\frac{1}{2}$ hours in a working day in physically writing down entries in account books, etc. (which in conjunction with the $1\frac{1}{2}$ hours for meals brings the $4\frac{1}{2}$ per cent. figure quoted above for an 8-hour working day down to about $1\frac{1}{2}$ per cent.). Furthermore, if one considers the case of literary authors (whom Shaw had above all in mind), the proportion is much less even than that, for the essence of writing of this kind lies in the meditation and mental cogitation upon exactly what to write, and many—perhaps most—authors do not write an aggregate of more than around 1,000 words per day (the physical committing to paper of which—with pen or type-writer—takes perhaps half-an-hour). This brings the saving down by a further four-fifths, to approximately $\frac{1}{3}$ per cent. (0·33 per cent.) which is a very different thing from the 20 per cent. claimed by Shaw. (For most authors, the saving would thus be about $1\frac{1}{4}$ days per year, not 73.)

Thus Shaw's reference in the quotation given on p. 458—to "authors, journalists, clerks, accountants, scholars, private correspondents and others writing continually and simultaneously all round the clock" has no valid significance, and the same applies to Shaw's frequent claims that if a phonetic alphabet had been available to them, Shakespeare would have written four or five more plays, and Dickens several further novels. The figure Shaw goes on to give of at least 500,000 years of time and labour being saved collectively by all the "scribes" in the world every year is also without basis.

Another statement of a similar kind was a letter by Shaw published in *The Times* of 15th April, 1941, referring to a *Times* leader which had appeared a few days earlier under the heading "A King's Spelling". (This had included references to the bad spelling of King George V, the poet Robert Bridges, and the artist Eric Gill, whose mistakes were often due to their tendency to spell phonetically (i.e. as the words sound). Prior to publication Shaw submitted his draft letter for comments to the Scottish printer of his books, Dr William Maxwell of R. & R. Clark Ltd. (whose reminiscences and letters—not including the following—were given in *Shaw the Villager*). Shaw apparently ignored his reply. Nothing similar from Maxwell appeared in *The Times*, and his letter to Shaw, first published here, throws further light on Shaw's capacity for miscalculation, and in addition, points to certain grave printing

difficulties which a new 40-letter alphabet would bring. Shaw
on this occasion had expatiated on the "immense" saving of
time, labour, and also in wear on machinery, which a phonetic
alphabet could (in his view) effect in the production of a typical
page of *The Times.* I give below an extract from Shaw's published
letter in *The Times* before giving extracts from Dr Maxwell's
letter to him commenting on the draft of it:—

. . . Let us see. The issue of *The Times* in which the article headed
"A King's Spelling" appeared was reduced by the war rationing of
paper to half the usual size. The leader page, including the article,
contained 54,369 letters. Each of the pages in the smaller type used
for advertisements contained 88,200 letters. As there were 10 pages
we have to multiply these figures by 10. Averaging them we get
712,845 letters as the content of a typical war-rationed 10-page
issue of *The Times.* For a normal peace issue of *The Times* we must
more than double this figure, which means that every 24 hours in
the office of *The Times* alone a million and a half letters must be
separately and legibly written or typed on paper, that someone
reading from the paper must monotype them on a machine which
arranges and casts them in metal, to be finally printed on huge rolls
of paper by another machine the wear and tear of which is in
proportion to the area of paper covered by the letters. This colossal
labour has to be repeated every working day in the year: that is
310 times, which gives us an annual task of writing, setting-up, and
printing-off four hundred and sixty-five millions of letters.

This for a single newspaper. But there are the other daily papers,
the Sunday papers, the weekly reviews, the magazines, and publications of all sorts, which make the figures astronomical and indeed
incalculable. In view of this, what are we to think of our device for
making every letter serve two purposes by doubling it? It is easy to
say "It takes only a moment to write a letter of the alphabet twice
instead of once." In fact it takes years, wears out tons of machinery,
uses up square miles of paper and oceans of ink. By shortening a
single common word instead of lengthening it, we could save the
cost of destroyers enough to make an impregnably guarded avenue
across the Atlantic for our trade with America.

It may interest you to learn that your leading article contains

2,761 letters. As these letters represent only 2,311 sounds, 450 of them were superfluous and could have been saved had we a British alphabet. The same rate of waste on the 465,000,000 letters printed annually by *The Times* gives us 94,136,952 superfluous letters, every one of which has to be legibly written or typed, read and set up by the monotypist, cast in metal, and machined on paper which has to be manufactured, transported, and handled. Translate all that into hours of labour at eight hours a day. Translate the labour into wages and salaries. I leave the task to *The Times'* auditors, who, after staggering the proprietors with it, should pass it on to the Auditor-General to be elaborated into an estimate of the waste in the whole printing industry of the nation.

It is, I suppose, for lack of such an estimate that we do not think it worth while to lift a finger to get an English alphabet. The King, who has to spend an appreciable part of his time in signing his name, which in southern English has three sounds, and should be spelt with three letters, has to write six (100 per cent. waste of his time),* with a result so equivocal that Herr Hitler speaks of him as King Gay Org. My surname has two sounds; but I have to spell it with four letters: another 100 per cent. loss of time, labour, ink, and paper. The Russians can spell it with two letters, as they have an alphabet of 35 letters. In the race of civilization, what chance has a Power that cannot spell so simple a sound as Shaw against a rival that can?

At present we are in such pressing need of more man-power that we are driven to transfer our women from their special natural labour of creating life to the industry of destroying it. I wonder some female mathematician does not calculate how many men would be released from literary industry for war work by spelling the common words could and should with six letters instead of with 11 as we insanely do at present. Battles may be lost by the waste in writing Army orders and dispatches with multitudes of superfluous letters. The mathematicians changed from Latin numerals to Arabic years ago. The gain was incalculably enormous. A change from Latin to British letters would have equally incalculable advantages, but we, being incorrigibly brain lazy, just laugh at spelling reformers

* Shaw is, of course, wrong. It would be 50 per cent. Furthermore, a Sovereign spends only a few minutes per day signing his or her name—very few documents requiring this.

as silly cranks. It took the Four Years' War to knock Summer Time into us. How many wars will it take to call our attention to the fact that there are shorter ways of spelling enuf than e-n-o-u-g-h?

Unfortunately, as most people write little and seldom, and read and spell by visual memory, not aurally, they are unconscious of any serious difficulty, and are only amused when some spelling reformer treats them to a few stale pleasantries about Frenchmen who, having been taught how to pronounce such a monstrosity as the spelling of though (six letters for two sounds), are then left to infer the pronunciation of through, cough, plough, &c., &c. We have endless exposures of the inconsistencies of our spelling and the absurdity of its pretence to etymology; but even professional writers who waste half their lives in blackening paper unnecessarily seem to have no grasp of the importance of our losses or the colossal figures into which they run.

Much work has already been done on the subject by inventors of phonetic shorthands, who have all had to begin by designing a 42-letter alphabet. The best of these, so far as I know, is that of our most eminent British phonetist, the late Henry Sweet, who had mastered all the systems, from Bell's Visible Speech to Pitman's; but, like all the rest, he proceeded to torture it into an instrument for verbatim reporting, and thereby made it difficult to learn, illegible, and useless for ordinary purposes. However, it is easy to discard his reporting contractions and use his alphabet in its simplicity. In my own practice I use Pitman's alphabet in this way with a great saving of time and labour for myself personally, but it all has to be transcribed and set up in the spelling of Dr. Johnson's dictionary.

The Orthological Institute has done invaluable service in calling attention to our waste of time by too much grammar through its invention of Basic English;* but though the interest for foreign students is great, no British Government will ever be stirred to action in the matter until the economics of a phonetically spelt scientific and scholarly Pidgin are calculated and stated in terms of time, labour, and money.

Yours truly,

G. BERNARD SHAW.

Ayot St. Lawrence, Welwyn, Herts.

---

* Invented and developed from 1926 onwards at the Orthological Institute in Cambridge by C. K. Ogden, the Institute's Director, and I. A. Richards.

Now follow the extracts I mentioned from Dr William Maxwell's letter to Shaw about the draft of the foregoing:—

. . . I cannot agree with your treatment of small type—you take the leader page as 54369 and the small type pages as 88200 and strike an average of 71284 overall but you ignore the large type adverts and space occupied by pictures. On a very rough and ready method I would cancel out one with the other, the small type and the emptier spaces (Contents, large type headings, liberally spaced advertisements, pictures, crosswords, adverts . . .) . . . I . . . would reckon the content of the leader page as the average all over, and that has a mighty effect upon your millions.

(4) So I sum up that side of the question by suggesting that you are (a) wrong in saying 54369 in leader page [I call it 40425] and (b) wrong in allowing 88200 letters per page for the small type and ignoring the "large open spaces". I therefore challenge your statement that "every 24 hours in the office of *The Times* alone a million and a half letters must be separately and legibly written or typed on paper" and suggest that the figure should be say 809000 in a 20-page issue.

. . . In effect I bring out that the ultimate figure on which your following argument is based falls to be reduced by about 45 per cent. and your final figure for letters per annum will have to be similarly cut down to a round figure of 250 millions. If there were more time I would have an actual calculation made to see how nearly I am right by setting off one against the other, the small type and the open matter, but I think I should prove not to be very far out; but when your "few million more or less" becomes a question of one million against half a million I do feel your letter needs drastic revision and if your letter appears as drafted I should have to cut in and try to prove your whole basis as wrong and that you would only have sufficient destroyers for the impregnable guarding of half the width of the Atlantic!

(6) Coming back to your statement that the article contains 2761 letters—you are approximately correct, but I think you ignore that blank spaces at ends of pars have to be filled up with metal and that the monotypist has to tap keys to fill out the line so I regard the blanks as equal to the number of "letters" in the article as

about 2950. But that is by the way—it does not affect the relation between the number of letters and the sounds. Your total of wasted letters is however very much affected. Your basis for the loss of 94,000,000 wasted letters is that 2761 letters give a waste of 450, so the proportion sum is

$$2761 : 465,000,000 :: 450,$$
$$\therefore\ 465000000 \times 450 \div 2761.$$
$$\text{Answer} \quad 75,750,000.$$

I can't make it 94 millions. Further as my figuring gives me only 250 millions in a peace time issue against your 465 your figure of wasted millions must be reduced proportionally and as your figure is corrected from 94 millions waste to only 76,000,000, the actual waste would be about 45 per cent. of the 76 so the wasted letters would be say 32 millions.

Your query as to how long a comp* would take to become proficient on a Monotype Keyboard in which the characters were 42 involves much technical consideration—the Keyboard, die case, etc., and the other equipment for the casting machine would require complete re-invention as the Keyboard has to be constructed on a minimum of five alphabets: Roman caps, Roman lower case, Italic caps, Italic lower case, Small caps; total of $42 \times 5 = 210$ [plus] accentuated letters Rom. and ital., say 30, Punctuation 10, Figures 10, Blanks for specials 12, Quads 6, [Total] 278, and the die case for the casting similarly re-equipped [sic], besides the necessity for reconstructing the casting machine itself to produce a much greater variety of characters than demanded from it on the 26 alphabet basis. There would be no difficulty in a comp attaining efficiency either in hand or machine work after say a month to get acquainted with the 42 character alphabet but it would be the very devil to change from the old to the new and the new to the old. If the new alphabet were universal and if infants of a generation began with it from their first day at school the idea would be perfectly easy and practicable, subject to the possibility of the reconstruction of the Monotype and the Linotype and other mechanical typesetting machines. . . .

Postscript.

Adverting to space occupied widely—advts, pictures, etc. In the 10-page issue there are 3700 square inches. Advts, pictures, &c.

* i.e. a compositor.

occupy about 860 square inches—this includes allowance for large type headings. These 860 sq. inches are equal to $2\frac{1}{3}$ whole pages which would have contained about 95060 words of leader page type.

P.P.S.

Since writing the foregoing yesterday I have had the opportunity of consulting my chief Monotype mechanician on the question of Keyboard, die case, and caster.

The normal die case for a five-alphabet lay out can hold 225 characters. Still adhering to a five-alphabet lay out it would (for your scheme) have to contain 278 characters. But in order to accommodate the equipment for certain special work, e.g. a Dictionary, we often use a 7-alphabet lay out. That would involve a die case of *over 400 characters*. I think the 278 could be managed but 400 would definitely involve the complete reinvention referred to earlier in this "essay".   W.M.

Although little or no notice of Dr Maxwell's comments was taken by Shaw in his letter as it finally appeared in *The Times* of 15th April, 1941, in fairness to Shaw it must be pointed out here that in his last (1950) Will he explicitly acknowledged that the precise saving which a new phonetic alphabet might effect was an open question. In this Will he specifically instructed that a statistical enquiry should be set up to investigate this aspect. Shaw's Will (and Mr Justice Harman's Judgement declaring the Alphabet bequests invalid) are given in full a little later in this book, but I will anticipate a little by quoting the following Clause which seems particularly relevant at this juncture:—

Clause 35. (1)

To institute and finance a series of inquiries to ascertain or estimate as far as possible the following statistics (*a*) the number of extant persons who speak the English language and write it by the established and official alphabet of 26 letters (hereinafter called Dr. Johnson's Alphabet) (*b*) how much time could be saved per individual scribe by the substitution for the said Alphabet of an Alphabet containing at least 40 letters (hereinafter called the Proposed British Alphabet) enabling the said language to be written without indicating single sounds by groups of letters or by diacritical marks instead of by one symbol for each sound (c) how many of these persons are engaged in writing or printing English at any and every moment in the world; (d) on these factors to estimate the time and labour wasted by our lack of at least 14 unequivocal single symbols; (e) to add where possible to the estimates of time lost or saved by the difference between Dr. Johnson's Alphabet and the Proposed British Alphabet estimates of the loss of income in British and American currency. The enquiry must be confined strictly to the statistical and mathematical problems to be solved without regard to the views of professional and amateur phoneticians, etymologists, Spelling Reformers, patentees of universal languages, inventors of shorthand codes for verbatim reporting or rival alphabets, teachers of the established orthography, disputants about pronunciation, or any of the irreconcilables whose wranglings have overlooked and confused the single issue of labour saving and made change impossible during the last hundred years. The inquiry must not imply any approval or disapproval of the Proposed British Alphabet by the inquirers or by my Trustee.

Despite the various criticisms which can be levelled at the details and practical difficulties of Shaw's phonetic ideas (and Shaw was never one to flee from fair criticism), it must be borne in mind that they by no means invalidate the *basic concept* of a reform in the British Alphabet. The saving which would at the very least result from using only one letter or symbol for frequently used words such as 'and', 'the', 'for', 'it', and 'to', and only two for 'though' and similar words, has obviously much to be said for it.

Some changes of this sort have, indeed, taken place in America, where the ending 'our' as in fav*our*, lab*our*, has for a long time been spelt *or*, and 'though' is frequently abbreviated to *tho*. Whether such abbreviations (*enuf* is another) are aesthetically pleasing is another matter, but it is perfectly legitimate to point out that we do not spell today—or even write today—as the Anglo-Saxons did (*vide* the tenth century *Beowulf*) or as three and half centuries later, Langland did in *Piers Plowman,* or Chaucer in *The Canterbury Tales.*   Marked changes have occurred even since Shakespeare's time, and indeed some spelling changes and pronunciations (if not alphabetic changes) have taken place even since the Victorian age.

It can also be legitimately pointed out that in parts of Ireland, a bi-alphabetic (as well as bi-lingual) state of affairs exists now, and has done satisfactorily for many centuries, among those who write (and speak) Gaelic in addition to English, and thus there would be no insuperable problem in the co-existence of a new English phonetic alphabet side by side with the traditional one.

Further examples are the various languages and alphabets of different parts of Yugoslavia (Slavonic, Serbo-Croat, and Macedonian), of India (Urdu, Tamil, Gujerati, etc.), of Africa, and of the U.S.S.R. (Soviet bank-notes have the amount in words printed simultaneously on them in the sixteen different languages, and in some cases alphabets, used in the different Republics). Many people in these parts speak two or more languages and also habitually write in more than one alphabet.

One can also point to the vast army of secretaries and business personnel who regularly write and/or read shorthand—who are obviously in a sense bi-alphabetic. And there is no doubt that Isaac Pitman's invention of Shorthand has saved the world an enormous amount of time, work, and money.

Furthermore, there is an obvious parallel between phonetic reform, and the reform of our British numerical system—as applied to weights and measures and distances. Numerical reform has had its advocates for at least as long as phonetic reform, and it has now achieved official acceptance, with the probability that during the next decade in Britain the decimal system will replace our absurdly antiquated and cumbersome pounds, shillings, and pence; our inches, feet, yards, furlongs, miles; our ounces, pounds, bushels, hundredweights, tons; our pints, quarts, gills, gallons, firkins, barrels, etc.—all of which use odd numbers such as 8, 12, 14, 16, 112, 1,760, and so on, instead of the decimal 10 and multiples thereof. The significant point in relation to Shaw's alphabetic ideas is that the objective in both cases is exactly the same—the saving of time, expense, and unnecessary work. That the decimal (metric) system has an enormous advantage in this respect over our own numerical system is the reason for Britain's impending change-over to it, and it is therefore not necessarily far-fetched or 'cranky' to advocate reforms in the realm of our equally archaic and illogical alphabet and language.

At the same time, phoneticians must of course concede that all languages have complexities of grammar, tenses, genders of nouns (in French and many other languages, if not in English) and of idiom which can never be entirely obviated; and of which even the partial removal would involve the loss of many individual quaint characteristics which are the essence of a language's character and charm. Thus the shortened spellings used in America (and proposed to be used in this country by Shaw, and on a much wider scale) are regarded by many English people as a good deal less pleasing aesthetically—and in some cases downright ugly—compared to the forms we are used to (with their roots in the past). But in these very words "forms we are used to" and "roots in the past" lies a central bone of contention, for what we like and what we don't, and what is considered good taste and what bad, is largely a matter of habit and convention. When radical changes are introduced, people resist them at first (often very strongly), but gradually tend to adapt to them, both consciously and unconsciously, so that after a time it can often be the old form that appears ugly, and not the new. (For example, much of Victorian architecture which not so very long ago was considered so revolutionary and 'progressive' appears to many today as heavy, over-ornate, in bad taste, and even hideous. Examples are the Albert Memorial and St. Pancras railway station. That many earlier styles, such as Tudor architecture or Italian Renaissance art, are still greatly admired today does not detract from the force of the foregoing argument. Few people will mourn the demise of our numerical system when the altogether more satisfactory decimal system takes over, which, indeed, it is in process of doing already.

Thus time will tell what measure of phonetic change may come about in the English language. Just as we do not write and speak today as we did 600 or 800 years ago, so it seems inevitable that English will not be spoken or written 600 or 800 years hence as it is today, and such changes as will take place will almost certainly include abbreviations and time-saving devices which will be at least a partial vindication of Shaw's basic objective. — A.C.

BERNARD SHAW'S WILLS

Shaw's last Will and Testament has already been referred to several times; notably in the contribution to *Shaw the Villager* by Harold O. White, the Luton printer who (with his wife) witnessed Shaw's signature to it; by Shaw's chauffeur Fred Day, who felt that he had not been provided for in the manner which he had gathered from conversations with Shaw he would be; by other associates and neighbours; and finally, in connection with the provision in it for the practical realisation of Shaw's proposed new alphabet, as described in the preceding pages.

I therefore think it may be useful and apposite to publish here in full Shaw's last Will. It is an interesting and important piece of Shavian writing (Shaw himself referred to it wittily as "my crowning masterpiece") which adds in an unusual way to the overall picture of his character with which this book is concerned.

However, before giving the text of this last Will, I propose to give extracts from Shaw's earlier Wills, partly in order to give perspective to the last one, in which they culminate, and partly because some of the clauses therein are quite different and of interest in themselves.

Although Shaw himself was undoubtedly the main author of these documents, there was inevitably some degree of collaboration between him and his solicitors in order to make the Wills comply with accepted legal practice. One cannot, therefore, expect to escape entirely the lack of punctuation, the repetitious phrases, and the frequent uses of words such as 'whereas', 'the said', and 'hereinbefore' which are inevitably found in many legal documents. I print here only the most significant parts of these *earlier* Wills, and, where indicated, have given the provisions of a clause or clauses in my own words, or in a condensed form, thus reducing the legal jargon to the minimum consistent with accuracy of meaning. Neverthe-

473

less, wherever I felt it necessary, I have reproduced the selected individual clauses word for word and complete.

WILL OF 1st JULY, 1901

The earliest Will made by Shaw which I have been able to trace is one dated 1st July, 1901. Shaw was then forty-five years of age and had been married just over three years. It is a relatively short document compared to his later Wills, though not less interesting in some of its clauses and the light they throw on Shaw. The main provisions included the following:—

The sole Executrix and Trustee was to be his wife Charlotte, and in the event of her death, Messrs F. L. Whelan, Sydney Olivier, and E. R. Pease (the last two were among the leading figures of the Fabian Society). If these three gentlemen, as well as Shaw's wife, should be deceased at the time of Shaw's death, or should they have refused to act, or be incapable of acting at Trustees, then Sydney Cockerell,* or failing him, Emery Walker (close associates of Shaw's friend William Morris), were nominated.

An annuity of £600 was to be paid to his mother; and in the event of her death, an alternative annuity, of £300, was to be paid to his sister Lucinda Frances ('Lucy'). In the event of his mother or his sister Lucy becoming not entitled to the stipulated annuities for technical reasons, there was provision for annuities to his friends Graham Wallas (a leading Fabian), M. E. McNulty (a friend from boyhood), and Henry Salt (Secretary of the Humanitarian League), at the acting Trustees' or Trustee's absolute discretion.

All Shaw's real and personal estate not specifically otherwise disposed of, including all his literary manuscripts and copyrights, were bequeathed to his wife Charlotte; and in the event

---

* It is noteworthy that when Shaw eventually died, in November, 1950, only Sir Sydney Cockerell (as he had become) was still alive out of the above-mentioned group of people. He read the lesson at Shaw's cremation at Golders Green. (It was a passage from Bunyan's *The Pilgrim's Progress*.)

of her death, to his friends Sidney Webb, Frederick Whelan, Sydney Olivier, Edward Pease, Sydney Cockerell, and Emery Walker UPON TRUST that they should pay his funeral expenses and administer his specific bequests. (There were legacies of £250 each to these friends in recognition of their services, if they acted as Trustees.)

The proceeds and income from his realisable assets were to be invested in "Government Securities or any security authorised by law for the investment of trust funds or on mortgage of any leasehold houses or land in England or Wales held for any term having not less than sixty years to run at the time of the investment or in or upon the debentures or preference stocks or shares of any Railway Company of the United Kingdom."

The specific bequests (apart from those already mentioned) which were to absorb the income derived from this investment were as follows:—

(A) The Advancement of education in and the promotion of the general knowledge of Economics Statistics Industrial History and any other branch or branches of Social Science or Political Science with power to transfer the trust premises or any part thereof or to pay the income of the same or any part thereof for any period or periods to the London School of Economics and Political Science of 10 Adelphi Terrace* in the County of London or to any other College or Institution now or hereafter to be established for either wholly or partially teaching or promoting the general knowledge of the last mentioned subjects or any of them upon such terms (including payment if thought fit) and in such manner as my Trustees or Trustee may from time to time determine (B) The teaching and promotion of physical culture oratory and the arts of public life including the study of phonetics† and the formation of a collection of records of spoken sounds with power to establish or endow

---

* The School's second address, shortly after its foundation in 1895 by Bernard Shaw and Sidney Webb.
† This proves that Shaw's extremely strong interest in phonetic reform existed for more than half a century. He was 45 years of age in 1901 (and must clearly have been interested for some years prior to this), and 94 in 1950 (the year of his last Will and his death).

or concur in establishing or endowing any College or Institution or any Readership in any College Institution or University for the purpose of giving instruction in or promoting either wholly or partially the study of the last mentioned subjects or any of them and of enabling members of public Authorities Clergymen Barristers Civil Military Naval and Marine Officers of all ranks Actors Lecturers and persons desirous of qualifying themselves for any employment or pursuit in which trained speech and personal bearing are needed to acquire such qualifications (but any such College or Institution is not to have for its sole object the inclusive or complete training in any single profession) . . . . (C) As a contribution to the National Gallery of Ireland or of any other permanent public Museum Gallery or other Exhibition now existing or hereafter to be established in Ireland and freely accessible to all citizens of works of fine art or of chosen examples of artistic craftsmanship applied to the industrial arts for the purpose of the maintenance of such exhibitions and the extension of their collections . . . . (D) Establishing maintaining or improving or assisting in the establishment maintenance or improvement of a publicly endowed Orchestra in Ireland (should it prove possible at any time to establish such an Orchestra) for promoting by means of performances of orchestral music of the highest class (not being exclusively or mainly choral performances of oratorios or of so-called Irish National music) a taste for and knowledge of music among the public generally any such orchestral performances to be freely accessible to all citizens (though not necessarily to the complete exclusion of places reserved for those who wish to contribute to the maintenance of the orchestra by paying for such places) or establishing maintaining or improving or assisting in the establishment maintenance or improvement of an endowed Theatre in Ireland for promoting by means of the performance of works of dramatic art of too high a quality to become profitable subjects of unsubsidized commercial theatrical speculation a taste for and knowledge of the highest forms of drama among the public generally . . . . (E) The promotion in any other way that may recommend itself to the judgement of my Trustees or Trustee of any work having for its object the bringing of the masterpieces of fine art within the reach of the Irish people of all classes in their own Country without discrimination or prejudice for or against any such masterpiece on the ground of the relations between its

Country of origin and the Irish people in the past or present (F) The promotion of all or any of the several objects C. D. and E. respectively hereinbefore referred to but as applicable to any part of the world and not restricted to Ireland or for the benefit of Irish people exclusively (G) The creation and endowment for all or any of the purposes hereinbefore referred to of one or more Professorship or Professorships Readership or Readerships Lectureship or Lectureships Fellowship or Fellowships Studentship or Studentships at any University College or other Institution (including the aforesaid London School of Economics) (H) The creation and endowment for all or any of the purposes hereinbefore referred to of a Library or Libraries Archive or Archives (whether for the preservation of written and printed or of phonographic or photographic or other records) with power for my Trustees or Trustee to cause to be written or translated and published or otherwise devised and manufactured any book or books or other works or records or recording devices relating or bearing upon any one or more of the several subjects hereinbefore referred to.

Shaw's property (cottages and land) in Carlow, Ireland, was to be administered by his Trustee or Trustees to assist in providing income to the estate, and new publications or performances of his works were also to be administered by them to the same end.

Shaw cut out with scissors his signature from the bottom of each sheet of this Will and wrote on the front of the first page, *Revoked by Will dated 3rd Aug. 1913.*

WILL OF 3rd AUGUST, 1913

Shaw appointed his wife sole executrix during her lifetime, and after that, for the first time, the Public Trustee. He bequeathed all his copyrights and literary estate generally to his wife, or, in the event of her death, Upon Trust to the Public Trustee (Clause 17).

Among other provisions, he left his body for medical dissection, and his skull or skeleton for possible preservation, and expanded his 1901 bequests concerning phonetics and putting the teaching of correct elocution onto a scientific basis.

Clauses of particular interest are the following (I have abbreviated or summarised some of them):—

Clause 3.

I DESIRE that after my death my body shall be reduced to ashes by fire if practicable and the ashes scattered unless any scientific use can be found for my body or any part of it in which case the nearest College of Surgeons or other Scientific Institution is welcome to dissect me and preserve my skull or skeleton or any part of my body that may be of scientific use or interest taking due care that the refuse be destroyed and scattered as aforesaid so that nothing shall remain capable of being identified as a relic. I have no objection whatever to either the omission or performance of any religious ceremonies whether Christian Mahometan Pagan or other on the occasion of my death or on any other occasion provided the ceremony be a cheerful and encouraging one or as in the case of the burial service of the Church of England have beauty enough to redeem its gloom and the witnesses well aware that most religions were alike to me inasmuch as they use common truths to give colour to their many errors and superstitions among which superstitions I dislike none more than those which treat the discarded body from which the eternal life has passed away as a person in a state of suspended animation who will revive later on and carry on his individual limitations and imperfections and recollections thereafter for ever. I also record here my strong objection to any visible monument or memorial in the shape of a cross or any other instrument of torture or death and to the exhibition of black fabrics or other conventional emblems of mourning and melancholy at my funeral.

Clause 4.

In this clause Shaw bequeathed the bronze bust of himself by Rodin to his wife, and after her death, "IN TRUST for the Trustees for the time being of the Shakespear Memorial National Theatre if they shall at my death or within five years thereafter have achieved their project of completing and endowing a National Theatre as a memorial to Shakespear. . . . AND in the event of the immediately preceding trust not taking effect or being determined then IN TRUST for the Trustees for the time being of the National Gallery in Dublin (in which many of the most pleasant and profitable hours of my boyhood were passed) absolutely . . ."

Clause 11.

"Subject and without prejudice to the bequests hereinbefore contained and subject also to the proviso in Clause 10 of this my Will contained" . . . Shaw bequeathed to his friends Sidney James Webb, Emery Walker, May Morris ("the daughter of the great Poet and Craftsman William Morris"), Sydney Carlile Cockerell ("Curator of the Fitzwilliam Museum of Cambridge University") . . . Henry Salt ("the biographer of Shelley"), Kate Salt his wife, and Harley Granville Barker . . . any of his chattels they might with the approval of his Trustees select as keepsakes for themselves, or for presentation to other of Shaw's friends who in their opinion might appreciate them, or for donation to Societies or Institutions in which Shaw had been interested, taking "sentimental considerations into account". Shaw added: "I express my regret that my means are not sufficient to provide for any material pledge of my regard for the many friends who as my Colleagues in the Socialistic movement or as Artists cooperating with me in the performance of my plays have not only made my career possible but hallowed it with kindly human relations." (A rider similar to that of the last six lines was to appear in all his future Wills, including the last.)

Clause 19.

In the event of his wife's death, Shaw's friend Harley Granville Barker was appointed dramatic executor, to grant permissions for the productions of his plays. Barker's remuneration was to be a commission of one-fifth of the gross receipts of such licensed performances (except when he produced any of Shaw's plays himself, as a theatrical manager) up to a maximum of £500 in any one year. The balance was to be handed over to the Public Trustee as income of the Residuary Estate.

Clause 20.

Similarly, Sydney Carlile Cockerell (later Sir Sydney) was appointed literary executor to control Shaw's manuscripts and the further publications of his writings, under the auspices of the Public Trustee. His powers included the right to give away individual papers or manuscript items—"at his reasonable discretion to persons who may in his opinion be fitly and graciously made recipients of such presents and to sell any of my manuscripts or other documents to other persons who will undertake to bequeath them to a public collection or one accessible to the public."

Clause 22.

An annuity of £52 was bequeathed to S. C. Cockerell during any time in which he should act as Curator and literary executor.

Clause 24.

The bequests to servants were as follows:—

All with over 7 years' service ..	..	2 years' wages
,, ,, 3-7 ,, ,, ..	..	6 months' ,,
,, ,, less than 3 years' service	..	2 months' ,,

Clause 25.

In addition, all servants with over ten years' service who were also over 45 years of age were to receive annuities of sums calculated to make up a total of £52 per annum each, after deducting any old age pensions from the State they might already be in receipt of.

Other annuities were:—

Clause 26.

To his sister Lucinda Frances (Lucy) ..   .. £750 p.a.

Clause 27.

To Georgina Musters, "(commonly called Judy) the daughter of my mother's half-sister Arabella Gillmore" ..   .. £156 p.a.

Clause 28.

To Kate Gurly (his mother's half-sister) .. £26 p.a.

Clause 29.

To Arabella Gillmore (his mother's half-sister) .. £104 p.a.

Clause 30.

To Charlotte Rogers (his mother's half-sister)
£81 18s. 0d. p.a.

Clause 31.

To Florence Farr .. .. £104 p.a.

Clause 32.

To Jane Patterson .. .. £104 p.a.

The last two named were ladies with whom Shaw had had early love affairs. The bequest to Florence Farr reads:—

I declare that if Florence Farr (who in One thousand eight hundred and ninety-four produced my play "Arms and the Man" at the Avenue Theatre in Northumberland Avenue London) formerly the wife of Edward Emery and now residing at . . .

And that to Jane Patterson:—

I declare that if Jane Patterson (whose kindness to me from One thousand eight hundred and eighty six to One thousand eight hundred and ninety two has been of enduring service to me and has always been held in affectionate remembrance and honor by me) now residing at . . .

Clause 33.

The last annuity was to his great friend from boyhood, M. E. McNulty. (£78 p.a.)

Clause 35.

This was to the effect that if the estate's income should temporarily be insufficient to pay all the annuities, that to his sister Lucy was to be paid in full, and the others "abated" as necessary, the Trustee having discretion to make up the reductions in later years if the income improved sufficiently to make this possible.

Clause 40.

In this Clause Shaw expanded on his 1901 provisions for the improvement of what he evidently regarded as an appalling state of mispronunciation of the noble English tongue by many who should know better. He went further (in Sections F to J) by for the first time broaching the subject of the formation of a new phonetic English *alphabet* to economise the *writing* of English.

From the Residue of the estate Shaw charged the Trustee to apply the funds to:—

. . . the founding endowing or promoting or assisting in the foundation or endowment or promotion of a combined Institute of Phonetics and School of Rhetoric, Oratory, Dress Manners and the Arts of Public Life (whether so entitled or not) with any or all of the following objects that is to say (A) Of conferring such certificates of proficiency in the art of private speech and the addressing of large public assemblies audibly effectively and gracefully or giving spoken orders to troops or crews or as may be demanded by bishops and sectarian governing bodies as a condition of ordination by Inns of Court as a condition of the call to the bar, by military naval and marine authorities as a condition of appointment to a command, by Hospital boards and educational authorities as a condition of appointments to professorships readerships lectureships or the like, by managers of theatres as a condition of the engagement of an actor or actress, by the Civil Service Commissioners as a condition of all appointments involving the exercise of judicial or other functions which demand public impressiveness and intelligibility or correct and refined address, as well as by the Auctioneers Institute by employers of shop assistants nursery and parlourmaids and other domestic servants and generally by all who though at present easily able to ascertain whether candidates for employment of any sort have learnt algebra or the Church Catechism have no means of finding out whether they can speak and behave themselves properly either in public or private life (B) Of the teaching and training necessary to enable persons of all ranks to obtain such Certificates as aforesaid (C) Of the substitution of a scientific training in phonetics for the makeshifts of so called elocution lessons by actors and others which have hitherto prevailed in the teaching of oratory (D) Of the formation of a collection of records of spoken sounds in all languages and dialects and the provision of instruments for reproducing them including records of the delivery of standard passages of rhetoric or distinguished actors and orators (E) Of cooperation with Academies of Letters and cognate institutions or taking independent action for the establishment of a standard English speech and the observation, and if necessary the protection and championship of its evolution by the sharpening of the sense of beauty in speakers or the discovery and practice of more convenient and fit forms no less than the resistance to its debasement by vulgarity slovenliness and ignorance (F) Of the preparation and publication of a phonetic transcription of the Bible and the plays of Shakespeare either complete or by such instalments as may be advisable according to a pronunciation which shall be neither that fashionable in London nor Oxford but rather that of famous speakers who have acquired metropolitan culture without losing the traditions of English speech which are better preserved in the provinces and in Ireland and Scotland than in London of which the best contemporary example I can name is the speech of the eminent Actor, Johnston Forbes Robertson (G) Of the improvement of the English Alphabet and the English script so as to render such phonetic transcriptions more fully possible both in print and manuscript with all designing and casting of types and the like that may be necessary for that purpose provided always that the scripts shall not be shorthands and that the enterprise be kept free of the existing pernicious confusion of the art of phonetic writing with the devices used to make possible the verbatim report of public speakers and the work of correspondence clerks by means of written memoranda (I) Of the establishment of scholarships in phonetics or research connected therewith (J) And generally of the activities which clearly belong to or follow from such a scheme of work as aforesaid . . . .

. . . And I declare that I make the foregoing bequest in the full knowledge that its scope far exceeds the financial means which my estate can offer towards its fulfilment but if there be sufficient money for two rooms and one enthusiast there will be enough to begin with as I am bequeathing not only property but an idea and the essential parts of a plan of action and nothing more is needed to form a nucleus for further endowment.

Clause 48.

I declare it to be my wish that the public Trustee shall be guided by his judgement and the experience of his office in the investment of my Estate and not by the statutory qualification of certain stocks as Trustees securities and I specially recommend to his preference the loan stocks and shares of co-operative enterprises such as those in which I have already invested so that as far as possible any capital of my estate shall be invested within the United Kingdom and applied particularly and directly to the creation of additional utilities instead of merely to the purchase of existing claims on established enterprises and that such consideration may be placed before the amount of revenue to be derived from any such investments.

This Will of 3rd August, 1913, had Shaw's signature on the final page only cut out, and beneath the aperture, he had written: *Revoked and Superseded by later Will dated* 28th *April*, 1921.

CODICILS TO WILL OF 28th APRIL, 1921 AND/OR A LATER ONE.

There is no copy of Shaw's Will of 28th April, 1921, in the British Museum, but there is a number of copies of Codicils on separate slips of paper, some of the more interesting of which I give below. (These Codicils are not dated, but the Clause numbers do not tally with those of the 1913 Will, and are proved to refer to the 1921 Will or to one of some years later by the reference in Clause 10 to T. E. Shaw—whom Shaw knew mainly in the 'twenties, and in addition, the dates of some are proved to be post-1925 because a note concerning Clauses 38, 39, 43, and 51 refers to the need to re-read them, to see if they are affected by the 1925 Property Act (Birkenhead).

I have slightly abbreviated and re-phrased some of these Codicils to avoid excessive repetition of legal jargon.

Clause 4.

A copy of the Rodin bust of himself "distinguished from the original by the omission from it of the shoulders and breast", was to go to the Royal Academy of Dramatic Art.

Clause 10.

"Add that if I survive my wife T. E. Shaw now an aircraftsman stationed at Mount Batten Plymouth and formerly famous as Colonel Lawrence of Arabia may select and keep for himself any books formerly belonging to my wife or specially associated with her in his memory in fulfilment of a clause in her Will which is operative only in the event of her surviving me."

Clause 11.

Mr and Mrs Higgs were to have all animals, birds, and other domestic pets they might care to accept.

Clause 29.

Mrs Georgina Musters was to have £130 p.a. during her mother's lifetime and £260 after her mother's death; this to be continued to her husband Harold Musters until his death should he survive her.

Clause 30.

Charlotte Rogers was to have £156 p.a. instead of £131-16-0.

A Clause number is not given with the rest of the amendments—as detailed below:—

To his chauffeur George Frederick Day, an annuity of £104 p.a.—to be continued to his wife until her death if she should survive him.

To his gardener Harry Batchelor Higgs, an annuity of £104 p.a.—to be continued to his wife (Shaw's housekeeper) Clara Higgs until her death if she should survive him; and a legacy of £100.

To his housekeeper Clara Higgs, an annuity of £104 to be

continued to her husband Harry Batchelor Higgs if he should survive her; and a legacy of £100. Shaw added that his intention was that the household income of £208 secured to the pair by this and the preceding Clause should not be diminished nor cease until both had passed away.

To the sisters Kate and Emma Hodgson (former maids), annuities of £52 p.a. each.

To Margaret Bilton and her daughter Alice (a former housemaid and parlourmaid) £156 p.a.—to be reduced to £104 p.a. plus a single payment of £25 for funeral expenses on the death of Margaret Bilton should she die before her daughter.

Shaw stipulated that all his bequests to his servants, active or retired, were not to become operative until his wife's death (if she survived him) and were to be subject to the deduction of any operative testamentary provision made for them by his wife, being duplicated in his own Will only in order to give the servants the security of his own estate in addition to Mrs Shaw's, and "to assure them that I fully share her gratitude to them for the services and sympathy which have set me free to devote myself to my own peculiar work."

Then followed bequests or amendments to bequests to relatives:—

To his first cousin, Emily Carroll—£156 p.a.

To Ethel Davies, daughter of his first cousin—£156 p.a.—to be continued to her husband if he should survive her.

To Aida Shaw, daughter of his first cousin—£156 p.a.

To Georgina Meredith, daughter of his mother's half-sister Charlotte Rogers, an annuity of £156, and a legacy of £50 to be paid to her on the death of her mother.

To Blanche Patch, his Secretary, an annuity of £260—to begin on the death of Mrs Shaw should she survive him: if not, on his own death.

(All the foregoing bequests were to be free of duty to the recipients.)

WILL OF 4th AUGUST, 1937.

The clauses of general interest are:—

Clause 4.

It is my wish that no memorial service or celebration concerned specially with me shall take place until a hundred years shall have elapsed after the date of my death thus leaving ample time for me to be forgotten but if for any reason my Trustee should consent to a public funeral (which as our monuments testify may happen to the unworthiest) and to the deposit of a handful of my ashes in some national or international fane I am indifferent as to the ritual to be observed (if any) as it is sufficiently well known that my religion is not ritual and that in my opinion and to the best of my knowledge all established rituals use common religious truths to give credit to many errors and superstitions among which superstitions I dislike none more than those which treat the discarded body from which the eternal life has passed away as a person in a state of suspended animation who will revive later on and carry on his individual limitations and imperfections and recollections thereafter for ever I also record here my strong objection to any visible monument or memorial in the shape of a cross or any other instrument of torture or death and to the exhibition of crepe fabrics or any conventional emblems of mourning and melancholy at my funeral except those which form part of the routine business of disposing of the dead and cannot conveniently be dispensed with.

Shaw gave all rights of dealing in his literary manuscripts and copyrights to his Trustees. He added (in Clause 9):—

AND I FURTHER DECLARE that my Trustee shall not in dealing with any such rights be bound by commercial considerations exclusively it being my desire that he shall give due weight to artistic and public and human considerations to the best of his judgement in the light of his conscience.

Clauses 16-22 *(inclusive)*.

Bequests to servants—apart from legacies and annuities to specified servants given in the ensuing clauses—were as follows:—

Those with over 7 years' service .. 2 years' wages

,,   ,,   3-7 ,,   ,,   .. 6 months' ,,

,,   ,, less than 3 years' service 3 months' ,,

To Harry and/or Clara Higgs (gardener and housekeeper) a legacy of £300 plus an annuity of £300.

The Higgs were also offered, if they so desired, any animals owned by Shaw at the time of his death. Shaw added: "I EXPRESS my wish that any horses birds or domestic animals which I may own at the time of my death shall be kindly treated and if necessary disposed of humanely."

To George Frederick Day (and/or his wife)—there was a legacy of £100 and £156 annuity.

To Kate Hodgman and/or Emma Hodgman (maids)— £52 annuities each.

To Miss Margaret Bilton (housekeeper)—£156 annuity.

To her daughter Alice Bilton after her mother's death— £104 annuity, and £25 towards funeral expenses of her mother.

Clause 22.

Shaw declared that all bequests to any servant or former servant of his contained in his current Will or any Codicil thereto were not to be paid or to become operative until the death of Mrs Shaw if she should survive him, and were to be subject to deduction of the amount of the benefit (if any) of any operative testamentary provision made for them by Mrs Shaw, such bequests being duplicated in his own Will only to give them the additional security of his estate, and to assure them that he fully shared his wife's gratitude to them for the services and sympathy which had set him free to devote himself to his own particular work.

Then came bequests to his relatives, and to his personal Secretary (Clauses 23-33 inclusive):—

To Arabella Gillmore (Shaw's mother's half-sister)— £144 annuity.

To Mrs Georgina Musters, daughter of the above—£144 annuity while her mother was alive, increased to £260 after her mother's death.

To Charlotte Rogers—£156-1-4 annuity.

To Eames Bagenal Rogers (son of the above)—£104 annuity.

To Georgina Meredith (daughter of Charlotte Rogers)— a legacy of £50 payable on the death of her mother and £156 annuity payable from the date of Shaw's own death.

To Emily Carroll—£104 annuity.

To Ethel Davies or her husband Sebastian Davies—£156 annuity.

To Adelaide Olivia Shaw—£156 annuity.

To Eva Maria Schneider—£120 annuity.

To Alma von Bank—£52 annuity.

To Blanche Patch, secretary—£365 annuity.

In this Will Shaw again amplified considerably his bequests relating to phonetics and the founding of an institution for the systematic teaching of correct elocution ("A School of Rhetoric" as he termed it). At this stage in his life his main concern was still with the very widespread *mispronunciation* of the English language in speaking, but in Section I he repeated the substance of his 1913 proposals for the formation of a new *alphabet* for writing—the forerunner of his later and far more detailed proposals in the press (as quoted in earlier parts of this book) and in his last Will of 1950.

Clause 44.

WHEREAS in the course of my political activities as a speaker at public meetings and my professional practice as a critic in the theatre and as a writer and producer of stage plays I have had special opportunities of observing the extent to which the most highly instructed and capable persons have their efficiency defeated and their influence limited for want of any organized instruction and training for the personal contacts whether with individuals or popular audiences without which their knowledge is incommunicable except through books and how the authority which their abilities should give them is made derisory by their awkward manners and how their employment in positions for which they have valuable qualifications is made socially impossible by vulgarities of speech and other defects as easily corrigible by teaching and training as simple illiteracy and whereas my experience and observation have convinced me that the lack of such training produces not only much social friction but grave pathological results which seem quite unconnected with it and that social intercourse is a fine art with a technique which everybody can and should acquire Therefore I declare subject and without prejudice to the trusts hereinbefore declared . . . that my Trustee shall stand possessed of my Residuary Trust Funds and the annual income thereof . . . UPON TRUST to apply the same (with power to transfer the same or any part thereof to and absolutely vest the same in the Trustee for the time being of any such School as is hereinafter referred to) in or towards the founding endowing or promoting or assisting in the foundation or endowment or promotion of a School of Rhetoric (whether so entitled or not) with the following objects that is to say (A) Investigating the discoveries made by artists who having found themselves disabled by their professional exercises and performances and having by a study of their own cases cured themselves and in doing so discovered not only harmless techniques for their particular professions but more general principles of self-control which have enabled them to achieve remarkable results in developing normality in children condemned as mentally defective and in treating cases classed as chronic disease and applying such techniques and principles in physical education (the published works of F. Matthias Alexander and Maria Levinskaya among many others will illustrate my intention) (B) Establishing the scientific authority and rank of the intuitions and methods of practising artists as distinguished from the routine of experiments on animals in physiological laboratories and the determinist and mechanistic doctrine which sees in the present and future of the universe only a physical consequence of its past (C) Specialising as a practical educational department or Arts faculty in the training of students for the personal contacts involved by their professions businesses or crafts by giving them a general command of refined speech and grace and effectiveness of manner (D) (More particularly) providing skilled instruction and of conferring such certificates of proficiency in the art of private speech and the addressing of public assemblies and congregations audibly effectively and gracefully or giving spoken orders to troops or crews or official evidence in Courts of Justice as may be demanded by (for example) bishops and sectarian governing bodies as a condition of ordination of ministers of religion, by Inns of Court as a condition of the call to the bar, by military naval and marine authorities as a condition of appointment to a command, by Hospital boards and educational authorities as a condition of appointment to professorships readerships lectureships or the like, by Managers of Theatres as a condition of the engagement of actors and actresses, by the Civil Service Commissioners as a condition of all appointments involving the exercise of judicial or other functions which demand public impressiveness and intelligibility of correct and refined address, by the British Broadcasting Corporation as a qualification for announcers, by the Auctioneers Institute, by employers of shop assistants, nursery and parlourmaids and other domestic servants, and generally by all who though at present easily able to ascertain whether candidates for employment of any sort have learnt Algebra or the Church Catechism have no means of finding out whether they can speak and behave themselves becomingly and efficiently either in public or private life (E) of the teaching and training necessary to enable persons of all ranks to obtain such Certificates as aforesaid (F) of the substitution of a scientific training in phonetics for the makeshifts of the imitative elocution lessons which have hitherto prevailed in the teaching of oratory (G) of the formation of a collection of records of spoken sounds and the provisions of instruments for reproducing them (H) of the preparation and publication of a transcription as phonetic as possible of the British Versions of the Bible the ritual services of the Established and Free Churches the plays of Shakespeare and other authors whose plays have taken permanent hold on the stage and generally of all books plays sentences proclamations articles and documents whatsoever prescribed to be spoken in public officially or professionally (the said transcription I would suggest to be made according to a pronunciation which shall be neither the 'Southern English' fashionable in Oxford nor London but rather that of speakers who have acquired metropolitan culture without losing such traditions of English speech as are better preserved in the provinces and in Ireland and Scotland than in London and which in any case shall without pretending to be 'the right' pronunciation be such as will qualify the utterer in respect of it for any employment or dignity howsoever distinguished (I) of the improvement of the English Alphabet and the English script so as to render phonetic transcription more fully possible both in print and manuscript with all designing and casting of types and the like that may be necessary for that purpose (but I prophesy disaster to this enterprise unless it be kept free of the existing pernicious confusion of the art of phonetic writing and printing with the modifications of shorthand used to make verbatim reporting possible) (J) of the establishment of scholarships and bursaries in phonetics or research connected therewith (K) And generally of the essentially artistic activities which belong to or follow from such a scheme of work as aforesaid with however the following strongly advised limitations (AA) That the School shall not undertake any specific professional or other training except that of the phonetician the orator and in the ancient Greek sense the musician that is to say shall not be a School of specific Political Science grammar languages law divinity military or naval tactics musical composition or the playing on artificial musical instruments acting fencing professional dancing any other specialization of art for the purpose of a single profession although the students should be free to form clubs to pursue any special subject and practice [sic] any special art they please and should be granted the use of the school premises freely for such clubs and encouraged in every possible way to form them and thereby test their tastes and capacities before choosing a profession (BB) That the Institute or School shall not be a commercial profit making enterprise . . . AND I DECLARE that as the full scope of the project sketched in this clause far exceeds the financial means which my estate can ever offer towards its complete fulfilment and also as it cannot be carried out by my Trustee it is my wish that when the time comes for putting this bequest into operation he shall communicate the contents of this clause together with a general statement of the funds available under it to the governing body of the University of London and to any other persons or bodies who may in his judgement be eligible to receive such information and he shall at the same time intimate that if no steps be taken or promised either by the said University officially or by the said schools professors readers teachers and persons or any of them to begin the carrying out of my idea on however modest a scale so as to provide at least a nucleus for further endowments my estate must pass into the hands of the Trustees of the British Museum in acknowledgement of the incalculable value to me of my daily resort to the Reading room of that institution at the beginning of my career AND subject and without prejudice to the trusts powers and provisions of and concerning my Residuary Trust Funds hereinbefore declared and contained I DECLARE that my Trustee shall stand possessed of my Residuary Trust Funds or so much thereof as shall not have become vested or have been applied under any of the aforesaid trusts powers or provisions UPON TRUST to transfer the same unconditionally to the Trustees of the British Museum.

Clause 47.

I DECLARE that my Trustee shall be at liberty to grant time or other indulgence to any debtor in respect of any unsecured personal loans made by me and (in particular when the loan has not in his judgement been a matter of business) to forego payment of and absolutely release all or any part of the amount of any such debts or loan without being answerable for any loss which may thereby arise and with regard to any such debts owing to me or claims I may have against any person or persons I express it to be my wish that my Trustee shall in the exercise of the aforesaid power deal kindly or leniently with all such debtors or other person or persons where a strict observation of the law would involve manifest injustice hardship or meanness (but no conventional distinction in this respect is to be made in favour of my relatives as distinguished from other persons) AND I ALSO DECLARE that certain bequests I had made in former Wills in favour of various persons I have now omitted to make not on account of any change of feeling on my part towards them but because deaths marriages and change of circumstances have rendered such bequests unnecessary and I also record my regret that my means are not sufficient to provide for a material pledge of my regard for the many friends who as colleagues in the Socialistic movement or as artists co-operating with me in the performance of my plays or otherwise have not only made my career possible but hallowed it with kindly human relations.

Clause 53.

WHEREAS it has been my practice on public grounds to encourage in every possible manner the performance of plays and the establishment of local societies for that purpose by school players and groups of local players who are not professional actors and cannot afford the fees demanded from amateurs by theatrical agents who in view of their remuneration by commission on the monies collected by them also cannot afford to deal in small sums and therefore refuse performing licences except on terms which are oppressive and often prohibitive and WHEREAS it is desirable on public grounds to allow the said groups and schools when playing for their own benefit professional terms scaled down to five per centum of gross receipts not exceeding fifty pounds per performance I must advise my Trustee that the management of this department of the business of my estate cannot be delegated to private agents who are unaffected by public interests.

In the 1937 draft Will there was a deleted clause (originally No. 8, then altered in pencil to 6) reading: "I BEQUEATH to my said wife if she survive me all my watches jewels trinkets personal ornaments and wearing apparel and all my furniture plate plated articles linen china glass printed books pictures prints musical instruments cameras wireless sets and other articles of household use and ornament wines liquors and consumable stores and provisions and all my horses carriages saddlery harness stable furniture Motor Cars and accessories live and dead stock plants and garden tools and implements and utensils not otherwise disposed of by this my will or any Codicil hereto (hereinafter called "my household and personal chattels") for her own absolute use and benefit and to be held and enjoyed by her as her separate property."

Shaw had crossed out this passage and, in a pencil note, proposed substituting the brief phrase: "all my personal chattels as defined by Section 55 (1) (X) of the Administration of Estates Act 1925." He added this comment in the margin:—

These lists are survivals from a time when a solicitors remuneration depended on the profuseness of his verbiage. They are legally objectionable because the lists cannot be complete and it may be argued that the missing items were not meant to be included. If I possess a horse when I die, it goes to my wife under the list. But suppose I possess a hippopotamus (which is quite as likely)! where does *it* go, not being on the list?

Another clause (originally No. 57) in the first draft of the 1937 Will began: "I declare that it shall be lawful for my Trustee to apportion as my Trustee shall think fit any funds which . . . etc."

Shaw's pencilled comment was: "Concerning this Clause 57, is there not a body of law determining the powers of trustees? If so, is it necessary to attempt a recapitulation? The words 'I declare that it shall be lawful' are enough to provoke any judge to upset the will. I cannot make anything lawful or unlawful. I can at best declare my intentions and wishes. I greatly prefer reliance on established law and practice to attempts at what is in effect special legislation."

CODICILS TO WILL OF 4th AUGUST, 1937

In a Codicil to his Will of 4th August, 1937, dated 13th August, 1937, Shaw among other things extended his proposals regarding a new alphabet. The following are the main provisions:—

Shaw revoked the bequests contained in Clauses 18 and 19 with the exception of the power of selection by Harry Batchelor Higgs and Clara Higgs or the survivor of them referred to in Clause 18, and in lieu thereof made the following bequests:—

(i) (a) To Harry Batchelor Higgs the sum of £150 and to his wife Clara Higgs the sum of £150, but if either of them should die before the date of payment referred to in this Will, the legacy of the one so dying should be payable to the survivor.

(b) To Harry Batchelor Higgs and Clara Higgs during their joint lives an annuity of £312 payable to them in equal shares of £156 each, and after the death of either of them the whole of such annuity of £312 should be paid to the survivor of them during his or her life.

(ii) (a) To his chauffeur George Frederick Day the sum of £100 if he should be living at the date of payment referred to.

(b) To George Frederick Day during his life and to his wife after his death if she should survive him, an annuity of £156.

The foregoing bequests or amendments to bequests were to be subject to the provisions of Clause 22 of the 1937 Will (given a page or two back).

In a *second* Codicil to his 1937 Will, dated 24th March, 1940, there were the following amendments or new clauses:—

Clause 16.
The word wages in this clause shall in the cases of servants in a service flat or other dwelling place in which the servants' wages are not paid by me be construed as regular gratuities paid to them by me and I HEREBY REVOKE the bequests to such servants in so far as their wages exceed the said gratuities.

Clause 21.
A sum sufficient to raise £104 to £156.

Clause 25.
A sum sufficient to raise £156-1-4 to £202.

Clause 26.
A sum sufficient to raise £156 to £208.

Clause 29.
A sum sufficient to raise £156 to £208.

Clause 33.
A sum sufficient to raise £365 to £400.

Clause 28.
Eva Glasgow being now deceased the contribution of £25 to her aunt Emily Carroll's funeral expenses may be made to the said Emily's executors instead.

Clauses 29, 30, *and* 32.

I call attention to the deaths of Sebastian Davis, Adelaide Olivia Shaw and Alma von Bank as having made my bequests to them inoperative.

Clause 22 of my said Will shall apply to the foregoing as if it were repeated herein verbatim.

The Will of 4th August, 1937, was superseded by later Wills dated respectively 25th September, 1940, and 17th April, 1946.

The following amendments or additional clauses appeared in a Codicil dated 26th September, 1947:—

1. I BEQUEATH to Mrs Alice Laden if she shall be resident in my service at the time of my death the sum of Two hundred and fifty pounds in addition to any sum to which she may become entitled under Clause 22 of my said Will.

2. I ALSO BEQUEATH to my Housemaid Margaret Cashin if she shall be resident in my service at the time of my death the sum of Fifty pounds in addition to any sum she may become entitled [*sic*] under Clause 22 of my said Will and an annuity of Fifty two pounds a year.

3. UNDER Clause 26 of my said Will I bequeathed to my chauffeur William Day and his wife Margaret Day a legacy of One hundred pounds and an annuity of Two hundred and eight pounds and as I have since enabled him to purchase his dwelling house I REVOKE both such bequests and in lieu thereof bequeath to them jointly an annuity of One hundred and fifty-six pounds to be continued to the survivor of them.

4. I BEQUEATH to Mrs Eleanor (Veronica) Wardrop now residing in London at 10 Park Village West the Swiss calendar watch presented to me by my brother-in-law the late General Hugh Cholmondeley which I have carried on my person ever since.

SHOULD my Secretary Blanche Patch survive me or should I be *non compos* at her decease I direct my Trustee to defray from my estate the expenses of her illness and of the becoming disposal of her remains.

A little later in this Codicil Shaw writes:—

It is possible that the Ministry of Education or other public authority may on its own initiative or at the instance of or in collaboration with the Pitman firm or other private enterprise anticipate my said Will by establishing in our public schools not an entirely new alphabet but an addition to the Twenty-six letters of the Johnsonese alphabet of the unequivocal vowels and missing consonants described in my said Will and given the rest a unique phonetic value besides perhaps discarding some letters as superfluous or ambiguous. In such an event much of Clause (39) and its sequels in my said Will would be more or less contra-indicated and Clause (43) come into operation accordingly. To what extent this may supersede my relevant bequest I must leave to the judgement of my Trustee subject to the following conditions.

The statistical enquiry described in Clause (39) Section 1 of my said Will may be financed and held and its conclusions promulgated in the Press as propaganda in any case.

No scheme of so-called Simplified Spelling (defined as all attempts to spell the English language in the Johnsonese alphabet by means of digraphs diacritical marks or use of two or more letters for one sound) shall be accepted or subsidized by my Trustee under my said Will.

Section 4.

This section I revoke because its object being to record the present pronunciation of the English language I have since ascertained that this has been sufficiently done by the phonetic Bibles of the late founder of the existing Pitman firm.

For the revoked list of books in Section 4. I empower my Trustee at his discretion to substitute the phonetic school primer I have myself designed and deposited in the custody of the Pitman firm.

Section 5 and 6.

These clauses shall stand and are hereby confirmed with the exception that the word . . . transliterations shall apply to only one of my works the purpose and object of the said clauses being the recording of an entirely new alphabet provided for under Section 3 as a sample of how an English text would look as a work of typographical art in an alphabet selected under the foregoing sections.

BERNARD SHAW'S

LAST WILL AND TESTAMENT

[This Will, dated 12th June, 1950, and granted Probate on 20th March, 1951, is given in its entirety, and includes Shaw's final phonetic alphabet proposals.—A.C.].

This is the Last Will and Testament of me George Bernard Shaw of 4 Whitehall Court in the County of London and of Ayot Saint Lawrence in the County of Herts   Author

1. I revoke all Wills and testamentary dispositions heretofore made by me.

2. I appoint the Public Trustee as the sole Executor and Trustee of this my Will who is hereinafter referred to as "my Trustee."

3. I desire that my dead body shall be cremated and its ashes inseparably mixed with those of my late wife now in the custody of the Golders Green Crematorium and in this condition inurned or scattered in the garden of the house in Ayot Saint Lawrence where we lived together for thirty five years unless some other disposal of them should be in the opinion of my Trustee more eligible. Personally I prefer the garden to the cloister.

4. As my religious convictions and scientific views cannot at present be more specifically defined than as those of a believer in Creative Evolution I desire that no public monument or work of art or inscription or sermon or ritual service commemorating me shall suggest that I accepted the tenets peculiar to any established Church or denomination [*sic*] nor take the form of a cross or any other instrument of torture or symbol of blood sacrifice.

5. I bequeath my copyrights performing rights filming rights television rights and all cognate rights now in existence or hereafter to be created with the manuscripts typescripts and other documents in which I have such rights to my Trustee Upon trust to apply the proceeds resulting from the exploitation

499

of such rights or the sale or other lucrative use of such documents as income of my estate.

6. I bequeath all papers and documents in my possession in which I have no copyright and which belong to me as material objects only to my Trustee to be examined as soon as conveniently after my death and divided as nearly as may be into sections as follows:—

Section A. Papers (if any) concerning my late wife's family or affairs.

Section B. Old Diaries account books Bank passbooks paid cheques and their counterfoils expired agreements box office returns and other records of my business operations and personal and domestic expenditure capable of being used by economic or legal historians or by biographers seeking documentary evidence as to prices and practices during the period covered by my lifetime.

Section C. Such letters and documents as might be worth preserving in a public collection such as that of the British Museum.

Section D. All documents needed for the administration of my estate and the carrying out of the provisions of this my Will.

Section E. Uninteresting documents of no use except as waste paper.

I bequeath the contents of these sections to my Trustee with the suggestion that the contents of Section A (if any) be presented to my late wife's niece Mrs Cecily Charlotte Colthurst or should she predecease me to such surviving relative of hers as my Trustee may select; that the contents of Section B be offered to the British Library of Political Science in Clare Market London for the purpose indicated and those of Section C to the British Museum or failing acceptance to any other suitable public collection whilst the contents of Sections D and E can be retained or destroyed by my Trustee as may be expedient. And I declare that if any doubt or disputes should arise as to which papers shall be thus dealt with the question shall be settled by my

Trustee whose decision shall be final Provided Always that my Trustee shall retain all or any of the aforesaid papers and documents for such period as shall in his opinion be desirable.

7. I declare that my Trustee shall manage and deal with my author's rights with all the powers in that behalf of an absolute owner (subject as hereinafter provided) for so long as may prove necessary or expedient during a period ending at the expiration of twenty years from the day of the death of the last survivor of all the lineal descendants of His late Majesty King George the Fifth who shall be living at the time of my death (hereinafter called "the Special period") bearing in mind that the licensing of theatrical performances and especially of cinematographic exhibitions and the like with the collection of royalties thereon will be a principal source of revenue besides continuing my practice in England of manufacturing my literary works at the cost of my estate and causing copies thereof to be sold on commission by a Publisher and shall make such other arrangements with Publishers and others as my Trustee shall think fit Provided always that my Trustee shall not sell assign or alienate such copyrights and other rights or any of them and shall not grant any licence or enter into any agreement or other arrangement in respect of the said copyrights and other rights or any of them which shall irrevocably bind or affect the same for a period exceeding five years (unless with power of revocation) at any one time calculated from the date of the execution of such licence agreement or arrangement but with power to renew or re-grant the same for any period not exceeding the aforesaid period and so on from time to time And I further declare that my Trustee shall not in dealing with any such rights be bound by commercial considerations exclusively it being my desire that he shall give due weight to artistic and public and human considerations to the best of his judgment and counsel.

8. I desire that my Trustee shall do all things and make out of my estate all payments necessary to preserve my aforesaid copyrights or any of them and to procure any renewal of the same that can be obtained And I authorise him to make such payments accordingly And for the guidance of my Trustee I record that with regard to my copyrights in the United States of

America (which are of considerable value) the same do not continue automatically for a period of fifty years from the author's death (as in England and other countries) but continue for a period of twenty eight years only from the date of first publication with a right of renewal for a further period of twenty eight years upon application being made and registered within one . year prior to the expiration of the first term.

9. I direct my Trustee without charging any payment to authorise Mrs Stella Mervyn Beech now residing at 122 Sussex Gardens in the County of London W.2 daughter of the late eminent actress professionally known as Mrs Patrick Campbell to print and publish after my death all or any of the letters written by me to the said eminent actress and in the event of Mrs Beech's death before such publication to give such authority (which is a permission and not an assignment of copyright) to Mrs Patrick Campbell's grandson Patrick Beech and without imposing any trust I desire that the proceeds of such publication should be reserved as far as possible by Mrs Beech or Patrick Beech for the secondary education of Mrs Campbell's grandchildren and their children (such being her own wish) and any legacy duty payable by reason of such authority being given shall be paid out of my estate.

10. Whereas I possess a bust of myself in white marble by the eminent Hungarian sculptor Sigismund Strobl and now in the custody of the London County Council I bequeath it to the as yet unbuilt Shakespeare Memorial National Theatre in London and I direct my Trustee to leave the said bust in the said custody until the opening of the said National Theatre.

11. Whereas certain portraits of myself in painting or sculpture are at present in public galleries or institutions as for example the marble bust by Rodin in the Dublin Municipal Gallery a painting by Augustus John in the Fitzwilliam Museum in Cambridge a bust in bronze by Paul Troubetskoy in the National Gallery of British Art at Millbank in London (known also as The Tate Gallery) and an earlier bronze by the same sculptor in the Foyer of the Theatre Guild at 245 West 52nd Street in New York City I bequeath all of them and any others that may be in the like circumstances at my death to the several institutions in

whose custody they stand save that in the case of the said
Theatre Guild which is not in its nature a permanent institution
I direct that on the Guild's dissolution or the winding up of its
business from any cause during the special period the bust shall
pass to the Metropolitan Museum in New York City or failing
its acceptance for immediate or future exhibition in that institution to the next most eligible (in my Trustee's opinion) American
public collection willing to accept it.

12. I bequeath absolutely the Crayon drawing of the late Harley
Granville-Barker by John Singer Sargent to the Trustees for the
time being of the National Portrait Gallery in London in whose
custody it now is.

13. I bequeath to the National Trust all that is mine of the furniture
cars and other contents except my cars and their appurtenances
of the house garage and garden and grounds in the village of
Ayot Saint Lawrence ordnance mapped as "Shaw's Corner"
now the property of the said National Trust to be preserved as
objects of memorial or artistic interest or disposed of or held in
reserve for the benefit of the said premises or the said village as
to the said Trust may in its judgment seem advisable

14. Whereas it has been my custom to allow the Actor's Orphanage to
receive and retain fees collected by the Collection Bureau of the
Incorporated Society of Authors Playwrights and Composers
for performance in the United Kingdom of my play entitled
"Passion Poison and Petrification" and I desire that such
arrangement shall be continued Now I hereby direct my Trustee
to continue such arrangement accordingly and to permit and
authorise the performance (but without expense to my estate)
of my aforesaid play at any time on the request of the Secretary
of the aforesaid Society or of the aforesaid Orphanage and for
the benefit thereof and to allow the aforesaid Society to continue to collect all fees in respect of the aforesaid play and pay
the same to the aforesaid Orphanage for the benefit thereof and
if any such fees as aforesaid shall come to the hands of my
Trustee then my Trustee shall hold the same upon trust for such
Orphanage absolutely And I declare that the receipt of the
Secretary Treasurer or other officer of the aforesaid Society or
of the aforesaid Orphanage for any such fees as aforesaid shall

be a sufficient discharge for the same and that any legacy duty payable in respect of the same shall be borne by the said Orphanage.

15. I authorise the Fabian Society of London so long as it shall remain an avowedly Socialistic Society and after it shall have ceased so to be if and whilst such avowal shall be contrary to law to print and publish for the benefit of such Society and its Cause all writing [sic] of mine which are or shall be at the time of my death included or with my consent about to be included amongst its publications and I direct my Trustee if necessary to grant to such Society such license as will give effect completely or as far as possible to the provisions of this Clause which however must not be construed as giving the said Society any sole or exclusive property in the copyrights concerned and any legacy duty payable by reason of such license being given shall be borne by the said Society.

16. I empower my Trustee to procure all necessary assistance and expert advice legal artistic literary or other for the discharge of his relevant functions and to pay its cost out of my estate.

17. Provided always And I declare that as my fashion of literary composition often obliges me to make my first draft without full and final regard to temperance of expression generosity or justice to individuals accuracy of history or public propriety generally and to remedy this imperfection by later corrections it is my wish and I charge my Trustee and all others under whose eyes any of my literary works and documents may pass not to publish or quote or suffer to be published or quoted any edition or extracts from my works in which any earlier text shall be substituted either wholly or partly for the text as contained in the printed volumes finally passed by me for press except in the case of texts which I may be prevented by death or disablement from so passing And further that in any critical or biographical notes that may from good reasons make public any passages written by me but subsequently altered or discarded heed be taken both to the credit and the feelings of any surviving person alluded to therein but no suppressions need be made for the purpose of whitewashing my own character or conduct

18. I bequeath to every indoor and outdoor servant or labourer including charwoman chauffeur and gardener (hereinafter

respectively referred to as such servant) of mine (other than any such as may be entitled to an annuity or pension under the provisions of the following clauses of this my Will) who shall be in the exclusive employ or in the case of my residing in a service flat the daily service of me at the time of my death and shall then have been in such employ for a continuous or virtually continuous period (that is to say only interrupted by illness or the like or military service and not by a formal discharge) of not less than seven years a sum equal to one year's wages or periodical gratuity of such servant and to every such servant of mine (other than as aforesaid) who shall be in the exclusive employ of me at the time of my death and shall then have been in my employ for a period of less than seven years but for a continuous or virtually continuous period of not less than three years a sum equal to six months' wages or periodical gratuity of such servant and to every such servant of mine (other than as aforesaid) who shall be in the exclusive employ of me at the time of my death and shall then have been in such employ for a period of less than three years a sum equal to three months' wages or periodical gratuity of such servant all such bequests as aforesaid to be in addition to any wages that may be or become legally due to any such servant as aforesaid Provided always And I further declare that whether the foregoing bequests shall become operative or not my Trustee shall have absolute power to act reasonably and generously in the case of any servant of mine or of my late wife who in the opinion of my Trustee is not sufficiently dealt with under the provisions hereinbefore made and accordingly to make to any such servant any such payment or additional payment out of my Estate as my Trustee shall in his discretion think desirable but without imposing any obligation upon him to make any such payment.

19. I declare that every annuity hereinafter or by any Codicil hereto bequeathed is bequeathed subject to the provisions relating to annuities hereinafter contained

20. I declare that if at the time of my death any person or persons who shall not then be in my employ but shall have formerly been in the employ of me or of my late wife and who shall not otherwise become entitled to any benefit under this my Will and shall

be in receipt of a pension or allowance from me then I bequeath to such person or persons an Annuity equal in amount to the amount of such pension or allowance of which such former servant shall be then in receipt

21. I bequeath to my retired gardener Harry Batchelor Higgs an annuity of One hundred and fifty six pounds and I direct my Trustee to see to it that the monument I have had erected in Windlesham Cemetery to him and his late wife shall on his death at the cost of my estate have its inscription completed and thereafter be cared for by the Cemetery authorities in consideration of an appropriate capital sum.

22. I bequeath to Emma Hodgman formerly in my service as Housemaid and now or lately resident at 130 Windmill Road in Gillingham Kent an annuity of Fifty two pounds.

23. I bequeath to Mrs Margaret Bilton now or lately residing at 48 Wilmer Road Tunbridge Wells and formerly in my service as housekeeper an annuity of One hundred and fifty six pounds to be continued after her death to her daughter Alice Bilton if surviving and on the respective deaths of the said Margaret Bilton and the said Alice Bilton I direct my Trustee to pay or apply for the benefit of the survivor of them or to such other person or persons and in such manner as he shall in his discretion think fit a sum of Twenty five pounds out of the capital of my Residuary Estate for or towards the funeral expenses incurred consequent on their respective deaths.

24. Whereas the annuities hereby bequeathed to Harry Batchelor* Frederick William Day and Margaret Day Mrs Margaret Bilton and Alice Bilton and Emma Hodgman are provided for as from my death by the Will of my late wife Charlotte Frances Shaw my bequests to them herein shall be subject to such reductions and increases as may bring their benefits to the same level as if only one Will and that the most favourable to them shall come into force at my decease.

* The surname, Higgs, was inadvertently omitted by the calligrapher. It may or may not be regarded as of some significance that Shaw did not notice this when he checked through and signed this Will on June 12th, 1950.

25. I bequeath to Mrs Georgina Musters the daughter of my mother's half sister Arabella Gillmore an annuity of Three hundred and sixty five pounds.

26. I bequeath to Eames Bagenal Rogers now or lately residing at 1249 Yale Street Santa Monica California the son of my mother's late half-sister Charlotte Rogers and to his wife after his death if she shall survive him an annuity of Fifty two pounds.

27. I bequeath to Georgina Meredith now residing at 34 Barrow Street in the City of Dublin daughter of my mother's late half-sister Charlotte Rogers an annuity of Fifty two pounds.

28. I bequeath to Ethel Gordon Walters at present residing at 34 Queens Gardens in the County of London W.1 daughter of my first cousin the late James Cockaigne Shaw an annuity of Two hundred and thirty four pounds.

29. I bequeath to my former housemaid Mrs Ronald Smith (born Margaret Cashin) a deferred annuity of Fifty two pounds a year should she survive or be separated from her husband Ronald Smith or a later husband if any.

30. I bequeath to my chauffeur and gardener Frederick William Day and his Wife Margaret Day jointly an annuity of One hundred and fifty six pounds to be continued in full to the survivor of them.

31. I bequeath to Eva Maria Schneider now residing at 196 Rivermead Court Hurlingham London S.W.6 an annuity of One hundred and twenty pounds in remembrance of her devoted services to my late sister Lucy.

32. I bequeath to my Secretary Blanche Patch Spinster an annuity of Five hundred pounds.

33. The following provisions shall apply to all annuities hereby or by any Codicil hereto bequeathed—

(1) The bequest of an annuity shall become operative only if the named annuitant shall not at my death have done or suffered anything whereby the bequeathed annuity or any part of it would become vested in or payable to some other person or persons and shall continue only until the annuitant shall become bankrupt or assign or charge the said annuity or any part thereof or do or suffer anything whereby the said

annuity or any part thereof would become vested in or payable to any other person and in the event of any annuity not becoming or ceasing to become payable by the effect of this subclause my Trustee may at his absolute discretion during the rest of the life of the annuitant apply out of the income of my residuary trust funds hereinafter defined any sums not exceeding in any year the amount of the relevant annuity for the benefit of the annuitant and for the purposes of sub clause (3) of this clause any sums which my Trustee decides to apply as aforesaid in any year shall be treated as if the aggregate of the same was an annuity.

(2) Every annuity shall be payable by equal quarterly payments payable in advance the first payment to become payable as at my death and to be paid as soon thereafter as my Trustee is in a position to pay the same.

(3) Every annuity shall unless and until a sum shall have been appropriated to provide for the same as hereinafter authorised or until the expiration of twenty one years from my death or the previous cesser whether partial or complete of the trust of the balance of the income of my Residuary Trust Funds hereinafter contained be payable only out of the income of my Residuary Trust Funds in each year from my death available for the payment thereof and if the income of my Residuary Trust Funds shall be insufficient to pay the said annuities in full the annuitant shall be entitled to be paid any capital sum in satisfaction of his or her annuity as a legacy but the said anuity shall abate pro rata for such period and to such an extent as shall be necessary having regard to the insufficiency of such income as aforesaid but if at the end of any year from my death there should be income available (after paying the full amounts of the said annuities for the time being payable for that year) to pay the amounts or part of the amounts by which the annuities then still payable had previously abated my Trustee shall out of such income pay the said amounts or such parts of the said amounts and rateably in proportion to such last mentioned annuities as such income shall be sufficient to satisfy. Upon the expiration of twenty one years from my death or the

cesser whether partial or complete of the said trust of the balance of the said income the annuities then subsisting if not then provided for under sub-clause (4) hereof and any amounts by which such annuities had previously abated if not made good shall be a charge on the capital of my Residuary Trust Funds.

(4) My Trustee may in his discretion at any time provide for the payment of the annuities for the time being subsisting by appropriating and retaining out of my Residuary Trust Funds and investing in the name of my Trustee in any of the investments hereinafter authorised (with power for my Trustee to vary or transpose such investments for others hereby authorised) such a sum as when so invested shall at the time of investment be sufficient by means of the income thereof to pay the said annuities And I declare that such appropriation as aforesaid shall be complete provision for such annuities and that in case the income of the appropriated fund shall at any time prove insufficient for payment in full of such annuities resort may be had to the capital thereof from time to time to make good such deficiency and the surplus (if any) of the income of the said fund from time to time remaining after payment of such annuities shall form part of the income of my Residuary Trust Funds And I declare that as and when any annuity provided for by means of the appropriated fund as aforesaid shall cease to be payable so much of the appropriated fund as my Trustee shall not think it necessary to retain to answer any remaining annuities shall revert to the capital of my Residuary Trust Funds.

(5) My Trustee shall have power if in his absolute discretion he thinks fit during the lives or life of any of the annuitants out of the income of my Residuary Trust Funds in any year not required for payment of such of the annuities as shall for the time being be payable or if he thinks fit out of the capital of my Residuary Trust Funds to make such additional payment to the annuitants for the time being living as in his opinion may be required to make good to such annuitants any decrease in the values of their annuities which shall be

due to an increase [*sic*]* in the purchasing power of the £ sterling after the date of this my Will.

34. I declare that all legacies (whether pecuniary or specific) and annuities bequeathed by this my Will or any Codicil shall be paid without deduction of legacy duty or any other duties payable in respect of the same and that the said duties including any duty chargeable by reason of an annuity arising on or being increased by the death of any annuitant shall be paid out of my real and personal estate hereinafter devised and bequeathed by way of residue.

35. I devise and bequeath all my real and personal estate not otherwise specifically disposed of by this my Will or any Codicil hereto and all property over which I have general power of appointment unto my Trustee Upon trust that my Trustee shall (subject to the power of postponing the sale and conversion thereof hereinafter contained) sell my real estate and sell call in or otherwise convert into money as much as may be needed of my personal estate (other than any copyrights which as provided by Clause 7 of this my Will are not to be sold) to increase the ready monies of which I may be possessed at my death to an amount sufficient to pay my funeral and testamentary expenses and debts estate duty legacy duty and all the duties payable on my death in respect of my estate or the bequests hereby made free of duty (other than testamentary expenses) and the legacies bequeathed by this my Will or any Codicil hereto or to make such other payments or investments or change of investments as in his opinion shall be advisable in the interest of my estate and shall invest the residue of such monies in manner hereinafter authorised And shall stand possessed of the said residuary trust moneys and the investments for the time being representing the same and all other investments for the time being forming part of my residuary estate (herein called my Residuary Trust Funds) and the annual income thereof Upon the trusts hereby declared of and concerning the same.

(1) To institute and finance a series of inquiries to ascertain or estimate as far as possible the following statistics (a) the

* Obviously this should read 'decrease'.

number of extant persons who speak the English language and write it by the established and official alphabet of 26 letters (hereinafter called Dr. Johnson's Alphabet) (b) how much time could be saved per individual scribe by the substitution for the said Alphabet of an Alphabet containing at least 40 letters (hereinafter called the Proposed British Alphabet) enabling the said language to be written without indicating single sounds by groups of letters or by diacritical marks instead of by one symbol for each sound (c) how many of these persons are engaged in writing or printing English at any and every moment in the world; (d) on these factors to estimate the time and labour wasted by our lack of at least 14 unequivocal single symbols; (e) to add where possible to the estimates of time lost or saved by the difference between Dr. Johnson's Alphabet and the Proposed British Alphabet estimates of the loss of income in British and American currency. The enquiry must be confined strictly to the statistical and mathematical problems to be solved without regard to the views of professional and amateur phoneticians, etymologists, Spelling Reformers, patentees of universal languages, inventors of shorthand codes for verbatim reporting or rival alphabets, teachers of the established orthography, disputants about pronunciation, or any of the irreconcilables whose wranglings have overlooked and confused the single issue of labour saving and made change impossible during the last hundred years. The inquiry must not imply any approval or disapproval of the Proposed British Alphabet by the inquirers or by my Trustee.

(2) To employ a phonetic expert to transliterate my play entitled 'Androcles & the Lion' into the Proposed British Alphabet assuming the pronunciation to resemble that recorded of His Majesty our late King George V. and sometimes described as Northern English.

(3) To employ an artist-calligrapher to fair-copy the transliteration for reproduction by lithography photography or any other method that may serve in the absence of printers' types.

(4) To advertise and publish the transliteration with the original Dr. Johnson's lettering opposite the transliteration page by

page and a glossary of the two alphabets at the end and to present copies to public libraries in the British Isles, the British Commonwealth, the American States North and South and to national libraries everywhere in that order.

36. I desire my Trustee to bear in mind that the Proposed British Alphabet does not pretend to be exhaustive as it contains only sixteen vowels whereas by infinitesimal movements of the tongue countless different vowels can be produced all of them in use among speakers of English who utter the same vowels no oftener than they make the same finger prints. Nevertheless they can understand one another's speech and writing sufficiently to converse and correspond: for instance, a graduate of Trinity College Dublin has no difficulty in understanding a graduate of Oxford University when one says that "the sun rohze," and the other "the san raheoze" nor are either of them puzzled when a peasant calls his childhood his "chawldid." For a university graduate calls my native country Awlind.

37. It is possible that the Ministry of Education may institute the inquiry and adopt the Proposed British Alphabet to be taught in the schools it controls in which event subsection 1 of Clause 35 foregoing and its relevant sequels will be contra-indicated as superfluous and Clause 40 come into operation accordingly but the adoption must be exact and no account taken of the numerous alternative spelling Reforms now advocated or hereafter proposed.

38. I hereby devise and bequeath the balance of the income of my Residuary Trust Funds not required during the period of twenty one years after my death to pay the annuities hereby or by any Codicil hereto bequeathed or for any other purpose upon which income of my Residuary Trust Funds may under the trusts hereinbefore contained be applicable Upon trust during the special period but subject to cesser as hereinafter provided To apply the same as follows:—

A. To remunerate the services and defray the expenses incidental to these proceedings and generally to the launching advertising and propaganda of the said British Alphabet.

B. To acquire by employment purchase or otherwise the copyrights and patents (if any) created by or involved in the designing and manufacture of the said Alphabet or the publication of the works printed in it without exploiting the said rights or for commercial profit.

C. To wind-up the enterprise when the aforesaid steps have been taken or if and when its official adoption or general vogue shall make further recourse to my estate and action on the part of my Trustee in respect of this charitable Trust superfluous

39. Pending the operation of the foregoing clause I direct that my Trustee shall for the said period of twenty one years from my death accumulate the said balance of the income of my Residuary Trust Funds in the way of compound interest by investing the same and the resulting income thereof from time to time in any investment in which my Residuary Trust Funds are authorised to be invested.

40. Subject to the trusts hereinbefore declared of my Residuary Trust Funds and the income thereof or if and so far as such trusts shall fail through judicial decision or any other cause beyond my Trustee's control my Trustee shall stand possessed of my Residuary Trust Funds and the income thereof but subject to a charge on the capital as well as the income thereof for payment of such of the annuities hereby bequeathed as shall be subsisting Upon trust as to one third thereof for the Trustees of the British Museum in acknowledgment of the incalculable value to me of my daily resort to the Reading Room of that Institution at the beginning of my career as to one third of the same Upon trust for the National Gallery of Ireland and as to the remaining one third of the same Upon trust for the Royal Academy of Dramatic Art at 61 Gower Street in the County of London and should any of these three institutions be permanently closed at the date when the trust to accumulate the said balance of income of my Residuary Trust Funds shall cease the others or other shall succeed to its share and if more than one equally.

41. I authorise my Trustee to postpone for such period as he shall in his discretion think fit the sale and conversion of all or any part of my real and personal estate hereinbefore devised and bequeathed in trust for sale and conversion notwithstanding the

same may be of a perishable or wearing out nature (but if any part of my estate shall be of a reversionary nature the same shall not be sold or converted into money until it falls into possession unless my Trustee shall think it probable that a loss will arise to my estate by postponing the sale and conversion thereof) and to retain any stocks shares or securities of which I may be possessed at my death whether fully paid up or not (but my real estate shall be impressed with the quality of personal estate from the time of my death) And I declare that the net income arising from any part of my real or personal estate previous to the sale or conversion thereof shall as well during the first year after my death as afterwards be applied in the same manner as if the same were income arising from such investments as are by this my Will authorised but that no reversionary or other property forming part of my estate not actually producing income shall be treated as producing income.

42. Should my Trustee have occasion to realise any of my investments in the shares and loan stocks of Friendly Societies not quoted on the Stock Exchange and therefore often sold by Executors and others at less than their value I direct my Trustee not to dispose of them without first offering them to the Directors of the said Societies they being commonly ready to liquidate such stocks at their face value.

43. I declare that my Trustee shall be at liberty to grant time or other indulgence to any debtor in respect of any unsecured personal loans made by me and (in particular when the loan has not in his judgment been a matter of business) to forego payment of and absolutely release all or any part of the amount of any such debts or loan without being answerable for any loss which may thereby arise and with regard to any such debts owing to me or claims I may have against any person or persons I express it to be my wish that my Trustee shall in the exercise of the aforesaid power deal kindly or leniently with all such debtors or other person or persons where a strict observation of the law would involve manifest injustice hardship or meanness (but no distinction in this respect is to be made in favour of my relatives as distinguished from other persons) And I also declare that certain bequests I have made in former Wills in favour of

various persons I have now omitted to make not on account of any change of feeling on my part towards them but because deaths marriages and change of circumstances have rendered such bequests unnecessary and I also record my regret that my means are not sufficient to provide for material pledges of my regard for the many friends who as colleagues in the Socialistic movement or as artists co-operating with me in the performance of my plays or otherwise have not only made my career possible but hallowed it with kindly human relations.

44. I declare that all monies liable to be invested under my Will may be invested in any investment or securities for the time being authorised by law for the investment of trust funds.

45. I authorise my Trustee to apportion as my Trustee shall think fit among the trust premises any charges deductions or outgoings whatsoever and to determine whether any money shall for the purpose of this my Will be considered annual income or not and the power of appropriation conferred by the administration of Estates Act 1925 shall be exercisable by my Trustee whether acting as personal representative or trustee and without any of the consents made requisite by that Act.

46. I declare that the Executor and Trustee for the time being of this my Will may instead of acting personally employ and pay a Solicitor Accountant Agent Literary Executor Bibliographer or any other person or persons to transact any business or do any act required to be done in connection with the administration of my estate or the trusts hereby declared including the receipt and payment of money and the keeping and preparation of books and accounts And I express it to be my wish (but without imposing any obligation) that my present English Solicitors the firm of J. N. Mason & Co of 41-44 Temple Chambers in the City of London my American Attorneys the firm of Stern & Reubens of 1 East 45th Street in New York City my Accountant Walter Smee now practising at 22 Shaftesbury Avenue West Central London, my British Publishers Messrs Constable & Co of 10 Orange Street in the County of London my Printers Messrs R. & R. Clark of Brandon Street Edinburgh, my present Secretary Blanche Patch, My Biblio-

grapher Fritz Erwin Loewenstein Doctor of Philosophy and Founder of the London Shaw Society (now residing at Torca Cottage in Saint Albans) whose knowledge of my literary affairs and interest in my reputation qualify him exceptionally for such employment shall be consulted and employed by my Executor and Trustee whenever their assistance may be desirable and available and that the Incorporated Society of Authors Playwrights and Composers shall continue to be employed as my Theatrical Agents on the special conditions now established between us. To this I add that my country Solicitor Ivo L. Currall of 2 Gordon Chambers 1 Upper George Street Luton in the County of Bedford is also familiar with my local affairs.

47. Having been born a British subject in Ireland in 1856 subsequently registered as a citizen of Eire and finally privileged to remain a British subject by the Home Secretary's letter dated the twenty seventh day of June One thousand nine hundred and forty nine I declare that my domicile of choice is English and desire that my Will be construed and take effect according to English law.

In Witness whereof I have hereunto set my hand to this and the thirteen preceding sheets of paper this twelfth day of June One thousand nine hundred and fifty.

Signed and acknowledged by the said George Bernard Shaw the Testator as and for his last Will and Testament in the presence of us who in his presence at his request and in the presence of each other all being present at the same time have hereunto subscribed our names as witnesses	*G. Bernard Shaw*

> *E. Marjorie White* Married woman
>   22 Compton Avenue, Luton, Beds.
> *Harold O. White*, Master Printer,
>   22 Compton Avenue, Luton, Beds.

This is the last Will and Testament

of me George Bernard Shaw of 4 Whitehall Court in the County of London and of Ayot Saint Lawrence in the County of Herts Author

1. I revoke all Wills and testamentary dispositions heretofore made by me.

2. I appoint the Public Trustee as the sole Executor and Trustee of this my Will who is hereinafter referred to as "my Trustee".

3. I desire that my dead body shall be cremated and its ashes inseparably mixed with those of my late wife now in the custody of the Golders Green Crematorium and in this condition inurned or scattered in the garden of the house in Ayot Saint Lawrence where we lived together for thirty five years unless some other disposal of them should be in the opinion of my Trustee more eligible. Personally I prefer the garden to the cloister.

4. As my religious convictions and scientific views cannot at present be more specifically defined than as those of a believer in Creative Evolution I desire that no public monument or work of art or inscription or sermon or ritual service commemorating me shall suggest that I accepted the tenets peculiar to any established Church or denomination nor take the form of a cross or any other instrument of torture or symbol of blood sacrifice.

17. Having been born a British subject in Ireland in 1856 subsequently registered as a citizen of Eire and finally privileged to remain a British subject by the Home Secretary's letter dated the twenty seventh day of June One thousand nine hundred and forty nine I declare that my domicile of choice is English and desire that my Will be construed and take effect according to English law. In witness whereof I have hereunto set my hand to this and the thirteen preceding sheets of paper this twelfth day of June One thousand nine hundred and fifty.

Signed and acknowledged by the said George Bernard Shaw the Testator as and for his last Will and Testament in the presence of us who in his presence at his request and in the presence of each other all being present at the same time have hereunto subscribed our names as witnesses

G. Bernard Shaw

E. Marjorie White Married woman
22 Compton Avenue, Luton, Beds.
Harold O. White, Master Printer
22 Compton Avenue, Luton, Beds.

Extracts from the first and last pages of Shaw's last Will (his "crowning masterpiece" as he called it).

MR JUSTICE HARMAN'S JUDGEMENT IN 1957, HOLDING INVALID THE ALPHABET TRUSTS IN SHAW'S WILL

[From *The Times Law Report*, February 20, 1957 (in *The Times* of February 21st), by kind permission of the editor.]

HIGH COURT OF JUSTICE

CHANCERY DIVISION

IN RE SHAW'S WILL TRUSTS: PUBLIC TRUSTEE v. DAY AND OTHERS

Before MR JUSTICE HARMAN

His LORDSHIP delivered a reserved judgment, holding invalid certain trusts relating to the alteration of the alphabet, on this summons, by which the Public Trustee, as executor and trustee of the Will of Mr George Bernard Shaw, who died on November 2, 1950, and whose Will, dated June 12, 1950, was proved on March 20, 1951, asked questions arising on the Will, several of which related to purposes connected with the alteration of the alphabet.

Mr Robert Lazarus appeared for the Public Trustee; Mr Mark Cockle for Mr and Mrs F. W. Day; Mr Charles Russell, Q.C., and Mr P. W. E. Taylor for the trustees of the British Museum and for the Royal Academy of Dramatic Art; Mr K. E. Elphinstone for the Governors and Guardians of the National Gallery of Ireland; and Mr E. Milner Holland, Q.C., and Mr Denys Buckley for the Attorney-General.

JUDGMENT

MR JUSTICE HARMAN, reading his judgment, said: All his life long Bernard Shaw was an indefatigable reformer. He was already well known to the English public when the present century dawned as novelist, pamphleteer, playwright, and during the ensuing half

518

century he continued to act as a kind of "itching powder" to the British public, to the English speaking peoples, and indeed to an even wider audience, reminding them of their follies, their foibles, and their fallacies, and bombarding them with such a combination of paradox and wit that he became before his death a kind of oracle—the Shavian oracle: he thus enjoyed the rare distinction of adding a word to the language.* Many of his projects he lived to see gain acceptance and be carried into effect and become normal.

It was natural that he should be interested in English orthography and pronunciation. These were obvious targets for the reformer. It was as difficult for the native to defend the one as for the foreigner to compass the other. The evidence showed that for many years Shaw had been interested in the subject. Perhaps his best known excursion in this field is *Pygmalion* in which the protagonist was a professor of phonetics. This was produced as a play in 1914 and had held the stage ever since and had invaded the world of film. It was indeed a curious reflection that this same work, tagged with versicles which I suppose Shaw would have detested, and tricked out with music, which he would have eschewed (see the preface to *Admirable Bashville*), was now charming huge audiences on the other side of the Atlantic and had given birth to the present proceedings. He (his Lordship) was told that the receipts from this source had enabled the executor at length to get on terms with the enormous death duties payable on the estate, thus bringing the interpretation of the Will into the realm of practical politics.

"UNFORTUNATE MIXTURE OF STYLES"

The testator, his LORDSHIP continued, whatever his other qualifications, was the master of a pellucid style, and the reader embarked

* The precise origin of the word 'Shavian' was given by the late Sir Sydney Cockerell in a letter to *The Times Literary Supplement* of 29th July, 1960, which he kindly permitted me to quote:—

SIR: It may interest your readers to know how the word shavian came about. William Morris, who died in 1896, told me a story one day of an English editor named Shaw of some Greek or Latin classic. This same classic was subsequently edited by a famous German scholar. The English editor looked eagerly through the Latin notes in the hope that some note of his own might be quoted. At last he came upon quite a long passage in a footnote, but it was followed by the words *sic shavius sed inepte.*

I told this story to GBS, who immediately adopted this Latin form of his name.

SYDNEY COCKERELL, Kew.

on his Will confident that he would at least find no difficulty in understanding the objects which the testator had in mind. This document, moreover, was evidently originally the work of a skilled equity draftsman. Unfortunately, it bore ample internal evidence of being in part the testator's own work. The two styles, as ever, made an unfortunate mixture. It was always a marriage of incompatibles: the delicate testamentary machinery devised by the conveyancer could but suffer when subjected to the *cacoethes scribendi* of the author, even though the latter's language, if it stood alone, might be a literary masterpiece. It was a long and complicated document made when the testator was already 94 years old* and it was rather youthful exuberance than the hesitations of old age that marred its symmetry.

The directions in clause 35 connected with what the testator called "the proposed British alphabet" prescribed no limit of time, but clause 38 showed that not more than the income of the first 21 years after the death was to be devoted to these purposes.

It appeared that the residuary estate was likely to consist of nothing but the copyrights and the royalties arising out of them. These were to devolve, at the end of the 21-year period, on the ultimate residuary legatees, the British Museum, the Royal Academy of Dramatic Art, and the Irish National Gallery, in equal shares. The first two of these now claimed that what might be called the "alphabet trusts" were entirely void and that the claimants were entitled therefore to come into their inheritance at once and to stop the accumulation of income. The grounds of this claim were, first that the trusts, being for an object and not for a person, were void trusts; secondly, that they were void for uncertainty. The Attorney-General appeared as *parens patriae* to uphold the trusts as charitable, and counsel for the Attorney-General, at his (his Lordship's) request, also supported the proposition of the executor that, even if not charitable, these trusts, not being tainted with the vice of perpetuity (as it was called) were a valid exercise by a man of his power of disposing of his own money as he thought fit. The claimants retort that these trusts were not charitable trusts.

---

* This is not strictly accurate. It was completed (signed and witnessed) on 12th June, 1950, six weeks *before* Shaw's 94th birthday, and most of it must have been drafted some months prior to this.

OBJECTS OF TRUSTS

The first of the alphabet trusts was to find out by inquiry how much time could be saved by persons who spoke the English language and wrote it by the use of the proposed British alphabet and so to show the extent of the time and labour wasted by the use of our present alphabet and, if possible, further to state this waste of time in terms of loss of money.

The second was to transliterate one of the author's plays, *Androcles and the Lion*, into the proposed British alphabet, assuming a given pronunciation of English, and to advertise and publish the trans-literation, in a page-by-page version, in the proposed alphabet on one side and the existing alphabet on the other, and by the dissemination of copies, and in addition by advertisement and propaganda to persuade the Government or the public or the English-speaking world to adopt it. This was described by the Attorney-General as a useful piece of research beneficial to the public because it would facilitate the education of the young and the teaching of the language and show a way to save time and so money.

It was suggested that the objects were charitable as being for education. The research and propaganda enjoined by the testator seemed to him (his Lordship) merely to tend to the increase of public knowledge in a certain respect—namely, the saving of time and money by the use of the proposed alphabet. There was no element of teaching or education combined with this, nor did the propaganda element in the trusts tend to do more than to persuade the public that the adoption of the new script would be "a good thing," and that was not education. Therefore he (his Lordship) rejected that element.

"POLITICAL PURPOSES"

It was very difficult to ascertain what were the limits of purposes held to be beneficial to the community "in a way which the law regarded as charitable." Who was to say whether this project was beneficial? That on the face of it was a most controversial question. He felt unable to say that the research to be done was a task of general utility. The testator was convinced, and set out to convince the world; but the fact that he considered the proposed reform beneficial did not make it so, any more than the fact that he described the trust as charitable convinced the Court that it was.

The objects of the ABC trusts were analogous to trusts for political purposes. They would involve a change in the law of the land. Such objects had never been considered charitable.

As to the question of uncertainty, once an object was charitable the law would provide the means of carrying it into effect by a scheme and it seemed to him (his Lordship) that the fact that the testator had not selected any particular form of alphabet for his experiment would not be fatal if the experiment itself constituted a charitable object.

The question of certainty became far more difficult if there was no charitable intent. The objection here was that the Public Trustee would not know how to direct his appointed statistical and phonetic experts to work.

His Lordship then considered the nature of the proposed alphabet, and stated that he would not have considered the testator's omission to choose a particular form of alphabet fatal, and continued: Could, then, this project be upheld apart from charity? He said that he felt bound to say at once that, as the authorities stood, he did not think that he was at liberty to hold that it could.

He then considered Houston v. Burns ([1918] A.C. 337), and In re Astor ([1952] Ch. 534). An object, he said, could not complain to the Court, which therefore could not control the trust and therefore would not allow it to continue. He felt some reluctance to come to that conclusion. He agreed at once that if the persons to take in remainder were unascertainable the Court was deprived of any means of controlling such a trust, but if, as here, the persons taking the ultimate residue were ascertained, he did not feel the force of this objection.

"INVALID AND MUST FAIL"

The result was that the alphabet trusts were invalid and must fail. It seemed that their author suspected as much, hence a jibe of his in them about failure by judicial decision. His Lordship answered that it was the fault, not of the law, but of the testator, who failed almost for the first time in his life either to grasp the legal problem or to make up his mind what he wanted.

Solicitors: Messrs J. N. Mason and Co.; Messrs Russell, Jones and Walker; Messrs Charles Russell and Co.; Messrs Bentley, Stokes and Lowless; Treasury Solicitor.

Editorial Note.—I will not add to the comment on the fore-going Judgement made by Barbara Smoker in her essay except to say that Sir James Pitman and some others felt that Mr Justice Harman had pre-judged the possible benefit in schools, and the national and individual saving of time, energy, and expense, which Shaw's alphabetic concepts might bring. They felt that these benefits would, in fact, constitute a 'charity' to society, as also would the free distribution to public libraries of copies of *Androcles and the Lion* transliterated in a new phonetic alphabet. On the more specifically legal aspects, their view was that Shaw's Will did set up a valid educational trust, and possibly also a limited and certain objective which, if it had been carried out, would have constituted a once-for-all completion of a testamentary disposition—i.e of a finite legacy of a memorial character. They therefore felt that the statistical enquiry Shaw provided for should have been carried out in order to produce evidence substantiating or refuting the saving in time, etc., Shaw had envisaged. However, the fact that the production of a new alphabet *was* eventually proceeded with, and a special edition of *Androcles and the Lion* translated into it published, has given a considerable measure of satis-faction to all interested in Shaw's ever stimulating ideas.

APPENDIX

Addendum to Chapter on War and Peace

In November, 1915, Shaw wrote a preface to a proposed reprint of his *Common Sense About the War* pamphlet. The reprint was never proceeded with, but the preface was set up in type, and a proof copy exists in the British Museum Library. It is an important document which appears to have escaped the attention of previous biographers, and I am glad therefore to give the chief points in it now, in supplementation of the details of the *Common Sense* pamphlet given in the chapter on War and Peace. Reference is made to the matter forming this Appendix near the foot of page 354.

Shaw in this preface quoted one of his critics (in fact, it was Henry Arthur Jones) who had gravely informed him that he (*i.e.* Jones) looked upon England as his mother, and regarded Shaw as having "kicked her on her deathbed". Shaw vigorously denied that he had done anything of the sort, pointing out that many of his criticisms of the Cabinet, the General Staff, the War Office, and the Foreign Office, etc., had by 1915 been taken up by numerous other people. He denied that England had betrayed her allies by failing to meet her obligations to them, or that he had ever implied that she had. He also denied that England had blindly and lazily allowed herself to be caught napping by the German army— on the contrary—Britain had gone beyond her obligations to France, and had been fully prepared for war during the previous five years.

Shaw added that when he had "made a present to the Germans of the easily answered electioneering official case for the war", and had stated the *real* case for it "stripped of every controvertible pretext", he had demonstrated the weakness of Germany's position as "the breakers of the peace of the West of Europe". As a result, he had been initially *condemned* by the Germans, not praised, and even told by them that his career as a playwright in Germany was finished for ever.

But, Shaw explained, the Germans had found to their surprise that his *Common Sense* pamphlet had been frantically denounced by the *British* press as pro-German, and they had then—and only then—"seized their advantage very intelligently", claiming him, Shaw, as on their side. This completely erroneous and distorted view of him as pro-German had then given added fuel to certain panicking British journalists and fanned their flames into the grossest travesty of the truth. Shaw also claimed that in 1915 his pamphlet still had "its work to do in getting rid of the silly and dishonorable travesty of the most formidable empire on earth [*i.e.* the British Empire] as the feeble and credulous dupe of a stage villain" [*i.e.* the Kaiser].

A further reason Shaw gave in this draft preface for having put the German case as well as the British was in order to appease American and Swedish opinion, which was incensed at what was regarded as hypocrisy on Britain's part over their loss of cargoes. Shaw pointed out that Britain's searching of American and Swedish trading vessels and occasional confiscations of their cargoes had led to strained relations with those countries which badly needed "some relief from the irritating anthems in our own praise with which we accompanied our seizure of their copper". He added that Britain's alliance with Russia did not include sympathy with Russia's extremely autocratic policies in Finland and elsewhere.

Shaw averred that his pamphlet had been written to suggest neither that all was ill with Britain, nor that all was well—but only to introduce some *facts* and *common sense* into the emotional and hysterical thinking which was rife in the early part of the war.

His attitude was to condemn "the childish romantic attitude that delights in figuring one's country as a persecuted, abandoned, duped, betrayed heroine, or as a little sailor in the melodrama fighting at fearful odds against a treacherous giant". He thought it monstrous that aspersions should be thrown by "the romantic fancies of England's least instructed patriots on our honorable fulfilling of our obligations to France". Shaw also stoutly defended Lord Haldane (who had been denounced by some sections of the public as a German spy!) as the man to whom Britain's preparedness for the war was in fact chiefly due. However, he also explained that Lord Haldane and Mr Churchill had not vindicated themselves regarding preparation for the war until some time after he had published *Common Sense*.

Another aim of the pamphlet, he explained in the preface, was to explode the legend that German militarism and army organisation were far superior to ours—even invincible. But, as he had pointed out, the partial unpreparedness of Germany had been proved when her army had been held up for ten days before Antwerp by a mere handful of Allied horse marines.

Shaw declared that *Common Sense* had been written with a view all the time to its effect abroad—especially in Germany, Sweden, and America—and without any pandering to the feelings of British readers of the type who "when they come upon any writing that does not flatter them and confirm all the outrageous nonsense they are said to have been talking, repudiate it furiously as unpatriotic".

Shaw also condemned the excessive censorship of news, which had resulted in our people, and our allies, filling up the void with their imaginations. Shaw observed: "I wish I could persuade the two Cabinets that the most awkward human realities do less mischief than the sugariest idealisations when they proceed from imaginations maddened by war."

Finally, Shaw emphasised that *The Times* and other newspapers had changed their criticism of his views to support, after the wild emotionalism of the first few months of the war.

INDEX

INDEX

NOTE: The word '(general)' after an entry indicates general references to a subject when specific aspects of it are listed separately.

Illustrations of subjects are included where possible and indicated by figures in italic type, the page numbers opposite or between which the illustration appears being given.

The Table of Contents and List of Illustrations should also be consulted if necessary, the entry for the chapter on general political themes on pages xv–xvii being especially detailed.

"Abatement" of annuities, 481, 508, 509
abbreviations (in spelling), 469, 471
ABC, the, 413–72, 522
abdication, 316, 321
Abel, 53
ability to govern, tests of, 338
abolishing, abolition (of war), 376, 400, 408
Abraham, 133
abroad, 332, 411
absolutism, 190
abstinence, 17, 234, 253
'abstract cause' (in law), 430, 433
absurdity, 376, 400, 401, 460, 465
Abyssinia, 391, 393, 402
'academic' attitude, 194, 219, 318
"Academies of Letters", 483
accentuated letters (in printing), 467
acceptance of many of Shaw's ideas, 519
accounts, 515
accountants, 458, 462, 515
account books, 500
acquirements, acquired capacity, ability, 339
actors, actresses, 339, 418, 427, 476, 482, 483, 491, 492, 502
Actors' Orphanage, 503–4
accuracy, 417, 473, 504
Acropolis, the, 369
address, notifications of Shaw's addresses, 7
Adelphi Terrace, London, 7, 475
Adler, Dr Friedrich, 188–90, 192–3, 195
Administration of Estates Act (1925), 494, 515
Admirable Bashville, The, 519

Admiralty, the, 355
adoption, political, 168
adulation, x
adult(s), adulthood, 86, 87, 257, 270, 442–3, 459
Adult Suffrage, 313, 324, 326, 331
Advanced Socialism for Intelligent People (1909), 243–4, 343
adventure, 307–8
adventurers, 236
Adventures of the Black Girl in her Search for God, The, 200–1
advert-ising, -isements, 420, 440, 466–7, 512, 521
advice, 368
advisers to the Public Trustee, 516
aeroplanes, airplanes, 389, 392, 394
Aeschylus, 36, 52
aesthetes, aesthetic, 419, 446, 469, 471
affection, 393, 481
Africa, 108, 135, 389, 470
age (old, middle, etc.), 360, 405–7, 410, 480, 520
agitation, agitators, 375, 427
agon-y, -ies, 392
aggression (military, international, etc.), 359, 369, 375, 396
agricult-ure, -ural, 207, 276, 309, 321, 333
aims of war, 376
A la Carte (revue), 61, 62–3, 69–70, 75n
Albert Hall, the, 236, 238
Albert Memorial, the, 471
aldermen, 339
Alexander, F. Matthias, 490
Alexander the Great, 377
algebra, 482
Algeciras, 367

Algiers, 109
Allen, C., 229–30
Allen, C. G., xiii
Allen, Clifford (Lord Allen of Hurtwood), 130
"Allerhöchst for life", Hitler as, 331
Allies, the; alliances, 199, 322, 346, 349, 351, 367, 370–1, 390, 396, 400, 412, 524, 526
allopathy, 406
allowances, 506
alphabet(s), (general), 418, 432, 452
alphabet bequests (in Shaw's Will), 429–31, 445, 468, 518, 520, 522
alphabet, phonetic, xi, 417, 422, 427, 433, 437, 449, 461–4, 467–71, 511, 522
alphabet, Pitman's phonetic, 27, 30, 414, 416–17, 465
alphabet, Shaw's proposed new British, 3, 20–2, 26–30, 413–22, 423, 425–7, 429, 432, 437, 442–7, 449–58, 464, 467, 469–73, 482–3, 489, 492, 495, 498–9, 511–3, 518, 520–1, 523, 450–1, 456
alphabet, the Latin, 435–6
alphabet, the Roman, 449, 467
alphabet reform, 425–7, 433, 436, 438, 469
alphabet, the Russian, 464
Alphabet, Sir James Pitman's Teaching, 449
alphabet, 'the standard English', 'traditional', '26-letter', 'Dr Johnson's', 'Phoenician', 30, 415–17, 419, 440, 442, 452, 455, 458–9, 468–70, 483, 498, 511, 520

alphabet trusts, 429–31, 443–5
Alsace-Lorraine, 378, 381
Amalek-ites, -itish, 226
amateur, the; amateurish, 390, 424–5, 469, 494, 511
amateur dramatic societies, 32–3, 494
ambiguity, 247, 498
ambition, 272, 285, 342
amendments (to Wills), 496
amends, 374
America, 1, 17, 27, 31, 61*n*, 83, 116, 148, 191, 198, 201, 206, 209–10, 250, 271, 281, 296, 311, 334, 348, 354, 356, 363, 370, 379, 384, 394, 397, 401, 403*n*, 408–9, 411–12, 415–17, 419, 463, 469, 471, 501–3, 507, 511–12, 525
American Civil War, x, 409, 412
American Declaration of Independence, 163, 182, *164*
Ames, Captain Lionel G., x, 103
ammunition, 355, 372
Amorites, the, 41
amusement(s), 273, 359
Anabaptists, the, 73
analogies, 269
analysis, vi
anarch-y, -ical, -ism, -ists, 69, 167, 171, 183, 191–2, 197, 216, 218, 284, 294, 297, 302–3, 305, 324, 340, 342
ancestry, 349
Androcles, 455
Androcles and the Lion, 60, bi-alphabetic edition, 423–4, 432, 442, 443, 445, 448–9, 452–5, 511, 521, 523, *450–1*
anecdotes, x
Anglesey, Lord, 284
Anglo-Saxons, 469
animal(s), (general), 16, 393, 485, 488
animal experiments, 496
Animal Farm (Orwell), 283
announcers, B.B.C., 491
annuities, 474, 480–1, 485, 487–9, 495–7, 505–7, 509, 513
anomalies, 460
anthems, 525
anthologies, works not available for, 10
anthropometric machines, 338
anti-clerical, -ism, 294
anti-climax, 394*n*
anti-democrats, 322–3

anti-Semitism, 186, 198, 200–1, 204, 210
anti-Shavians, 424
'antis', 406
Anti-Socialist League, the, 174
Antonines, the, 168, 170
Antony, Mark, 186–7
Antwerp, 381, 526
Anschluss, 395–6, 402
'Anybody', 326
anxiety, 301
apiarist, ix
apoplexy, 348
Apostles, the, 225
apostrophe, Shaw's non-use of the, 25*n*
appeal (at law), 431
appeal of war, 375
appearance, personal, 125, 274
Applecart, The, 341
apprentice(s), -ship, 273, 324
appropriation of Trust Funds for investment, 509
appropriation, power of, 515
Aquinas, St Thomas, 72
Arabic numerals, 427, 434, 443, 464
arbitration, 410
Arc, Joan of, 48
Archbishops, 254
Archer, William, 348
architecture, 471
archives, 471
"Are We Bolshevists?" (1919), 233–4
'aristocracy of talent', 327
aristo-crats, -cracy, 153, 169, 193, 217, 240, 290, 292, 307, 337
Aristophanes, 184
Aristotelian Society, the, 378
Aristotle, 41, 49, 55, 184, 248
arithmetic, -al, 38–9, 257, 282, 415, 457
Armageddon, 369
Armistice, 396
Armistice Day, 386
arms, arming, armaments, 237–8, 349–50, 359, 386, 390–1, 401–2, 444
Arms and the Man, 429, 481
Army, the; armies, 127, 156, 278, 283, 291, 357–9, 372, 377, 385, 389, 401, 411, 464, 476
arrest, 236, 336
Articles, The Thirty-nine, 42
artisans, 284, 413–14
arts, the; artists, vi, 65, 73, 204, 210, 250, 252, 268, 275, 279, 281–2, 314–15,

327, 414, 418, 420, 425, 429–30, 440, 476, 479, 487, 490, 492–3, 498–9, 503–4, 511
Aryan race, 185, 198
ascenders (typographical), 441
ashes, 478, 487, 499
Asia, -tic, 198
Asquith, Herbert (Earl of Oxford and Asquith), 118, 150, 152, 206, 256, 351–2
assassination, 192, 194, 370, 374
assemblies, public, 482, 491
assets, liquid, 428
assets, realisable, 475
assignment (of copyright, annuities, etc.), 501–2, 507
Assyria, -n, 248
Astor, In re ([1952] Ch. 534), 522
Astor, Lord and Lady, 311, 429
Astronomer Royal, the, 277
asylum, lunatic, 268–9
Ataturk, Kemal, 17, 340, 393
atheism, atheists, 218, 222, 294
Athenaeum, the, 256*n*
Athens, 149–50, 184
Atlantic Charter, the, 321
Atlantic ocean, the, 463, 466
Atlantic Pact, the, 399
atomic bomb, x, xii, 408, 412, 444
Atonement, the, 73, 133–5, 136, 155–6
atrocit-y, -ies, 22, 181, 242, 340, 363, 376, 397, 400, 407
attack, military, 363, 369, 380, 394, 396
Attorney-General (London), the, 430–1, 518, 520–1
Attorney-General (Dublin), the, 237
Auctioneers' Institute, the, 482, 491
audiences, 490, 519
Auditor-General, the, 464
auditors, 464
Augustine, Saint, 71–2
Augustus, Emperor, 186–7, 340
Aurelius, Marcus, 168
"Author as Manual Laborer, The" (1944), 413–22, 426
authoritarian,-ism, 184
'authority', authorities (representative, public, etc.), 285–6, 404, 481, 482
authors, 275, 413–14, 416, 419, 428, 454, 458, 460–2, 491, 516

Authors, Society of, 14–15, 31–2, 84, 329, 413, 421, 430, 503
auto-crats, -cracy, 170–1, 185, 197, 221, 225, 329, 333–5, 340, 408
autographs, refusal of, 10, 14
automatons, 376
Austin, John, 206
Australia, 15n, 29, 198, 459, 471n
Austria, -n, 181–2, 188, 192n, 370, 381, 384, 396, 402
Austrian Nudists, the, 96
avenger(s), -ing, 392–3
Avenue Theatre, London, 481
Ayot St. Lawrence, ix, x, directions for reaching, 33–4; 45; infatuated girl rents cottage in, 93; Shaw's Corner, 499; Shaw's Corner, National Trust and, 503
Ayrshire, 444

baby, babies, 82, 86, 267, 270, 275, 348, 392, 395
Bacchantes, the, 361
Back to Methuselah, vi, 55–6
bad debts, 267
Baghdad, 373
Bakunin, Mikhail, 216, 220
balance between democracy and dictatorship, 330
balance of power, 367, 370, 380
Balderstone, Caleb, 418
Balfour, Arthur, Earl, 118, 256
Balkans, the, 136
ballyhoo, 312, 395
bank(s), -ing, 194, 196, 298, 368, 500
bankruptcy, 202, 328, 383, 507
"Banner of Peace", 391
Bar, the, 482, 491
barbarism, 383
barber(s), ix, 290
Barker, Sir Ernest, 306, 308
Barker, H. Granville, 83, 87n, 217, 479, 503
Barlow, George, 105
Barnato, Barnett, 264, 284
barons, 317
barracks, 376, 405
barrage, 380
Barrett, Pauline M., 440–1
barrister(s), 177, 268, 270, 285, 427, 476
Basic English, 29–30, 465
Basic Income, the, 275–7, 279–82, 301, 303, 327–8

Bath, 428
battlefield, 383, 394
battles, 269, 359, 371, 373, 388–9, 394, 404
battleships, 389
Bax, Belfort, 216, 218
bayoneting, 347, 380
B.B.C., the,—See British Broadcasting Corporation
B.B.C. Committee for Spoken English, the, 29
beadles, 358
bearing, personal, 476
bears, 393
beauty, 48, 478, 483
Bebel, Ferdinand August, 220n
Becket, Thomas à, 192, 196
Bedford Debating Society, the, 301
Bedfordshire, 518
bee(s), beehive, 308, 392
Beech, Patrick, 502
beer, 17, 406
Beerbohm, Sir Max, 43
Beethoven, Ludwig von, 263, 392, 405
behaviour (individual, mass, human, national, etc.), 364, 404, 482
Belgium, Belgian, 346, 353–5, 366
beliefs (general), 406
bellicosity, 369
belligerents, 380–1
Belloc, Hilaire, 217, 244, 247–53, 252
Bell's Visible Speech, 465
Belsen, 403
beneficiaries (of Shaw's Will), 427, 430, 433, 444
benefits (social), 265
'benevolent' dictators, 330, 335, 339–40
Bennett, Arnold, 107, 217, 349
Bentham, Jeremy; Benthamite, 343
Bentley, Richard, 264
Bentley, Stokes & Lowless, 522
Beowulf, 469
bequests in Shaw's Wills (general), 413, 433, 473–523, 486–7, 489, 493–7, 505–6, 514–15
bequests, alphabetic, 413, 426, 429, 433, 473, 483, 492, 498, 510–11, 520
Beresford, Michael, xiii, 309
Berlin, 369, 376, 392, 396, 400, 406–7
Bermondsey, 406
Bernard Shaw on Peace (c. 1948–9), 210–11, 282, 330

Bernhardi, von, 356, 382
Bethel, 292
betrayal, 86, 375, 525
Beveridge Report, the, 318
Bevin, Ernest, 399
bi-alphabetic editions, conditions, 424, 432, 443, 470
Biarritz, 109
Bible, the, 24–5, 42, 47, 56, 65, 73, 216, 253, 483, 498
Bible Society, the, 73–4
bibliographer, 515
bicycle, learning to ride a, 159
bigotry, 348
bi-lingual conditions, 470
Bilton, Alice, 486, 488, 506
Bilton, Margaret, 486, 488, 506
biograph-y, -ers, 1–2, 479, 500, 504, 524
biolog-y, -ical, -ists, 185, 201, 308, 424
birds (general), 273, 393, 485, 488
birds of paradise, 393
Birley, Mr, 459
Birmingham, 120
birthday, friends urged not to celebrate his, 12
bishops, 75, 250, 482, 491
Bismarck, Prince von, 221, 340, 376, 378, 381
'bitter-enders', 378n
bitterness, 385, 388
blackguards, 234
Black Sea, the, 108
Blackshirts, the, 194
Blake, William, 284
Bland, Hubert, 292, 333
blanks (typographical), 467
blasphemy, 386
Blatchford, Robert, 218
Blenheim, 350
blockade(s), blockaders, 356, 383, 397
blood sacrifice, 499
bloodshed, 180–1, 236, 239, 381, 398
"bloodthirsty guttersnipe" (Hitler), 399
Bloody Sunday (1887), 236
'blow-below-the-belt', 401
Blumenfeld, R. D., 174
blunders, in war, 349
Blyton, Enid, 443
Board of Works, the, 421
'bodies',—see 'public bodies, associations, societies'
body, Shaw's, 477–8, 487, 499
Boers, the, 410
Boer War, the, xii, 409–11
Boganda, the (African tribe), 135
Bohemian, -ism, 324

bold type, 447
Bolsheviks, Bolshevism, 200, 213, 230–1, 234–6, 239, 241–2, 278, 294, 395. *229*
bomb(s), -ing, 186, 194, 392, 400–2, 407–8
Bonapart-ist, -ism, 170, 197
book-keepers, 461
bookmakers, 288
books, 8*n*, 9, 12, 33, 261, 278, 280, 308, 375, 405, 415, 419–20, 427, 458, 477, 485, 490–1, 494, 498, 501
booksellers, ix
Booth, General, 47
boredom, as one of the causes of war, 375
borrow-ing, -ers, 379
Borzoi dogs, 185
Bosnia, 381
Bosphorus, the, 108
Boston Sunday Post, the, 353–4
Boswell, James, 264
Bourbons, the, 174, 191, 333
bourgeois, -ie, 193, 216–22, 226, 229–30, 278, 318, 333
boustrophedon writing, 442
boyhood, Shaw's, 479, 481
Bradlaugh, Charles, 175
braggart(s), 356
Brahminism, 132
'brains' (i.e. intelligence), 266, 269, 301, 304, 361
Bramwell, Lord, 180
bravery, 350, 383
bread, communisation of, 205
Breakages Limited, 317
breathed/voiced figural relationship, 447
Bremen, 400
bricklayers, 268, 328
Bridges, Robert, 414, 426, 462
Bright, John, 322
brilliance, vii
Britain, British (general), 21, 103, 189–90, 192, 197–9, 202, 204, 208–9, 214, 228, 231, 233*n*, 234, 258, 260, 276, 281, 284, 296, 303, 305, 312–14, 316, 328, 330, 336, 346, 348, 353, 355, 357–8, 360, 366–71, 374, 376, 378–9, 381, 384–5, 389, 390, 392-3, 396–7, 399–403, 406–11, 414, 417, 420, 460–1, 464–5, 469–70, 484, 491, 512, 516, 519, 521, 524–5
Britanski Soyuznik, 302
British Alphabet, new—See Alphabet, proposed new British
British Broadcasting Corporation, 29, 36, 182, 199*n*, 326, 391*n*, 491

British Commonwealth, the, 27, 313
British Council, the, 30, 421
British Empire, the, 358, 368
British International Press Ltd., 395
British Legion, the, 386
British Library of Political and Economic Science, xiii, 3, 500
British Museum, the, xiii, 3, 172, 208, 210, 213, as Shaw beneficiary, 427, 430, 431, 443–4, 493, 500, 513, 518, 520
British Museum Reading Room, Shaw's use of, 493, 513
British Socialist Party, 130
Brittain, Vera, vii, xiv
Brobdingnag, King of, 44
bronze, 478, 502
brother-in-law, Shaw's, 497
'Brother Jonathan', 235
brothers, 377
Brown, Begonia, 313
brutality, 194, 238, 398, 400
Bucket, Inspector (Dickens character), 290
Buckingham Palace, 364
Buddhism, 132, 190
Budget(s), 259
buffer states, 362
building, municipal, 125
'bunk', speeches of Ramsay MacDonald described by Shaw as, 298
Bunyan, John, vii, 206, 406, 474*n*
bureau, -cracy, -cratic, 212, 221, 226, 272
burial service, 478
Burne-Jones, Sir Edward, 43
Burns, John, 223
bursaries, 492
"Bury the Hatchet" (1919), 383
business, -man, b. personnel, etc., 201, 203–4, 217, 275, 470, 490, 493, 500, 514–15
busts (sculptures), 478, 485, 502–3
Butler, Nicholas Murray, 426
Butler, Samuel, 70, 217
Butt, Alfred (later Sir Alfred), 62, 69, 73, 75*n*
buying and selling, 206, 258, 268
Byron, Lord, 350

Cabinet, the; Cabinets, 144*n*, 189, 192, 211, 275, 278, 324, 342, 366, 397, 404, 524, 526
cacoethes scribendi, 520

cad(s), 338
Cad, definition of the, 246; in war, 364. *365*
Cadbury family, 250*n*
Cadbury, George, 249–50
Caesar, Julius, Caesarian, 36*n*, 167, 170, 186–7, 196, 264, 340–1, 377, 394, 410
Cain, 53
cajolery, 235
Calais, 372
calamit-y, -ies, 361, 376–7, 399
Californian Shavian, the, 423
calligraph-y, -ers, 30, 420, 438, 506, 511
callousness, 187*n*, 379
Calvin, John, Calvinism, 174, 225
Cambridge University, 479, 502
Campaign for Nuclear Disarmament, the, 407
Campbell, Mrs Patrick, 502
Campbell, Rev. R. J., 131, 141, 146, 155–6, 157, 159, 161
camp-followers, 383
candidates' deposits (elections), 324
candidates, political, 309, 313, 324
Candid Friend, The, 26*n*, 216
cant, 324
Canterbury, Archbishop of, the, 142, 151
Canterbury Tales (Chaucer), 469
canvassing, 313
capacity, human, 277, 283, 285, 301
Cape Times, the, 299
capital (general), 110, 114, 116, 122, 178–9, 200, 211, 215, 229, 243, 411, 484, 509
Capital Gains Tax (1962 and 1965), 211
Capitalism, Capitalist system, 110, 113–14, 115, 116, 169, 181–2, 186, 195, 196–7, 200, 203, 206, 209–10, 211, 213, 215–16, 219–20, 222–5, 227, 229–30, 231–2, 280, 287–9, 293, 295, 296, 298–9, 301, 311, 318, 319–20, 322–5, 333, 347, 351–2, 353, 394–5
Capitalism, Ulster Protestant, 22
Capitalist(s), 116, 222, 227, 232–4, 249, 254, 274, 287, 320, 325
capital letters, 435, 441, 447, 457, 467

Capital (Marx), (*Das Kapital*), 208, 214, 216, 221, 222, 224, 288
capital punishment, 3, 18–19, 403
Carlow, Ireland, 477
Carlyle, Thomas, 235, 330
Carnegie, Andrew, 17, 426
Carnegie Trust, the, 421
Carnot, Lazare, 385
carpenter(s), 254, 392
Carpenter, Edward, 218
Carroll, Emily, 486, 489, 496
cars,—See motor-cars
Carson, Edward, Baron, 173, 238
cartels, 248
"Case Against Chesterton, The" (1916), 304–5
Casement, Sir Roger, 373–4
"Case for Equality, The" (1913), 254–71, 280n
Cashin, Margaret, 497, 507
casting (in printing), 467–8, 492
castor oil, 186–7, 190
catchwords, political, 328
Catechism, the Church, 482, 491
Catherine, the Empress, 377
Catholics, Catholicism, 73, 96, 100, 198, 207, 212, 247, 252, 256
cats, 273, 429
Cavalcade (magazine), 203
celebrations, 487
cells (of organic whole), 261
Celts, the, Celtic, 200, 364
censorship, 3, 58, 59–60, 61–2, 63–77, 315, 355, 363, 526
centenarians, 275
Central Empires, the, 369, 371, 378
centralised power, 214
Central News Ltd., 247n
"centres of rest and culture" (in Russia), 276
century, centuries, x, xii, 419, 426, 433, 436, 449, 452, 487, 511, 518–19
ceremonies (religious, etc.), 478
Certificates of Proficiency, 483, 491
cesser, 508–9, 512
Ceylon, 458
chain stores, 116n
Chamberlain, Sir Austen, 385, 391, 410
Chamberlain, Houston, 186, 198
Chamberlain, Joseph, 219
Chamberlain, Neville, 397
Chamberlain, the Lord, 58, 62–3, 72–4

Chancery Court, the, 240, 427, 430, 443, 518, 521
Chantilly Psalter, the, 28
character (general), 380
characters (typographical), 450–1, 453, 455, 457, 467–8
charges, deductions or outgoings on Shaw's estate, 515
'charitable object' (legal), 522–3
charitable trusts, 520–2
charities (general), charitableness, 9, 14, 33n, 178, 234, 421, 427, 430–1, 519, 521, 523
Charities, the Official Protector of, 430
Charity Commissioners, 417
Charles I, 182, 331
Charles II, 174
Charter, the Atlantic, 321
Charter, the Great (*Magna Carta*), 168
charwomen, 269, 504
chastity, 234
chattels, chattel slavery, 291, 297, 479, 494
Chaucer, Geoffrey, 469
chauffeur(s), ix, 459, 473, 485, 486–7, 504, 507
Cheke, Sir John, 426
Chelsea, 282
chem-ist, -istry, -ical science, ix, 404
Cheops, Pyramid of, the, 341
cheques, 500
'Chesterbelloquacity', 247
Chesterton, G. K., vii, 173, 217, 244, 245–7, 251, 341, 252
Chicago, 198
child, -ren, -hood, xii, 21, 37, 86, 87, 90, 201, 257, 261, 267, 274–5, 277, 280, 289, 302, 337, 342, 344, 390, 392–3, 409–10, 420, 433–4, 436, 438, 440, 442–3, 452, 458–60, 490, 502, 512, 525
China, Chinese, 29–30, 65, 198, 386, 392, 408, 459, 460n. 65
chivalry, 134, 362, 383, 401
Chocolate Soldier, The, 429
choice, 247, 323, 330–1
Cholmondeley, General Hugh, 497
choral music, 476
'Chosen Race', the, 'Chosen Race theory', 201, 398
Christian Church, the, 50, 53, 60, 65, 74, 133, 347
Christian Commonwealth, The, 256n
Christian economics, 130–61, 162, 242, 254, 343–4

Christian Economics, (speech), 130–61, 162, 254 343–4
Christian European Society (Belloc), 248
Christianity, 19n, 70–1, 123, 130–61, 217, 221, 225, 242–3, 248, 253, 292, 302, 377, 478
Christian Socialist, The, 176
Christ, Jesus, 59, 65, 131–3, 139, 156, 159–60, 161, 221, 253, 302, 386, 388
churches (general, various denominations, etc.), 14n, 221, 301, 334, 338, 347, 349, 369, 406, 491, 499
Church of England, the, 60, 62, 71, 74, 76, 197, 250, 386, 406, 478
Church, Hayden, 282n
Churchill, (Sir) Winston, 203, 208, 213, 239, 241, 295–6, 310, 346, 355, 369, 393, 399, 402
churchmen, 216
churches and war, the, 347 369, 377, 386–9
C.I.D., the, 212, 399
cinema, the, cinematographic exhibitions, 375, 501
circumstances, 493, 502
cities (general), 392, 400, 402, 406
citizens, citizenship, 21n, 163, 166, 322, 324, 336, 342, 357, 359, 399, 404, 476
Citrine, Sir Walter, 318
'City', the, City of London, 174, 406
City Temple, the, 146, 161, 344; Literary and Debating Society, 131
civilians, 348, 352, 356–9, 366, 374–5
civilisation(s), 16n, 19, 132, 154, 169, 179, 204, 207, 243, 248, 264, 274–5, 280, 308, 319, 322–7, 333, 342, 375, 380, 382, 389, 394–5, 399, 404, 411, 424, 464
Civil Rights, citizen rights, 351, 357, 359
Civil Service, Servants, xiii, 126, 283, 332, 407, 476, 482, 491
civil war, 180, 193, 236, 296, 299, 303, 394. 295
"C.K.C.", 70
claims against debtors, 493, 514
Clapham, 367
Clarion, the, 217, 219, 221, 256n, 290

Clarion Vocal Union, the, 105
clarity, clarification, x, 452
Clark, R. & R. Ltd. (printers), 462, 515
classes (general, social, various, class war, etc.), 156, 162, 176–7, 180–1, 219–22, 226, 229, 234, 237, 240, 242, 245, 255–6, 258, 275, 278, 285, 287, 289–90, 292, 303, 307–8, 311, 314–15, 318, 320–1, 327, 395, 476, 479
classless society, a, 162, 230, 257, 285
clauses (in Wills, etc.), 390, 402, 445, 468, 473, 478, 484–7, 492, 494–8, 504–5, 508, 510, 512, 520
cleanliness, 247
Cleopatra, 91
clergy, the, 334, 476
clerks, 454, 458, 461–2, 483
clothes, clothing, 98–101, 257–8, 261, 270, 277–8, 280, 282, 406
'clown' in Shaw, vii
clubs, 492
coalition, -ists, 295
coarseness, 274
Cobbett, William, 189
Cobden, Richard, Cobdenism, 213, 321, 322–5
Cockburn, Sir John, 247, 253
Cockerell, Sir Sydney, 474–5, 479–80, 519n
Cockle, Mark, 518
Cockney, 418, 425
cocoa, 249, 250
"Code of Decent Pugnacity", 364
Codicils (to Wills), 484, 494–7, 505, 510, 512, 515
coercion, 22, 32, 166, 168–9, 171–2, 181, 235, 245, 289, 329–32, 336
coinage, 420
Cole, G. D. H., 213, 298
colleagues, 479, 493, 515
collections, public (of art, etc.), 476, 480, 483, 491
collective farming, 208–9, 309
collective ownership, 224
collective security, 367, 368–9, 385
Collectivism, 152–3, 183, 245, 252, 292
colleges (general), 252, 422, 427, 475–7
"College of Surgeons", a, 478
Collier, Jeremy, 45–6
Collings, Jesse, 208

Cologne, 406
Colonies, 381
"Colossal Labor Saving" (1947), 26–30
Colour Question, the, 151, 266, 268
Colthurst, Cecily Charlotte, 500
combat, -ants, -ancy, 362, 380, 392, 405–6, 410
combination, military, 390
comfort, 251, 261
Comintern, the, 234
commerce, commercialism, commercial considerations, 135, 217, 250n, 267, 376, 379, 380, 383, 411, 430, 459, 476, 487, 492, 513
"commercialised cad", the, 375
commission, 479, 494, 501
committee(s), (general), 309, 427
Committee of One Hundred, the, 408
Committee for Public Retrenchment, the, 368
common ownership, 229
common sense, 361, 384, 409, 525
Common Sense About the War, 7, 346–9, 351, 354–5, 357, 385, 408, 411, 524–6
Commons, House of, 17, 118–19, 121, 152, 178, 235, 313, 316, 402, 443
Commonwealth, the British, 27, 212, 313, 342, 415, 419, 512
Communism, x, 3, 46, 137, 140–1, 142, 185–6, 190, 193, 197, 200, 203, 204–6, 207–15, 225, 227, 228–9, 230–1, 233, 239, 242, 243, 247, 274, 276, 284, 294, 297–9, 302, 305–12, 315, 317–18, 320, 322–5, 328–9, 343–4, 383, 385, 395, 398–9, 405, 408. 303.
Communist Party, the British, 210, 214
community, the, communities, 128, 165, 176, 180, 186, 195, 201, 204n, 237, 246, 249–51, 254, 261, 265, 268, 289, 295, 308, 343, 357, 376, 382, 521
competition (commercial, general), 177, 262, 270, 375–6, 379, 410, 420, 427, 433
"Complete State Regulation", 314–15
composers, composition, literary, 504

composers, composing, musical, 492, 314–15, 354
compositors (printing) 416–17, 419, 467n
compulsion (general), 307, 332, 359, 420, 427
compulsory industrial and civil service, 293, 295, 357
'Compulsory Labour', 231–2, 293, 297–8. 303
compulsory military service, 297, 347, 352, 357
"Compulsory State Service", 406. 295
Comte, Auguste, 318, 333
concentration camps, 403, 408
Concert of Europe, the, 382
"Conclusive Peace", the, 362
Concordat, 334
conduct, 36–44, 55, 183, 279, 323, 329, 343, 504
confession (religious, etc.), 388
"conflicting private interests", 299
conformity, social, 314
confusion, 203, 264, 267, 294, 301, 321, 345, 360, 370, 433, 469, 483, 492, 511
conquer-or(s), -ing, 381, 388
conquest(s), 202
conscience, 329, 334, 342, 376–7, 405, 487
conscientiousness, 241, 304, 343
conscientious objection, 294, 373, 377, 392, 404–8.
conscription (general, industrial, etc.), 295, 363, 372, 405, 408
conscription, military, 352
'consent, consciousness of', 167
consent (of the people, of the governed, etc.), 167, 171, 335–6
Conservative (attitudes, Party, Conservatism), 103, 144n, 174, 216, 224, 278, 285, 287, 289, 292, 295, 298–9, 308, 318, 324, 328, 344–5, 353, 364, 408
consonants, 20, 27n, 435, 498
conspirac-y, -ies, 294, 338, 420
Constable & Co. Ltd., 515
Constantinople, 108, 381, 392
constituenc-y, -ies, 310, 339
Constitution, the, constitutional, -ism, 123, 173, 189, 234, 236, 317
Constitution, the Soviet, 309

Consumers (v. producers, etc.), 197, 292
contemporaries, 416-19
contractions (shorthand, etc.), 416–19, 446–7, 465
contradiction(s), 361, 397, 402
'contradiction in terms', 283 306
contra mundum, 351
'Control of Trust', 522
controvers-y, -ial, xii, 269, 274, 342, 521
convention, -al, 334, 470, 493
conversation, xii, 512
convictions (general), 389, 398
co-operation (party, social, of the governed, etc.), 251, 335–6, 342
co-operative enterprises, 484
co-operative farming, 209
Cooper, Gladys, 48
Copernicus, 41
'copy' (for the printer), 414
copyright(s) (general), xiii, 417, 428, 430–1, 444, 474, 477, 487, 499–501, 504, 510, 512, 520
Copyright Act (1911), the, 11
Corfu, 189
Coriolanus (Shakespeare), 216
"Corporate State", the, 197, 210
correspondence, 356, 432; lack of response to, 8, 11–12
corruption, 171, 191, 216, 301, 310, 322, 330, 350, 411, 417, 419
Cossacks, the, 238
cottages in Ireland owned by Shaw, 477
Cotterill, Erica, 80–95. 80, 81, 85, 88–9
Coué, Professor Emile, 56
Council Chamber, the, 410
councils (general), 427
counsel (legal), 266, 520
country gentlemen, 338
coup(s) d'état, 187, 333
coupled alphabetical strokes, 438, 441, 445
coupled votes, 285
courage, 199, 253–4, 350, 362, 378, 384, 386, 393
Court of Chancery,—See 'Chancery Court, the'.
Courts of Justice, 491
cousins, Shaw's, 486
Covenants (of League of Nations, etc.), 390, 401
Coventry, 406
Coventry Herald, the, 344
coward(s), -ice, 166, 361, 371, 390, 401

crafts, -manship, 315, 424, 476, 479, 490
Craies, C., 70
cramming (for examinations), 42
cramp, writers', 415
Crane, Walter, 218
cranks, 414, 465
Creative Evolution, 425, 499
creative life, the, 315
Crécy, 136
creeds, 340, 382
cremation, 268, 412, 474, 499
Crimean War, the, xii, 409, 412
crimes, criminal(s), 16n, 18–19, 189, 206, 284, 304, 312, 319, 332, 375, 381, 397, 401
"Criminal Direct Action", (political), 294. 294
Cripps, (Sir) Stafford, 318
critics, criticisms, of Shaw, x, xii, and passim.
Cromwell, Oliver, 168–9, 189, 198, 336, 340–1, 358, 377
Cross, the, 388, 478, 487, 499
Crossman, Miss Yvonne, xiii
Crown, the, 286
"crowning masterpiece", Shaw's, 473
Crown Prosecutor (Dublin), 237
Crucifixion, the, 133, 136, 156
crudity, 383
cruelty, 169–70, 174, 181, 195, 340, 344, 378, 381
culture, cultural, 275–8, 280, 309, 319–20, 327, 363, 483, 491
cupidity, 362
Currall, Ivo L., 516
Currency Cranks, 326
Current Shorthand, 446, 448
cursive style of writing, 446
Curzon, Lord, 231
cynicism, 227, 237, 410

Dachau, 403
Daily Chronicle, the, 374, 377, 385
Daily Citizen, the, 7, 217, 351–3
Daily Express, the, 174, 357
Daily Herald, the, 80n, 222n, 227–8, 237–8, 320, 396
Daily Mail, the, 127, 400
Daily News, the, 186, 188, 190, 193, 250n, 256n, 282–3, 349, 383, 411
Daily Sketch, the, 357
Daily Telegraph, the, 354
Daily Worker, the, 210, 212, 213

Dalton, Charles, 45
Danakils (tribe), 393
dancing, 492
danger(s), 86, 348, 379, 397
d'Annunzio, Gabriele, 236
Dardanelles, the, 10n
daring, 169–70
Darwin, Charles, 27n, 56, 222–4
Das Kapital (Marx),—See Capital (Marx)
Das Programm (music journal), 68
Davies, Ethel, 486, 489
Davies, Sebastien, 489, 497
Day, Frederick William (chauffeur), 473, 485, 488, 496, 506–7, 518
Day, Margaret, 497, 506, 507, 518
day(s), amount of writing possible in, etc., 419, 458, 460–3
Deans, Jeanie, 41
death, 16n, 18, 19n, 134, 179, 183, 192n, 231–2, 259, 267, 364, 368, 374–5, 378, 388–9, 392–3, 397, 399, 422, 425, 428, 437, 474, 475, 477–9, 485–9, 493, 496–7, 499–500, 502, 504–6, 508, 510, 512–15, 519–20, 524
Death Duties, 259
death, fear of, 20n, 134
death warrants, 192–3, 232
debasement, of English language, 483
debates, 244–53, 301–2
debt to Society, 128–9, 267, 270, 293, 342
debts (general), debtors, 240, 428, 457, 493, 510, 514
'decent men', 234, 342
decimal systems, 423, 470–1
Deck, Richard, 27n
Declaration of Independence, the American, 163, 182. 164
declaration of war, 396, 402, 405
decrease in value of annuities, 509
decrees, 317
defeat (in war), 361, 364, 410
Defence, A (1927), 188–90
defence (in war), 358, 375, 380
Defence of the Realm Act, the, ('D.O.R.A.'), 368, 388
deferred annuity, 507
de Gaulle, General, 333, 336n
delegates, 230, 309
Deliverance (divine), 386

INDEX 535

delusions, 171, 314
demagogue(s), 167, 305, 307, 338
democracy, 101–3, 144–5, 148–50, 153–4, 162, 163–70, 171–5, 184–6, 190, 193, 195, 197, 201, 202, 212, 225, 235, 240–1, 245, 255–6, 259, 272, 280, 285–6, 288, 293, 297, 304–14, 316–17, 321–4, 326, 330–1, 333–4, 337–9, 342, 351–2, 367, 370, 383, 385, 395, 397–8, 405
"Democracy and the Apple Cart" (1930), 316–17
"Democracy as a Delusion" (1927), 165–70, 171
"Democratic Aristocracy", 327
"Democratic Communism", 405
"Democrat who is not also a Socialist is no Gentleman, The" (debate, 1911), 244–7
demolition, 392, 407, 424
demoralization, 323, 398
Denikin, 385
Denshawai massacre (1907), 130, 150
Department of Scientific and Industrial Research, the, 421
dependence (women's economic dependence on men), 260
De Quincey, Thomas, 206
Derby, Lord, 410
descenders (typographical), 441
Deserted Village, The (Goldsmith), 206
Deslys, Gaby, 61, 62–3, 67, 69–70, 71, 75n, 76. 64, 65
Despard, Mrs Charlotte, 237
despot(s), -ism, 167–8, 170, 175, 184, 191, 302, 331, 333, 397, 399
destroyers, 463, 466
destruction, 389, 404, 464
deterrence, deterrents, 16n, 18–19
'deterrent idea', the, 407n
De Valera, Eamon, 173
devastation, 375, 381, 386
Devil, the, 71n, 251
Devil's Disciple, The, 156
diacritics, 437, 440, 469, 498, 511
Dialectical Materialism, 318
dialects, 458, 483
Dickens, Charles, 17, 19n, 27, 49, 79, 175, 183, 201, 217, 239, 240–1, 290, 398,

415–16, 417, 436, 458, 459, 462
dictator(s), -ship, 167–9, 172–3, 175, 187, 189, 190, 202–3, 236, 297–8, 308, 312, 322, 330–1, 334–5, 339–40, 408. 303
'Dictatorship of the Proletariat', 236, 308
"Dictatorship of the Proletariat, The" (1921), 181–2, 294–5
dictionaries, 418, 465, 468
digraphs, 436–7, 440, 498
Digswell, 297
Dinard, 276n
dinners, 282, 303, 348
Diocletian, the Emperor, 197
diphthongs, 27n, 36n, 439, 447
diplomacy, diplomats, 166, 199, 338, 366, 370, 391, 399
Diplomacy after the War (1915), 366–7
Diplomacy (Scribe), 54
'Direct Action', 294
direction of labour, 279
Directors ('Instructed', etc.), 276–7, 280–1, 315, 327, 337
Directory, The, 191, 333
disablement, 323, 401, 504
disappointments, 87, 335, 398
disarmament, 349, 358–9, 383, 389, 392, 401, 407
discussion(s), 202, 420
disease, 24n, 406, 490
disfranchisement, 287, 324
disillusionment, 292, 388
dismissal of rulers, 324
dispatches (military), 464
Disraeli, Benjamin (Earl of Beaconsfield), 216
dissection (medical), 477–8
dissolving Parliament, 316
distance, measures of, etc., 394, 423, 470
distortion of letters, in phonetic writing, 441, 446
distortions, Shaw's, 269
distressed areas, 397
distribution, industrial, etc., re-distribution, 207, 224, 243–5, 247–8, 249, 252, 258, 260–1, 264–5, 267, 275–6, 279–80, 282, 294, 312, 325, 377, 395
Dives (Biblical character), 405
dividends, 124, 298
divine right, 331
Division (in House of Commons), 316, 321, 335
division of labour, 323

divorce, 425
dock labourers, dockers, 268, 284
doctor(s), ix, 290
documents (general), 415, bequeathed by Shaw, 500, 504
dole, the, 182, 298, 395
Doll's House, A (Ibsen), 54–5
domesticity, domestic matters, 291, 380
Don Juan, 54
Don Quixote, 134
'Don't Know' class, the, 413
D.O.R.A. (Defence of the Realm Act), 368, 388
Drake, Sir Francis, 388
Drama, the (general), 476
Drama, Elizabethan, 50, 52–3
Drama, Greek, 48–52
Drama, Religious, 48, 50, 52–3, 55
Drama, Restoration, 53–4
Drama, Seventeenth Century, 50
Drama, Victorian, 53
dramatic societies (local, school, etc.), 494
dramatists, ix, 425
Dramatists' Club, the, 348
drawing(s), 441, 460, 503
dreams, dreamers, 320, 452
dress, -ing, 326, 482
drilling (military), 407
drink, -ing, 16–17, 35, 274, 288, 326
drowning, 197, 379
drudgery, 261, 273, 277, 293, 414
drugs, 406
drunkenness, 243. See also 'drink'
Dubb, Henry, 313
Dublin, 237–9, 502, 507, 512
Dublin Municipal Gallery, 502
Duff Cooper, Alfred (Lord Norwich), 199n
dukes, 110–14, 141, 191, 290
Dürer, Albrecht, 56
duty, 234, 355, 388
dynast-y, -ies, 350

"E.A.B.", 70–2
eagles, 347, 409
earthquakes, 361, 379
East, the, Eastern civilisation, Eastern bloc, etc., 311, 367, 369, 371
Easygoers, the, 303
eating, 302, 326
Ecclesiastes, Book of, the 216
Economic Association, the, 421

economic dependence, women's on men, 260
Economic Order in Production, 299–301
economics (general), economists, 166–7, 206, 252, 285, 304–5, 309, 343, 383, 414, 418, 420, 424, 465, 475, 500
economics, Christian, 130–61, 162, 254
econom-y, -ical (i.e. saving, avoiding waste), 361, 368, 417, 419–20, 447, 454, 457, 460–5, 468–70, 511, 521, 523
ecstatics, the, 361
Eddy, Mrs Mary Baker, 56
Eden, Anthony (Lord Avon), 203, 318
Eden, Garden of, the, 50
Edinburgh, 515
education (school, political, general), 28, 36–44, 82, 115–16, 119–20, 172, 182, 201, 216, 251–2, 264, 266, 276, 278–9, 281, 288–9, 291, 303, 309, 319, 324, 338–40, 342, 384, 401, 420, 431, 436, 438, 443, 449, 475, 482, 490–1, 498, 502, 521, 523
educational trust, 523
Education, Minist-er, -ry, of, the, 28, 498, 512
Education Year Book (W.E.A.), the, 338
Edward II, 168
Edward III, 199
Edward VII, 355
Edwards, Enoch, M.P., 105
efficiency (social, industrial, etc.), 281, 330, 434, 438, 491
egalitarianism, 191
egotism, xi
Egypt, -ians, 151, 179, 220, 248
eighteenth century, the, 410
Einstein, Albert, 199–200, 280, 392
Elba, 332
"Election Prospects", 324. 325
election(s), -eering, electoral systems, elected bodies, etc., 168, 170, 226, 235, 240, 308, 311–12, 316, 319, 321, 323, 330–2, 334, 337, 339
electoral system, the Russian, 212
electorate, the, 153n, 169, 172, 298, 338, 408
electro-mechanical readers, 449

Elgar, Sir Edward, 43
Elijah, 138
élite, the, 331
Elizabeth I, 167, 267, 340, 436
Ellis, Alexander, 426
elocution, 477, 483, 489, 491
Elphinstone, K. E., 518
emblems, 388, 478, 487
Emerson, Ralph Waldo, 262
Emery, Edward, 480–1
emotion-al, -ism, 385, 392–3, 402, 433, 525–6
Empire, the British, 117, 119, 386, 388, 391, 394, 395, 400
empires (general), 149, 182, 381, 385, 391–2
employers, the employing class, 186, 237, 262, 289, 292, 296, 311–12, 319, 379
employment (public, private, etc.), 126, 253, 261, 308, 414, 476, 482, 490–2, 505, 512, 516
emulation, 362
encirclement, 369
Encyclopaedia Britannica, the, 296
endocrine tests, 338
endowment (private, public, etc.), 476–7, 482, 484, 490, 493
ends and means, 194
enemy, the, enemies (personal, during war, etc.), 332, 349–51, 368, 380–1, 383, 399, 402, 407
energy, 259, 362, 364, 454, 522
enfranchisement, 149, 326
Engels, Friedrich, 220–1, 343
Enghien, Duc D', 191, 195
England, the English, English language, institutions, etc., 20, 29, 40, 65–6, 107, 109, 127, 141, 150, 176, 185–6, 191, 196, 207, 210, 213, 229, 235, 239, 249, 251, 292, 304, 313–14, 316, 318, 322, 341, 343, 349, 350–1, 354, 356, 358, 364, 372, 374, 380–2, 385, 389, 393–4, 399, 410, 414–19, 422, 425, 428, 430–3, 435, 452, 458–9, 464–5, 468–72, 475, 482–3, 489, 492, 498, 502, 511–12, 516, 518–19, 521, 524
enjoyment, 72n
enterprise (private, public enterprises, etc.) 158, 173, 203, 204, 207, 225, 249, 253, 273n, 285, 301, 317, 320, 323–4, 484, 492, 513
enthusi-asm, -asts, 226, 484

envy, 301, 362–3
Enzyklopädisches Wörterbuch (Muret-Sanders), 346n
equality (general, physical, religious, political, etc.), 245, 260, 262–6, 271, 277, 281, 283–5, 287, 326, 333, 337–8, 350, 367, 380
Equality Merchants, 326, 327
equality of income, 3, 142–3, 145, 156–7, 162–3, 207, 242–5, 247, 249, 251, 254–85, 299–301, 308, 315, 327–9, 337
equality of opportunity, 261, 264, 266, 273, 280, 285
Erewhon (Butler), 70
error(s), 399, 478, 487
Essex Hall, Strand, the, 205
Estate Dut-y, -ies, 428–30, 486, 510
estate, Shaw's (general), 419, 429, 430–1, 444–5, 474, 477, 481, 483–4, 488, 492–3, 500, 502–4, 510, 513, 515, 519
estate, Shaw's real and personal, 510
eternity, eternal life, 478, 487
"Ethical Principles of Social Reconstruction, The" (1917), 378–83
ethics, ethical principles, etc., 379–83
ethnology, 185–6, 198, 201
Eton (school), 144n, 182, 323, 381
etymolog-y, -ical, 213, 419, 459, 465, 469, 511
eugenics, 145–8, 256–7, 280, 301
Eurasia, 385
eurhythmic principles, 438
Euripedes, 36, 52
Euripedes (Murray), 149, 361
Europe, -an, 135, 192, 198, 208, 227, 231, 242, 248, 308, 322, 347, 350, 367, 369–70, 372, 381, 383–4, 390, 392, 397, 399, 401, 435, 524
"European Commission", 401
Evening Standard and St. James Gazette, the, 359
'Everybody', 313, 314, 326
Everybody's Magazine (New York), 209–10
Everybody's Political What's What, 2, 5–6, 285, 316, 345, 404–7
'Everyman', 326
Everyman (morality play), 53
Everyman (periodical), 368

"Everything - or - Nothing - All-at-Once-Brigade", 209
'Everywoman', 326
evil(s), 134, 141, 162, 206, 244, 246, 253, 260, 263, 265, 269, 282, 296, 304, 379–80, 384, 410–11
evolution (biological, social, etc.), 154, 222, 260, 306, 322, 343, 371
examinations, 40–2, 265, 338, 368
Exchequer, the Chancellor of the, 121, 420, 428–9
exclusiveness, 504–5
execution(s), -ers, 19, 192, 195, 290, 373
executives, 427
executor(s), executrix, 422, 428, 430, 445, 474, 477, 496, 499, 514–16, 519–20
exertion, degrees of, relative rewards for, etc., 265–70
exhortation, 393, 410
expenditure, Shaw's personal and domestic, 500
expenses of administration of Shaw's estate, 512
experiment(s), (general), 204, 282, 325
exploitation, 182, 219–20, 258, 318–19, 398, 411, 499
explosives, 347, 406–7
export(s), -ing, 208, 257
expropriation, 289
expulsion, 348
extermination, xi, 16, 197–9, 231, 288, 323, 327, 329, 402, 408
extra-marital sex, 79–80
extravagance(s), -antly, 273, 363, 404
exuberance, 424, 520
exultation, 378, 392

"Fabian Basis, The" (1908), 205–6
Fabian Election Manifesto (1892), 288
Fabian Essays, 227, 229, 316, 319, 327
Fabian News, 398
Fabian Quarterly, 317, 398
Fabian Socialism (Cole), 213
Fabian Society, Fabian Socialism, vii, 7, 103–4, 121, 127–8, 130, 166, 170, 172–3, 185, 203, 207–8, 213, 214, 216, 219, 221–2, 227–9, 231–2, 236, 239, 243, 253n, 262, 278, 280n, 284, 291–3, 298, 301, 305–8, 317–18, 319–20, 322, 327, 404, 474, 504

"Fabian Successes and Failures" (1944), 317–19
facetiousness, viii
factories, factory conditions, f. operatives, etc., 233, 276, 309, 319, 321, 328
Factory Acts, 182
facts, vi, 360–1, 364, 393, 399, 404, 409, 458, 525
Facts for Socialists (Fabian Society), 121
fads, 417–19
failure(s), (general), 385, 404, 421, 434
failure of alphabetic bequest, possibility of, 513
'Fair Shares for All', 328
fallac-y, -ies, x, 260, 262, 283, 423, 433, 519
fallibility, 403
"Falling Market in War Aims, The" (1918), 377–8
Falstaff, 263
fame, 37
family, the, families, 166, 234, 252, 275–7, 279–81, 291, 327
famine, 379
fanatic-s, -ism, 181, 348
farmers, ix, 321, 379
Farnell, W. (Conservative Party agent), 103
Farr, Florence, 481
Fascism, 184–94, 196–7, 199, 200, 204, 210, 213, 236, 307, 313, 318, 320, 322–4, 329, 333, 391, 395, 397–8, 408
Fascist salute, the, 391, 396n, 402
Father, the (God), 388, 393
fathers, 278, 331
fear(s), 183, 293, 330, 371, 391, 428
feelings, 493, 504, 515
fees (for performing Shaw's plays), 30–33, 494, 503
Fellowships, 477
fellow-Socialists(Shaw's),398
Feminism, 286
fervour, patriotic, 348–9, 364
Feudalism, feudal inequality, etc., 192, 225, 255, 289, 333, 383, 410
fic-tion, -titious, 46, 48–9, 363, 380
fiends, 234, 380, 389
Fifth Column, 397
fight-s, -ing, 293, 310, 351, 358, 363–4, 366–7, 369, 371, 375–7, 390, 394–7, 401, 405–7, 409–10. 365
fighting services, the, 347
films, film stars, 273, 519
Finance Act (1894), the, 428n

finan-ce, -cial, -ciers, 166, 275, 279, 296, 312, 317, 338, 376, 411
financial appeals, Shaw's refusal of, 8–9, 14
"fine phrases", 235, 391
finite legacy of a memorial character, 523
First World War,—See 'War'.
Fisher, Admiral Lord, 355
fish, flesh or fowl, 15, 16n
fitness to rule over others, 338
Fitzroy Square, London, Shaw's home at, 7
Fitzwilliam Museum, Cambridge, 479, 502
flags (national, military, etc.), 347, 388, 411
Flanders, 355–6, 366
'flapper vote, the', 313
flats, service, 496, 505
fleets, 389, 411
flibbertigibbert(s), 357
flogging, 150–1, 358
"flop of Fabianism" the, 320
Florence, 138
Fluellen, 418
flunkeys, 234
foe, the, 386, 388
food, feeding, 16n, 144n, 257–8, 260–1, 265, 270, 277, 280, 384, 406–7
fools, folly, foolishness, 86, 235, 284, 326, 330–1, 343, 377–9, 384, 388, 390, 395, 400, 405. 519
Foote, G. W. 136, 148
Forbes-Robertson, Sir Johnston, 483
force, 200, 316, 359, 369, 379–80
forcible feeding, 152, 238n, 286
Ford, Henry, 167, 281
foreign affairs, 368–9
foreigners, 368
Foreign Office, the, 219, 346, 352, 355, 524
foreign opinion, 363
foreign policy, 352, 399, 411
foresight, 253, 371
Fortnightly Review, the 236n, 354
fortune, Shaw's, 413
founding (School of Phonetics, Institute of Rhetoric, etc.), 482, 489, 490
Fox, George, 460n
fox hunt(s), 321
France, French, 29, 36, 61, 108, 173–4, 191, 271, 316, 333, 341, 346–7, 353–5, 360, 366, 369–72, 376,

378, 381, 390–1, 396, 400, 402, 437, 465, 471, 524
France Libre, La, 331
franchise, the, 255, 310, 325
Franco, General, 393–4
Franco-Prussian War, the, xii, 409
Franklin, Benjamin, 384, 426, 435
fratern-ity, isation, 191, 226, 271, 319–20, 333, 350
freakishness, Shaw's alleged, 349
"free contract", 297, 324
freedom, 153, 175, 182–4, 190, 201, 209, 212–13, 248–50, 252, 287–8, 291, 293, 297, 301, 304–5, 308, 311, 314–15, 318, 324–6, 342–4, 358–9 404
Free French, the, 336n
free speech, 195, 202, 311, 364
Freethinker, the, 136, 256n
Freethought, 169
Free Trade, 213n, 294
French Empire, the, 174
French, Sir John (later Earl of Ypres), 355
French Revolution, the, 173–4, 333
friendly societies, 204, 514
friends, x, 479, 493, 515
Friends House, Euston, 175n
Friends, the Society of, 460n
frightfulness, 406
Front, the (military), 374–5, 394
frontiers, 381, 390
Führer, the,—See Hitler, Adolf
Fundamentalism (religious), 169
fundamentals, the, 391
funds, 492, 495
funerals (public, expenses, etc.), 475, 478, 486–8, 496, 506, 510
funk, -ing, 235, 390
Further Meditations on Shaw's Geneva (c. 1938), 313, 404
future, the, 358–9, 385, 490

'Gaberlunzie', the, 304
'Gaby Glide', the, 61
Gaelic, 470
Galileo, 59
galleries (art, public, etc.), 476, 502
gallery, the, 269
Gallipoli, 370, 373
Galsworthy, John, 52, 217
gambl-ers, -ing, 272, 288
Gane, Charles, 23
garden(s), -ers, ix, 289, 488, 494, 499, 504, 506–7

Garibaldi, Giuseppe, 375
gas chambers, 403, 408
gas, poison, (in war, etc.), 372, 389, 392–3, 403n, 406
Gas and Water Socialism, 243
"G.B.S", ix
General Election, the, 118, 235, 298, 360
generalisations (general), 269, 318
generations, 350, 357, 360, 420, 432, 467
Genesis, the Book of, 222
Geneva, 184, 313n, 403
genius(es), ix, 17, 78–9, 204, 217–19, 260, 277, 324–6
"genteel brigands", 291
genteel life, 290
Gentiles, 132, 200
gentleman, Shaw's definition of a, 110, 206, 231–2, 234, 246, 251, 258–9, 266, 290, 337, 364. 365
George V, 255, 462, 464, 500, 511
George, Henry, 216
geometric style writing, 438, 442, 446
Germany, the Germans, 40, 115, 127, 170, 182, 186, 188, 198, 200, 217, 219, 221, 223–4, 281, 314, 318, 332, 341, 346–8, 351, 354–6, 361–4, 366–7, 369–74, 376, 378–82, 384–6, 389–90, 392–3, 396, 399–400, 402, 406, 408, 410, 437, 443, 519n, 524–6
German Social Democracy (Russell), 224
Gerrard, Frank, 14n
"Gestapos" in Britain, the Commonwealth, and other countries besides Germany, 212, 324, 332, 397, 399
gesticulation, 402
Getting Married, 51
getting things done, 286
Gettysburg, 165, 322, 393
ghetto, 217
Gibeon, 41
Gill, Eric, 462
Gillmore, Arabella, 480–1, 488, 507
Giotto, 27n, 43
G.K.'s Weekly, 185
Gladstone, W. E., 213n, 321
Glasgow, 109
Glasgow, Eva, 496
glory, glorification, 290, 347, 350, 361, 373, 384, 388
glorymonger(s), 332
God, 25, 41, 53, 70, 101, 129, 135, 137–41, 153n, 154–5,

165, 167, 174–5, 239, 242, 246, 251, 297, 305, 343–4, 347, 361, 370–1, 386, 388–9, 392, 396. 303
'god, a', 'gods, the', 87, 200, 215
Goering, Hermann, 198
Goethe, 341, 405
Golders Green, 33, 412, 474n, 499
Goldsmith, Oliver, 206, 216
golf, 304
Gollancz, Sir Victor, 345n
good (versus evil, etc.), 71n, 379
goods and services (economic), 320
goodwill, 341, 388
Gordon, R. Howard, xiii
governess, Shaw's, 39
governing class(es), the, 219, 234
government(s), character, art, and functions of; governing, government departments, governing bodies, the governed, etc., 21, 152, 153n, 165, 168–9, 171–3, 183–5, 191–4, 201–2, 207, 226–7, 229, 235, 237–9, 241–2, 245–6, 255, 263–4, 279, 287–8, 294–5, 297, 304, 307–10, 312–14, 316–17, 320–1, 322–4, 326–7, 331, 334–5, 336, 338–9, 341–2, 360, 368, 381, 384–5, 390, 394, 397–8, 404, 410, 417, 421, 426, 444, 449, 465, 475, 482, 491–2, 521
"Government by the Unfittest", 327
"grab - and - keep - whatever-you-can" attitude, 411
'gradualness', Fabian policy of, 208, 228, 235, 243, 306, 317
grammalogues, 417
grammar, 14n, 459, 465, 471
grandchildren, 502
Granville Barker, Harley,—See Barker
gratuities, 496, 505
Great Expectations (Dickens), 175
Greece, the Greeks, 149, 179, 492, 519n
Greek Drama,—See Drama
Greenwood, Hamar, 236
Gregg's shorthand, 27–8, 416–17
Grey, Sir Edward (Viscount Grey of Falloden), 346, 352
grouse-shooting, 144n

"Guardian Class", the, (Plato), 281, 337
guilds (general), 252, 427
Guildhall, London, 75
Guild, the London City, 421
Gujerati, 470
Gulliver (*Gulliver's Travels*), 44
gun(s), 186, 194, 392
Gurly, Kate, 481
Gurney's shorthand, 416
Gustavus Adolphus, 242
Gyges, ring of, 269

Habakkuk, 240
Habeas Corpus Act, the, 189
habits, 362, 471
Haig, Earl, 374
Haldane, Viscount, 355, 525
half-sisters, 481, 486, 488, 507
Hamburg, 406
Hamilton, Alexander, 384
Hamlet, x, 52
Hamon, Auguste, 291–2
Handel, George Frederick, 27n
handwriting, manuscript, 438, 441, 446, 454–5, 457, 483, 492, 512. *456*
Handy Andy, 418
hanging, 18–19, 137, 290, 400
Hanley (Staffs.), 104–7, 120
happiness, 165, 263, 265, 307–8, 394
Hapsburgs, the, 385
Hardie, James Keir, 118–19, 319
hardship, 194, 493, 514
Hard Times (Dickens), 240
Hardworkers, the, 303
Hare scheme, the, 339
harlequinading, Shaw's, 349
Harman, Mr Justice, 431, 468
Harrow (school), 144n, 323, 381
harshness, 274, 305, 330, 340, 344, 411
haters, hatred, hate, 249, 330, 349, 356, 362–4, 380, 393
'Have' nations, 400
'Have Not' nations, 400
headings, newspaper, 466, 468
health, 234n, 260–1, 270, 406
Hearst, William Randolph, 174
Heartbreak House, 356
Heart of Midlothian, The (Scott), 41n
Heaven, 50, 53, 120, 137–8, 151, 183, 251–2, 383, 386, 393

Hegel, -ianism, 194, 227–8, 314, 395
hegemony, a European, 381
Helena, St, 196, 332
Hell, 50, 53, 183, 251–2, 340, 375
Henderson, Professor Archibald, 1, 236, 295–6, 354–7
Henry VII, 135
Henry VIII, 197
Henry Dubb, 235
heredity, 168, 331
hero-es, -ic, -ism, 374, 383, 392
hero-worshippers, 219
Hertfordshire, ix, 1
heterodoxies, political, 325–6
Hibberd, Stuart (B.B.C. announcer), 459
hierarch-y, -ies, 321, 338
Higgins, Professor Henry, 426
Higgs, Clara (housekeeper), 485–6, 488, 495, 506
Higgs, Harry Batchelor (head gardener), 485–6, 488, 495, 506
Hill, Rowland, 30
Hindhead, 357
histor-y, -ians, 190, 193, 199, 220, 248, 252, 275, 323, 336n, 340, 349, 385–6, 395, 403, 452, 475, 500, 504
Hitler, Adolf, x, 17, 184–5, 186, 197–200, 202–3, 210, 312–3, 321–2, 334, 385, 390, 393, 395–6, 397–400, 402–3, 408, 464
Hobhouse, Professor L. T., 263, 265–71
Hodgman, Emma, 486, 488, 506
Hodgman, Kate, 486, 488
Hohenzollern régime, 'Hohenzollernism', 170, 298, 372, 385
holidays, 268, 291, 304, 461
Holland, 316, 354, 410–11
"Holy Alliance", a, 401
Holy Ghost, the, 294, 388
Home Guard, the, 405
Home Journal, 224
Home Office, the, 421
homeopathy, 406
Homer, 42. *42*
Home Rule Act for Ireland, 321
Home Secretary, the, 18, 516
homicide, 362, 379, 393
homunculus, Shaw described as a freakish, 349
honesty, 233, 283–4, 308, 322
honour, -ableness, 87, 357–8, 375, 378, 391, 481
Hornby, C. H. St. John, 306–8

horror(s), 209, 231, 348, 363, 366, 398, 400, 444
horse(s), 347, 488, 494–5
horse-breeding, 145–6, 263
hospitals, 400, 482, 491
Hottentot(s), 151
hours, 419, 461, 471, 479
house(s), housing, 258, 475, 497, 503
household staff, ix
housekeep-ers, -ing, ix, 286, 488, 506
House of Lords, 169
housemaid(s), -ing, 277, 486–7, 506
Houston v. Burns ([1918] A.C. 337), 522
Howard, Sir Ebenezer, ix
Howell, James, 426
Howells, William Dean, 426
"How to Talk Intelligently about the War" (1940), 314, 396
Hughes, M.P., Emery, 444
Hughes, W. R., 57
Hugo, Victor, 192
Hull Daily Mail, 359
human being(s), 87, 449
human capacity, ability, capabilit-y, -ies, 277, 283, 285, 301, 489–90, 492
human considerations, 430, 487
humaneness, 20n, 406–7, 488
"humane type of poison gas, a", 403
Humanitarian League, the, 474
humanity, humanitarianism, vi, ix, xi, 246, 260, 262, 288, 330, 334, 350, 380, 397
human nature, 192, 285, 307, 357, 375, 393, 404
human race, the, 159, 176, 179, 181, 197, 322, 338, 382, 393, 412
human relation(s), -ships, 356, 479, 494, 515
humbug, 234, 304, 310, 322
humiliation, 269, 385
humility, ix, 246, 388
humour, xi
hunger, 239, 273
hunger-strikes, 286. *295*
"Huns", the, 348
husband(s), 86–7, 286
hustings, the, 312
Hyde Park, 202
Hyndman, H. M., 214, 216–18
hypocrisy, 35, 234, 346, 348, 399, 424, 525
hyster-ia, -ical, 351, 525

Ibsen, Henrik, 46, 54–5, 56, 345

ideal citizen, the, 163
ideals (general), idealists, idealism, 173, 194, 217, 226, 234, 262, 271–2, 277, 283, 299, 308, 313, 380, 425, 439–40, 525
ideas, xi, 404, 424, 469, 484, 523
idiocy, 210, 313
idle, idlers, idleness, 117, 206, 213, 228, 231, 243, 266, 269, 289, 292–5, 297, 304, 307, 310
'idle rich', the, 289, 295
idols, idolatry, 170, 172–3, 175, 214, 255, 258, 288, 291, 337—8, 340, 357, 370–1
ignorance, (general, political, etc.), 242, 269, 274, 288–9, 292, 310, 313–14, 323, 326–7, 340, 369, 380, 483
illegibility, 416, 446, 465
illiteracy, 278, 319, 490
illness, 257, 497, 505
illogicality, 460, 471
illusions, illusory, 224, 226–7, 319, 360–4, 380. 387
imagination, 364, 368, 371, 414–15, 526
Immanence of God, the, 137–41, 151, 154
imperfections, 478, 487, 504
Imperial Eagle (of Germany), the, 347
Imperial Economic Committee of the Home Office, the, 421
imperialism (general), 334, 355, 370, 391, 397, 400–1, 409–11
"impetticose the gratillity", 420
'impossibilism', 223
imposture, 314, 338
impotence (political), 317
"Imprint" type, 454
imprisonment, 192n, 195, 236, 238n, 240, 286, 364, 385, 406, 408
incivility, reason for among the poor, 274
income(s) (general), 'real', taxation of, utilisation of, etc., 259–63, 265–7, 269–70, 274, 285, 287, 289, 294, 302–3, 327–8, 427, 468, 475, 477, 481–2, 486, 500, 508–15, 520
Income, Basic, the, 275–6, 277, 279–82, 301, 303, 327–8
income, earned and unearned, 121, 272, 296
income. equality of, 3, 142–3, 145, 156–7, 242–5, 247,

249, 251, 254–85, 299–301, 308, 315, 327–9, 337, 345n
Income, inequality of, 143–4, 148, 219, 230, 255–6, 257, 260, 264–5, 269, 272–4, 284
income, national, the, 207, 267, 275–6, 279, 304, 327
incompetence, incompetent, the, 168, 170–1, 174, 191, 193, 310, 330, 360
'inconclusive' peace, 348
inconsistency, 324–6, 408, 416, 436, 465
Incorporated Society of Authors, Playwrights, and Composers, the,—See Society of Authors, the
indemnit-y, -ies, 376, 381
independence, national, individual, etc., 373–4
independent incomes, 297
Independent Labour Party (I.L.P.), the, 7, 104, 130, 173; Summer School (1929), 297
India, Indians, xii, 151, 169, 198, 397, 400, 412, 458, 470
Indian Mutiny, the, x, 412
individual, the, individualism, individual differences, 204, 209, 221, 225, 269, 273n, 274, 284–5, 297, 301–2, 305, 308, 309, 403, 405–8, 478, 487, 489, 504, 511, 523
individuality, human, 262–3
indoctrination, political, 232
inducements to housemaiding work, 277
indulgences to debtors, 493, 514
industr-y, -ial, 127, 165, 182, 194, 196, 200, 203, 215, 220, 232, 237–8, 243–4, 247–50, 262, 270, 272, 276, 277–8, 296–7, 299, 309–10, 313, 316, 319, 399, 458, 464, 475–6
inefficiency, 330, 398, 400, 436
inequality (general, human, social), 260–1, 264–6, 268, 271–3, 277, 284, 338
inequality of income,—See income, inequality of
inevitability of 'gradualness', Fabian policy of, 208, 228, 236, 243, 306, 317
infallibility, 403
infant education, 443, 467
infant schools, 434
infatuated admirer, advice to, 80–93

inferiority (individual, social, moral, physical, etc.), 284–5
"infinite variety" (Belloc), 252
Inge, The Very Rev. W. R. (Dean), 206, 240, 293
inhabitants, 406, 412
inheritance, 298. 303
initiative, 204, 273n, 400
injur-y, -ing, 393
injustice, 219, 259, 493, 514
innocence, 87
Inns of Court, 482, 491
inoculation, 406
inquisitions, 186, 242, 350
inscriptions, 499, 506
insecurity, 323, 328
insight, 385, 412
insincerity, the Church's, 388
inspectors, factory, 321
instincts, 86, 362
institutes, institutions (general), 388, 427, 475–9, 483, 489, 492, 502–3
Institute of Journalists, the, 14
"Institute of Phonetics and School of Rhetoric, Oratory, Dress, Manners, and the Arts of Public Life", Shaw's proposed, 482
"instructed director class", 280–1, 315, 337
instruction,—See teaching
instruments, musical, 492, 494
instruments of torture,—See torture.
insult(s), 337, 399
intellect as a passion, 79
intellectuals, the intellectual approach, x, 199, 236, 287, 292, 294, 315, 343, 357, 361, 380
"intellectual proletariat", the (in Russia), 276
intelligence, 284–5, 288, 310, 317, 323, 335, 402, 404
intelligentsia, the, 170, 278, 337
Intelligent Woman's Guide to Socialism and Capitalism, The, 230
intelligibility, 418, 459, 482, 491
intemperance, 16–17, 66, 273–4
interest (financial, economic), 184, 214, 216, 221, 360, 428
interest(s), (general), 285, 424–5
intermarriageability (social), 242, 257, 277, 281, 285, 327, 337

international, -ism (general) 229, 305, 347, 375, 487
international aggression, 359
international arrangements, 411
'international combination of nations', 359
international communication, 436
international court, 402
international finance, 338
international language, 459
international police force, 359, 367, 386
international politics, 411
international relations, 410
"International Socialist League", an, 223
'International, the' 220, 227
interview, conditions for, 12–14
intimidation, 379
inurn-ing, -ment, 499
invalidity (legal), 431, 468, 518, 522
invasion, 202, 350, 385, 410
invent-ors, -ions, 299, 324, 389, 413, 422, 426–7, 465, 469, 511
investment, 211, 368, 376, 411, 475, 484, 509–10, 513–15
Iran, 332
Ireland, the Irish (general), x, xii, 21–2, 173, 181, 192, 198, 199n, 200, 238, 256, 321, 349–50, 373–4, 397, 410, 424, 430, 459, 470, 476–7, 483, 492, 512, 516
Ireland, model postcard on, 22
Irish Statesman, The, 335
irrationalism, 404
Irrational Knot, The, 2
Irving, H. B., 68, 70
Ismail, 406
-isms (general), 398
Israel, 200
italic, 446, 467
Italy, 186, 190–2, 194, 196, 198, 204, 318, 332, 371, 381, 384, 391. 400, 408, 471
"itching powder", Shaw described as, 519
Ivan the Terrible, 174

Jamaica, 334
James II, 168
Japan, -ese, 198, 371, 382, 408
jargon, legal, 473, 484
Jarrow, 397
Jefferson, Thomas, 384
Jenner, Edward, 42
Jensen, Nicholas (typographer), 28

Jerusalem, 320, 331
Jevons, William Stanley, 215, 224–6, 256
Jews, 133, 139, 186, 197, 199–200, 216–17, 398, 402, 408
"jibe at the law" (in Shaw's Will), 522
jingoes, jingoism, 294, 349, 351, 361n
Joan of Arc, 48
Job, 27n
jockeys, 273, 289
Joel, 240
John, Augustus, 502
'John Bull', 235
John Bull (magazine), 242, 285
John Bull's Other Island, 357
John, King, 182
John O'London's Weekly, 25n
Johnson, Dr. Samuel, 264
Johnson, Dr. Johnson's alphabet, 26–28, 419, 465, 468–9, 498, 511
Johnson, W. Branch, xiii
joining of alphabetic letters, 438, 440–1, 445–6, 457
joint stock companies, 116, 225
joke, Shaw's alphabet ideas regarded as a, 425, 437
Jones, Henry Arthur, 55, 63, 348–9, 356n, 524
Joshua, 41, 221
journal-ists, -ism, 181, 199, 203, 221, 226, 246, 458, 462, 525
Journal of the War Years (Weymouth), 199n, 397
Jowett, Benjamin, 271
"Joy Riding at the Front" (1917), 374–6
judge(s), 151, 156–7, 250, 337, 373
judgement, 361, 468, 476, 484, 487, 492, 498, 514, 518, 523
judicial decision, 513, 522
"judicial homicide", 19n
judiciary, the, judicial functions, 275, 491
Jupiter, 90
jur-y, -ies: trial by, etc., 226 250, 258, 373
'Jusqu'aubout-ist', -ism, 378
justice, 144, 181, 183, 246–7, 249–50, 252, 260, 265–6, 280, 285, 320, 330, 340, 354, 363, 374, 380, 386, 388, 405, 410, 504
jockeys, 273, 289

'Kaffir boom' in 1895, the, 284n

Kaiser, the, 187, 331, 364, 368, 409, 525
Kant, Immanuel, 379, 407
Kautsky, Karl, 192
Kean, Edmund, 17
keepsakes, 479
Kelvin, Lord, 226, 263, 283
Kensington, Bishop of (1913) (The Right Rev. J. P. Maud), 62, 63–4, 65–8, 70. 64
Kent, 394
Kerensky, Alexander Feodorevitch, Kerenskyist, 187
keyboard (monotype), 467–8
keys to the Shaw Alphabet, 448, 451
Kharkov, 406–7
kicking, 364, 384, 398, 401
Kiek, Rev. E. S., 105, 123, 129
killing (slaying, etc.), 18–19, 134, 196, 199, 232–3, 242, 270, 289, 336, 363, 366, 370, 392–3, 395, 405, 410. 233
Kimpton, ix
kindergarten, need to teach the Shaw alphabet in, 449
kindness, kindliness, xi, 479, 481, 488, 493–4, 514–15
King, the, kings, 118–19, 131, 153, 167–8, 172, 316–17, 333, 337–8, 350, 464
King Albert's Gift Book, 354
"kingdom of Heaven on earth", the, 332
King Lear (Shakespeare), 216
King's Hall, Covent Garden, 170, 294, 360, 366, 369
"King's Spelling, A", 462
Kingsway Hall, the, 165, 302–3, 340
Kipling, Rudyard, 37
Kirkwood, David (Baron), 189
kissing, 86, 87
Kitchener, Lord, 360, 389. 365
Klein, Julius, 373
Klootz, Anarchasis, 382
knowledge, 424, 475–6, 487, 490
Koltchak, Alexis, 385
Kropotkin, Prince Peter Alexeivitch, 216, 218
Ku Klux Klan, 198, 236
Kunowski, Felix von, 443, 447
Kut (Iraq), 370
labour (general), 201, 214, 217, 223, 275, 279, 292, 296, 301, 322, 324, 351, 395, 411, 413–14, 417, 419, 454, 457, 458, 462–5, 469, 511, 521

542   SHAW—"THE CHUCKER-OUT"

labour-ers, -ing classes, 268,
270, 278, 321, 326–7, 329,
379, 395, 413–14, 504
Labour Exchanges, 291
Labour Leader, The, 233,
256n, 287n
labour leaders, 316
Labour Monthly, the, 181,
220, 227, 232, 293–4, 314
Labour movement, the, 173,
258, 345, 352–3
Labour Party, the, 104, 117–
19, 121, 173, 186, 188, 197,
258, 287, 290–1, 292–4,
296–8, 301, 317–18, 320,
328, 345, 352–3, 399,
408
labour-saving (devices,
schemes, etc.), 26, 413,
420, 459, 469, 511
Labour and Socialist International, the, 188
Lacey, Rev. T. A., 71–2
Laden, Mrs Alice, 103, 403,
497
Lady Chatterley's Lover
(Lawrence), 61n, 76–7
laisser-faire, 185, 195, 197,
280, 324–5
land, -owners, 110–12, 114,
152, 176, 179, 194, 200,
209, 248, 250, 333, 395,
475, 477
landlord(s), -ism, 110, 112–
13, 122–3, 178–81, 200,
225, 227, 254, 274, 312,
321, 379, 424
Langland, William, 469
languages, 435–6, 443, 447,
452, 458–9, 461, 469–72,
482–3, 489, 492, 498, 511,
519–21
Lansbury, George, 237
Larkin, Jim, 144, 237
Lassalle, Ferdinand, 216,
218
"Last Spring of the Old
Lion, The" (1914), 349–51
Latin, 426, 435, 464, 519n
Latin races, 185
Laval, Pierre, 336n
lawbreakers, 336
Lawrence, D. H., 61n, 76–7
Lawrence, T. E. ('of
Arabia'), (T. E. Shaw),
484–5
laws, the law (general), law
courts, 'law and order',
lawyers, 'legal matters',
etc., 168, 180–1, 194–5,
212, 223, 231, 234, 237–8,
241, 248, 250n, 254, 283–
4, 294, 301, 304–5, 336–8,
340, 361, 386, 388, 399,
401, 404–5, 408, 427–8,
430–33, 473, 482, 491–3,

495, 500, 504–5, 514–16,
521–3
laws (economic, scientific),
261, 263
Lazarus, 221, 405
Lazarus, Robert, 518
lazy people, laziness, 166,
262, 273, 286, 288, 314, 464
Leader, The, 285
leader page (in newspapers),
466, 468
leader(s), -ship, 167, 196,
236, 298, 313, 316, 318,
321, 330, 341, 364, 384,
400, 403
League of Nations, the, 198,
342, 359, 382, 386, 390–1,
401–2, 411
League of Western Civilisation, 367
learning, 459
leaseholds, 475
Lebensraum, 400
Lecky, James, 425
Lecture Recorder, The, 184n,
211
lecturers, lectureships (university, institute, etc.),
476–7, 482, 491
Lectures on Jurisprudence
(Austin), 206
Left, the (general), 345
"Lefts who are never right",
326
left-wing factions, different,
230, 318
lega-cies, -tees, 421, 431,
443–4, 475, 485–9, 495,
497, 508, 510
legacy duty, 502, 504, 510
legality, 363, 444–5
legibility, 416, 418, 442, 448,
458, 463–4, 466
legislat-or(s), legislation,-ure,
293, 304, 319, 321, 342,
358, 382, 420. 295
Leibnitz, Gottfried Wilhelm,
264
leisure, 184, 196, 201, 204,
276, 279, 301–2, 304, 311,
314–15, 325, 395
Leith (Ireland), 239
leniency, 493, 514
Lenin, Vladimir Ilyich, 187,
192, 208, 211, 228, 231,
235, 242, 305, 307, 384,
399
Leonardo da Vinci, 41
letters (of the alphabet), 415,
417–19, 434, 436, 440–3,
445–6, 448, 452, 457–8,
460–1, 463–4, 466–7, 469,
498, 511
letters (correspondence), bequests concerning, 500,
502

letters (correspondence) to
Erica Cotterill, 80–95
letters, printed, 23–34
levellers-up, -down; levelling
(social), 225, 259, 261,
278, 281, 285, 328
Levinskaya, Maria, 490
Lewis, Maurice, 298
Liane de Pougy, Mlle, 284
Liberal, -ism, 117–18, 128,
168, 186–7, 191, 195, 197,
213n, 219, 221, 224–5, 250,
261, 286, 292, 321, 324,
345, 408
Liberal and Social Union,
the, 176
libertine(s), 86
liberty, 153, 165, 168, 171,
174–5, 181–4, 186, 191,
195–6, 201, 223, 260, 271,
280, 287, 293, 301, 306,
310, 313, 321, 322–6, 333,
342–3, 350, 357, 367, 380,
388, 395
libraries, 422–3, 432, 448,
477, 512, 523–4
licensing (of performances of
Shaw's plays), 30–3, 479,
494, 501, 504
Liebknecht, Karl, 188, 216
Liège, 353, 373
lies, literature and, 47
life (general), lifetime, etc.,
x, 16n, 36–44, 219, 223,
229, 259, 263, 265, 267,
270, 302, 307, 364, 378,
383, 393, 412, 415, 425,
458, 460, 477–8, 482, 487,
500
life beyond, the, 129
*Life and Death of Mr. Bad-
man* (Bunyan), 206
Life Force, the, 86–7
life, higher and lower forms
of, 154, 158, 271
"Life More Abundant"
(motto), 293
Lille, 373, 381
Limerick, 369
limitation(s) (personal, individual, of schemes, etc.),
285, 478, 487, 492
"Limitation Conference,
'The' (1921), 385
limited and certain ob-
jective, 523
Lincoln, Abraham, 163, 165,
322, 377, 393
lingua franca, 459
lino-type, -typists, 416, 419,
467
Lion, the British, 350
lip-reading, 459
liquidation of undesirables,
the, 19n, 201, 319, 394,
402–3

Listener, The, 182, 389, 457
Lister, Lord, 42
literary composition,—See composition
literary critics, 391
literary estate, Shaw's, 477
literary executor, Shaw's, 480, 515
litera-ry, -ture (general), 47, 268, 418, 420
literary manuscripts, Shaw's, 480, 487
literary style, 24–5, 26*n*
Literature, English, 36, 412, 419, 428
"Literature of the Theatre, The" (1924), 45–57
lithography, 511
Little England, -ers, 294, 410
"Live and let live", 394
liver injections, 16*n*
Liverpool Courier, the, 368
Liverpool Fabian Society, the, 329
living, earning a, 272, 278
Lloyd George, David (later Earl), 173, 236, 259, 372, 393
loan stock, 514
loans, unsecured personal, 493, 514
local authorities, 399
local councils, 332
local government, 342; Local Government Boards, 23, 223
Locarno Pact, the, 385, 390, 411
lock-outs, 296, 299
Lodge, Sir Oliver, 283
Lodge, Oliver (junior), 70
Loewenstein, Fritz Erwin, 25*n*, 516
logic, -al, 345, 404, 442
Logic of Political Economy (de Quincey), 206
logographic systems of writing, 437
Lohengrin, 372, 390
London, 21, 75, 124–5, 272, 392, 407, 475, 483, 491–2, 498, 502–4, 507, 513, 515
London, Bishop of, the, 74–5
London County Council, the, 502
London Diocesan Council for Preventive and Rescue Work, 75
London, Lord Mayor of, the, 272
London School of Economics and Political Science, xiii, 475, 477
London University, 492
longhand, 416, 457–8
Lonsdale, Frederick, 348

looting, 361, 407
Lord, the, 388
Lord Lieutenant of Dublin, the, 239
lotteries, 272
Louis XIV, 316
Louis XVI, 173
Louvain, 366
love (general), 3, 78, 226, 249, 360, 393
love affairs, 481
love, falling in, 87, 146, 258
love, making, 86–7
"Love panacea", the, 320
loyalty, 353, 364, 386, 410
Lucifer, 392
Lunacharsky, Anatoly Vasilievitch, 229
lunatic asylum, 16*n*, 268–9
lunatics, 198
Lusitania, s.s., 348, 355–6
Luther, Dr Martin, 27*n*, 242
Luton, 516
Luxemburg, Rosa, 188
luxur-y, -ies, 179, 243, 256, 275, 278, 285
Lynch, Colonel Arthur, 376
Lytton-Bernard, Dr Bernard, 161

McCarthy, Sir Desmond, 391, 402
McCarthy, Lillah, 87*n*
MacCarthy, Professor P. A. D., 441–2, 448
Macaulay, Thomas Babington (Lord), 206
MacDonald, James Ramsay, 298–9
Macedonia(n), 470
McFie, Ronald Campbell, 69–70
MacGowan, Rev. Dr W. S., 62–3
machine age, the, 434
machinery, 414, 419, 437, 463, 467
Macmillan, Harold, 428
McNulty, M. E., 474, 481
magazines, 375, 463
Magdeburg, 406
Magna Charta, 182
Magrath, J. F., 440–1
Mahomet, -an, 59, 478
maids, ix, 488
Major Barbara, 47
majorit-y, -ies, 153*n*, 166, 169, 180, 193, 230, 235–6, 240, 307, 314, 316, 328, 331, 337, 409
Majorocracy, 166, 168–9
Malthus, Thomas Robert, 206
Mammon, 347
man, a better sort of, 260

Man and Superman, vi, 26*n*, 55, 71, 183, 341
Manchester, 109, 265, 309
Manchester Guardian, The, 188, 193–5, 340, 383
Manchester School,—of Individualists, of Capitalists, 407–8
Manchuria, 120
man-in-the-street, the, 170, 202, 245
mankind, 176, 249, 251, 253, 262, 328, 332, 343, 355, 404, 412, 424
manners, 260, 278, 289, 357, 482, 490
manœuvring (political, etc.), 391
manufacture of own books, Shaw's, 501
manufactur-ers, -ing, 299, 477, 513
manuscript (See also handwriting), 492. *253*
manuscripts (literary), Shaw's, 474
manuscripts, Shaw's refusal to advise on others', 8, 14
Marcus Aurelius, 168
Margate, 197
marriage, 78–9, 83–4, 86–7, 147–8, 260, 291, 323, 393, 493, 515
Marson, Rev. C. L., 101
martial law, 236, 363
Marx, Karl; Marx-ian, -ist, -ism, 130, 192, 197, 203, 208–9, 214–24, 227–9, 230, 235–6, 239, 278, 295, 303, 317–18, 321, 333, 343, 384. *228, 253*
Mason, J. N. & Co., 515, 522
mass-appeal, Hitler's, 385
mass-communication, 169
masses, the, 180, 235, 279, 293, 310, 403
Massingham, H. W., 259
masterpieces, 276, 520
master(s), the master class, 18, 178, 182, 244, 253, 273, 302
material-ist, -ism, 215, 222, 226, 318
mates, mating, 260, 393
Mathematical Society, the, 421
mathematic-s, -al, -ians, 228, 264, 275, 285, 327, 414, 418–19, 434, 457, 464, 469, 511
Matriarchy, 287
Matteotti, Giacomo, 186–7, 191, 194–6, 331
Maud, the Right Rev. J. P. (Bishop of Kensington, 1913), 62–8, 70

Maunsel & Co., Dublin, 376n
Maxwell, Dr William, 413, 462, 466–8
Mayor, Lord, the, 273
Mazzini, Giuseppe, 191, 375
M'Cormick, Mr, 386
meanness, 493, 514
means of production, the, 179
means, Shaw's financial, 479, 483, 492–3, 515
measurement, 265–6, 268, 339
measures (political, social, etc.), 167–8, 259, 316, 318, 383, 420
meat-eating, 16, 408
mechanistic (social) doctrine, 490
medical profession, medicine, 261, 424
megalomania, dictatorship as, 330
Mehrwerth (surplus value), 215, 221
Mein Kampf (Hitler), 200
Memorial Hall, Faringdon St., 244
memorials, memorial services, 487, 503
men (general), 257, 260, 267, 285–7, 322, 358, 383, 392–4
mental defectiveness, 490
Mephistophele-s, -an, 218, 304
mercy, 231, 388, 406
Meredith, Georgina, 486, 489, 507
merit(s), 262, 316
Mesopotamia, 388
'Messiah', the, 331–2, 333
metaphysic-s, -ians, 215
Methodists, 294
"metropolitan culture", 483, 491
Metropolitan (magazine), 271
Metropolitan Museum, New York, 503
Michelangelo, 392
middle class(es), 110, 112, 114–17, 119, 121, 181, 217–19, 223, 226, 236, 292, 319
Mikado, The, 393
militancy, 286, 366
military affairs, military authorities, militarism, 194, 241, 291, 323, 346–7, 358–9, 366, 372, 381, 401, 419, 476, 482, 491–2, 526
military service, 357–9, 407, 505
millionaires, 144n, 277–8, 281–2, 284n, 407

Millionairess, The, 444
millions, 458, 463–4, 466–7
Mill, John Stuart, 330
Milner-Holland, E., Q.C., 518
Milner, Lord, 410
Milton, John, 347, 426
mines, miners, 273, 276, 294
minimum social standards, 262, 283
Minimum Wage Act (proposed), 291
Minister of Peace, 366
Ministers (of Cabinet, State, etc.), 316, 317
ministers of religion, 491
Ministry of Labour, the, 421
Ministry of Production, 421
minorit-y, -ies, 166, 168, 204, 235–6, 241–2, 249, 307, 319, 331, 409
minutes (time), 416, 419, 457–8, 460
miracles, 134, 136, 155, 159, 452
Miraculous Birth of Language, The (Wilson), 446
Miraculous Revenge, The (Shaw) (a short story), 56
Misalliance, 51
miscalculation, 462
miscegenation, 199
mischief, 86, 220, 322, 349, 400, 405, 407, 411
misconceptions, x, 424
miser-y, -ableness, 376, 392–3
mispronunciation, 482, 489
mistrust, 293, 321
"mixed social methods", 204
mob, the, 331
Modern Drama, 423
"Modern Education" (1937), 36–44
"Modern Spelling Primer, A" (1947), 459n
modesty, 432
Mohammedanism, 132
Molière, 54
Monaco, 108–9
monarch(s), -y, -ies, 174, 316, 326, 369–70, 376, 385
monetary systems, 423
money, 8–9, 12, 14, 109, 112, 122, 128, 141, 143–4, 156–7, 160, 173, 177, 193, 204n, 206, 217, 223, 242–3, 246, 253, 257, 260–1, 263–6, 270, 274, 280, 281, 302–3, 308, 312, 316, 320, 323, 327–8, 336, 354, 359, 368, 375, 419–20, 425–9, 431–2, 443–4, 465, 469–70, 483, 492, 494, 510, 515, 520–1

monopolies, 414
monotyp-e, -ists, 419, 454, 463–4, 466–8
'Monsieur Tout le Monde', 332
Monte Carlo, 108–9
months, 480, 488, 505
Montreal, 70
monuments, 478, 487, 499, 506
'Moralised Capitalism' (Comte), 318
moral(s), -ity, 3, 45, 55, 58–60, 61–77, 78–91, 96–102, 134, 153n, 194, 219, 231–2, 246, 262, 273, 284–5, 289, 307, 340, 347, 361–2, 363, 374, 380, 392, 397, 402, 409–10. 233, 365
Morgan, Pierpoint, 220n
Morning Post, the, 247n
Morris, May, 479
Morris, William, 28, 209, 216–18, 227–8, 315, 474, 479, 519n
Morris, W. R. (Lord Nuffield), 281
mortgages, 184, 475
Moses, 138, 151, 220
Mosley, Sir Oswald, 199–200, 398
mother(s), -hood, 278, 286, 301, 331, 348, 392
motor-cars, 258, 281, 347, 494, 503
mourning, 478, 487
mouth, fighting with the, 364. 365
Mozart, Wolfgang Amadeus, 54
Mrs Warren's Profession, 59
muddleheadedness, 399
municipal (enterprises, employment, etc.), 123–5, 193, 342
munitions, 348, 356
murder, 20n, 24, 59, 136, 187, 191, 204, 266, 361, 366, 373, 386, 388
Muret-Sanders, 346n
Murphy (newspaper editor), 174
Murray, Professor Gilbert, 50, 149
Museum, British,—See British Museum
music, musicians, 269, 278, 476, 492, 519
Mussolini, Benito, x, 167, 169, 184, 186–7, 188–94, 196–8, 202, 210–11, 236, 312–13, 321, 331, 391, 393, 395–6, 398–9, 402–3
Musters, Georgina, 480, 485, 489, 507
Musters, Harold, 485

mutiny, 152, 291, 351
'My Country Right or Wrong' attitude, 348
My Fair Lady, 429–30, 444
mystery plays, mediaeval, 52–3
mystic, -al, -ism, 255, 343

naïveté, 460
'namer' dots, 447
names of alphabetic letters, 437
Naples, 406
Napoleon, -ic, 17, 167–9, 190–1, 195, 197, 216, 264, 331, 333, 341, 377, 389–90, 399, 410
Napoleon III, 170, 192, 220–1, 340, 376
Nares Owen, 48
Nash's Magazine, 311, 338
Nation, The, 256n, 259–71, 385
National Anthem, the British, 388
National Anti-Vivisection League, the, 23
National Assembly (the Russian), 242
national cash, the, 338
national control, of land, capital, and industry, 200
National Council of Social Service, 421
National Gallery of British Art (Tate Gallery, the, 502
National Gallery (London), the, 68
National Gallery of Ireland, Dublin, as Shaw beneficiary, 427, 430–1, 476, 479, 513, 518, 520
National Government, the (1931), 299
national income, the, 207, 267, 275–6, 279–80, 304, 327
nationalisation, 9, 180, 204, 207, 213, 272, 296, 298, 317. 228
National-ists, -ism, 303, 320, 373, 476. 228
nationalit-y, -ies, 381–2
National Liberal Club, 254, 257, 259
National Portrait Gallery (London), the, 503
National Reformer, The, 214
National Savings Committee, the, 421
nationalistic sentiments, 363
national service, 407
National Service Department of the Ministry of Labour, 421

National Socialism, 199, 210, 318
national sovereignty, 342, 382
National Theatre, a, 425
National Trust, the, 503
"Nation of Villagers, A" (1907), 209–10
nations, 225, 330–2, 361, 394
NATO alliance, 386
NATSOPA (trade union), 329
natural capacity, ability, 339
Nature, 183, 193, 275, 287, 293, 314, 322–5, 330, 371, 392
nature, man's 'higher' and 'lower', 234
Navy, the; naval affairs, battles, etc., 127, 355, 389, 476, 482, 491–2
Nazi, Nazism, 199, 201, 320, 400, 408
necessit-y, -ies, 243, 256, 275, 278, 285, 287, 326, 360, 362, 377, 418
needs (individual, social, etc.), 259, 261–2, 268, 275, 282
Negroes, 198, 269
neighbours, ix, 267, 312, 324, 336, 375, 379, 473
Nelson, Lord, 17, 42
Nero, 197
neurosis, 66
neutral, -ity, 354, 362, 374
New Age, the, 173, 256n, 289
"new being", a; "new sort of man", a, 155, 256
Newcastle, 123, 127
Newcastle Fabian Society, 104, 121, 127–8
New Commonwealth, the, 256n
New Deal, the, 182
New Democratic Freedom and the Democratic Freedomain, The (pamphlet), 163
"New Economic Policy" (Lenin), 208, 228
New Leader, the, 200
New Republic, The, 183n, 201n, 342–3
News Chronicle, the, 250n, 256n
newspapers (general), xii, xiii, 248, 251, 256, 263, 312, 339, 361, 375, 409, 414, 416, 419–21, 426, 463
New Statesman, the, 7n, 256n, 280, 285, 301, 304, 325, 326–7, 345–6, 349
New Testament, the, 42, 155
Newton, Sir Isaac, 215, 264, 266, 269, 392

New Witness, The, 173, 340
New York, 502–3, 515
New York Herald Tribune, the, 295
New Zealand, 119
Nickson, Miss M. A. E., xiv
Nietzsche, Friedrich Wilhelm, 347, 379
Nightingale, Florence, 284
nineteenth century, the, 194–5, 267, 310, 370
Noah's Ark, 55–6
noble, -ness, 375, 379, 383, 482
No Conscription Fellowship, 130
Noddy books (Enid Blyton), 443
nomenclature, political, 203
nomination, 286, 309
non-combatants, 405
non compos, possibility of Shaw becoming, 497
Non-Intervention Committee (re Spanish Civil War), the, 395
non-resistance (pacifist), 394
nonsense, 361, 380, 386, 391, 396
non-specialist, the, 424
Nordic characteristics, 186, 198, 199–200
normality, 519
Norman, C. H., 130, 205n, 244
Northcliffe, Lord, 173–4
'Northern' English, 511
North Staffordshire Labour Party, the, 104
notations, 434, 436
novel(s), -ists, 416, 418, 436, 462, 518
nudism, 96, 99
Nuffield, Lord, 281
numbers, 455, 457, 467–8, 470
numerical systems, reform of, 470–1
nurseries, nurserymaids, 400, 482, 491
nurses, 273
nursing, 348
nymphomania, 91

Oates, Titus, 398
obedience (social, political, etc.), 337–8
obiter dicta, viii
object, an; cannot complain to the Court, 522
objects of Shaw's alphabet trusts, 521–2
obscen-e, -ity, 351
Observer, the, 274–5, 279, 283
occupations, 254, 401, 405

octogenarians, 394
Oedipus, 36n, 51–2
Oedipus (Sophocles), 50–1, 52
officers (army), 358, 384
'official case for the war', the, 524
officials (State, government, etc.), 252, 360
Ogden, C. K., 465n
Oh, You Beautiful Doll (revue), 263
old age pensions, 119, 258, 265, 480
"Old Gang" (the Fabian Society's), 319
Old Testament, the, 149
oligarchs, oligarchy, 169–70, 189, 225, 241, 307, 310, 313, 323, 337
Olivier, Margaret (Lady), 333
Olivier, Sydney (Lord), 292, 318, 333–4, 474–5
Olympic Theatre, the, 17n
omniscience and omnipotence, 167
once-for-all completion of a testamentary disposition, 523
"One Party or Totalitarian State, the", 303, 309, 311, 334
one-sound-one-letter alphabet, 433
opera, 50
opportun-ists, -ism, 169, 298
opportunity (general), 268, 288, 384, 391
opportunity, equality of, 261, 264, 266, 273, 280, 285
opposition (the political, party, etc.), 303, 310, 312, 317, 410
oppress-ion, -ors, 181, 350, 381, 405, 408, 494
oracle, Shaw as, 519
Orage, A. R., 173
Orange rebellion, the, 373
oratorios, 476
orators, oratory, 203, 363–4, 404, 475, 482–3, 492
orchestras, 476
order of letters in alphabet, 435, 437
orders (government, military, etc.), 324, 336, 384, 464, 482, 491
ordinary people, folk, ix, x
ordination (religious), 482, 491
Origin of Species (Darwin), 56
originality, 424, 426
orthography, 426, 428, 433, 460, 511, 519

Orthological Institute, The, Cambridge, 30, 421, 465
Orwell, George, 283
Osborn, Sir Frederic, 45
Ottoman Empire, 182
Ouida, 217
outlaw(s), 357, 366
overcrowding, 327
overtime, 303, 405
Owen, Robert, 206
Oxford, 366, 483, 491
Oxford, Earl of, 206
Oxford University, 414, 422, 459, 512

pacif-ists, -ism, iii, xii, 346, 366, 374–6, 381, 393–4, 399
Paganism, 478
pages, 466, 468
pain, -fulness, -lessness, 392, 403
Paine, Tom, 59, 384
paint-ers, -ing, 314, 427, 502
Pakistan, 458
palaces, 337
Palace Theatre, the, 61–6, 68, 72–4
Palestrina, Giovanni, 43
Pall Mall Gazette, the, 85, 284, 355
Palmer, Mitchell, 236
pamphlet(s), -eers, 412, 518, 525
Pan Anglicanism, 382
Panel of Experts (to judge Shaw Alphabet competition), 432
Panels (of 'tested persons'), 338
Pan Germanism, 382
Pankhurst, Sylvia, 197, 201, 237, 286
Paper Economic Committee of the Ministry of Production, the, 421
Paradise, 193
paradox, -es, *passim*
paralogisms, 306
paralys-ing, -is, 366, 382
"parasitic proletariat", the, 289–90
parasitism, 175, 231, 275, 289, 293–4, 303
parens patriae, 520
parent(s), -age, 35, 79, 81–2, 267, 270, 275, 290, 392
Paris, 107, 392
Parliament, -ary, 58, 118, 120, 122–3, 150, 167–8, 175, 178, 196–7, 227, 237, 256, 267, 286, 289–92, 295–6, 298, 310, 313–14, 316, 321, 331, 333, 335, 339, 341–2, 368, 395, 398–9, 409, 411, 415

parlourmaids, 482, 486, 491
parochialism, 313
'pars' (paragraphs), 466
Parties, political (general), 234n, 280n, 335, 345, 399
partisan(s), 322
Party labels, 345
party system, the, 313–4, 316, 335, 342, 398
"Party System and Socialists, The" (1944), 303, 334–5
Pascal, Blaise, 399
passbooks (bank), 500
Passey, E. H., 283–4
Passion, Poison and Petrifaction, 503
passions (primitive, secondary, martial, etc.), 70, 362–3
past, the, 471, 477, 490
Pasteur, Louis, 42
Patch, Blanche (secretary), 486, 489, 497, 507, 515
patent(s), -ee(s), 299, 412, 469, 498
pathological results of bad speech, 490
patience, 253, 284, 286
patriot(s), -ism, 234, 346, 348–9, 355–6, 363, 373, 379, 383–9, 411
Patterson, Jane, 481
Paul I (of Russia), 331
Paul, St, 138, 178
paupers, 275, 277, 295
Pax Germanica, 372
payments, 475, 481–2, 488–9, 493, 510, 514
peace (general), 226, 330, 347–8, 352, 359, 366, 371, 374, 376–80, 383, 388, 391, 396–7, 399
"Peace Conference Hints", 411
"peasant proprietary civilisation" (Chesterton), 247
peasant(s), -ry, 208, 230, 247, 251, 333, 376, 512
Pease, Edward R., 7, 474–5
Peckham, 368
peer(s), 278, 316, 339
penalt-y, -ies, 183
penitence, 388
pensions (old age, army, etc.), 119, 258, 265, 284, 358, 480, 505–6
people, the, 165, 167–8, 171, 174, 183, 191, 193, 200–1, 240–1, 235, 248, 256, 304–5, 307, 310, 312–13, 320, 322, 327, 330, 335–7, 378, 388, 399
People's Palace, Mile End, the, 75

people, "specially capable", 275
"people's will, the", 310
percentages, 278–9, 304, 330, 332, 429, 457–8, 461–2, 464, 494
perfection, 258, 293, 459
performance(s), (of artistic works), 477, 479, 493–4, 503, 515
perjury, 187, 195
'permeation', Fabian policy of, 236, 292
permutations, 415, 418
'Perpetua' type, 454
perpetuity (legal), 420
'perpetuity period, the statutory', 427
persecution, 202, 204, 218, 220, 278, 311, 393, 398, 404, 525
persons (pioneering, superior, conservative, average, backward, inferior, etc.), 285, 491
pessimism, 216, 404
Pétain, Henri Philippe, Marshal, 336n
Peter the Great, 174, 370, 377
Peter the Hermit, 200
Peter, St, 138
Pethick-Lawrence, F. W. (Lord), 237
petition, 130
Petrie, Sir Flinders, 395
pets, 273, 485
Phaeton, 339
Philistin-es, -ism, 217–18
philolog-y, -ists, 426
philosoph-y, -ical, -ers, 153n, 221, 223, 227–8, 275, 281, 308, 327, 333, 343, 379, 382–3, 395, 424
phobias, 197–8, 200
Phoenician alphabet,—See alphabet, the Standard English, etc.
phonemes, 435, 452
Phonetic Alphabet Society, London, the, xiv
phoneticians, 418, 427, 431, 437–8, 440, 445, 457–8, 469, 492, 511, 522
phonetic reform, 413, 423, 431, 470, 475n
phonetic relationships, 437
phonetics (general), 458, 472, 475, 477, 482–3, 489, 491–2, 498, 511, 519
phonetics, applied, 426
phonetics, as theme of Pygmalion, 429
'phonetic school primer', Shaw's, 498

Phonetics, Oratory, etc., Shaw's proposed school of, 482
phonetic spelling, 20, 26–30, 36n, 415–22, 423–72, 475, 482–4, 489, 491–2, 498, 511–13, 518–23
phonetics, science of, the, 425, 437
phonetic writing, 417, 492
Phonotypy, 426
phraseograms, 417
physical culture, education, 475, 490
physical force, 200, 237
physiological laboratories, 490
Pickwick, -ian, 286
pictographs, 434
pictures, 33, 278, 280, 466–7, 494
Pidgin English, 29–30, 459, 465
piece-work, 299
Piers Plowman (Langland), 469
Pilate, Pontius, 50, 133
pilfering, poverty the reason for, 273
Pilgrim's Progress, The (Bunyan), 474n
Pilgrim Trust, the, 421
Pinero, Sir Arthur W., 348–9
pioneer(s), -ing, 285, 320
pirate(s), 308, 388
Pisgah, 226
Pitfold, Haslemere, Shaw's home at, 7
Pitman, I. J. (now Sir James), 428, 431n, 438, 448–9, 523
Pitman, Sir Isaac, 426, 470 498
Pitman, Sir Isaac & Sons, Ltd., 498
Pitman's phonetic alphabet, 27
Pitman's shorthand, 27–8, 416–17, 419, 426, 465, 470
Pius IX, Pope, 192
Plan for Germany ("Victory's"), 401
Plan of Campaign for Labour, A, 320
platitudes, 402
Plato, -nism, 41, 271, 281, 308, 337, 379
play performances, terms and conditions, 30–3, 494
plays, 54, 305, 405, 415, 419, 424–5, 429, 436, 443, 458, 462, 479, 483, 491, 494, 503, 515, 519
playwright, Shaw's aims as a, 58–60
playwrights, 291, 418, 518
pleas, pleading, 377, 406

pleasure(s), 71n, 291
plebiscite, the, 167
Plebs (magazine), 228
pledge of regard, 479, 493, 515
pluck, 360
plunder, 361, 381
Plunkett, Horace, 173
plutocracy, 117–18, 172, 209–10, 212, 240, 255–6, 289–90, 312–13, 316–17, 322–5, 337
Plymouth, 406, 485
Poel, William, 53
poet(s), -ic, -ry, 250–1, 264, 353–4, 361, 479
"pogroms", 408
Poincaré, Raymonde, 29, 191, 236
'point' sizes (typographical), 452, 454. 453
poison, -ous, 234, 356, 389, 393, 403, 406
Poitiers, 136
Poland, Polish, the Poles, 200, 312
police, the, policemen, 156–7, 167–8, 173, 194, 220, 236, 237–9, 323–4, 329, 336, 358, 368, 385, 398
Police State, the, 212
political homogeneity, fatal want of, 369
political incapacity of the masses, 293
political maturity, 230
'Positive Philosophy' (Comte), 318
political purposes, trusts for, 522
Political Quarterly, the, 312, 317
Political (or Social) Science, 475
politics (general), politicians; political parties, science, factors; political, 169, 171–2, 195, 199, 202, 209, 218, 221, 236, 274, 288–9, 292, 305, 309–10, 312–14, 321, 337, 340, 342–3, 349, 371, 373–5, 381, 383, 386, 391, 394, 399, 404, 408, 420, 475, 489, 492, 519, 521, 522
"Politics of Unpolitical Animals, The" (1933), 184–5
poor, the, poverty, 17, 162–3, 171, 181, 219, 227, 234, 237, 239, 242, 246, 256–7, 261, 263–4, 267, 269, 272–4, 279, 286, 289–92, 297, 303–4, 323, 327, 329, 338, 344, 405
Poor Law, the, 291

Pope, the Popes, 96, 98, 100, 167, 192, 211, 338, 377
popularity, 363, 375
population (movements, aspects of, etc.), 215, 243, 275–6, 278, 336, 341
Porson, Richard, 264
Portugal, 371
Positivism, 218
postal services, 204, 420
'postcards, printed',—See 'printed postcards'
post-Marxian Bonapartism, 197
postmistress, village, the, ix
Potteries, the, 105–7, 109, 111, 122–3, 126
Pougy, Mlle Liane de, 284
power (industrial), 276n
power(s), 171, 178, 226, 258, 272, 287, 310, 316–17, 320, 331–2, 336, 339, 340, 350, 367, 380, 384–5, 398, 405, 408
Power (Russell), 214
practical (quality of being), —working in practice, etc., 286, 345, 404, 418, 438, 440, 446–7, 452, 467, 469, 478
"practical professors of political science like Lenin and Stalin", 305
practice, learning by, 159, 416, 455, 457
pray-ers, -ing, 347, 349, 376, 386, 388
prefaces (general), 3, 425, 448
prefaces to unpublished works, 8–9
Preference Stocks, 475, 484
prejudice(s), 256, 342, 449, 476, 479, 490, 493
preparedness for war, 525
present(s), -ation, 480, 512
President(s), 167–8, 338
Press, the, 12, 169, 172, 174, 186, 202, 238, 250, 301, 306, 323, 352, 358, 364, 425, 445, 457, 489, 498, 525. 228
Pretorian Guard, 196
prevarication, 346, 398
prevention (of war, etc.), 389, 405
pride, 234, 246, 362, 378
pride in work, 315
priests,172,211-12,337-8,377
Prime Minister(s), 131, 143, 151–2, 168, 183, 275, 291
primitive, -ness, 275, 380, 383, 394
Primrose Hill, 263
principle(s). (social, individual), 225, 264, 302, 383

'printed letters', 23–34
'printed postcards', 6–23, 346, 403, 413, 432, 439. 13
print-ers, -ing, ix, 415–16, 418, 436–8, 452, 454–5, 458–60, 462, 463–4, 469, 473, 477, 483, 492
printing operatives, 328–9
Prior's Field, Godalming, 231
prison(s), -ers, 20n, 21n, 137, 206, 336, 406–7
prisoners-of-war, 373
private enterprise, 195, 203–4, 207, 210
private interest, 321
privation(s), 347
privilege(s), 221, 225, 263, 272, 290, 313–14
"Privileged Beggar", the, 304
Privy Council, the, 421
Prize Competition for new alphabet, 431, 437–42, 445–7, 452
probate, Probate Court, the, 428, 499, 518
Procrustean, Shaw describes the law as, 284
producer, the (v. the consumer), 292
production (industrial, means of), productivity, etc., 220, 223–4, 245, 248–50, 252, 259, 275–7, 280, 285, 293, 299, 301, 303, 320, 325, 327, 336, 395, 407, 414, 458
profession(s), -al, p. classes, etc., ix, 33n, 202, 246, 278, 280–1, 285, 289, 294, 323, 328, 338, 469, 476, 489–90, 492, 511
professor(s), -ships, 267, 477, 482, 491, 493–4, 519
proficiency, 482–3, 491
profit(s) (financial), 124, 204n, 214, 216, 235, 237, 267, 299, 316–17, 319, 411, 429, 476, 492, 513
profiteers, 317
pro-Germanism, 399, 525
progress, human, artistic, etc., 452, 471
Prohibition (in America), 198
proletariat, the, proletarian, 174, 190, 201, 216–17, 219–20, 222–3, 227–8, 231, 235, 247, 274, 280, 288–90, 293, 296, 303, 305, 308, 318–20
promiscu-ous, -ity, 243
promises, political, 310
promot-ing, -ion (political, etc.), 312, 481–2, 491

pronunciation, 436, 458–9, 465, 467, 469–70, 482–3, 489, 491–2, 498, 511, 519, 521
propaganda, 425–6, 498, 512, 521
propagation, 443, 445
proper names, 447
property (general, private, public, etc.), 178–9, 195, 206, 208, 220, 227, 229, 235, 245, 247–53, 259, 265, 289–91, 301, 320, 336, 340, 351–2, 417, 420, 477, 484, 494, 504, 510
Property Act (Birkenhead) 1925, the, 484
"Property and Slavery" (debate, 1913), 247–53
proph-ets, -ecy, 235, 240, 242, 291, 330, 331, 333n, 385, 412, 492
Proportional Representation, 169, 339
propriet-or(s), -ariat, 176–8, 181, 231–2, 252, 303, 333, 464
prosperity, 322, 336, 407
prosti-tute(s), -tution, 243, 246, 273, 291, 424
Protestant(s), -ism, 198, 242, 256, 294, 337
Proudhon, Pierre Joseph, 333
Providence (Divine, etc.), 147, 275, 322, 388, 392
provinces, 483, 492
provincial visits, Shaw's, 7
Prussians, the, Prussianism, 174, 194, 341, 351, 369–70, 372, 382
psychia-try, -trists, 198, 440
psycholog-y, -ists, 49, 199, 238, 362, 382, 436, 438
Ptolemy, 41
public, the, x, 296, 368, 420, 434, 476, 480, 518, 521
public action, enterprise, control, etc., 195, 201, 204, 207
public activities, cessation of, 12
publican(s), ix, 288
publication(s), 414, 420, 477, 480, 491, 501–2, 504, 513, 523
Public Authorities, 476, 498
public benefit, the, 421, 431
public bodies, 9, 14n, 368, 417, 421, 492
public collections, 500, 503
public 'G.B.S.' personality, Shaw's, ix
public impressiveness, 482, 491
public interest, the, 303, 494

publicity, 426–7, 433
public life, 226, 353, 475, 482, 491
public meetings, assemblies, 426, 482, 489, 491
public opinion, 256, 263, 293, 310, 368
public organisation(s), 281, 309
public ownership, 319
public schools, 298, 381–2, 420. 303
public serv-ice(s), -ants, 275, 312, 328
public speak-ing, 24–5, 27n, 483
"public-spirited gentle-man", the, 375
public-spiritedness (general), 260, 343
Public Trustee, the, 417, 421, 427–31, 437–8, 440, 445, 448–9, 452, 469, 477, 479–81, 484, 487, 490, 492–3, 495, 497–501, 504–6, 504–6, 508–10, 512–15, 518, 522
public welfare, 321, 335
public work, 309, 339
Puck, x
Pugmire, Dr S. L., 440, 442
pugnacity, 246, 286, 310, 347, 364, 375, 377, 393. 365
punctuality, 234, 332
punctuation, 24–5, 467, 473
punishment, 16n, 18–19, 136, 139, 140, 254, 401, 460
purchasing power of the £, 510
Purdom, C. B., ix, 7n, 45, 61, 346
"purges" (general), 408
"purges", Soviet, 305
Puritan(s), -ism, 73, 76
"purring", Shaw's, 366
Pyat, Felix, 217
Pygmalion, 425–6, 519
pyramid of Cheops, 341

Quads (typographical), 467
Quakers (Society of Friends), the, 198, 284, 460
qualifications, 476, 490
quarrel(s), -someness, 346, 374, 379
Queen's Hall, London, the, 247
"Quelle Sera la France de Demain?" (1944), 331–3
Quick, Oliver C., 307–8
quirk (in Shaw's character), 403
quotations from Shaw, his punctuation followed, 4

racialism, 197–200, 201
racial prejudice, 201, 218
radical, -ism, 239, 250n, 256n, 269, 292, 471
Radical party, the, 181
Railway Companies, 475
rank (senior, junior, hum-blest, highest, etc.), 283, 414, 476, 483, 490–1
rank-and-file, the, 276, 311, 327
rape (in war), 366
rapine, 100, 407
rascality, 233
rate(s), -payers, 110, 120–1, 124, 204, 393
Rathenau, Walther, 188
rational behaviour, argu-ments, etc., 404
raw material, Marx's mis-conception of, 214
Raymond Savage Ltd., 389
Readerships (University, etc.), 476–7, 482, 491, 493
reading, 420, 434, 436, 438, 443, 458–9, 519
Read, R. Kingsley, 440–2, 445–8
real and personal estate, Shaw's, 513–14
realit-y, -ies, 313, 383, 390, 403, 410, 525
"Real Socialist Party, A", 291
re-armament, Shaw advo-cates, 347
reason, -ing, -ableness (rat-ionality), 87, 121, 269, 362–3, 369, 374, 376, 405, 442, 449, 457, 505
"Rebuilding Babel" (1948), 203–4
receipts (box office), etc., 30–1, 479, 494, 500
recklessness, 364, 369, 397
reconstruction (of society, after war, etc.), 241, 381–4
recording instruments, de-vices, 477, 483, 491
records (official, national, etc.), 420
records (written, photo-graphic, general), 477, 483, 491, 498, 500
"recreants", Shaw's attitude to, 310
recreation, 261
recruiting, 349, 358
Rector of Ayot, the, ix
Red Flag, The, 210
Redmond, John, 118
reductions and increases in bequests to servants, 506
Reeves, Mrs Edith, vi
Referendum, the, 169

reform, -ers (See also social reform), 209, 376, 395, 519, 521
Reformation, the, 316
Reform Bill (1867), the, 174
regicide, 187
regimentation, 323
regiments, 372, 394
regional authorities, regarded by Shaw as "Gestapos", 399
rehearsal(s), x, 86
"Reign of Terror", 310
relationships, perception of, 436
relatives (general), 421, 487, 493, 500, 514
relatives (Shaw's), provision for, 486
relics, cremation of Shaw's body to leave no, 478
religion, 47–8, 50, 52–3, 55, 59, 61, 64, 66, 70–1, 73, 128–9, 130–62, 175, 202, 218, 227, 232–4, 242, 246, 251, 254–5, 258, 289, 291, 294, 305, 322, 337, 343, 362–3, 369–71, 373, 394–5, 408, 478, 487, 491, 499
religious ideal, Shaw's, 128–9
religious intolerance, 62–77
reminiscences, ix, x, xii
remuneration, 267–8, 270, 479, 494, 512
Renaissance, the Italian, 471
renewal of licence (for per-formance of Shaw's plays), 501–2
rent, 125, 144n, 177, 180, 184, 214–15, 221, 256, 274, 281, 298, 303, 314
rentier(s), 196
repertory theatres, 217
reporters, xiii. 416
reporting shorthand, 459
representation, representa-tives, 166, 168, 256, 312, 339
repression (Soviet), 305
reprieve, 20n
republic(s), republicanism, 173–4, 182, 186, 218–19, 226, 369–71, 376, 385, 394, 410, 470
Republican Presidents, 338
Republic, the (Plato), 271, 281
research, viii, 483, 492, 521
resentment, 184, 393, 395
residue of estate, residual trust funds, residuary lega-tees, 427, 479, 482, 490, 493, 506, 508–10, 512–13, 520
'resistance movements', 336n

respectability, 234, 251, 395, 424
responsibility, 183, 232, 233n, 237, 239, 270, 287, 308, 310, 313, 329, 397, 401
"Responsibility for the War" (1915), 353–4
Restoration comedy, 53–4
restriction (social, governmental, etc.), 322–4
results (of war), 377
retaliation, 19n
retirement, 302–3, 342
retribution, 19
returns (box office),—See receipts
revenge, 19, 36, 136–7, 139–40, 393
revenue, 421, 484, 501
reversionary nature of part of Shaw's real or personal estate, 514
revival (after death), 478, 487
revocation (of Wills), 477, 484, 496–9, 501
revolution, revolutionary, 189, 191–2, 203, 217–19, 223, 229–31, 236, 239, 253, 270, 281, 297, 306, 333, 343, 471
Revolution, the French, 173–4, 333
Revolution, the Russian, 173, 228, 230–1, 347
rewards, 129, 159, 268, 270, 374
Rheims, 369
rhetoric, 208n, 345, 364, 482–3, 489–90, 492
Rhineland, the, 390
Rhodes, John Cecil, 264
Rhondda, Lady, vii
rhythm of handwriting, 454
Ricardo, David, 206, 215, 256
'rich, the' (wealthy, the), riches, 144n, 171, 183, 234, 242–3, 246, 255–6, 257, 263–4, 267, 272–4, 290, 297, 303–4, 323, 327–8, 359
Richard II, 168
Richards, I. A., 465n
'rider' to Shaw's Wills, 479
ridicule, Shaw's power of indiscriminate, 269
Right, the (general, political), 345, 353
righteous indignation, British, 347
rights, Shaw's, in literary and other works, 499–501
Ring, The (Wagner), 55
risk(s), 253, 272

ritual, ritualism, 333–4, 487, 491, 499
rival(s), rivalry, 391, 397, 464, 469, 511
robber(s), robbing, 178, 227–8, 398
'Robber Caste, the', 294
Robson, Frederick, 17
Rodin, Auguste (his bust of Shaw, etc.), 478, 485, 502
Rogers, Charlotte, 481, 485–6, 489, 507
Rogers, Eames Bagenal, 489, 507
rogue(s), roguery, 233, 376, 380
Rolls Royces, x
Roman Catholic Church, 211–12, 242, 256, 294
roman-ce, -tic, 361–2, 364, 425
Roman numerals, 427, 434
Romanoffs, the, 385
Rome, the Romans, 133, 179, 186, 341, 392
Romeo and Juliet (Shakespeare), 65, 70
Rossetti, Dante Gabriel, 390
Rousseau, Jean-Jacques, 217, 326
routine, -ers, 39, 262, 268, 339, 375, 417, 461, 487, 490
Rowley, Charles, 218
Royal Academy of Dramatic Art (as Shaw beneficiary), 427, 430–1, 485, 518, 520
Royal Commission for the Exhibition of 1851, the, 421
Royal Prerogative, the, 286
Royal Progress, the, 167
Royal Society of Arts, the, 421
Royal Society of Literature, the, 14n
royalties (on literary works), 428, 445, 501, 520
royal-ty, -ists, 316, 372
Rugby (school), 382
rul-ers, -ing, 170, 172, 193, 197, 200, 230, 302, 313, 317, 323, 330, 336–8, 340–1, 388, 403
rules of war, the, 401
ruling class, the, 190, 240
Rumania, 371, 381
Ruskin, John, 206, 217, 228, 239–40, 241–2, 284
Russell, Bertrand (Earl), 214, 224, 360, 408
Russell, Charles, Q.C., 518, 522
Russell, George ('A. E.'), 173, 237
Russell, Jones & Walker, 522

Russell, Sir John, 209
Russ-ia, -ian, the Russians, 22, 152, 173, 182, 187, 190–3, 208, 210, 212–14, 228–31, 235–6, 242, 276, 278, 298, 303, 305–6, 308–11, 319, 327, 332–4, 342, 347, 367, 369–71, 381–2, 384, 386, 394–5, 399–401, 405, 408, 445, 464, 470, 524
Russia, model postcard on, 22
Russian Revolution, the, 173, 228, 230–1, 347
Russo-German agreement (1939), 396–7
ruthlessness, 191, 204, 231, 294, 316, 324

sabot-age, -eurs, -euses, 286, 301, 310
sacredness (of life, treaties, etc.), 226, 362, 390, 397
sacrifice(s), 16n, 134, 364, 370, 380–1, 383
Saint Joan, 48
St Albans, 516
St Augustine, 71–2
St Helena, 196, 332
St John's Gospel, 139
St Michael, 392
St Pancras Railway Station, 471
St Paul, 138, 178, 232
St Paul's Cathedral, 68, 240
St Peter, 138
St Thomas Aquinas, 72
salaries, 276, 328, 464
sale or conversion of Shaw's real and personal estate into money, 513–14
Salisbury, Lord, 370
Salome, 68
Salt, Henry, 218, 474, 479
Salt, Kate, 479
Salvation Army, the, 46–7
Salvemini, Professor Gaetano,
Sanctions, 403
Sanders, G. H., 16n
San Francisco, 370
sanitation, 120, 308, 368
sanity, 415, 436, 448, 464
Sargent, John Singer, 503
Satan, 304
satisfaction(s) (general), 362–3, 381, 392
satisfaction, personal, 259, 263, 265
Saturday Review, the, vii
satyromania, 91
Sault, Joseph, W., x, xii, 56, 61, 103
savager-y, -ies, 188, 393
savages, 320, 339

saving,—See under economy
savio(u)rs, 291, 312
Scandinavia, 363
scenery, dramatic, 49
Schneider, Eva Maria, 489, 507
scholar(s), -ships, 458, 462, 483, 492, 519
school(s), -ing, 14n, 43, 275, 280, 301, 322, 395, 400, 419, 434, 442, 449, 467, 490, 492–4, 512, 522
school editions, Shaw's works not available for, 10
"School of Rhetoric", Shaw's proposed, 489–90, 492
Schrecklichkeit, the German, of 1915, 406
science (general, political, social, etc.), scientific, 201, 204, 210, 226, 245, 268, 275, 277, 279, 282, 317, 319–20, 327, 339, 341, 371, 379, 403, 425, 434, 440, 452, 465, 477–8, 483, 490–1, 499
Scientific Advisers Division of the Ministry of Production, 421
Scot-land, -tish, 65, 73, 303, 483, 492
Scott, Capt. Robert Falcon, 158
Scott, Sir Walter, 41n, 303
Scribe, Augustin Eugène, 54
'scribes', 415, 454, 458, 460–2, 468, 511
script (handwriting), 418, 420, 438, 440, 442–3, 446, 483, 492, 521
scriveners, 415, 421
sculpture (see also busts), 502
sea, the, 350, 397
Second Advent, the, 320
seconds (time), 416, 458, 460
secretar-y, -ies, 351, 416–17, 470, 486, 488–9, 497
sects, different socialist, 292
secular case for equal incomes, the, 254
securities, 484, 514–15
security, 184, 201, 250–2, 261, 308, 351, 370, 375, 475
sedition, 152, 236–9, 291n, 311
selection of rulers, 169, 330–1, 338, 341
self-criticism, 16, 269, 363
self-defence as an illusion of war, 380

self-development, 271–2
self-government, 342
Self-Help (Smiles), 273n
selfishness, 206, 267, 363, 379
self-possession (individual, national, etc.), 361
self-preservation in war, 379
self-sacrifice, Shaw's view of, 233
self-trumpeter, Shaw described as a, 356
Semele, 90
Semites, 200
Semitic languages, 437
sentimental-ity, -ists, 181, 286, 288, 479
Serb-ia, -ians, 192n, 370–1, 381
Serbo-Croat, 470
Sermon on the Mount, the, 393
servants (general), 273, 323, 326
servants, Shaw's, 421, 480, 482, 486–8, 491, 496, 504–6
servants, Shaw's bequests to his, 480, 485–6, 487–8, 495–7
service(s), (social, to the community, etc.), 249–51, 253, 258, 267, 302
Service for Economic Action, the, 421
services, years of, 480, 488
Servile State, The (Belloc), 249
servility, 253, 288
servitude (general, penal, etc.), 177, 178, 248, 253
settlement out of court, 431, 445
Seven Ages of Man, the, 37
seventeenth century, the, 50, 220, 394, 406
Severn, the, 316
sex (general), sex differences, sex equality, etc., 3, 86, 268, 406, 410, 425
sex appeal, 97–101
sex relations, 78–93
sexual attraction, 257
sexual barriers, 266
sexual emotion, 64-72, 75-6
sexual reform, 96–102, 162
sexual selection, 257, 260
Shakespeare, William, vii, x, 27, 36–7, 50, 52–3, 69, 216, 240, 264, 392, 415, 419, 436, 458, 462, 469, 478, 483, 491
Shakespeare Memorial National Theatre, the proposed, 478, 502

sham, 172, 316, 331, 367, 397, 401
shame, -ful, 86, 237, 240
shapes of alphabetic letters, 434–5, 438, 440–2, 445–7
shares (in companies), 475
Sharp, Cecil, 101
Shavian, the, 35, 423
"Shavian", origin of the word, 519n
Shavians, 424
Shaw, Adelaide Olivia, 489, 497
Shaw, Aida, 486
Shaw, Charlotte Townshend (Mrs Bernard Shaw), 23, 79, 84, 93, 286, 474, 477–9, 485–6, 488, 494, 499, 500, 505–6
Shaw estate,—See under estate
Shaw, George Bernard, passim. [Since references to Shaw occur on every page, the following broad guide is necessarily arbitrary and limited. Individual references to the numerous other aspects of Shaw's life and personality dealt with in the book are to be found elsewhere in the Index, and also in the list of CONTENTS at the beginning of the book].
'in the witness box', 2–3; attitude to his detractors, 2; his wit and humour, 5; his intellectual brilliance, 5; gifts and donations, 6; reads all correspondence personally, 6; often, but not always, said 'No' to correspondents, 6; his character and outlook, 6; not a professional lecturer, 7; his home at Pitfold, Surrey, 7; —at 29, Fitzroy Square, London, W., 7; —at 10, Adelphi Terrace, London, W.C., 7; —at 4, Whitehall Court, London, S.W.1, 8; —at Ayot St. Lawrence, Herts, 8; cannot undertake extra literary work, 8; cannot always reply to letters, 8; cannot help his readers financially, 8–9; cannot read literary manuscripts, 8, 14; cannot contribute prefaces, 8; his donations to undenominational bodies, 9, 14; not a millionaire, 9; attitude to taxation, 9; nationalised

his landed property, 9; attitude to giving autographs, 10, 14; serialisation of his books, 10; broadcasting of his plays, 11; cannot always acknowledge donations of books, 12; cannot advise literary beginners, 14; will not give sittings or receive visits except from intimate friends, 14; will not send Messages for publication, 15; his vegetarian diet and the slaughter of animals, 15–16; on temperance, 16–17; on capital punishment, 18–21; on phonetic spelling and proposed new alphabet, 20–2, 26–30 (See also under alphabet, spelling, etc.); on Ireland, 22; on Russia, 22 (See also under Russia); acknowledges expressions of sympathy on wife's death, 23; on vaccination, 23–4; on punctuation, literary style, and public speaking, 24–7, 104; licensing of his plays, 30–3; route to Ayot St. Lawrence, 33–4; his early years, 35, 38–9; parents' attitude to, 35; admits "not grown up" at 81, 38; some educational experiences, 39, 43; his artistic temperament, 43; advocates being "a good hater", 44; his new 'discussion' type of play, 55; aims as a playwright, 58–60; attacks stage censorship, 61–77; a strict moralist, 76; capacity for sexual sublimation, 78–9; conventional respect for marriage, 80; pursued by infatuated girl, 80–95; "an expert in sex appeal", 97–8; critics of his social views, 103; his technique of public speaking, 104; vain about personal appearance, 125; his socioreligious ideal, 128; does not profess to be a Christian, 131; but gives "the best, noblest . . . sermon ever given anywhere", 161; complex and paradoxical nature of his social and political views, xvi, 163; [N.B. re pages 162–345,—See also list of

running half-titles in CONTENTS, pp. xv–xvii]; criticised for Fascist sympathies, and his replies, 184–200, 202; confusion regarding his political and social beliefs, 203; calls himself a Communist, 203, 207, 209, 211, 214, 284; but in practice perforce a Capitalist, 209, 211; claims "British Communism" made "constitutional and practicable" by himself, Sydney Webb, and fellow Fabians, 208; subscriber to the Daily Worker, 210; views on Karl Marx and Marxism, 214–24, 227–30, 239, 303, 317–18, etc. (See also under Marx); confesses himself "weak in mathematics", 228; described as a "bourgeois thinker", 229; charged with being "anti-Socialist", 230; advocates violent methods of Bolsheviks in England, 231; his unusual conception of Bolshevism, 233–5; risks imprisonment for sedition, 235–9; advocates armed insurrection, 237; escapes prosecution because "rich and influential", 238; attitude to social views of Ruskin and Dickens, 239–41; claims that all Socialists are Tories in a sense, 241; advocates equality of incomes, 242–85, 299–300, 303–4, 326–9; his briefer definitions of Socialism, 243–5, 285, 299; his debates with Chesterton and Belloc, 244–53; his conception of the gentleman and the cad, 246, 364; brought up not to play with children of shopkeepers, and to regard Roman Catholics as eternally damned, 256; "is out for fun and knows he can get it", 269; his wit criticised, 269; accused of lack of self-criticism, 269; described as winning battles but losing campaigns, 269; his unique personal political faith, 284; views on women in politics, 285–7; attacks the Labour Party, 287, 290–1, 293–4, 297–8, 320, 352;

criticises the working class, 288–90; criticises tradesmen and lower professional classes, 289–90; wants his own political party catering for his own social class, 290–1; criticises Trade Unions, 292, 294–9, 319, 352; advocates making strikes illegal, 294–5, 297; advocates compulsory labour (industrial conscription), 295–8, 407; praises Soviet régime, 299, 303, 305, 308–10, 334, 347; complains about having been misunderstood for 30 years, 301; his view that "Russian Communism is Fabian Socialism" criticised, 305–6; advocates that free elections be made criminal offence, 312; his apparent volte face from Fabian denunciation of Marx, 317; advocates extermination of believers in what he had himself believed in 30 years previously, 327; the $64-billion billion question, 330n, 339; praises General de Gaulle, 333; described as a Tory, 335; advocates tests of fitness to be rulers, 338–9; admits civilisations ultimately dependent on consciences of governors and governed, 342–3; one of his definitions of liberty, 343; religious basis of his social views, 131–61, 343–4; misinterpretation of his words, 345, 348; declines, like Ibsen, to adopt any political label, 345; his love of rhetoric and questionable logic, 345; recommends closing down of churches in war-time, 347, 349, 369; unpopularity of his war views, 348 et seq.; expulsion from Dramatists' Club, 348; feels some patriotic war fervour despite intellectual objectivity and detachment, 349; subscribes to War Loan, 359–60; his views misrepresented by the Press, 364–6; his "purring" and his "snarl", 366; visits the front, 374; proposes Locarno Pact, 385; urges that people be 'liquidated' if they will not 'live and let live', 394; advocates sending octogenarians like himself to war instead of young men, 394; his freedom of commentary, but lack of experience of statecraft, 404; his excessive faith in human rationality, 404; appeal for a new British alphabet a failure in his lifetime, 421–2; described as a brilliant interpreter and propagandist rather than original thinker, 424; valuation of estate and copyrights, 428–9, 444; fiasco of memorial appeal, 429; his alphabet trusts set aside, 430–3, 440, 443, 518–23; prize competition for suitable alphabet, 431–2, 438–42, 445; designed no actual alphabet himself, 432; hatred of mispronunciation of English language and of general British inefficiency, 436; criticised for not tying up alphabet bequests with infant education, 443; his alphabet project gets less than 1 per cent of his estate's funds, 444; bi-alphabetic edition of *Androcles and the Lion* published, 448–9; the Shaw Alphabet criticised as saving less time than he envisaged, 452–72; his Wills, 473–516; phonetic reform bequest as early as Will of 1901, 475–6; leaves body for medical dissection, 477–8; leaves skeleton and skull for possible preservation, 477–8; objects to black emblems of mourning and visible monuments, 478, 487, 499; his busts and portraits, 478, 485, 502; bequests to former mistresses, 481; later phonetic reform bequests, 482–3, 489–92, 498, 510–13; desires no memorial service until he is forgotten, 487; trustees not to be bound by commercial considerations exclusively, 487, 501; criticises legal verbiage, 495; his Last Will and Testament, 499–516; desires ashes mixed

with wife's in garden, 499; birth and death as British Subject, but citizen of Eire for a time, 516. *Frontispiece, 42, 43, 65, 80, 228, 229, 252, 387*
Shaw, George Carr (father), 256
Shaw, James Cockaigne, 507
Shaw, Lucinda Carr (mother), 474
Shaw, Lucinda Frances Carr (sister), 474, 480–1, 507
Shaw Memorial Appeal, 429
Shaw Review, the, (U.S.A.), 61*n*
Shaw's Corner, vii, 429, 499, 503
Shaw Society of America, 1
Shaw Society (of England), London, xiv, 516
Shaw, T. E.,—See Lawrence, T. E.
Shaw the Villager, and Human Being, vi, vii, ix, xii, 1, 7*n*, 12*n*, 36, 45, 61, 78, 103, 346, 403, 413, 462, 473
Sheffield Daily Telegraph, the, 364
Shelley, Percy Bysshe, 264
shells (military), 372-3, 404-6
Sheridan, Richard B., 24
Shewing-up of Blanco Posnet, The, 58, 60
ships, 276, 405
shirkers, 319
shooting, 183, 201, 230, 242, 358, 361, 399, 405, 408
shop assistants, 482, 491
shortened (American) spellings, 471
shorthand(s) (general, as opposed to longhand, diff. types, etc.), 27–8, 416–20, 425, 433, 438, 446, 465, 469–70, 483, 492, 511
'Shorthand, Current' (Sweet's), 446, 448
shrine, Shaw's home as, 429
Siberia, 401–2
sight, children's learning by, 459–60
signature, Shaw's, 10*n*, 477, 484
Simplified Spelling, 26–30, 418, 433, 438, 498
sin, 294, 338
sincerity, Shaw's, 398
sinecur-e, -ist, 332
Single Tax Campaign (1882), 216
Sinn Feiners ("Shinners"), 198
Sixteen Self Sketches, 26*n*, 27*n*, 79

sixteenth century, 73, 426
sixth century, 434
$64-billion billion question, the, 330*n*, 339
$64,000 question, the, 330
skill, 301, 341, 357
skull, Shaw's, provision in his will for preservation of, 477
slaughter, 356, 384, 392, 394, 407
slavery (industrial, economic, etc.), 16*n*, 165, 175–84, 213, 216, 243–4, 247–8, 250, 277, 291, 293, 297, 323–6, 342–4, 357, 359, 378
Slavs, 200
sleep, 302, 326, 461
slums, 125, 180, 207, 375, 424
Smee, Walter, 515
Smiles, Samuel, 273*n*
Smith, Mrs Ronald,—See Cashin, Margaret
Smith, Warren S., 61*n*
Smoker, Barbara, xiv, 423–52, 457, 523
"snarl", Shaw's, 366
snob(s), -bery, -bishness, 175, 289–90, 313, 319, 342
"snobocracy", 313
Snowden, Philip, 298
snubbing, 267
sobriety, 177
social abuse, 240
social barriers, 260, 282
social benefits, 265, 281, 319, 521, 523
social change, 201, 335
social conscience, 240, 442
"Social Danger of Inequality", The (1890), 272–4
"Social Democratic Federation", 214
Social Democrats (European), 231
Social Democrats (German), 186
social disorder, 312, 332
social equity, 234*n*
social evils (general), 269
social experiment(s), 282
social inequality, 260
social instinct(s), 234, 339
social intercourse as a fine art, 490
socialisation, 281, 319, 325, 407
"Socialised Toryism", 200
Socialism, x, xi, xii, 104–29, 130–61, 162–3, 169–70, 173, 176–85, 186, 188, 191, 193, 195, 201, 203–6, 207, 209–10, 213, 216–33, 236, 239–40, 243–7, 250, 254, 270, 272, 280, 285, 287–93,

294, 296–305, 307, |311, 313, 317–20, 323–5, 327, 329, 335, 337, 342, 344–5, 347, 350, 352–3, 378, 404, 407–9, 411, 425, 479, 493, 504, 515. *233, 294, 295, 300, 302*

"Socialism and Human Nature" (1890), 232–3

Socialism in a Single Country (Stalin), 229–30

"Socialism in our own time", 298

Socialist Leader, the, 256*n*

Socialist League, the, 225

"Socialist Movement is only the Assertion of our Lost Honesty" (debate, 1884), 301–2

Socialist Societies, 319

social levelling, 225, 259

social measures, 259

social obedience, 255

social order(s), 219, 306

social organisation, 269, 405

social prejudice, 256

social problems (general), social questions, 223, 244, 256, 332, 404

social reform, -ers, 58, 259, 262–3, 383, 425, 518

social responsibility, sense of, 234*n*

social rule ("Live and let live"), the, 394

Social Science, 475

social service, 246

social snobbery, 289

social standards, 285, 307

social stratification, 285

social subordination, 255, 337

social theor-y, -ies, 206

societies (general), 422, 426, 479

society (general), 86, 153*n*, 229, 260, 262, 403

society, debt to, 128–9, 267, 270

society, a scientifically organised, 276

society, solvency of, 267

sociologists, professional, 153*n*, 340

soldier(s), -ing, 21*n*, 177, 223, 242, 246, 297, 336, 348–9, 364, 372, 374–6, 384, 390, 394, 405–6, 410

solicitor(s), 290, 495, 515–16

"Solidarity of Social Democracy, The" (1904), 220*n*, 221

"Some Illusions of the War" (1915), 360–6

Somerset, 414

Song of Solomon, 65

Sophocles, 36, 50–2

sounds, 418, 435–40, 446, 448, 459–60, 464, 467, 469, 475, 491, 498, 511

'sound-writing', 446

South Africa, 15*n*, 284*n*, 297, 409, 411

South America, 332, 512

'Southern English', 491

South Place Ethical Chapel, The, 331

South Western Star, the, 367*n*

sovereign nationality,—See national sovereignty

Sovereigns, 464*n*

Soviet (general, régime, ideas, etc.), Soviets, 187, 207–9, 213, 228, 293, 344, 384, 399

Soviet Constitution, the, 309

space(s), 438, 448, 452, 454–5, 466–7

Spain, Spanish, 29, 182, 332, 392, 394, 412, 437

Sparrow, John, xiii

specialising, 424

"special period", the, 501, 503, 512–13

specific professional training precluded by Shaw in his 1937 Will for all subjects except those of phonetician, orator, and "musician in the ancient Greek sense", 492

Spectator, the, 206

speculation, 284, 411, 476

speculators (in war), 352

speech (general, trained, art of, etc.), speaking as opposed to writing, speakers, 420, 436, 471, 476, 482–3, 491, 512

"speech, refined", 490

speech-sound frequency, 437

speed (in writing, shorthand, etc.), 416–17

speed of writing, Shaw's, 419, 446, 457

Speenhamland System, the, 298

spellers, bad, 462

spelling, spelling reform, 20, 26–30, 32*n*, 52*n*, 310*n*, 415–18, 420, 422, 425–6, 433, 436, 438, 442, 447, 457, 460–72, 482–4, 511–12

spelling changes, 470

spelling, phonetic, 20, 26, 438, 462, 464

spelling, shortened, 471

spelling, simplified, 26

Spencer, Herbert, 326, 379, 426

spies, 336

spiritual values, 308

spite, 362, 383

spoils (of war), 381, 383

Spoken English, B.B.C. Committee for, 29

Sprechspur, 447

squabble(s), 374, 380, 397

Squeers, Mrs Fanny, 23, 235

squire-arch, -archy, 216

Staffordshire Sentinel, the, 104

stage censorship, —See censorship

stage morals, 61–77

stalemate, 380, 382

Stalin, Joseph, 203, 208–9, 211–13, 228–9, 303, 305, 307, 327, 397, 399, 403. *228*

Stalingrad, 406–7

"standard English speech", Shaw's proposed, 483

standardisation, 281

"standard Socialist day", the, 302. *302*

standards, social, 285

Stanley, Sir Henry, 135

Star, the, 202

starv-ing, -ation, 267, 293, 375, 379, 383, 397, 405

State, the, States, 19*n*, 166, 168–9, 179, 182, 192, 197, 204, 210, 212, 219, 221, 225, 232, 241–5, 247–9, 251–2, 279, 282, 307, 311, 314, 318–20, 323, 334, 339, 341, 359, 381, 406–7, 420, 443, 480. *228, 233, 294, 295*

State-aided enterprise, 204, 249, 320

State Capitalism, State-aided Capitalism, State-financed Capitalism, 311, 318–19, 322–4

statecraft, Shaw's lack of experience of, 404

State regulation (general), 319

"State Regulation, Complete", 314–15

statesmen, 236, 310, 332, 377, 382

State- Social-ists, -ism, 219

statistical enquiry re Shaw alphabet, 432, 449, 468, 498, 523

Statistical Society, the, 421

statistics (general), statisticians, 418, 443, 469, 475, 510–11

status, social, 251

Statute Book (the English), 388

stealing, 140

Stern & Reubens, New York, 515
Stetson, Mrs, 334
Stock Exchange, the, 514
"Stock Exchange British Imperial patriot", the, 410
stocks and shares, 211, 484, 514
stocks; recommended that Shaw be put in the, 349
Stopes, Dr Marie, 96
stories, war, 375
Strand Magazine, the, 146
Stratford-upon-Avon, x
strike, the right to, 294–6
strikes, striking, 227, 238, 294–7, 299, 312, 405. *294*, *295*
Strindberg, Auguste, 56
Strobl, Sigismund, 502
strokes used in writing, 'coupled strokes', etc., 434, 438
Stuart monarchy, the, 316
students,—at Shaw's projected school, 492
studentships, Shaw's endowment of, 477
stupidity, 267, 380, 393, 395, 400, 460
Stürgkh, Count Karl von, 192*n*
style, literary (general), 26*n*–27*n*
style, literary, Shaw's, 26*n*, 519–20
subjugation, subjugatory clauses, 390, 398, 402
subsid-y, -ies, 317, 476
subsistence, 246
"suburban professional man", the, 328
success(es), 332, 360, 368, 385, 442
'successful man', Shaw's view of the typical, 234
sufficiency, 247, 285
suffrage, the, adult suffrage, 174, 286, 307, 313, 323, 326, 331
Suffragettes, the, 159, 238*n*, 286, 348
Suffragists, the, 286
suggestive stage performances, 61, 64, 66–7
Summer Time, 465
Sun, the, 512
Sunday(s), 348, 406, 463
Sunday Chronicle, the, 366
Sunday Dispatch, the, 282*n*
superficiality, 382, 385
superiority (individual, social, moral, physical, etc.), 277, 284–5, 380
supermen, 145, 154, 260, 307, 322, 340–1

supernational-ists, -ism, 303, 334, 342, 367, 382
"Superstate", the, 399
superstition, 358, 478, 487
supertax, 259
superwomen, 260
supply and demand, 215, 268, 320
suppression(s), (of criticism, etc.), 363, 379, 408, 504
supremacy, Britain's, 350
surfeit, 274
surplus value (economic), 214, 221, 223–4, 227
surtax, 286
survival after death, 478, 487
"suspended animation", state of, 478, 487
Suvarov, General Alexei Vasilievitch, 406–7
sweated wages, etc., 314
Sweden, 525
Sweet, Henry, 22, 27–9, 417, 422, 426, 442, 446, 465
Swift, Jonathan, 216, 412
Switzerland, 370
sycophantism, 294
Sykes, Sir Tatton, 263
Sylvaines, the Vernon, ix
symbols (alphabetical), 432, 434, 437, 440–2, 447, 455, 469, 511
sympathy, 87, 468, 488
symposium, advantages and disadvantages of, etc., x, xii, 1–2
syndical-ists, -ism, 191, 305
Syria, -n, 410

Table Talk of G.B.S. (Henderson), 296
tactic(s), -ians, 319, 492
Tagblatt (Vienna), 359
tailors' bills, x
take-over bids, 116*n*
Talavera's Plain, 373
talent(s), 204, 254, 259, 272, 275, 278, 293, 305, 315
talking with tongue in cheek, vii, xi
talk-writers, 449
Tamil, 470
tariffs, Tariff Reform, 108*n*, 219
taste(s), 257, 283, 471, 476, 492
Tate Gallery, the, 502
tax-ation, -payers, 9, 14, 113, 115, 121–3, 183, 204, 211, 259, 286, 296, 328, 332, 359, 405, 420, 444
Taylor, P. W. E., 518
Tcheka, the, 187
teach-ers, -ing, 42–3, 281, 395, 419–20, 438, 443, 459–60, 469, 476–7, 482–3, 489–91, 493, 511, 521

Tebramund, 372
Teheran Conference, the, 401
television rights, 499
temperance, 3, 16–17, 273
tenants, 180, 379
Ten Commandments, the, 379
Tennyson, Alfred Lord, 382
terms for ending First World War, 367
terms, political, 203
territor-y, -ies, 381, 400, 410
terror(s), 181, 329, 362, 376, 401
"testamentary expenses", 510
test of "sufficient" equality of income, 277
tests, of physical and intellectual capacity, fitness to rule, etc., 265, 323, 338–9
Tewson, W. Orton, 359–60
Thames, the, 368
"That the Socialist Movement is only the Assertion of our Lost Honesty" (Lecture, 1884), 301
theatre, the, 305, 476, 482
theatre agents, 289, 494, 516
theatre critics, 489
Theatre Guild (U.S.A.), the, 502–3
theatre, the literature of the, 45–57
Theatre, a National, 425
theatre managers, 479, 482, 491
theatres (general), 425
Thiers, Louis Adolphe, 192, 220
theocrac-y, -ies, 196, 322
theor-y, -ies, -ists, 181, 229, 236, 404, 440, 452
thief, thieves, thieving, 86, 140, 253, 284, 342. *252*
Thirty Years' War, the, 136
Thompson, Alex M., 366
Thorndike, Dame Sybil, vii, 80, 95
though, 21, 415, 418–19, 436, 438, 448, 460–1, 465
thought, 262, 390, 424, 461
"three day week", a, 303
thrift, 112–13, 177, 273
Throne, the British, 316
thunderbolt(s), 87, 379
tides, Shaw's scheme for harnessing the, 276
Tillett, Ben, 237
Tilly, John Tzerclaes, Count of, 406–7
time, 376, 413, 416, 432, 434, 438, 443, 454, 457–8, 462–3, 465, 468–72, 493, 511, 514, 520–1, 523

Time and Tide, vii, 96, 197, 321–5, 390–1
time and piece work, 266, 268, 270
Times, The, 19n, 23, 60–76, 122, 137, 203, 207, 209, 213, 221, 305–11, 324, 327, 342, 352, 355, 398, 409, 412, 414, 431n, 462–4, 468, 515–22, 526
Times Literary Supplement, the, 519n
Timon of Athens (Shakespeare), 216
"Tipperary", 394
tipping, Shaw's view of, 246
toleration (in religion, politics, sexual morality, etc.), 66, 202, 324
Tolstoy, Count Leo; Tolstoyan, 225, 374
Tom Jones (Fielding), 53
'top 5 (or 10) per cent of the population', 278–9, 304, 330, 332
'top' people, 328
Torquemada, Tomás de, 186
torture, 187n, 238, 478, 487, 499
Tory, -ism, Tories, 241–2, 294. 299
"Tory Communism", 239, 241–2
"Tory oligarchism", 241
totalitarian, -ism. 212, 303, 321, 322–5, 330, 334, 399
"Totalitarian Democrat", the, 322, 330
trade(s), traders, ix, 246, 281, 285, 321, 357, 394, 405, 459
trade secrets, 299
tradesmen, 289, 323
Trade Union(s), -ism, 173, 204, 213, 219, 227, 268, 284, 287, 289, 292–8, 309, 312, 318–20, 329, 352, 357, 379, 405, 414. 228
trading, municipal, 123–4
traditional English speech, 483, 492
Trafalgar, 182, 350
Trafalgar Square, 236, 349
training, 476, 482–3, 459–92
trains, 276, 332, 347
traitor(s), -ousness, 385, 399
transcriptions, 416, 419, 465, 483, 491–2
translation(s), 477, 523
transliterations, 419, 422, 442, 498, 511, 521, 523
transport, proposal to nationalise, 298
Transylvania, 381
treacher-y, -ousness, 363, 397

Treasury, the, 444
Treasury Solicitor, the, 522
treaties, 354, 362, 367, 369, 380–1, 390
trenches, the, 352, 356, 380, 394
Trentino, 381
"triangle" situations, 80, 83
tribes, African, 389
tribunal(s) (international, etc.), 374, 382, 405
Tribune, 213, 221n
tricolor (of France), 347
"Trinitarian Gladstone", the, 321
Trinity College, Dublin, 414, 512
Tristan and Isolde, 65
triumph, -ant, 364, 390
Troilus, 447
Trotsky, -ists, -ism, 229, 303, 305, 326, 385
Troubetskoy, Paul, 502
trustee(s) (general), 284, 474–8
Trustee, the Public,—See Public Trustee
Trustees securities, 484
trust premises, 515
Trusts, private, joint, trust funds, etc., 417, 422, 427, 433, 490, 493, 512–13, 515, 518
truth(s), 175, 260, 269, 283, 354, 356, 361, 399, 425, 478, 487, 525
Tsar(s) (Czars), -ism, 168, 185, 193, 231, 278, 305, 384
Tudor architecture, 471
Tukes, the (family), ix, 12n
Tupholme, J. H. S., 104
Turkey, Turks, the, 10n, 332, 370, 373, 382
Twain, Mark, 426
twentieth-century, the, 199, 452
Twentieth Century Molière, The (Hamon), 291
twenty-first century, the, 444
types, type faces (printers'), typography, 420, 425, 438, 448, 452, 454–5, 459, 466–8, 483, 492, 498, 511. 453
type setting, 464
typists, 416, 419, 459
tyranny, 152–3, 165, 174, 186, 191, 201, 204, 213, 242, 301–2, 304, 307, 310, 337, 366, 384

Ulster Protestant Capitalism, 22
ultimatums, 396
"Unavoidable Subject, The" (1940), 199–200

uncertainty, trusts void for, 520, 522–3
Uncle Sam, 235
"Underdog Authority", 327
understanding, xii
undeveloped countries, 411
unearned income, 121
uneducated, the, 323
unemployment' the unemployed, 122, 126–7, 201, 257, 267
unhappiness, 165, 265, 273, 323
uniformity, human, 261, 307–8
Unionist Party, the, 118, 128, 336
Union Jack, 347
United Kingdom,—See Britain
United Nations, the, 358, 382, 386
United States of America,—See America
unities, dramatic, 49–51
unity (political), 319
universal, -ity, 458, 467, 469, 511
Universe, the, 86, 160, 214, 490
universit-y, -ies (general), 280, 314, 338, 476–7, 512
University of Cambridge, 479
University of Leeds, 441n
University of London, 492
University of Oxford, 414, 422, 459, 512
unphonetic spelling, 436
unpreparedness for war, 354 526
unproductiveness, 293
Unreason, 349, 383
unskilled labour (wages of, etc.), 329, 414
'Unsocial-ists', -ism, 310, 319, 338
untrustworthiness the result of poverty, 274
upper class(es), the, 117, 119–20, 216, 258
uppishness, 267
Urdu, 470
U.S.A.,—See America
"U.S.F.S.R." (Union of Soviet Fabian Socialist Republics), 213
U.S.S.R. (see also 'Russia', 'Soviet'), 208, 384
usur-y -ers, 379
utility (general, public, etc.), 204, 362, 484, 521
utility (economic), 226, 261, 265
Utopia, -n, 191, 210, 229, 255, 268, 332, 335, 414

vaccination, 23–4, 406–7
validity (general), 363, 462
validity (legal), 427, 469, 523
value, valuation (general), 381, 428, 514
value (economic theories of, etc.), 215, 220–2, 228, 255–6, 272
vegetarianism, 3, 15–16
vengeance, 362, 378
Venice, 170
Venus de Milo, 70
verbatim reporting, 417, 465, 469, 483, 492, 511
verbatim reports of speeches, original style and interpolations retained, 4
verbiage, legal, 495
"vermin, social", 231
Versailles Treaty, the, 186, 200, 383, 385, 390, 396, 400, 402
vested interests in drunkenness and prostitution, 243
vestryman, Shaw as, 404
Veto, the Russian, 382, 386
Vicar of Wakefield, The (Goldsmith), 206
Vichy government, the, 336n
vice, 59–60, 254, 273
Victoria and Albert Museum, the, 65
Victoria, Queen; Victorianism, V. era, 174, 222, 369, 470–1
victor-y, -ies, 351-2, 362, 374, 381, 383, 390, 392, 396, 407
"Victory" (pen-name), 400, 402
Vienna, 193, 392
Vietnam, 403n
Vieurkleur, the, 410
villagers of Ayot St. Lawrence, vi
villain-y, -ies, 188, 210
violence (violent revolution, etc.), 181, 193, 195, 231, 236, 239, 253n, 257, 274, 291n, 297, 329, 398, 408
Virgil, 42, 70. 42
virtue(s), 234, 246, 254, 273, 288, 376, 379–80, 398
visits, no longer allowed by Shaw, 14
visual memory, 459, 465
vitality, Shaw's, 424
vivisection, 490
vocabulary, 419, 436
void trusts, 520
'volcanic blowholes', 276
Volkswagen car, the, 281
Voltaire, 60
von Bank, Alma, 489, 497

vote(s), -rs, voting; the vote, 159, 169, 172, 182, 184, 240, 265, 285–6, 308–10, 312–13, 316, 321, 324, 330, 338–9, 347, 390, 399
vowels (general), 414, 416, 418, 435, 437, 439–40, 447, 459, 498, 512
vowel sounds, v. symbols, 414
vulgarity, vulgar people, 337, 483, 490

wages, 183, 206–7, 223, 229, 238, 259, 276–7, 291, 294, 296, 314, 328–9, 357, 414, 328–9, 357, 414, 464, 480, 488, 496, 505
Wages Boards, 182, 259
Wages Paradox, The, 327–8
Wagner, Richard, 54–5, 263
Wales, Welsh, 117, 198, 475
Walker, Emery, 474–5, 479
Wallas, Graham, 474
Walters, Ethel Gordon, 507
war(s) (general), 130, 149, 158, 180, 188, 235, 242, 316, 321, 322, 330, 332, 336, 346–412, 524–6. 365, 387
war criminals, 332, 401
Wardrop, Eleanor (Veronica), 497
'War to End War', the 362, 375, 378
war fever, 363
War, First World, the, xii, 130, 359–60, 378, 384, 389, 399
War and the Future (Wells), 341
War Issues for Irishmen (1918), 376–7
War Loan, the (1915), 359–60
warmongers, 351
War Office, the, 346, 352, 355, 358, 524
War, Second World, the, xii, 336n, 385, 389–91, 399–400, 408, 465
washing bills, x
washing, time involved in, 302, 326
Washington Conference, the, 411
Washington, George, 41, 377, 384
waste, 206, 259, 261, 263–4, 361, 393, 395, 419, 432, 436, 458, 464–5, 467, 469, 500
Waterloo, 182, 350
Waterloo Bridge, 204
waywardness, Shaw's, 349
Waziristan, 397

wealth, 248, 259, 264, 282, 378, 395
wealthy, the,—See rich, the
"weapon of the strike", 295
weapons, primitive and modern, 389
wear on machinery, possible saving through the Shaw Alphabet, 463
Webb, Beatrice, 280, 294, 475n
Webb, Sydney (Lord Passfield), 168, 173, 184, 208, 213, 217, 227–9, 231, 262, 280, 292, 294, 298, 320, 333, 475, 479
Webbe, Sir Harold, 335
weight, pulling one's (in society), 269
weights (general), 420, 423, 470
welfare (social, general), 321, 323
Weller, Sam, 418
Wellington, Duke of, 377
"well-made play", the, 54
Wells, H. G., 217, 276, 281, 341
Welwyn, Herts., 386
Welwyn Garden city, Herts., ix, 33–4, 45–8, 57
Welwyn Times, the, 386
West, the, Western Civilisation, Western world, Western Powers, etc., 248, 299, 308–9, 311–13, 321, 322, 369–72, 382, 386, 405, 443
Western Mail, the, 364
Western Socialist, the (Boston, U.S.A.), 229
Westminster, 321
Weymouth, Anthony, 199n, 397
What I Wrote About the War, 411
Wheathampstead, ix
Whelan, F. L., 474–5
Whigham, H. J., 271n
'whimsical arguments', Shaw's, 269
Whip, the Party, 321
Whisky, 17
White counter-revolutionaries, the, 305
White, Harold O., 473, 516
White, Marjorie, 516
Whitehouse, J. Howard, 239n
white races, the, white world, the, 367, 370–1
White Slave Traffic Bill, the, 75
whitewashing of Shaw's character, 504

"Whither Britain" (1934), 389
Whittington, Dick, 272
wholesalers, attitude of Shaw's father to, 256
"Why Not Abolish the Soldier?" (1899), 357–8
wickedness, 349, 378, 395, 401
widows, social provision for, 291
wife, wives, 86, 87, 274, 326, 344, 348, 380, 435
Wilde, Oscar, 2, 263
Wilhelm II, 187
Will of 1901, Shaw's, 474, 477, 482
Will of 1913, Shaw's, 477–84, 489
Will of 1921, Shaw's, 484–6
Will of 1937, Shaw's, 487–97
Will of 1940, Shaw's, 497
Will of 1946, Shaw's, 497–8
Will (of 1950), Shaw's Last, 413, 417, 419, 423–4, 428–9, 431–3, 437, 445, 448–9, 468, 473, 475n, 489, 499–523. 517
"will to conquer", 381–2
William III, 174, 316
William IV, 174
Williams, James, 61
Wills, earlier, 473
Will's, former, 493, 514
Wilson, R. A., 446
Wilson, President Woodrow, 372, 382
Winchester (public school), 381
Windlesham Cemetery, 506
winning fights, wars; ethical and practical aspects of, 401
wireless, the, 169, 172, 312, 324

wise, wisdom, 253, 265, 324, 330–1, 340, 360, 385, 404, 408, 452
wit, ix, 269, 519
wolf, wolves, 397
womanliness, 234
women, vi, 86, 159, 234n, 238, 255, 257, 260, 267, 285–7, 366, 392–3, 405, 410, 425, 464
women, emancipation of, the, 151–2, 285–7
Wood, John, xiii
words, 460–1, 463, 467
word-signs, 447
work, 110–12, 157, 182, 246, 265–6, 268, 269–70, 302–3, 312, 314–15, 332, 337, 339, 342, 344, 394, 398, 405, 407, 414, 444, 454, 461, 463–4, 467, 470–1, 476, 483, 486, 488, 492
workers (general, different kinds of, societies of, etc.), 260, 262, 273, 282, 288, 292, 299, 309, 320, 324, 328, 353
Workers' Educational Association, the, 338
"work glutton", the, 303
workhouse, the, 182, 206, 273, 395
working class, workers, the, 110, 114–16, 117, 119–20, 173, 211, 216–19, 229–30, 234n, 237, 264, 287–92, 295–7, 315, 351, 353
working day, the, 415, 461–2
work-man, -men, ing men, 226, 240–1, 289–90, 345, 384
works, Shaw's literary, dramatic, etc., 504
work tests, 265

world (the new, old, whole of the, rest of the, etc.), x, xii, 335, 351, 359, 381, 410, 413–14, 457, 462, 476–7, 511, 521
World League for Sexual Reform, Third International Congress of (1929), the, 96
'World Revolutionists', 326
wounds, 369, 375
Wrangel, Karl Gustav, Count, 385
wrangling, political, 319, 332
wranglings, re Shaw's proposed new alphabet, 469, 511
wrestling, 391, 401
wretched, -ness, 288
writ-ers, -ing, 281, 314–15, 329, 405, 413, 419–20, 424–5, 434, 458, 461, 465, 472, 477, 480, 482, 504, 511

Yankee(s), 346
years, 419, 458, 460–3, 469, 475, 480, 482, 487–8, 502, 505, 508, 514, 520
yellow races, yellow world, the, 367, 370–1, 386
"Yesmen and Nomen", 321
Yomiuri Shimbun, 321
Yorkshire, 414
Yorkshire Evening Post, the, 10n
Yorkshire Telegraph, the, 366
Yugoslavia, 470

Zangwill, Israel, 341
Zeitgeist, 424
Zeppelin(s), 348, 366
zero, 434, 452